# Men at Work

# THE IRWIN-DORSEY SERIES IN BEHAVIORAL SCIENCE IN BUSINESS

## Editorial Committee

ARGYRIS  *Interpersonal Competence and Organizational Effectiveness*

ARGYRIS  *Organization and Innovation*

ARGYRIS, DUBIN, HAIRE, LUCE, WARNER, WHYTE, & STROTHER (eds.)  *Social Science Approaches to Business Behavior*

GUEST  *Organizational Change: The Effect of Successful Leadership*

KUHN  *The Study of Society: A Unified Approach*

LAWRENCE & SEILER, WITH BAILEY, KATZ, ORTH, CLARK, BARNES, & TURNER  *Organizational Behavior and Administration: Cases, Concepts, and Research Findings*  Revised Edition

MASLOW  *Eupsychian Management: A Journal*

MASSARIK AND RATOOSH  *Mathematical Explorations in Behavioral Science*

RUBENSTEIN & HABERSTROH (eds.)  *Some Theories of Organization*

SCOTT  *The Management of Conflict*

WHYTE  *Men at Work*

WHYTE & HAMILTON  *Action Research for Management*

# MEN AT WORK

by

## William Foote Whyte, Ph.D.

PROFESSOR OF NEW YORK STATE SCHOOL
OF INDUSTRIAL AND LABOR RELATIONS,
CORNELL UNIVERSITY

1961

## RICHARD D. IRWIN, INC.

AND

## THE DORSEY PRESS, INC.

HOMEWOOD, ILLINOIS

90,169

# ACKNOWLEDGMENTS

THIS book is the fruit of many others besides myself. In some cases, a whole chapter or part of a chapter is based upon the research project of another scholar. I shall acknowledge these contributions as the material appears in the book.

My first exposure to the field of human relations in industry came through association while at Harvard (1936–40) with Conrad M. Arensberg, Eliot D. Chapple, and F. L. W. Richardson, Jr. In the same period, I was fortunate in being able to take a small seminar with Elton Mayo and also became acquainted with F. J. Roethlisberger and the monumental research he carried out in association with Mayo at the Western Electric Company. While at the University of Chicago (1944–48) and as a member of the Committee on Human Relations in Industry, I worked closely with W. Lloyd Warner, Burleigh B. Gardner, and Everett C. Hughes. This experience provided rich opportunities to develop my work in industry and my thinking about it.

While I had known George C. Homans in my period at Harvard, it was only much later that I began making use of his ideas on the scale indicated in this book.

Chris Argyris, George Homans, John Mee, George Strauss, and Abraham Zaleznik all read earlier drafts of the book, and their cogent criticisms led to very substantial revisions, which, I hope, have made this a better book than when they saw it.

Some of my colleagues at the New York State School of Industrial and Labor Relations have read parts of the book in draft form and been most helpful in their criticisms. I benefited from discussions with Henry A. Landsberger, Frank B. Miller, Temple Burling, Ralph Campbell, Felician Foltman, Robert Risley, and Wayne Hodges.

For aiding my research in many ways, I am indebted to Alec Winn of Aluminium Company of Canada.

I tried out much of the first draft of this book on a graduate student seminar and benefited greatly from the criticisms of the following seminar members: Vernon Buck, Richard Dunnington, John Hinrichs, Stuart Klein, Theodore Lisberger, Signe and Craig Lundberg, Victor Murray, and Richard Ritti.

Major parts of this book were typed—over and over again—by my secretary, Katherine Anderson. Josephine Richards also did a substantial share of the typing.

I read the first draft aloud to my wife, Kathleen King Whyte, and my daughter Joyce sat in on some of this. Their criticisms were most helpful.

I add the traditional statement to the effect that the good ideas in this book came from others and the author alone is to blame for the shortcomings.

**W. F. W.**

# TABLE OF CONTENTS

## PART I. HISTORICAL AND THEORETICAL BACKGROUND

CHAPTER                                                                 PAGE

INTRODUCTION . . . . . . . . . . . . . .   1

1. ORGANIZATIONAL RELATIONS AS A FIELD OF STUDY . .   5
Discovering What Wasn't True. The Rude Awakening. Theoretical
Formulations. Research Methods Used.

2. TOOLS FOR ANALYSIS . . . . . . . . . . .  17
Activities, Interactions, and Sentiments. The Identification of Sentiments. An Attempt at Concept Clarification. The Symbols to Which
Men Respond. The Characteristics of People. Symbolic Acts. Words
as Symbols. Situational Determinants of the Meaning of Symbols.
What Things Mean. Activities and Conditions of Work. Symbols for
the Organization. Summary on Symbolism.

3. THE INDIVIDUAL IN HIS ORGANIZATIONAL ENVIRONMENT .  38
What Is Joe Like? The Impact of Impersonal Forces. Reciprocity and
Rewards and Punishments. Human Relations in the Workplace. Visu-
alizing Human Relations. Where Do We Go from Here.

## PART II. THE SOCIAL AND ECONOMIC ENVIRONMENT

INTRODUCTION . . . . . . . . . . . . . .  55

4. THE WORK WORLD IN INTERCULTURAL PERSPECTIVE . .  57
The Concept of Culture. The Meaning of Work. Culture and Communication. The Japanese Factory. In Conclusion.

5. INDUSTRY AND THE COMMUNITY . . . . . . . .  68
Social Structure, Technology, and Unionization. Social Structure and
Economic Progress. Ethnic Influences. Absentee Ownership and Com-
munity Power.

6. FORMAL ORGANIZATION STRUCTURE . . . . . . .  81
Size and Structure: A Restaurant Case. Organization Structure and
Patterns of Supervision. Functional versus Product Organization.
Specialization and Organization Structure. Conclusion.

7. IMPACT OF THE ECONOMIC ENVIRONMENT . . . . .  98
Incentives as Economic Symbols. Individual Differences. Group Behavior. Pavlov and Piece Rates. The Measurement of Work. Problems
of Rate Changes. Incentives and Foreman-Worker Relations. Inter-
group Relations. A Broader Base for Incentives? Job Evaluation.
Economic Environment and Social System.

## PART III. THE TECHNOLOGICAL AND PHYSICAL ENVIRONMENT

INTRODUCTION . . . . . . . . . . . . . . 123

8. FROM KITCHEN TO CUSTOMER . . . . . . . . 125
Status, Sex, Layout, and Equipment. Communication Systems. The
Crying Waitress. The Role of the Supervisor. Conclusion.

9. FROM STEEL SHEETS TO BARRELS . . . . . . . 136
   Technology and Work Flow. Vertical and Intergroup Relations.
   Personnel Changes. The Economic Environment and Work Flow Re-
   lations. Worker and Union Relations. Analysis of the Case.

10. TEAMS OF ARTISANS . . . . . . . . . . . 149
    Team Composition and Work Operations. Historical Perspective.
    Team Leadership. Work Flow Problems. Quantitative Measures of
    Leadership. Work Group Cohesion. Management-Worker Relations.
    Working Conditions and the Job Itself. The Card-Ranking Method.
    Creativity. Achievement. Pressure and Timing. Amount of Work.
    Variety. Contribution. Personality, Status, and Human Relations. The
    Context of Work Process Satisfaction. The Pattern of Job Satisfaction.

11. MEN ON THE MOTOR LINE . . . . . . . . . 179
    Technology and Work Flow. Sentiments toward the Jobs. The Role
    of the Foreman. Work Groups and Social Groups. Conclusions.

12. MAN AND PROCESS . . . . . . . . . . . . 198
    The Man Who Walked Off the Job. Technology and Process. Personal
    and Organizational History. The Union Drive. Sloan's Last Six Weeks.
    ANALYSIS. 1. Explaining Joe Sloan. 2. Technology, Work Process,
    and Symbols.

13. TOWARD THE AUTOMATIC FACTORY . . . . . . . 218
    Technology and Physical Conditions. Early Reactions. Pay and Pro-
    duction. Changes in Interaction, Activities, and Sentiments. Conclu-
    sion.

## PART IV. UNION-MANAGEMENT RELATIONS

INTRODUCTION . . . . . . . . . . . . . . 235

14. ENTER THE UNION . . . . . . . . . . . 237
    In the "Good Old Days." The Company Union. The Masters Crack-
    Down. The Situation at Hi-Test. New Supervision at Hi-Test. The
    Campaign. Local Management's Counteroffensive. The Farewell Party.
    Negotiating for the Company Union. Management's Eleventh-Hour
    Effort. Analysis. Long-Run Changes. Changes in Interpersonal Re-
    lations.

15. WHO GOES UNION AND WHY . . . . . . . . 268
    1. The Social Background in Voting Intention. 2. The Social Char-
    acteristics of the Job. Special Ties with Management. Analysis.

16. THE EVOLUTION OF UNION-MANAGEMENT RELATIONS . . 280
    The Rise and Fall of Frank Vitucci. The Decline of the Steward.
    The Union Meeting. How Much Centralization? The Meaning of
    Grievances. The Evolution of Rules. Loyalty: Dual or Divided. Con-
    clusion.

17. WORK GROUP COHESION AND MILITANCY . . . . . 300
    1. Smelting versus Chemical Division. The Case of the Caustic Plant.
    Post-War Adjustments. The New Management Approach: 1953–57.
    Conflict Cases. Analysis. 2. The Rise and Fall of the Grinders. The
    Environment. The Social System: 1941. The Union Enters. The
    Fruits of Organization. Technological, Physical, and Personnel
    Changes. A Cut in Prices. Management's New Offer. State of the So-
    cial System. Analysis.

18. THE COLLECTIVE BARGAINING PROCESS . . . . . . 324
Seven Keys to the Negotiating Process. The Role of the International
Representative. Getting the Contract Accepted. Launching the Agree-
ment. The Problem of Manipulation. Conclusion.

19. PATTERNS IN UNION-MANAGEMENT RELATIONS . . . . 352
A Scheme for Analysis. Union-Management Reciprocity. Problems
at Lower Levels. The Scheme as a Guide to Data.

20. HUMAN PROBLEMS OF LARGE-SCALE BARGAINING . . . 363
Is Large-Scale Cooperation Possible? The General Electric Approach.
Impact on Union Leaders. Success Under What Conditions? Conclu-
sion.

## PART V. THE MANAGERIAL PROCESS

INTRODUCTION . . . . . . . . . . . . . . . 375

21. THE FIRST-LINE SUPERVISORY POSITION . . . . . 377
*The* Foreman Does Not Exist. The Changing Nature of Foreman
Positions. Moving Up From Worker to Foreman. The College-
Trained Foreman. Status Symbols in the Supervisory Relationship.
Conclusion.

22. THE MAN-BOSS RELATIONSHIP . . . . . . . . 390
Reciprocity in Rewards and Punishments. Reciprocity in Initiating
Activity. Conditions for Effective Initiation. Criticizing Subordinates.
Communication: Written or Oral? Conclusion.

23. MANAGERIAL SUCCESSION . . . . . . . . . . 408
The Managerial Process under Potter. The Managerial Process under
Stanton. Impact of the Change in Managers. The Managerial Process
under Ellis and Geiger. The Role of the Assistant Supervisor. The
Impact Hits Bottom. Personality and Managerial Behavior.

24. BUILDING INITIATIVE IN MANAGEMENT . . . . . . 429
Stimulating Upward Communication. Rewarding and Penalizing. Ex-
tending the Pattern Down the Line. Results Achieved. Costs of Success.
Planning for Organizational Development. Conclusion.

25. ON THE MEANING OF DELEGATION . . . . . . . 449
Measuring Delegation. The Picture Two Years Later. What Accounts
for the Changes? Toward a Definition of Delegation.

## PART VI. SERVICE, STAFF, AND CONTROL ACTIVITIES

INTRODUCTION . . . . . . . . . . . . . . 461

26. MAINTENANCE AND OPERATING ORGANIZATIONS . . . 463
The Standardization Program. The Area Coordination System. The
Struggle at Milo. Conclusions.

27. ENGINEERS AND THEIR INNOVATIONS . . . . . . 481
Fred Fisher's Group. Going into Production. Development Engineers
Take Over. Analysis. On the Process of Innovation.

28. COST CONTROL, PRODUCTION, AND PEOPLE . . . . . 493
What Do Budget Symbols Mean to People? Problems with Budgets.
The Impact on People. The Budget-Making Process.

29. THE ROLE OF THE PERSONNEL MAN . . . . . . . 501
The Evolution of the Personnel Department. A Case of Organizational
Mobility. The Paradox of the Personnel Department. The Personnel
Man as Human Relations Consultant. Conclusion.

30. AN ACTION RESEARCH PROGRAM FOR THE PERSONNEL
MAN . . . . . . . . . . . . . . . . 511
The Action-Research Team. What Were the Problems? Beginning in
Food Service Departments. Other Studies. Top Level Problems. Re-
sults. The New Role of the Personnel Man. The Role of the Research
Director.

## PART VII. A THEORETICAL RESTATEMENT

INTRODUCTION . . . . . . . . . . . . . . 527

31. THE INDIVIDUAL . . . . . . . . . . . 529
The Personality of Workers. The Personality of Managers and Supervisors. How Fixed Is Personality? The Individual and the Organizational Environment. The Organization Man Problem.

32. THE GROUP . . . . . . . . . . . . 539
A Theory of Work Group Cohesion. Who Gains from Cohesion? The
Utilization of Management Groups.

33. THE ORGANIZATION . . . . . . . . . . . 551
Organizational Products. Authority or Integration? Rewards and
Penalties. A Systems Approach to Organization. The Strategy of Or-
ganizational Change.

## INDEX

INDEX . . . . . . . . . . . . . . . . 581

# PART I  Historical and Theoretical Background

## INTRODUCTION

THIS is a new kind of book. It undertakes to present research cases, the analysis of cases, and a theoretical scheme to guide students in such analysis.

Books in the field seem to fall in one of three categories: *monographs*, research studies of a particular case for a particular scientific problem; *casebooks* in which human relations cases are presented to students—but no analysis is provided; and *textbooks*, which cover a wide range of topics and may present a number of theoretical ideas—but undertake no integrated theoretical scheme.

The attempt to combine cases, analysis, and theory all in one book presents many difficulties in the writing. If the effort is successful, students should find in this book a rich learning experience. If the effort fails . . . , but let us get on with the effort, and hope for the best.

In the 1930's at Harvard, Lawrence J. Henderson, a noted physiologist, offered a course in "Concrete Sociology." If it seems peculiar for a physiologist to be teaching sociology, I can only add that the title of the course was even more peculiar in that period. It was a time when much sociological work was global in its interests and rather far removed from any concrete data. Henderson did not seek to provide much of the data himself, but he invited men who had been involved in field studies or field experience to present their own concrete data and see what kind of analysis they could work out of it.

L. J. Henderson's specifications for the sociologist at that time appear to me equally compelling now. Judging from his own work and that of others in the natural sciences, Henderson proposed these requirements for progress in the scientific study of society:

The sociologist, like the physician, should have first, intimate, habitual, intuitive familiarity with things; secondly, systematic knowledge of things; and thirdly, an effective way of thinking about things.[1]

When the student first goes out to study human relations in industry,

---

[1] *Sociology 23: Introductory Lectures*, 2d ed., revised in October, 1938, mimeographed, p. 18.

he may have the impression that each situation he encounters is unique. As he continues working, case after case, in a variety of situations, he develops that intuitive familiarity of which Henderson speaks. He begins to see similarities and differences and is thereby able to move on to more systematic work.

This book presents cases from the restaurant, hotel, steel and other metals, automobile, glass, and petroleum industries—plus some others which are not identified for reasons of maintaining company anonymity. Most of these cases are drawn from my own field research experience.

In making such a selection, I am not assuming that these are the best cases available in the literature. I am just assuming that my own immersion in them will enable me to present them more effectively to the students and will enable me perhaps to pass on some of my own familiarity.

There is, of course, no adequate substitute for firsthand field experience with research problems in human relations, but I hope that this approach will be the closest thing to such an adequate substitute that can be put between the covers of a book. I hope with this approach that students will experience vicariously what life is like out in the work places where we have been studying organizational behavior. I would like them first to get a feel for the variations and then for the uniformities to be found in comparing one situation with another.

I should also like to show that the abstract propositions that represent scientific progress are based upon the behavior of living individuals, groups, and organizations. Therefore, in this book the student will not encounter only generalizations and brief illustrative material concerning nameless individuals and groups. He will get acquainted with worker Joe Sloan, Foreman Tom Walker, Manager John Dyer, Personnel Man Meredith Wiley, Industrial Engineer Fred Fisher, and many others. He will also meet the work groups around the glass furnace, the group in the centerless grinding department, and a number of others.

We will get, eventually, to some broad and general statements regarding human relations in industry, but we will approach them by means of examining the experience of particular individuals, groups, and organizations.

What do we mean by a "systematic knowledge of things?" In any field, we must first ask what the relevant things are, for no one can study systematically all of the "things" that may be present in a given situation. Part I, the theoretical introduction to this book, presents the categories of "things" that I assume to be both relevant and important to the study of human relations in industry. In the following parts of the book, on a case-by-case basis, I seek to present these "things" as systematically as I can. There will be glaring gaps in the presentation.

To present all of the cases most effectively, we would have to have the same categories of data filled in for each case. Since other researchers in some cases were looking for other "things" than I and since what I was looking for changed as I went on, Case A may be strong in certain categories of data and weak in others, while Case B may be strong where Case A is weak, and vice versa. Nevertheless, if the book shows the value of the systematic knowledge I seek to present, students can at least learn what the relevant "things" are so that, in their own later experience or research, they can try to fill in the types of data that I cannot always provide for each case.

The effective way of thinking about things should come to the students in three stages. Part I presents the conceptual or theoretical tools that are to be used. These tend to point out the relevant "things" on which we need systematic knowledge, as I have already noted. The tools themselves also give a preliminary picture of the way different types of data may fit together, so that we can begin thinking about them more effectively. The second stage comes with the presentation and analysis of cases. This involves the application of the conceptual tools to concrete field problems. It also involves a process of analysis—to a limited degree. The analysis is necessarily limited because, in this part of the book, a separate analysis is developed for each case, with only occasional references to other cases. Such an analysis, of course, is of only limited value. We assume that no case is a law unto itself. We shall therefore be needing to compare case with case, to sort out for similarities and differences, to tackle general problems present in a number of the cases, and finally to attempt to state whatever scientific generalizations or uniformities we can reach. The final stage of analysis brings us to the level of some general and abstract propositions which, hopefully, the student can apply to his own organizational experience.

The final stage of analysis in this book does not of course present any final or definitive view of the field. It is still a highly tentative ordering and analysis of data which will be modified and refined by future research men. While emphasizing the tentativeness of the conclusions, however, I do not wish to oppress students with a sense of ignorance regarding this field. Of course, we all feel that we know only a small fraction of what needs to be known. Nevertheless, in recent years I have had increasingly strongly the feeling that the data and generalizations of various studies are beginning to fit together into a pattern that offers prospects for important practical application and accelerated theoretical progress. At least I shall undertake to present this pattern here and let students judge for themselves the extent to which they can find the pattern useful in organizing their own organizational experience.

This book is written in the first person, whenever I deal with one of my own cases or one of my own opinions. It is customary for the writer to say "this author found" instead of "I found" or "This author believes" instead of "I believe." I find this a clumsy way of writing. Perhaps the use of the first person in such a book will make me subject to charges of unbecoming egotism, but the book is necessarily a very personal production. I have lived through a great part of it in my work since 1942 in my various field studies, and it would simply give a misleading impression if I presented my data and conclusions in the traditional impersonal manner. Students should be on guard in any case against the personal biases and blind spots of the author. Perhaps this writing style will help to place them on guard.

# Chapter 1 *ORGANIZATIONAL RELATIONS AS A FIELD OF STUDY*

WHAT factors account for conflict or cooperation in organizational relations—between man and boss, within management, within the union, and between union and management?

What conditions lead to high morale among organizational members? What conditions lead to high productivity? Do morale and productivity vary together? Or do we find high morale associated with low productivity and vice versa?

What does the job mean to the worker? How do workers react to the variety of types of jobs found in modern industry?

What conditions account for the cohesion of work groups? Why is it that in Group A the members "stick together" and act in concert while in Group B the members are divided against each other and are unable to advance any group cause?

How do men in organizations react to changes—to what changes introduced in what ways? Is it possible to introduce changes in such a way as to avoid disturbance of individuals and groups and the resistance they often manifest to change?

These are some of the questions to be discussed in this book. Such questions fall into the field called industrial sociology or human relations in industry.

Neither title for the field is entirely satisfactory. Industrial sociology implies that all or most of the contributions in the field have been made by sociologists. In fact, while sociologists have played a major role, important contributions have also been made by anthropologists, psychologists and economists. The term "human relations" has been used to apply to everything from sex education to race relations. When we tack the phrase "in industry" onto it, we focus our attention somewhat more, but we still find people giving widely varying interpretations to that term. To some it seems to mean "how to win friends and influence people" in an organization. To others it means how to be nice to people. To still others, it means an attempt to build scientific knowledge regarding the behavior of individuals and groups in organizations.

5

I shall not attempt now to rename or redefine the field of study. So long as we are in general agreement regarding the types of questions we want answered, the student can make up his own mind, as he goes through this book, what sort of a field of study this is and what are its possibilities and limitations.

But before we get into the presentation and analysis of what has been learned so far, let us put the field in perspective by noting how it has evolved.

While anyone preoccupied with tracing the geneology of ideas can trace the origin of any social science field back to Aristotle, more or less, the period of intensive development of our current field of study had its beginnings in the early 1930's. Up until that time, organizational behavior was the almost exclusive concern of students of "scientific management" and industrial psychologists.

The leading exponent of "scientific management" was Frederick W. Taylor, the engineer whose work gave rise to a whole school of thought and management activity. Taylor began his work in the late nineteenth century period, when industrialization was proceeding rapidly in the United States, and yet a professional approach to management was unknown. His studies convinced him that there were gross inefficiencies in the organization of work and the motivation of workers in even the most prestigeful corporations of the age.

What Taylor accomplished need not concern us in a book of this type. In tracing the stream of intellectual development, we are primarily concerned with the assumptions on which Taylor's work was based.

Taylor assumed that the industrial man was an individualist, reacting to his environment simply as an individual and without regard to any ties with other people. He assumed also that man was primarily, if not exclusively, motivated by money. Therefore, the way to get the maximum productivity from the individual was to base his pay upon the amount he produced—in other words, establish a system of piece rate payments.

While any industrial plant necessarily involves a division of labor and specialization of tasks, Taylor believed that increases in efficiency depended in large measure upon increasing the specialization of the workers and managerial personnel. If the worker could be confined to one or a very few simple tasks, he would develop a speed at performing these tasks that was thought to be unobtainable if his job were more varied.

In the eyes of Taylor and his associates, standardization went along with specialization. There was thought to be a "one best way" to do any job. It was the role of the industrial engineers to study the job in question, to design the best operating method, to instruct the worker in it, and to see to it that the work got done in the prescribed fashion.

The extreme development of standardization and specialization required the support of managerial control and discipline, so that individual variations would not disrupt the engineering plan. This meant building a logical and abstract structure of the formal organization, relating job to job and placing all jobs within a structure of authority.

Taylor also had a notion regarding functional supervision. One foreman might be responsible for organizing the work, another for training the workers, another for establishing the best method of doing the job, and so on. This particular aspect of his thinking need not detain us for long, because it was soon abandoned by his followers, and has long since ceased to have any influence in industry. The other notions, described above, did indeed have a tremendous impact upon industry, and that influence is still being felt.

The first psychologists in industry were concerned with measuring men's mental and physical abilities and their physical stamina. Tests were devised and applied for certain types of skills. Studies of the effects of fatigue and monotony were undertaken.

The now-famous Western Electric Company–Harvard Business School research program began in the late 1920's with a rather traditional focus of interest. The researchers were concerned with studying the effects of varying physical conditions upon worker productivity. The illumination experiments involved introducing changes into lighting and measuring productivity under these varying lighting conditions. Down to what the experimenters called "bright moonlight," the workers proceeded much as they did under better lighting conditions. We can assume that a prolonged period of inadequate lighting would have led to eye strain and thus to lowered productivity. We can also assume that, if the experimenters had left the workers completely in the dark, productivity would have dropped drastically. This study showed, however, that for a considerable range of lighting conditions and over short periods of time, there was no direct relationship between illumination and productivity.

The experimenters now sought to test the effects of rest periods and refreshments upon productivity. For this purpose, they set aside a special room for the relay assembly experiment. Six girls already in the employ of the company were selected for this project. The girls were not selected because they were either high or low producers, nor were they told that they should make an effort to produce as much as they could. In fact, the experimenters emphasized that they should simply work at a pace which seemed natural to them. However, they did know that their productivity in the assembling of telephone relays was to be precisely measured.

The test room girls were officially under the supervision of a foreman, but he was occupied elsewhere and gave little attention to the test room. An observer had his desk in the room, and noted down conversational and other behavior of the girls. It was emphasized that the observer had no authority over the girls, and that his data would be kept confidential. After the girls had been allowed several weeks to become accustomed to their new work site and social conditions, the experimental changes were introduced.

For periods of several weeks each, the experimenters tried one and then another pattern of rest periods and refreshments, and also variations in the length of the working day. As the experiment proceeded through eleven periods and almost a year's time, productivity rose substantially above the base period before changes were introduced. The incautious experimenter might have concluded from these results that rest periods, refreshments, and a certain amount of shortening of the working day were indeed responsible for higher productivity, although the quantitative results did not clearly indicate which experimental conditions were optimal for productivity. Rather than accepting this general conclusion regarding the "success" of the experiment, Elton Mayo, director for Harvard in the research program, determined upon a twelfth experimental period in which the girls were to return to the original conditions—no specified rest periods, no refreshments, and a working day of the regular factory length. Productivity in this twelfth period rose to a new high!

The birth of our field of study might be dated from the twelfth experimental period of the Western Electric research program. Elton Mayo argued that the results of this period could not be explained away as being due to some chance variation. The results showed dramatically that the girls were not responding solely to the variations in conditions introduced by the experimenters. Whatever the effects of the changes in working conditions, there were apparently other and more powerful forces at work, uncontrolled by the experimenters. What were these forces?

Some students have explained the results in terms of the "Hawthorne effect" (Hawthorne being the name of the plant in which the work was conducted). According to this theory, the girls felt that they got special recognition through being part of the experiment and thus were responding more to the prestige gained through participation in the experiment, than to the specified experimental conditions. Others have noted the drastic differences in the social situation of the workplace enjoyed by these girls compared with what prevailed regularly in the factory. We have already noted that the foreman did not supervise them in the manner that he did girls in the regular department. In fact, he had little contact with them at all. The observer developed an informal, friendly relationship with the girls and even consulted them at several points regarding the course of the experiment. That this consultation was more than an idle gesture is shown by the fact that on occasion the girls were allowed to veto ideas the experimenters wanted to try out.

However the explanations might differ in detail, the results of the twelfth period clearly showed the importance of social influences on productivity. Mayo and his associates, F. J. Roethlisberger and W. J. Dickson, now went on to design studies into the social influences in work groups operating under more usual factory conditions. These studies, together with the test room report, have deservedly become classics in social science research.

It is not my concern to review here all of the major findings of this research program.[1] For our purposes, it is only important now to point out the main ways in which the Western Electric program clashed with previously popular assumptions regarding organizational behavior and established some new assumptions of its own.

The assumptions of F. W. Taylor were challenged at crucial points. The Western Electric study showed without any question that workers did not respond simply as isolated individuals, but were strongly influenced by the social relations they experienced. They worked for money, to be sure, and yet they restricted output well below the level that their skill and endurance alone would have made possible. Apparently workers developed social "norms" regarding what amount of productivity was socially acceptable. (The phenomenon of "restriction of output" had been noted and described before, but the Western Electric study of the Bank Wiring Room was the most systematic study of this phenomenon yet to appear.)

The traditional industrial psychologists fared no better in their clash with the Western Electric findings. Workers in the Bank Wiring Room were tested for mechanical aptitude, and the test results were compared with production records for each individual. The results showed no significant correlation. One of the lowest producers had one of the highest aptitude scores, and one of the highest producers had one of the lowest aptitude scores. The tests admittedly did not take into account worker motivation and group processes, and these aspects of the work situation were to assume commanding importance in future research.

While the Western Electric Company inplant studies were proceeding, W. Lloyd Warner, a social anthropologist who was a consultant to the project, developed his own community study of Yankee City, a small New England industrial city. Part of this community research program involved a study of the unionization of the shoe factories, which took place during the period of the Warner study. Thus, the field of social research was broadened to include industry-community and union-management relations.

---

[1] For Mayo's interpretation, see particularly *The Human Problems of an Industrial Civilization* (New York: The Macmillan Co., 1933). For the major research report on that program, see F. J. Roethlisberger and W. J. Dickson, *Management and the Worker* (Cambridge: Harvard University Press, 1939). For a very useful analysis of *Management and the Worker* and the controversies surrounding it, see Henry A. Landsberger, *Hawthorne Revisited: Management and the Worker, Its Critics, and Developments in Human Relations in Industry* (Ithaca, N.Y.: The New York State School of Industrial and Labor Relations, 1958).

The leads turned up in the Western Electric research program were not immediately followed up by the researchers. While the major reports on the Western Electric program were published between 1935 and 1939, field work at Hawthorne had terminated in 1932, and no new major efforts at human relations in industry research were to be noted until more than a decade later.

In 1943, the Committee on Human Relations in Industry, of the University of Chicago, was formed, with W. Lloyd Warner as chairman and Burleigh B. Gardner as executive secretary. Over the next five years, the Committee carried on an active program of primarily inplant studies. I began my own research in industry in 1942, when at the University of Oklahoma, and joined the Committee on Human Relations in Industry in 1944.

In 1944, E. Wight Bakke organized the Labor and Management Center at Yale University, to develop this line of research there. Bakke had begun his research career with studies of the effects of unemployment on workers. This interest naturally led him to examine the meaning of work to the worker. While the unemployment studies were necessarily carried on in the community, the Labor and Management Center concerned itself primarily with plant and union studies.

In 1946, Rensis Likert founded the Institute for Social Research at the University of Michigan. From its inception, the Institute has been active in organizational studies.

Other centers of research soon followed, and by 1950, research in organizational relations was proceeding in many of the leading universities in the country.

## DISCOVERING WHAT WASN'T TRUE

While recognizing the importance of the Western Electric research program, we should note that its primary intellectual impact was in demonstrating to us what was *not* true—not in demonstrating what was true. The Mayo group also coined the term "informal organization," to point to the tendency of human beings, when thrown together in an organization, to develop relations with each other that are not specified by the formal organization structure and that sometimes seemed to develop in opposition to these formal channels. In other words, the researchers demonstrated that the student who seeks to understand organizational behavior through giving his attention exclusively to the formal structure of the organization will receive only a partial and a highly misleading view. Just what role formal organization structure plays, however, was left unclear.

The Western Electric program did give rise to concentrated study of face-to-face relations in industry. In contrast to the formalistic view of the organization, this was certainly constructive. Unfortunately, reaction against one unsound approach often leads men into the opposite extreme, which may be equally unsound. Thus the preoccupation with face-to-face relations led some of us into the implicit assumption that these relations could be studied and understood quite apart from economic forces, technology, the work flow, organization structure, and plant-community relations.

This concentration on face-to-face relations led us to assume that the more harmonious organizations would be led by individuals who had superior skills in human relations. This led to the further assumption that training supervisors in human relations could lead to the building of more effective and harmonious organizations. Such assumptions led to the tremendous proliferation of supervisory training programs in human relations that grew up in the 1940's and 50's.

## THE RUDE AWAKENING

This line of thinking has been severely jolted by several significant studies.[2] Clark Kerr and Abraham Siegel put to us the following embarrassing question: If cooperation in industry depends primarily on the skill and understanding of the key people involved, how do you explain the fact that there has been consistent conflict in the longshore industry in this country, and even internationally, while relations in the clothing industry have been reasonably peaceful?[3] Can it be that the key people in Industry A just happen to be skilled in human relations, whereas their opposite numbers in Industry B are a bunch of bunglers?

This would be hard to believe, and as a matter of fact we do not believe it. We have had to recognize that there are certain forces operating that are more powerful than the human relations techniques of individual executives or union leaders. Along this line, Kerr and Siegel emphasize the homogeneity or heterogeneity of worker groupings on the job or in the community.

Strike-prone industries, they argue, are those in which most workers work in close proximity on the same or similar jobs, and in which they live in close association in communities where they are cut off from intimate contact with other types of workers or with management people. At the other extreme, heterogeneity leads to more peaceful union-management relations: workers who do a wide variety of jobs and are scattered through the community, among other types of people, are less likely to strike.

This is an oversimplification of the Kerr–Siegel argument, but for our

---

[2] This section from W. F. Whyte, "Human Relations Reconsidered," W. Lloyd Warner and Norman H. Martin, *Industrial Man* (New York: Harper & Bros., 1959), pp. 315–16.

[3] "On the Inter-Industry Propensity to Strike," in Kornhauser, Dubin, and Ross, *Industrial Conflict* (New York: McGraw-Hill Book Co., Inc., 1954).

purposes, it need not be presented in detail. It is enough to note that they have drawn our attention to the powerful influence of job structure and community organization upon human relations on the job.

A second major blow came from research evaluation of the impact of supervisory training programs.

In recent years, two solid pieces of research have been done along this line. In each case, the workers were given a questionnaire, dealing with their relationship with their supervisors, before the training program was administered to the supervisors. The same questionnaire was given to the workers some months after the conclusion of the training program. The result? Disappointing, to say the least.

Edwin A. Fleishman, Edwin F. Harris, and Harold E. Burtt, at Ohio State, found that the International Harvester Company program had effected no gain in these supervisor-worker relationships—and perhaps it had even resulted in a slight loss.[4] The University of Michigan Survey Research Center's study of a training program in two divisions of the Detroit Edison Company showed a small over-all gain.[5] However, it was found that there had been a loss of ground in one division, which was more than compensated for by gain in the other.

How can we account for these results? Were the programs in themselves no good? No doubt better training can be given, but probably these courses were a good deal better than the average in industry today.

We find the best explanation by looking at the two divisions in the Detroit Edison study. The researchers found that in the division where progress had been made, the foremen were led by a higher management which supervised them very much in line with the principles developed in the course. On the other hand, in the division which lost ground, the foremen were under superiors who directed them in a manner which was entirely out of harmony with the program.

These findings suggest that the effectiveness of a training program for lower-level supervisors depends in a very large measure on the way that program is supported at higher levels in the organization. Nor can that support be simply verbal. Real success depends on the actions of top management in its day-to-day behavior.

What about training in human relations for the higher-ups?

Years ago, management tended to make the foreman a sort of scapegoat for all human relations difficulties. It was assumed that if the foreman were only as good a leader of men as the president or vice-president of the company, then there would be no problem. Today few management people are that naive. They are ready to recognize that a change in

---

[4] *Leadership and Supervision in Industry: An Evaluation of a Supervisory Training Program* (Monograph No. 33) (Columbus: Bureau of Educational Research, The Ohio State University, 1955).

[5] See Norman A. Maier, *Principles of Human Relations* (New York: John Wiley & Sons, Inc., 1952), pp. 184–92.

behavior at higher levels may be necessary too, if the foreman is to do the skillful job of supervision expected of him. So it makes sense to direct training at these higher levels.

Nevertheless, we are becoming increasingly doubtful whether training can do the job here. We often assume that people high up in management are free agents. If they put pressure on their subordinates in a way that hinders cooperation and lowers morale, we may assume that this is because they do not have the necessary human relations skills, or because they have some personality difficulties. But the truth is that the big wheels are not free to do as they please. They too are under pressure.

The plant manager is in competition for advancement with other plant managers. He is struggling to meet a budget that is deliberately set tight so as to demand his best efforts. He works with accountants and cost control people who, as Chris Argyris has explained, gain their successes through discovering and reporting the failures of production people.[6] Faced with rising material costs and wages, the manager must spur his organization to greater efficiency, so that the plant produces in greater volume and still keeps costs down and profits up. He has design engineers, industrial engineers, personnel men, and other specialists to help him and his production men do this, and yet he finds much of his time and energy devoted to untangling the snarls that arise among the people who make up the complex and sensitive organism which he directs.

At still higher levels, the company executive may be under less direct pressure from above, but he generates his own pressure in response to his ideal of the successful American executive. That ideal demands that he not be content with today's achievement, that he be constantly pushing to improve or expand the organization. Progress may require him to gamble millions of dollars on projects whose payoff is years away. Responsibility is a heavy weight in itself.

Our problem involves certain things that are bigger than the individual and his social skills. What are these things? As we shall see in later chapters, the behavior of men in industry is shaped to important degrees by money, technology and workflow, organization structure, and the social environment of the community in which the organization is located. This does not mean that the individual human being is simply the pawn of these forces. It does mean that his powers of changing the situation are severely limited if he can only operate on a face-to-face basis and without any control over money, technology, organization structure, and community environment.

In this book, we are not attempting to determine which is more important: money or face-to-face relations, technology or face-to-face relations, or organization structure or technology, and so on. It will do us no

---

[6] See Chapter 28, "Cost Control, Production, and People."

good to try to measure the impact of each element, because the elements fit together into a combination or pattern. It is our task to present, understand, and analyze this pattern.

## THEORETICAL FORMULATIONS

Since our field of study has diverse disciplinary origins, theoretical ideas in current use naturally reflect this diversity. Any author who hopes to bring theory to bear on this subject, therefore, has two possible choices. He can seek to present all of the theoretical notions that seem to have relevance to the problems under discussion. Or he can limit himself to one line of theoretical development.

Either course of action has its advantages and its limitations. The comprehensive theoretical approach has the advantage of relative completeness. Given the fact that this field is not yet "jelled" into a commonly accepted body of knowledge, concepts, and theoretical propositions, a comprehensive approach has the advantage of introducing students to all of the theoretical tools that may later prove to be useful. But this approach has the disadvantages that go with comprehensiveness—and heterogeneity. The student may indeed be introduced to everything now known which appears to be relevant. He is presented with all the tools, *but* he has very little opportunity to make systematic use of any of them.

The choice of one theoretical approach presents the obvious disadvantage of bias and incompleteness. The student will not be introduced to some perfectly respectable and perhaps even important theoretical ideas. The data may perhaps be selected to fit the particular theoretical scheme, instead of the scheme being selected because it fits the data. There is even the danger that the theoretical scheme will provide a "slanted" interpretation of the data—that an alternative scheme would fit the data just as well if not better.

In spite of these obvious limitations, I have chosen to present and analyze the data in terms of one (more or less) coherent theoretical scheme. Insofar as this decision can be logically defended, it is based upon the assumption that it is better for students to have an opportunity to apply one set of theoretical ideas systematically than to be exposed superficially to a wide variety. The cutting edge of theoretical tools cannot be assessed unless we have the opportunity to dig deeply into the data with them.

While some limitations cannot be avoided in the approach I am taking, I can at least provide students and teachers with one important safeguard. This book presents a large body of data, much of it in considerable detail. The cases we are to discuss are presented in sufficient detail so that it is possible for students and teachers to apply to them theoretical ideas not contained in this book. In fact, I urge them to approach the book in such a critical frame of mind.

The theoretical approach to be here used is commonly known as "interaction theory," although that term seems unduly limiting to the framework as it is now developed. The first publication representing this approach appeared in 1940.[7] Eliot Chapple and Conrad Arensberg had worked together in W. Lloyd Warner's Yankee City study. When Arensberg returned from a field study in rural Ireland, the two men set about to examine the Yankee City and Irish materials to find some kind of theoretical scheme that would stand scientific tests. After they had developed, tested, and abandoned four earlier schemes, they began concentrating upon the observation and measurement of human interaction: the frequency and duration of interpersonal contacts and the origin-response ratio or the proportion of interactions initiated by A to B, compared with those from B to A.

They stated the theory first in highly abstract form. It was first applied to industrial organizations in a study by Conrad Arensberg and Douglas McGregor.[8]

The theory was further elaborated and modified by George C. Homans in *The Human Group*.[9] A further development of this line of thinking is represented in Homans' *Social Behavior: Its Elementary Forms*,[10] which I have had the advantage of reading before publication and which has influenced my own thinking substantially.

I used the Chapple-Arensberg approach in my first field study in an urban slum district and have later applied it to all of my work in industry. I do not wish to give the impression that I am presenting what is commonly agreed upon as a standard "interactionist" approach to the field. There are differences in point of view among those using this general approach. However, these are of more interest to the advanced student of organizational theory than they are to students who are receiving their introduction to the field.

Students should be further cautioned that what I am presenting is by no means a majority point of view of those studying organizational relations. This is distinctly a minority view. But the value of the approach is not in the long run to be determined by majority vote. The best test comes from the application of this body of ideas to the data in our

---

[7] Eliot D. Chapple, in collaboration with Conrad M. Arensberg, *Measuring Human Relations: An Introduction to the Study of the Interaction of Individuals* (Genetic Psychology Monograph No. 22) (Princetown, Mass.: The Journal Press, 1940).

[8] "Determination of Morale in an Industrial Company," *Applied Anthropology*, Vol. I, No. 2 (January–March 1942), pp. 12–34.

[9] New York: Harcourt Brace & Co., 1950.

[10] New York: Harcourt Brace & Co., 1961.

field of concern. The student himself, as he goes through the book, should be able to assess this utility.

## RESEARCH METHODS USED

Since conclusions can be no better than the data upon which they are based, it is important for students to know the origin of the case material presented here. Detailed discussions of research methods can be found elsewhere.[11] A brief summary must serve our purposes.

These data come out of the process of social exploration. The primary characteristic of researchers in this area is that they have gone out actively into the field to observe interpersonal events and to interview participants in those events. Written documents have been of secondary importance—and have sometimes been unduly neglected.

Data have come from both participant observers and nonparticipant observers. The participants have been students who have worked at actual industrial jobs, but have also sought to keep a work diary regarding the events taking place around them. The nonparticipants have sought to fit themselves unobtrusively into the scene so that they could observe events in as natural a setting as possible.

Interviewers have not been concerned primarily with attitudes or sentiments—with how the informant feels about the organization or various individuals. They have been concerned particularly with the events themselves, seeking to find a pattern in this flow of interpersonal events. This concentration of interest on events has meant that generally the data do not arise out of questionnaires—instruments ill-adapted to tap the flow of events. However, at several points in this book, questionnaire data are presented to supplement the data from other approaches.

I have already noted that one of the major studies involved a field experiment. The student will find, however, that relatively little of our data come from experiments—if that term is used in its "pure" sense—involving the control of certain variables and the manipulation of a single variable. In the field of social behavior, such experimental conditions are extremely difficult to meet, for we are likely to find, as was found in the Western Electric program, that change depends upon movement among several variables and that no single one accounts for the result. We have thus been limited on the one hand, but on the other hand, there is in the record an abundance of material regarding rather self-conscious efforts to introduce change and to observe and record what happened in the process. If pure experiments have been few, the researchers have nevertheless often worked with an experimental spirit. I hope such a spirit will pervade this book.

---

[11] For the research methods primarily used in studies reported in this book, the best treatment will be found in Richard C. Adams and Jack J. Preiss (editors), *Human Organization Research: Field Relations and Techniques* (Homewood, Ill.: The Dorsey Press, Inc., 1960).

# Chapter 2 *TOOLS FOR ANALYSIS*

TO GO beyond common sense discussion of human problems in industry, we need some tools of analysis. The social scientist uses words and numbers as such tools. The key words he uses he calls concepts: words pointing to the leading ideas of his theoretical system.

Theory, particularly in this stage of development, requires that the concepts we use be relatively few and that they be closely integrated. If we use a large number of concepts, our scheme becomes too complex to handle. If the concepts are not interrelated, we have no system. We simply have a set of words that refer to presumably important aspects of the subjects we are discussing. We can use the words to point to data, but we cannot use them as an aid in manipulating data.

For conceptual tools to be useful, they must be capable of application to concrete situations. The best way, then, of defining the concepts is to show how they concretely apply. At the same time, if we demonstrate the tools in terms of an actual case, there is the danger that we will become so preoccupied with the details of the case that we will fail to appreciate the general applicability of the concepts. To avoid this pitfall, I shall present the tools in their application to Joe Member, a hypothetical participant in the organization. We shall consider how he got to be the way he is and what he reacts to in his present situation.

In a book concerning groups and organizations, it may seem strange to start our discussion on this individual basis. We begin with the individual because he is the unit that feels, thinks, and acts, and whose actions, at least, can be observed. Even when we report what we see of a group in action, we are in effect dealing with a summary of the individual behavior we observe. However, even as we start with the individual, we want to know how he fits into the group, how collective action arises on a group basis, and how individuals and groups fit into the larger organization. From our examination of Joe, the individual, we will develop a scheme to apply to the analysis of groups and organizations.

## ACTIVITIES, INTERACTIONS, AND SENTIMENTS

We will be concerned first with Joe's activities, interactions, and sentiments.

By *activities*, we refer to certain things that Joe does. For example, he works at his job and sometimes engages in horseplay. We may also

17

see him drinking a cup of coffee and smoking a cigarette during the morning coffee break, and playing cards with a few friends during the lunch period. These activities can be objectively described and even to some extent measured. In some types of jobs (but not in others) it is possible to measure the productivity for which Joe is directly responsible. While horseplay cannot be measured, at least the amount of time spent in that activity can be added up.

We are also interested in the *initiation* of activity. Some people characteristically initiate changes in activity for others, whereas some seldom initiate such changes. Does Joe have opportunities to initiate activities for others while he is at work? Does he, in fact, take this initiative?

*Interaction* refers to certain aspects of interpersonal relations that we can observe and quantify. How often does Joe talk with other workers while he is in the plant? Does he talk with many of them, or are his interactions limited to a few? How often does he interact with the foreman? With the superintendent? With the time study man? And so on.

We can also note who characteristically *initiates* the interaction. Does Joe start the conversation or other social activity with other workers? Or does he tend to wait for others to initiate the interaction?

Such observations reveal to us the composition of informal groups in the workplace and the structure of leadership they have developed. This charting of interactions also may tell us a good deal about which men tend to act together.

*Sentiments* refer to the mental and emotional reactions we have to people and physical objects. Sentiments have the following three elements:

1. An idea about something or somebody; that is, a cognitive element.
2. Emotional content or affect.
3. A tendency to recur, upon presentation of the same symbols that have been associated with it in the past.[1]

I regard sentiments as a personal frame of reference, through which the individual perceives, interprets, and evaluates the world around him and his place in it. Many schemes of classification of sentiments are possible. For our purposes, I find it useful to set up these categories:

1. Self-concept.
2. Evaluation of activities.
3. Personal identification.
4. Ranking.

We shall be concerned primarily with these three aspects of the *self-concept*: status, personal worth, and level of aspiration. Status involves

---

[1] I am indebted to discussions with Alexander Leighton for this approach to sentiments. See particularly Chapter VII and Appendix A (with Jane M. and Charles C. Hughes) in his *My Name is Legion* (New York: Basic Books, Inc., 1959).

Joe's own conception of his prestige position in society. As he begins work, this self-evaluation is likely to be strongly influenced by the status of his parents in the community and by the status of those with whom he is customarily associated outside of the workplace. Perhaps his father is a skilled worker, and Joe is inclined to think of himself as at least a slight cut above those who come from families where the father was unskilled, and perhaps only sporadically employed.

Personal worth involves the individual's own evaluations of what he is good at and what he is not good at. For example, Joe may consider himself one of the most skilled men on his particular job, and may also take pride in his tinkering at home.

Level of aspiration refers to the objectives Joe hopes to reach. These hopes tends to be limited by what Joe thinks is—or should be—possible, providing Joe is a normal individual. That is, if you ask him whether he would like to have a million dollars, he will give an affirmative answer, but Joe does not expect to have a million dollars, and is not going to be frustrated by his inability to acquire this fortune. On the other hand, if you ask him whether he would like to have the job immediately above him in the line of promotion, his response will be more closely related to reality. Perhaps he not only expresses an interest in having that job, but says that he will be seriously disappointed if he does not have the opportunity of moving up within the next year. He may go on to say that he would like to become a foreman, even though he recognizes that most foremen in his company are college graduates and he has not had a college education. In that case, he recognizes that he probably won't be able to achieve his ambition, and yet the job is so close to his present experience that he can't help aspiring to it and feeling frustrated at his lack of progress.

Status, personal worth, and level of aspiration tend to be related to each other, but may also vary independently of each other. For example, the man who thinks of himself as having high status is likely also to place a high evaluation upon his personal worth, but this may not always be the case. He may recognize that his family and friends have high status and yet still lack confidence in his own abilities. Similarly, a man who considers himself very good at his work is likely to aspire to promotion, but we do encounter individuals who tell us, in effect, "Sure, I am good at this job, but this is a job I like to do, so why should I want to move up?" In this book, we will be concerned with each of the three aspects of the self-concept and with the ways in which they move together or move independently.

*Evaluation of activities* involves Joe's judgment about which activities are good or bad, right or wrong. For example, Joe may believe that a hundred units a day is a "day's work" in his job. He could produce more and is sometimes tempted to do so, but he feels that this would not be the right thing to do. He may believe that it is good to swap jobs with fellow workers to break the monotony, even though this is against management rules. He may believe that the activities of the time study man are bad and that any worker who gives him accurate information is doing the wrong thing.

The reader may be familiar with the concept "norms" and feel that this is what we are talking about. That is not the case. At this point, we are considering the evaluations that Joe as an individual makes.

To be sure, his evaluations are importantly influenced by those of his fellows, and this influencing process will be a major concern in this book. We speak of *norms* only when we find members of a group agreeing, at least implicitly, as to what activities should be carried on and what should be avoided, and when we find them taking action to show disapproval of the one who violates these group evaluations. In other words, a *norm* involves a collectively agreed upon evaluation of activity. Joe may make a number of individual evaluations which are not shared by members of his work group and therefore do not contribute to the establishment of group norms.

*Personal identification* involves Joe's feelings as to who are his friends and who are his enemies. He may consider all members of his work group friends, but even in that case he will probably acknowledge that he is "closer" to some than to others. Or we may find the work group seriously divided, so that Joe considers only some of them for him and with him, whereas others he feels are against him. He makes similar evaluations of management people.

On the individual level, it is probably not enough to speak simply of liking or disliking. We often hear people distinguishing between liking and respecting. I assume that liking and respecting go together more often than not, but we should be alert for situations in which they do not; therefore, we should keep our eyes open to both aspects of interpersonal sentiment.

We can also speak of personal indentification at the level of group, department, and organization. Does Joe feel really a member of his work group? Does he feel that his is a good department to work in? How does he feel about the company? We will be concerned with all of these aspects of personal identification as we proceed in this book.

*Ranking* involves Joe's evaluation of the relative prestige of those he sees around him. Within Joe's department, we find both formal and informal ranking among workers. Formal ranking is determined by the job classification scheme in effect in the department. Everyone knows that job A is a better job than job B, so that we may say that the man who works on job A has a higher rank than the man who works on job B. This formal ranking generally has a strong influence on the informal rankings accorded to departmental members by their fellows. Informal group leadership within the department tends to be assumed by workers holding high formal rankings. However, this is not uniformly true, so we must always be concerned with the personal evaluations of rank that are given fellow workers by Joe and the other members of the department.

While we speak of ranking again on an individual basis, it has been shown that there tends to be a high degree of agreement among people in the same community or organization about the relative prestige ranking of their fellows.[2] While Joe and his fellow workers do not talk explicitly about ranking, their conversation is interspersed with casual or pointed comments that express approval or disapproval of, or liking or disliking of, individuals around them. As the expression of these sentiments is exchanged among members, a collective ranking arises.

Joe also ranks members of management. Here the formal titles play a role perhaps even more important than at the work level. But again, they do not completely determine the way Joe ranks members of management. For example, he may feel that his own foreman does not "carry much weight" with higher management, whereas the foreman of an adjoining department "carries a lot of weight." In effect, he is saying that he ranks the other foreman above his own.

## THE IDENTIFICATION OF SENTIMENTS

How are we to know that sentiments Joe has? His activities and interactions can be directly observed and to some extent measured. Not so with sentiments. We identify his sentiments by what he tells us about them and by the inferences we make from the behavior we observe. For example, if we see Joe and another worker talking and laughing together, we are inclined to assume friendly sentiments of personal identification between them. To be sure, appearances can sometimes mislead us. For example, the union members of a contract negotiating group may speak with great vehemence regarding a certain contract clause, leading us to assume that they feel very strongly about this one. We may learn later that this was a clause of little importance to the union and one on which they expected to make no progress. They made a big fuss about it, hoping to make management people feel guilty about their unwillingness to concede, so that management would be softer on the next point which was really of major concern to the union.

While we can all think of examples of such discrepancies between the way people feel and the sentiments they appear to be expressing, we must recognize that if we were not able to assume a correlation between internally felt and overtly expressed sentiments in most cases, it would

---

[2] See W. Lloyd Warner, Kenneth Eells, and Marcia Meeker, *Social Class in America* (Chicago: Science Research Associates, 1948). Also Joseph Kahl, *The American Class Structure* (New York: Rhinehart & Co., 1957).

be impossible for us to live a coherently organized social and economic existence.

We must always proceed with caution in our interpretations regarding sentiments, yet we will find it impossible to deal with human relations and human organization without having some way of handling sentiments.

## AN ATTEMPT AT CONCEPT CLARIFICATION

Up to this point, I have undertaken to define the terms sentiments, activities, and interactions, and show how I intend to use them. Since the terms have been used in other ways in the past even by those operating within the general interaction framework, it may be helpful to compare the present usage with that which has prevailed earlier.

First, let us try to be clear regarding the difference between interaction and activities, for they are often mixed together, and I myself have been guilty of some of this confusion. The field observation situation itself invites such confusion, for in most cases we see interaction and activities going on simultaneously, although the overlap is not complete. Whenever individuals interact, they are also carrying on some activity, even if only conversation, while activity can be carried on by the worker alone, without any interaction. In effect, what the research man does in the field is observe what is going on and abstract from this the interactions and the activities. That is, he observes who is interacting with whom and what activities the two or more men are carrying on.

A more serious confusion, of which I have been especially guilty, has been the failure to distinguish between *initiation* of *interaction* and *initiation* of *activities*. Sometimes the two go together, as when the foreman approaches Joe and tells him, "I want you to start on job X now," and we see Joe changing his activities in order to undertake job X. But often this correspondence is not to be observed. For example, Joe might approach his foreman and ask, "What do you want me to do now?" The foreman says, "I want you to do job X now." In this case we say that Joe initiated interaction for the foreman, and the foreman initiated activity for Joe. Or let us say that the foreman approaches Joe and says, "How's it going?" Joe replies, "This machine isn't working right. How about getting the repairman over?" The foreman nods, and we see him going off apparently in search of the repairman. In this case, the foreman has initiated interaction, but it is Joe who has initiated activity for the foreman.

The reader who is familiar with the writings of George C. Homans may note that although Homans' approach has influenced my thinking significantly, I have made no mention of his concepts of *internal* and *external system*. The omission has been deliberate, for I suspect that here Homans has introduced an unnecessary complication. Let us first consider what Homans means by the two systems, and then examine the complications involved in using these concepts. Homans says:

> The external system is the state of these elements (interaction, activity and sentiments) and of their interrelations, so far as it constitutes a solution—not necessarily the only possible solution—of the problem: How shall the group survive in its environment? We call it external because it is conditioned by the environment; we call it a system because in it the elements of behavior are mutually dependent.[3]

He defines the internal system as "group behavior that is an expression of the sentiments towards one another developed by the members of the group in the course of their life together."

In Homans' formulation, we find interaction, activity, and sentiments in the internal system and in the external system. Furthermore, there is a mutual-dependence relationship between the two systems so that a change in one affects the other, and vice versa.

I have stated very briefly a rather complicated idea. I do not wish to go into further detail at this point, because I suspect that Homans has here introduced an unnecessary complication.

First, I question whether the concept of two systems, external and internal, is useful and applicable. The idea underlying the distinction does indeed seem to have some value. We all recognize that people have to do certain things in order to get the job done and to meet the formal requirements of the organization. We recognize that they do not limit their behavior to these formal requirements of organization and technology, but always elaborate additional behavior, which has sometimes been called informal and which Homans now describes as the internal system.

However, if we go beyond the general statement and try to distinguish observationally between the two systems, we run into difficulties. Can we distinguish between external and internal activities? Probably this is the easiest of the three distinctions to make, since the activities involved at work are clear cut. Not so with interactions. In some work situations we see people carrying on at the same time interactions growing directly out of the work and the more informal interactions coming out of sociability needs. Finding the distinctions between sentiments in the internal and external systems is even more difficult, since the worker's sentiments on the job he is doing are intimately involved with the sentiments toward the people with whom he is working. Homans now writes that he has abandoned this former distinction between internal and external system.[4]

---

[3] *The Human Group* (New York: Harcourt Brace & Co., 1950), p. 90.

[4] See his review of my *Man and Organization* in *Administrative Science Quarterly* (December, 1959). In his latest book, Homans does not use this distinction. See *Social Behavior: Its Elementary Forms* (New York: Harcourt Brace & Co., 1960).

## THE SYMBOLS TO WHICH MEN RESPOND

We can describe Joe in terms of the interactions and activities he emits and the sentiments we infer that he holds. If we wish to go beyond description and explain why Joe behaves as he does, we then have to use some concept that relates Joe to his social and physical environment. He reacts to something "out there." What is "out there" for Joe? And how can we describe systematically what it is to which he reacts?

To be sure, Joe reacts to the interactions and activities others direct toward him, but that is not all which is "out there" for Joe, and even the interactions and activities may be accompanied by important symbolic elements.

Past experience, plus what he has heard from others, furnishes Joe with the cues whereby he recognizes the situation confronting him and responds to it in an appropriate manner. Even when the actor is not explicitly aware of the nature of the cues, it is possible for the social scientist to identify them. As we identify and analyze these cues, we see some of the forces that channelize human relations.

These cues I shall call *symbols*. Symbols are words, objects, conditions, acts, or characteristics of persons which refer to (or stand for) the relations among men, and between men and their environment.

Men use verbal symbols to express their sentiments; their perception of symbols in the world around them activates or reinforces certain sentiments. Symbols may also serve to trigger certain activities and interactions without any prior impact upon sentiments.

The definition requires illustration.

## THE CHARACTERISTICS OF PEOPLE

Let us begin with the characteristics of people. We recognize, of course, that an infinite number of characteristics of people can be pointed to if we have enough different observers doing the pointing. We are concerned, rather, with the cultural and biological uniformities which imply certain responses on the part of other actors.

The most obvious of such characteristics is *sex*. Now, we do not think it necessary to tell a student how to recognize the difference between a man and a woman. That point is that, when Joe recognizes another individual as a woman, he does not simply make a biological judgment. He assumes, without reasoning it out, that certain jobs are appropriate for this individual, certain activities are appropriate for her to perform, and certain relations are appropriate between them depending upon time and situation. In organizational life, the way in which people respond to a given position may determine whether a woman or a man will hold that position. Examples of this will be found in Chapter 8 on "From Kitchen to Customer."

Differences in *age* may also have important social consequences.

Anthropologists refer to this phenomenon as *age grading:* the organization of social life in terms of the ages of the participants, so that people of one age participate in one set of activities and people of another age participate in a different set. In a few societies, age grading appears to have been the primary scheme of organization; with the division from one age grade to the next sharply marked, with ceremonial activities performed to induct individuals into the higher age grade, and with men associating much more with their own age mates than with others. In our own society, age distinctions are much less emphasized, and yet we cannot afford to ignore them altogether, for we find that people do recognize age distinctions and adjust their behavior to some extent to these distinctions. In some situations (as in Chapter 10, "Teams of Artisans") age differences seem to be importantly involved in the social problems of an organization.

There is an industrial form of age grading—seniority—that operates alongside the system based on biological age. At least at the work level, in most situations, the individual's seniority date may be one of the most important social characteristics he has.

Seniority means simply length of continuous service. The simple definition becomes more complex as we seek to determine what continuous service means; that is, how long an individual may be laid off without losing the right to count his seniority from his initial hiring date. The situation becomes still more complex as we consider the unit in which the individual holds seniority. For purposes of promotion, transfer, demotion and layoffs, the individual's seniority may be company-wide, city-wide (covering the plants of that company in a given city), plant-wide, on a departmental basis, or it may be figured in terms of a given promotional ladder (a series of jobs graded so that the worker moves up or down the sequence).

This is not the place to discuss various seniority systems. My only purpose is to suggest that seniority is an important characteristic attached to people on the job. Fellow workers are much aware of their places on the seniority roster and, as we shall see, these seniority differences may have important effects on their relations with each other.

Ethnic and community status differences may also have an impact on the workplace. People are identified as Irish, Polish, Italian, Jewish, or Negro according to the characteristics of the name, facial features, hair color, skin color, and so on. On occasion, common ethnic membership may serve to draw people together and differences in ethnic identification may stir rivalries.

Differences in status in the community are not so readily identified in the plant, and yet there may be behaviors that suggest such differences. There tends also to be an associated characteristic: education. Organization members tend to learn how much education a given individual has had and to respond to him to some extent in terms of that degree of education.

## SYMBOLIC ACTS

The actions and the words of an individual provide symbols through which others assess their relations with him.

For example, John Gossett, new vice-president of Inland Steel Container Company, was awaited by a delegation of local union leaders just as he was taking over his new position. When Gossett came out of his office to announce that he would not meet with this delegation at this time and place, Lucius Love, union president, stepped forward to shake hands. Gossett put his hands behind his back.[5]

In our society the shaking of hands is such a common ceremonial gesture that we endow it with little symbolic meaning. The refusal to shake hands is something else again. Gossett meant only to indicate by this gesture that he did not recognize the right of the union to demand to meet with him at this time and in this situation. Love and his fellow union officers interpreted the gesture as a declaration of war on the union. Since Love was a Negro, Gossett's refusal of his hand also suggested that the vice-president was anti-Negro. Love confirmed this interpretation in the first grievance meeting when he introduced a white union officer, who had not been present in the original delegation, to Mr. Gossett. Gossett shook hands without any hesitation (by which he intended to mean only that he was willing to meet with the union on grievances).

The interpretation of this symbolic act to the workers by union leaders served to reinforce already negative sentiments toward management and to establish John Gossett as the arch enemy of the union. Here the symbolic act influenced sentiments of personal identification.

A symbolic act may also serve to bring people closer together, to open up increasing opportunities for interaction, and to pave the way for the development of positive sentiments. Consider the case of S. Buchsbaum and Co. and the United Chemical Workers Union. Using a labor spy, President Herbert J. Buchsbaum had broken a strike in 1935 and destroyed the union. When a union was again organizing in 1941, Buchsbaum was just as determined to resist. The strike came at a time when inventories were high and orders slow. Management could have kept the plant closed for a month or longer with little damage, and yet Buchsbaum changed his mind and signed a contract after a three-day strike.

What caused the change? The story is told in detail elsewhere.[6] Here I shall simply present a symbolic act which had a far-reaching effect

---

[5] Actual names used in this case. For description and analysis of the case, see my *Pattern of Industrial Peace* (New York: Harper & Bros., 1951).

[6] Actual names used in this case. A. H. Whiteford, W. F. Whyte, and Burleigh B. Gardner, "From Conflict to Cooperation: A Study in Union-Management Relations," special issue of *Applied Anthropology*, Vol. V, No. 4 (Fall, 1946).

upon Buchsbaum's sentiments. We see the act as described by Sidney Garfield, union business agent, and then by Herbert Buchsbaum. The key symbols are italicized in each case.

This is Garfield's story:

I think something that made him (Mr. Buchsbaum) trust me was rather interesting. During the strike, things were pretty rough for a while and we had a number of clashes when people tried to get into the plant. One time one of the men came flying down the street about sixty miles an hour in a car and ran right up on the sidewalk to the doors of the plant and tried to let people in that way. He might easily have run over some of our boys standing around, but they got between him and the door of the plant and had him trapped there. The strikers were all for taking care of him quickly right then and there and turning the car over in the street, but I knew enough to realize that that would be a bad move because of *the great American tradition of respect for property*, so I made them leave the car alone. I don't mean that I was easy. There was one fellow who was trying to sneak in, and I pulled him out of his car and just kicked him down the street.

When this incident came up, the chief company detective was standing right inside the door with a gun in his hand, but he was afraid to use it, and I found out later that he was impressed by what had happened and had gone up and told Herb Buchsbaum about my respect for property, which apparently made some impression on Herb, too. It's the little things which make the difference.

Let us see how this situation looked to Mr. Buchsbaum.

There was quite a bit of *violence and sabotage in our 1935 strike*. Expensive equipment was smashed, sand was thrown in bearings, materials were destroyed, and there were some bricks thrown through the windows.

The 1941 strike was quite different. A few people got beaten up, but *the company suffered no property damage*. The union had good discipline on that point. There was one time when some of our people were trying to get through the picket line into the plant. They drove up in a car onto the sidewalk and right in front of the plant entrance to get the people in. That car endangered the lives of some of the picketers, and they rushed up and wanted to turn it over. Garfield stepped in then and wouldn't let them do anything to the car. That made an impression on me when I was told about it. I felt that these were *responsible people*. I didn't agree with them, but I could see that they were going out of their way not to harm the company.

Acts may also be symbolic of the individual's social ranking. Does the individual drive his car into a parking space marked with his name, or just anywhere in a parking lot? Does he go to eat in the executive dining room, or in the employees' cafeteria? Does he go to the executive washroom, or doesn't he have that treasured key?

If he works in a hotel, can he sign his name to an officer's check in one of the restaurants? This question was the key to a problem described to us by a general manager of a hotel:

I put a new man on as chief engineer last year. I agreed to pay him 50 cents a day more than his predecessor got, but he wasn't to take his lunches. In the hotel business we find that if people are just free to eat what they want, they don't appreciate it, and it's really wasteful. Besides the 50 cents, this man got a $700 bonus at the end of the year that his predecessor didn't get, so he was doing much better.

When we talked it over at the start, it was all right with him, but I noticed as time went on that he wasn't really getting into the spirit of the organization. He was just going through the motions of his job. He was generating the electricity and the steam, but that was about all. Finally I was going away for a couple of weeks' vacation, and I didn't want to leave it that way, so I called him into the office, and I said to him, "Look here, you and I don't seem to be getting along together. I'd like to know what's the matter."

"Well," he said, "I want my lunches." I pointed out to him that he was getting 50 cents a day for those lunches, and he was getting a $700 bonus his predecessor didn't get.

He said that was all true, but he still said, "I want my lunches."

"Well," I said, "I can't see your point, but maybe I'm wrong. Tell me, why do you want your lunches?"

He said, "How can I be an executive if I can't go into the dining room and sign a management check like the other executives?"

Well, I gave him his lunches and after that everything was all right. Now, that may seem like a little thing, but if I'd taken care of that right in the beginning, he would have been worth a thousand dollars more to us.[7]

In most cases of symbolic acts having status or ranking implications, some physical object will be associated with the act: the parking lot, the executive dining room, the key to the executive wash room, the management check, and so on. The symbolic significance of objects will be discussed further at a later point in this chapter.

### WORDS  AS  SYMBOLS

When we consider the symbolic aspects of words, we run into difficult problems of classification and analysis. Not all words refer to the relations among men or between man and physical objects, but a large proportion of words used in speech do have such implications. What, then, are we to do with words?

Our problem here is not an inability to observe. In many situations, we can observe what is said, making detailed notes on oral statements; on some occasions we can even tape-record conversations so that we have a complete record of content. But gathering the data may be only the beginning of our problems. For example, one researcher was able to tape-record a series of collective bargaining and mediation sessions. The transcribed data on this one case ran to 5,000 typwritten pages. This was rich data, to be sure, but analyzing it required developing categories that would permit some general statements about what was happening in this situation.

The most comprehensive scheme for categorizing oral interaction is

_____

[7] From my *Human Relations in the Restaurant Industry* (New York: McGraw-Hill Book Co., Inc., 1948), pp. 345–46.

that developed by R. Freed Bales at Harvard.[8] His scheme involves classifying each utterance, gesture, or facial expression in terms of its assumed intent from the standpoint of the speaker. He uses six categories to represent the emotional expressions of agreement or disagreement, solidarity or tension, and six others centering around the task problems of asking or giving suggestion, opinion, or orientation. The Bales method also involves noting who speaks to whom, and in this way is related to methods concentrating strictly on the quantitative pattern, without verbal content.

The Bales method has given rise to a series of significant studies, but in nearly all cases the research has been confined to experimental group situations studied in the laboratory. While the future may see more use of the method in studies of organizations, its great complexity makes its use difficult in most field situations. Since we do not yet have more than small fragments of data to report from organizational studies by this method, we will not be dealing with the approach further in this book.

A simplification and modification of the Bales' method has been used with considerable promise by Paul Lawrence and his associates in *The Changing of Organizational Behavior Patterns*.[9] Lawrence was studying the attempt of a supermarket chain to decentralize authority and responsibility. He needed to have methods of observing behavior which would enable him to determine the extent of decentralization that had taken place. The link between the main office and the stores was the district manager. The Lawrence study involved observation of a number of district manager–store manager pairs.

A research man followed each pair and observed them throughout the period when the district manager was in each store. The method developed enabled the researchers, in addition to recording the total talking time of each man, to categorize each statement under one of four categories: question, information, opinion, or suggestion or direction. The observer simultaneously recorded whether the topic involved people, merchandise, record systems, physical plant, or small talk.

In cases where the district manager did most of the talking and where most of his comments would be categorized as opinions, suggestions, or directions, it could be said that he was not delegating authority and responsibility. This method enabled the researchers to compare one district manager with another, and to compare the behavior of one district manager over different points of time to see whether increasing degrees of delegation did take place. The findings of this study will be discussed later in Chapter 25, "On the Meaning of Delegation."

The Bales and Lawrence methods involve schemes of classification

---

[8] *Interaction Process Analysis: A Method For the Study of Small Groups* (Cambridge: Addison-Wesley Press, 1950).

[9] Boston: Harvard University Graduate School of Business Administration, 1958.

designed to apply to the total flow of verbal and gestural interaction. What we might call the *significant symbol* approach tackles the study of verbal and gestural expression from an opposite point of view. The researcher makes no attempt to categorize all of the content he observes, but he notes that certain marked behavior changes follow upon emission of certain verbal or gestural symbols. In some cases, the behavioral changes observed are so marked that it would be impossible to explain them without taking into account the specific words or gestures used in the moment preceding the behavior change.

Although the researcher can hardly accept as fully satisfactory any scheme which leaves nearly all of observed verbal and gestural content unanalyzed and unclassified, at the same time he sees equally compelling arguments against methods which would lump that occasional but crucial set of symbols which leads immediately to a significant behavior change together with the large mass of symbols to be observed in any conversation. The student of *significant symbols* begins by observing that, on a certain occasion, A says to B a few words which seem to result in an immediate and marked change in B's behavior and relationship to A. The student analyzes the particular symbols in terms of the past relationship between the two men and the nature of the new behavior and relationship. Perhaps then he observes a change in a different direction in the relations between C and D. He examines this, as he did with A and B before, and files his two cases away for later attention. When a number of cases of such changes have been assembled, the student is in a position to make some tentative classifications regarding types of significant symbols and their impact upon human relations.

In examining words, we shall be particularly concerned with the symbols that suggest ranking or personal identification and are thus linked to the corresponding set of sentiments.

Titles are words that obviously symbolize status. We take this for granted with titles at high levels, but we need to recognize this also for low-ranking positions. In positions at the bottom of organizations, even the title itself may be a source of problems. For example, a restaurant manager once told us about a problem he had with a woman employee who came in to announce that she was quitting. His interview with her elicited no expressions of dissatisfaction with the job and the work situation. Why then did she want to quit? She told him that the night before she had become involved in an argument with some friends and relatives. In the heat of the argument, one of them pointed a finger at her and called out, "You dishwasher!" No adjective was used with the term. Apparently, none was thought to be necessary.

Words may have an important bearing upon the development of friendly or hostile sentiments. Symbols may represent similarity or dissimilarity among people, or, more directly, friendly or hostile sentiments among them.

The two categories are likely to have the same meaning for people. When we hear one man say of another, "We have a lot in common," we take the statement also as expressing positive sentiments. In general, when A sees similarities between himself and B in characteristics important to A, this perception tends to be associated with positive sentiments toward B. This suggests that when A has been assuming that he and B were totally dissimilar and he is then exposed to symbols pointing out similarities, these new symbols may make possible a shift to more favorable sentiments.

In more general terms, we recognize certain words as implying friendly sentiments and other words as implying negative or hostile sentiments toward us. Subject to the qualifications to be introduced shortly, if a man emits friendly symbols toward us, we increase our friendly sentiments toward him, interact with him more often, and are more inclined to respond to initiations of activity from him. If he emits hostile symbols, we are inclined to react with negative sentiments, to decrease our interactions, and to resist his efforts to initiate activities for us—unless outside pressures require us to interact and respond. (The negative sentiments would arise in any case.)

If there were no qualifications to these statements, the task of manipulating men would be simple indeed. We could reduce it all to one proposition: sweet talk will get you anything.

Let us now add the complications that realism requires.

## SITUATIONAL DETERMINANTS OF THE MEANING OF SYMBOLS

The social meaning of the verbal symbols cannot be determined simply by analyzing the words themselves. The meaning will depend upon the preexisting relationship between speaker and listener, the situation in which the words are uttered, and the way in which they are spoken.

We often hear good friends say to each other words that would be considered offensive and insulting by men who did not have such a friendly relationship. This downgrading of one's friends is part of the American kidding pattern which we use—if we are wise—only among our friends.

We are all familiar with the traditional frontier admonition: "Smile when you say that, pardner." Social meaning clearly is influenced by facial expression, tone of voice, and gestures accompanying the words.

Nor do apparently friendly words necessarily symbolize a set of favorable sentiments. When we hear such words from an individual toward whom we hold hostile sentiments, our first interpretation is likely to be that he is trying to trick us, and we try to think what move he is planning against us under cover of the sweet talk.

For once we can say that a popular maxim has general applicability:

actions speak louder than words. If we have observed no actions that symbolize for us a friendly relationship, then we are inclined to be skeptical of the friendly words. Only as the actions and words seem to go together do we let down our guard and interpret the friendly words as suggesting favorable sentiments. This is illustrated in the following case.

During World War II, one particular management had been having some trouble in holding on to its labor force. As part of a personnel program to meet this problem, management set up an employee library. The idea was to make it very convenient for employees to pick up reading matter to take home with them. The library was stocked with detective stories and other light fiction. As an afterthought, management added a few technical books, just in case some workers wished to study up in connection with the work they were doing.

Several months later, when management people were assessing the use of the library, they were surprised and discouraged to find that practically none of the light fiction books had ever been taken out. On the other hand, the technical volumes were constantly in demand. But, in spite of the large number of workers taking the technical books home, those books remained in extraordinarily good condition.

When Burleigh Gardner was called in to advise management on this situation, a few interviews with employees gave him the explanation. There had previously been many conflicts between workers and management. The workers were strongly hostile to management. It followed from this that an apparently friendly act by management must have some evil intent. What could it be? It must be a scheme to find out which workers were really seriously interested in their jobs and therefore should be considered for promotion. The library could readily provide management with the names of those who had taken out the light fiction and the names of those who had taken home the technical books. Obviously, the light fiction readers were not going to get any consideration from management. Therefore, the workers avoided the light fiction and signed up for the technical books. But it was not necessary to read a technical book. All that was necessary was to get your name on the library card for that book.

Needless to say, management had no intention of using the library for this purpose. Nevertheless, according to the "logic of the sentiments" held by workers toward management, their theory of the purpose of the library was quite reasonable.

## WHAT THINGS MEAN

That physical objects can symbolize status is now just as well known to the layman as to the sociologist. We all recognize that the size of the desk, and the design and material used in its construction, can symbolize the status of the executive in the organization. We are told in advertisements that "a title on the door rates a Bigelow on the floor," but we find in firms that do provide executives with carpets, that not just any old title will do. The man may have to be quite high up in order to rate a carpet.

A telephone on the desk is not just a means of communication. It also serves to point out that the man who has one is more important than the man who lacks one. The interoffice communication system (squawk box) may have even more marked status implications. Since only a few channels are available for such a box, the executive who makes the decisions on these matters includes only those with whom he feels it is important to be able to communicate instantly. The man who is on the box is generally thought to be more important than the man who is not.

The clothes people wear have status significance, as we see especially in the distinction between "blue collar" and "white collar" workers.

The objects people work on or with tend also to have status connotations. Mary, the working supervisor of the fish station in a large restaurant, found the status symbols attached to her job particularly distressing. While management people considered her skill to be above that of women involved in preparing chickens, vegetables, and salads, and although she was paid accordingly at a higher rate, she could not escape from the negative evaluations many workers gave to the food on which she worked. She resented it bitterly when people walking by her station would sniff, wrinkle up their noses, and make unpleasant faces. She told me that she objected to being called the "fish woman." The proper title should be "seafood station supervisor."

These reactions of fellow workers so distressed Mary that she finally left the restaurant, looking, presumably, for some place where the true value of fish—or seafood—would be properly appreciated. Management people in the organization were aware of her problem to some extent. In fact, one of them told me that fresh fish do not "smell"; they have a "savory aroma." But management was unable to protect Mary from the symbolic evaluation of her status that she suffered at the hands of other workers.

## ACTIVITIES AND CONDITIONS OF WORK

The activities people perform on their jobs tend to be interpreted symbolically as reflecting the status or social ranking of the individuals. That is, the people who hold what are considered to be the more desirable jobs tend also to be accorded more prestige from their fellow workers. Activities thought to involve high degrees of skill, judgment, and responsibility tend also to have high status. In general, there is a close relationship between pay and worker status evaluations of jobs, but the correlation is rarely perfect, and there may often be serious discrepancies that give rise to problems between workers and management.

The conditions associated with the job tend to have symbolic status implications for that job. Other things being equal, a clean job outranks a dirty job.

Research in recent years indicates that working conditions in themselves may not be an important influence on the satisfaction of the worker with his job or with management, but this finding may be due to the general high level that working conditions have reached in the United States in recent years. We may assume that, within a given range of possibilities, working conditions will simply be accepted by workers without having a noticeable effect upon their job satisfaction. We should assume, however, that exceedingly poor working conditions would lead to negative sentiments both toward the job and toward management.

Two qualifications to that general statement should be added. The goodness or badness of working conditions can be to some degree a relative matter from culture to culture. In an underdeveloped nation, industrial conditions that would be thought outrageous by American workers may be taken for granted by workers who have never experienced anything better. Even within a single society, workers do not seem to have absolute standards of the social meaning of good or bad working conditions. If men are working under difficult conditions but feel that, given the technology and work process, management can do nothing to improve the conditions, then the conditions themselves do not serve to symbolize management's sentiments toward workers. On the other hand, if workers experience difficult conditions which they feel could reasonably be improved by management, then the conditions serve to symbolize lack of management concern for workers, and perception of these symbols reinforces negative worker sentiments toward management.

## SYMBOLS FOR THE ORGANIZATION

So far we have been talking about symbols having a bearing upon the relations of individuals to each other. We have considered how symbols tend to rank people in an organization and to classify them as hostile or friendly to each other.

We should recognize that the individual does not identify himself solely with other individuals. He also identifies himself, positively or negatively, with the organization as a whole and perhaps with a certain subunit of it.

In an organization, there must be some symbols that stand for the organization as a whole to its members. In the military, the symbols are readily recognized: the type of uniform identifying a particular branch of the service, the insignia on the uniform indicating more particularly the unit of membership (as well as the rank in it).

In business firms, the total organizational symbols (beyond the trademark) are not so obvious. The executive who does not recognize the symbols of his organization may blunder into a good deal of trouble.

The point is illustrated in the following case, which involved a clash between Mr. Jefferson, the new manager of Everbest Restaurant, and the assistant manager, Miss Lucas, who had been with the organization for many years. Everbest was an old established organization well known for its high-quality foods. But it had been losing money, and Jefferson was sent in "with a free hand" to change things. He described in this way some of his difficulties with Miss Lucas:

> I'll tell you, I had a hard time with her. When I came in, Everbest had been losing ground in competition, and I had a free hand to make changes. Well, I went ahead and changed things right off the bat. That was my mistake. I tried to do it all myself, too. One thing I went to work on was the menu. I went ahead and simplified the menu, and then I changed the price structure. That caused a lot of disturbance.
>
> I'll tell you though what upset her most. At the time I came in, Everbest had served nothing but U.S. prime beef. Any beef on our menu was always U.S. prime. Of course, we want to serve good meat, but I didn't think we had to serve that particular grade every time, so I changed it.
>
> Well, at the same time I changed the chocolate sauce. I'm telling you, we were serving a brand of chocolate sauce that they would have been ashamed to serve in a cheap restaurant. It was terrible. I went ahead and put in a much better grade of chocolate sauce.
>
> You see, I wasn't running down the quality. But when I changed that U.S. prime beef, Lucas got terribly upset. You'd have thought the world was coming to an end. That was a terrible thing to do. She didn't think that Everbest could survive without serving U.S. prime beef.[10]

Even without consulting Miss Lucas, we can readily see that the manager and assistant manager viewed the problem from quite different angles. To Jefferson, this was simply a practical problem: What quality of foods should be bought and what prices should be charged in order to enable the restaurant to cope with competition most successfully? Taking this approach, he could not see that it was necessary to serve U.S. prime beef all the time. He felt that the type of meat purchased should be determined in line with the over-all business requirements of the organization. The same reasoning called for an improvement in the quality of the chocolate sauce. So, according to Jefferson, he made changes resulting in a slight lowering of standards in one item and a considerable improvement in another.

What Jefferson overlooked was that to Miss Lucas this was not primarily a practical problem. Without realizing it, he was attacking a symbol that represented Everbest restaurant to Miss Lucas and gave meaning to her connection with it. That restaurant had stood for U.S. prime beef for years, and U.S. prime beef had come to stand for the Everbest restaurant in the thoughts and feelings of Miss Lucas. She had come to take pride in being associated with a restaurant that served

---

[10] *Human Relations in the Restaurant Industry, op. cit.*, p. 336.

nothing but the very best. And when she thought of the very best, she didn't think of chocolate sauce. She thought of a few items that she considered especially important. These were the symbols of the restaurant. Her reactions to Jefferson showed that U.S. prime beef had become for her one of the chief Everbest symbols.

Our study of status in the kitchen showed that the highest status jobs were associated with the preparation and cooking of meat. It does not take a special study to show that, in this country, beef has the highest status of all meats. If beef has such symbolic significance, then the quality of beef served becomes a vital concern, and U.S. prime beef can readily become one of the symbols by which the members identify their organization.

Suppose we wish to shift the identification of individuals from organization A to organization B. Must we seek to undermine the symbols associated with A and promote a new set of symbols to be associated with B? Or can we preserve the set of symbols to which people have been orienting their behavior and build the old symbols into the new organizational relationships?

One answer to these questions was provided by Pope Gregory VII as long ago as the year 601. At this time the Church had been attempting to convert the heathen Britons, and two of the missionaries, finding that they were making little progress, wrote to Rome for advice. The Pope responded with these words:

> We must refrain from destroying the temples of the idols. It is necessary only to destroy the idols, and to sprinkle holy water in these same temples, to build ourselves altars and place holy relics therein. If the construction of these temples is solid, good, and useful, they will pass from the cult of demons to the service of the true God; because it will come to pass that the nation, seeing the continued existence of its old places of devotion, will be disposed, by a sort of habit, to go there to adore the true God.
>
> It is said that the men of this nation are accustomed to sacrificing oxen. It is necessary that this custom be converted into a Christian rite. On the day of the dedication of the temples thus changed into churches, and similarly for the festivals of the saints, whose relics will be placed there, you should allow them, as in the past, to build structures of foliage around these same churches. They shall bring to the churches their animals, and kill them, no longer as offerings to the devil, but for Christian banquets in name and honor of God, to whom, after satiating themselves, they will give thanks. Only thus, by preserving for men some of the worldly joys, will you lead them more easily to relish the joys of the spirit.[11]

This case suggests that skillful administrators have always recognized the significance of symbols in organizational behavior—though few have ever spoken of them so explicitly as did Gregory the Great. It is our task in this book to make the symbols explicit, to deal with them systematically, and to relate them effectively to interactions, activities, and senti-

---

[11] My translation from Giuseppe Pitré, *Feste Patronali in Sicilia.*

ments. If we are successful in this, the knowledge can be used both by students of organization and by men of action.

## SUMMARY ON SYMBOLISM

Let us now put our conclusions on symbols in general terms.

Symbols serve to represent the relations among men, and between men and physical objects. They thus serve to orient us as to the social meaning of the world around us, indicating what sentiments, interactions, and activities are appropriate for a given situation.

Symbols may trigger certain interactions and activities without any prior change in sentiments taking place. In other situations, we note first an impact of symbols upon sentiments, with changes in interactions and activities following upon the sentiment change.

A symbol does not have an absolute meaning. Its meaning is dependent upon the context of the situation in which it appears. The context should be examined in terms of time as well as in terms of the characteristics of the present situation. The individual will interpret a given symbol in terms of his pre-existing sentiments and the interactions and activities of his past experience. He will also interpret the symbol in terms of the current context of interactions and activities. However, a symbol which does not fit into this context may open up possibilities for change in sentiments, interactions, and activities. Later chapters will provide many examples of symbols that played important roles in the behavior of workers and management people.

# Chapter 3  *THE INDIVIDUAL IN HIS ORGANIZATIONAL ENVIRONMENT*

TO EXPLAIN the behavior of an individual in an organization, we need to have the answers to the following three questions:

1. What is Joe like? In other words, what is it in the way of customary patterns of sentiment, interactions, and activities that he brings into the work situation?
2. What impersonal forces in the work environment are influencing his activities, interactions, and sentiments?
3. How do others in the workplace directly influence Joe's activities, interactions, and sentiments?

## WHAT IS JOE LIKE?

How shall we answer the question: What is Joe like?

It is often said that, in dealing with the individual and the organization, we are operating on two different levels and therefore must use two different sets of concepts. There might be no serious objection to this point of view if means were provided for linking the two sets of concepts, but more often we find the student of personality and the student of organization operating so independently of each other that their ideas never meet.

It is my aim to use the same set of concepts on both personality and organization. Since my main focus of attention is upon the organization, I shall not attempt the depth of analysis that would satisfy the specialist in personality study. On the other hand, my approach provides for the linkage between personality and organization, and this, I feel, is an important advantage.

I assume that the personality Joe brings with him to the organization is one of the important determinants of his behavior in the organization. I also assume that, by the time he is an adult, Joe's personality is rather firmly shaped. The personality may be subject to modification by the situation in which the individual works, and yet no adult personality can be completely refashioned so as to adjust it better to the work situation.

38

There are some individuals who can adjust to a variety of situations and others whose flexibility is extremely limited, but I assume that no one can adjust to the full range of work situations to be described in this book. It is therefore important to examine both the personality Joe brings to the job and the social requirements the job places on Joe. If we can describe personalities and social requirements of jobs in the same terms, we can advance our knowledge of the relations of individuals to organizations. As we concentrate upon the organization in this book, we shall only attempt a few preliminary steps toward this integration of personality in organization.

Looking at personality in the same way as we do organization, we shall be concerned with the pattern of interactions, activities, and sentiments that Joe has developed before coming to work. We shall ask some of the same questions already asked regarding Joe's behavior in the organization.

Is Joe accustomed to interacting with many or few individuals? Has he customarily interacted with a high or low frequency? Does he tend to initiate interaction with others, or does he tend to sit back and wait for others to approach him?

We need to know something regarding the types of activities Joe has carried on in the past and also the social context for these activities. Has he tended to act alone, with a single other individual, or as part of a group? When involved in activities with others, has he tended to take the initiative in getting these activities going, or has he been mainly a follower who responds to the initiative of others?

We assume that Joe's reactions to authority figures, to peers, and to subordinates will be influenced by the experiences Joe has had in the process of growing up. To the child in the family, the parents represent authority, and his relations with them are bound to influence his later relations with authority figures. But the individual does not interact exclusively with parents. He may also develop peer group associations: a group of friends within which he interacts frequently. Life experiences are not uniform in this respect. Some individuals lead a highly active peer group life from early years, whereas others never develop strong peer group ties. These differences should make a difference in the individual's integration into the work group in later years.

To some extent we can gain answers to these questions regarding interactions and activities through intensive interviews with Joe and with others who have known him. Such interviews should enable us to distinguish between extremes: for example, between the individual who is socially isolated, having little participation with others in interaction and activities, and the individual who has a high rate of interaction and social activity. We find that precise quantitative measures of personality cannot be provided by such an approach, and yet they are not beyond our reach if we wish to pursue this line of study.

Eliot D. Chapple has developed the Interaction Chronograph which enables us to place personality assessment on a quantitative basis.[1] The Chronograph provides us with what might be called micromeasures of interaction, in contrast to the gross measures we can get through counting the number of times A interacts with B and the amount of time they spend in each other's company. The Chronograph is designed to measure the interpersonal activity that goes on within a single interpersonal contact.

As the Chronograph has been most generally applied, the subject whose interaction pattern is being measured is given an interview of approximately half an hour's length by a trained interviewer. The interview is not standardized as to content, but is highly standardized as to interactional form. That is, there are five periods within the total interview, with the first, third, and fifth being adjustment periods. During these the interviewer seeks to encourage the subject to talk and tries to avoid interruptions or failures to respond to the subject. The second period is the silent period in which the interviewer fails to respond to the subject for a specified number of seconds. In the fourth period, the interviewer systematically interrupts the informant and maintains the interruption for a specified number of seconds.

While this may sound like an artificial situation, experience seems to show that people in general are so little aware of the form of interaction that the structure of the interview does not become apparent to them. Each mode of interaction is common in our society. Some individuals regularly behave in the adjustment pattern which avoids interruption or failure to respond. Others consistently interrupt. Still others are consistently slow in responding. The only unusual thing about the interview situation is the combination of all three types of conversational behavior within the same interview. This provides opportunities to test the reactions of the subject to the three types of interactional situations. Since the form of interaction is standardized from one interview to the next, the method also enables the researcher to make quantitative comparisons of the interaction patterns of one individual with another.

An observer to the interview operates the Chronograph. When he observes individual A active in speech, gesture, change of physical posture or facial expression, he presses down the key assigned to A. Pressing another key enables him similarly to time the interactional behavior of B. When both A and B are active at the same time, the observer presses down both keys. When neither is active, neither key is pressed.

The Chronograph makes its own measurements, in time units, of

[1] See E. D. Chapple, "The Standard Experimental (Stress) Interview as Used in Interaction Chronograph Investigations," *Human Organization*, Vol. XII, No. 2 (Summer, 1953). See also E. D. and Martha F. Chapple and Judith A. Repp, "Behavioral Definitions of Personality and Temperament Characteristics," *Human Organization*, Vol. XIII, No. 4 (Winter, 1955).

periods of activity and inactivity of each individual, and of the synchronization of their interactions.

The results achieved by this method can be put to a variety of uses. For purposes of this book, the most interesting possibility is that of relating the measured interaction pattern of the individual to the interactional requirements of a particular job. The results already achieved by Chapple in this field suggest the utility of his method. Unfortunately, not enough work has been done so that we can talk very systematically about the interactional requirements of jobs and how they relate to interaction patterns of individuals. This discussion, therefore, is designed simply to indicate one of the important ways in which the study of the individual personality may be more effectively linked to the study of the organization.

Let us now turn to the sentiments that make up another aspect of Joe's personality. We assume that some of Joe's sentiments regarding management, unions, appropriate rates of pay, and an acceptable rate of progress in the organization are shaped to a considerable degree by his experiences in family and community. We shall be concerned with the fit between the sentiments he brings to the job and the influences of the job situation itself.

With that much background, let us return to the question: What is Joe like?

We can start painting the picture with a broad brush and work toward a more detailed analysis. To begin with, Joe is the way he is because he is an American—a citizen of the United States. We tend to take this for granted, but we have only to study behavior in other countries to realize that many of Joe's sentiments, and even some of his activities and modes of interaction, are items he has acquired from his own culture. In Chapter 4, "The Work World in Intercultural Perspective," we shall seek to show how differences in culture lead to different beliefs and behavior.

Joe has also been shaped by the social structure of the community in which he has grown to maturity, and by the position of his parents and immediate associates in that structure. Some of these influences will be examined in Chapter 5, dealing with "Industry and the Community."

We shall also wish to take a look at Joe's particular personality in terms of the role he plays in industry. We shall look at him in the role of subordinate and also in the role of superior, in each case seeking to relate his personality to the behavior he manifests on the job.

In Chapter 8, "From Kitchen to Customer," we shall see what difference personality makes to the ability of a worker to adjust to a difficult combination of interactions and activities.

In Chapter 15, "Who Goes Union and Why," we shall seek to fit together the worker's early social experience with his response to a unionization drive.

In Chapter 23, "Managerial Succession," we will be concerned in part with the personality of the individual who plays the role of supervisor. We shall seek to demonstrate some of the ways in which early social experience affects the pattern of supervisory behavior the individual manifests in the organization.

The material in those chapters will simply be suggestive of various possible interconnections between personality and organizational behavior. This will not be a major focus of our interest. We assume that a large part of the individual's behavior in the organization is to be explained in terms of his membership in a particular work group. Through examining the relationships developed within the group and the forces impinging upon the group from the outside, we shall seek to determine why Joe acts as he does—even as we recognize that personality differences from one Joe to another will introduce some variability in his responses.

## THE IMPACT OF IMPERSONAL FORCES

Strictly speaking, we might say that no impersonal forces impinge on Joe in his workplace. The factory was built by men; the machines were built and installed by men. The wage payment and incentive system was installed by men. Altogether, Joe works in a man-made environment.

Nevertheless, we will find it useful to distinguish between those man-made forces which strike him in an impersonal fashion, and the interactions and activities which he directly experiences with and from other men.

On the impersonal side, we can regard the organization structure, the economic reward system, the work flow and technology, and the legal framework of the shop.

The organization structure establishes the positions of individuals in the organization and the responsibilities attached to the various jobs. This structure not only defines Joe's position, but has important effects upon his interactions. For example, whether the foreman supervises three men or thirty men will have an important effect upon the interactions between Joe and the foreman. These structural influences are explored in Chapter 6, "Formal Organization Structure."

Everyone recognizes that behavior in industry is influenced by money, but just how behavior is influenced is a large and complex question. In Chapter 7, we will consider a preliminary framework for handling the impact of money upon men, and nearly all of the cases discussed in the following chapters will deal with some aspects of this man-money problem.

The technology and the organization of the work flow can have pervasive and profound influences upon behavior and relations. This technological framework may determine whether Joe interacts with few or many in his job, and will even channel within certain limits just who the individuals in his interaction range will be. This framework will determine whether Joe is working with a number of individuals who are doing the same thing together, whether he is working on an individual machine in a department manned by other workers also working individually on similar machines, or whether he is in a department surrounded by men doing quite different things. The physical conditions at work and the variety or routinization of the job will effect his sentiments toward it. These various influences stemming from the technology and work flow will be explored in Chapters 8–13.

Joe's behavior is also affected by the legal framework prevailing in the plant where he works. The term "legal" here is not limited to the laws enacted by Congress, or by state or local authorities. In any workplace, a set of rules and regulations arises governing required, optional, and proscribed activities. For this legal code to have a direct effect upon Joe, someone or some group must intervene to punish him when he violates a rule. However, Joe does not learn what the rules are simply through direct personal experience. He hears them discussed, and he observes or hears about cases where other individuals have been penalized. In this way he learns to respond to the set of symbols that we call the legal framework—to recognize that violation of some rules will bring almost sure punishment, whereas violation of other rules may involve little if any adverse consequences.

The impact upon Joe of impersonal influences may be either direct or symbolic. For example, the work flow and technology have an immediate and direct effect upon him, determining within limits his work activities and even his interactions. But when a technological change is about to take place, Joe may begin reacting to this change well before the new machine or new arrangement of the work flow has been introduced into the department and has, therefore, had a direct effect upon him. When he hears that a technological change is proposed, he perceives the change symbolically in terms of his own past experience with technological change, and also in terms of the sentiments expressed to him about such matters by fellow workers.

## RECIPROCITY AND REWARDS AND PUNISHMENTS

The normal individual is an active and gregarious fellow. He would rather be doing something than doing nothing, at least for a good part of his waking hours. While individuals vary greatly in their interactional requirements, the normal individual is not happy to be left by himself for long periods of time.

Thus, without any imposed plan, we could expect a certain amount of activity and interaction to take place among individuals who are at the same location, just because of the intrinsic rewards that activity and

r. However, while being active and seeing people can be
nds in themselves, this is true only to a very limited degree.
he motive power to get work done, management must link re-
n certain classes of activities and interactions. To discourage
ypes of behavior considered contrary to management goals,
ement seeks to associate certain activities and interactions with
hment.

In general, we may say that in his life in the plant—as well as elsewhere—Joe seeks to earn rewards and escape penalties. This statement
by itself tells us nothing, for we can always explain whatever a man
does by saying that he is either seeking to win a reward or to avoid a
penalty. It is only as we begin to explore systematically the nature of
rewards and penalties in the organization that the generalization becomes
of some value.

Before proceeding further, we should note two cautions. In the first
place, we should not assume that all items of behavior are generated by
specific and immediate offers of rewards or threats of punishment. While
direct rewards and penalties play an important role in teaching the
infant and small child what to do and what not to do, by the time the
child has grown up and gone to work, he has "internalized" his sentiments about behavior. In other words, he will do what he thinks is good
without expecting or demanding an immediate reward. Similarly, he will
avoid doing what he considers to be bad even when he is confident that
he can escape the penalties. (We are not here concerned with how the
sentiments Joe brings to the workplace were formed.)

Even as we acknowledge the importance of "internalization," we must
recognize the importance of rewards and penalties in reinforcing Joe's
tendencies to do what he thinks is right and in extinguishing his tendencies to do what he considers wrong. If he does over and over again
what he thinks is good and nobody ever rewards him for this behavior,
in time he is likely to do it with diminishing enthusiasm, if indeed he
continues at all. Similarly, if he observes others around him doing what
he considers wrong and escaping penalties, he is eventually likely to say
to himself, "Why should I be a sucker when those fellows are getting
away with it?"

Joe's visualization of himself as a "sucker" introduces the concept of
*cost*. He can hardly regard himself as a "sucker" if he sees no alternative
courses of action worth considering. It is only as he keeps on doing what
he thinks he should while seeing attractive alternative possibilities that
we can say, with Homans, that the continuation of the current activity in-
curs for him a *cost:* the cost of foregoing alternative activities. As the
externally offered rewards for his current activity come to seem small or
nonexistent to Joe, and the potential rewards for an alternative activity
seem to grow larger, we can say that the cost of continuing the current
activity seems to increase. As the *cost* increases, so does Joe's tendency to

regard himself as a "sucker" if he continues what he has been doing.

Rewards and penalties are important in getting Joe to change his sentiments regarding appropriate behavior. Joe's sentiments regarding what is right and wrong may be well formed by the time he goes to work, but most of these sentiments do not have any obvious and easy application to the work situation. He develops with experience a new set of sentiments to cover that situation. This means that sentiments do change with experience, and the rewards and penalties Joe receives play an important part in the shaping process.

We must also recognize that there will be individual differences in what is found rewarding or penalizing. In the extreme case, the masochist takes pleasure in experiences that everyone else finds punishing. While this is true, it is not of much importance to us. Few people are masochists, so that for most situations we can disregard that possibility. As a practical matter, we can assume certain broad similarities among men in what they find rewarding or penalizing—and then make certain allowances for individual differences. For example, we can assume that everyone in the plant likes money, and therefore the offer of money will be regarded as a reward. We recognize, however, that there are individual differences in the dedication to money. While everyone likes to have it, for some individuals it ranks very high in the scale of values, whereas with others it ranks relatively low. For some problems, we assume a similarity of sentiments regarding money and disregard individual differences. For other types of problems, individual differences will be important. These matters will be explored more thoroughly in Chapter 7.

Most rewards and penalties are offered, directly or indirectly, by people. Following Homans again, we may speak of human relations involving an exchange of values among men. This is illustrated in Marcel Mauss' *Essay on the Gift.*[2]

In all the tribes Mauss examined, he found that the presentation of a gift from A to B created in B the sentiment that he is indebted to A until he has been able to return the gift with an object of like value. We might enlarge this conception of gift exchange, for it would seem to apply to the exchange of services or activities as well as to the exchange of physical objects. In other words, the activity performed by A in behalf of B establishes with B a more favorable sentiment toward A, and also

---

[2] Glencoe, Ill.: The Free Press, 1954. The puzzle is that this set of ideas has not been more effectively integrated in human relations thinking before now. My own study of *Street Corner Society* (Chicago: The University of Chicago Press, 1943 and 1955) makes a great deal of this exchange of favors in the street corner gang. I have a chapter on the exchange of favors in my *Human Relations in the Restaurant Industry* (New York: McGraw-Hill Book Co., Inc., 1948). However, it was only as I read George Homans' *Social Behavior: Its Elementary Forms* (New York: Harcourt Brace & Co., 1960) that I began to see how these ideas fitted in with the social system of my scheme.

activitates a sentiment concerning an appropriate activity: that a favor given should be returned. The persistence of these sentiments requires that they remain implicit. If A, in calling for a service from B, tells B that he owes it to A, this generally leads to a denial on the part of B of the obligation, and to negative sentiments toward A.

I would only add that the same logic applies also to the exchange of penalties. We might state it more generally this way: The provision of goods and services that are positively valued from A to B tends to elicit positive sentiments from B to A and to lead further to the provision of goods and services that are positively valued from B to A. These same reciprocities seem to hold for negative values, although here we are presumably dealing with a withholding of goods and a provision of activities that are negatively valued.

In the informal group, if an exchange of negatively valued activities continues for long, the group breaks up. The members withdraw from interaction that is punishing rather than rewarding. In the hierarchical organization, we often find men engaged in interaction over an extended period of time during which they are engaged in the exchange of negatively valued activities.

One of the purposes of this book is to explain the development of such a pattern of exchange, and also to show the ways in which such a negative exchange may be transformed into an exchange of positively valued activities, with the accompanying growth of favorable interpersonal sentiments.

## HUMAN RELATIONS IN THE WORKPLACE

Up to this point, we have sketched the forces that have created the personality that Joe brings with him into the workplace and the impersonal forces that make up his working environment. We have also noted the exchanges that may take place between Joe and others in the workplace.

It is as if we had described an actor and then set him on the stage in settings representing a street corner, a drawing room, or the conference room of a business office building. When we know the characteristics of the actor and of the setting in which he is to act, we can make certain predictions as to what he is likely to do. However, these predictions will be of a very general nature until we bring other actors onto that same stage and observe our actor engaging in interactions and activities with them. That is, we can predict that our actor will probably not be observed shooting craps in the drawing room or drinking cocktails in the conference room, but even if we could be 100 per cent sure of such predictions—which we cannot—this limited information would hardly enable us to make the kinds of predictions that we would like to make regarding the actor.

Let us now set Joe on the stage of his factory department in interactions and activities with fellow workers and member agement. So as to begin at the simplest level, let us consider on., relations between Joe and one other individual, the departmental foreman.

The first observation we can make regarding activities between the two men is that sometimes they are initiated by the foreman and sometimes by Joe. That is, sometimes we may observe the foreman telling Joe what job to do and perhaps how to do it. At other times, we see Joe pointing out to the foreman a defect in the machine and proposing a change in work activity, which the foreman accepts. While we normally expect more activity to be initiated from foreman to worker than in the other direction, we have learned to expect to find negative sentiments among workers who have practically no opportunity to initiate activities for foremen (when the foremen initiate frequently for them), or among workers who experience a sharp reduction in the ratio of their initiations of activity to the foreman. The significance of these phenomena will be illustrated time and again in later chapters.

The same observation can be made regarding interaction: sometimes it is initiated by the foreman to Joe and other times by Joe to the foreman. We do not necessarily expect that the initiation will be predominantly with the foreman. Apparently this depends not only on the formal positions occupied and the personalities of the two men, but also upon the nature of the technology and work flow. On the automotive assembly line, as we shall see in Chapter 11, workers may be expected to initiate interaction more to the foreman than he initiates to them. We are far from being able to say what is an appropriate distribution of initiations between foreman and worker for a healthy organization, even when we try to limit our generalizations to one particular technology. We can, however, say that if we observed a marked change in this ratio, we should expect to find sentiment and activity changes associated with it.

For both activities and interactions, we will speak of two aspects, which we will call the *direct* and the *symbolic*. We speak of the one as direct because it is open to direct observation and, within our definition, it requires no interpretation of its meaning. The symbolic aspect involves the social values attached to the activities and interactions.

Let us illustrate the two aspects in a sample activity. Let us say that we observe the foreman assigning a job to Joe. On the direct side, we can count this as an initiation on the part of the foreman. We can identify the job by name and go on to describe the activities Joe emits in doing the job. But symbolic meanings also go with the activities. One symbolic dimension involves the skill that is thought to be required to do the job assigned. If Joe is given a job which is thought to require more skill than his customary run of jobs, he is likely to react with favorable sentiments toward the job itself and toward the foreman who assigned it to him—assuming that he is fully confident of his ability. On the other hand, if the job is thought to represent a level of skill well below Joe's own evaluation of his own skill (and if Joe has been getting no assignments above this particular level and, further, if more skilled jobs are available in the department and being assigned to men he considers no more skilled than himself), then Joe is likely to react with negative sentiments toward the job itself and toward the foreman who assigned the job to him.

The economic environment may constitute a particularly important symbolic dimension of job assignment, particularly in those departments having piece rates, as we shall see in more detail in Chapter 7. Suppose the job is known as a "stinker," one on which little or no bonus earnings can be made. We can expect Joe to react with negative sentiments to the job itself. Whether this assignment contributes to negative sentiments toward the foreman will depend upon the relation of this particular job assignment to Joe's past experience and to the pattern of assignment in the department. If Joe feels that he has been getting his "fair share" of the good jobs, then he may say to himself philosophically that somebody must take a turn at the "stinkers" and it is perfectly all right for the foreman to assign him one. On the other hand, his past experience may have led him to the conclusion that most of the good jobs go to the foreman's "favorites," and the assignment of this "stinker" will only reinforce his negative sentiments toward the foreman.

Let us apply our notion of reciprocity to the relations between Joe and his foreman. The foreman performs a positively valued activity for Joe (helps him to master a difficult job, which may improve his chances for promotion or lead to greater incentive earnings). Joe responds with a more favorable sentiment toward the foreman. He is prepared to reciprocate on the appropriate occasion (he puts out extra effort when the foreman tells him he has a rush job).

Similarly, let us say that the foreman performs a negatively valued activity toward Joe (gives him a "stinker" for his next job). Subject to the qualifications noted earlier about the relation of this event to past events, Joe responds with more negative sentiments toward the foreman and with negatively valued activities at the appropriate opportunity. Perhaps he slows down as much as he dares.

When Joe is presented with the "stinker," does he immediately direct a negative activity toward the foreman? Probably not. The two men are not interacting and exchanging activities in a vacuum. How Joe responds depends in large measure upon how others respond to his situation. Thus, his immediate response to the foreman may be just a minor change in work activity beyond that caused by the new job assignment itself. That is, he may reduce his normal work tempo somewhat and find more than the usual opportunities to leave the job. He may seek out interactions with fellow workers—and perhaps with the union steward

—to communicate his negative sentiments regarding the foreman. If the symbols he emits describing his own sentiments evoke responses of approval from other workers and from the steward, we may find a further chain of activities taking place, involving the processing of a grievance initiated by Joe. Or perhaps the interactions and activities initiated by Joe toward fellow workers may lead to some kind of collective activity; for example, a group slowdown.

If Joe receives no positive response in his interactions and activities with other workers, he may still try to express his negative sentiments toward the foreman in some kind of negative activity, but the activity will be more limited and carried out on an individual basis. For example, Joe may reduce the tempo of his work activity, but he is unlikely to go as far in this direction as he would if he were confident of the support of fellow workers. His activity responses may take the form of withdrawal from the situation—increased absences and possibly even quitting the job.

In this book, we are not satisfied simply with knowing how Joe feels about his foreman. Nor are we satisfied with discovering how Joe expresses that feeling toward the foreman with some sort of activity. In fact, we find we cannot explain what Joe does in response to an activity of the foreman unless we examine Joe in his interactions and activities with the work group. Furthermore, we are not concerned simply with the relationship between the individual and *the* work group, for we find that there are great differences from group to group—differences along the dimension that we shall call *cohesion*. In some groups it appears that almost any problem the individual faces wins support from other group members, so that individual problems rapidly become collective problems. It is this type of situation which Leonard Sayles refers to as having high *resonance*.[3] It is as if the worker called out to his fellows, "I've got problem X," and received from them a quick response, "We've got problem X too," or "Your problem is our problem."

In other groups we have an opposite situation. The individual's problem remains his individual problem; at least, no one is inclined to help him do anything about it. Members complain that "these fellows don't stick together."

Whether he is a member of a high or a low resonance group will make a great deal of difference in Joe's activities and interactions. It will, therefore, be one of our important concerns to explore the forces leading to high or low cohesiveness in work groups. The forces determining work group cohesion will be noted in several chapters and dealt with more systematically in Chapter 17, "Work Group Cohesion and Militancy." In our theoretical discussion of Part VII, I shall undertake to state some general propositions regarding work group cohesion.

---

[3] *Behavior of Industrial Work Groups* (New York: John Wiley & Sons, Inc., 1958).

### JALIZING HUMAN RELATIONS

may help the reader if we put in chart form what we have been
to express in words. Still concentrating on Joe, the picture is as
shown in the accompanying diagram.

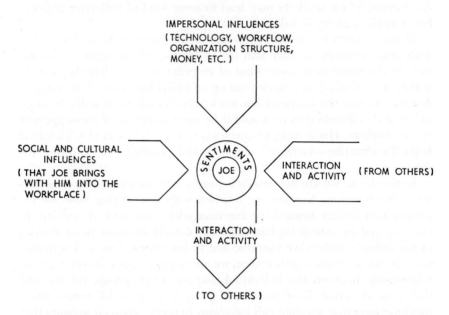

No scientific value should be attached to the chart by itself. It is simply
a way of summarizing in a visual manner what has so far been put
into words. The chart is intended to tell us that the sentiments, interactions, and activities of Joe in the job situation are resultants of:

1. The social and cultural influences that have shaped the personality he
   brings to work with him.
2. The impersonal forces operating on him in the plant environment.
3. The interactions and activities directed to him by others.

### WHERE DO WE GO FROM HERE?

It is important for the reader to recognize at this point what has and
what has not been attempted. I have not presented a theory of human
relations in industry. Rather, I have sought to present an introduction
to a theory of human relations in industry.

I have presented the concepts or theoretical tools that I expect to use
in examining cases in the chapters that follow. But here I have done no
more than describe the tools and furnish a few illustrations of the way in
which they may be used.

The chapters following in Parts II through VI will provide us with exercises in using these tools. As each situation is presented, we shall sharpen up these conceptual tools on particular bodies of data. In the analysis in each chapter we will use the tools as effectively as we are able to use them. Nevertheless, the analysis in each chapter will be of a limited nature, applying primarily to the particular data in that chapter.

It is only as I reach Part VII and undertake a theoretical restatement that I shall attempt to pull out of the individual chapters their limited generalizations, and combining them with research data from other studies, present more far-reaching and integrated propositions regarding the organization of human relations in industry.

We shall begin with what Joe brings to the plant from the social and cultural environment, and then show the effects upon him and his fellows of the impersonal forces of the plant environment. While the union will figure prominently in some of the cases in Parts II and III, it is in Part IV, with our discussion of union-management relations, that we will undertake to deal with this field more systematically. Parts V and VI will take us into the managerial process, to the study of leadership from the level of foreman up to higher management, and to the integration of specialized activities into management.

The reader should note, however, that I do not talk solely about the impact of technology on workers in the chapters dealing with technology, nor do I talk about managerial leadership entirely apart from the union-management relationship. In human relations in industry, we are dealing with a variety of forces coming to bear at the same time, in the same situation, with varying degrees of impact. It is impossible to treat one force in isolation from all others. The best we can do is to think in terms of foreground and background. The force on which we are concentrating at the moment we place in the foreground of description and analysis, but we nevertheless note that other important forces are operating on our case in the background.

In this field, we face a problem, because while we can only talk about one thing at a time, we must necessarily think about several things at the same time. That is what is meant when we speak of a *social system* or of a *pattern* of interactions, activities, and sentiments. We are not looking for *the* cause of any event in the workplace. We are assuming a relationship of *mutual dependence* among interactions, activities, and sentiments, such that, if a change is introduced in one, we can expect to observe changes in the other two.

In Parts II–VI, we shall examine a number of sequences of changes within our interaction-activity-sentiment social system. In the final chapters, I shall try to state some systematic propositions regarding the behavior underlying these concepts.

Lists of both readings and discussion questions are arranged according to parts of the book, since the material in each part is intended to fit closely together. The reading list is not comprehensive. It includes a small number of items that seem to fit well with the text. The instructor may wish to assign parts of these or select others.

Most of the questions proposed are of a type requiring considerable discussion. Some could be used for written assignments. The instructor may add, if he wishes, more specific shorter-answer questions.

Students might also be required to write their own questions—and answer them. I have argued that good questions are more important to research than good answers. A research man of average ability can find the answers to good questions. It is a more exacting task to formulate a good question, for that question points us toward the more significant aspects of the field under study.

Many of the questions to follow require the student to deal with the material in more than a single chapter. So that he will not seek to answer a question referring to material beyond the point of his reading assignment, I have used the chapter numbers in the left-hand column to indicate that the particular question can be answered without going beyond the chapter against whose number it appears.

## Collateral Readings

CHAPPLE, ELIOT D., and SAYLES, LEONARD. *The Measurement of Management.* New York: Macmillan & Co., 1961.

HAIRE, MASON (ed.). *Modern Organization Theory.* New York: John Wiley & Sons, Inc., 1960.
Various points of view are represented.

HOMANS, GEORGE C. *The Human Group.* New York: Harcourt Brace & Co., 1950.

———. *Social Behavior; Its Elementary Forms.* New York: Harcourt Brace & Co., 1961.
These two books by Homans, and the one by Chapple and Sayles, are closest to my own theoretical point of view.

LANDSBERGER, HENRY A. *Hawthorne Revisited: A Plea for an Open City.* Ithaca, N.Y.: New York State School of Industrial and Labor Relations, 1958.
Present a valuable critique of the work in this field.

ROETHLISBERGER, FRITZ J., and DICKSON, WILLIAM J. *Management and the Worker.* Cambridge, Mass.: Harvard University Press, 1939.
The study that gave birth to this field is reported best in this work.

RUBENSTEIN, ALBERT H., and HABERSTROH, CHADWICK J. (eds.). *Some Theories of Organization.* Homewood, Ill.: Richard D. Irwin, Inc. and the Dorsey Press, Inc., 1960.

## Discussion Questions

1    1. How have popular conceptions of the nature of the field of industrial sociology or human relations in industry changed in the course of its evolution? How would you define the field now?

2    2. Define the following terms: interaction, activity, sentiment, symbol. Illustrate each with examples.

2    3. What is the difference between initiation of activity and initiation of interaction? How significant is this difference?

2    4. If you were studying an organization, what methods would you use to gather data on interactions, activities, sentiments, and symbols? What difficulties would you expect to encounter?

3    5. What are the characteristics of a good theory of organization (or of human relations in industry)?

3    6. How will you be able to test the theory being developed here?

3    7. What kinds of propositions would you expect to be able to develop from this approach? Give examples.

3    8. Compare the theory being developed here with some other theory of human behavior. What are the main similarities and differences?

# PART II The Social and Economic Environment

THE interactions and activities Joe engages in while at work do not occur in a vacuum. They arise in a particular social, economic, technological, and physical environment. Joe's behavior can only be understood against the background of this environment.

Part II deals with some of the social and economic aspects of this environment. First we place Joe's work situation in international perspective, noting some of the ways in which culture affects behavior on the job. Then we look more closely at certain aspects of American society, noting how the social structure of the community may affect behavior within the plant and between management and union.

Next we move into the plant to examine influences specifically planned by management which can be taken as part of the environment for the individuals and groups we study. We see some of the ways in which the organization structure may affect worker and managerial behavior. Finally we look at the all-pervasive economic influences to show how rates of pay and incentive systems affect relations of workers to each other, to management, and to the union.

# Chapter 4 *THE WORK WORLD IN INTERCULTURAL PERSPECTIVE*

WHY does Joe behave as he does? He behaves that way, in part, because he is an American—because he has grown up in the culture of the United States.

Ask Joe to describe the culture of the United States, and he won't know how to begin. His difficulties will not be due entirely to the technical term, "culture." Even when we define the term—as we shall shortly—his difficulties are not resolved. He has trouble because he is trying to talk about things he takes for granted.

It is said that the most important things to know about a group of people are the things they themselves take for granted. Yet it is precisely those things that the people find most difficult to discuss.

We need perspective in order to understand ourselves. International comparisons may help us to attain that perspective. For example, after spending a year in Venezuela, I felt that I had learned at least as much about the United States as I had about Venezuela. The differences in culture that demanded my attention prodded me to ask much more searching questions about my own culture than I could when I had experienced no points of comparison.

While this books deals primarily with the United States, let us begin by putting Joe—and the members of management in his company—in international perspective.

## THE CONCEPT OF CULTURE

What do we mean by culture? We must first recognize that the word is used in several senses.

In the sense often encountered in conversation, culture refers particularly to music, art, and literature. A cultured individual is one who knows what is supposedly best in music, art, and literature—and also behaves according to the social customs of other "cultured" (or "culti-vated") people. A man who does not have these attributes can be said to be "uncultured."

57

I shall use the word in quite a different sense—the technical meaning that it has in anthropology and sociology. This refers to the patterns of belief and behavior of a given society. It includes music, art, and literature, but these are only a small part of the concern of the anthropologist as he studies the culture of a given group. In this sense, every human group has its own culture. We cannot say that one group or individual has more or less culture than another group or individual. We can, however, compare cultures from group to group, noting their similarities and differences.

The individual is not born with culture. He learns the culture of his own particular group in the process of growing up. When we say that culture is learned, we also note that it is subject to change. In fact, cultures are constantly changing all over the world. In some cases, changes come quite rapidly, but rare indeed is the situation in such a state of flux that the student is unable to provide a coherent description of the culture of the people in question.

Culture is often thought of in esoteric terms. A given people have a religion very different from ours, they have food habits that seem strange to us, and they also dress quite differently. These are indeed matters of culture, and they are not without importance. However, such differences are so obvious that they can hardly escape attention. We shall be concerned here with the way culture influences the day-to-day behavior of people in organizations and even the way in which they build their own organizations.

## THE MEANING OF WORK

This is what work meant to a highly successful U.S. inventor and businessman:

> I often tell my people that I don't want any fellow who has a job working for me; what I want is a fellow whom a job has. I want the job to get the fellow and not the fellow to get the job. And I want that job to get hold of this young man so hard that no matter where he is the job has got him for keeps. I want that job to have him in its clutches when he goes to bed at night, and in the morning I want that same job to be sitting on the foot of his bed telling him it's time to get up and go to work. And when a job gets a fellow that way, he's sure to amount to something.[1]

Ponder carefully this statement by Charles F. Kettering. It was made in America, and indeed there are few other countries in the world where such a statement could be made and given wide currency.

This is not to suggest that Kettering's is a typical U.S. view of the meaning of work. When I first came upon this gem of wisdom, I posted it on the bulletin board outside of my university office. Within a short

---

[1] Charles F. Kettering, quoted in *Coronet*, September, 1949, p. 72.

time it had accumulated penciled comments from graduate students and secretaries—all derogatory. The critics did not seem to take the advice seriously.

Even as we recognize the Kettering statement to be extreme, let us not discount it altogether. It represents the pure, distilled essence of what the eminent German sociologist, Max Weber, has called the Protestant ethic.[2] In this view, work is not only a means of getting ahead, but it is considered to be of positive moral value. Note that Kettering is not simply saying, "If you work hard, you will have a better chance of getting ahead than if you don't work hard." Such a statement could conceivably be subjected to a scientific test which would probably prove it to be true more often than not. But one doesn't test moral principles scientifically, and the Kettering statement bears the stamp of a strong moral admonition on the intrinsic value of work.

Weber called this view the Protestant ethic because it seemed to gain currency in the Western world at the time of the Reformation and grew out of the views of some of the leaders of the Protestant movement. The view is no longer exclusively associated with one church. In the United States today few Protestants would subscribe to such an extreme view, although there may be some broad differences between average Protestants and Catholics in their feelings on the value of work, as one study described in Chapter 7 will suggest.

In our own country, we should expect to find that views on the value of work vary with class differences. Workers are not as likely to place the same value on work in itself as might management people. In fact, many management people are concerned with giving more meaning to the work workers do. As we shall see in later chapters, some factory jobs seem to offer little inherent interest to the workers and the moral value of work is not a strong motivating force for them.

If we compare individual to individual and group to group in our society, we will find a wide range of sentiments regarding work, but this should not obscure the fact that there are more important differences between our culture and some others regarding the value of work.

All over the world most people must work for a living. But in some societies work is regarded as simply a means to an end. If one has enough money to live in the style of his own social group without working, then he doesn't work. He has others do the work for him.

Not so in the United States. The millionaire playboy may be a familiar phenomenon in the newspapers, but he is also the butt of strong public censure. We wonder how he can justify his existence if he doesn't work. In fact, most millionaires keep right on working, piling up more money or giving it away—or both. Even when we criticize some of the causes

---

[2] See Talcott Parsons' translation of *The Protestant Ethic and the Spirit of Capitalism* (Glencoe, Ill.: The Free Press, 1948).

to which the millionaire gives his money, we recognize that he is working hard at giving it away and we respect him for that.

In other countries there are culturally determined sentiments regarding the type of organization in which the individual may work and the type of position he may hold. In most of Latin America, at least until recent years, it has not been considered appropriate for the son of an upper-class family to have his career within a large company. At most, he may work for a short time in a large company—perhaps a U.S. concern —in order to learn something about modern business methods. He will then leave the company to take up the position of running or helping to run the family business. "The organization man," as we know him here, just does not fit into the upper-class pattern of life in such countries. This means that companies cannot go beyond the stage of a small family organization without recruiting children of middle and lower class parents for managerial positions. Thus on the one hand, these upper class sentiments regarding organizational membership may retard progress in economic development. On the other hand, as industrialization nevertheless does proceed, it tends to raise up to social prominence people who could never have risen except through such organizations.

Culture also creates sentiments regarding the appropriate type of economic enterprise for a given individual. In parts of Latin America as well as a number of other countries, the traditional aristocracy is based upon land ownership. For example, in the family which owns a large hacienda devoted to cattle raising or farming, the owner is traditionally expected to do little work. He employs a manager or overseer to run the hacienda for him, and his own managerial functions are limited to inspections of progress. In fact, the owner often does not live on the land. He prefers to live the life of leisure in the capital city and make only occasional trips to the hacienda.

As long as his land holdings are large and provide him with an income adequate to maintain his family's style of life, the owner has no incentive to increase the productivity of his enterprise. In fact, most such enterprises are probably highly inefficient according to current U.S. standards of agricultural methods and productivity of workers.

How do new economic enterprises develop in a country where the social leadership is tied to the traditional exploitation of land and labor? Everett Hagen, of the Center for International Studies at Massachusetts Institute of Technology, provides us with a case study that helps to answer this question.[3]

In his studies of personalities and social backgrounds of economic innovators in Colombia, Hagen found that a disproportionately large number of these men came from in and around the city of Medellin in the

---

[3] "The Entrepreneur As Rebel Against Traditional Society: A Research Note," *Human Organization*, Vol. XIX, No. 3 (Winter, 1960–61).

valley of Antioquia. As he traced the history of Colombia back to the era of first settlement, he gained some clues as to the preponderant influence of Antioqueños in Colombian economic life.

Medellin and the valley of Antioquia were among the first areas settled by the Spaniards. Other areas that were settled early were appropriate for large-scale farming and cattle raising. The Spanish settlers in these areas were able to take over lands and become landed aristocracy, with Indians and other servants or slaves doing the work for them. In this way, the hacienda pattern was established.

Not so in Antioquia. In that valley, the land was not suitable for large-scale agriculture or cattle raising. The valley did, however, possess one important resource: gold. With Indian slaves, the Antioqueños began exploiting the mines. The Indians could not stand the rigors of this new type of work and the treatment they received, and so this particular labor force died out. The Antioqueños then imported slaves from Africa, but this again was no solution. Importation was expensive, and the mines were not so rich as to cover the continuing costs of importation of slaves and constant replacement of those who died out. So at last the Antioqueños faced a most unhappy decision. They would either have to abandon the mines—their only source of wealth—or else they would have to go in and dig out the gold themselves. They chose to dig. In this way, over several generations, the Antioqueños were able to gain themselves a reasonably good living.

This experience naturally conditioned their sentiments regarding work. While the landed aristocrats from the other towns regarded them as an inferior people grubbing the ground, the Antioqueños began to gain some appreciation of the dignity of hard work and of the values of building up industrial enterprises. These sentiments have carried over to this day, so that the sons of the social leaders of Antioquia have an outlook regarding work and industrial organizations that is quite different from that of the landed aristocracy.

This is not to say that only the Antioqueños built the thriving industry now to be found in Colombia. Many others have participated in that development. However, Hagen argues that where these others have been of upper class origin, they have also been, for one reason or another, rebels against their class. They have not accepted the traditional standards. Somehow they have believed that there was indeed dignity in industrial and commercial enterprise.

The same points can be illustrated historically. In England, it was not the landed aristocracy which ushered in the Industrial Revolution. With few exceptions, members of this class looked down upon the new industrial pursuits and upon those who engaged in them. That revolution depended upon new groups of people coming forward from lower status levels.

Culture also has a strong influence upon the way in which work at lower levels of the organization is viewed. We find a distinction between white collar and blue collar jobs, between office jobs primarily involving the handling of papers and shop jobs involving the handling of machines and other physical objects.

While some distinction is universally observed, the magnitude of the status distinction between the two classes of jobs varies greatly from society to society. Our own society tends to minimize this distinction. From earliest times, most of our forefathers had to work with their hands to some extent in order to establish homes and gain a living. A landed aristocracy, with servants or slaves to do the manual work, developed only in a few sections of the country. This background helped to clothe working by hand with dignity, even when office workers were recognized as superior in status.

It seems likely that the status difference between the two classes of work has declined further in recent years with the relative gain in earnings of blue collar workers and improvements in the physical conditions of the factory. The blurring of lines between the types of jobs may be carried further by the progress of automation which creates new classes of jobs, located in factory-like areas, which involve no real handwork but require instead the observation of a highly technical process.

In Latin America, the line between white collar and blue collar workers is much more sharply drawn. This is illustrated even in the two languages, English and Spanish. We can use the one word, "employees," to refer to office and factory workers alike. The other common word, "workers," does not make the distinction explicit either. It is more generally used to apply to factory workers, but when a person uses that word, it is not clear that he is referring only to factory workers. To make the distinction in English, we have to use rather cumbersome language. The terms "office workers" and "factory workers" will serve in some situations, but what about the cases where the men who work with their hands don't work in factories? Perhaps the most useful terms are "white collar workers" and "blue collar workers"—but note that we have to use three words in each case to make the distinction clear. Not so in Spanish. That language offers one word for each of the categories. A white collar worker is an *empleado* and a blue collar worker is an *obrero*.

Along with this linguistic difference go important differences in the handling of these classes of people. In countries such as Peru, the distinction is basic to the labor laws of the country and the *empleados* have substantial government protection, whereas the *obreros* are given little attention at all.

This distinction is constantly reflected in daily behavior in Latin America. For example, consider the case of a U.S. professor who was teaching in a Venezuelan university. He had just received a shipment of supplies from the United States and was eager to open up the wooden crate as soon as possible. He called upon the janitor to bring him a hammer. When the janitor returned, the professor, without thinking, reached for the hammer. The janitor did not give it to him. The professor then asked for the hammer, but again the janitor refused to give it to him. The crate was opened only when the professor stepped back and allowed the janitor to open it. The work involved lasted only for a moment and involved a minimum of physical effort. The janitor responded quickly to any *appropriate* order the professor gave him, but he felt strongly that it was not fitting that a man with the status of a professor should do the slightest bit of work suitable for an *obrero*.

In the United States, a middle-class man may shine his own shoes, wash his own car, paint his own house, and so on if he feels inclined to do so. He may have various reasons for not undertaking such tasks, but the fear of losing social status will not be one of them. Doing physical work on one's own house and possessions is not considered beneath the dignity of a middle-class man in this country. He may even enhance his personal reputation by doing a good job in these fields. However, there are many countries in which a middle-class man who can ill afford to pay to get such tasks done will still feel that he cannot undertake them himself. He will not feel right himself about doing the jobs, and he will fear losing status in the eyes of others.

A sharp line of social distinction between white collar and blue collar jobs can be a very serious obstacle to the economic development of a country. In underdeveloped countries, with broadening educational opportunities and new job openings in industry, most young men and women who have learned to read and write want to become office workers. Thus these countries are faced with an oversupply of clerks and a critical shortage of skilled workers. This presents a problem not only to management people and government officials concerned with economic development, but also to the employees themselves. In many of these situations of early industrialization, most clerical jobs will be dead end jobs, whereas a good man starting in the plant or field may move up steadily to the top skill classifications and then perhaps a step or two beyond this into the lower ranks of supervision. However, wherever there is a sharp distinction between office and shop, even those people who see the advantages of potential progress in the shop job will hesitate to forsake the job classification which establishes them as respectable people from the outset.

## CULTURE AND COMMUNICATION

Culture also affects the pattern of communication among individuals.

If you disagree with someone, do you thrash it out with him face-to-face? Do you keep it to yourself? Or do you take it up with some third party?

In union-management relations, the grievance procedure as we know it is rare inside Latin American plants. To a much greater extent than in the United States, the government becomes involved in the handling of all kinds of labor problems.

These differences seem to be clearly related to the culture and social organization of Latin America. There we find that society has been much more rigidly stratified than it has with us. As a corollary, we find a greater emphasis upon authority in family and community.

This emphasis upon status differences makes it difficult for people at varying status levels to express themselves freely in discussion and argument. In the past, the pattern has been for the man of lower status to express deference to his superior in any face-to-face contact. This has been the case even when everyone knows that the subordinate dislikes the superior. In fact, the culture of Latin America seems to place a great premium upon keeping personal relations harmonious on the surface.

In the United States, we feel that it is not only desirable but natural to speak up to your superior, to tell the boss exactly what you think, even when you disagree with him. Of course, we don't always do this, but the important thing is that we think we should do it, and we feel guilty if we fail to speak our minds frankly. When workers in our factories are newly elected to local union office, they may find themselves quite self-conscious about speaking up to the boss and arguing grievances, but many of them quickly learn to do it—and enjoy the experience. As our culture emphasizes thrashing out differences of opinion in face-to-face contact and de-emphasizes the importance of status differences, we find ourselves in a cultural environment which makes it possible to build our institutions for the handling of industrial disputes on the basis of the local situation and direct discussion by the parties immediately involved.

In Latin America, where it is exceedingly difficult for people to express their differences face to face, and where status differences and authority are much more strongly emphasized than here, it is quite natural for workers to look for some third party—the government—to take care of their problems. If they have difficulty in thrashing out their problems with management, they find no difficulty in telling government people how they feel about management.

Consider the case of a Venezuelan drilling foreman with a large U.S. oil company in Venezuela. A man of very little formal education but substantial ability, he had worked himself up to the position of supervisor over a drilling crew. His classification was higher than that of the first-line foreman, who was a member of the "junior staff." This man had reached a "senior staff" position and so had "arrived" as a bona fide member of the management.

I found the Venezuelan supervisor highly satisfied with his job on all points except one, which involved communication. He said he had advanced much higher in the company than he had ever expected. He spoke of his North American superior with real enthusiasm. He described the superior as an able, sympathetic, and understanding person, and added, "He actually speaks better Spanish than I do." How then could there be a problem of communication between the two individuals?

The Venezuelan described his problem. No sooner would he have the men on his crew trained so that he had a good team working for him than one or another of them would be transferred to some other crew. His superior made the decisions on these transfers, and the Venezuelan didn't understand why the transfers were made so frequently.

I asked, "Have you ever complained to your superior?"

The Venezuelan seemed startled at the very idea: "Oh, no, no!"

"Well," I tried again, "perhaps I put it the wrong way. Have you ever discussed the matter with your superior?"

He said he had not.

"Have you ever thought that some time you might bring it to his attention?"

The Venezuelan paused to give that question some thought. Finally, he answered, "Well, maybe some time when we are talking about something else, I might indirectly bring it in." But than a happy thought struck: "But Mr. Jones has the same job I have and he has exactly the same problem. I think he is going to bring it up to the boss."

We might say that when a man fails to speak up to his boss, it is because he is afraid of what the boss will do to him. Certainly, fear played a part in establishing the culture pattern in the society as a whole. In a highly stratified society where all powers are concentrated in the hands of the superior, the subordinate learns that it can be dangerous to question a decision of the superior. In this type of situation, people learn to behave submissively—at least in the presence of the boss. They do not learn to thrash things out with him, face to face. Then, when there is no reason to fear, they still do not feel that it is natural to speak up.

In this case, the Venezuelan spoke most cordially of his boss and gave not the slightest indications of fear. Furthermore, as he well recognized, his position in the organization was completely secure. Nevertheless, it somehow did not seem natural for him to speak up even to a sympathetic and understanding superior. He did not even have to make his criticism direct. He might simply have asked the superior to explain the reasons behind his decisions on transfer of workers. But even that was too much.

We can sum up the difference in this way. In the United States, subordinates do not just automatically speak up to their superiors. The superior needs to behave in such a way as to make it clear that he will not retaliate in response to criticism. If he gets that point across, he can be confident that real communication will flow upward, because people in our society are primed to speak up to the boss whenever the situation seems right. In Latin America and in other more highly stratified societies, it is not enough simply to remove the fear of retaliation. The manager who wants his subordinates to speak up to him must provide incentives to help them to learn this type of communication.

In the United States, the pressure for upward communication is always present. The superior needs only to take the cork out of the channel of communication. In Latin America, the superior, in addition to removing the cork, must provide some sort of suction to bring this sort of communication up to him. We shall explore a case along these lines in a later chapter. (See Chapter 24 on "Building Initiative in Management.")

### THE JAPANESE FACTORY

For a final example of the impact of culture upon organizational life, let us consider a case entirely outside of Western civilization, *The Japanese Factory*, as discussed by James Abegglen.[4]

The impact of cultural differences does not seem to pass away before advancing industrialization. Japan is a highly industrialized nation, and yet as Abegglen points out, her factories are organized according to a social logic quite different from ours.

Japanese workers are hired for life. They are practically never fired. Promotions go largely by seniority even at managerial levels. The incompetent executive moves up with advancing years to positions with titles appropriate to his age—even when this means devising types of duties that will keep him from interfering with the progress of the firm. The pay of workers bears no relation to their productivity. The pay envelope is the sum of a complex set of factors, in which length of service and number of dependents figure prominently. All management decisions are made on a group basis—at least nominally. If an individual were credited with a certain decision that turned out to be unwise, then the individual would lose face. To spare management people from such humiliation, to all appearances the group as a whole shares responsibility in all decisions.

If we were to see such a system being established in a company in the United States, we would confidently predict that it would not work. No doubt that prediction would prove correct, because the Japanese system would not fit into our own culture. However, the important point to note is that the system does work in Japan. That is not to say that there are no sources of inefficiency in the system. Indeed, Abegglen points out some of the inherent difficulties. At the same time, however, he points out that Japan's industry has advanced just as rapidly as ours in the last century.

Clearly, a United States management expert attempting to advise Japanese industrialists would have to make sure that his recommenda-

---

[4] Glencoe, Illinois: The Free Press, 1958.

tions fitted into the culture and social organization of Japan and were not simply homemade United States recipes, automatically applied.

## IN CONCLUSION

The individual brings part of his culture with him into the workplace. A knowledge of the culture will therefore be helpful in understanding his behavior.

Since culture is, in part, learned behavior, and since there are differences among the parts of a large and complex society, we should expect to find individual differences in what people within the same society learn from their culture. At the same time, we should expect to find similarities in beliefs and behavior within a given culture and contrasts when we compare it with another culture. In this book, we shall be exploring both these similarities and differences.

# Chapter 5  *INDUSTRY AND THE COMMUNITY*

THE organization does not exist in a vacuum. Not only does it share in the culture of its society, as indicated in the previous chapter, but also it is more specifically influenced by the community in which it is located.

Life in the plant may be influenced by these community factors:

1. The class structure.
2. Kinship and clique relations.
3. Ethnic group membership.

We shall illustrate these influences with several cases. While much of our material in this chapter is drawn from New England, our aim is not to describe New England as it was at the time of the various studies nor as it is now. Some of our material goes back as much as thirty years, and yet the general principles it illustrates are not bounded by time. Let us examine these influences in particular cases.

## SOCIAL STRUCTURE, TECHNOLOGY, AND UNIONIZATION

The best starting point for our view of the social structure of New England is the monumental study of Yankee City carried out by W. Lloyd Warner and his associates in the early 1930's.[1] Yankee City is a small industrial town (about 17,000 population) just beyond easy commuting distance from Boston. It is an old city, having been founded in 1630. The period around the turn of the nineteenth century marked the high point in the development of the city, for then it was an important center of shipbuilding, whaling, and ocean commerce. By the time of the Warner study, all of these activities were far in the past and Yankee City had become a small manufacturing center, with the production of shoes the most prominent industrial activity.

The Warner group found six social classes in Yankee City, to which they gave the names of upper-upper, lower-upper, upper-middle, lower-middle, upper-lower, and lower-lower. The upper-upper people were

---

[1] See especially Vol. 1, *The Social Life of a Modern Community*, Yankee City Series (5 vols.; New Haven: Yale University Press, 1941–59).

members of the old family aristocracy. The families of the members had been prominent in the economic and social affairs of the city for several generations. The lower-uppers represented the newly rich, who were currently prominent in many of the affairs of the city. They mixed with the upper-uppers on many business and social occasions but were not invited to the small discussion clubs which were the most exclusive social groupings in the city.

The upper-middles were largely business and professional people and their families. Into the lower-middle classification fitted the small shop-keepers and some skilled artisans.

The upper-lowers were "poor but honest," skilled and semi-skilled workers, who worked steadily at their jobs whenever work was available. At the bottom were the lower-lowers, who lived off sporadic employment, relief payments, or digging for clams on the clam flats.

This class pattern was reflected in the ecological distribution of people in the city. The upper-uppers and the lower-uppers tended to live on or near Hill Street, whereas the lower-lowers were concentrated in the Riverbrook area near the clam flats. However, the correlation was by no means complete. Some people were commonly referred to as "Hill Streeters" when they did not, in fact, live on Hill Street but belonged to the top segment of the society that was associated with that area. Similarly, some people referred to as "Riverbrookers" did not actually live in that section but were so identified by the Yankee City people because they fitted at the bottom of the social structure.

The Warner group found a correlation between income and status, but the correlation was not nearly as high as is commonly supposed. In fact, the lower-uppers averaged a somewhat higher income than the upper-uppers. However, they lacked the lineage necessary for the top prestige position in Yankee City. (This may be peculiar to New England and certain other sections which emphasize lineage. The Warner group, studying a small midwestern city, could find no clear dividing line between upper-upper and lower-upper.[2] They described a five-class system with simply an upper class at the top.)

The lack of correlation between income and status is seen not only in these broad comparisons but also in many individual cases. For example, the man with the highest income in town, a factory owner who had come up through the ranks, was found to occupy an upper-middle class position. His wealth would have enabled him to buy a house in the Hill Street area and to mix in the social activities of the two upper classes; to become accepted as a lower-upper. However, he did not care to move out of the "side street" home in which he had begun living when he was poor. Furthermore, he showed no interest in mixing in the social activities of the two upper classes.

---

[2] *Democracy in Jonesville* (New York: Harper & Bros., 1949).

The ethnic distribution of the population influenced the placement of families in the class system. The upper-upper class was composed exclusively of Yankees, people who traced their ancestry back some generations, predominantly of English stock. The lower-upper class was predominantly Yankee, but a few Irish were included—and no others. Over 80 per cent of the upper-middle class were found to be Yankees, but some French Canadians, Jews, Italians, Armenians, and Greeks, along with the Irish, were members of this class. For the lower-middle class, the Yankee proportion dropped to 67.1 per cent, while among the upper-lowers it was 38 per cent. It is interesting to note that the lower-lower proportion of Yankees rises somewhat to 42.9 per cent, indicating that a substantial number of people who could trace their ancestry back through a number of generations of Yankee stock (like the upper-uppers) were in this depressed segment of the population. Long residence of a family in Yankee City did not in itself confer prestige. The family had to have been associated with several generations of prominence in the social and economic affairs of the city.

Let us look now at the impact of this community and its class system upon a problem of human relations in industry: the unionization of the shoe workers of Yankee City. Changes within the community were by no means the only force in bringing about this unionization. In fact, it is one of our problems in the analysis of human relations that we rarely encounter a situation where a change comes about as a result solely of one type of force.

In this case, changes within the community were accompanied by changes in technology and job content, and by social and economic changes taking place beyond the community.

This was in the early period of the CIO organizational drive, and unionization activities elsewhere, coupled with governmental support of the right to unionize, undoubtedly had important effects in encouraging the shoe workers to organize and go out on strike.

To understand the other influences, we must go back to the community and the shoe industry a generation or two before this crisis and then note how conditions had changed.

In the earlier period of the shoe industry in Yankee City, the jobs were hierarchically organized as to skill and pay. In those days, the young worker entered on a non-skilled job and, by dint of diligent work, increasing skill, and years of experience, rose to higher positions within the work ranks and even to lower supervisory positions. In those days, the cutters were the aristocrats of the working force. In accordance with this reputation, they once used to come to work in top hats.

In those early days, the shoeworker could see himself fitting into a definite place in a graded social and economic hierarchy of skill. Even if his place was low, he could see prospects of moving up step by step to higher status positions. He looked up to the cutters at the top of the prestige hierarchy, and the cutters, in turn, were accorded due respect by the lower supervisors, who were men who had come up through the ranks like themselves. Furthermore, the factory owners, then of the upper-upper class, knew the cutters personally and took a paternalistic interest in them.

Technological changes destroyed the old pattern of social and economic arrangements within the plant. Mechanization destroyed the old skill hierarchy, minimizing the differences in skill—and pay—among the various jobs. Upon entering the shoe plant, the worker could look forward only to slight increases in skill and pay in response to his own efforts and to the investment of his working years. Pay increases beyond this minimum were dependent upon general pay increases for the factory as a whole. This lack of social and economic differentiation among the workers contributed to their solidarity and to their response to unionization efforts.

In the old days, the worker who had risen to be a cutter was assumed to have acquired a large part of the knowledge needed by a foreman, and therefore, promotions from worker to foreman were quite common. When mechanization in the plant had reduced the job skills to a minimum, working at the bench was no longer viewed by management as a valuable preparation for supervision.

Along with technological changes came changes in the ownership of the local plants. Not being able to survive as independent units, they were sold to corporations having headquarters far from Yankee City. This meant that, whereas in the earlier period the top men in the Yankee City shoe industry were members of the upper-upper class, at the time of the study the men were simply hired managers of outside interests, occupying nothing higher than an upper-middle position in the community class system. This had effects before and during the strike. Before the strike, it meant that the managers did not hold the high community positions that would have given them prestige and would have helped them to dominate the working force—and to get their domination accepted. During the strike, it meant that management no longer had the full support of the top status people, as would have been the case with such a crisis in an earlier period. In fact, many high prestige community leaders expressed open sympathy for the strikers and also aided them in material ways.

The crisis was not, therefore, defined by many people in the community as a conflict between classes in Yankee City. Rather, they looked upon it as a struggle between Yankee City and outside interests, thus allying together Yankee City people of all social classes in opposition to the big city management. In fact, local sentiment against the "foreigners" was so strong that two of the factory managers themselves openly expressed sympathy for the strikers.

This situation seems to have sapped the self-confidence of management men who tried to stand firmly with higher management in the crisis. Warner makes the point in the following way:

> One of them damaged the cause of management when he tried to fight the head of the union during a peace conference. Everyone said he blustered and acted badly when he used such tactics. He was under the control of higher management and occupied an inferior managerial position where he had little freedom to assume command and take leadership. Yet he had learned from "one of the grand old men" of the last period, when he worked for him, how his kind of man should act and he knew that an owner and manager should assume control. It seems a reasonable hypothesis that the conflict between his beliefs on how a manager should act and what he was permitted to do by his status greatly contributed to causing his unfortunate act, an act which materially aided the union. He tried to take command in a situation where it was impossible to do so, and instead of commanding he could only "bluster."[3]

## SOCIAL STRUCTURE AND ECONOMIC PROGRESS

Analysis of the social structure may also contribute to our understanding of the economic rise or fall of a community. Consider the case of New Bedford, Massachusetts, as described by Seymour Wolfbein in the *Decline of a Cotton Textile City*.[4]

During the depression of the 1930's, almost two thirds of the textile mills in this once-thriving industrial city closed down. While the depression was clearly the main cause of such a catastrophic loss, the textile industry of the city was actually declining through the 1920's. "The crisis was brought to a head in 1928 by the longest and severest strike in the city's history, a six-month strike in response to a 10 per cent wage cut. When the mills reopened in 1928, they employed only half the number of workers they had employed in 1927, and the value of the cotton textile products produced by these mills was cut one third."[5]

How can this sharp decline in the textile industry in New Bedford be explained? The common explanation is Southern competition. It is said that Southern communities offered cheaper labor, freedom from unions, and large tax concessions to lure the textile industries into their area. These influences are certainly of great importance, but are they the whole story?

The advantages were not all on one side. The New Bedford plants had an already skilled labor force, and they were much nearer to the major mass markets for their products than were the Southern mills.

On balance, we must conclude that the economic advantages were indeed with the Southern mills and that, even if the New Bedford mills had been managed with a high degree of efficiency, they would have

---

[3] Chapter 3, "The Factory in the Community," William F. Whyte (ed.), *Industry and Society* (New York: McGraw-Hill Book Co., Inc., 1946).

[4] New York: Columbia University Press, 1944.

[5] *Ibid.*, p. 11.

suffered some decline in relation to the growing industry of the South. But was the loss of almost two thirds of the mills an inevitable response to economic factors? Before we accept this simple answer, let us look at the managements of the mills.

Through the period immediately preceding World War I, throughout the war, and during the immediate post-war boom, the New Bedford mills were exceptionally profitable. During this prosperous period, dividends paid actually went far beyond the point that would have been justified by a realistic appraisal of earnings. The author of our study comments:

> Since depreciation was not taken into account, profits were overstated and large dividends were consequently paid out of partly fictitious earnings. The result was that many mills found themselves without sufficient funds to provide for replacement of worn-out equipment and modernization of plant. Resulting obsolescence played an important part in adding to the South's differential advantage over New England.[6]

Take, for example, one mill which at the time of going into bankruptcy had no machine in its plant less than twenty years old. A firm of cotton brokers, studying the proposed liquidation of the company, made these comments:

> Much of the machinery is of almost historic value. . . .
> This was seen from the fact that the renowned Henry Ford found in the plant some specimens that he thought were of sufficient interest to purchase for his museum. How the officers of this corporation can justify their operation of the plant is difficult to see.

Clearly the management of many of these mills was carried on in a highly inefficient fashion, but what has this got to do with the social structure of the community? Wolfbein makes this comment:

> Not only were the cotton mills and financial institutions of New Bedford closely interlocked, they were also joined by a comparatively small number of persons belonging to the more important families of the city. Throughout New Bedford's history the familiar pattern of son succeeding father who, in turn, had succeeded his father to important positions in the mills and banks, has gone on with great regularity.

There was one exception to this pattern: Walter Langshaw, president of the Dartmouth Manufacturing Corporation. Beginning as a textile mill worker in New Bedford, Langshaw rose through the ranks to become head of a successful company which he founded with the aid of outside capital.

During the strike of 1928, the managements of the struck companies were seeking to persuade the public that the decline of textiles in New Bedford was primarily due to the union high-wage policies and that a 10 per cent wage cut was necessary to re-establish business on a

---

[6] *Ibid.;* all quotes from Wolfbein which follow are taken from pp. 91–98.

sound foundation. Mr. Langshaw was not a member of the Manu-
facturers' Association of the city and did not cut wages as did the rest of
the mills. His company was not struck.

At a critical point in the strike, Langshaw wrote a long letter to the
*New Bedford Standard* in which he argued that the unions and wage
rates were not the main problem at all. Instead, he attacked the interlocking system of financial and family control of the struck companies—
noting that his name was nowhere to be found on the list of these directorates in spite of the fact that he was one of the largest investors in the
city. He went on to strike this blow:

> The cotton business has suffered more because official salaried positions
> have been given to sons or friends of those who had pull, and whose invest-
> ments were negligible, without regard to qualifications in any respect. There
> are many who have been drawing $10,000 to $25,000 a year as officials in
> the cotton manufacturing business whom I would pension rather than have
> them in the employ of the Dartmouth Manufacturing Corporation.

This kind of talk did not endear Langshaw to the social leaders of the
city. He described his own position in this way:

> While I have been very happy in my work and knowledge that I was suc-
> cessful and able to take care of myself, in some respects I have been as lone-
> some as a salmon would be in a mill pond surrounded by suckers and tad-
> poles.

After presenting us with all of the material given here, Wolfbein
comes to a curious conclusion:

> The system of family control and interlocking directorates was not a major
> cause of the troubles that beset New Bedford and its leading industry. In fact
> many of the mill managements have been and are progressive. They have
> made sincere efforts to solve the industry's problems; replacing out-of-date
> equipment, overhauling obsolete merchandising and distributing methods,
> carefully conserving and guarding their fund of technical skill and experience,
> diversifying their products, and adapting machinery to the manufacture of
> rayon goods and rayon and silk mixtures. *And many of these efficiently op-
> erated mills have survived.* (Italics mine.)

The conclusion is a curious one, because in a book devoted to explaining why two out of three of the mills in New Bedford failed, one would
think that a scholar would have to base his analysis on the factors accounting for the failure of these particular mills. It certainly proves nothing to
argue that the efficiently operated mills survived.

Having given us substantial evidence of the importance of family control in the failure of so many mills, why does the author shrink from
drawing the conclusion that apparently follows from his data? On this
we can only speculate, but the table of contents of this book provides one
reasonable clue. In a book 176 pages long, Wolfbein devotes only 7
pages to the matters here under discussion. Furthermore, they simply
form a sub-head entitled "Ownership, Management, and Control" in a

chapter entitled "Other Factors in New Bedford's Decline." The explanation seems to be that the study was undertaken as a piece of economic research. All of the traditional economic factors in the situation were carefully canvassed, but this did not seem to cover quite everything. The author then threw in a brief chapter on "Other Factors" and reassured himself that these factors were not very important. However, we are very much indebted to him, for his own data very clearly show the impact of the community social structure on the economic decline of the city.

Let us now see if we can provide some integration between the economic and social forces accounting for New Bedford's decline. Let us begin by acknowledging the great importance of Southern competition, but then seek to put this into perspective.

Through interlocking directorates, the banks and most of the mills of New Bedford were controlled by a few important families. If we can assume that the social structure of New Bedford was similar to that of Yankee City, this means upper-upper families, with probably some admixture of lower-uppers. A new man coming up from the ranks, like Langshaw, was not accepted into this group, no matter what ability he displayed. He had to go outside for capital. Fragmentary evidence suggests that he must have held an upper-middle class position in New Bedford in spite of his wealth and ownership of one of the mills.

Within this tightly knit group of controlling families, the interests of family and friends came to dominate over "pure" economic or technical considerations. This was shown both in staffing and promotions, and in depreciation and investment policy.

In many cases, men were apparently appointed or promoted to important positions in one of the mills more in recognition of their family connections and social relations than in terms of criteria of business competence.

The family system can be expected to show its influence also in dividend, depreciation, and investment policies.

Currently accepted theories of business management require that everything be subordinated to the company. The company is the *real* thing. This means that every effort must be made to maintain the health of the plant. Since machines are constantly in the process of wearing out and newer and more efficient machines are becoming available, the health of the organization requires that money be set aside for depreciation and new machines be purchased and installed whenever costs can be significantly lowered by this step.

Since the company is looked upon as having a perpetual life, high profits at one period are not considered an excuse for failure to set aside money for the maintenance and improvement of plant and equipment. In fact, a "good" management will make even more generous provision for improvements in prosperous periods.

If the family is the *real* thing, and the company is viewed as a supporting institution, then a different logic prevails. In that case, the choice between higher dividends and prudent reinvestment of funds in the business is likely to be resolved in favor of money for the families. In fact, some of these companies paid out dividends at fabulous rates in periods of prosperity. Wolfbein gives us an illustrative case:

> The mill started operations in 1911 and paid its first dividend in 1913. In the fourteen years from 1913 to 1926 inclusive, stockholders received a total of almost two million dollars on an investment of $800,000. An idea of this mill's prosperity can be gained by noting that in 1922, for example, stockholders not only received their regular 8% dividend plus extra dividends of 32%, but also received a 50% stock dividend at the end of the year.

If the mill managements had pursued the "pure" business policy of making regular investments in new machinery and plant improvements, then when the depression came and Southern competition proved so menacing, the New Bedford mills would have been in a strong position to fight for their existence. Furthermore, having already invested so much in keeping the plants up to date, the stockholders would have been exceedingly reluctant to abandon the mills.

When the funds necessary to keep the mills up to date were drawn off instead into higher dividends for the controlling families, these families increased their wealth greatly and became able to make substantial investments—elsewhere. Then when the crisis came for each mill, the owners had a choice that could only be made in one direction. To keep a mill running would have required a large immediate investment in new equipment in order to bring an obsolete plant up to date, and even then there would be no assurance of success in the face of the increasing Southern competition. Since the investment funds were in the hands of families and not in the coffers of their New Bedford companies, these families could invest the same amount of money required to modernize a New Bedford mill into a mill in the South and have a new mill with all its attendant advantages. When events had reached the point of this choice, the game was already lost for the mill workers of New Bedford.

## ETHNIC INFLUENCES

Just as a man's ethnic identification influences his status in the community, so does it also affect him in the plant. Two other New England studies document this point.

Orvis Collins reports as a participant observer on a steel cable plant in which he worked for a number of months.[7] The top management people were all Yankees. The foremen and a high proportion of the skilled work-

---

[7] "Ethnic Behavior in Industry: Sponsorship and Rejection in a New England Factory," in Robert Dubin, *Human Relations in Administration* (New York: Prentice-Hall, Inc., 1951), pp. 243–49.

ers were Irish. The Italians and other groups were thoroughly concentrated at somewhat lower levels. There was, of course, no official recognition of ethnic affiliation as a factor in job rights. Furthermore, there was a union and a contract giving emphasis to seniority in promotion. However, the union officers were predominantly Irish. This is not to suggest that they had a deliberate policy of favoring the Irish. When there were clear-cut differences in seniority or other important objective factors, ethnic identification did not determine job rights, but in doubtful cases the Irishmen got the benefit of the doubt.

These influences even extended to the appointment of foremen. While the union had no contractual rights to concern itself with the appointment of foremen, Collins describes one case in which workers and union officials successfully resisted the appointment of a Yankee who had come up through the ranks. It did not help that this man had an ethnic identification with a superior ranking in the society as a whole. By custom, foremen's jobs belonged to the Irish. Of course, the ethnic matter was never brought out directly in official discussions of the case, but Collins reports that some of the workers said privately that this was what the argument was all about.

A later study by Abraham Zaleznik, Robert Christenson, and F. J. Roethlisberger, with the collaboration of George C. Homans, attempts to predict the informal group organization of workers and the group leadership within a particular factory department.[8] For data on which to make their predictions, they used the location of the worker's work station, job classification, sex, age, education, and ethnic identification. While all of these factors proved to be of some importance, being Irish was the best indicator of the individual's membership in a high status group and of his possibility of being an informal leader of such a group.

This is not to suggest that the Irish must necessarily be the dominant group in the ranks of the workers. That appears to depend upon the status system of the surrounding community and upon the history of the various groups within the enterprise in question. In a study of a highly skilled glass blowing department, Frank Miller and I found that the Swedes had been in control of all the top positions. The workers who were not Swedes had to make their way against this strong barrier.

Ethnic identification tends to be an important influence in local union elections. This is not to say that the Irish worker just automatically votes for the Irish candidate, the Italian for the Italian, and so on. There are nearly always other factors involved. However, when these other factors are evenly balanced, ethnic divisions in the voting can be expected.

Here we are talking about things which are not officially recognized in the ideology of a democratic society—like social class. All men are created

[8] *The Motivation, Productivity and Satisfaction of Workers* (Boston: Harvard Graduate School of Business Administration, 1958).

equal, and we are expected to reward them on their individual merits without regard to social class or ethnic identification. In fact, as we all know, these influences do have effects, but the effects tend to be officially denied while they are tacitly acknowledged.

This is not to say that our democratic ideology is of no importance. Since it holds a strong place in the sentiments of most Americans, direct or indirect appeals to this ideology are powerful weapons in the hands of those seeking to break through social class barriers or to disregard ethnic identification. In fact, it is important to note that you cannot state the discriminatory argument openly. You can't say: "This man should have the job because he is an Irishman." In fact, if your behavior suggests that this is the real reason behind the position you are taking, your opponent can shame you with the charge that you are allowing un-American sentiments to influence your judgment.

The pattern of ethnic status may be expected to vary from one part of the country to another. Furthermore, the importance of ethnic identification may also be expected to vary regionally and through time. In the places where I have studied workers of mixed ethnic backgrounds, the lines of ethnic identification seemed still to be strong, but they were presumably a good deal stronger during the periods of mass immigration. As we deal with second-, third-, and fourth-generation Americans, we can expect a diminution of these influences. On the other hand, whenever a new group arrives in large numbers, such as is the case with the Puerto Ricans in New York City, we can expect the ethnic lines to be more sharply drawn.

## ABSENTEE OWNERSHIP AND COMMUNITY POWER

Let us return for further exploration to one aspect of our Yankee City case: the impact upon community life of a change in the locus of ownership of industrial plants.

Fifty to one hundred years ago our small and medium sized cities abounded with locally owned and managed manufacturing plants. As we have seen in Yankee City and in New Bedford, these old family-owned and locally managed concerns have been fading from our scene. As in New Bedford, some of the firms have simply gone out of existence. As in Yankee City, many of them have been taken over by large corporations, whose top management is located in one or another of our major cities.

This change has involved a significant shift in power relations within the community. In Yankee City, we saw that some of the leading citizens of the community were openly sympathetic to the shoe workers in their organization efforts and highly critical of the absentee top management.

In some cities and towns, the growth of unions led to changes in political control. As the Steel Workers Organizing Committee took over one company-sponsored union after another to build a strong international, in many cases the men who rose to leadership at the local level went into politics and won control of city hall.

The growth of unions also led to union representation on some of the boards of civic agencies and community fund drives. If worker contributions provide a major part of the support for community projects, it becomes hard to deny representatives of labor the right to sit on the boards involved in raising and distributing the funds.

Noting such changes, some spokesmen of business have sought to give the impression that labor has become dominant in this country and that businessmen have become politically impotent. The facts hardly support this view. They show businessmen exerting strong influence at every governmental level from local to federal. Nevertheless, there has been a change, and the change has been such that it can leave the management of a given plant politically and socially isolated in its community.

The owner of the plant is generally a man of well-established position in the community. The manager for an absentee owner may move from job to job and community to community every three or four years, so that he can hardly put down roots in the community and match the man who has grown up there.

I have seen situations in which the local management of a plant was looked upon with suspicion in a community even by the local business people. Recognizing that such isolation can arise, the top managements of some large concerns have recently been emphasizing the community relations responsibilities of local managers. The manager is expected to be active in local organizations—and not just the country club. He is expected to know and to be able to work with local business people and political figures. In fact, some companies are even beginning to encourage members of their organizations to become active in politics, though this has by no means become the common pattern.

Some may regard this sort of activity simply as self defense, from the standpoint of the corporation. When a crisis arises—a strike, for example—management is in a much better position, as we shall note later, if its local management people have strong ties with the business community and some political influence.

Whatever the motives for such participation, some management people are coming to feel that it is good public relations—and public relations are more highly regarded than in previous times. Furthermore, some managements are beginning to see that public relations need not be limited to the pious publicity releases that sound so pleasant to company officials and make so little impression on anybody else. In a few cases, the company's public relations program is organized around the civic activity of management people, supplemented by financial support to some of these civic activities. In some cases the activity involves urban renewal, in other cases it may involve unpaid service on a school board, and so on. No clear pattern has yet emerged, but it is significant that a process of searching is going on.

No longer do businessmen generally feel that they can justify their leading position in the community simply through doing a good job in the plant. Increasingly, this justification is being sought in community affairs.

The same process seems to be going on within organized labor. As the wages of members of some unions have risen to the level of the earnings of many small business and professional people, the union leader can no longer justify his role simply as champion of an underprivileged minority. The search for new values is going on within unions too.

# Chapter 6 *FORMAL ORGANIZATION STRUCTURE*

SO FAR we have been dealing with environmental influences that reach the work group from outside of the organization itself. As we move inside the plant, let us continue our exploration of forces that can be considered in the environment, as far as a particular work group is concerned.

The formal organization structure provides the human framework within which group life takes place. By formal organization, I refer to two elements: (1) the officially determined structure of positions in the organization, with the officially established channels of who-reports-to-whom, and (2) the activities officially assigned to each position.

The rapid growth of interest in human relations in industry has served to deflect attention from the formal organization structure, but now we are again recognizing the importance of this environmental influence. The administrative theorists of the scientific management school aimed to devise organization structures and procedures in such a way that behavior within organizations could be controlled within very narrow limits. They were preoccupied with drawing geometrical charts of relationships and calculating the number of individuals who could be effectively supervised by a single supervisor in terms of mathematical formulas. This was all done on an *a priori* basis, with the theorists making logical deductions from certain untested initial assumptions and only sometimes bringing in cases from experience to justify their conclusions.

As the human relations field grew up out of empirical field work in organizations, we could easily see that there were wide variations in behavior within the same formal organization structure. This led us for a time to neglect formal organization structure and to concentrate upon the relations that grew up among people as they worked together day by day. Some called this the "informal organization" to indicate that it was not officially established by management, but simply represented a human adaptation to the working environment.

In this book, I am not utilizing the popular distinction between formal and informal organization. The justification for this decision is much the same as the one I have given in Chapter 2 for my refusal to use Homans' distinction between external system and internal system.

If we were to go out in the field to observe behavior and then categorize our observations under formal and informal organization, we would quickly get into insoluble problems. At the extremes, it may seem easy enough to distinguish between formal and informal behavior, but we actually find a large part of the behavior we observe falling between these extremes, where we can make no clear-cut distinctions.

For purposes of this book, the key word in our definition of formal organization structure is "officially." We are dealing with positions *officially* established and activities *officially* assigned to each position.

Such a definition makes no assumption that there will be any particular type of correspondence between formal organization structure and the behavior to be observed in the organization. What the relation is between formal organization structure and behavior is not to be assumed in advance of investigation. Research is required to determine the impact formal organization structure has upon behavior. This chapter will begin our exploration of this relationship.

We shall explore four aspects of formal organization structure:

1. Impact of size on an organization structure and on relations within the organization.
2. Impact of different types of structure (holding size constant) on patterns of supervisory behavior and superior-subordinate relations.
3. Implications of types of organization structure at the shop level in manufacturing activities.
4. The growth of specialization and its impact upon organization structure and organizational relations.

## SIZE AND STRUCTURE: A RESTAURANT CASE

To examine the relationship between size and structure—and the problems in human relations that develop with increasing size—let us consider the story of Tom Jones, restaurant man, who starts at the bottom and reaches the top.[1] He is a fictitious character, but the human problems he faces are representative of those that go with organizational growth everywhere.

The success story can be told in five stages. Jones begins with a small restaurant where he dispenses short orders over the counter (stage 1). He has two employees working for him, but there is no division of labor, and all three work together as cooks, countermen, and dishwashers.

The business expands, and Jones finds it necessary to move to larger quarters and hire new employees. Here we see the beginning of the division of labor (stage 2). He now has a staff of cooks, dishwashers, and waitresses to serve the customers over the counter or in their booths. But the staff is still small, and there is only one supervisor, Jones himself. He

---

[1] From W. F. Whyte, *Human Relations in the Restaurant Industry* (New York: McGraw-Hill Book Co., Inc., 1948), pp. 21–29.

keeps track of everything and frequently pitches in to work when he is needed at one of the stations.

In these early stages, the restaurant is characterized by the informality of its human relations. Jones is close to all his employees. They are few enough for him to know them well, and the fact that they work together so closely forms a good basis for friendship.

There are few formal controls in evidence. The workers know what the boss expects of them, and they know what to expect of the boss. The organization rolls along in a comfortable, informal manner.

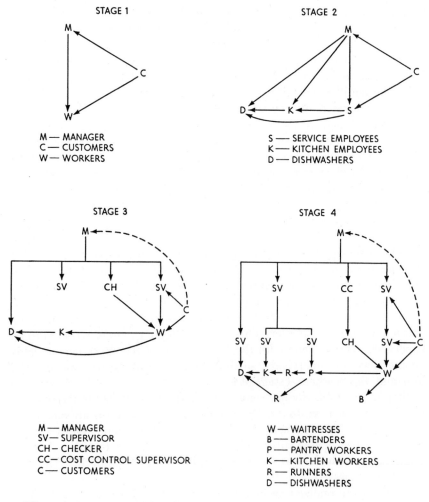

STAGE 1

M — MANAGER
C — CUSTOMERS
W — WORKERS

STAGE 2

S — SERVICE EMPLOYEES
K — KITCHEN EMPLOYEES
D — DISHWASHERS

STAGE 3

STAGE 4

M — MANAGER
SV — SUPERVISOR
CH — CHECKER
CC — COST CONTROL SUPERVISOR
C — CUSTOMERS

W — WAITRESSES
B — BARTENDERS
P — PANTRY WORKERS
K — KITCHEN WORKERS
R — RUNNERS
D — DISHWASHERS

There is just one problem in stage 2 that Jones did not have to face in stage 1. Now, if the organization is to function smoothly, the work of waitresses, cooks, and dishwashers must be coordinated. Sometimes Jones observes that there is friction among these various workers, but he is nearly always on the spot when trouble arises so that he can step in to smooth things over. The problem, therefore, is relatively simple at this point.

The first two stages are also characterized by the close relationship between Jones and his regular customers. He finds that his restuarant has become something of a social center in his neighborhood, and he has become an important local figure. The regular customers are his friends. They come in to eat, but they also come in to talk with him. In the regular course of business activity, he hears of the successes and failures, of the family and business affairs, of the local people. When they are in trouble, they tell him, and if he can help them, he does.

Tom Jones serves good food and has his own style of menus and service. This helps to account for his success, and yet, if you cross-examine his regular customers, they will admit that some of his competitors do just as good a food job. They go to the Jones restuarant because they enjoy the familiar, friendly atmosphere of the place and because they are personally loyal to the owner-manager.

Now the business continues to expand, and Jones again takes over larger quarters. No longer is he able to supervise all the work. He hires a service supervisor, a food-production supervisor, and places one of his employees in charge of the dishroom as a working supervisor. He also employs a checker to total checks for his waitresses and to see that the food is served in correct portions and style (stage 3).

In time, he finds that he can take care of a larger number of customers if he takes one more step in the division of labor. Up to now, the cooks have been serving the food to the waitresses. When these functions are divided, both cooking and serving can proceed more efficiently. Therefore, he sets up a service pantry apart from the kitchen. The cooks can now concentrate on cooking, the runners carry food from kitchen to pantry and orders from pantry to kitchen, and the pantry girls serve the waitresses over the counter. This adds one more group of workers to be supervised, and to cope with the larger scale of the operation, he adds another level of supervision, so that there are two supervisors between him and the workers (stage 4).

Stages 3 and 4 introduce some very significant changes in the position and activity of Tom Jones. He is no longer able to keep up such close relations with his customers. There are too many of them, and they come and go too fast. To be sure, he knows a large number by name, but the relationship is much more formal: "Good evening, Mr. Smith." "How are you, Mr. Jones?"

He comes to realize that he can no longer count on personal relations with customers to build up his business. He cannot sell the good will of the restaurant directly. He must sell it through his supervisors and workers. They represent him to the customers, and he must teach them to maintain the distinctive atmosphere and style which the customers find attractive. With the personal touch of the owner carrying less direct weight, he must give special attention to improving standards of food and service, so that customers who have never seen him will eat in his restaurant because "it's the best place in town."

This expansion also gives rise to new problems in the relationship between the manager and his subordinates. As the number of employees grows, Jones finds that he no longer has time to get to know them well. With those who were with him in the early days, he manages to maintain a cordial personal relationship even though he has much less time for them than before. But those more recently hired are little more than names and faces to him.

He has the uncomfortable feeling that he no longer knows his organization as he once did. He overhears one of the newer employees saying, "There's a clique of old-timers in here. You can't get a fair break unless you belong to the old gang. The boss plays favorites."

This worries Jones. He has always prided himself upon his relationship with his employees, and he is determined to solve this problem. But he does not have time to get to know the new people as he did the old. And the loyalty of the older employees has been responsible for a large measure of his success. That must be worth something. He does not feel that it is right to break off relations with the old-timers just to meet the charge of favoritism. So what can he do?

He also faces new problems. One day Frank, an employee of some years' service, comes in to complain that Miss Markley, his supervisor, has discriminated against him. He had been expecting a promotion to a higher paying job, but the supervisor told him that his work was not up to standard and that he could expect nothing better than his present job. Frank appeals to the boss to overrule Miss Markley.

Jones thinks it over. He has always had the impression that Frank was doing a good job, but Miss Markley is in a better position to know the facts of the case. Still, he does not feel that she has always used good judgment in handling workers in the past, so it is quite possible that she has been unjust to Frank. Perhaps he should tell Frank that he will take care of the case for him, but that would undermine the authority of his supervisor. So perhaps he must simply tell Frank to accept Miss Markley's decision as final. But then Frank will probably quit. That in itself may not be so serious, but as workers fail to get a hearing from Jones, they will stop coming to him with their problems and he will be completely cut off from them.

If that happens, the morale of the workers will be left entirely to his supervisors. Perhaps that is inevitable in the long run, for as the organization continues to grow and executive responsibilities pile up, there simply is not enough time left in the day to keep in direct touch with the employees.

While this is a natural result of growth, it raises new problems for the owner-manager. He wonders how he can select supervisors who are capable of doing a good personnel job. He knows how to evaluate their knowledge of food production or service, but skill in human relations seems so much more difficult to measure. He interviews the applicants for supervisory positions, and he sizes them up on the basis of his own experience. He feels that his judgment is above average, and yet he sometimes doubts his whole procedure. Perhaps he is just choosing people who make a good impression on him, thus assuming that the workers will react in the same way. Yet he knows very well that there are supervisors who manage to make a good impression on management, but are highly unpopular with the workers. The ideal supervisor is able to adjust well to subordinates and superiors alike—but how is he to be located?

Of course, people are not born with supervisory skill, nor can they be expected to have it when they take on their first supervisory job. Such skill grows with experience and training. Perhaps the deficiencies of Jones' selection procedure would not be so serious if he could provide new supervisors with the sort of experience and training that would make the most of their talents in handling people. That, he realizes, is a major problem.

When Jones was beginning, he could state his personnel problem in very simple form: How can I get the cooperation of the workers? As the organization grew, he found he had to leave that problem more and more in the hands of his supervisors. His problem was: How can I get the cooperation of my supervisors? At first he did not recognize this as a problem. He assumed that anyone who was a part of management would naturally give his best to the organization. In the course of time, he learned that this was not so. Not that supervisors willfully refused to do their best. Under certain circumstances, they were simply unable to perform at full capacity. Through observing his supervisors, he found that their efficiency was much higher when they were happy and well-adjusted in their jobs than when they were facing nervous tensions. That was enlightening, but it solved no problems. Instead, it posed a new one: How can I make supervisors happy and well-adjusted in their jobs?

As the restaurant organization expanded, Jones discovered that it also moved toward standardization. When he himself worked behind the counter, he did not need to worry about elaborate financial controls. He knew his workers and he trusted them. He knew, from day-to-day experience, just about how much business he was doing, so that if the cash register was ever short, he could check up on it right away.

With a large organization, such informal controls necessarily break down. Jones had to build up a system of cost control, and the old employees had to learn new ways.

In the kitchen, there was a larger problem. Jones made his name through maintaining a certain standard of food and service. In his single restaurant, the quality of the food depended upon the chef. If the old chef went out and a new chef came in, the character of the food changed. One man seemed too slender a thread from which to hang the future of his restaurant.

With stage 5 in development, the chain restaurant, this problem became more acute.

From the customers' standpoint, there is little justification for a chain except in the advantage it gives them in knowing what type of food and service to expect, no matter which unit they patronize. This cannot be done without standardization, and that means standard recipes as well as standard service procedures.

Jones approached the problem of standardized recipes tentatively at first. He told the chef of his first large restaurant that he had a secure job with the organization for as long as he was able to work, but in case he were lost through illness or other causes, it would be a great loss to the restaurant to have his secrets leave with him. Would he be willing to write down some of the chief recipes upon which the restaurant depended?

The chef did not respond very well to this request. He said he was very busy and besides, he just did these things by heart and would not know how to put them down on paper. Jones was sure that the chef could furnish the information if he really tried. The owner-manager became aware of another factor in the situation.

Operating without written recipes, the chef was king of the kitchen. The manager might find fault with some of the dishes, but not knowing how they were made, he could only bring the matter to the chef's attention and hope for the best. If recipes were furnished, the manager could then supervise the chef much more closely. He could check to see that the recipes were being followed. He could bring in new recipes and revise old ones.

Furthermore, this standardization would tend to take the skill out of the job and much of the prestige with it. It had taken the chef years to learn his craft, and now, in a restaurant down the street, cooks were being trained through standard recipes in a matter of weeks. And women were taking over those jobs, too. It all went against the grain, and the chef did not want to be a party to it. So he balked. And Jones wondered whether it would be possible to change the chef's attitude or whether a kitchen with standardized recipes required a fresh start, with inexperienced workers and a college-educated food-production manager to train them.

That was a major problem and there were others like it. Increasing size required standardization of procedure, and that involved important changes in work routines and human relations. Unless these changes were made skillfully, the morale of the organization would deteriorate. Within limits, standardization was clearly necessary for business reasons, and so he faced another problem: How can I gain the benefits of standardization without losing employee morale and cooperation?

In later chapters we will consider some possible ways of dealing with the human problems that Tom Jones faced. My purpose at this point is simply to show how increasing size leads to changes in organization structure, and how size and structure together affect the social system of activities, interactions, and sentiments.

## ORGANIZATION STRUCTURE AND PATTERNS OF SUPER-VISION

Suppose we hold constant the type of organization and the number of employees. What variations seem to be associated with differences in organization structure?

The best case along this line comes from the experience of Sears, Roebuck and Company.

This story begins in the Spring of 1949, when a sudden recession hit the retailing business throughout the country.

In examining the company's response to this crisis, the personnel researchers gave particular attention to their department stores of intermediate size. Prior interviewing and observation pointed to the organization structure as an important research focus. There were enough stores of this size throughout the country so that it was possible to examine differences in organization structure and separate these factors from differences in geographical location and other influences. Such stores had approximately thirty-two departments. Without any management planning in this particular respect, the stores had grown up with two different types of management structure. In the one that we will call type X, there was a store manager, an assistant manager, and thirty-two division managers. The assistant manager shared the duties of the manager in various ways, and the two of them constituted a management team. In the other type of structure, type Y, there was a store manager and five or six second-level managers, each one having four to six division managers reporting to him. Thus type X had two levels of authority above the salesmen, while type Y had three. The statistics on costs and profits showed that type X was a much more effective model from an economic standpoint. Furthermore, Sears' personnel department found that type X stores produced much more than their proportionate share of management personnel considered promotable to higher levels, whereas type Y stores produced less than their share.

How can we explain these results? Here we see the connection between closeness of supervision and organization structure. In the type Y store, the store manager had only six or seven people reporting directly to him. Therefore, he was able to supervise their work in considerable detail. In fact, if he did not supervise closely, we might ask what he did with his time. His immediate subordinates had only four to six people reporting to them, and therefore, could provide close supervision of the work of the division managers. This meant that the division manager could check a decision of any importance with his superior and was not encouraged to back his own judgment and initiative.

On the other hand, in store type X it was literally impossible to provide close supervision. No manager can supervise closely the work of thirty department heads. He must choose division managers who have some initiative, judgment, and organizing ability, and then he must be willing to trust them to run their departments. He will expect his department heads to make mistakes, but he will also expect that, in his general review of operations, the most serious mistakes will come to his attention. Thus, the reasons for the mistakes will eventually be diagnosed and discussed with the department heads. Furthermore, he will expect a man to learn much more from the mistakes that are his individual responsibility than from the mistakes on which his boss made the final decision.

The first superficial conclusion to be drawn from this study was that all of the intermediate size stores should be converted into organizational structures of the X type. However, before making this recommendation, the Sears personnel people went to stores representing both types to conduct interviews, and particularly, to study the store manager in action. In this phase of the study they discovered a very interesting relationship between the personality of the store manager and the type of structure that he directed.

The manager of the X type store, who worked with an assistant to supervise approximately thirty division managers, appeared to be an individual with an optimistic view of people. He spoke freely of his faith in his subordinates. He seemed to take pride in the successes they achieved on their own initiative. On the other hand, the manager of the Y type store seemed to have a much more pessimistic outlook. He felt that it was very difficult to get good, hard-working people any more. Young people these days were being spoiled by the government or the educational system. James C. Worthy comments, "These managers often seemed to expect the worst of their people and generally found their fears justified. They found that people had to be watched, that their work had to be checked closely—otherwise no telling what might happen."[2]

We might ask here whether the personalities had created the organization structure, or vice versa. In this case, the personalities seemed to come first. The researchers found that when a manager who had been effective in an X type store was transferred to a store of the Y type, he soon was reporting to higher management that he did not need all the management people he had on hand. He was trying to get his middle management people transferred to other units, so that he would eventually

---

[2] This case is adapted from my bulletin, *Modern Methods in Social Research* (Washington, D.C.: Office of Naval Research, 1952). It is based upon an unpublished manuscript of James C. Worthy, formerly vice-president, Sears, Roebuck and Co.

have under him the X type organization in which he was comfortable and effective. On the other hand, when the manager from the Y type of structure was transferred to a store with the X type organization, he soon reported that to meet very specific problems in that situation he needed to have a man who would take over the supervision of several of his divisions. In time he too created the type of structure in which he functioned most comfortably.

Worthy concludes his analysis of personality and organization structure in these terms:

This, of course, poses a critical question: If the structure of the organization is of such basic importance, and if changes in structure can be accomplished only through character changes on the part of the top men, what hope is there of any significant progress? After all, personality changes of any magnitude in adults are extremely difficult to bring about and likely to require the equivalent of psychoanalysis or religious conversion. In terms of the problems facing industry, either of these processes, whatever its value otherwise, is slow and its results uncertain. If changes in character were the only way to accomplish needed changes in the functioning of organizations, we should be in a very poor way indeed.

Fortunately, there appears to be an alternative; or, rather, there appears to be another factor at work as a determinant of organization structure which is relatively independent of the character and personality of the key people in it. This is the generally accepted body of organization principles developed under the aegis of scientific management: the principles of the functional organization, the limited span of control, etc. Many businessmen have set up their organizations along these lines, not so much because that is the way they might have done it if left to follow their own instincts, but because these are the accepted ways of how an organization *should* be set up. Many of these men, if given an alternative theory of organization, could readily adapt to it. It is for this reason that the development of a more adequate system of principles is of such vital importance.[3]

Long before human relations research began, we had theories of formal organization structure. We are now returning to theorizing along these lines. There is a difference, however. The older generation of theorists proceeded on an *a priori* basis without reference to research. Having discarded the old theories but recognizing again the importance of formal organization structure, we are just beginning to develop empirical research on that structure.

James C. Worthy has been one of the chief management spokesmen for the conception of the flat organization structure—one with relatively few levels of authority in relation to the number of organization members. Sears, Roebuck and Company has been particularly identified with this point of view. The conception has been applied to the retailing end of the Sears business to a spectacular degree. It is noteworthy, however, that the large Sears mail order plants resemble the traditional hierarchies of

---

[3] *Ibid.*

large factories. This suggests a re-examination of the impact of the type of mission upon the possibilities of flattening the hierarchy.

What are the factors in the Sears B stores, for example, that make it possible for one manager and an assistant to direct the work of thirty-odd division heads? At least three factors seem to be of importance.

1. *Independence of Units.* The various selling divisions of the store can operate with a high degree of independence from each other. There is no flow of work from division to division and very little influence of any kind from one division on another. The manager can leave his division head alone with the assurance that, if the man does make mistakes and gets his division into difficulties, the problems will be localized within that division. In an organization where there is a flow of work from unit to unit, a problem within any one unit may soon involve the whole organization.

2. *Simplicity of Technology.* The selling end of the business involves a very simple technology. Problems of maintenance are minimal compared to those experienced in a plant having complex machines and processes. There are no engineers, production planners, inspectors, and other specialists whose work must somehow be integrated with the line organization.

3. *Measurability of Results.* This involves the system of accounting symbols designed to measure the performance of the organization and its various units. All organizations develop figures designed to measure results, and some figures are always provided. However, in many situations, there is a serious question as to whether the figures that are available adequately reflect the performance of the unit under management's scrutiny.

For example, consider the problem of operating a large oil field. The results of the operation as a whole are indeed subject to some measurement. The number of barrels of oil produced at a given market price can be compared with the wages and salaries, costs of materials and equipment, power, taxes and so on for a given time, providing some overall measure of results. But even this figure provides no sure guide to the effectiveness of the organization. No oil field is just like any other. Suppose the profits are down in one particular field, but local management claims that it has been meeting unusually difficult problems in drilling. The decision as to whether, considering these conditions, management's performance was good, fair, or poor remains a matter of interpretation. The figures themselves do not tell the story.

If it is difficult to evaluate the performance of the organization as a whole in a particular oil field, the problem of evaluating the performance of its various units becomes immeasurably more complex. In the oil field, only the drilling, production, and pipe line units are directly involved with producing the product and making it available for distribution, and yet it may be that only one third of the personnel in the field is directly involved in these units. The others are involved in maintenance, construction, and other services to the field, and in the technical engineering and theoretical work that goes with oil production.

How then can the performance of a given unit be evaluated? Not in terms of its own output if it only services producing units. Of course, comparisons are always made of the costs of a given unit compared with that same unit for previous months and with other similar units in the company, and efforts are made to measure the amount of work done. However, there are always important questions of judgment left unresolved by the figures provided.

In the B store situation, the problem of result measurement is incomparably simpler. These hundreds of stores throughout the country have a uniform accounting procedure. Each store is a self-contained unit. The results from one store can be compared at a glance with the results from another. Past experience will indicate what allowances should be made for the wealth or poverty of the market. Within a given store, comparisons of costs and sales can be made with equal ease within each division.

Decentralization may be said to depend to some extent upon the abilities of superiors to judge by results. The philosophers of decentralization argue that the superiors should not supervise in detail but should judge as to the necessity of their intervention according to the results being achieved by their subordinates. If the results are good, the superior does not need to intervene in any detail. If the results are bad, the superior needs to come in and scrutinize the operation carefully. But in some types of operations the accounting figures readily provide a useful measure of performance, whereas in others they simply do not. If the performance of a subordinate unit does not provide any direct measure of results, the superior is inclined to involve himself much more heavily in the details of operation of that unit. Without having any neat record of results to go by, he may feel that if he can assure himself that things are being done in the right way (that is, his way) the unit will be functioning well. This necessarily involves close supervision.

While some of the differences between organization structures can be charged to the different missions of the organizations, nevertheless, within each type of organization, whether in the oil industry or the retail industry, there is room for variation as between a flatter or a longer hierarchy. The organization structure that evolves may be to that extent a result of the philosophy of the management people who establish it. It is argued that one man can only supervise adequately the work of five or six subordinates if their tasks are of any complexity and require any cooperation among them. This, however, assumes that adequate supervision means close supervision, that men will not perform well unless they are closely supervised. If we make the contrary assumption, that men perform better when they have less detailed supervision, then greater numbers can be supervised by one individual, and management can build flatter organization structures.

## FUNCTIONAL VERSUS PRODUCT ORGANIZATION[4]

The structure of the formal organization may be organized at the shop level along functional lines, along product lines, or with some combination of the two.

A small plant making a complete product cannot be organized around functional lines because there will be too few machines of a given type to be put together in one department. It is the larger plants which have the choice.

The functional principle calls for putting together in one location and under one supervisor all machines of a given type. For example, there may be one department for milling machines, another for punch presses, one for drill presses, and so on. The product principle of organization calls for groupings of machines and operations in terms of a particular product or part of a product. In such an organization, we may find several milling machines, drill presses, punch presses, and so on in the same department.

The principle of organization selected has important consequences for the functioning of the organization. We shall not try to strike a balance between advantages and disadvantages but will simply note the impact of each organizational type.

The functional organization provides for specialization by workers and their foreman on a particular type of machine. The foreman can be particularly skilled on this machine and thus able to step in on any technical difficulty, and to provide training and operating advice for workers. Workers can start on the simple jobs in the department and work up in a steady progression to the most skilled.

The foreman is free to devote his time to the technical problems of machine operation because the coordination of the production on various machines is handled outside of his own department. On the other hand, this means the foreman's experience is confined to narrow technical problems. He does not learn on the job the skills of coordinating diverse activities; in other words, he does not learn skills essential to management at higher levels. The workers may develop considerable skill on a particular machine, but their skill also is confined within narrow channels. They are isolated from other types of operations.

Finally, the functional organization completely divorces the worker from the product which he helps to make. He tends to think in terms of a particular skill. He cannot identify himself with the making of the prod-

---

[4] In this section I have drawn heavily upon Burleigh B. Gardner and David G. Moore, "The Techniques of Organization," *Human Relations in Industry* (3d. ed.; Homewood, Ill.: Richard D. Irwin, Inc., 1955).

uct when his own part fits in at some point that may be unknown to him.

In the product organization, the foreman cannot be skilled in all the operations he supervises, and this may be a serious deficiency, depending upon the level of skills and ingenuity of the men working for him. On the other hand, his job puts an emphasis upon the skills of coordinating diverse activities. If he can develop these skills, he not only contributes to organizational efficiency, but at the same time gathers the experience that can help him to handle more complex coordinating problems at higher levels. If he does not develop such skills, then the product organization cannot function effectively.

The workers in the product department are not likely to become specialists on a particular type of machine as in the functional department, but under certain conditions, they may be able to develop a wider range of skills. If there is a line of promotion from one machine or operation to another, then these diversification possibilities are present. On the other hand, this movement from one type of machine or operation to another presents management with problems of training. Furthermore, since the foreman is not a specialist in all of the machines, he can do relatively little on the technical side of the training process. How serious this is depends in part upon the technical complexities of learning new jobs. Where the new job is simple and easily learned, there is no problem, but where considerable skill is required, the product type of organization presents serious problems.

Finally, organization on product lines promotes the identification of workers—and foremen—with a particular product. This creates a sense of belonging that contributes to higher morale.

The effects of the two principles of organization are not felt simply at the shop level. They have important consequences for organization structure at high levels also. The functional type of organization tends to be associated with a longer chain of command. Where coordination is not accomplished within the department, management has to build a structure around the various departments to provide coordination on higher levels.

The two principles of organization are also likely to produce different impacts upon the cohesion of work groups. The product principle builds a department that is heterogeneous as to job operations, skills, pay and so on. The functional principle builds a department which is much more homogeneous as to types of operations, skills, pay and so on. Since workers in the functional department share the same relationship to the technological and economic environment, they are also likely to share the same sentiments and to respond as a group to changes in this environment. In the product department, workers do not share the same relationships to the technological and economic environment and are likely to be less cohesive in their responses to it.

Cohesiveness of a work group can be an advantage or a disadvantage

to management. If management has some success at getting the cooperation of the workers in a given department, then cohesion among the members can be a strong asset. If there is a running conflict between workers
and management, then a cohesive department is a threat to management
and a department more heterogeneously oriented is a distinct advantage.
The problems of supervising work groups will be discussed later. For
present purposes, I am concerned only with showing the impacts of various aspects of formal organization structure upon the behavior of workers
and supervisors.

## SPECIALIZATION AND ORGANIZATION STRUCTURE

So far, our discussion has concentrated on what is commonly called the
line organization: the direct channel of authority from top management
down to the people who produce the product in the shop or sell the goods
in the store. Years ago, there were many organizations in which the
line management made up all or nearly all of the managerial personnel.

This is no longer true. We live in an era of increasing specialization,
so that we find companies operating today with a variety of specialists
who relate themselves to the line organization in ways which should be
studied. These non-line management people are classified under several
terms; most commonly, staff, service, and control.

I shall make no attempt here to define these terms, for I feel that much
literature is misleading in this respect. In Part VI, which deals with
"service, staff, and control groups," I shall attempt to explore this field
systematically.

For present purposes, it should be enough to enumerate some of the
main specialist groups, briefly describe their functions, and indicate
some of the problems of integrating them with the line organization.

There is often an inspection department set up to watch over the quality
of production. There is an accounting and cost control group involved in
measuring costs and establishing budgets for the operation of the company.

There are engineering groups (with various sub-specialties) involved
in the design and installation of new products, processes, and production
methods. Among our specialist groups, the engineers are expected to be
the chief agents of innovation, and we will have several occasions to
examine the impact of their innovating activity.

Nearly every organization will require a maintenance department. As
we shall see in Chapter 26, "Maintenance and Operating Organizations,"
maintenance can be organized in various ways, and each pattern involves
its own distinctive set of human and technical problems.

Finally, there is the personnel or industrial relations group, which is
charged with devising and administering the systems whereby men are
placed in the organization, compensated, and evaluated. The personnel

organization usually has some responsibility for handling appeals of line management decisions, particularly when unions are involved.

The first general point to make about specialist groups is that in some cases, relations between specialist and line manager may be highly predictable, given knowledge of the formal positions involved and the officially assigned activities. For example, Eliot Chapple has commented that there is one easy way for a research man or a consultant to establish himself with management as a perceptive and knowledgeable individual. Without having any prior knowledge of the manufacturing organization, he can safely say, "I suppose you are having some trouble with your relations between the production department and the inspection department." The prediction will rarely turn out to be wrong, and the guess may help to establish the reputation of the predictor.

It is not only the nature of the activities performed by the specialists, in relation to the line, that influences the relations between the two groups. There is also a question as to where the specialist activity is to be tied into the line organization, with different results to be expected from different structural decisions.

For example, take the case of one company which established a dual system of authority in each of its manufacturing plants. The plant controller was officially independent of the plant manager at each location. He was directly responsible for managing the office force and for providing his superiors—in the Controller's Department at the divisional office—with the operating figures of the plant.

Through our research, we were familiar with the situation in three of the company's plants; two of them were in the same city as the divisional office, the third was about 250 miles away. We learned that there was almost constant friction between plant controller and plant manager in the first two plants. In the third plant, relations between the two departments seemed to be reasonably harmonious.

The high level of friction between the two departments in each of the first two plants seemed to be due to the independent position the plant manager and the plant controller occupied in each plant. The difference between the situation in the first two plants and that of the outlying plant became clear when we added to organization structure the impact of geography and accessibility of communication channels. In the divisional office city, each plant manager interacted frequently with the production manager, his immediate superior in division management. Each plant controller interacted frequently with his immediate superior in the Controller's Department in the divisional office. When any problem arose between controller and manager at the plant level, it was an easy matter for each man to take the problem up with his boss. He needed only to pick up the telephone or to take a few minutes' drive into divisional headquarters.

In the outlying plant, the situation was quite different. The controller and manager at the plant level saw their immediate superiors only once every two or three months. The telephone was available, but this was a highly cost-conscious company where all expenditures were carefully scrutinized. It was understood that long distance calls were to be limited to matters of real importance.

Therefore, the plant manager and plant controller in the outlying plant had no alternative but to try to work out their problems together. As it happened, the two men had worked together in another plant, and the man who was now controller had worked directly under the man who had become plant manager. In the outlying plant, the relationship that had been previously established on a formal basis continued to exist on an informal basis. The observer who was not familiar with the formal organization structure of the company would have assumed in this plant that the controller was subordinate to the plant manager—as indeed he was in behavior.

This case suggests that a certain type of structural arrangement may tend to promote friction between certain parts of it. We also see that certain other forces (in this case, geography and lines of communication) may modify the relationship that could otherwise be predicted.

## CONCLUSION

In this chapter we have seen that the formal organization structure tends to have an important impact upon the behavior of people in the organization. It tends to limit possible behavior in certain directions and to provide channels within which other types of behavior may more readily develop.

It is a mistake to think of formal organization structure as positively determining behavior. At the same time, we should be aware of the strong influences on behavior provided by the structure. The skillful executive will not only think of ways of behaving that will modify the impact of a particular structure. He will also think of ways of reorganizing the structure so as to promote the type of behavior he seeks to develop in the organization.

# Chapter 7  *IMPACT OF THE ECONOMIC ENVIRONMENT*

THIS chapter will illustrate some of the ways in which the economic environment affects workers and certain ways in which they respond to this impact.[1]

We take man's concern with making money as natural and inevitable. We do not stop to think that this interest, like others, is culturally determined. Man is not born loving money. He learns to take a strong or a weak interest in money through the experiences he has in the process of growing up in his own society.

In the beginning stages of industrialization in underdeveloped countries, management often faces a problem of getting the workers sufficiently interested in money to assure regular attendance on the job. Workers coming into plants from rural areas have had little experience with money and have not learned to desire the wide range of things that money can buy. They find that their wages give them much more money than they need in order to maintain their customary standard of living. It is only as such people raise their aspirations regarding their own standard of living that they become greatly interested in gaining increased pay for more work.

## INCENTIVES AS ECONOMIC SYMBOLS

It is sometimes said that the high wages in American plants lead to high productivity. Whatever connection there may be is exceedingly indirect and remote. Management people may say that increasing worker productivity will enable management to pay higher wages, but wage rates do not respond rapidly to changes in worker productivity, so that the worker sees no economic reward in producing more. The wage rate may therefore only provide an incentive for the worker to keep his job. Keeping the job will require meeting management's minimum standards of production, but will hardly tap the resources of energy and ingenuity that the worker can bring to bear on the job if he is strongly motivated.

[1] This chapter is based largely on my *Money and Motivation* (New York: Harper & Bros., 1955). For a full discussion of economic incentives, see that book.

Noting that the wage rate itself provides no direct incentive for production, many management people have sought to use money with greater emotional effect by relating the economic symbols of pay directly to work activities: the more work turned out, the more pay. Such schemes are often known as "piece work" because they involve setting a price upon each piece produced. Management offers workers guarantees of protection as well as rewards for additional effort and ingenuity. They are guaranteed that they will always receive their regular hourly rate even if their incentive earnings fall below it, and they are further guaranteed that high incentive earnings will not lead to a cut in the piece rate (the price established by management for each piece produced).

Individual piece rates, the incentive approach most commonly applied in American industry today, are something more than a technical arrangement. They also represent a theory of the nature of man. In his life within the organization, he is thought to be primarily if not exclusively interested in maximizing his economic gains. Furthermore, he can be counted on to respond individualistically to the economic symbols management sets before him. Management initiates, the worker responds. And he responds as an individual. The logic of individual piece work includes no consideration of the worker's relations with his fellows.

The economist knows very well that these assumptions about economic man do not hold in the actual world. Experienced executives also sense that the theory of behavior underlying piece rates is imperfect and incomplete, to say the least. Having no other theory to put in its place, they tend to accept the theory of economic man as if it were indeed true, and to act accordingly. It is my aim, through examining worker response to incentive systems, to lay the foundations for a more adequate theory of man's response to economic symbols. A new theory is necessary because we see, wherever we look, that men are not behaving as the old theory says they do.

In our re-examination of "economic man," let us first consider individual differences, and then go on to discuss group behavior.

## INDIVIDUAL DIFFERENCES

Individual differences in worker response to money have been most systematically explored by Melville Dalton, who carried on a study of a large factory department where workers were paid on an incentive or piece rate basis. In this 300-man department, Dalton selected for intensive study 84 workers all of whom had been on their jobs for seven years or more. While this did not eliminate differences in skill, at least none of the men were handicapped by lack of experience. Furthermore, Dalton found that some of the lowest producers had been given a Class A rating by management before the introduction of the incentive system. This suggests that skill differences played a minor role in production records.

In this shop, bonus payments started when the worker reached 66 per cent. The norms of the work group required that no one should produce more than 150 per cent on any job.

Production records of these men provided Dalton with three categories into which they could readily be classified. Nine of the men were called "rate-busters" by their fellows, since they frequently went beyond the 150 per cent ceiling. There were 50 men who averaged more than 100 per cent, but never exceeded the 150 per cent ceiling. They were clearly motivated to earn incentive money, and yet they abided by the group norm. We may call them "middle-performers." The remaining 25 averaged under 100 per cent. They appeared to make little if any effort to make bonus, and we can call them the "under-motivated." For certain purposes in the subsequent analysis, we shall consider the middle-performers and the under-motivated together, calling them "restricters." The only division socially recognized by the men was that which divided "rate-busters" from the rest.

In examining social background, social participation, spending and saving behavior, politics and religion, Dalton found interesting differences between these categories of workers. In background, he found that the nine rate-busters had all either grown up on farms owned by their parents or had been children of middle-class parents in towns or cities. The restricters predominantly grew up in an urban environment and had a working-class background.

In social participation, the rate-busters were of course socially isolated in the shop, but even outside of the shop we see marked differences in social participation, with the restricters being much more socially active with family, friends, and clubs. All of the rate-busters except two appeared to be social isolates in the community. One of the two active rate-busters was a member of the Masons, a predominantly middle-class organization.

Although the rate-busters, of course, made more money than anyone in the shop, those who collected for the Red Cross and other charitable activities reported to Dalton that it was harder to get money from these men than it was from any others in the department. Quite a different situation prevailed in the purchasing of war bonds. There rate-busters were always at the top of the list.

In politics, Dalton estimated that something over 70 per cent of the men in the shop as a whole were Democrats. In the unmotivated category, 22 out of 25 (88 per cent) were Democrats. The 50 middle-performers were more divided, but still predominantly Democratic. Eight out of nine of the rate-busters were Republicans, and we might classify the ninth as a "regional Democrat." This lone Democrat came from the Deep South, and his political views corresponded with those of conservative southern Democrats. If we divide the 84 men according to political affiliation, we find Republicans averaging 123.3 per cent and Democrats averaging

95.8 per cent (critical ratio 4.0). However, a good part of this difference can be accounted for by the eight Republican rate-busters.

Dalton found Protestants averaging higher in production than Catholics, and he reported that of the 98 practicing Catholics in the 300-man department as a whole, there was not a single rate-buster.

Comparing the men according to country of origin, Dalton found that the foreign born averaged 90.6 per cent, whereas the native born averaged 108.7 per cent (critical ratio of 3.5), in spite of the fact that the foreign born averaged slightly longer in years of experience in the shop. The figure seems to reflect two interrelated forces; acculturation to American life, and social class position and mobility. The more the worker fits into our way of life and our status system, with its emphasis upon social mobility, the more interest he displays in earning money.

So far we have been reporting Dalton's data regarding the behavior and expressed sentiments of these men. Dalton goes on to report one set of observations regarding the internal physical and psychological adjustment of the workers. Nine of these eighty-four men reported that they were under treatment for ulcers or for incipient ulcers. All nine were found among the middle-performers.

While we must treat with caution a single set of such observations—and one based upon informant reports to the social scientist and not upon independent medical examinations—nevertheless, this concentration of a physical condition thought to be related to emotional stress, found entirely among the middle-performers, may well reflect the pulls of conflicting forces felt particularly within that category. The middle-performers wanted to earn money and strove to do so, but they also wanted to retain the goodwill of their fellows, and therefore they stopped short of 150 per cent. The rate-busters were single-minded in their pursuit of money. To Dalton they expressed themselves most vehemently against the restricters in general. The rate-busters were socially isolated, to be sure, but they made it quite clear to Dalton that they had no desire to be considered members of a work group made up of restricters.

At an earlier period the unmotivated workers had tried to make as much bonus as they could up to the informal group ceiling, but they reported that they had abandoned this struggle. They reasoned that the additional money was not worth the emotional frustration involved in trying to beat the incentive system. In effect, they had simply renounced the bonus.

We see from this brief review of Dalton's findings that the response to the incentive is by no means automatic. Not only do individuals respond in different ways to the same incentive, but these differences are associated with differences in social background, participation, spending and saving, politics, and religion.

For some problems, these individual differences will be important to us. However, we should not allow our concentration upon the individual differences to obscure the general pattern. With few exceptions, workers do reach informal agreements as to the amount of bonus it is safe and desirable to earn, and these norms govern their behavior.

## GROUP BEHAVIOR

Let us assume that the work group has arrived at 150 per cent as the productivity norm: the worker is not supposed to produce more than 150 per cent on any job. As soon as the newcomer acquires the skill that enables him to approach the 150 per cent figure, he is initiated into the secrets of the work group. He is told that it is not safe to go beyond the group norm, that management will cut rates or that other dire consequences will follow earnings above this norm. If he does not respond to casual suggestions, negative sanctions will be applied by the work group. The man will be called a rate-buster, or other uncomplimentary names. He will be socially ostracized by his fellow workers—a heavy penalty, except for those few who prefer to isolate themselves. This means also that the worker will be cut off from the circulation of the informal know-how of factory production. On many jobs, experienced workers have developed short cuts in methods and have built jigs and fixtures that enable them to work faster—and with no additional effort—than would be possible if they followed the methods established by the time study men when they studied the job and set the piece rate. On a given job, the rate may be very "tight" when the management-approved method is followed, and the worker may have to put out great efforts to make even 115 per cent of his base pay. Armed with the secrets of the work group, the same man may be able to raise his output easily up to 150 per cent. The worker who goes beyond 150 per cent on easy jobs will not be let in on the secrets that enable him to approach 150 per cent on the jobs which seem to have "tight" rates.

Although in general a piece rate system does bring forth more production than straight hourly pay, these gains are not without cost. We often find a piece rate system accentuating conflict between workers and management and between the union and management. The grievances and other complaints against management often seem to revolve around the incentive system.

Why is it that the piece rate system yields only limited gains of production and tends to add to the conflict in the social system?

## PAVLOV AND PIECE RATES

Before pursuing our examination of worker behavior, let us look at another body of theory that may be applicable to these problems: the theory of conditioned response developed by Ivan Pavlov, the great Russian psychologist.[2] Pavlov worked with dogs, but other experimenters have achieved similar results upon other animals. In some of these experiments a piece of food served as reward and a mild electric shock as punishment. The sound of the bell was designed to indicate that food would shortly be offered, whereas a different sound signalized the approach of an electric shock. After only a few exposures to these auditory stimuli, the animal made the appropriate discriminations. When the bell sounded, and even before the food was offered, the animal would salivate and give other signs of anticipating a rewarding experience. For the other sound, it would crouch, lift up the leg that was to be shocked, or assume some other apparently withdrawing or defensive reaction.

One condition should be noted in connection with such results. It has been found in various conditioning experiments that the animal does not continue indefinitely to respond in a vigorous manner to the stimuli. After repeated exposures, it reacts in a more lethargic fashion—as if losing interest in the whole business.

So far (if we overlook the condition just noted) the experiment seems to lend support to the reward-punishment theory. However, let us complicate the picture with reports on further conditioning experiments. In one case Pavlov presented to the animal two lighted discs of markedly different shapes. Upon presentation of one, food was forthcoming, whereas the other was followed by the shock. When the conditioned reflex had been established—that is, when the animal responded consistently and appropriately to each of the two symbols—Pavlov began to modify the shapes of the discs so that they became more and more alike. At first the animal reacted much as before. As the symbols became more similar, it continued making the appropriate behavior discriminations but with increasingly marked signs of agitation. Finally a point was reached where the animal failed to respond to either disc in the accustomed manner; instead, it displayed such signs of agitation as barking, panting, cowering, struggling to escape, and so on. Furthermore, it was found that this reaction was not a momentary one. The animal that had so broken down in the experiment could not be led to respond to the experimental stimuli again until after a rest of some months or even years. Its behavior outside of the experimental situation also showed signs of abnormality.

Other researchers have repeated the experiments and achieved the same results. In fact, the experimental neurosis has become a well-known psychological phenomenon.

We cannot safely reason from analogy concerning the behavior of ani-

---

[2] *Ibid.*, pp. 195–98. See this book for a fuller exposition of these ideas. For a useful research review, see H. S. Liddell, "Conditioned Reflex Method and Experimental Neurosis," J. McV. Hunt, *Personality and the Behavior Disorders* (New York: Ronald Press, 1944).

mals in a laboratory to the behavior of men in a factory. Research must be done at many intervening points before we can make such a jump on the basis of scientific evidence. Nevertheless, certain analogies may be suggestive.

The first stage of the conditioning experiments suggests that consistent association of a given symbol with a reward establishes an appropriate response to that symbol, whereas consistent association of another symbol with punishment establishes an appropriate response to that symbol. However, we note that even consistent associations, when repeatedly made, seem to have a "wearing off" effect. We seem to see this effect in the factory also. We hear many complaints from management that an incentive system that once stimulated a vigorous response seems now to be taken for granted and has little stimulating effect.

Our chances of eliciting desired responses with a reward-punishment approach depend upon our ability to establish a definite and consistent association between symbols that stand for rewards and the rewards themselves, and similarly in the case of punishments. We have seen what happens when the animal becomes unable to discriminate between the reward symbol and the punishment symbol. When a given symbol can stand for either reward or punishment, the animal's behavior becomes disorganized.

It is the thesis of this chapter that many piece rate situations resemble much more closely the conditions of the experimental neurosis experiments than they do the experiments in which reward and punishment symbols are clearly differentiated.

I am not trying to say that factory workers are neurotic individuals. I am simply suggesting that many incentive systems place them in a conflict situation where they are unable to determine whether the symbols presented them stand for expected rewards or for expected punishments, or for some combination of rewards and punishments. Some of the defensive and aggressive behavior of workers must be understood in these terms.

In the piece rate situation, the connection of the economic symbol with a given unit of reward is much more complex than a connection between the sound of a bell and the offering of a chunk of meat. Let us now explore this complexity.

## THE MEASUREMENT OF WORK

The effectiveness of the incentive system depends in large measure upon the price that is established for each unit produced. If the price is too high, then workers will be able to make high earnings without bringing to bear any more effort and ingenuity than they would devote to a job on hourly pay. If the price is too low, the workers will be able to make little if anything beyond their hourly pay. They will then complain to management. If management does not respond by setting a higher price per piece, workers will soon turn to holding back production so that the incentive earnings drop far below the hourly rate which is guaranteed and paid to them. In other words, the incentive becomes a "decentive." Instead of simply responding to the economic symbols management sets before them, workers themselves take up the manipulation of economic symbols to put pressure on management. If they can turn in incentive earnings of perhaps a dollar to $1.50 an hour on jobs for which their guaranteed base pay is two dollars an hour, the workers assume quite correctly that this would be a serious worry to management.

The rate, then, should be "just right"—but how can that be achieved?

The responsibility for setting the rates falls generally upon the time study man. As he studies a new job, his first responsibility is to see to it that the job is being performed in the most efficient manner—"the one best way" sometimes referred to in the textbooks on scientific management. (Whether there is a "one best way" for many jobs is certainly a debatable point. Workers argue that since they themselves are not standardized, what is the best way for one worker may not be as good as some variation on the method for another.)

Having standardized the work methods he plans to study, the time study man then makes systematic observations of worker performance on the job. He is expected to observe fast workers, slow workers, and average workers, so that his rate can be based upon his estimate of what the average experienced worker can do. The rate is not based entirely on these observations of performance. The time study man recognizes that the machine will not be running for a steady eight hours a day. He makes certain customary allowances for "personal time" (for coffee breaks, to go to the wash room, and so on) for fatigue, and for machine breakdowns. These allowances are necessarily arbitrary, since they can be based only in part upon observation of worker behavior. Thus, at best, the percentages allowed for these arbitrary factors can make the difference between rates being too loose or too tight.

A more serious element of personal judgment enters in with the allowance for percentage efficiency of operation. The theory, in its pure form, made no provision for such an allowance. It assumed that, while he was being observed and timed, the worker would carry on at the "normal" pace he would follow if the same job were being paid on day rates. If this were true, then the rate could be set so that the "normal" pace that the operator would apply if he were on hourly pay only would yield 100 per cent of that hourly pay, whereas, if he put out the additional "incentive effort," he could earn approximately 130 per cent. However, management people soon learned that workers who are being time studied do not continue to work at a "normal" pace—not if they can help it! Occasionally, an inexperienced worker under the observation of the time study man becomes so nervous that he cannot help speeding up. Experienced workers avoid this error and pride themselves on their ability to slow down while still appearing to work fast. They add unnecessary motions when possible. They pretend that the job is much heavier and more difficult than it is. They argue that the machine speed called for by the time study man is too fast and will damage tools or materials. When he challenges this conclusion, they run the machine at the speed he requires and produce the damage to tools or materials that they have predicted, through subtle operating tricks they have learned through years of experience—or from the advice of other skillful workers.

The experienced time study man is not fooled by such maneuvers. He knows that the workers are trying to fool him, and therefore he makes allowances for the play-acting he observes. He notes how much the worker is producing during the observation period and estimates what percentage this is of what a man would do if he were working at a "normal" pace. For example, let us assume that the worker, while under observation, is producing forty units an hour. The time study man estimates that the worker is only producing at 80 per cent efficiency, which means that a "normal" pace would enable him to produce 50 units an hour. The price will then be set on the basis of fifty units an hour yielding approximately the hourly rate, with the assumption that an "incentive effort" will enable the worker to produce about sixty-five units an hour.

In other words, the time study man undertakes to guess how much he is being fooled by the worker. If he guesses right, the resulting rate will be acceptable to both worker and management. If he underestimates the extent to which the worker is fooling him, the resulting rate will be loose. The workers will be happy, but management people will be unhappy, because they will be paying for additional effort and skill they are not receiving. If he overestimates the amount the worker is fooling him, the rate will be too tight. In that case, both parties will be unhappy; the workers because they are not making any money, the management people because they aren't getting the production.

Whatever the outcome, note that the rate setting process, while beginning with scientific observation of work activity, ends up with a series of allowances that convert the process into something of a guessing game. Under these circumstances, it seems remarkable indeed that mutually acceptable rates often do get set.

Appearances are deceptive on this score. Sometimes a tight rate on a job performed by the methods on which the rate was set becomes a rate paying acceptable earnings when the workers devise shortcuts and improvements in the methods of work. Such inventions are commonplace occurrences of factory life. At the other end, when workers restrict incentive earnings at a certain point, management people are often not fully aware of how loose a given rate may be—of how much workers could produce if they cared to "go all out." In a situation where 130 per cent was the informal ceiling on incentive earnings, Donald Roy tested out a number of jobs for brief periods and found that he could go up as high as 300 per cent on some of them—and he did not count himself as skillful as some of the workers around him.

A time study man's job is difficult enough when he is free to do it in his own way. Many times that is impossible. The time study man argues that he cannot do a realistic study on a new job until the workers have had some time to get accustomed to it and to develop some skill. The length of this practice period is a frequent source of conflict between workers and management. If the workers have been previously working on incentive jobs, it is a severe economic loss for them to be working on their regular hourly pay while they await the setting of an incentive rate. Naturally, therefore, they pressure management to get the rate set as soon as possible. Furthermore, what is to be done with jobs that are only going to last a limited length of time? If the job itself is expected to run out in about six weeks, the time study man can hardly be allowed to require the men to take a month to get used to the job before he sets his rate.

Our discussion so far may suggest that workers know how much they can produce on a given job and therefore, it is the task of the time study man to find out what they already know. The workers may indeed know for old established jobs the possibilities they have had ample opportunity to explore. Their knowledge is much less exact regarding the possibilities of new jobs, particularly when they are involved with management in an argument over the rates. In this situation, they are deliberately holding back and exaggerating the difficulties of the job.

We have seen many cases in which workers were arguing with management that it was impossible to make acceptable incentive earnings on a particular job unless the piece work price was increased. For example, while the workers would admit to a research man that their statements to management were exaggerated, at the same time they apparently were sincere in their belief that the rate in question was unfair. They would argue to management that even their greatest efforts would not raise production beyond the 100 per cent base pay, while they would acknowledge to friends and students that it might be possible to get the pay up to 110 or 115 per cent—but they felt this was still far short of acceptable earnings. In such situations, a deadlock develops and is maintained for some period of time, with the workers producing well below 100 per cent, trying to get the piece rate increased. Meanwhile, the workers lose money every day at this reduced rate of production. As time goes on, some of the men become convinced that no matter what they do, management is not going to increase the price. At last, one worker gets tired of the waiting and pressure game and decides to "give it a whirl." He goes to work and finds, to his surprise, that he can make 110 per cent immediately and that 130 per cent or more is well within reach as soon as he acquires the skill—or learns the shortcuts. At this point, the dam of resistance breaks. The workers all buckle down to the job. Before long, they have reached a point where they have to restrict output so as not to go beyond the informal ceiling.

This suggests that it is very difficult, when a worker is not trying to produce, for him to give a realistic estimate of what he can produce if he does try. Should management, therefore, just stand firm on its rate decisions and expect time to work in its behalf? The problem is not that easy. Sometimes, when the workers say that they cannot "make out" on a particular rate, they are only stating facts. They may even try out the job at full speed for several hours and find that they fall so far short of earning incentive pay that it is a hopeless task. In that situation, there is every reason for them to hold production down well below 100 per cent indefinitely—if they do not resort to more direct action.

When the workers claim they cannot "make out" on a job, is the claim fact or fiction? That is a very difficult question for management to answer, and the workers themselves cannot always really know the answer.

## PROBLEMS OF RATE CHANGES

Let us assume that in spite of all these difficulties, acceptable piece rates have finally been set. If technology and work processes remained static, the problem would now be solved. In a dynamic economy like ours, technology and work processes are constantly subjected to change.

The logic of the incentive system requires that a change in technology or job methods that would enable the worker to produce more with the same effort and skill calls for a new time study and a new rate. Workers sometimes feel that management has introduced a minor and insignificant change in the job simply as an excuse for cutting the rate. To meet this problem, many union contracts state that a rate cannot be changed unless there has been a "major" or "substantial" change in job methods or content. This helps to maintain worker confidence in the incentive system, although there is still a good deal of room for argument as to what constitutes a "major" change.

But what of a series of minor changes, spread over the course of many months? Apparently, this is a frequent source of incentive difficulties. As workers and management gain experience with a particular job, minor improvements are introduced; some by the engineers, some by the workers themselves. Both parties may agree that no single change can be considered "major." Nevertheless, the cumulative impact of a series of such changes can transform a mutually acceptable rate into one that is so loose that the workers can produce up to the informal ceiling with a minimum of effort.

There seems no easy answer to the question: How many minor changes equal a major change? With each minor change, management may consider intervening with the new time study and a new rate, but any such action would precipitate a clash with the union. Management is often tempted to keep the peace by letting the old rate stand. In a competitive industry, this cannot go on forever. At last it reaches a point where, as management people say, "the incentive system has just broken down." By that they mean that the rates have become so loose that management is simply paying premium rates for no more than the amount of production that could be brought forth in a similar plant where the workers have always been on straight hourly pay. What to do now? To suddenly abandon the incentive system, thus cutting worker earnings drastically, is to invite a long and bitter strike. To "tighten up" the rates gradually on job after job is to invite a running battle with the union throughout the plant.

The magnitude of job changes is not the only issue. An equally difficult one involves the authorship of the changes that are introduced. When changes are introduced by management, workers do not argue over management's right to set a new rate—though they may argue about the magnitude of the change. But, as we have already noted, the workers often devise shortcuts and invent mechanical aids that result in really major changes on the job. Who "owns" the fruits of these changes?

One company handled the problem in this manner. Workers were invited to write up all improvements that they devised on suggestion blanks and drop them in the suggestion box. If the management committee decided an improvement was worthwhile, then the worker who submitted the suggestion would receive a financial reward—but also, the time study men would come in and re-study the job with the new methods and establish a lower rate for all of the workers doing that job. On the other hand, if a worker chose to keep his improvement secret from management to get the payoff for himself and his friends in increased earnings or lessened effort, he could try to keep his invention secret. However, if the time study men chanced to observe the worker doing the job with the improved method, they would move in and make a new study of the job and establish a lower piece rate price—and the worker would get no suggestion reward for his improvement.[3]

Either course of action promised the worker punishment as well as a reward. As long as he kept his invention a secret from management, he and his fellows could profit. But if the invention were discovered, then he and all of his fellow workers were summarily deprived of rights of ownership of the idea and faced a rate cut. On the other hand, if the worker put in his invention as a suggestion, he might get an award (of an unpredictable amount), but he could count on getting a lower rate set on the job and incurring the enmity of fellow workers who shared in the rate cut but not in the suggestion award. And what of the worker who

---

[3] I am indebted to Robert Kahn of the University of Michigan for this example.

puts in the suggestion box an invention that is not his own? Some inventions are known and used among a group of workers for many months without coming to management's attention, and it is not at all clear who the original inventor was, if indeed it was a single individual and not several men pooling their ideas.

The ownership of ideas presents a particularly touchy question from the standpoint of the workers. The "air hose" case, described in detail elsewhere, illustrates this problem.[4]

The case came up at a time of intense antagonism between management and union in the Inland Steel Container Company's Chicago plant.

It involved a grievance concerning a change in rates on two jobs on a particular punch press. This punch press blanked out covers from sheets of steel to be used on the pail line. When the job was first run, there was a tendency for the cover pieces to stick to the machine; the operator then had to tap them loose, which slowed up the machine considerably. One of the workers on the job connected an air hose to a compressed-air connection so that the hose would blow air upon the covers from above to push them loose onto an inclined plane out of the machine.

This change had been in effect for some time without any change in rates when a time study man observed it and consulted the operator about it. The time study man reported the matter to the engineering department, which installed a metal pipe to blow air on the underside of the punch press. Management claimed that this was a major improvement in machine and method justifying a revision in the piecework rate; the price was thereby reduced by nine cents a thousand pieces on one job and by eleven cents a thousand pieces on another. The worker in question and all the union people were incensed at this change. One of them said, "They held us up on that just as if they had stuck a gun at us. That's what I thought then and I still think so."

The union officers charged that management had cut the rate on a punch press job in violation of the contract. They seized upon this grievance as representing the most outrageous example of unprincipled and oppressive management action. The case was argued heatedly through the first three steps of the grievance procedure.

The union claimed that blowing the air from the bottom instead of from the top was simply an excuse for rate cutting and was therefore not justified. Furthermore, the original idea had come from a worker and not from management, and the job already had been run with an air hose for some time.

Management argued that the rubber air hose never worked properly and had been disconnected for some time before the metal air hose was

---

[4] See my article, "Economic Incentives and Human Relations," *Harvard Business Review*, Vol. XXX, No. 2 (March–April, 1952).

put in the new position. Therefore, this constituted a major change, which justified a re-study of the job. Furthermore, management claimed that earnings on this job had increased since the rate change.

In this plant, there were at the time many types of conflict between union and management, but to many of the workers the air hose case seemed to symbolize all of their problems. Why should that have been the case? Not because they had sustained economic losses. That particular job was run rather infrequently, and furthermore, management presented figures to show that incentive earnings were actually 33 to 34 cents an hour higher after the installation of the metal air hose and the cutting of the rate than they had been on the old rate.

In the sentiments then prevailing between workers and management, the workers and union officers were in no mood to treat the earnings figures as simple factual data. It was only after a substantial change in the patterns of sentiments, interactions, and activities that such figures could be accepted and the grievance readily resolved. The nature of this change will be discussed later. For present purposes, it is significant that the particular case that seemed to symbolize for many workers the immorality and untrustworthiness of management should revolve around this very question of the ownership of ideas.

Even when workers and management can agree that a major change has been introduced (and on the initiative of management), the problem of rate changes is not resolved. Let us assume that on the job in question workers had been earning 150 per cent, whereas the plant-wide average is around 130 per cent. Quite apart from the difficulties of measurement, should the time study men attempt to set the new rate so that the workers can earn 150 per cent or 130 per cent? The workers and union officials naturally argue for 150 per cent, claiming that anything less really represents a rate cut and is not in line with the spirit of the agreement guaranteeing against rate cuts. Management people are naturally inclined to feel that 130 per cent is adequate and that if they are bound to replace each "loose" rate by one equally loose, they will be losing control of the incentive system.

## INCENTIVES AND FOREMAN-WORKER RELATIONS

Piece rates can have a marked effect upon foreman-worker relations. Under a system of hourly rates, the foreman has a constant problem of motivating his workers to produce. Some workers will go along at a steady pace, whether or not the foreman is present, because of the sentiment they have toward "a fair day's work," but some will "goof off" if the foreman is not on the job to check them. The foreman may be faced with difficult disciplinary problems involving differing interpretations as to acceptable levels of work effort.

Under an incentive system, at least in cases of those rates that have been reasonably well established and accepted, there is no problem of keeping the men on the job. To be sure, they restrict production at the level of their own informally established ceiling, but if the foreman has been a worker himself, he understands and accepts this. Furthermore, as long as the workers produce at close to this ceiling level, the record will be acceptable to higher management and will not bring down upon the foreman any great pressures for higher production.

As a matter of fact, if the workers did produce as much as they could, this would disturb the stability of the foreman's relations with higher management. As long as most of the jobs are yielding 125 to 135 per cent earnings, and this continues over a period of time, higher management gets the impression that the situation is well under control. If incentive earnings varied all the way from 60 per cent to 250 per cent, and the same job paid radically different amounts on different days (according to the personal variations in skill and health of the workers), then higher management would really be concerned, and the foreman would visualize all sorts of experts coming in to try to find out what is going on.

The foreman does have a problem with the "tight" rates, where workers are producing below 100 per cent. However, he does not have to shoulder the whole responsibility of this problem. In many cases, he can stand aside and watch the struggle between time study, the workers, the union, and higher management—even as he claims that everything would run smoothly in his department if it weren't for those time study men.

In the types of departments where there is a wide variety of incentive jobs to be assigned to workers on a day-to-day basis, the foreman faces difficult problems in making these job assignments. He can reward those he considers to be good workers and friends of his with more than their share of "gravy jobs" and assign an extra quota of "stinkers" to the "trouble makers." On the other hand, this will lead to charges of favoritism, and the foreman may find the situation getting out of hand.

How can he avoid these charges of favoritism? Jobs may be assigned on the basis of an objective standard such as seniority, with the high seniority people getting their choice of the better jobs. Under this system, no one can accuse the foreman of favoritism as to individuals, but it is likely to be very demoralizing to the low seniority people who get nothing but the "stinkers." They may accept the justice of an arrangement which gives high seniority people more of the "gravy jobs" than they themselves receive, but they will hardly accept a constant diet of "stinkers."

Furthermore, this apparently simple system may lead to a good deal of administrative confusion, as was the case in one punch press department.[5] There, at the beginning of each day, a schedule of the jobs to be

---

[5] Case described in more detail in my article, "Interviewing for Organizational Research," *Human Organization*, Vol. XII, No. 2 (1953).

run was posted, and individuals were free to choose according to their seniority ranking. It was understood, however, that if the job selected ran out during the day, the worker would then have to accept whatever job the foreman assigned him at that point.

On the previous day, the foreman made up his own tentative job assignments based upon his predictions of which jobs would be chosen by which people. Unfortunately, his predictions were not very accurate, so there was always a period of delay and confusion at the start of the day while the workers argued with each other and with him, and a union representative also came in to try to straighten out the confusion.

If the foreman had needed only to estimate how the jobs ranked in the minds of the workers, he would have been right most of the time, for there was a high degree of consensus on this matter. However, the problem offered a second and independent variable: the number of pieces to be run for each particular job. To simplify the illustration, let us assume that there were 24 jobs in question, which were ranked in the order of worker preference from A to Z. When the worker had to choose between job A and job H, other things being equal, he would always choose job A. But suppose job A called only for the amount that he could produce in about two hours, whereas job H was going to run all day. If he chose job A, after two hours he would have to take his chances on whatever was assigned to him. It might be another job approximately equal to H, in which case he would have been better off starting with A. On the other hand, he might get X, Y, or Z. With which job would he then choose to begin? The foreman was not able to answer this question with a high enough batting average so as to avoid confusion and conflict.

## INTERGROUP RELATIONS[6]

So far I have been concentrating upon the reaction of individual workers and work groups to incentives. As the relation of one group to the economic environment has been changed by the introduction of incentives, so also has the relation of this group to other groups in the plant been changed. As I have already pointed out, workers are not only concerned with their earnings in an absolute sense. They are also very much concerned with where their earnings place them in relation to other individuals and groups in the plant. In this sense, one group can lose ground even while its own earnings remain constant, if other groups around it at the same time are gaining in their relation to the economic environment.

[6] For my ideas on inter-group problems in industry, I am much indebted to Muzafer Sherif. Since the cases used in *Money and Motivation, op. cit.*, grew out of Leonard Sayles' work particularly, I did not realize at the time the extent to which my analysis of such cases was influenced by Sherif's work. I am glad to make this belated acknowledgment.

This kind of problem arises most commonly between maintenance and production departments. In most situations, maintenance workers are more skilled than production workers. Men in some classifications have reached their positions only after going through a period of apprenticeship training, whereas production workers may be quite competent on their jobs after a few hours to a few weeks of training. The maintenance workers have higher status, or social prestige, within the plant and in the community. In line with this status evaluation is their hourly pay, which is generally significantly higher than that of the production workers.

In most cases, the contribution of the maintenance workers cannot be directly measured. Therefore, they are seldom placed on incentives—although it is possible to work out indirect incentive formulas, and these are being applied in an increasing number of cases.

When production workers are put on incentive, this narrows the gap between their earnings and those of the maintenance people, and in some cases production workers even achieve higher earnings. This change in relative positions in relation to the economic environment results in changes in sentiments, interactions, and activities in and around the maintenance department. Though they may have been satisfied with their pay before, maintenance workers now begin to complain to management and union officials that they are unfair prey to "inequities." The problem comes to a head particularly around the time of contract negotiations, when union and management seek to agree not only on how many cents per hour is to be granted by management, but on what proportion of this overall figure shall be set aside to take care of these presumed inequities in the maintenance department.

The logic of collective bargaining does not provide for any necessary relationship between the earnings of maintenance and production workers. Therefore, management and union negotiators bring in elaborate figures to show that the workers in each maintenance category either are or are not underpaid in relation to men of the same skill and classification in the surrounding area. Even as they talk about these outside comparisons, both parties are likely to be aware of the rub of friction between different parts of the work force. Under these circumstances, management is often willing to concede increases for maintenance workers even when management figures indicate that these employees are at or above area rates—providing this does not raise the cost of the overall financial settlement. (For example, if the parties get together on ten cents an hour, they may also agree that eight and a half cents is to be added to the hourly pay of every employee in the plant, and the balance of one and a half cents per employee is to be utilized to take care of the supposed "inequities.")

The task of negotiating inequities is not done once and for all. Where production workers have a lucrative incentive, maintenance workers are likely to feel that even the succession of pay adjustments they get over a period of years does not really re-establish the pay differential that correlates with superior skill.

Between negotiating periods, this inequity situation is likely to plague interdepartmental relations. The production workers are dependent upon the maintenance workers for fast and efficient repairs and other services in order to keep the production going and the incentive pay coming in. Production workers and their foreman are likely to complain that the maintenance people are neither responding to their needs fast enough, nor working diligently enough when they do finally get on the job. On the other hand, we hear maintenance people ask why they should break their necks—or some other part of their anatomy—just to help the production workers make a few extra dollars.

Intergroup problems can also arise between groups of production workers, even when both are on incentive. Let us say that workers in group A are earning $2.00 an hour on hourly rate, while workers in group B are earning $1.90 an hour. The groups work close together in the same department, and the line of promotion calls for men to move from group B to group A. Now let us assume that they are both put on incentive, and to make things easier for management and the union, that the incentive goes in at the same time for both groups. If the system works perfectly, the men in group A will be able to earn around $2.60 an hour, and the men in group B will be able to make slightly under $2.50. In that case, there will be no problem between the two groups. However, given the inaccuracies necessarily involved in the rate-setting process, we are almost as likely as not to come out with a situation in which group A members are making $2.40 an hour and group B members are making $2.75 an hour. Group A members immediately begin to complain over the "inequity" and demand that their piece work price be increased so that they can again make more than the group B members. Group B members raise no complaint, of course, but they also refuse to allow the foreman to "promote" them into a group A job. Having come out with a piece rate considerably looser than intended for group B, management is reluctant to make peace simply by allowing for a similar loosening in the group A rate. Furthermore, there are not just these two work groups to think about. As group A and group B move up, this changes their relations to other work groups, and management is beset with pressure to take care of other "inequities" claimed by other groups.

The union as well as management encounters problems in the area of intergroup relations. Consider the case of the men in the labor pool of a steel mill, who were engaged in putting together a steel container for the armed forces. Many of these men had held jobs at higher levels in the plant, but because of a reduction in the work force, they had been bumped out of their regular departments and dropped into the labor pool, where they were not on incentive and where their hourly pay was at the bottom of the plant range. Naturally, these men were discontented with their earnings, and at the same time, management was unhappy with the amount they were producing. Under pressure to fulfill the defense contract, management was only getting five completed tanks out of this particular work group in an eight hour day.

Most of the workers on this job were welders, and they urged the union president, who was himself a welder, to get management to put the job on incentive. Management agreed, although somewhat reluctantly, because the group operation presented difficulties from the time study standpoint.

While the time study men were studying the operation, the union president made a point of making his own observations and talking confidentially with the workers. The president thought that he was on good terms with these men, and since he was thoroughly familiar with the work they were doing, he thought that he could not be fooled by them. They swore to him that eight units a day was the absolute maximum possible production, and his own observations seemed to confirm this figure. After considerable argument with time study men and management, the union president was able to persuade management to offer the men a rate per unit that was based on the assumption that eight units was indeed the maximum possible production. This meant that a hundred per cent was set at about six units a day.

Now the men went to work to see what they could really do. Production rose at once to twelve units, and it finally levelled off at sixteen per day.

Why didn't the men restrict output to some informally established ceiling? We don't know the real answer to that question. It may have been because some of them were short-service employees in the plant, without thorough indoctrination in the ways of factory life. It may have been because the defense order was considered a temporary run and the men themselves were looking forward to moving back to their regular departments and out of the labor pool. However, we are not concerned so much with the reasons for their actions as with the consequences of those actions.

The men who had been at the bottom of the plant in earnings now suddenly found themselves at the top. This created an intolerable situation for management, other work groups, and union leaders—particularly the president.

The president felt personally outraged. These workers had made him look like a fool. Other more skilled and senior employees were demanding that they be allowed to bump down and into this department and onto the lucrative job. There was a general demand for renegotiation of all incentive rates.

What to do about the incentive rate on the steel containers? The union could hardly urge management that a piece rate be cut. However, the union officers did gather together arguments on a number of other piece rates in the plant that they claimed were too tight. When they presented these claims to management, the management people agreed to raise these prices somewhat providing the union would agree to cutting the price on the steel containers. The union president found he could agree with this move without any difficulty at all.

The men working on the steel containers were outraged and vowed they would get even with the union president. Their opportunity came a few months later in the annual election for officers, when they united in a body behind the insurgent candidate to help defeat the incumbent. The votes of this group alone were not enough to make the difference, but those votes hurt the president's cause, and his handling of the case damaged his reputation among other workers throughout the plant.

## A BROADER BASE FOR INCENTIVES?

So far I have been talking primarily about individual piece rates, although the discussion of intergroup relations applies equally well to group piece rates, where the individual pay-off is based upon the output of the group. It has occurred to a number of people that it might be possible to eliminate many of the problems arising under individual and group piece rates by using a broader base for the incentive. Why not base the incentive pay-off on the performance of the entire plant?

This has been done in a number of cases, the best known being those that follow the Scanlon Plan. In the area of symbols, this involves attaching the pay-off to improvements in the labor costs as compared to some base period. If, for the given period, labor costs in relation to the sales dollar are below the base period, the difference is paid out according to a formula previously agreed on between union and management.

Later we shall examine in more detail the workings of the Scanlon Plan. In this chapter, I am simply concerned with illustrating various ways in which the symbols of economic incentives affect human relations. For this purpose, we need to note especially that the impact of a plant-wide incentive is quite different from that of an individual or small group incentive.

Whatever the difficulties involved in the individual piece rate, from the standpoint of worker motivation it offers one great advantage. The worker can see a direct connection between his performance and his incentive earnings. Under a group incentive plan, the connection is not quite so direct, and yet the individual can at least observe the performance of others who share the group rate with him and exert some influence over them. The smaller the group on which the incentive is based, the closer the connection between the individual's performance and his incentive earnings.

Under the plant-wide set of symbols, the connection between individual performance and incentive earnings is exceedingly remote. If there are hundreds to a thousand or more workers in the plant, whether one of them produces little or much will have an infinitesimal effect upon his own incentive earnings. The Plan will therefore only be effective in motivating higher performance insofar as individuals and small groups are effectively integrated into a plant-wide social system, which is then attached to the plant-wide incentive symbol system. To explain what this means would require us to examine the processes whereby individuals and groups are integrated into a total organization. When we have explored this process in later chapters, we shall return to the examination of the relationship between the symbol system and the social system of the plant.

## JOB EVALUATION

In this chapter, we have been concentrating upon incentive systems, for they provide us with the clearest cases for tracing the relationship between economic factors and worker behavior. However, we should recognize that in this country more workers work on straight hourly pay than on incentives. And even in the case of piece rate jobs, there is always the problem of setting the basic hourly rate which provides the guaranteed minimum earnings for incentive jobs.

Management people have long recognized that alleged "inequities" in the pay relations among various jobs are a potent source of ill will from workers to management and among groups of workers. It is therefore important that management give systematic attention to the pay relations among the various jobs, and this is often done through what is known as a job evaluation program. Through studying the various jobs, personnel people attempt to evaluate them along dimensions such as skill, responsibility for equipment, physical hazards, working conditions, and so on. Difficulties in job evaluation often arise, since the evaluation of jobs in the various dimensions depends upon personal judgments that have a large degree of subjective element in them. But this is not the only evaluation difficulty. We often find problems arising when official evaluations of jobs run afoul of other important considerations. In the minds of workers, a clean job outranks a dirty job in prestige, a physically light job outranks a heavy one, and a job performed in cool and comfortable surroundings outranks a job performed under hot and unpleasant conditions. Nevertheless, under some conditions, management must increase the rewards for the low-ranking jobs in order to get people to do them.

This problem arose during World War II in a large plant in the metal industry. In a sense, the smelting division is the heart of the operation, yet the jobs in this division are relatively low in skill and are considered to be dirty, hot, and heavy. In a period of wartime labor shortage, a pay scale based primarily upon skill simply was not good enough to bring in and retain the required labor force in smelting. When they could take jobs elsewhere in the plant that paid as much or more, conferred higher social status, and involved more pleasant working conditions, why should new workers want to come into the smelting division?

To relieve this labor shortage in smelting, management sought to increase the pay in the division. Blocked by wartime regulations against wage increases, management resorted to a subterfuge. An incentive system, based upon the weight of the product produced in the division, gave the men an indirect increase in pay. Since the connection between the efforts of the men and the production of the division was very tenuous, this could hardly be called a true incentive system, but it did serve the purpose of offering sufficient pay to maintain a working force within the division.

With the end of the war, the labor market in the area changed radically. At this point, it would have been possible to hire all the necessary employees for the smelting division on a pay scale without the incentive added. Furthermore, in the postwar period the relatively high earnings of the smelting division workers were a source of some dissatisfaction to workers in other divisions who considered themselves more skilled, and therefore, entitled to higher pay. In every negotiating session with the union since the war, management has sought to cut down on the smelting division's production bonus—while granting general pay increases. Naturally, this has always been resisted by the union. Over the years, management has been successful at cutting a few cents off the production bonus, but only at a cost of some bitter collective bargaining struggles.

While job evaluation was not mentioned in our discussion of worker response to incentive rates, it should be evident that many of the intergroup relations problems discussed earlier arise out of a conflict between incentive and job evaluation systems. For example, the job evaluation system establishes skilled maintenance workers at a substantially higher rate than semiskilled production workers. The incentive system then destroys the differential, and the parties have to contend with the resulting "inequities."

Students who are accustomed to thinking of management people as acting in rational and consistent fashion would do well to recognize the existence of such systems which function at cross-purposes. There is problem enough when the two systems are administered by the same department. The situation is likely to become even more complicated and difficult when, as is often the case, the incentive system is administered by the industrial engineering department and the job evaluation system is administered by the personnel department.

## ECONOMIC ENVIRONMENT AND SOCIAL SYSTEM

In this chapter, I have posed a number of problems that arise out of the impact of the economic environment upon the social system. We have seen economic symbols giving rise to changes in sentiments, interactions, and activities, as workers and management people respond to these symbols. At the same time, we should not assume that a given set of economic symbols just automatically has a predetermined effect upon the social system. The impact depends in part upon the state of the social system at the time when it is exposed to a given set of symbols. Limiting ourselves for the moment to the symbol-sentiment relationship, we can show that a given set of economic symbols, when presented in a situation of intense hostility and distrust between workers and management, will be interpreted by workers as representing the hostile actions and intentions of management. This will bring forth a mobilization of interactions and activities aimed at resisting management. When the same set of economic symbols is offered in a situation marked by cordial sentiments between workers and management, the worker response will be very different indeed.

This is not to say that, given harmonious sentiments between the parties, workers will just trustingly accept any set of economic symbols management presents to them. It means that, when a new piece rate is presented to them, they will approach it with the expectation that it is likely to turn out to be a fair rate, and they will try to see what they can do with it. If their job activities indicate, after a time, that they cannot make under this piece rate the earnings to which they have been accustomed, they will take the initiative in interaction with management or with the union in an effort to get the rate changed. Given the pre-existing pattern of cordial sentiments between the parties, the chances of working out the problem through discussion will be good. However, if the process does not lead to any solution reasonably satisfactory to the workers, then this in turn will affect their sentiments negatively toward the incentive system and toward management. Several experiences of this nature will lead to a deterioration of the pre-existing cordial sentiments, so that workers will no longer approach a new piece rate with the assumption that it will be equitable.

To press farther with this analysis, we need to study the forces that lead to hostile or cordial sentiments within the social system, as we shall in succeeding chapters.

## Collateral Readings

ABEGGLEN, JAMES. *The Japanese Factory*. Glencoe, Ill.: The Free Press, 1958.
    Gives a picture of human relations in a highly industrialized country with a culture far different from our own.
FORM, WILLIAM H., and MILLER, DELBERT C. *Industry, Labor and the Community*. New York: Harper & Bros., 1960.

A comprehensive discussion of industry-community relations.

WARNER, W. LLOYD, and LOW, J. O. *The Social System of the Modern Factory.* New Haven: Yale University Press, 1947.
> The classic industry-community study of the Yankee City Series.

GARDNER, BURLEIGH B., and MOORE, DAVID G. *Human Relations in Industry*, chaps. 2–6, 11–13. 3d ed. Homewood, Ill.: Richard D. Irwin Inc., 1955.
> A realistic picture of human relations problems.

STRAUSS, GEORGE, and SAYLES, LEONARD. *Personnel: The Human Problems of Management*, chaps. 25–28. Englewood Cliffs, N.J.: Prentice-Hall, Inc., 1960.
> Combines personnel and human relations approach.

WHYTE, WILLIAM FOOTE, and others. *Money and Motivation.* New York: Harper & Bros., 1955.
> An analysis of worker response to money incentives.

## Discussion Questions

4    1. Suppose you were sent out on a technical assistance mission to help an underdeveloped country speed its process of industrialization. What are some of the main social problems you might expect to encounter? What would you try to do about these problems?

5    2. In a community you know and for a given company, where would you place the following in status: top management, middle management, foremen, staff specialists such as engineers and personnel men, and union leaders? What evidence do you use in placing them? How does community status affect behavior in the plant?

5    3. On your own campus, is there a commonly agreed upon status hierarchy of fraternities, sororities or clubs? What is the evidence for your answer? What difference do status differences among organized groups make in the behavior of students?

6    4. The span of control refers to the number of subordinates directly supervised by a given superior.
   *a*) What conditions lead to a broad span? A narrow span?
   *b*) What are the consequences in behavior you would expect to be associated with a broad or a narrow span?

7    5. Under what conditions do workers respond most strongly to a money incentive? Under what conditions would you expect a weak response?

7    6. Compare the Scanlon Plan with individual piece rate systems. If the Scanlon Plan is to be successful, how should the pattern of interactions, sentiments, and activities differ from that prevailing under piece rates? What leadership problems does this present for management and union?

# PART III The Technological and Physical Environment

CHAPTERS 8 through 13 will explore some of the ways in which the technological and physical environment affects human relations in the organization.

We shall not be able to isolate the impact of technology and physical environment, for these always have their influence along with a number of other environmental factors. In Part II we have already considered at length the impact of the social and economic environment, and this will figure again in the subsequent discussion.

An organization is commonly thought of in vertical terms: as a series of man-boss relationships. This is an important part of the story, but some discussions of organization lead us to think it is the whole story. To balance this overemphasis upon the vertical, let us give special attention to some of the other important sets of relations to be observed. Here we shall concentrate upon the work flow; upon those relations among individuals and groups that necessarily arise as the work moves from one work station to another and from one department to another.

There are many other horizontal relations that do not arise directly out of the flow of work, but work flow relations are likely to be the most repetitive and patterned of all the relations that occur in the horizontal direction. When placed together with the vertical relations of the organizational hierarchy, they make up a large part of the organizational framework.

The work flow may take many forms. At the high extreme of technological determination, we find arrangements such as the automotive assembly line, (Chapter 11), where parts move down a conveyor belt at a fixed rate of speed, established by management, and workers perform their simple and routinized operations as the parts come to them. Somewhat less technologically determined are production or assembly lines, where parts flow from worker to worker down the line but at a speed controlled by the workers—directly, at least. The barrel department case (Chapter 9) is an instance of this type. In still less technologically controlled cases, parts do not flow from worker to worker directly, but are taken from one work station to another by truckers, supply men, or others holding different titles but performing the same functions.

We have a situation of a distinctly different type when the worker himself, as well as the product, moves from work station to work station. The restaurant industry presents cases of this type, which we shall explore in "From Kitchen to Customer" (Chapter 8).

The six chapters of Part III also illustrate other aspects of man's relation to the technological and physical environment of the workplace.

Chapters 10 and 11, "Teams of Artisans" and "Men on the Motor Line," present an extreme contrast in technology and job skills which points up differences in job satisfaction. The chapters also show how technology may affect work group cohesion and informal leadership.

Chapters 12 and 13, "Man and Process" and "Toward the Automatic Factory," examine worker responses to semi-automated jobs. In the first case, we are dealing with a chemical process industry, where workers watch charts and gauges and make periodic adjustments in controls. In the second case, we deal with a mechanical process that has been partially automated, with the workers observing and making adjustments in the controls. In both cases, we see that the jobs have relatively low requirements in physical labor, but high requirements in the responsibility the worker bears for the functioning of the process.

In Chapter 13, furthermore, we can compare the new job with the old and examine some of the problems of introducing change, a topic which will be dealt with more extensively in a later chapter.

# Chapter 8 *FROM KITCHEN TO CUSTOMER*

THE restaurant is both a production and a service unit.[1] It produces a highly perishable product for immediate distribution and sale on the premises. The smoothness of the operation of the work flow depends in part upon managerial skill in coordinating demand and supply, minute by minute, throughout the working day. If an oversupply of food is prepared, the mechanical aspects of the work flow will run most smoothly, but there will be a deterioration of the quality of food that is kept waiting for long periods of time, leading to customer complaints. Oversupply also leads to a large volume of leftovers, which present an economic as well as a menu-planning problem to the restaurant.

If food production is running behind demand, there will be long delays in getting the food to the customer, leading to friction between the customer and waitress and between waitress and employees in the service pantry.

Following the waitress, let us note the key points in the work flow, and then analyze the problems that tend to arise at each point. The flow begins when the waitress gets her order from the customer. If the restaurant serves drinks, she may have to call at the bar first. In a large restaurant, she then calls at the service pantry to place her order for the food. When she has picked up the food, in some restaurants, she must stop at the checker stand before returning to the dining room. The checker totals her check and stamps it on the cash register; she also inspects the tray. Then the waitress finally returns to the customer with the food. Of course, this cycle may be repeated several times for a table of customers for each meal. (See the accompanying figure for the work flow in a large restaurant, as reproduced from Chapter 6.)

The particular problem of the large restaurant is to tie together its line of authority with the relations that arise along the flow of work. In the first instance, this involves the customer relationship, for here is where the work flow begins. The handling of the customer relationship

---

[1] This chapter based on my article, "The Social Structure of the Restaurant," *American Journal of Sociology*, Vol. LIV, No. 4 (January, 1949), and my chapter, "When Workers and Customers Meet," William F. Whyte (ed.), *Industry and Society* (New York: McGraw-Hill Book Co., Inc., 1946).

A LARGE RESTAURANT:

WORK FLOW AND ORGANIZATION STRUCTURE

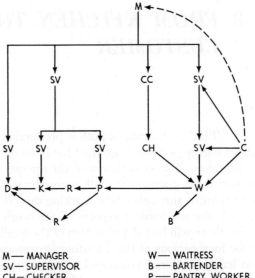

M — MANAGER
SV — SUPERVISOR
CH — CHECKER
CC — COST CONTROL
     SUPERVISOR
C — CUSTOMER

W — WAITRESS
B — BARTENDER
P — PANTRY WORKER
K — KITCHEN WORKER
R — RUNNER
D — DISHWASHER

is crucial for the adjustment of the restaurant personnel, and a large part of that problem can be stated in strictly quantitative terms: who originates action for whom and how often? In a large and busy restaurant a waitress may take orders from fifty to one hundred customers a day (and perhaps several times for each meal) in addition to the orders (much less frequent) she receives from her supervisor. When we add to this the problem of adjusting to service pantry workers, bartenders, and perhaps checkers, we can readily see the possibilities of emotional tension—and in our study, we did see a number of girls break down and cry under the strain.

The customer relationship is, of course, only one point along the flow of work which brings orders from dining room to kitchen and food from kitchen to dining room. In a large restaurant operating on several floors, this is a long chain which may break down at any point, thus leading to emotional explosions in all quarters. The orders may go from waitress to pantry girl and then, as the pantry girl runs low in supplies, from pantry girl to pantry supplyman, from pantry supplyman to kitchen supplyman, and from kitchen supplyman to cook. And the food comes back along the same route in the opposite direction. Where drinks are served, the bar must be tied in with this flow of work, but there the chain is short and the problem less complex.

The checker presents a work flow problem deserving special notice.

This employee is a combination clerical worker and inspector. As inspector, if she finds anything on the waitress' tray which in her judgment is not correct, she has the authority to send the waitress back to the kitchen.

This interruption of the anticipated pattern of activity for the waitress is a common source of friction with checkers; it also leads to delays in service which may involve the waitress with more friction with service pantry people and customers. Even when the checker simply totals the checks, this function may create a traffic problem, which in turn can give rise to problems in human relations. When business is slow, waitresses may move through the checker station with only a few seconds' delay. During the rush hour, we often observe several waitresses waiting in line to have their checks totaled and their trays inspected. While they wait, the hot food begins to cool and the cold food begins to warm up. This can lead to friction between customers and waitresses.

We have here a social system whose parts are interdependent in a highly sensitive manner. Thus the emotional tension experienced by waitresses is readily transmitted, link by link, all the way to the kitchen.

## STATUS, SEX, LAYOUT AND EQUIPMENT

Besides the work flow, we should note these other factors which affect the relations among employees: status, sex, layout and equipment. I would propose the hypothesis that relations among individuals along the flow of work will run more smoothly when those of higher status are in a position to originate for those of lower status in the organization, and conversely, that frictions will be observed more often when lower status individuals seek to originate for those of higher status. (This is, of course, by no means a complete explanation of the friction or adjustment we observe.)

While more data are needed on this point, we made certain observations which tend to bear out the hypothesis. For example, in one kitchen we observed supplymen seeking to originate action (in getting food supplies) for cooks who were older, of greater seniority, more highly skilled, and much more highly paid. This relationship was one of the sore points of the organization. Still, we discovered that there had been one supplyman who got along well with the cooks. When we got his story, we found that he had related himself to the cooks quite differently than had the other supplymen. He sought to avoid calling orders to the cooks, and instead just asked them to call him when a certain item was ready. In this way, he allowed them to increase the frequency of their origination for him, and according to all accounts, he got better cooperation and service from the cooks than any other supplyman.

Much the same point is involved in the relations between the sexes. In our society most men grow up to be comfortable in a relationship in which they originate for women, and to be uneasy—if not more seriously disturbed—when the originations go in the other direction. It is therefore a matter of some consequence how the sexes are distributed along the flow of work. On this question we gave particular attention to the dining room–service pantry and dining room–bar relationships.

In the dining room–pantry situation there were four possible types of relationships by sex: waiter–counterman, waiter–pantry girl, waitress–pantry girl, and waitress–counterman. We were not able to give much attention to the first two types, but we did make intensive studies of two restaurants illustrating the third and fourth types. Ideally, for scientific purposes, we would want to hold everything else constant except for these sex differences. We had no such laboratory, but the two restaurants were nevertheless closely comparable. They were both large, busy establishments, operating on several floors, and serving food within the same price range in the same section of the city.

Perhaps the chief difference was found in the dining room–pantry relationship itself. In restaurant A, waitresses gave their orders orally to the pantry girls. On the main serving floor of restaurant B, waitresses wrote out slips which they placed on spindles on top of a warming compartment separating them from the countermen. The men picked off the order slips, filled them, and put the plates in the compartment where the waitresses picked them up. In most cases there was no direct, face-to-face interaction between waitresses and countermen, and indeed, the warming compartment was so high that only the taller waitresses could see over its top.

These differences were not unrelated to the problems of sex in the flow of work. One of the countermen in restaurant B told us that in all his years' experiences, he had never before worked in such a wonderful place. Most workers who express such sentiments talk about their relations with their superiors or with fellow employees on the same job or perhaps about wages, but this man had nothing to say about any of those subjects. He would discuss only the barrier that protected him from the waitresses. He described earlier experiences in other restaurants where there had been no such barrier and let us know that to be left out in the open where all the girls could call in their orders was an ordeal to which no man should be subjected. In such places, he said, there was constant wrangling.

This seems to check with experience in the industry. While we observed frictions arising between waitresses and pantry girls, such a relationship can at least be maintained with relative stability. On the other hand, it is difficult to prevent blowups between countermen and waitresses when the girls call in their orders. Most restaurants consciously or unconsciously interpose certain barriers to cut down waitress origination of action for countermen. It may be a warming compartment as in this case, or as we observed in another restaurant, there was a man pantry supervisor who collected the order slips from the waitresses as they came in and passed them out to the countermen. There are a variety of ways of meeting the problem, but they all seem to involve this principle of social insulation.

The rule that all orders must be written serves to cut down on interaction between waitresses and countermen, but this in itself is not always enough to eliminate friction. Where there is no physical barrier, there can be trouble unless the men who are on the receiving end of the orders work out their own system of getting out from under. We observed such systems at one bar and at one of the serving counters in restaurant B. The counter in this case was only waist high. While the girls wrote out their orders, they were also able to try to spur the men on orally, and there was much pulling and hauling on this point, both at the bar and at the pantry counter.

The men who did not get along in this relationship played a waiting game. That is, when the girls seemed to be putting on special pressure for speed, they would very obviously slow down or else turn away from the bar or counter and not go back to work until the offending waitresses left their order slips and stepped away themselves. Thus they originated action for the waitresses. While this defensive maneuver provided the men with some emotional satisfaction, it slowed down the service, increased the frustrations of the waitresses, and thus built up tensions to be released in larger explosions later.

One bartender and one counterman not only enjoyed their work, but were considered by waitresses to be highly efficient and pleasant to deal with. Both of them had independently worked out the same system of handling the job when the rush hour got under way. Instead of handling each order slip in turn as it was handed to them (thus responding to each individual waitress), they would collect several slips that came in at about the same time, lay them out on the counter before them, and fill the orders in whatever order seemed most efficient. For example, the bartender would go through the slips to see how many Martinis, Old Fashions, and so on were required. Then he would make up all the Martinis at once before he went on to the next drink.

When the work was done this way, the girl first in was not necessarily first out with her tray, but the system was so efficient that it speeded up the work and the girls were content to profit this way in the long run. The men described the system to us simply in terms of efficiency; but note that, in organizing their jobs, they had changed quantitatively the relations they had with the waitresses. Instead of responding to each waitress, they were originating action for the girls (filling their orders and sending them out as they saw fit).

## COMMUNICATION SYSTEMS

Along with our consideration of layout and equipment in the flow of work, we should give attention to the communication system. Where the restaurant operates on one floor, the relations at each step in the flow can be worked out on a face-to-face basis. There may be friction, but there is also the possibility of working out many problems on a friendly, informal basis.

When a restaurant operates on two or more floors, as many large ones do, face-to-face interaction must be supplemented by mechanical means and each possibility has its difficulties.

People can try to coordinate their activities through the house telephone. Without facial expressions and gestures, there is a real loss of understanding, for one does not generally respond solely to people's voices. Still, this might serve reasonably well if the connection between kitchen and pantry could be kept constantly open. At least in the one restaurant where we gave this subject special attention, that solution was out of the question, as one call from kitchen to pantry tied up the whole house phone system and nobody could call the manager, the cashier, or anybody else on this system as long as that call was being made. Consequently, the telephone could be used only to supplement other mechanical aids (in this case, the teleautograph).

The public address system has the advantage over the telephone because it can be used all the time, but it has the great disadvantage of being a very noisy instrument. Busy kitchens and service pantries are noisy places at best, so that the addition of a public address system might be most unwelcome. We do not yet know enough of the effect of noise upon the human nervous system to evaluate the instrument from this point of view, but we should recognize the obvious fact that surrounding noise affects the ability of people to communicate with each other and therefore becomes a problem in human relations. The teleautograph makes no noise and can be used at all times, yet it has its own disadvantages. Here, we have an instrument in the service pantry and one in the kitchen. As the pantry supplyman writes his order, it appears simultaneously on the kitchen teleautograph. The kitchen's replies are transmitted upstairs in the same way. The machine records faithfully, but it does not solve the problem of the meaning of symbols. We may pass over the problem of illegibility of handwriting, although we have seen that cause serious difficulties. The more interesting problem is this: How urgent is an order?

When the rush hour comes along, with customers pushing waitresses, waitresses pushing pantry girls, and pantry girls pushing supplymen, the supplyman is on the end of the line so far as face-to-face interaction is concerned, and he is likely to get nervous and excited. He may then put in a larger order than he will actually use or write "rush" above many of his orders. If he overorders, the leftovers come back to the kitchen at the end of the meal, and the kitchen supplymen and cooks thus learn that the pantry supplyman did not really know how much he needed. They take this into account in interpreting his future orders. And when everything is marked "rush," the kitchen supplymen cannot tell the difference between the urgent and not-so-urgent ones. Thus the word becomes meaningless, and communication deteriorates. Stuck in this impasse, the pantry supplyman may abandon his machine and dash down to the kitchen to try to snatch the order himself. The kitchen people will block this move whenever they can; so, more often, the pantry supplyman appeals to his supervisor. In the heat of the rush hour, we have seen pantry supervisors running up and down stairs trying to get orders, trying to find out what is holding up things in the kitchen. Since they have supervisor status, the kitchen workers do not resist them openly, but the invasion of an upstairs supervisor tends to disrupt relations in the kitchen. It adds to the pressures there, for it comes as an emergency that lets everybody know that the organization is not functioning smoothly.

## THE CRYING WAITRESS

Let us now return to the crying waitress, whom we mentioned earlier. In a study of one restaurant I gave special attention to the crying waitress for reasons which I hope were scientific as well as human.

The study took place during World War II, at a time when this particular restaurant was doing a rush of business and was hard-pressed to provide enough employees to keep up with the customers. All of the waitresses spoke of the nervous tension involved in the job, and yet it was only a small minority of the girls who would occasionally break down into tears and have to leave the service floor.

Assuming the cooperation of the management and the girls, a medical doctor with his instruments might have been able to make quantitative measures of the state of internal agitation felt by the waitresses, thus enabling us to make comparisons from case to case. Lacking such refined measures, I had to fall back upon a discrimination which, if crude, was at least objective. Some girls cried, others did not. Through interviewing the girls themselves, it was possible to determine who fitted into each category. I could then ask myself: "What makes the difference between the crying and the non-crying waitress?"

The broadest generalization we can make is that crying behavior is related to length of waitress work experience. There are a number of reasons why this should be so. In the first place, there is a selective process at work, with girls who break down under the strain tending to drop out of the industry. The more experienced girls have more skill in organizing their work and have had practice in coping with almost any problem that may arise. Furthermore, in some restaurants where stations are assigned on a seniority basis, the more experienced girls tend to work in the same general location, where they are able to help each other. Inexperienced girls may be concentrated together too, but they generally have their hands so full with their own work that they can't provide each other with the help over rough spots, which is so important when the pressure is on.

As a rule, the more experienced girls are much more aggressive toward service pantry workers and bartenders, so that they are able to get some of the pressure off in that direction.

There is also an important difference in relations with customers and with supervisors. In this restaurant, waitresses moved by seniority to the more desirable locations, where the steady customers came. Sometimes these relationships became cordial; then the appearance of a steady customer would completely change the situation for a waitress who had been in difficulty with strangers. Even when the steady customer was an unpopular one, at least he was not an unknown quantity, and the waitress knew what to expect of him.

Experienced waitresses make their adjustment to the standards of the restaurant and do not make many mistakes in their work. Thus they are less subject to criticism and enforcement of rules from supervisors. In fact, where we have observed it, the comparison is quite striking. The experienced waitresses proceed with little if any regulation of their behavior by supervisors, whereas inexperienced girls tend to be subjected to a good deal more attention from the supervision.

Experience accounts for a great deal, but it does not tell the whole story. I found an occasional experienced waitress who sometimes broke down and cried, and there were, of course, many inexperienced waitresses who did not break down.

Taking another step in analysis, I sought to find pairs of inexperienced waitresses, as closely matched as possible in seniority, social, and family backgrounds, but different in their responses to tension. I found two pairs of twins, who had come on the job at the same time. I also studied two pairs of close friends; in each case, the pair came from the same small town and entered the restaurant together.

In all four pairs, I found a very marked leadership pattern with (let us say) Mary speaking up for Jane, telling Jane what to do, and managing Jane's relations with the outside world. In each of these four cases, it was Jane, the dependent individual, who occasionally broke down and cried; whereas it was Mary, the leader, who withstood all the tension without giving way.

This observation suggested taking a new look at the interactional world of the waitress on the job. Observations and interviews indicated that the management slogan, "The customer is always right," gave a highly misleading impression of waitress behavior. The slogan implies that the waitress plays a passive role, simply responding to the wishes of the customer. Actually, it appeared that the waitress who maintains her own emotional equilibrium plays a very active leadership role with the customer. She does not simply respond to the customer. She takes the initiative to control his behavior. Even when she is so busy that she cannot spend time with new customers to take their orders, she gets to the table for a moment, makes herself known to the people, gives them the menu, and tells them that she will be with them shortly. Having thus been reassured, the customers are much less likely to wave at her, clink glasses, and engage in other behavior that waitresses find annoying. When she does get to the customers, she is again quick to take the initiative when the opening arises. She knows the dishes that will require a long wait in the service pantry and tells the customers what to expect. When she finds the customer hesitating as to what to order, she is quick to come in with a suggestion. This may make the customer feel better. In the rush hour at least, the suggestion is also likely to be a dish that the waitress knows she can get out rapidly.

For the waitress, holding the initiative does not depend only upon these concrete actions. Waitresses themselves speak of the importance of setting the emotional tone of the relationship at the outset. If the waitress appears timid and harassed, the customers are likely to be uneasy and to expect the worst from her. The expectations on both sides are then generally met. On the other hand, if the waitress approaches the customers in a cheerful and self-confident manner, the customers tend to assume that everything will go well and leave themselves in her hands.

There are other relations for the waitress to manage in the service pantry and with fellow waitresses. The organization of mutual assistance among several waitresses can lighten the work load and greatly ease the emotional tension for all concerned. In fact, the dependent waitress seems able to maintain her emotional equilibrium when she is part of a closely knit working group led by someone else. In one of our pairs, Jane did not break down as long as she was working at a station next to Mary. The breakdown occurred only after she had been transferred into another room.

We see, therefore, that the same leadership abilities that a girl displays in her social life enable her to organize the work world so as to ease her emotional tensions and maintain her equilibrium.

## THE ROLE OF THE SUPERVISOR

Let us now turn to the role of the supervisor in this particular work flow situation. It should now be apparent that especially during rush hours, the waitress experiences far more work flow interactions (with customers, service pantry workers, bartenders), and interactions with fellow waitresses than she does with her supervisor. The effective supervisor recognizes that this interactional situation makes her own position far different from that which may prevail in some production organizations. She tries to confine her initiative and interaction with the waitresses to times before they go on the floor or to periods before the rush hour begins. When the rush is on, she does not correct them or give them instructions except in unusual situations. If she observes behavior that seems to call for criticism, she withholds action until the rush hour pressure is off.

The effective supervisor recognizes the pressure problems the waitresses face and does what she can to relieve the pressure. When she seats customers on a station whose waitress is in the service pantry, the supervisor herself may take the first steps to establish control over the customers and make them feel that they are getting proper attention. She sees to it that they get the menus, and if the waitress is still delayed in the service pantry, the supervisor may even begin taking the orders. If the delay promises to be really serious, she may even get new orders to the waitress while she is waiting in line so that she can put two sets of orders together, speed up her work, and get some of the pressure off.

Important are not only the concrete things that the supervisor does in this relationship, but also the feeling waitresses have that the supervisor is looking out for them and trying to help them. They speak warmly of this type of supervisor. They speak caustically of the hostesses who look pretty on the floor but do not have any concern about the problems the waitresses are facing.


## CONCLUSION

Since we are accustomed to thinking in terms of hierarchical authority, I have begun Part III with a case where work flow relations dominate the work situation for employees.

We even find that relations with the supervisors are relatively unimportant for the experienced waitresses. They are fully occupied with the work flow relations and have little interaction with supervisors. The inexperienced waitresses find the supervisory relationship much more important. However, note that even here it is the skill the supervisor displays—or lack of skill—in easing the stresses in the work flow that carry the major weight in determining the sentiments waitresses hold toward the supervisors.

We have seen that the impact of the work flow can be modified by layout and equipment, and by the status and sex of the interacting individuals. The impact may also be modified by reorganizing job activities, thus changing patterns of interaction and of the initiation of activities.

The chapter also enabled us to explore certain aspects of the relationship between individual personality and the interactional and activity requirements of the job. While the job of waitress is ordinarily thought to be low-skilled, we see that it can require interpersonal skills of a high order. In a large and busy restaurant, if the waitress is to maintain her emotional equilibrium, she must be able to handle a large number of interactions at a very high frequency, and to initiate activities for others. We have seen that girls who have displayed such a leadership skill in community affairs make a better adjustment to the pressures of waitress work than those who have been highly dependent upon the initiative of others.

# Chapter 9 *FROM STEEL SHEETS TO BARRELS*

TOM WALKER, foreman of the barrel department in a steel fabricating plant, was a brilliant success in 1948 and a failure in 1950.

In the years 1947–48, Walker's department set production record after production record. In 1945 he had taken over a department that lagged far behind the same departments in the corporation's two other fabricating plants, and by 1948, Walker's department had the best cost and production record of the three. His relations with workers and with the union were also excellent. Even in a period of intense union-management conflict that lasted into 1947, Walker had been considered a relatively good foreman by union officers. The years 1947–48 marked a sudden change to cooperative relations throughout the plant. No one credits Walker with having played a major role in bringing about the plant-wide change, but higher management acknowledges that he did an especially good job in building cooperative relations in his own department. The 1937 strike that led to the organization of the union began in the barrel department, and ever since that time the barrel department has seemed to be the bellwether in union-management relations. If the union-management problems of the barrel department had not been solved, the over-all cooperative relations could not have been established. All in all, Walker looked like an important man and a highly successful man in 1948.

By the spring of 1950, productivity was down and costs were up in the barrel department. There was growing friction among the workers, between the workers and the foreman, and between Walker and other members of management. The union officers turned against Walker. Finally management transferred him to a less important department. He took a substantial cut in pay and found himself supervising fifteen men instead of seventy or more.

How can a man be a hero in 1948 and a bum in 1950? What happened to Tom Walker?

To explain that change, we will examine three interrelated types of data; the technology and work flow, the formal organization of the plant, and the relations of the foreman with the various categories of people with whom he came in contact.

136

## TECHNOLOGY AND WORK FLOW

There were three production lines in the barrel department; the main line, the aux (auxiliary) line, and the side line. On most days both main and aux lines operated. The side line was used just for special jobs that come up less frequently.

The main and aux lines were similar and the following description holds for both of them.

These were called assembly lines because the barrel shells moved from work station to work station as the successive operations were performed. However, they differed from automotive assembly lines in that the operator himself had direct control over the speed of production. The job could be performed at different speeds at different points on the line, so that barrel shells might pile up waiting at one point and be clear at other points. Men worked in pairs on either side of the line at most points.

The line began where men known as rollers took sheets of steel and put them on a machine that shaped them in circular form. The shells then rolled to the welders who welded the two sides together. Then the testers checked the welding for leaks. Next came the beader men, who put the shells on a machine that put the beads (protruding ribs) into them. The shells then rolled into a spray booth, where their insides were sprayed with paint or lacquer. The double seamer operators attached both ends of the barrel. The barrel might then go on to another spray booth where an outside coat of paint or lacquer would be applied. Some orders called for a baked enamel finish, and the barrels were carried through bake ovens on conveyors for that purpose. Conveyors carried the completed barrels directly into the shipping department. There were numerous variations of this procedure, depending upon the specifications of the order, but those were the basic steps.

## VERTICAL AND INTERGROUP RELATIONS

The foreman of the barrel department had an assistant working with him. The foreman reported to an assistant production supervisor and a production supervisor. There were two additional levels of line authority; vice-president in charge of production, and president of the subsidiary.

The foreman received his orders as to what sort and number of barrels were to be produced from the production control department. These orders covered a period up to two weeks, within which time he could make adjustments in his own schedule. On the basis of these orders, he requisitioned the sheets of steel he would need from the steel storage department and the number and types of covers for barrels from the punch press department. At the other end of the line, he notified the foreman of the shipping department as to the number and types of barrels to be produced, and the destination of the orders.

Foreman Walker also dealt with the accounting, maintenance, and inspection departments. The accounting people handled timekeeping and rate setting for the barrel department. While no new rates were set in the 1948–50 period, the timekeeping job was a daily function. One maintenance man was regularly assigned to the barrel department, but much maintenance work required the assignment of extra men. The inspector carried out the customary job of enforcing quality standards.

Since the plant was unionized, Walker also dealt with the steward and other union officers.

This, then, was the technology, work flow and organization structure that provided the setting for Tom Walker in 1948. What had changed for Walker over the two succeeding years? We shall note a whole series of interrelated changes.

## PERSONNEL CHANGES

We shall first examine the relations Walker had built up in the period up to 1948, and then describe the changes in each set of relations between 1948 and 1950.

Walker became foreman in 1945 under general production supervisor Al Short. Short had been a barrel department foreman in another plant before taking up his more general duties, and the barrel department was his chief interest in this plant.

It was the practice of John Northrup, vice-president in charge of production, to recognize every departmental production record with a personal letter or telegram to the foreman, expressing congratulations to all the men. Such communications were placed on the bulletin board. Northrup also had posted in a department a plaque giving the record number produced, the date, and the names of all men working on the crew at the time.

In addition to this higher management recognition, Al Short personally rewarded the barrel department foreman and assistant foreman with bottles of whiskey and bought cigarettes and cokes for all the men in the crew. According to Northrup, Short followed this practice only for the barrel department. The other foremen got a "thank you" and nothing more. Northrup felt that this gave rise to resentment against Walker and Short.

Northrup said that Walker was a hotheaded fellow who got into arguments with every other management man with whom he dealt. When these arguments came to Short's attention, he tended to support Walker. Tom Walker felt that he had a dependable ally in Al Short.

In June, 1948, Short left the company. He was succeeded by Jess Wiley, who had been a superintendent at a smaller plant. As soon as Wiley learned his way around the plant, he discovered that Walker was involved in tangles with inspectors and timekeepers, and with the foremen of the machine shop, punch press, steel storage, and shipping departments. Wiley reported that his aim was to handle such arguments in this way: He would rebuke the two parties for getting excited over the issue and tell them they were being childish. He would then advise them to settle such problems among themselves.

Wiley gave this illustration. He found Walker engaged in a furious argument with a timekeeper—over six cents. Wiley listened to the stories of the two men and decided in favor of the timekeeper. Walker then protested that he could not make any record for himself when his boss acted that way. Wiley countered by saying that six cents didn't mean anything, and he should be thinking of more important matters.

Wiley also exercised closer control over Walker than had Short—at least in one respect. Walker had been free to answer grievances according to his own judgment and was required to consult his superiors only when in doubt. Higher management felt that this practice allowed some departments to get "out of line" with others. All foremen were thereupon required to check the answer to each grievance with general production supervisor Wiley, even though the foreman might be certain he knew the right answer. Wiley felt that Walker resented this control and blamed Wiley for it personally.

Northrup, who had worked his way up from the bottom in this plant, felt that he knew Walker well and spoke of going on hunting trips with him, but these apparently had not been recent events. Northrup said that he liked Walker personally and had been anxious to "straighten him out." Northrup illustrated by telling this story. He had been in the office of Lou Fisher, assistant to general production supervisor Wiley. The phone rang and Fisher picked it up. Northrup said he could not understand what was being said, but noticed that the voice was so loud it drove Fisher away from the receiver. Northrup picked up the other phone in the office to listen in. He reported that he had never heard anyone so explosively raked over the coals as Walker was then raking the man who was his immediate superior. Finally Northrup broke in and told Walker to come up to his office. Walker came up somewhat chastened, and Northrup told him that it was outrageous for a man to talk that way to anybody, let alone his boss. They talked at some length, and Walker agreed that he had been "out of line." But Northrup did not notice any change in Walker's behavior after this talk.

Walker had come up through the ranks in the barrel department. At the time he was a group leader, he had Ed Hodges (union president, 1940–48) working in his crew, and the two men developed a high regard for each other. Hodges was colored and Walker white.

When Walker became foreman, he and Hodges did their best to work out informal adjustments even while higher management and the union were struggling. Hodges reported that he could go to Walker and get action on any reasonable request that was in the foreman's province.

Walker reported similarly that he could get help from Hodges. This reciprocal relationship was strengthened as the over-all union-management relationship in the plant improved.

Lou Halsey, a friend of Hodges, was steward in the barrel department. While Hodges was in the plant, he performed as steward informally, and Halsey had little to do. When Hodges left in August, 1948, to go on the staff of the international union, Halsey became more active.

## THE ECONOMIC ENVIRONMENT AND WORK FLOW RELATIONS

Walker's relations with certain members of management were particularly affected by certain production changes that took place in late 1948 and in 1949. Up to this time, throughout the period of Walker's foremanship, the company had operated in a seller's market. When large orders were readily available, there was no need to take on small orders or orders that were complicated from a production standpoint. Throughout the period when Walker was making his production records, he was favored by long runs on the same types of barrels.

Walker's superiors had always felt that he was weak on the planning side of his work, but when the department was making the same barrel for a week or more at a time, there was relatively little planning to do.

In late 1948 and 1949, the market situation changed radically. Customers reduced their inventories and placed smaller orders. To keep the plant operating, salesmen went out and sold more small orders and complicated orders. This multiplied the difficulties in planning and in production. It meant more paper work for Walker and increased the frequency of his contacts with foremen in steel storage and punch press and in the shipping department. These contacts had always been fraught with conflict.

These production changes also affected Walker's relations with the maintenance foreman and with inspectors. More frequent change-overs on the production lines increased the frequency of machine breakdowns, and led to more insistent demands from Walker to the maintenance department.

When the buyer's market set in, customers began setting quality standards that they previously had been unable to insist upon. The inspector was instructed to tighten up his standards. This led to more rejects of barrels, and that in turn led to more frequent clashes between Walker and the inspector.

During the period of the seller's market, the work force in the department had averaged fifty-eight men. When the work of the department became more and more complicated, with shorter runs and new types of products, the normal complement rose to seventy-one. About twice a week, ten or twelve additional men were brought in from other departments.

All these various changes resulted in a falling off of production and a rise in costs in the barrel department. Northrup reported that he recog‧ nized that the market changes made it impossible for Walker to meet in 1949 the production records he had made in 1947 and 1948. He said he told Walker that he did not expect records any more. He would be satisfied with good, steady production. But he sensed that Walker was still straining at the old records. ( Walker denied this. )

## WORKER AND UNION RELATIONS

It was difficult to get a picture of Halsey's new activity. Walker reported spending more time with Halsey than he ever had with Hodges. But he added that they had a lot of arguments that didn't seem to get anywhere. Jim Carter, Halsey's successor as steward, reported that Halsey and Walker did not seem to get along very well.

One important change in the barrel department did come about through discussion between foreman and steward. (Accounts are conflicting as to whether Hodges was still in the plant when the decision was made.) When a man's particular job on the production line ran out during the day, the practice had been to try to place him in another department. If no such opening were available, he would be sent home for the balance of the day. Halsey arranged a system whereby a man whose job had run out could bump men of lesser seniority if they were performing the same work on another production line. Those other men would then have to be placed elsewhere or else go home.

The international representative reported that this change gave rise to great resentment within the department, especially among the men who did not have long seniority. He said they blamed the decision on Halsey's selfishness, as he had very long seniority and would be one of the chief beneficiaries of the bumping procedure. The international representative and the new president of the local agreed with the protesting group in this case and maneuvered a meeting at which the rank and file cut loose in criticism of Halsey. The steward then resigned, and Jim Carter was elected in his place. This change took place shortly before Walker's demotion.

The best account of Walker's growing difficulties with the workers was given to me by Jim Carter, the new steward. He began by saying that personally, he had always liked Walker.

In the first place, it made a lot of difference when Hodges left that department. When you have a president in the department, he carries a lot more weight than just a steward. People listen to him, the foreman really listens to him. When Hodges left that made a lot of difference. The steward in that de-

partment never had done very much. He didn't do very much after Hodges left.
I don't think Walker listened to him.

You know Walker had been in that department for many years. He worked
himself right up and at first the men were pleased when he got the job. Besides
that, after that long strike (1946) they really wanted to work and make some
money, so he was in a position to make a good record. And those production
records he began making in that department made trouble for him in the long
run. The men thought that those records were all right, but not as an everyday
proposition. They didn't like it when he expected them to do every day what
they had done once as a special thing. It was all right after that six-months'
strike, but it went on and on, and the men were getting tired.

Walker would go after the men who slowed down. You know, in that production line there are some men who have easy jobs and some men who have
hard jobs. The fellows with easy jobs can go a lot faster, and they pile up the
production where they are and roll the barrels down the line to the next fellow
after them.

Carter explained that there had been no problem of one man urging
another man to speed it up, but people who worked faster passed their
production along to the next point and the foreman could easily tell
where the bottleneck was. Then he would come around and say, "What's
the matter?" The worker would reply, "I'm going as fast as I can." Then
Walker would tell him that he knew that wasn't true because the man
had done more before and he would cite the production record. He would
say, "What's the matter, are you sick? If you are sick, you ought to go
home. If you can't get out production, I'll have to take you off here and
put somebody in who can." Carter said that the man might speed up for
the moment but he would resent Walker for it and he would also resent
the other men on the line who had made him look bad.

Another thing, Walker used pretty rough language. People would come to
me and complain that he was cursing them out. Now you might listen to him
and you could tell that the cursing wasn't really addressed at the men. Mr.
Walker was just cursing, but still people took offense. You know, he used to
talk that way all the time and nobody paid any attention. They would say,
"That's just the way Tom is. It don't mean nothing."

Now when the men wouldn't get the production up and things were going
bad, Mr. Walker would get excited. He would lose his temper before the men
would. And that's bad. He would become more and more excited when he
couldn't get the production up.

It got so that people were only doing what they had to do. You know, on a
line like that, all the jobs fit together and you need to work along with the
other fellow in order to do a good job. But it got so that it was just every man
for himself. Every man was doing just what he had to do and nothing more
and the whole line suffered. Another thing, in the old days when Mr. Walker
would give an order and a worker would know that there was a mistake in it,
he would bring it up to Mr. Walker so that they could make a correction and
the mistake wouldn't go through. But when Mr. Walker got so excited pushing for that production, it seemed like he wasn't interested any more in what
the men thought. He was just telling them what to do and it got so that they
would go ahead and do it even when they knew it was wrong, and they'd be
glad it was wrong so they could show him up.

A couple of times Mr. Walker called me in and told me that a certain individual wasn't doing the job he should do. I went over and watched the man. If a man is really laying down on the job or sabotaging or something like that, I'm supposed to talk to him. But the man would be just doing what he had to do and nothing more, but nothing less either. In a situation like that I couldn't help the foreman. If he wants the men to do a little more, he's got to win their cooperation. There is nothing I can do for him.

Vice-president Northrup added that it was especially the new people and the extra people who complained against the foreman's strong language.

## ANALYSIS OF THE CASE

Before proceeding with our analysis, it would be most helpful to have Tom Walker's own version of what happened. Unfortunately, this is not available.

In the 1948 period, when I was carrying on an intensive study of union-management relations, Walker talked with me frankly and freely. When I returned to the plant for a brief visit shortly after his demotion, he greeted my opening interview question with a broad grin and this statement: "Well, you know how it is, Doc. There are a lot of things I could tell you, but you know you talked to a lot of people when you were here last time, and some of them aren't here any more."

He was referring particularly to Al Short, his former general production supervisor, who had been fired shortly after I left the plant in 1948. The firing grew out of conflict between Short and the union, in which top management became convinced that Short had deliberately failed to live up to certain agreements negotiated with the union. I was not even aware of any such difficulties until I was informed that Short had been discharged, but the coincidence between the termination of my study and the discharge gave rise to suspicions in the mind of the demoted foreman that I was unable to overcome. He simply laid all of his difficulties to mechanical problems and said that no one could have done a better job keeping those machines running.

While we cannot see the situation through Walker's eyes, we can examine the forces playing upon him that led to failure and demotion.

Did Tom Walker change? Or did the situation change?

First we should note that certain aspects of Tom Walker's behavior remained the same from 1948 through 1950. In 1948, he was known to be weak on paper work and on the planning of his production. He did not get along well with most other management people. He used profanity profusely within the department—and sometimes even outside.

In the period of 1945–48, these characteristics of the foreman simply did not matter much. In the period where most of the department's production consisted of long runs, many of them lasting a week or more, there was very little planning for Tom to do. Long runs also meant few interactions with other management people. Approximately once a week he had to requisition steel sheets from the steel storage department and covers from the punch press department. With about the same frequency, he would have to notify the shipping department foreman what order was being run on each line and to what customer it was to be shipped. Long runs also meant that it was seldom necessary to introduce mechanical changes into the lines, and production lines that are not tinkered with are subject to less mechanical troubles. Thus Walker had little occasion to require maintenance service that was not immediately available from the maintenance man assigned to his own department and under his own supervision.

According to steward Jim Carter, the profanity did not really matter in this time either. The men would explain to each other: "That's just the way Tom is. It don't mean nothing."

These characteristics of the foreman gave rise to trouble as the situation underwent marked changes. Changes in key personnel happened in this case at approximately the same time as changes in the types of production going through the department. Let us examine the impact of these changes.

Al Short was a former barrel department foreman himself, having held that position in another plant. While he had responsibility for the total production in the plant, somehow he continued to see the performance of the plant primarily in terms of the barrel department, as shown by the recognition he gave to records in that department beyond what he gave to others.

The love that Short and Walker shared for barrels played an important part in the handling of Walker's conflicts with other management people. When Walker got into arguments with other management people, he could generally count on having Short on his side.

Equally important to Walker was his relationship with Hodges, the local union president. As a result of the key role he played in the resolution of a bitter union-management conflict, Hodges had tremendous prestige within the plant. Over the years, first as fellow workers and later in their official roles, the two men had developed a friendly and mutually supporting relationship. They were able to work out their mutual problems together. Furthermore, Walker's status in the management group was increased by the effectiveness of his dealings with the union president.

Perhaps if all else had remained stable, the replacement of these two key men in Walker's social orbit would not have caused great difficulties. But everything else seemed to change at the same time, and Walker faced these changes without the support of the two men with whom he had established close working relations.

Changes in the economic environment external to the plant led to important changes in types and volumes of products manufactured. This put unaccustomed pressure on the planning activities of the foremen. In the earlier period, his general schedule from the production planning department for a two-week period might contain only two or three orders. Now he might receive a schedule calling for him to run ten or twelve orders, which involved him in scheduling each of the orders among the various lines and at various time periods of the two weeks.

These production changes also multiplied the interactions Walker was having with other management people—who already had hostile sentiments toward him. He had to order supplies much more frequently from steel storage and punch press. He had to check much more frequently with the shipping department on order numbers and addresses, and sometimes he forgot to do this, leading to further complications. (On one occasion when the shipping department foreman had not been informed what order was coming through, he complained to Walker, and Walker shouted back: "Well, you can see it coming down the line, can't you?") Note also that this increase in interactions primarily involved Joe taking the initiative. Such sharp increases in initiations are likely to lead to resistances on the part of those to whom the interactions are directed.

The more complicated production and the frequent changeover of machines led to an increased frequency of machine breakdowns and much more frequent calls from Walker to the maintenance department foreman. In view of his sentiments toward Walker, the maintenance foreman was not inclined to rush his men into the barrel department when he also had work to do elsewhere in the plant, and there was no Al Short around to see that barrels got taken care of first.

In the earlier period, the inspector has been a functionary of minor consequence. The change in the market situation, leading to top management's emphasis upon quality, converted him into a powerful figure who frequently told Walker what he could and could not do.

We can sum up the pattern of management relations by saying that at a time when the nature of the work required Walker to initiate for other management people with increasing frequency, he experienced ever greater difficulty in getting the responses that he had received when he had the support of Al Short.

In his relations with the workers, Walker suffered particularly from the loss of Hodges, union president. When Hodges was in the department, the work group appeared to be united behind him, and Walker had a key man through whom he could deal with the department.

Walker's agreement with the union and the department on seniority and bumping rights served to break up the department into two contending factions. The agreement must be seen against the context of the changing production situation.

In the earlier period, it would have had little if any effect. When the department was on a steady program of long runs, it was a rare occasion when one long run was finished in the middle of the day and men had to be transferred out of the department or sent home for the balance of the day because the next run did not call for them. In the first place, the long runs generally called for much the same complement of personnel and skills. In the second place, even when changes were called for, the long runs made them infrequent.

Under the new situation, Walker was constantly having to shift from one product to another, so that bumping became a daily possibility.

Under the old arrangement, when men were dropped off the line because the next product did not require someone at their work stations, there was no one they could blame for their loss; they were simply the prey of impersonal forces. Under the seniority bumping rights arrangement, the low seniority men often had the experience of being dropped off the line when work at their station was to continue. They could see higher seniority men looking around for someone to bump. This tended to divide the department along seniority lines into a privileged and underprivileged group.

This factional issue led to friction along the production lines. It had always been true that some work stations were easier than others, and thus provided greater production possibilities. In the earlier period, the men at these easy stations held back so as to maintain a smooth flow down the line. Now this smooth pacing disappeared. If the men at an easy work station had something against the men at the next and more difficult work station, they could just cut loose and pile up barrel shells waiting for them. This tended to put psychological pressure on the men who were behind, and it showed the foreman just where the "trouble" was. When the foreman intervened to try to spur production at the bottleneck point, he not only stirred up resentment against himself but also against the workers at the preceding station who had, in effect, called the foreman's attention to the bottleneck.

In the earlier period, Walker had been known as a man who would listen to workers and respond to their suggestions and complaints. Now, caught in these new pressures, he seemed no longer able to listen. Instead, he was constantly seeking to initiate for the men—to spur them on toward heightened activity.

At the same time, the workers were not making the same incentive earnings that they had in early 1948. While each type of barrel was supposed to have an incentive rate adjusted to the possible speed of production, the common experience with incentive systems shows that the men make more on long runs than they do on short runs. Short runs do not provide for the development of skills and work rhythms making for high production. Furthermore, they lead to increased machine breakdowns with their attendant losses of incentive. Thus the men suffered in their relations to the economic environment, both in lowered incentive earnings and in more frequent job transfers or losses of part- or full-days' work.

The effect of all these changes was to shift worker sentiments toward Tom Walker in a markedly negative direction. This was shown particularly in two ways. In the earlier period, workers had taken the initiative in calling to Walker's attention costly errors in planning and organizing that he was about to make. For a man as unsystematic as the foreman, this was an invaluable aid. Under the new conditions the aid was withdrawn, and the men simply stood back to watch Walker get into trouble.

Worker reaction to his profanity marked the second change. This was particularly noted for the new workers in the department and for those who came in twice a week on special jobs. Having had no opportunity to get really acquainted with "good old Tom," they bridled at the words he used at them—or in their presence. But now even the old-timers ceased to regard the foreman as "good old Tom" and, in this new context of interpersonal sentiments, the profanity could no longer be regarded as a neutral or even colorfully attractive characteristic of the man.

Let us put the analysis in more general terms.

We see in this case how technology and work flow determined within limits with whom Walker interacted and also how often. The change in products produced impelled Walker greatly to increase his attempts to initiate activities for other management people. That led to a situation which may be put in the form of the following proposition:

If A greatly increases his attempts to initiate activities for B, without responding increasingly to B's initiations, *then* (1) B's sentiments toward A will become more negative, and (2) B will seek to reduce his responses to A *unless* outside pressures on B induce him to continue responding.

In the present case, other management people apparently bore negative sentiments toward Walker before the change took place. We may assume that the change made these sentiments more intense, but we have no measure of intensity. Changes in intensity of sentiments are more difficult to identify than changes from positive to negative or vice versa.

Regarding the condition specified under (2) above, the situation is much more clean-cut. Other management people were no longer under pressure from the general production supervisor to give special attention to Walker's attempted initiations. Therefore, they responded with increasing resistance.

Given the pre-existence of negative sentiments toward Walker on the part of the other management people, the above proposition must be viewed as tentative for that relationship. The same proposition seems to apply in a much less equivocal manner in the foreman-worker relationship. Walker increased his initiations of activities for the workers and at the same time decreased his responses to their attempted initiations to him. The result was a shift from positive to negative sentiments and a withholding of activities positively valued by Walker. The pattern of reciprocity broke down.

We note here also the role played by four significant symbols: barrels, whiskey, six cents, and curse words.

The first three have the same significance. Al Short's attachment to barrels, and his favoring of the barrel department with bottles of whiskey for the foreman and assistant foreman when production records were made, tended to build up Tom Walker's sense of self-importance. These symbols also indicated to other management people that Walker was an important person to contend with. They might not like him—and indeed they didn't—but these and other symbols indicated that they had better respond to his demands upon them. The six cents illustrates the opposite end of the status evaluations. Wiley considered six cents of no consequence, but it was symbolically important to Walker. It showed him that the man who had once won arguments with other department heads was now even losing points to as lowly a management man as an inspector.

What is the function of such symbols? They serve as cues or stimuli to set off certain interactions and activities and inhibit others. They also evoke sentiments. They do not, of course, function in a vacuum. Each symbol must be seen in its social context.

The attachment of Short to barrels is relevant to our interests only insofar as it influenced his interactions and activities. A bottle of whiskey can mean many different things in different times and situations. If every foreman in the plant had received a bottle of whiskey when his department made a production record, then Tom Walker's bottle would not have had any status significance. It was symbolic in this way because it set him above fellow foremen. Finally, we see that the words used— even curse words—must be interpreted in terms of the prevailing pattern of interactions, activities, and sentiments. The same words that evoke smiles in one situation may evoke anger in another.

# Chapter 10  *TEAMS OF ARTISANS*

WHEN we think of American industry we tend to think in terms of mass production. This type of production has indeed characterized much of our economy, and yet, in seeking to explain the behavior and reactions of workers in mass production industries, we are always comparing them, explicitly or implicitly, with the skilled craftsmen of other eras. While we recognize the gains of mass production in raising our standards of living, we wonder what human values have been lost in the substitution of mechanization for handcraft skill.

We cannot go back to an earlier era to make our comparative studies, but we shall do the next best thing. We shall look at teams of modern craftsmen, blowing and shaping fine glassware which will be sold as objects of art. The data come from a study carried out by Frank Miller and me during the years 1952–53 in the Benton Division of the Shawcross Corporation.

We shall be concerned with worker responses to the job itself: to the mental and physical activities involved in producing the glassware. But these reactions can only be understood against a background of knowledge of the social setting in which the work takes place. The social relations are particularly important in this case for two reasons: (1) the work process allowed much freedom of physical activity and interaction among the men, and (2) changes in the community and union environment of the plant resulted in significant changes in worker-worker and worker-management relations just prior to our study.

The historical background is necessary for an understanding of interactions and activities on the job. Description of those interactions and activities lead us to an examination of the satisfactions or dissatisfactions workers find on the job.

We shall discuss technology and work flow first, then fill in the historical background of social changes. After an examination of relations among workers and between workers and management on the job, we shall consider what it means to be an artisan in a mass production world.

## TEAM COMPOSITION AND WORK OPERATIONS

The work of the team (or shop, as it is called in this industry) is carried on around a circular furnace, which has four circular openings or "glory holes." Four work benches are attached to the furnace extending out in the spaces between the glory holes. A metal bar protrudes parallel to the work bench, to provide support for the glass worker as he rolls and manipulates the iron holding the glass.

The Benton plant has five furnaces, arranged in the pattern of the number five on a pair of dice. In some cases all members of the same team work around the same furnace, but in other cases a team may be divided between two adjoining furnaces. Thus it is possible to have six work teams or shops working on the five furnaces.

From the top down, in the order of skill, pay, and prestige, the teams consist of gaffer, servitor, gatherer, bit gatherer, stick-up boy and carry-in boy. Some shops may contain seven or eight members, since some pieces may require an additional bit gatherer or an additional servitor or gatherer.

The work cycle begins when the gatherer goes to pick up a piece of molten glass on the end of a hollow blow iron. He may rotate or "marver" the piece on a smooth metal stand, he may "block" it in a cup-shaped wooden tool, and he may begin the process of blowing it up. While he works, he is likely to push the piece through his door of the warming furnace, or "glory hole," in order to maintain the proper temperature for working the glass. As he finishes his part of the work, he carries the piece around to the servitor and generally reheats it so that it is ready for the servitor. The servitor brings the piece closer to its final shape by blowing and by the use of hand tools. When the piece has reached the basic shape of the final product, except for ornamentation and the finishing of its top, the stick-up boy steps forward with a solid metal rod with a piece of molten glass at the end and fixes the rod to the bowl at the opposite end of the servitor's blow iron. The servitor then breaks off the bowl at the end of his blow iron, leaving the bowl open at the end where it has been broken from the iron. The glass, firmly cemented to the solid rod, is taken by the stick-up boy to the gaffer's bench. The gaffer then opens up the bowl, shears it, and shapes it with iron tools, assisted by the carry-in boy, who sometimes holds a wooden paddle against the piece. If the design requires smaller pieces of glass for handles or ornamentation, the bit gatherer brings them to the gaffer and puts them on the bowl under his direction. When the gaffer completes the piece, the carry-in boy slips an asbestos-covered fork under it and the gaffer cracks it off of the iron rod, whereupon the carry-in boy carries it to the kiln or lehr where it goes through a gradual annealing process.

The work process goes on, so that at any one time there may be two or more pieces in various stages of production. The work sequence outlined here would not hold for all pieces, since there are some large pieces on which the servitor, instead of the gaffer, affixes the bits. Furthermore, in the production of stemware (wine glasses) the gatherer performs the servitor functions observed on other shops, and the servitor attaches the stem and foot with bits furnished him by the bit gatherer.

## HISTORICAL PERSPECTIVE

An historical review in most factories would give major emphasis to technological and process changes. Not so here. While all of the knowledge and skills of chemical engineering have been brought to bear upon production of an absolutely clear crystal glass and the development of rigid temperature controls over the gas furnaces, the basic material is still fabricated according to methods that are centuries old. There has been only one technological change of any significance in recent years. In the old days, the gatherer had to make his gather out of a large pot of molten glass, so that he had to estimate the amount of material that he would be using. Today, the molten glass is provided him by the gob machine. At this machine, a constant stream of molten glass flows at a uniformly controlled rate so that the number of seconds of flow determines the weight and volume of the glass. The gatherer now calls into a public address system "forty seconds"—or whatever amount required. When this amount is provided him in a metal mold, he simply sticks his iron in, rotates it, and pulls the glass out. This assures that a uniform amount of glass will be used on each piece. Beyond this point the blowing, shaping, shearing, and ornamentation are all done by hand.

Although there has been very little technological change, there have been tremendous changes in the social organization of the blowing room. Years ago, the craftsmanship of Benton glassmaking was almost entirely a Swedish monopoly. It was widely believed that only the Swedes had the skill and artistic sense to reach the top in this difficult craft. Naturally, the men of Swedish extraction supported this view. In general, they offered no help to young Italian-Americans or indeed to young workers of any other than Swedish stock. In fact, some of the glassworkers today speak of how the old Swedes used to get together and talk in Swedish so that the non-Swedes were completely shut out of their conversations.

While today a man may be encouraged to "frig" (experiment with the different phases of glass-making) during his lunch hour or at odd times when he is not needed on production, in the old days the controlling Swedes would not allow any of the younger glassworkers to perform any operation that was not strictly part of the job.

The Swedish gaffer in those days was a man of great prestige in the community as well as in the factory. The old-timers today say that you used to tip your hat to the gaffer when you met him on the street.

Within the factory, the control of the old gaffer was well-nigh absolute. Discipline was sometimes enforced physically—a kick in the pants to one of the young men seemed part of the accepted way of doing things.

The gaffer had almost complete control over the membership of his work team. While the assignments and promotions were made officially by management, every effort was made to give the gaffer the people he wanted to work with, and we have never heard of instances where a gaffer was forced to accept a man that he did not want. Thus, a man could be refused an increase in pay or a promotion if the gaffer who had the vacancy on his shop did not want that particular individual.

Since the Swedes in Benton started at a very early age and displayed remarkable longevity, the progress of younger men was very slow. Many shops worked together for years without any changes in personnel. Thus, a very settled social system developed.

When the situation in the blowing room did change at last, it seemed that everything was changing at once and with extraordinary rapidity. The old Swedes began to die or retire. Their sons did not succeed to their positions as might have been the case in Sweden, for in this country the sons of the craftsmen went on with their education and advanced into technical, professional, and managerial positions.

The new generation of non-Swedish glassworkers rose rapidly to positions of control. However, as these new men rose to the top, they discovered that they did not have the control that had been exercised by the old Swedes. There seemed to be several factors responsible for this change.

A union came into Shawcross in 1943. While the Benton workers had taken little, if any, part in the organization process, they were included in a union shop contract. Until the union came in, the gaffer at Benton regarded the organization of the factory as having a step-by-step series of gradual gradations of prestige and authority from shop boy up through gaffer, foreman, plant manager, and so on. The gaffer did not have to decide whether he was a worker or a member of management, and no one decided it for him. The coming of the union drew a horizontal line through the factory. You were either a worker and union member, or a member of management. This did not mean that the two groups were necessarily in conflict; it did mean that you could belong to only one group. So far as the union was concerned, the gaffer became a glassworker like other glassworkers. He might even be represented before management by someone lower than himself in pay and prestige.

The entrance of the union also meant that seniority became the dominant factor in promotions. Thus today the gaffer may want a certain individual on his shop, but if the man does not have the requisite seniority, there is nothing that management can do in acceding to the gaffer's wishes. Furthermore, when the gaffer does not want a certain individual on the shop, management will seek to take his preferences into account. Nevertheless, the man may have the seniority that entitles him to a chance to make good on this shop and the gaffer may have to accept him.

In representing the interests of the men, the union representatives deal with foremen and higher management people as the men in authority. They do not deal with the gaffer; in fact, they may question decisions and preferences of the gaffer.

With the opening in 1951 of a new plant which had a gallery for visitors, Benton experienced a very considerable expansion of its operations. Up until this time, the glassworkers had always worked one shift, eight to four. Now the expansion necessitated two shifts—six to two and two to ten. Since the expansion came in the period of rapid retirement of the old Swedish glass workers, the company went into a period of extraordinarily rapid promotions.

At the time of our study (1952–53), there were gaffers in their fifties and sixties who had worked from thirty to forty years in the trade, but had reached the gaffer position only within the last three to seven years. On the other hand, there were men in their forties or even late thirties who had reached the top within the last two to three years. While these men had fifteen to twenty-five years of service in Shawcross, none of the three youngest gaffers had more than seven years of experience inside Benton. Since one local union represented all of the over seven thousand Shawcross workers in this city, and since the seniority system provided for a common seniority system for all Shawcross workers, it was possible for men to move over into Benton and carry with them ten to twenty years of seniority gained in another part of the works. This seniority enabled them to rise rapidly as openings developed.

## TEAM LEADERSHIP

The entrance of new people, the rapid changes in shop composition, and the promotions of relatively inexperienced men have changed the social system, so that the gaffer faces problems of leadership and control far different from those experienced by his predecessors. At the same time, he faces younger people who have grown up in an environment where authority is questioned far more than it was many years ago. This seems to be true throughout our society. Children at the dinner table are no longer expected to speak only when they are spoken to by adults. And in many ways the strict controls over the young have been relaxed year by year. There has arisen a generation of workers which is no longer conditioned to give automatic response to authority.

Against this background we can see that the gaffer today has an extraordinarily difficult leadership job. At one time, the old-timers who are now at the top had to submit passively to the very heavy subordination that was required of them over the years by the old-time Swedish craftsmen. Now, they themselves are at the top, and they recognize that it is not possible for them to exercise authority as it was exercised upon them. They are not bitter about this. In fact, we find them quite openly critical of the strict controls that were exercised. They recognize that times have changed and they feel that times should have changed, although they wonder whether the pendulum has not swung too far against authority. But even as they accept the changes intellectually, they are in an uneasy and uncertain position. They know that the leadership that was exercised upon them can no longer be practiced, but they have had no experience in any other approach.

The young men never served under the old system of tight control, so they are perhaps more free to devise new ways for meeting a changed situation. At the same time, their task is not an easy one either technically or socially. On the technical side, they have had to learn the skills of the craft much faster than was ever before thought possible. At the same time, they have had to find a place for themselves socially among the older gaffers who have always believed that it takes twenty to thirty years in the trade to become a really skilled craftsman. In a sense, as the young man proves that he can do an adequate job in working up to be a gaffer in five years, he is demonstrating that the craft is not as difficult and exalted as the old men have claimed it to be. In this situation, it is hardly surprising that the young gaffer receives little advice and encouragement from the older men whose technical skills and experience could save him countless mistakes.

The gaffer of old had his control of the shop built into the legal environment. Today he finds himself in the ambiguous position of many of his counterparts elsewhere—group leaders, straw bosses, or working foremen, as the position is variously known. He has responsibility for the performance of his shop, and yet lacks formal authority to run the shop.

There are effective ways of meeting this situation, as we will see in the case of Jack Carter, one of the younger gaffers, who had risen very rapidly to that position. In effect, Carter had built a social leadership to take the place of the technical-legal system which supported earlier gaffers. This was evident in his handling of both technical and disciplinary problems.

In the old days, when a technical difficulty arose on the shop and the gaffer could not correct it in words, he would "go back" and demonstrate to the servitor, gatherer, or bit gatherer how he wanted the work done. During the period of our study, even the older gaffers seemed reluctant to do this. Lacking the formal supports of the old system, they seemed also to lack confidence in themselves. It might have been years since the gaffer had done any gathering. Was he sure now that he could do it just right? Furthermore, particularly in this type of work, there is no "one best way" of handling the job. Different men can perform the same operation in different ways and get equally good results. The oldtime gaffer would have had the confidence to insist that his way was the best way, but if some of the older gaffers we observed had sought to demonstrate an operation, they might have been greeted by a comment from a subordinate to the effect that "Johnny Jensen used to do it different." Jensen, who had retired shortly before the beginning of our study, held the highest prestige of the oldtime Swedish gaffers.

For the younger gaffers, there was just no possibility of demonstrating the way the work should be done by the servitor, gatherer, or bit gatherer. They had moved up through these positions so rapidly that they just did not have the requisite skills.

Jack Carter met these technical problems through directing a group discussion among the members of his shop. Whenever any new problem came up, he would call the group together for a pooling of ideas. Although the men under him all had less experience than he, their experience spread throughout the blowing room. Some of the shop members had worked under oldtime Swedish gaffers and had observed how things were done by these master craftsmen. Even if he was not performing the operation himself, an alert worker could learn a great deal from observing a skilled man. In this situation, Jack Carter directed the discussion and made the final decision, but there was a vigorous sharing of ideas before the gaffer made the decision.

We never observed anything like this with the older gaffers. They took as their model the oldtime Swedish gaffers, for whom it would have been inconceivable to ask for technical opinions from subordinates.

How does the gaffer handle criticisms to his own subordinates? In the old days, when the gaffer was the acknowledged boss, this seems to have been much easier to do. Today, when the gaffer has no formal authority and still works so closely with his men, he often seems to be so concerned about being accepted by them that he finds it difficult to address criticisms to them. But refraining from these criticisms does not solve the interpersonal problems any more than it solves the technical problems, as the following case indicates.

As the foreman was observing the shop, he noticed that the men seemed to be having difficulty and that the gaffer was getting very upset. The foreman approached the gaffer and asked for an explanation. The gaffer shook his head and said, referring to his gatherer, "Joe isn't blowing it up straight."

The foreman looked at the piece and noted that the observation was correct. But then he asked, "Have you spoken to Joe about it?"

The gaffer again shook his head and said, "No, that wouldn't do any good. He just can't get it right."

The foreman now started around the glory hole to speak to the gatherer, but he had only taken two or three steps when the gatherer approached him and said, "What's *he* complaining about now?"

The foreman explained. The gatherer grunted and went back to the next piece. This particular piece came out perfectly straight, so the foreman was hopeful that the immediate problem had been solved. However, when he returned to talk to the gaffer, he was met with a request to change the job assignment to another piece. The gaffer said that things just weren't going right. Knowing from past experience that this particular gaffer was likely to get "on the hog" (to get into a rut where nothing seemed to go right) and then to "fire over" with his shop (go home in the middle of a shift), the foreman reluctantly agreed to the change.

The gaffer in this case was a young man of a good deal of promise. He was thought by management people to have the technical possibilities which would make him as good at the gaffering operations as the best of the oldtime Swedes. His inability to handle interpersonal problems directly on his shop slowed down even his technical progress and made it difficult for him to resolve his nervous tension.

Jack Carter handled similar situation quite differently. He sought to take direct action before the foreman noticed that anything was wrong. If the foreman did find something wrong, Carter insisted that the matter be brought to his attention first. Then he would take direct action. It was not always easy.

Consider the case of Don, the obstreperous bit gatherer. He had a reputation for being a wise guy who would not let anyone tell him what to do and who would do as little work as possible. He had been moved from shop to shop because of complaints lodged against him. When Don was moved into Jack's shop there was trouble again, but this time it was shortlived. Within a week after the transfer the gaffer gave me this account:

We're getting along all right now. I had it out with him on the first day. I would tell him how I wanted things done, and he was always giving me an argument about it. It seemed that every time I would say something to him he would take it as a personal criticism.

So finally I had it out with him. I told him: "Don, when I tell you I want you to do things different, that's no personal criticism. I'm just telling you the way I work best. Now, I don't want an argument every time I tell you what to do. I want you to do it my way even if I'm wrong."

Well, at first he didn't like it. He went around sulking and saying that he was going to put in for a transfer to another shop. Then he comes up to me and says: "You've never heard anybody else complain about my work, have you?" That's what gave me the opening to lay it on the line for him. I said to him: "Good God yes. I've heard everybody talking against you. Why do you think you've been transferred around here so much?"

Well, that really set him back. He was really surprised. He said to me, "Nobody's ever told me about it." I told him, "That's what I mean. Some fellows around here will complain about you to each other and they'll talk against you to the foreman, and they will never tell you anything to your face. Now, if I've got something against you, I'll tell it to you right to your face and I won't go around talking against you. The way I feel about it, what you do on this shop is between you and me and shouldn't concern anybody else, and if I have anything against you I'm not running to the foreman. I'll take it right to you and we'll straighten it out that way. That way it'll be better for you and better for me too."

Well, he said he'd think it over. I guess he's changed his mind now. It took him just a couple of days. Yesterday he came to me and said: "Jack, if I tell you I won't ask for a transfer, will you ask them to keep me on this shop?" I told him I wasn't going to ask anybody for anything. I told him that I didn't want him to be obligated to me or me be obligated to him. It was all right for him to work on this shop as far as I was concerned, but it didn't need to go beyond that.

A few days later I had a chance to get the reaction of the bit gatherer. He put it this way:

I like this shop all right. I really think this is the only good shop in the place. When you're doing something wrong here, Jack or Tom (servitor) will tell you to your face and they keep it right on the shop. This is the only shop where they treat you like a human being. When they take it to you that way, they make you feel like you're part of the team.

Very occasionally, there were problems that Jack Carter could not re- solve directly; that called for an appeal to the foreman. However, in such cases, he always insisted that the subordinate in question go into the foreman's office with him so that they could put the case to the fore- man together. No one enjoyed going into the foreman's office in this way, but the men valued the assurance that Carter would never complain to the foreman about them "behind our backs." On Jack Carter's shop, you always knew where you stood with the gaffer.

Taking action on mistakes is difficult enough to handle when the responsibility for a particular mistake is clear. The problem becomes much more difficult on those frequent occasions when responsibility is not clear. As he spends most of his time at his own bench, the gaffer has limited opportunity to observe the performance of subordinates and to check on questions where there may be doubt as to responsibility.

Under these circumstances, what can the gaffer do? He may wait until he has accumulated enough evidence to make sure of the nature of the difficulty. This is certainly better than jumping to conclusions, but the process may take considerable time and it may be a source of annoyance to the gaffer as he deals with imperfect pieces to such an extent that it upsets his own emotional equilibrium.

There is still another alternative: to present the difficulty to other members of the shop as a problem to be solved. Consider this example from the Carter shop. The shop had been having trouble with what are called mold marks—marks left on the glass by the mold used in blowing up the piece. We asked the gaffer for the source of the difficulty. He said he thought that the shop boy had not been holding the mold tight as his servitor blew up the piece. Immediately after giving me this explanation, Carter walked over to show the imperfect piece to the shop boy. They conversed for perhaps two minutes in a good-natured fashion. The shop boy asked the gaffer what he thought was the source of the difficulty. The gaffer said that there were several possibilities, that he was not sure, but one possibility was that the shop boy was not holding the mold tightly shut. The shop boy responded by saying that that was a possibility, but he had the impression that he had been keeping it tightly shut. At this point, the servitor joined in the conversation. After he had looked at the piece in question, he said that it was entirely his own responsibility. He had been blowing the piece up too fast.

There are several interesting aspects to this incident. In the first place, the gaffer thought he knew what the trouble was, but he happened to be mistaken. If he had acted directly on his mistaken impression, he would only have upset his relations with the stick-up boy and stirred up a very defensive reaction.

Instead of telling the worker that he was wrong, the gaffer simply listed various possibilities. It was noteworthy that, although the stick-up boy did not think he was at fault, he nevertheless seemed to be willing to consider that possibility calmly without being defensive about it. And finally, the servitor was perfectly willing to take over the responsibility himself. In approaching the problem this way, the gaffer avoided defensive reactions and made it possible for his men to look upon the problem objectively. As they handled it harmoniously, they also strengthened themselves technically.

By his own leadership skill, Jack Carter built high morale on his shop. The men took pride in their team membership. They wanted to work with Jack. So strong was this effect that the servitor, who had seemed to us an ambitious young man, turned down a promotion that would have increased his pay by eight dollars a week, because it would have meant moving to another shop. As he explained it:

> Well, I've been working for Jack for five years now and we have always got along good together. I just didn't want to make the change. I remember how it was when I was working for this other fellow. I was on edge all the time. Then when I would go home at night I would get in arguments with the wife and kids. It's different today. I get along good on the job and I get along good at home. It isn't worth eight dollars to me to make that change.

Carter's experience suggests that, even without the formal supports of authority, it is possible for a gaffer to become a strong team leader. However, his case was exceptional. We can say that the situation allowed such leadership to arise, but we cannot say that it provided any formal supports for such leadership.

## WORK FLOW PROBLEMS

The performance of a shop depends not only upon the technical skills of each of its members. It depends also upon the organization of a smooth flow of work so that the piece of glass arrives at the right place at the right time. The work flow is complicated by the chemistry of the glass. It can only be worked effectively within a certain temperature range.

If it is worked when too cold, imperfections will show up in the annealing process, and the piece will have to be discarded. Even with the most efficient work flow, the glass will have to be warmed in in the furnace several times in the course of operations. If the work is not well co-ordinated, additional warmings in will have to be added, which means extra work for certain members of the team for the same amount of finished production. When the pieces are heavy, this extra work becomes particularly onerous.

The work flow has its psychological effects also. When the work is running in a smooth and well-coordinated fashion, each worker can develop his own rhythm of work. When coordination breaks down, work rhythms are destroyed, and this is likely to lead to technical as well as emotional difficulties.

We tend to take work flow coordination for granted, but its importance becomes apparent when it breaks down. We observed one striking inci-dent of this nature between a servitor and a bit gatherer. It involved a large and rather heavy piece on which the servitor had to affix a series of bits brought to him by the bit gatherer. The servitor noted that he was having to lift up the heavy piece to warm it in after each bit, whereas he could get at least two bits on before the warming in became necessary if the bit gatherer would move faster.

The servitor told the bit gatherer to bring the bits in faster. The bit gatherer replied that he was working just as fast as he cared to. The servitor insisted with increasing vehemence, and the bit gatherer replied equally heatedly that the servitor was not going to make him move any faster. Finally, the servitor passed the piece on to the gaffer and slugged the bit gatherer.

This was an extreme case of incoordination and conflict. It was the only fight we observed or heard about during the eighteen months of our study. However, it illustrates the tensions that can and do arise along the line of the work flow.

Atypical as it is, the case nevertheless illustrates other points we have been making regarding the changing nature of shop leadership. In the old days, it would have been unthinkable for a bit gatherer to resist the directives of a servitor. If the servitor had been less than satisfied with the cooperation he was receiving, he probably would have taken the matter to his gaffer. The gaffer could then have told the bit gatherer that he would either have to cooperate, or else the gaffer would have him taken off the shop. In this case, it would have been no help for the servitor to appeal to the gaffer because the gaffer was one of those who just could not bring himself to make a criticism directly to a subordinate.

In most cases coordination of work activity is achieved without argu-ment—and even without verbal or gestural communication. Making a quantitative study of interactions on four Benton shops, Frank Miller started with the assumption that, for each interaction, there must be an originator and a responder—that is, for each pair interaction, one man acts first and the other responds to him. Whenever the interaction involved words or gestures (such as hand signals or head nods), one could readily observe who acted first. However, Miller noted large numbers of interactions in which no such communication took place. Apparently two men came together and acted together in response to their observation of the condition of the glass and the stage reached in the manufacturing cycle. On any design that was a familiar part of the shop repertoire, such interactions labeled "situational" by Miller outnumbered those in which verbal or gestural communication was involved.[1]

While we do not have sufficient quantitative data on this point, observations might be expected to show a pattern of relations between situational and "free" contacts when the work and personal relations are going smoothly. When the shop is "getting on the hog," we might expect to see changes in the pattern of free interactions and a marked increase in the proportion of free interactions in relation to situational ones.

There is another aspect of the work flow that is important to the emotional equilibrium of the men. Individuals reported to us most satisfaction with a flow in which they could "get ahead" and have free time for relaxation before the next operation, or in which the next piece of glass arrived at their station momentarily after they had passed on the preceding piece. Individual tastes differed as to whether it was better to get ahead and relax or to work in a continuous flow. On the undesirable conditions, there was general agreement. The worker felt under pressure when the next piece arrived before he had completed work on the preceding one. This did not mean that a piece would be offered to him before he could take it. It meant that, as he was trying to finish a piece, he could see out of the corner of his eye his predecessor in the work flow holding the next piece in readiness or warming it in again to keep it ready. While many men welcomed the free time that came with getting ahead, time in which you had to wait for a co-worker while you had your iron in your hand was definitely not welcomed. This kind of waiting time meant additional labor in warming-in, as we have noted in the fight between servitor and bit gatherer.

Since one man being ahead often means that he is crowding the pace for the next man, it is not an easy task to smooth the work flow on a shop. The pace is influenced in large measure by the nature of the piece being produced. On one piece an individual may have little to do and often find himself ahead. On another he may have a much longer work cycle and may drop behind. Since different pieces exert pressures at different places on the shop, the reactions of shop members to the same piece may be quite varied.

---

[1] See his "Situational Interactions: A Worthwhile Concept?" *Human Organization*, Vol. XVII, No. 4 (Winter, 1958–59).

These work flow problems present delicate tasks of coordination, particularly for the gaffers. They also present problems for the foremen who need to note chronic cases of incoordination, so as to transfer men in the hope of building more compatible teams.

## QUANTITATIVE MEASURES OF LEADERSHIP

Can leadership be described in quantitative terms? Miller made observations that will enable us to quantify some of the ideas we have been discussing.[2]

He observed four shops in samples of twenty-minute periods, totaling four hours each on two pieces, or eight hours of observation time per shop. Only four out of the twelve shops had their men located so that Miller could observe all shop members simultaneously, which meant that some interesting shops had to be left out of this phase of the research. The sample did not include Campisi, the top status man among the old-timers. Three lesser status gaffers, Kurt Larson, Gus Pinelli, and Carl Schultz were included. The sample included only one of the young gaffers, but that was Jack Carter, with whom we are already well-acquainted. These data covered a total of twenty-three men on the four shops.

For each man, Miller noted the number of situational interactions ($S$), interactions originated ($O$), and interactions responded to ($R$) within the shop. For interactions with men outside of his own shop, originations and responses were also noted. (There were, of course, no situational interactions between men on different shops, since the work flow was confined to a single shop.)

For interactions originated within one's own shop, Carter had the highest number of all of the 23 men; 160 in 8 hours, or 20 per hour. He totaled 103 responses, tying for fourth place among all 23 men, but placing first among the 4 gaffers. His situational interactions (213) were lowest of the 4 gaffers observed. (Since situational interactions vary greatly with work classification, it would not be meaningful to compare Carter with men in other classifications.)

These figures for Carter seem to result from a combination of task, skill, and personality factors. The particular designs observed gave him some free time to move around—and originate interaction. The designs were relatively new to the shop, and the men were relatively inexperienced; this tended to raise the proportion of free, as against situational, interactions. And finally, Carter was an exceedingly active person socially. He made the most of the interactional opportunities offered by the work.

Gus Pinelli presented an extreme contrast to Carter. His designs of ash trays and plates presented few technical problems and moved very fast. This gave him the highest number of situational interactions (433)

---

[2] *Ibid.*

of all the gaffers. It also served to pin him down to his bench most of the time, thus limiting his free interactions. Only the servitor came in contact with him in situational interactions. They could have talked together, but seldom did. For interaction with other men, they would have had to seek these men out—and generally they did not. For 8 hours, Pinelli had 33 originations and 14 responses. (Compare this with 160 and 103, respectively, for Carter.)

These quantities fitted in well with the sentiments we heard expressed toward Pinelli. He was accorded little respect as a workman. He was thought unimportant in the informal organization of the department. He was considered a disagreeable fellow to work for; you avoided contact with him when you could.

The quantities do not tell us such a clear story for gaffers Larson and Schultz. In this early stage of such quantitative studies, we might expect the figures to be more revealing at the high and low extremes. Further research might give us comparative data that would enable us to make more of the Larson and Schultz figures.

Jack Carter, the top originator of in-shop contacts, was also top man in originating and responding to out-of-shop contacts. Gus Pinelli ranked at the very bottom in originating and responding to out-of-shop contacts, reflecting again the sentiments held toward him in the department as a whole. For the four teams, Miller found that the individual's rank in originations within his team correlated at .98 with rank in out-of-team contacts (originations plus responses). The very close correspondence between interaction counts in-shop and out-of-shop suggests that individuals have characteristic patterns of interaction. The active man on the shop is also active outside.

## WORK GROUP COHESION

We may be inclined to think of the workers in a given department as constituting a work group with its own leadership and norms of behavior. There are departmental groups of this nature, but there are also departments in which workers are divided into contending factions, and we cannot speak realistically of the *work* group.

In any case, the degree of cohesion or factionalism within a department is not something to be taken for granted. That is a subject for research. Let us consider Benton as a case for preliminary analysis and for some tentative conclusions, which we hope to develop further at a later point.

In most respects, we could say that the personnel of the blowing room showed a minimum of cohesion, but there were instances when the men stood together. We shall examine both instances of cohesion and of noncohesion.

The forty-odd men on each of the two shifts of the blowing room could be divided roughly into two factions; the old-timers and the young men.

The old-timers were the men in their fifties and early sixties who had come up slowly through the ranks in the period when the old Swedes were still in control. The young men ranged from mid-forties down to early twenties. Even the gaffers among them were only in their late thirties or early forties. They had made nearly all of their progress in the period since the retirement or death of the old Swedes.

The importance of age grading in the traditional blowing room is indicated by the title of the top man. "Gaffer" is an old English term for grandfather.

The young gaffers were looked upon with contempt by the old-timers. They were not thought to be real glassworkers. They were not maintaining the real quality standards of Benton (though management seemed quite satisfied with their performance in this respect). Furthermore, they were not all-around glassworkers; they could not do skillfully all of the operations on the shop.

When the young men had difficulties with a new and more complicated piece, the old-timers watched from a distance with ill-concealed satisfaction. They did not volunteer helpful advice. When their advice was requested, they found themselves to be "too busy" to go to the other man's shop to discuss his problem and to observe his work. At other times, they responded to requests for advice with suggestions that they knew would lead the young men into further technical difficulties. At the time of our study, we learned about this advice-giving through interviews, but the situation was already a matter of the past. Young men no longer asked the old-timers for the secrets that would advance their progress.

The young men reacted by taking a negative view of the personalities and skills of many of the old-timers. There were at least three old-timers whose skills were universally respected, but there were a number of others whom the younger men considered to be bungling workers in spite of their long years of experience.

The separation of the men into two factions could be observed both on and off the job. For a time, we made observations of who was seen with whom during the lunch period or just before or after the working day. To a very high degree, the old men tended to cluster together, and so did the young men. The work allowed many of the men some free time between their job operations, so there was opportunity for social contact on the job. Most of these contacts were channeled within a single age group.

A lack of cohesion was shown in the failure to arrive at any department-wide production norms. This was particularly evident when a given design was shifted from a shop of old-timers to one of younger gaffers. This happened on several occasions when work was shifted from Al Campisi's shop to that of Jack Carter. Since management, like the workers, rated Campisi most skilled of all the old-time gaffers, he was assigned nearly all of the exhibition pieces, and also many of the more complicated regular designs, as they were introduced into the line in the spring and fall.

To take on these new pieces, Campisi had to be relieved of some of his old items. These were passed along to the gaffers who were coming up, such as Jack Carter.

In the eyes of the old-timers, Jack Carter should not have been able to make these newly assigned pieces at all. If he did, after an appropriate period of failure and struggle, his production should level off below that regularly attained by Campisi. Under no circumstances should he make more than Campisi had made.

Jack Carter did not share these views of either his abilities or his social obligations. He took pride in raising the quality and quantity of his production rapidly. He sometimes did run into technical difficulties that threatened to take him out of the status competition, and one of these incidents we will discuss later. However, in general, Carter was able to raise his production to that attained by Campisi in an outrageously short time. In fact, in some cases he even went beyond Campisi's records. Not much beyond, but just enough to show that he and his men could do it.

This was the source of considerable annoyance to Campisi and his friends. The old gaffer had been the chief protégé of Johnny Jensen, the last of the great Swedish gaffers. Jensen was remarkable not only for the great skill with which he worked the glass, but also for being an exceptionally fast worker. Campisi was thought to have acquired most of the skill of Jensen, but he was not nearly so fast as the old Swede. Therefore, he could be overtaken in competition on some pieces, even as he moved on to new items of production.

While at the time of our study most of the men were well satisfied with their jobs, there were a number of them who had complaints about various matters, and particularly about their failure to receive merit increases in pay as soon as they were eligible for such consideration.

In most cases, such men kept their complaints to themselves or just shared them with a friend or two. There was the general feeling that a man would not get any backing from his fellows on any problems he might take up.

If there was to be any concerted action among the men, we might have expected it to be directed against Jim Dayton, assistant production manager and immediate superior of the foremen. He was regarded by the men as the real boss of the blowing room. A young man of industrial engineering training, he was frustrated by the apparently easygoing pace of life in the blowing room and sought ways to establish greater control over this area. In the fall and winter 1952–53, Dayton made three moves that stirred up antagonism in the blowing room.

The first move, without any prior discussion, was a memorandum addressed to the blowing room foremen, with carbon copies to the plant guards, which was placed upon the bulletin board for all workers to read. The notice read as follows:

Within recent weeks there has been an increase in the number of finished and unfinished pieces missing. To help eliminate this deplorable condition, we must prohibit all unauthorized persons from entering the finishing area. In the future, if there are pieces of ware which in the foreman's judgment should be shown to blowing room personnel, those pieces of ware should be taken by the foreman to the person, or that person should be escorted by the foreman into the finishing area.

This notice was offensive to everyone in the blowing room, and particularly to the gaffers. While up to this point there had been no restriction on movement into the finishing area, it had been the gaffers particularly who had availed themselves of this freedom. A gaffer might wander in now and then to see how the pieces his shop made looked as they were inspected and put through the finishing process. The gaffers claimed that it was a considerable aid to their work to be able to see the pieces at these later stages. They felt that it was demeaning to have to call upon their foreman to accompany them for this purpose. The gaffers were no more pleased at the idea of having the foreman bring the pieces to them. Such actions seemed to advertise to the whole blowing room that the gaffer had been making mistakes.

On the day the memorandum was posted, one of the men added to it a penciled comment stating that the assistant production manager should go back to the army, where such notices were more appropriate. However, while the notice provided the research interviewers with many heated anti-Dayton comments from the men, no concerted action was forthcoming. The new rule remained in effect, and the agitation simply died down.

In late January, Dayton took two further actions of general significance. One night he searched the lockers of the blowing room men for cups and saucers from the company cafeteria and for pieces of Benton ware. As Dayton told us later,

Boy, there was a lot of excitement. That is, the people who had glass in their lockers made a lot of fuss. The people who didn't have glass found in their lockers, I guess they didn't care much one way or another. It's a funny thing. The one who made most of the fuss had most of the glass in his locker, and he was the one who had the most expensive stuff. The only really expensive stuff we found was in his locker.

The next night Dayton had the outside door of the blowing room bolted shut, so that the men entering or leaving the blowing room had to use the door at the far end of the finishing area, a hundred feet or more distant. This action was taken on orders of higher authority, following the vice-president's chance observation of a tourist stepping through the door into the blowing room to get a closer look at the process. But as far as the men were concerned, Dayton deserved all the blame for the idea.

The men were strongly resentful, both over the locker search and the door welding. There was a feeling that the lockers were the men's private property and that management had no right to enter them; that in the event of a search, management should have had a representative of the men present. Regarding the value of the ware found in the lockers, there were conflicting points of view. Dayton called some of it "semi-finished— in the process of being finished." The men in whose lockers such glass had been found argued that it was only ware that had been discarded in inspection. Such disagreements arose because of the nature of the inspection process. At that point, some pieces were immediately discarded but others were set aside as doubtful, and the final determination was made only at the end of the day.

The men regarded the door welding as unwarranted interference with their freedom of movement and further evidence that Dayton regarded them all as potential thieves.

What was done by the men about the locker search and the door welding? As far as we could tell, the men took no action at all on their own initiative. Within a week, men in the blowing room were saying that as far as they could tell, all of the excitement had died down and nothing was going to happen.

A few days later, management did call a meeting of gaffers (at the suggestion of the researchers) to discuss some of the changes then in prospect. At this time some of the gaffers did vent their feelings regarding the two incidents. At this meeting, the production manager announced that management had decided to open the door once again. He defended the locker search. (However, within management, it was agreed that if any searches were to be made in the future, a management man would be accompanied by a union representative on this mission. This decision was not known to the men.)

Why was the door opened? Apparently because one of the safety inspectors from the main office considered this locked exit a hazard in case of fire.

While the general picture was that of a divided department with little power for concerted action, there were indeed two occasions on which all of the men stood solidly together. The first arose before our research began and at the time the men moved into the new plant, with its gallery for visitors to watch the work process. Since Sunday was the best day for visitors, management scheduled Sunday as a regular working day and made Monday the day off for the men. For equally obvious reasons, the men did not care to work on Sunday. The representatives of the men and union officers met with management to argue the case. The result was a compromise which gave the men most of what they wanted. Instead of operating a full schedule on Sunday with five shops each on two shifts, management scheduled only one shift to coincide with visiting hours and settled for just two shops on that shift. This meant that instead of working every Sunday, each worker was off four Sundays out of five.

If we can judge from interviews with workers and management people, the workers stood solidly united on this issue. If management had insisted upon its original work schedule, it seems likely that the men would simply have refused to work on Sunday.

The second incident involved working on election day in 1952. It was management's interpretation that the morning shift would have ample time to vote after quitting time, and the afternoon shift, before coming in to work; therefore, there was no need to give the men two hours off with pay. A notice to this effect was posted on the bulletin board. It seemed to contain some loophole for claims for time off in the case of men who might have difficulty in getting to the polls. The notice was posted late on the day before election day, and was worded in an exceedingly ambiguous fashion.

Just to test out what the notice meant, Jack Carter put in a written request for time off. When he came in to work on election day, Carter was informed by his foreman that his request was not to be granted. By this time, it was already evident that the two hours' pay had become a popular issue in the blowing room, and Carter decided to see it through. He demanded to have the union president brought in. At first the president interpreted the notice on the situation in the same way as had management, but finally Carter insisted that there must be a law to cover this situation. The union president telephoned the Vice-president for Industrial Relations in the main office, and he in turn consulted the company attorney. Sure enough, the attorney found that there was indeed such a law, and that the men were entitled to take two hours off. The decision came through after election day, but the result was that all the men in the blowing room—and in the other plants too—received two hours' extra pay.

While Carter was highly unpopular with some of the old-timers in the blowing room, on this particular issue they were all behind him.

That united front broke down just a year later, again on election day. Curiously enough, management did not reach a decision on how election day should be handled until the last minute, when it was decided that the 6 to 2 shift should get off at noon and the 2 to 10 shift should come in at 4 o'clock. In order to keep some activity going between noon and 4 o'clock for possible visitors, the foreman got two of the morning shift shops to work a regular schedule—with two hours of additional straight-time pay plus two hours more of overtime pay.

When Jack Carter came in at 4 o'clock on the afternoon shift and found that another shop had been working straight through, he kidded the men, calling them "scabs." Just how seriously this was intended we do not know, but the old-time gaffer to whom it was addressed was bitterly resentful and the other men of his age group sided with him. On this issue, Carter did not even have the full support of the younger men. The other gaffer involved was one of the younger men and other young men had received overtime pay on the shops in question.

How can we explain the cohesion observed on some issues and the lack of integration in others? For this purpose, we should look at both the position of the men and the nature of the issues, presented in terms of heterogeneity or homogeneity.

We were observing a highly heterogeneous department both in skills and age. Skills ranged from unskilled up to a level of a master craftsman. The department was further divided markedly into age groupings. This meant that a benefit the individual sought, such as a merit increase or additional overtime work, was mainly of concern to himself alone, or at most, to his shop. In a few cases, a man's gaffer might speak up for him on the merit increase question, but he received no general support.

Given the heterogeneity of the department, even some issues that appeared to have a department-wide impact actually affected some individuals much more strongly than others. The notice barring men from the finishing area primarily affected the gaffers. They were the ones who were accustomed to entering that area. A servitor might very occasionally have gone in, but the lower ranking men hardly ever entered the area.

The locker search also had an uneven impact. No one in the blowing room defended Dayton's action, but those who were most bitter about it were indeed the ones in whose lockers some glass had been found— even though no disciplinary action was taken against them. The ones who had not been caught with the glass could view the event with much less concern. In fact, since the man whose locker contained the most glass was one of the high-prestige old-timers, some of the younger men even got a bit of satisfaction through seeing him embarrassed. In any event, there was no concerted move against management. The only actions that arose were of an individual nature, with some men threatening to buy their own private locks.

While the door welding case was resented by everyone, the door was used primarily by men working close to it. In good weather, they could step outside when there was a delay between operations. (The main door had to be used anyway at the beginning and end of the shift, since the time clock was located there.)

The issues of Sunday work and election day pay were quite different. No one wanted to work on Sunday, and everyone welcomed an additional two hours' pay. On the second election day issue, however, the impact on the men was no longer homogeneous, and group cohesion broke down. While all of the men benefited at least to the extent of two hours off with pay, some were thought to have benefited more than others through their overtime work, and this issue split the department.

## MANAGEMENT-WORKER RELATIONS

The nature of the work in the blowing room made it difficult, if not impossible, for management to exercise the control that is possible in other work situations. In fact, the frustrations over these problems may have led Assistant Production Manager Dayton into some of the issues already described.

A man with training in industrial engineering naturally thinks of production problems in terms of discovering the best job operations and then standardizing their use for the whole department. This calls for time and motion studies. In his early period at Benton, Dayton did indeed toy with the idea of having such studies made, but he either abandoned the idea of his own volition or was warned off by higher management.

Time and motion studies in the blowing room would have encountered two problems. In the first place, they would have created an issue with a homogeneous impact upon all of the men in the blowing room, and united resistance could have been expected. In the second place, time and motion studies in the blowing room would have faced unusual technical problems. The industrial engineer could observe and time each movement made, but how could he determine how many movements were necessary? This applied to the movements a man made in working the glass, and even more, to the warming in periods. An additional warming in or two could add markedly to the duration of the work cycle, and yet how could the industrial engineer say just how many times a piece needed to be warmed in? The servitor or gaffer made this judgment by the appearance and feel of the glass, based on long years of experience. If the men were required to speed up their pace, they could spoil piece after piece, and it would be impossible for management to prove that it had been done on purpose.

Management did try to establish control over the work pace through setting production standards; so many pieces per hour for a given design. Without observing the same situation with production standards removed, it was impossible to say what the effects of these standards were. Perhaps on balance they brought forth more production, but on some individual jobs they seemed to raise production, and on others to depress it.

At one time in our study, Dayton reported that production was averaging about 70 per cent of production standards. The range was around 40 per cent to 100 per cent, with a shop going over 100 per cent only very occasionally.

Acknowledging the difficulties of making accurate estimates of production possibilities, management people reported that they would have been quite happy for the workers to be under 100 per cent on some pieces and over on others. The workers interpreted the standards quite differently. When they were making 100 per cent or close to it, they would tell us that they were doing all that management had asked them to do. Why do any more? On jobs that ran well below 100 per cent, they would complain that the production standards were ridiculously high and that it was impossible to meet them.

Management considered the possibility of revising downward those production standards where workers fell far short, but this was not done. There seemed to be two main reasons for such a decision. In some cases, management could argue that failure to approach the production standard was due to deficiencies in skill and experience of members of the shop. Hopefully, they would be able to come closer in the future. In a few cases, management could show that the old Swedes years ago had met the production standard. This was not possible to demonstrate in most cases because new designs were added twice a year and very few pieces remained in the line year after year. Furthermore, since 100 per cent was interpreted by the men as the maximum they should produce, management people were afraid to drop any of the standards for fear that this would limit possibilities of improvement.

Even when the men looked upon a particular production standard as unrealistically high, they could not afford to ignore it altogether. Pay increases within a given classification were not automatic at Benton. A man became eligible for "consideration" for a merit increase every six months until he reached the top of his classification, but these increases did not come automatically. A man had to persuade his foreman that he was showing progress. While promotions to higher classifications were restricted by seniority, a man also had to show that he could do the work, and he might fear to take on a higher job if he had not been able to persuade management that he was doing well at his current job.

The task of determining merit is difficult in any case and especially in a work team. A good man may be working on an inferior team or a poor man may be carried along on a good team. How is the foreman to assess the contributions each man is making to his team? This was an issue continually arising between individuals and the foreman.

The foremen we observed had risen through the ranks in other plants of the company, so they had had no direct experience with the kind of craftsmanship being practiced in Benton. This meant that they were severely limited either in training men on the job or in criticizing the work done, because they could neither speak from experience nor demonstrate the operations.

The foremen made up the work schedules and assigned the designs to be made by each shop, within the general production plans presented them by the assistant production manager. They had to bring the gaffers reports on imperfect work done, but they had to be quite tentative in suggesting the sources of the difficulties. When the gaffer's control over his own men broke down, the foreman had to intervene, but he was never sure as to how much initiative he should take with subordinates on the shop and how much he should work directly with the gaffer. He had to learn to vary his approach with each gaffer.

The foremen spent some of their time out on the floor observing the men and their work, but given limitations of craft knowledge, just what they should do on the basis of these observations was not an easy question to answer. At one time, Assistant Production Manager Dayton, believing that the men would work harder if the foremen were on the floor more often, moved the foremen's desk and telephone out of the room next to the blowing room and placed them right out in the open, on the edge of the blowing room itself. This was looked upon by the foremen as a blow to their status. It provided further practical difficulties, since the desk was located in a dirty and noisy area where the foremen had trouble understanding telephone conversations, could not keep their records clean, and could not carry on a conversation that would not be observed by everyone in the blowing room. This move was likewise resented by the workers, who knew at once why it had been made. Within a short time the foremen had their own office back, but were still under pressure to spend more time on the blowing room floor.

Just what effect, if any, the foremen's presence had on productivity seemed a highly dubious point to us. On the other hand, opportunities to observe and interact with the men made possible two important functions. The performance of a shop depended upon teamwork. As the foremen got to know the men, they learned to spot friction points and to transfer individuals from one shop to another. All three foremen prided themselves on utilizing their knowledge of the workers in this way.

Observation also enabled the foremen to offer technical assistance in some exceptional cases. At first we did not see this as a possibility, and indeed there seemed to be only one foreman who had both sufficient observational skill and skill in relating himself to the workers to be of real help. The foreman demonstrated this at a critical point in the work career of Jack Carter.

Early in Carter's tenure as a gaffer, his shop was working on a design that had been handled by the top-prestige Campisi shop. This design was more difficult than anything Carter and his shop had done heretofore. After a promising start, Carter ran into trouble. For two days, nearly every piece his shop made was rejected in inspection. Carter and his shopmates were exceedingly worried and nervous; when things went wrong in this way, there was always the danger that the men would lose confidence in their ability to do a job. Carter knew that the old-timers had been saying he would never be able to master this design. Carter was not inclined to give up, but he felt himself blocked at every point.

It was at this time that one of the foremen spent two hours observing him and talking with him. On the basis of his observations on this shop and others involving this and similar pieces, plus his observations of Carter's technique, the foreman suggested several changes in technique to Carter. Some of these were entirely the foreman's ideas, while some evolved from the discussion between the two men. As Carter put these new ideas into practice, he found the work smoothing out almost immediately. Rejects in inspection dropped rapidly, and within a few days the Carter shop had mastered this particular piece.

In this case, the technical points contributed by the foreman were certainly of significance, but perhaps equally important was the emotional support that he gave Carter in the crisis situation. It helped Carter to feel that there was someone working with him, sympathetic to him, and trying to help him at every step. He always spoke warmly of that particular foreman.

## WORKING CONDITIONS AND THE JOB ITSELF

The workers' relations with foremen and other management people are always of some importance in building the sentiments attached to the job, but they are not the whole story. How do these men feel about the conditions of their work and about the actual job activities? Their sentiments toward working conditions can be summarized in simple terms because they were highly uniform. Compared with all of their previous experiences in the old Benton plant or elsewhere, this new plant offered ideal working conditions. It was light and clean and well-ventilated—an important point when men have to work around furnaces.

The men who had worked in other types of glass manufacturing were particularly enthusiastic about working conditions. They spoke of their earlier jobs as being hot and heavy, whereas they recognized the jobs in the blowing room to be physically light and relatively clean work.

They considered the pay good, particularly in the top brackets. The period of rapid expansion had been particularly rewarding economically to the younger men, who had moved up in classification and pay.

But what did it mean to these men to become craftsmen in a mass-production world?[3]

When we tried to get at worker reactions to the mental and physical processes involved in the work itself, we had great difficulty in getting any meaningful answers. For example, we wondered whether the men experienced aesthetic satisfactions—had feelings of creativity—in their work. We found we could not tackle this question directly without embarrassing ourselves and the workers. Such matters are not easy to talk about in the factory.

## THE CARD-RANKING METHOD

Frustrated at our direct approach, we devised an indirect approach through asking the gaffer or the servitor to arrange a set of cards, each one representing a job his team performed, in order of preference. (We are indebted to Assistant Production Manager Dayton for the suggestion that cards might be used in this matter.) When the glassworker had placed the cards in order of preference, we asked him to explain why he ranked them the way he did.

---

[3] This discussion is based on William F. Whyte, "On Asking Indirect Questions," *Human Organization*, Vol. XV, No. 4 (Winter, 1957).

We found that we got no data of any particular value out of the ranking itself, but when the men were called upon to explain their rankings, most of them talked in a manner that revealed much more of their feelings about the work process itself than we had been able to elicit in the ordinary type of interview.

It should be noted that some of the men found it difficult to make any rankings. Thus the method could not be used in a standardized fashion but served as a useful supplement to other methods.

The evaluations made by the men seemed to fall in the following categories. We made no effort to rank them in order of importance, because there was a good deal of difference from man to man.

### CREATIVITY

One gaffer made these comments regarding jobs that he ranked high on his preference scale: "When you get done, you've got a nice piece of work there . . . it really looks like something . . . when I can say I made that piece, I really swell with pride."

Another gaffer, after commenting on aspects of a piece he disliked, said, "That little mug don't look like nothing when you're done."

Still another gaffer commented on his favorite piece, "When you're finished, you've got something."

Concerning the piece he rated at the bottom, a gaffer said, "The trouble with this thing is you don't have anything when you're finished. Until it is ground and polished in the finishing room, it doesn't look like anything; so it is just a lot of work for nothing."

Apparently, just playing a part in the creative process is not enough. The men feel a need to bring the process to completion and "have something to show for it." (All pieces go on to the finishing department, where all are polished, some are ground, and a few are engraved. However, some pieces look much more finished than others when they leave the gaffer's hands.)

### ACHIEVEMENT

A young servitor, still uncertain of his skill, made this comment on one piece: "This is a good job. It comes pretty good for me. It looks like I like best the ones I can make. Maybe with some of those others, if I could make them better, I would like them better."

Another young servitor, who was still at the low end of the pay scale for his classification, described all his top-ranking pieces in the same way: "These are class A jobs."

On a job that he ranked next to last, a young servitor made these comments: "This is the God damndest thing. I'd give $500 to get ahold of that blueprint and burn it up. You've got three candle cups here and they've

gotta all look alike. If they don't, the candelabra looks like the devil . . .
I don't know how to make the cups just as they should be done. That's
my trouble."

### PRESSURE AND TIMING

One gaffer made this comment on a piece he ranked toward the bottom: "You've gotta hurry . . . you can't take your time to work on it
and make it come out good."

A servitor said about his most disliked piece, "This job is no good.
When I am on this job I feel like I have that iron sticking up my hind
end all the time. You've got to hurry all the time."

The feeling of pressure was related to the size of the pieces made and
to the production standards set by management. On small pieces, management naturally expected the men to turn out a larger number. However,
the actual percentage of production standard achieved did not seem to be
the controlling factor. We found men expressing more frustration regarding pressure and inability to achieve the production standard when they
were making nine pieces an hour on a small object whose production
standard called for ten, than they expressed regarding a larger piece
where they were making four an hour against a production standard of
five. (Small pieces were generally disliked for reasons that fall in the creativity category. We received many comments to the effect that these
small pieces "didn't look like much.")

The feeling of pressure was not simply a matter of the speed expected
by management in relation to the difficulty of the job. It also involved the
steadiness of the work pace and the coordination of activities among members of the team.

One gaffer commented: "This is a real nice piece, and time goes faster
working on it." Another gaffer called one of his favorite pieces, "A good
time-flier." The workers felt that time went fast—and pleasantly—when
they had a job on which they worked smoothly and steadily and never
felt they were behind, with other people waiting for them to finish their
part of the job.

If steady work were not involved, the men valued a job on which they
could "get ahead and then take it easy." A servitor commented on one of
his favorite jobs: "For this one I just blow the bulb. I get a ten-minute
break after doing one of these jobs. The gaffer has most of the work to do
on this, so it is a pretty good job for me."

There were numerous comments regarding the undesirability of a job
in which the individual was frequently "behind"—that is, had other people waiting for him to finish his operation. Since one worker would be
"ahead" and another "behind" on the same piece, the two were inclined
to evaluate the piece differently, from this standpoint.

## AMOUNT OF WORK

While the men generally commented that work in Benton was less taxing physically than most other factory jobs, there was nevertheless a considerable difference among jobs in the amount of physical effort required. While the men did not generally like the very small pieces which required fast work and did not give an impressive appearance, they also expressed some reservations about some of the largest pieces, which required a good deal of physical effort. This factor was not always sufficient to give a low rating to a piece, because sometimes the larger pieces were highly evaluated in terms of the skill required and the appearance of the finished product.

Some jobs were highly evaluated because they were easy to do and "moved right along" without presenting any particular mental or physical problems to the worker.

## VARIETY

Even though the workers regarded some jobs highly because of the ease with which they could handle them, apparently they also felt the need for some challenge in the working situation. Several men rated certain pieces high because they represented a different type of work and product from their usual line.

## CONTRIBUTION

This factor came into the evaluation of only one man, but it seemed quite revealing in his case. This gaffer said of his favorite piece, "This is our bread and butter. They tell me that this piece of ware has paid more wages than any other piece in Benton's history. I like to make the olive dish because if I have a couple of bad days on other ware and haven't made much production, I know I can make the olive dish and make it up." This was one of the older gaffers who, in terms of years of experience, might have been expected to rank toward the top in prestige. However, he was not regarded by management or by his fellow workers as very skillful, and his repertoire was limited to relatively simple pieces. He got some of his satisfaction from the contribution he assured himself he was making to the company.

## PERSONALITY, STATUS AND HUMAN RELATIONS

So far we have been looking at these reactions in general terms. The following case indicates how this approach can throw light upon the sentiments and relationships of a particular individual.

Jack Carter evaluated his first four choices in the following way:

1. Gustafson (high-prestige gaffer, then retired) said that this was a son-of-a-bitch. Sometimes he refused to make it and would put it off until another week. He said it would take anybody a year to learn how to make it. (Carter said he made a few of the right quality the first time and that he was finding it going very well.)

2. The fellow that used to make this (Campisi) said that nobody else could make it. . . . Well, I proved I could make it. I got a few the first time and I'm doing better now.

3. Jessup (old gaffer, not of the highest prestige) said it would take at least three months to learn how to make this. (Carter added that he had been able to make it almost from the very start.)

4. This was supposed to be hard to make. The first time I made it, I found out later that some of the young fellows had bets on that I wouldn't get one out of the first three that I tried. Well, I found that I could make it all right.

It is interesting to note that in Carter's case his pride in achievement and his competitive rivalry with the older men dominated his feelings regarding the work.

## THE CONTEXT OF WORK PROCESS SATISFACTION

Even when we concentrate our questioning on the man's relations to the physical and mental processes of his job, we see that he does not react to those processes in a social vacuum. To be sure, he does react to the monotony and fatigue of the job, as illustrated in our categories of "Amount of Work" and "Variety." However, he also reacts in terms of *work flow* and of *status* or prestige relations.

The men are much concerned with the problems of "Pressure and Timing," which involve work flow relations among workers—and also worker-management relations (production standards). Status is reflected in four of our categories. "Creativity" is related, at least in part, to status, for the men reported this feeling particularly in the case of objects having high prestige with fellow workers. The "Achievement" theme is particularly prominent among the young men who are beginning to claim equality with the older, established glassworkers. "Variety" involves not only monotony but also status, for the low-status gaffers tend to be confined to designs that are quite similar to each other. (This does not apply to the "wine shops." While stemware designs are necessarily less varied, high skill and speed are required for these delicate operations.) Our one case under "Contribution" shows a gaffer seeking the satisfactions of status in one channel when he has been unable to achieve them through the ordinary channels.

Thus we see that worker reactions to the work process can only be understood against a background of knowledge of the social system. At the same time, these reactions help to illuminate the role and status of the individual and the functioning of the social system itself.

## THE PATTERN OF JOB SATISFACTION

We can now pull together the various factors contributing to the Benton workers' sentiments toward their jobs.

Pay was mentioned in a mildly favorable manner by some of the men as they discussed the good features of the job, and we had no complaints against the pay scale in general. Since the younger men were moving up rapidly, they naturally expressed satisfaction with progress. The rapid movement nevertheless had two negative aspects. It was resented by the older craftsmen who felt that the young men were moving up much too rapidly. It also led to dissatisfaction on the part of individuals who were not getting merit increases at regular intervals. As has been found in other studies, when upward movement is rapid, there may be more dissatisfaction expressed about up-grading opportunities than in situations where advancement is seldom achieved.

All of the men spoke warmly about the working conditions in their new plant. They were also favorably impressed with the inclusion of the gallery which focussed public attention upon them.

Especially noteworthy was the freedom from control either by the technology or by management. The work flow and the design of the product made provided certain limitations in the interactions of workers. We have seen, in comparing the quantitative observations of Jack Carter and Gus Pinelli, that some of the differences between the two men could be accounted for by these factors. Nevertheless, the technology and work flow allowed more latitude for free interaction than is found in most work situations. This did not mean that there were no human problems involved in getting the work done. As we have seen, there were many—and sometimes serious—frictions arising among the men. The work situation placed upon the men themselves the burden of organizing their relations with each other. These relations were influenced by the technology and by management action only to a very limited degree.

The work situation made it possible to develop strong informal leadership within a given work team, although as we have seen, the external changes that had taken place had weakened the position of the gaffer. At the same time, the existence of wide differentials in age and status and the lack of correlation between age and formal status tended to create rivalries within the department, so that the cohesion of the total department was generally low.

The work situation was not without psychological "pressures" for the men, but the pressures did not seem to stem primarily from either controls provided by the technology or by management. The workers themselves were able to control their own pace, and since they held a monopoly on skills of glassmaking, it was very difficult for management to intervene effectively to change work behavior.

The pressures felt seemed to be directly related to the responsibilities of the task. The men themselves commented that glassmakers were a temperamental lot. There was always a chance that when things started to go wrong on one job, the situation would go from bad to worse, so that soon there was nothing to do but "fire over," thus abandoning the job and the work situation for the rest of the day. But note that the men had this release from emotional tensions within their own control. Walking off the job in a work group in most other work situations is considered to be a wildcat strike, likely to lead to a sharp clash between union and management. In this case, the walkout was defined quite differently. The management people did not approve of "firing over," and foremen would always try to take some steps to smooth things over when a walkout was imminent. However, once the men had made such a decision, management neither intervened at the time nor penalized them later—short of withholding wages for the hours not worked. The management people recognized quite well that it was impossible for them to exercise direct control over this situation. If they had insisted that the men remain on the job, the workers might have produced only defective ware, so that management's actions would have been self-defeating.

As we approached the meaning of the actual job operations themselves, we were impressed by the variety of meanings they had for the workers. The jobs did provide the satisfactions of creativity and achievement for many of the workers. They also carried a number of other meanings specified earlier.

At first we were concerned because we did not seem to get any uniformity in our probing of the satisfactions men found on their jobs. Then we came to recognize that this lack of uniformity was perhaps in itself a significant finding. It suggested that the worker in this situation might find ways to satisfy his own personality far more than was possible in most other work situations.

In our examination of workers on the assembly line, we will find a much more uniform response to the particular job situation and a much more constricted area of freedom of action.

# Chapter 11 *MEN ON THE MOTOR LINE*

TO MANY people assembly lines stand for modern mass production industry. There are two things to say to qualify this point of view.

1. Actually, the assembly line is only one among a large number of types of technology, some of which we have been examining. It would be a mistake to consider the assembly line typical of American industry.
2. There is some variety among types of technology that come under the heading of assembly lines.

There are long tables at which workers sit, performing their operations and pushing the completed pieces to the next person. This allows for some variation in work tempo, since there is space for a certain number of units to be placed next to each individual, and that number can vary. Even on the barrel line discussed earlier, the barrel shells only rolled on from point to point as they were released by workers performing each operation. There was thus some room for variation in work tempo also. The distinctive feature of the automotive assembly line is that the work objects move on a conveyor whose speed is mechanically controlled and set by management. It is the impact of this particular type of technology that we will now examine.

Work on the automotive assembly line has the following characteristics:

1. Mechanically controlled work pace.
2. Repetitiveness. The worker performs only a few operations, and he performs them again and again.
3. Minimum skill. Though the worker may have extreme difficulty in adjusting himself to other aspects of the work, it only takes him a few hours, or at most a few days, to acquire the manual skills involved in most assembly line jobs.
4. Predetermination of tools and techniques. The worker has no say as to the tools and techniques he uses.
5. Minute subdivision of product. The worker deals only with a very small part of the total operation.
6. Surface mental attention. The work is so simple and repetitive that it presents no challenge to the worker's mind. At the same time, he will make mistakes if he does not give it his almost constant visual and mental attention.

To this we might add one further element which seems necessary in automotive assembly work: work load variations. We should not picture assembly line work as always involving exactly the same motions for the individual worker on a line that always moves at exactly the same speed. Workers and management people alike are constantly concerned with the problems of "balancing the line." The line speed must be thought of in relation to the number of men on the line, the number of operations they perform, and the time necessary for each operation. Within limits, line speed can be increased by adding men to the line and giving each man a shorter work cycle. Similarly, as the line is slowed down, men can be dropped from the line and the remaining men given a longer work cycle. Thus a drop in demand for the car can be met by running the plant on shorter hours a week without changing line speed, or by reducing the speed of the line and laying off some of the men. Similarly, an increased demand for the car can be met by operating the plant longer hours, or by speeding up the line and adding more men to it.

When a model change-over occurs, it is customary to start the line at a relatively slow speed and increase the speed as the men gain experience on the new operations.

Even while the line speed remains constant, the same individual worker may find it easy or difficult to keep up with the line, according to what he has to do on the different models that flow past him. One motor may require a standard transmission, the next one an automatic transmission, and so on. Inevitably his work on one will be more difficult than on the other and will take longer. Management seeks to meet this problem by alternating the sequence of models on the line so that a worker who has a hard job on one model will have an easy job on the next one. However, this is not always easily arranged, and there may be a tendency for a certain type of model to "bunch up" on the line. If a given worker does a long job on this model, he will get "in the hole," feel himself under particularly heavy pressure, and even have to let an occasional unit go by him. (At the end of the line, models are inspected, and those with faulty or incomplete work go to what is euphemistically called the car conditioning department, where the work is done over again.)

Working on more than one model might introduce a slight but welcome variety into the worker's life, but the value of this variety is outweighed by the line balancing problem it produces. Workers find it hard enough to put up with mechanical pacing, but having to put up with more difficult tasks that put one in the hole seems to be a most distressing experience.

Those who have philosophized about man's work always have suspected that the automotive assembly line is a particularly unpleasant work environment. Until recently we might have believed this meant simply that intellectuals would find this type of work unpleasant; perhaps the average workingman might have no such feelings.

Thanks to the work of Charles Walker and his associates on the Yale Technology Project, the automotive assembly line is now the most thoroughly researched work environment we have (and this chapter is based entirely upon their work). The Walker group finds that the average assembly line worker does indeed dislike just about everything connected with his job except the high pay and other material benefits he receives. Furthermore, his sentiments toward the work itself seem to affect other sentiments, so that he tends to have a negative reaction toward management and also, in certain respects, a negative reaction toward the union.

To examine in more detail the impact of this particular type of environment upon a work group, let us turn to a study by Arthur N. Turner.[1]

## TECHNOLOGY AND WORK FLOW

For introduction to the technology and work flow of the motor line, let us follow this description provided by Turner:

Essentially, the motor line is a rectangular area about one hundred feet long and forty feet wide; the most prominent feature is a moving S-shaped overhead conveyor from which the motors being assembled are hung at about four foot intervals. Figure 1 is a diagram of the general layout. The different areas of the motor line are designated by Roman numerals I through IV. (The longest straight section of the conveyor, III, is divided into IIIA and IIIB.) The physical characteristics of the motor line and the general work process can be described together in simplified terms as follows.

There is a large "rack" where motor blocks are stored, which is outside the motor line area, adjacent to I. The rack contains three vertical "layers" of motor blocks, and runs almost the whole length of I. The motor blocks are delivered in freight cars on the other side of the storage rack, and lifted onto it by an elevator (operated by a member of the materials handling department). There are three basic models of motor blocks, each with several variations, and each must be placed at the correct location (horizontally and vertically), on the rack. They slide down a slight incline to the other side of the rack, so that a sufficient number of all models and types is (theoretically) always available as required by the motor line's schedule.

On the motor line side of the rack there are two elevators, only one of which is usually in operation at a time. The elevator runs on tracks horizontally along the length of the rack as well as vertically. According to the scheduled order of motor models the elevator is used to fetch the correct model from the rack and deliver it to the beginning of I at the right time. The motor block is taken from the elevator and placed on the conveyor by means of an electric hoist.

While the motor block is on I, such parts as carburetors, starter cables, power steering units, fuel pumps, starters, and distributor wires are attached to it. Some of these parts have been built up as sub-assemblies on stationary benches near I.

After turning the corner at the end of I, a few additional assembly operations are performed at the beginning of II, such as securing distributor wires

---

[1] "Personality and Group Membership: A Case Study of an Automobile Assembly Line" (Ph.D. thesis, Cornell University, 1958).

### FIGURE 1

#### The Motor Line

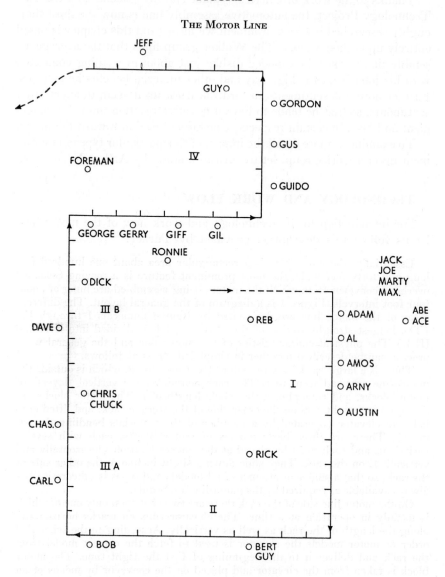

and carburetors. On the far side of II the various models of automatic and manual transmissions are stored. During the first part of the study these transmissions were lifted by an electric hoist and placed on a "transmission line" at the beginning of III, from which they were lifted and installed on the motors. Other parts, including fans and fan belts are installed on IIIA. On IIIB and around the bend at the beginning of IV, numerous transmission bolts are tightened, and parts such as transmission housings and extra exhaust pipes are installed. On the rest of IV, generators and a number of smaller parts and linkages are installed and adjusted, and fluid inserted in the transmissions and tested for leaks. Finally "repair" operations are performed at the end of IV, after which the assembled motors are lifted by the conveyor over an aisle and lowered to a point on the main chassis line called "motor mount," where they are installed on the chassis. Almost everything connected with the motor and transmission is supposed to be in working order when it leaves the motor line.

Figure 1 gives the usual work locations of each man on the motor line as of the beginning of the study. Their spacing along the line was such that they made up three main "work subgroupings," I, IIIA, and IV. In addition, there were three relative "isolates," Dave and Dick on IIIB and Bert on II. (Bob, although really on II, was considered part of the IIIA subgrouping.)

The names of the men as given in Figure 1 and throughout the study are of course fictional, and follow an alphabetical scheme designed to help the reader recall their various work stations.

In addition, the foreman, Frank Melotti, was usually but never continuously in the area, as were a sweeper, Max, and a materials handler, Marty. Occasionally the motor line was visited by one of the two general foremen, Tony Kahl or Tom Maynard, or by various labor relations or work standards department people.

To get an idea of work assignments on the assembly line, let us consider one case in detail. This is the job of Austin Thorsen, one of the more prominent figures in the work group, who had been grievance chairman of the local union and was still active in union affairs. Reporting that the job was typical of motor line operations, Turner described it in this way:

On model A Austin took eight distributor wires from eight bins near the line and attached them, one to each spark plug, gathering the wires together with a "spreader." After (sometimes before) that, he took a metal rod and bolt from the other side of the line and attached the rod to the carburetor linkage. On model B (on which the distributor wires were already on the motor block), Austin took up two "guns" (hand, power-operated wrenches) and tightened a bolt which secured a gas line to the carburetor and four bolts which secured the carburetor itself. Then he attached five brackets used for gas lines which were later installed by someone else, running up two bolts for each bracket. On those model B motors which were not to be equipped with dual exhausts, he attached a metal cover over the exhaust opening on one side of the motor, running up three long bolts with another "gun." On model C, his operations were similar to those on model A; the bar linkage to the carburetor was different and installed somewhat differently, but the distributor wire operation was much the same. Other than a certain degree of dexterity and ability not to get flustered by the pace of the line, the job required no particular skill. A week at the most was regarded as sufficient for an "average" worker to be able to perform all of these operations at the speed required by the pace of the line (thirty to forty motors per hour). Since more work was required on some models than others, the order in which the models were scheduled was important to Austin. Like most men on the motor line, he had difficulty keeping out of the hole when the schedule "ran heavy on his rough jobs" (e.g., model B with single exhausts).

In addition to the jobs at fixed stations on the assembly line, there were two other types of jobs in the department. Reb, Rick, and Ronnie worked on "bench jobs," putting together sub-assemblies for use on the line. Since the operator was always engaged in building more than one model of a particular unit, he could use his own judgment about when to shift from one model to another and also could vary his work pace to some extent. These three men had nearly 20 years' seniority each. As a general rule, only top seniority men are found on these stationary sub-assembly operations, which suggests that an auto worker will get off the assembly line whenever it is possible.

Jobs in the category of relief man, utility man, and repair man were held by Jeff, Jack, and Joe, who also had long seniority in the department. While these jobs were generally preferred to fixed assembly line jobs, they were not as highly valued as the bench jobs. In fact, while the variety of the work was appreciated, it was thought that these men were subjected to a good deal of pressure. While each of these three men sometimes changed off in functions for the other two, the job descriptions were quite distinct. The function of the relief man was to take over each job on the line for ten minutes in the morning and ten minutes in the afternoon, in order to provide the "personal relief" to which each operator was entitled. The utility man was supposed to know all the jobs on the line also, and to be able to fit in anywhere when someone was absent on this or even in adjacent sections. The repair man stood at the end of the line, going over the supposedly completed motors. He decided what if any additional work was needed and carried out that work. In this he was aided by men on the line, who made chalk marks to indicate that they had been unable to complete a certain operation.

## SENTIMENTS TOWARD THE JOBS

We have already noted that the men on bench jobs and other jobs without fixed line assignments tended to be happier in their work. Let us now examine the reactions of those men who were pinned down to fixed positions on the line.

First, we note the men's reactions to restrictions in interaction imposed by the technological environment. Except for brief periods of relief and at lunch time, the worker cannot seek out people with whom he might want to converse. His position on the line becomes his social orbit while on the job, limiting him to the man above and below him on his side of the line and one to three men on the other side. In this particular case, few men had more than one or two others with whom interaction on the job was possible, and some were completely isolated spatially. Furthermore, the noise of line operations was such as to make conversation very difficult.

As one man on the motor line put it:

> The job is monotonous, at least sometimes it is, but if you can look up at another fellow and say something to him, that breaks up the monotony. But if you can't, then you have that pressure on top of the monotony and that's what's bad. You get the two combined. You go in that place and you come out of it at the end of the day just a plain dummy. That's what happened to me; that's what causes your sickness and your nerves.

As other studies have shown, men have different interactional needs. Some can go with little interaction for a long period of time without feeling any deprivation, whereas others need much more frequent interaction. In another study, Frank J. Jasinski found an interesting relationship between reported need for interaction and sentiments toward the company and toward the immediate job.[2] In response to the question "Does the company do what it can for the workers?" almost two out of three of those who reported that they valued opportunities to talk on the job replied that the company did nothing for the workers. Of those who expressed indifference about talking on the job, less than one of three reported that the company did nothing at all. In response to the question, "Is your job interesting?" those needing to talk showed the same tendency toward negative answers, but the contrast was not quite so marked in this case.

In Jasinski's sample, 125 men fell into the category of appreciating opportunities to talk, whereas only 49 fell into the category of indifference to conversational opportunities. This suggests what we might expect; that most workers do require interaction on the job and do feel deprived when it is not available to them.

All of the men complained about the pressures of keeping up with the mechanically paced line, and particularly about the difficulties of being in the hole. One man put it this way:

> You get in the hole and that fouls you up and you can't get caught up again. It makes you feel miserable and then you come home and you are miserable. That happened to me last year for a while.

The interest a man finds in the job seems to be related to the number of operations the individual performs. The fewer the operations, the more monotonous and uninteresting the job appears to be. This is illustrated in a study by Walker and Guest.[3] They asked 180 assembly line workers this question: "Would you say your job was very interesting, fairly interesting, not too interesting, or not at all interesting?" Response showed the pattern found in the following table:

OPERATIONS PERFORMED CORRELATED WITH DEGREE OF JOB INTEREST, PRESENT JOB

| Operations Performed | Very or Fairly Interesting | Not Very or Not at All Interesting | Total |
|---|---|---|---|
| 1 | 19 | 38 | 57 |
| 2–5 | 28 | 36 | 64 |
| 5 or more | 41 | 18 | 59 |
| Total | 88 | 92 | 180 |

$X^2 = 16.23$    $n = 2$    $P < .001$

---

[2] "Technological Delimitation of Reciprocal Relationships: A Study of Interaction Patterns in Industry," *Human Organization*, Vol. L, No. 2 (1956).

[3] Charles R. Walker and Robert H. Guest, *The Man on the Assembly Line* (Cambridge, Massachusetts: Harvard University Press, 1952), p. 54.

Carl, one of our motor line workers, expressed his feeling in this way:

It's the monotony that gets you down. If I had a chance to, I would like a
job where today you do one thing and tomorrow something else. I would like
to work the whole line. You would learn a lot that way. I would like to be
able to work on any job in the line. Right now I only know three jobs: hanging
transmissions, Chas' job, and the fan job. I would be interested to know all
the jobs around the line so that today if I came in and wanted to I could
change jobs. That way there would be something different and it wouldn't
be monotonous. Frankie wanted to do that; he spoke to me about it. He
would like to give every man a chance to work at the end of the line so that
he could see what came off the line and get to know the whole motor line
that way.

While research seems to demonstrate that Carl is right, that men
would be better-adjusted to their jobs if they had a greater variety of
experience, Turner is not convinced that the men in general would welcome such a rotational plan. He finds the men so concerned with their own
problems of keeping out of the hole on a particular work station that
rotation might seem to pose even greater threats of getting behind.

One of the men put to Turner this question:

I want to ask you something; do you think that a job like this can affect a
man's mind after a while? Sometimes I think when I am just doing this job
over and over again, I can't think as well as I used to be able to. What do
you think of that?

If workers have such negative feelings toward the job, why should
they have any concern for the quality of their work? Wouldn't a man want
to do a job that would just get by? Apparently not. Turner found the men
on the motor line very much concerned about quality. While their main
concern with mechanical pacing was the pressure it put upon them, they
also complained that at times it made it impossible to do a quality job, and
this left them with a feeling of frustration. One man expressed it this way:

It's something inside the man. Most guys don't feel right if they don't do
the job right. When you have a job, you like to do it right and not shirk on
it. No matter how you might feel about the company you still like to do the
job you have in the right way; otherwise, you don't feel right inside.

In spite of their strong feelings against management and the immediate job, workers seemed to need to take pride in being able to do as good
a job as the environment allowed.

The men were also oppressed by a feeling of helplessness. There
seemed to be very little the individual could do to help himself when he
was in trouble, and the technology made it impossible to rally the support of other workers on the job without precipitating a wildcat strike.

The significance of these sentiments of helplessness are illustrated particularly from the experience of Chris, who in the course of the study left
the motor line and got a job on the "unloading dock." After expressing his

strong preference for the new job, Chris described some of the valued aspects of it to the researcher with obvious relish:

The other day they had 3000 wheels to unload from a freight car. Two foremen and the general foreman were standing around all the time trying to get the men to get them unloaded. Every hour they would send over two more men. At the end of the day they still had 300 wheels in the car, because any time the foreman looked the other way the men would stop working. They did it just because they didn't like being watched over all the time. The foremen and general foreman couldn't figure out how with all those men they weren't getting the wheels unloaded, but they were scared to come in the car to look because then they might get a pile of wheels on them.

Much as he preferred his present assignment to the motor line, he claimed that another unloading dock was even preferable to his own in this important respect:

On the other dock the men *really* stick together. On this dock they don't stick together so good, because there are some older men who may be afraid for their job or afraid of the foreman. But on the other dock, when the foreman tried to make them work up to the whistle, they would do it; but they would time it so that after the whistle blew the foreman would have to close the doors of all the freight cars and lock them himself. Well, that was a hell of a job for him, so after a while he forgot about making them work until the whistle blew and the men closed the doors for the foreman and things were better. They could quit earlier.

On the assembly line, collective action is not impossible, but it can only be brought about through means of a work stoppage, which is in itself an extreme measure. In many other work environments, like the unloading dock, men have a wide freedom to organize self-defensive and aggressive actions against management short of the extreme of a work stoppage.

As men talked about their work careers, they very generally expressed the feeling of being trapped. The pay and other fringe benefits were good. For men of some seniority, the work was secure and reasonably steady. As a man grew older on the assembly line, he feared more and more that he would not be able to keep up. At the same time, he accumulated the seniority that might eventually get him off the line—and yet jobs off the line were relatively few. With increasing age, he recognized that his chances of getting a good job elsewhere were declining. He had learned no marketable skills. If he dropped out of the assembly line job, he might have to take something with much less pay and security.

As Ely Chinoy has shown, assembly line workers frequently talk and think about quitting their jobs.[4]

Many express a desire to work for a smaller company. In part, this represents a desire to get off the assembly line, but even where there are assembly lines in smaller companies, they are thought to move more

---

[4] *Automobile Workers and the American Dream* (Garden City, New York: Doubleday, 1955).

slowly. The men are also contrasting the impersonality of their lives on the assembly line of a large corporation with an idealized picture of life in a small company where "it would be more friendly" and where, for example, "you have one or two guys at the top who own it . . . and they will share with the workers everything they make; but with a big corporation it's not like that."

Even more desirable from the standpoint of the men was the possibility of working for oneself; as a small store owner, a television repairman, and so on.

The flavor of these feelings of being trapped is well represented by the following quotation from a man who called Turner and poured his troubles out to him:

I'm quitting; I'm through with this — — place, I'm going to California. . . . I'm going as soon as the summer is over, . . . I decided over the week-end. . . . I don't care how my wife feels about it, I'm leaving. If she doesn't want to come, that's too bad, I'm still going. I've made up my mind; I'm not getting any place here, and I'm through with this — — place. I'll go to California and be a salesman. I can always pick oranges.

I was in California in the Army. A baseball player I know out there told me to stay; he'd fix me up with a good job. But my wife wouldn't move. She wouldn't leave this area, so I had to come back here.

I'm not bitter against this company; I'm bitter against myself.

In the war my wife was sick. She had to stay in bed six months. That used up all my money. I wanted to use my G.I. benefits to study to be an electrician or something, but after the war I was sunk. The doctors had taken all my money so I had to come back here. It's always been like that with me. I'm going. With my parents it was the same. I wanted to be a jockey. I was only ninety pounds, but my mother was afraid something might happen to me so I had to stay at home. I was the oldest son and I always had the — —. I couldn't go to high school. My family was poor; I saw how it was. I got a job at seven dollars a week. I couldn't afford the clothes to go to high school anyway. Now I've got no education and what can I do?

Yes, I'm bitter against myself. I'm over forty, and who wants you? There are lots of jobs I could have had, like research and that. But they ask you how much school you've had and I say seventh grade. What the — — good is that? They don't want seventh grade. I'm not dumb. I got as good a brain as the average guy, but without education they don't want you. No math, no science; that stuff is important. We get these students in here. They do these jobs for a while, but they are going somewhere, you know?

I tell my son, "Study all you can; get all the education you can, it's very important." Every day I tell him that; it's for his own good. He's got a job now keeping score for the baseball games. He likes sports; he likes outdoor things. I tell him to be a high school coach or something like that. What's wrong with that? But you've got to study.

Anyone can do this job I'm doing. I'm not indispensable. I'm just bitter at myself that I didn't do something else before this. Here I am, and what can I do? But I'm getting out of here. Couldn't be any worse. Where you see you're doing something or getting somewhere.

Note that on three occasions the man says "I'm bitter against myself." However, this bitterness does seem to extend to management and the union in most cases. A man can hardly live with himself if he accepts all the blame for the conditions to which he is subjected on the assembly line.

Management is the natural target for men's resentments because it is management which has established the systematic coercion of the assembly line. Furthermore, the assembly line worker has little if any personal contact with members of management above the level of foreman. His relations with the foreman will be discussed shortly.

Management is generally seen as concerned only with squeezing out of the worker every ounce of effort that is humanly possible. From the vantage point of the assembly line, each change in local management seems to be a change for the worse. As one man said:

> Each time they get a new manager it seems to be worse. They get more of these men around clocking the men and seeing if they can put a little more work on them, like that guy you see standing there. The way it is is like this; I come home and my wife says, "How about going for a ride?" I say, "I don't want to do that; I'm too tired." I've done nothing around the house for the longest time because I just am too tired when I get home from this place, the way it is now.

This reaction is particularly interesting because it followed a change that had apparently brought in a new manager who was much more concerned with people and human relations problems than his predecessor. There was indeed some evidence of improvement brought about by this new manager: absenteeism and rate of grievances had dropped; production quality had increased. But under the pressure of his immediate job, the worker could only see the new manager as bringing in changes, and the changes as representing efforts to load more work upon the men and tighten up controls over them.

Actually assembly line technology presents management with exceedingly difficult technical questions of balancing the line. Typically, failures to balance a line properly were not attributed to errors in judgment on the part of management functionaries but were charged to the deliberate intent of management people to squeeze more work out of the workers. Such reactions are described in this way by Turner:

> The extent to which this pressure tended for many workers to pervade their total attitude came out very strongly in several of the responses to the question on the impact of changes in management. The typical opinion was that the recent management change, and by extension any management change, had resulted in efforts to cut back on manpower and to increase the amount of work required of each individual.
>
> Actually the standard amount of work expected of each man had not changed. On an overall basis, increases or decreases in manpower were proportionate to increases or decreases in the line speed. But to the typical worker on the motor line any change in the production schedule seemed to result in more work. When the line speed increased, it seemed that you had to work faster, even if in fact you had somewhat fewer operations to perform. When the line speed was decreased, what was most noticeable was the increased

number of operations assigned to each individual. Both increases and decreases in production had occurred under the new manager, and both gave rise to the feeling that there was a new effort to decrease costs by cutting down on manpower at the expense of the amount of work expected of each man. As a matter of fact there had been equally or more severe fluctuations in production under the old management, and these too had presumably given rise to temporary dislocation in the equitable distribution of the work. Because of the fact that three separate types of motors were being assembled, with many minor modifications for each type, as well as because of other complexities, it was extremely difficult to adjust to changes in schedule without at least a temporary period of trial and error before the line was properly "balanced." However, it was unusual for the men to acknowledge that these inequities were in fact temporary and inadvertent. By many men they were interpreted as a conscious effort of the new management to squeeze as much work out of each man as possible.

Regarding the union, the general feeling was that you had to have a union or else conditions would be much worse. Except in the cases of Austin and a few other men who participated actively in the union, there was no feeling on the part of the men that the union was currently working to improve conditions of the men. Such a reaction might be expected. If the assembly line itself is the most serious problem to the workers, then the only real solution to the problem is the elimination of the assembly line. The workers well recognize that the union cannot possibly bring this about.

There was a feeling that those individuals who most aggressively complained might get some redress through the union, whereas those who were more willing to accept conditions just got ignored. Even for the aggressive individuals, there was some feeling that the union would push some grievances and drop others simply for purposes of bargaining with management. Finally, there was a particular difficulty in the handling of work load grievances. There were so many changes taking place in the schedules of work and men that by the time a man's grievance reached the point of decision, the conditions to which it referred might have been changed independently of his action. This tended to frustrate the handling of grievances.

## THE ROLE OF THE FOREMAN

Frank Melotti, the foreman of the motor line, had come up through the ranks and was fairly popular with the men, but nevertheless he was now regarded as "on the other side." The changes in feeling toward the foreman as he moved into management are well described by Al, who had been an old friend of Frank's. Here is how Al responded when Turner asked him how frequently he and the foreman talked with each other during an average day:

Some days three or four times, some days not at all. It's a funny thing, Frankie and I used to be more chummy before he was a foreman. I used to go to his house quite often. Since he is a foreman I can't find myself at ease with him. It's not that exactly, but I feel uncomfortable some way. I see Frankie in the bar or something like that, not in the shop but outside, and we talk together but I don't know. . . . (It's as though now he is a foreman you can't be friends together in the same way?) Well, now I feel I don't know how he would take it up. Before we would kid around and say things, but now I don't know how he would take it. I'm not built in that way that I could say to him, "So and so has a rough job." Before I would, but now he could say, "It's none of your business," or something like that. I see Frankie at the club and he has a few friends around this block here and when he is passing he stops in or when I am going by his house I stop in and say, "What are you doing?" and he says "I'm mowing the lawn or clipping the hedges" and we talk a little bit about things like that.

The men's feelings toward the foreman were colored by their recognition that he had a difficult job to do. Several of the men in the department had turned down opportunities to become foremen, and when Turner asked them which one among their number would make the best foreman, he had difficulty in getting the question answered. The most common reply was "I wouldn't want to wish that job on anybody." The reaction seemed to be that the foreman, like themselves, was trapped in the technology.

How did the foreman interact with his men? For Frank Melotti, we do not have a quantitative picture, and we will discuss other aspects of his relations later. First let us look at the quantitative picture for another foreman in another assembly line unit, as presented in *The Foreman on the Assembly Line*.[5] (See accompanying table, p. 192.)

In this case, note the large number of interactions during a working day, the numbers of people interacted with outside of the foreman's work unit, and the short duration of the average interaction, particularly with his own workers. The picture we get is of a foreman moving around quite rapidly, being contacted by or contacting large numbers of people and communicating with them very briefly. Interactions are short; there is no time for discussion.

Note also that less than 40 per cent of the foreman's interaction time is spent with his own workers. This has implications that we shall explore later.

While more quantitative studies are needed before we can generalize regarding the interactions of the assembly line foreman, the figures presented here are probably fairly representative. We find further that in relation to his own workers, the foreman may be contacted by them more often than he contacts them. In other words, they may call upon him for help in dealing with the problems of technology more often than he initiates interaction with them. These interactional ratios are probably of

[5] Charles R. Walker, Robert H. Guest, and Arthur N. Turner, *The Foreman on the Assembly Line* (Cambridge, Massachusetts: Harvard University Press, 1956) p. 86.

Nearly half of the foreman's time was spent in direct contact with other people. This involved verbal and non-verbal interaction (hand signals, nods, performing work together) with someone else. These interactions are summarized in the table.

| Contact | Number of Incidents | Total Min- utes Spent | Per Cent of Total Time | Average Time per Incident (mins.) |
|---|---|---|---|---|
| OWN Men: | | | | |
| Regular operators........... | 87 | 67 | 13.8 | ¾ |
| Utility man................. | 14 | 10 | 2.1 | ¾ |
| Repair man................. | 13 | 12 | 2.4 | ¾ |
| PEERS: | | | | |
| Other foremen.............. | 23 | 33 | 6.9 | 1½ |
| SUPERIORS: | | | | |
| General foreman............ | 7 | 28 | 5.8 | 4 |
| Department Supt............ | 3 | 15 | 3.0 | 5 |
| General Supt. or higher...... | 0 | 0 | 0 | 0 |
| SERVICE PERSONNEL: | | | | |
| Maintenance.......:....... | 20 | 24 | 4.8 | 1¼ |
| Materials handling.......... | 5 | 5 | 1.1 | 1 |
| Inspection................. | 8 | 10 | 2.1 | 1¼ |
| Work standards............. | 1 | 1 | .2 | 1 |
| OTHERS: | | | | |
| Other hourly............... | 6 | 4 | .8 | ¾ |
| Observer.................. | 30 | 20 | 4.2 | ¾ |
| All others................. | 11 | 10 | 2.1 | 1 |
| NO CONTACT.............. | 176 | 244 | 50.7 | 1½ |
| TOTAL............... | 404 | 483 | 100.0 | |

considerable importance in explaining worker sentiments toward the foreman, as we shall see in the case of Frank Melotti.

The men saw the foreman in a favorable or unfavorable light insofar as his interactions with them seemed to relieve or intensify the pressures of the assembly line. The minority who expressed unfavorable opinions of Frank Melotti accused him primarily of favoritism, insincerity, and an occasional tendency to respond to the pressures on him by "blowing his stack" or "losing his temper too quickly." One of them put it this way when asked how often he talked with the foreman:

. . . only when he comes up and says something to me. If they would just come and ask what had happened when you missed something because you couldn't get it, why you would talk about it. That's okay. But when they come up and right away start yapping their big mouth about something, I just turn away and go about my work. I don't feel like talking with them when they act like that.

While all the men recognized the foreman's tendency to get excited, they did not feel, in general, that he took it out on them. One man contrasted him favorably with other foremen in this way:

I think Frankie is a little more (pause)—like some of the foremen if a man misses something, they want to lay into you right away, which is not fair. Frankie is a little more lenient about it. He tells you about it and says to watch it next time, but he doesn't give you a reprimand right away. Then when I see a wrong motor on the line or something like that I tell him about it. There are many wrong motors that I have caught and told Frankie about.

How does the foreman help to relieve the pressure of the line? Particularly by stepping in to help out a man when he is in the hole. As one man said:

Some of them get along with him good; about 10 per cent don't. (Does how the foreman gets along make much difference to your job?) It makes a lot of difference; that's the most of the difference. I'll tell you about Frank. He used to be on Dave's job. He used to be a worker, so he understands what the men go through on the job. Of the foremen I've had I got along with Frankie better than any of them. If he can do something to help you he will. Like sometimes I have trouble . . . (with my job). Frankie will notice and try to help me out. The other foremen are not like that.

Another said:

Frankie's a good foreman because he tries to help everyone. He wants no trouble with the guys because if they have a complaint, then time study comes over, and Frankie doesn't want that, so he helps as much as he can. . . . Some foremen are different. We had one foreman who quit. Everybody didn't like him, so they made trouble for him. He would never help. If you had trouble he would say, "Come to my desk and make out a grievance." Frankie is never like that. If he sees you are in the hole, he helps you right away. If you miss something and everyone makes a mistake sometimes, he says nothing about it, he fixes everything all right.

The union contract prohibits a foreman from doing the work of a worker except when demonstrating the operation to the men. When workers dislike a foreman, they can readily give him trouble by lodging grievances against him when he works on the line. As long as he is generally well accepted by the men and limits his stepping into the line to helping out his men in emergencies, then his actions are seen as relieving the pressure of the line and are welcomed by the men.

Apparently the foreman can also serve to provide the only touch of personal relationship with management in an impersonal environment. One man expressed the point in this way:

The foreman has a lot to do with the morale of the men. If you come in in the morning and the guy's puss is a mile long it makes you feel funny. If Frankie didn't say hello in the morning I felt funny—something must be wrong—but if he has a pleasant personality, then you know that he doesn't think of his people as just cattle but as people and that makes you feel better. I went two years in there without one fellow ever saying hello to me. . . . That gave me the most insecure feeling I ever had in my life. . . . I give Frankie credit for that, he always goes down the line and needles each of the guys a little bit about something or other.

"Does it make much difference to your job what sort of a fellow the foreman is?" In response to this question, fifteen men answered yes, one gave a qualified yes answer, two were doubtful, and only two said no.

Although it may seem to the outsider that the foreman does not have the power to add or subtract much of the pressure of the line, what little he can do does apparently make a good deal of difference to the men. However, a favorable sentiment toward him does not carry over any favorable sentiments toward the company.

## WORK GROUPS AND SOCIAL GROUPS

The technology severely limited the interactions possible among the men during the work process, compared with a number of other technologies. What interactions were possible were channeled by the locations of men in space into what Turner has called three working subgroupings, positions I, IIIA, and IV on the chart. Three men, Bert, Dave, and Dick had positions that left them relatively isolated. The isolation seemed to be particularly difficult for Bert. He had a job that was hard to keep up with in the first place, and he suffered under the complete lack of social support while working. In the latter period of Turner's study, Bert was home sick with what the men described as a nervous breakdown.

It was only when they were not working that the motor line men had any freedom to take up their own social groupings. From observations before the line started, during the mid-morning ten-minute coffee break, and during the half-hour lunch period, Turner found two principal non-work subgroupings that he called the card players and the conversation subgroup. The card playing group was built around Chris, Austin and Al who played pinochle every lunch hour. Rick, Joe, Guy, and Gil usually watched the game. During the morning coffee break, Chris, Austin, Al, and Rick met at a particular location in the middle of the motor line area. They were often joined by Reb and less regularly by a number of others such as Gus, Jack, or Joe.

Dick and Guido were the center of the conversation subgroup, getting together every day for lunch and coffee and engaging in an animated conversation on a wide variety of topics. At lunch they were usually joined by Gus and often by Reb and Chas. During the coffee break, Dick and Guido met together in another location, more often than not by themselves.

What was the leadership structure of the motor line? Turner's questions and observations suggested that there were three criteria for leadership, and which individuals were cited depended upon which criterion was used.

When men were asked to say which of their fellows did the best work on the motor line, choices centered on the conversation subgroup, with Dick receiving eight choices and Guido, six.

This seemed to be a significant question to the workers. Turner readily got answers from all but five men on the question. Dick and Guido themselves spoke with pride about their ability to handle the work, and

Turner heard a number of other comments expressing respect for their abilities.

Friendship choices might be considered another criterion of leadership, the highly chosen men being key people in this respect. The responses to the question, "Who are your two or three best friends in the plant?" conformed in general to the actually observed card-playing and conversation groups except that a number of men chose friends outside the department, said everyone was his friend, or refused to choose.

A third criterion for leadership might be perceived ability to represent the group before outside bodies. When Turner asked the men which of their number had the most influence with higher management or with the union, those willing to reply at all named Austin for both areas of representation. That this evaluation was realistic was indicated by the organization of the one concerted protest noted by Turner in his thirteen months with the motor line. Let us follow his own account of what took place:

> There was a sudden "cutback" in production, while Frank Melotti was on vacation. Fred Brewer, a younger, less experienced foreman ran into difficulty in increasing the operations assigned to each man in order to reach the scheduled decrease in manpower.
>
> On the day of the change, many men got into the hole and there was a noticeably tense atmosphere throughout the motor line. The foreman thought that he had talked most of the men out of submitting grievances until they had tried the new schedule out a while longer. However, four days later, Frank Melotti came back to the motor line to find that five grievances had been submitted over the new work loads, and that there had even been talk of an unauthorized walkout. Several of the jobs were retimed, and Frank made a number of readjustments in individual assignments, as a result of which most of the grievances were soon dropped, and in about a week Frank had eliminated most of the "tight spots."
>
> It appeared to the observer that Frank came back to the motor line just in time to prevent some serious trouble. The "hard time" all the men had been giving Fred Brewer and the five simultaneous grievances were part of a concerted protest directed against three things in particular:
>
> The decrease in manpower which was believed disproportionate to the decrease in line speed;
>
> The distribution of the new job assignments between the men, by the inexperienced foreman;
>
> The alleged activities of Jack in talking with the foreman about the new job assignments.
>
> Resentment on all three counts had come to a head at a special meeting at the union hall organized by Austin and Chris, which had no formal standing as far as the union was concerned.

The "special meeting" was seldom discussed in the interviews. It took place before the observer was sufficiently well known to be invited himself. However, it was described in some detail by both Chris and Austin. Chris regarded the purpose of the meeting as being primarily "to punish Jack," who had been helping Fred "set up the jobs," for "telling the foreman one thing and us something else."

Austin arranged it mostly, because on something like that we let Austin organize it because he is familiar with the union. Mostly it was Austin and me and the Tailor (Al)—we decided about it. We told all the guys except Jack about this special meeting. We didn't tell them why. We gave them several days so everyone could come. Everyone came except Gil and Dick. Gil is a funny guy, sort of two-faced. I don't know why Dick didn't come. . . .

Chris went on to describe how the union officers at first objected to a meeting with no union representative present, but were persuaded to let the motor line have its private meeting first, and then call the union officers in.

We had our meeting and we decided that we would like to get Jack right out of the union. We finally called the union guys back in and we told them what we had decided and also we told them to get busy on the motor line and get the jobs straightened out or we would all walk out.

According to Chris, there were two results. The union did concentrate on getting an acceptable settlement on most of the motor line grievances (but not on Bert's job, because "he is not the type of man to be persistent about it"). And Jack "changed completely" after he heard what the meeting had been about, and "stayed away from the foreman for a couple of weeks . . . so we kind of forgot about it."

Austin's description of the meeting was equally interesting but quite different. He saw it primarily as a protest against the new job assignments in general, and especially against the extra work which Fred had been short-sighted enough to give to Austin himself:

If there was only a 10 per cent decrease in line speed it was obvious that it wasn't right to put all that extra work on me. The men seen what occurred. In the meantime Fred is looking around to see what more men he can pull out and he doesn't use any caution or reason about it. Personally, Fred was not a bad guy, but I don't think he understood the fundamentals of time study or standards. Well, on my operations when that occurred, the men rallied to my defense because they figured, "If he is going to do it to *him*, Holy Christ, what chance have we got? This guy has been a committeeman and in the union. What will they do to us, if they can do that to him?" Immediately there was talk about let's walk, let's strike, and this and that.

Austin then described how he had persuaded the men that it would be illegal and dangerous to stage a walkout. He strongly blamed the union for not "educating" the men better on what is and what is not permissible under the contract. "I have to explain to them, 'Look, we can't walk off; if we do we get discharged and no one can help you.' "

It was interesting that this effort to calm the men down and to persuade them against an unauthorized walkout was the main thing which Austin remembered about the special meeting. He went on to show unusual understanding of the conflicting feelings typical of such a time:

I have to explain all of that every time. I think what it is, it's that the guys are mad. They want to do something about it, but again they don't want to. They want to show themselves that they are ready to get tough about it, but they kind of want to be told that they shouldn't do it. They want to be ready to take action, but they don't want the action really to occur. I know they know in their hearts that they don't want to do it (walk out), but I have to go through that and explain it every time.

## CONCLUSIONS

The various studies show that the environment of assembly line technology is so oppressive in its impact on activities and interactions as to produce negative sentiments not only toward the job itself but also toward management and the union.

While we will not be sure until we have a number of other studies as intensive as Turner's in using the same methods, the impression we get is that in this work environment one does not find the strong group cohesion that is observed in certain other types of work environment. The environment severely limits interaction while the work is proceeding, and it leaves some individuals totally isolated. The men have no opportunity to exert collective pressure against management in the actual performance of their jobs—in contrast, for example, to the situation described by Chris on the unloading dock. Any protest must be organized when the line is not running, as was the case with the special meeting.

This does not mean that we should expect assembly line workers to be passive instruments of the technology and of management controls. The technology does make it difficult for them to organize themselves effectively, but the technology also puts extreme pressure on the individuals, thus creating needs for protest. This would seem to lead to an uneasy balance between apathy and agitation.

The impact of the environment upon foreman—worker relations is equally marked. Here again we are handicapped in comparisons because we do not have much quantitative data for foremen in other work environments. However, we have the impression that the assembly line foreman's job is distinctive in the large number of interactions for a working day, and also in the brief duration of those interactions, particularly those with the workers. Mechanical problems may arise at any moment on the line, so that he spends much of his time moving up and down the line, responding to the initiative of workers calling for help or calling matters to his attention, or intervening directly himself. He also has constant problems of relating his line to the rest of the plant, and this involves him in a range of interactions outside of his own work crew.

The technological environment is so overwhelming that nothing the foreman can do would really make the workers like the work they do. Nevertheless, it is possible for him to modify to a degree the impact of this environment upon workers. To the extent that he does so, he can build favorable sentiments toward himself. These favorable sentiments do not extend beyond the immediate personal relationship.

# Chapter 12 *MAN AND PROCESS*

IN OUR examination of the impact of the technological and physical environment, we have been dealing primarily with manual work in various forms, mostly with mechanical operations. In the petroleum and chemical industries, many of the jobs involve controlling the processes by observing various indicators, making periodic checks or tests on operations, and manipulating instruments. In such jobs, the physical labor involved is trifling. The activity is of quite a different nature. As automation progresses, more and more jobs in industry will be of this nature. Therefore, the present case and that presented in the next chapter deal with matters of growing practical importance.

How does a worker adjust to the process and the activities that go with it? How do changes in the process affect him? I shall not seek to answer these questions in general terms. An intensive examination of the experiences of one individual will certainly not present a typical case, but it will enable us to illustrate some of the common problems involved in this type of work environment.

This is the case of Joe Sloan. First, I shall present his problem as it comes to a crisis, and then I shall go back over the events and influences leading up to this crisis.

## THE MAN WHO WALKED OFF THE JOB

On the morning of Monday, April 12, 1943, Joe Sloan, a poly (No. 1) operator at the Hi-Test Aviation Gasoline Plant, walked off his job.[1] Why did he do it?

Johnny Hudson had been on tour (shift) with Joe Sloan at the time of the incident. He explained that they had been in process of shifting over from production of iso-heptene to the regular product, iso-octane, which, blended with other hydro-carbons, yields aviation gasoline. To make the shift, they had to empty the pipes of iso-heptene, venting the vapors and liquids onto the floor of the control room. Hudson said that for a few minutes, until the liquid evaporated, it was all over the floor and its fumes filled the air. He went on:

---

[1] This chapter is based on my "Engineers and Workers: A Case Study," *Human Organization*, Vol. XIV, No. 4 (1956).

It was really a hazard, but I didn't know what Joe was going to do until he just tapped me on the back and says, "Johnny, I am leaving you with it." I sure was sorry to see him go.

The foreman, Tom Lloyd, gave this account:

I was down at the catalyst plant when Sloan called me. He says, "Come on up here. I have something I want to show you." When I got there, he was purple in the face, and he shook his finger under my nose. He says, "I have told you about this time and time again. I have told you to do something about this, and you have done nothing. A man ought not to have to work in conditions like this."

Now, he was in the right about it. We should have connected those lines up outside so that the place wouldn't have been flooded. We have done that now. It was just one of those things I hadn't got around to although I had always meant to do it. But that thing had happened fifty times before, and the men had just taken it so when Sloan made such a fuss about it, I couldn't help thinking it was funny. I must have smiled, but I tried to keep a straight face. I says to him, "Now you get off me." After that he calmed down a little but he said, "I don't think a man ought to have to work under such conditions." I says, "That's right. He don't have to." Sloan walks around the pump a couple of times and then he comes back to me and says, "I don't think I will work under such conditions." Then he taps Johnny Hudson on the shoulder and says the same thing to him. After that he goes up and talks to Jess (Jess Douglas, plant manager). From what Jess said to me, I don't think Sloan had anything against me personally. He just said, "I got fed up and decided to leave."

The foreman was asked whether Sloan would be allowed to return.

Well, I don't know about that. If he had waited until we got that pump going, it would have been different. But he just left his fellow workmen on the spot. That was bad. Anyway, I don't think he wants to come back.

Lloyd went on to say that he thought Sloan had been sorry that he had turned down an aircraft factory job offered him some time before and had used this incident to force the company to give him his release so that he could take the job after all.

Plant Manager Jess Douglas made this comment:

That certainly hit me like a ton of bricks. Sloan has been a very good operator. I knew he had a hot temper. He had had one run-in before with the superintendent here before me. I never found out just what it was. I knew he was unhappy in his work. I told him there would be some possibility of getting in another line when he got his correspondence course finished. Franklin (personnel man) and I had talked with him yesterday afternoon. I wasn't really able to satisfy my curiosity about his reasons for quitting, but at least we got it settled on an amicable basis. It will go on the records that he resigned for ill health. He will get two weeks' sick pay before he is out, and then we will give him recommendations for any job that he applies for. I told him that I did not think a man of his caliber should have flown off the handle that way and he admitted it.

On April 15, Joe Sloan was interviewed as he came in for his paycheck. He began by showing a letter from his doctor saying that he was suffering from "a severe occupational neurosis probably due to a fear of explosions." He went on:

I didn't really resign, if that's what you want to know. I got out under pressure. When I came up to talk to Douglas on my way home, I didn't think I was quitting, but when we were about half way home, he told me he didn't think I ought to come back. When he and Franklin talked with me at home yesterday, Douglas said, "If I were you, I wouldn't have the face to come back in the plant after leaving in the face of hazard." I says, "Do you mean that you wouldn't do anything about that?" And he says, "I wouldn't have the face to go back in the plant after that." I told him I had called it to the attention of Tom several times, and he had done nothing about it. This time there was gasoline on the floor and gas vapors in the air. The windows were open and the wind was blowing from the north toward the furnace. I said to him, "It looks like a man has to quit or get roasted like a pig to get any action, don't it?" And he says, "I wouldn't say that." But right after I left they did fix up that connection outside the control room.

Sloan was asked what it was about this *particular* incident that had made him take drastic action. (The change-over from iso-heptene to iso-octane occurred about once a month.)

Well, I jumped out Tom about it and he just said, "Get off me." so I took that to mean that he wasn't going to do anything about it. I had just stood enough. That was all.

He added that he thought he had been let out because management had identified him as being active in the CIO drive to organize the plant but said he could not prove this.

He said that this was the first time in six months that he had awakened in the morning without a headache. His doctor had put him on a strict diet of milk and custards to guard against stomach ulcers.

The Sloan case aroused much comment among the workers, some of which is presented here. Said Ed Logan, a hydro-stillman (No. 2) operator and one of the most popular men in the plant:

It's too bad. Joe has always been a little hot-headed, but I've never known him to do a man an injustice. Now there are some men in here that are already talking against him. It is that selfishness that you see all over here. Now I stand to gain more out of this than anybody else. But I would be tickled to death to see him come back. I talked with him for an hour and a half at his house last night about it.

Frank Swanson, a fractionator (No. 3) operator who had worked under Sloan for many months, had this to say:

He was a smart boy, but there must have been a cog loose somewhere. A man shouldn't fly off the handle like that.

Mark Walling, a poly (No. 1) operator on another tour (shift), made this comment:

Sloan will be hard to replace. This place is losing a damn good operator. . . . They just say the man blowed up. But why does a man blow up like that? They ought to try to find that out.

Walling puts the problem of this case very well: Why did Joe Sloan blow up? And we might ask, what was Joe talking about when he said, "I had just stood enough."

To the men of Hi-Test plant, that was a real puzzle. While some of them had their theories, no one was able to explain it even to his own satisfaction—not Plant Manager Douglas, not Foreman Lloyd, and not fellow workers. Even Joe Sloan himself could not go much beyond describing the emotions he experienced and the actions he took in the crisis.

To solve the problem, it will be necessary to fill in some general background about the company and plant, examine Joe Sloan's relations with employees and management, and review some of the events of the months leading up to his walkout. The subsequent materials will be focussed on Joe Sloan as much as possible, but it will be necessary to include some data bearing upon much broader problems.

## TECHNOLOGY AND PROCESS

Let us now present the physical setting in which this drama took place.

Hi-Test consisted of three operating units which, to the layman, presented a veritable technological wonderland.

The motive power for the process was generated in the engine room where six huge engines pounded away ceaselessly. They were in the charge of an engine operator, who worked alone with the machines and the noise.

Near the engine room was the catalyst plant where an operator with a crew of ten men handled the chemical process that produced the catalyst used in making the gasoline.

The heart of the operation was the control room where the wall was lined with sensitive automatic meters to record every change in the process. Here worked the poly (polymerization) operator (No. 1), hydro-stillman (No. 2), and fractionator operator (No. 3).

On its way from gas to iso-octane, the principal component of aviation gasoline, the gas-liquid traveled through hundreds of yards of steel tubing. The tubes carried it through a cracking furnace where it was subjected to a temperature of 1300 degrees Fahrenheit. Two cooling towers ran water over the tubes, four fractionating columns separated lighter from heavier parts, several stills distilled the substance, and so on, until it ran off at the end into storage tanks.

The catalyst plant was a chemical manufacturing unit, not connected with the steel tubing which linked the engine room with the control room. The latter two units were directly dependent upon each other in both technical process and human action.

The work duties of the control room were largely divided between the fractionator operator (No. 3) and the hydro-stillman (No. 2). When the works was opened, the poly operator (No. 1) was responsible for control room, catalyst plant and engine room, but there were charts in the control room registering the engine room operations so little human contact was necessary there. The poly operator rarely walked over to the engine room. The engine operator usually came into the control room once a day to join the others at lunch and perhaps once more during the working day. There was nothing to take the poly operator into the catalyst plant except his responsibility for checking on work activity. The catalyst operator was rarely seen in the control room.

The work of the three control room men (for each shift) is difficult to describe; except for regular hourly samples of product for testing to be drawn from various pieces of equipment, the activity depended very largely upon the condition of the process. When operations were going smoothly, the men had little to do but watch their charts. When operations were not going quite right, there were adjustments to be made almost constantly. Since any adjustment made by the fractionator operator affected operations in the area of the hydro-stillman (and vice versa), this would be a period of accelerated interaction between them and with the poly operator.

An emergency would generate greatly accelerated activity. For example, if one engine broke down, the control room men had to respond quickly in order to lighten the load on the other five. Otherwise, the other overloaded engines might all go down, and the process would come to a very costly halt.

The poly operator had a large and heavy responsibility, but few specifically assigned duties. Every hour he was required to look into the cracking furnace from both sides, to check the condition of the tubes. Grey shadows on the white-hot tubes indicated carbon deposits that might cause a blowout, pouring vapors into the furnace and setting off a fire that would play over the outside of the furnace. If these carbon deposits could be blown out, the life of the tubes would be prolonged. While the poly operator had certain other checks to make, his job consisted primarily of coordinating the activities of the other two men.

It was *technically* possible to operate the control room with only two men, and in fact, the plant was set up on this basis. However, the company found it necessary to set up the poly operator position to assure a proper coordination between the other two men.

## PERSONAL AND ORGANIZATIONAL HISTORY

This was a young and rapidly growing company. Joe Sloan was a young man—only twenty-nine when he walked off of the job—and he had expected to grow with it. Indeed, he had gotten off to a rapid start.

An only child, he had been forced to drop out of high school after three years by the death of his father. He was bright and eager to get ahead, and at first it seemed that the company was wide open with opportunities for him.

Sloan had been only a few years on the job when management set up a pilot plant to test out the possibilities of making aviation gasoline from natural gas. The men selected to work in the pilot plant were chosen solely in terms of management's estimate of their ability, and Sloan was among them.

When the Hi-Test plant was put into operation in 1938, management continued to consider the work there of a difficult and experimental nature. In its other operations, management had generally been following seniority in promotions, even though there was no international union in this situation with a contract emphasizing seniority. Feeling that the skills necessary to operate the new plant were not generally available in the work force, management manned Hi-Test at first entirely without regard to seniority. It was only somewhat later that men began moving into Hi-Test on the basis of their seniority.

Thus Sloan found himself in the top operating position of the new plant at the age of twenty-four. Everything looked rosy to him at the time. He found the new job challenging and interesting. He assumed that when he had shown he could master this job, a promotion into management would not be long in coming.

But poly operator was as high as Joe was ever to get in the company. Shortly after he had attained this position, a new general manager of the Natural Gasoline Department laid down a new policy: only college graduates were to be appointed to positions such as foreman and staff engineer. (Actually the policy was changed in 1944, under pressure of exceedingly rapid wartime expansion and manpower shortage. But that was too late to do Joe Sloan any good.)

Joe did not give up hope of advancing at once. At the time, management had not made it entirely clear whether a man who satisfactorily passed a correspondence school course in chemical engineering might be allowed to cross the barrier. Management encouraged workers to take such courses but made no commitments as to promotions. When I first met him early in 1943, Sloan was within half a year of completing his International Correspondence School course in chemical engineering, reportedly with high grades. Nevertheless, he was pessimistic about the future. He described his feelings in this way:

> I feel like I am just bumping my head against the ceiling here. There isn't much chance of getting a better job. I would like to get an engineer's rating. There are always new things to do and it is interesting work. But if I can't get that kind of job, I won't stick to this company for life. If I can't get ahead after this war, maybe I will go into business for myself. I have been thinking about getting into the cosmetics business. With what I know about chemistry, I think I might make a go of it. I thought of quitting once before, but then the army began getting close to married men. I'm only here to stay out of the army.

As Sloan remained on the same job, his sentiments toward the job itself changed. He said:

The first year I found it interesting. There was a lot to learn. But after that it got monotonous. Now it is just routine. Of course, from time to time the process is changed, and that gives you something to work on, but otherwise it is just routine and I get sick of it. . . .

While Joe Sloan remained in the same official position for a period of five years, the status of that position declined as the difficult and experimental operations became routine. Sloan describes the change in these words:

When we were chosen, we had a meeting with Bill Jones (foreman) and the superintendent. Bill told us we were supposed to be above the men, that we could not belong to the company union, we were really supervisors. At that time we were in charge of the catalyst plant. Bill told us to go down there every once in a while and see if anybody was not working and report to him. The men resented that snooping. I wouldn't snitch on the men myself, but we had one snitcher among the poly operators. I don't blame the men for the way they felt about that. One time Gasper (poly operator) and Thompson (catalyst plant operator) got into a fight and as a result of that Bill Jones told us we weren't over the catalyst plant any more.

There used to be poly operator meetings with Bill Jones. We would get together and talk over things. If we had discussed operations, it might have done some good, but Gasper would lead off with some crackpot idea. Chester and Martin would take one side and Walling and I would take the other side. We were pals then; that was before he double-crossed me.

At that time the poly operators in Texas had got a couple of raises and we had not been raised here at all. When the plant started out, we were supposed to get within ten dollars of what they got in Texas (per month). We got together and asked to discuss the salary with the company. I was appointed spokesman. They knew I wasn't afraid to talk, and they thought Gasper would talk too much.

I talked about the responsibilities of the job. They were expecting us to act like supervisors but still we were not getting that pay. After that, they decided to cut out some of our responsibilities. They didn't give us a raise at that time. That was when the poly operator meetings were dropped. We had been coming in on our own time like supervisors. If we were just operators like the rest, they would have had to pay us extra for those meetings.

In the first four years at Hi-Test, Sloan served under two foremen, recently graduated chemical engineers, who were highly unpopular with most of the men. This presented problems to Sloan, because while these foremen had a strong distrust of the abilities and sense of responsibility of the other operators, they did have some confidence in Sloan's ability and also in that of Mark Walling, the second-youngest poly operator. In other words, the young foremen were thought to favor the young and ambitious poly operators.

Sloan described his relations with foremen and fellow workers in this way:

I was plenty unpopular when I came on this job at first. I was very young then, and I was an only child in my family. My wife was one of ten children. She didn't know anything about psychology from the textbooks, but she was able to help me a lot.

This was my first job handling men. I made a lot of mistakes. I was too conscientious. The trouble was I believed what Jones and Fitch (former foremen) told me. They told me that I should push the men, that I should stand behind them and keep them working. I don't think I was nasty about it, but the men didn't like it. Then I saw that Walling's crew was producing less than any of us, and he was getting all the credit, so I changed my motives. Then one man on my crew squealed on Edwards (fractionator operator) to Bill Jones. Edwards knew I got along good with Jones so he thought I had squealed, and he wouldn't talk to me for a month. That's all straightened out now. Those men know that whenever I have a complaint about them, I will take them with me to the foreman.

Then I got in trouble too because I didn't smoke on the job. The men used to step outside to sneak a smoke. When the supervisors caught onto it, they thought I had squealed. I just didn't think it was right to smoke around a gasoline plant, but I never did squeal. Then when the men were taking gasoline, I didn't want to do that either and when I didn't do it, they were afraid I would squeal on them. Then I got into some trouble down at the catalyst plant. I really didn't have anything to do with it but I just got roped in on it. The fight was between Thompson (catalyst operator) and Gasper (poly operator at Hi-Test), but Thompson had been claiming that I hadn't been labelling the used catalyst right. I don't know who made the mistake there. It was such a little thing that I didn't pay any attention to it. But that got taken out on me.

Being the youngest man here, I have been very careful about handling the men. Whenever a man gives me an idea, I try to tell it to the foreman in his presence. The men know that so they give me plenty of ideas. Now Johnny Hudson has had no technical education, but he has a good practical mind, and he will think of something good maybe once a week.

Those poly operator meetings never did any good. The men would just get together and gripe about the operators on their tour. The poly operator would get down on some man, and he couldn't do anything right. Whenever they began tearing down a man, I would say, "Put him on my tour, and I will make it a good tour." Then the supervisor would tell me they put the new men on my tour because if they couldn't do the work, I could. That way, I have always got the newest operators. Johnny Hudson is a good man. He is a good hydro-stillman. His only trouble is that sometimes he gets excited and wants to do the wrong thing, and I have to stop him. They wanted to put Swanson on another man's tour and that man wouldn't have him, so I got him. I have never known a man who was more willing or more stupid. You tell him how to do a thing a hundred times, and he doesn't know any better the ninety-ninth time than he did the first time. (Swanson was a man in his fifties with long seniority but little experience relevant to Hi-Test.) . . . .

Bill Jones used to listen to what the men would say about other operators. He trusted me, and so some of the men suspected that I was snitching on them. That's what Charley Lester (hydro-stillman) thought when Bill got down on him, but I never did it.

For a time both Sloan and Walling seemed to enjoy a favored position with management. They were good friends. Then a change occurred to leave Sloan somewhat isolated insofar as the poly operators were concerned. He describes it in this way:

Chester and Martin had the most seniority. I was the youngest so I knew I couldn't get anything by myself. But Walling was the next youngest, and while we stuck together, that balanced things out. At that time the poly operators rotated working with different crews and getting different days off. Chester and Martin didn't want to rotate. Naturally, they had the seniority, so with this system, they could choose their days off. They talked to Walling and they finally persuaded him. So Chester picked Friday and Saturday, Martin got Sunday and Monday, Walling Wednesday and Thursday, and I got Monday and Tuesday. (By this time Gasper was doing office work and was not included.) We were off two days one week and one day the next (averaging forty-four hours a week). I knew I wouldn't get anything because I didn't have the seniority, but I didn't like the way they did things. Whenever there was any change, I wouldn't be consulted, I would just get what was left. That is what I would have got anyway, but it would have been a nicer way to do it if they had consulted me first.

About a year before his walkoff, Joe Sloan's career was very nearly terminated abruptly. While Sloan was looking into the cracking furnace, examining the white-hot tubes for carbon deposits, a tube blew out *outside* of the furnace and burst into flames just a few feet behind them. If the accident had happened closer to him, he could have been severely and perhaps fatally burned. Sloan confessed to me that after this experience he never again looked into the cracking furnace from this particular side, though he continued to check the other side. He freely admitted that there was just as much danger on the other side, but he could not bring himself to take up again the position he was holding at the time of the accident. Several weeks after his walkoff, Sloan commented to me in this way about his accident:

I had that accident a year ago. Ever since that time I didn't feel right about that equipment. Not just the cracking furnace. I was more afraid of that 750 pound (pressure) equipment. . . . We used to have a couple of weeks of testing work around the yard every so often. I remember I always used to feel better in that two weeks. The rest of the time, for the last six months, I worked in the plant. I always used to wake up in the morning with a headache.

## THE UNION DRIVE

Management had provided its workers in this area with a company union in 1935. A CIO union had made two previous attempts to organize Hi-Test and other plants of the company in this area. Late in 1942, a new organization drive was begun.

At about the same time, higher management, having become aware of friction between workers and local management, made some strategic replacements. Tom Lloyd came in as foreman for Hi-Test and the catalyst plant, and Jess Douglas came in as plant manager immediately above him.

At the time of my study, both men had become highly popular with the workers. Lloyd was a chemical engineer, like his predecessors, but at thirty-six he was a good deal older and more experienced than Jones and Fitch had been. Furthermore, having had no previous experience with Hi-Test, he had to trust the workers to handle the operations effectively. He respected them and they respected him.

Sloan describes the response of the poly operators to the unionization drive in this way:

> When this latest CIO drive got started way back in the fall, the poly operators went to Douglas (plant manager) and asked him to give us a new classification. We didn't ask any more money. We just asked to be called shift foremen, and then we wouldn't have to take a stand one way or another in this union business. Douglas wouldn't even discuss the matter with us, so if we go for the CIO, they can't complain. We are all for the CIO in here except for one man. I would do more organization for the union if I didn't have to watch my step because I still have hopes of going up.

In early February of 1943, the poly operators in particular and the other Hi-Test operators in general suffered another blow to their status. It occurred at a time when the company, stimulated by the CIO drive, had begun negotiating a new contract with the company union. The previous contract had not included any provisions regarding wage rates, and it was said that the contract currently discussed would be more comprehensive.

Along with fellow workers at Hi-Test, Joe Sloan had no faith in the company union, but naturally developments in the current "negotiations" were matters of keen interest to the workers. Furthermore, the men asked themselves: What have we got to lose? In fact, the poly operators might stand to gain something out of these discussions, for their representative, a fractionator operator, was arguing with management that poly operator pay should be increased. He was claiming that, in view of the great skill and scientific knowledge required of the poly operators, they should be paid the same as the top operators in the company's refineries.

Management was not yielding on this point, but the discussion proceeded calmly enough to the end of the formal meeting. It was after the formal meeting that Masters, chief company negotiator, speaking casually to some of the men, made the remark that hit the Hi-Test plant and the whole works area with dramatic effect. The Hi-Test representative reported it in this way:

> Did you hear what Masters said about us? He told us that we were only watchmen. He said, "Down there in that plant you have got automatic controls and charts. If anything goes wrong with the meters, you just call a meter man. If anything goes wrong with the engines, you call a repairman. If anything goes wrong with operations, you call an engineer, and he tells you what to do. There is no skill in that work. You just have to watch the charts."

Foreman Tom Lloyd, in commenting on the incident, shook his head and said:

> We work for months to smooth out our relations with the men and get everything in the groove. Then he comes along and throws everything out of line. This is not the first time it has happened either. . . .

My data do not show how Sloan himself responded to this statement. However, the statement was resented bitterly by all of the men with whom I discussed it. Given Sloan's youth and ambition, we can safely assume that he felt strongly about it. This symbolic blow seemed to show just to what extent management had downgraded the status of the poly operator since the opening of the plant, when he was considered really a part of management.

## SLOAN'S LAST SIX WEEKS

On March 1, long awaited transfers of Hi-Test men to the synthetic rubber plant in Texas were carried through. There was no worker criticism of the way the transfers were handled. The company had asked for volunteers, and the plan had been explained in a company union meeting.

At the same time, the company announced a lengthening of the work week from forty-four to forty-eight hours, to meet the manpower shortage. Since only one Hi-Test operator elected to make the transfer, the new work schedule left the plant with a manpower surplus. One of the poly operators would have to serve as a hydro-stillman for half of his six days. The new schedule also meant that the regular three-man teams which had been together for months were now broken up.

Management elected to make the personnel changes on a strict seniority basis, so the demotion fell to Sloan. However, Plant Manager Douglas explained to him that he would retain his poly operator classification and rate of pay. With the additional four hours of overtime at time-and-a-half, his monthly income was substantially increased.

Shortly after this, Sloan took his two-week vacation. My first opportunity to interview him again on the job following his demotion came on March 23. Sloan was hydro-stillman on evening tour (3 P.M. to 11 P.M.) under poly operator Walling.

Sloan said that he had been offered a job as a chemist in an aircraft plant. He had gone to talk with the personnel man there and had been shown through the plant. The money would be somewhat less than he was now getting, but "it would be a clean job and the chances for advancement might be better." He did not take it, he said, because he wasn't sure what the job would look like a year from now.

I went to see Franklin (personnel man) on this to find out how I stood with the company. This was the first time I have ever gone to talk with Franklin. It was amusing and aggravating at the same time. He spent the first half hour telling me that he had never told a lie, then he talked for about an hour telling me how important engineers were to the company. He wanted to make me feel satisfied with my job. Then when I brought out that letter that he had signed congratulating me on my ICS course, and saying that there would be a possibility of advancement if I got through with it, he had to talk himself all around those things that he had been saying. I'm sure he hadn't remembered signing that letter at all, and he didn't give me a chance to bring it in until he told me all this about the college men. He didn't want to say that he had lied in this letter or that he was giving a different picture in talking to me, so he just talked around in a circle for a while. I didn't get any satisfaction out of that.

I went and talked with Douglas (plant manager). I know I can count on him to tell me the truth. I asked him if he thought this letter Franklin had written me was a lot of ballyhoo. He said, "It kind of looks that way, don't it?" He didn't build me up or tear me down. He just told me where I stood with the company. He told me there was no danger of me being bumped back (into a lower pay and status classification). I felt better knowing that.

Now, I am satisfied with what I am doing. I don't worry about it any more.

I asked if that last statement did not represent a change in his feelings about the job. He agreed. I asked him to explain the change. He said he couldn't, except that perhaps he felt better knowing where he stood.

Later in this same week poly operator Martin went to the hospital for an operation. It was expected that he would be out for two months. Sloan assumed that in this case he would be returned to full time on the poly operator job, but Tom Lloyd decided that the job should be open to bids and filled on a seniority basis. Johnny Hudson, the hydro stillman who had worked under Sloan for many months, had much more seniority than Sloan and was awarded the poly operator position. Sloan retained his poly operator classification and pay but continued to divide his week between poly operator and hydro-stillman positions.

Commenting on this change after he had left the plant, Sloan said that he had indeed felt discriminated against, but he added,

That didn't bother me. I won't say I understood the reasons for that decision, but I didn't complain about it because I thought too much of Hudson. He was my best friend in the plant.

On April 4, the representation election was held, and the CIO union lost by a narrow margin. (The watchman statement had by now receded into the background.)

The union drive will be discussed in Chapter 14. For present purposes, our only concern is its effect upon Sloan. He said that the CIO defeat was a disappointment to him, although he had had no great hopes that things would be different if the union came in.

On Tuesday, April 6, at 6:30 p.m., Tom Lloyd received a telephone call from the main office with the order to start the tri-iso-butylene run as soon as possible. He had known some time in advance that a product of this nature was to be made, but it was not until this time that he was given the exact specifications (initial boiling point and dry point temperatures). Lloyd asked if he could start the run the following morning, but he was told that this was a rush order so that it was necessary to start work immediately.

Since Lloyd was not familiar with the detailed operations of the fractionating column, he telephoned Dan Benton, his staff engineer, and asked him to return to the plant to take charge of operations at once.

The fractionating column in which the product was to be made was under the direct charge of the fractionator operator, but having had a good deal of fractionating experience, the hydro-stillman was naturally interested also, and both men normally worked under the supervision of the poly operator.

To this group were added Lloyd and Benton, who ordinarily spent little time within the plant. During the run, Lloyd spent most of his time at Hi-Test, consulting with Benton and the operators. He also took samples from the fractionating column up to the laboratory in order to run distillation tests on them. When he went home to sleep, he called in Catalyst Operator Thompson to do the distillations.

Benton was in active charge from Tuesday night until Friday morning. During that period, he was in the plant almost continually, getting only ten hours of sleep. At the start, he took over the No. 3 fractionating column himself and directed the fractionator operator in all changes. Since the plant was operating in a routine manner otherwise, there was little for the poly operator and the hydro-stillman to do except watch Benton and the fractionator operator.

Benton had certain definite ideas as to how the run should be started, and it appeared that by Thursday morning he had been successful. The product at that time tested to specifications, but by the time the test results were reported, the column had become flooded and was no longer making the product. Having been unsuccessful in this effort, Benton listened to the suggestions of the operators and tried out a number of their ideas.

At the start of the daylight tour (7 A.M. to 3 P.M. Friday) fractionator operator Kendall gave his opinion to Lloyd that no further progress could be gained along the lines then being pursued, and went on to outline his ideas as to how the fractionating column should be handled. Lloyd had a high regard for Kendall and therefore decided to turn the column over to him without restrictions or supervision. By now Benton was physically and mentally exhausted, and Lloyd sent him home.

At the end of Kendall's tour, he still had no results, but he was able to convince Lloyd that he was moving in the right direction. Lloyd ordered Kendall to work another eight hours, remaining in charge of the key column. Walling was poly operator on evening tour (3 P.M. to 11 P.M.). Lloyd instructed Walling to pay close attention to the way Kendall was operating the column.

At the end of evening tour, the product was still to be made. Lloyd sent Kendall home and held Walling over for another eight hours, ordering him to take exclusive charge of the column. Early Saturday morning, twenty-two hours after Kendall began trying his plan, the product came over, and shortly the brief run was completed.

One operator expressed the general viewpoint of the workers when he said:

It wasn't until they left it to the operator that they got the thing lined out. Sure, it would have gone much faster if they had made it that way in the first place. The operator knows these columns better than the technical man.

During the week of the run, Sloan had worked Monday through Wednesday on graveyard tour (11 P.M. to 7 A.M.) as a hydro-stillman under Walling. Thursday through Saturday, he worked as poly operator, but when the product was finally being made, he found Walling held over to retain charge of the key column, so Sloan had nothing to do with the making of this experimental product.

Some weeks later I asked Sloan to tell me particularly about his reactions to the tri-iso-butylene run. He said it had not bothered him particularly. He went on,

Now I don't have anything against Benton. I like Dan. But we hadn't been accustomed to having an engineer supervise operations like that. He was around all the time telling the fractionator man what to do. Lloyd was there most of the time too. He didn't really do anything. He would just talk to Benton and with the rest of us, figuring out what to do. Then he spent some of his time running distillations. . . .

One night when I was on tour, we had Thompson in there from the catalyst plant running distillations for Lloyd while he slept. We had never had a man from the catalyst plant work in there with us before. Thompson (a company union representative) and I got into a hot argument about the company union and the CIO. It didn't really amount to anything, but I didn't like to have Thompson around all the time. He has the type of overbearing personality that don't appeal to me. . . .

One night Tom Fitch (Lloyd's predecessor as foreman) called the plant at 2 A.M. He had something to do with the run from the main office end . . . Fitch knows the operations here a lot better than Lloyd . . . Lloyd was in the plant with us at the time. I asked him why he thought Fitch had called. "Oh," he says, "he probably just wanted to show he was interested in his job." I said to Lloyd, "Then why are you down here now? For the same reason?" He didn't have anything to say to that.

On this particular week, Sunday was Sloan's day off. He returned to work Monday on daylight tour as hydro-stillman under Johnny Hudson. This was the first time Sloan had worked under his former hydro-stillman. It was this morning that the control room was flooded in the course of the changeover from iso-heptene to iso-octane, and Sloan walked off the job.

## ANALYSIS

### 1. EXPLAINING JOE SLOAN

Why did Joe Sloan walk off the job?

It will be helpful to divide this into two questions: Why was Joe Sloan dissatisfied? What led him to take such drastic action?

Sloan's negative sentiments toward the job and the company certainly contributed to his action, and we shall begin by explaining these negative sentiments. However, a man can have negative sentiments toward his job in the company for a long time without quitting, and in fact Sloan had no intention of quitting. After examining the sources of his dissatisfaction, therefore, we shall move on to review the events that brought these sentiments to the boiling point.

Why the negative sentiments? The main explanation comes from reviewing Sloan's position in the company over a period of years. He had moved up rapidly to the top operating position at an extraordinarily early age. This naturally served to raise what social psychologists call the level of aspiration. The individual's sentiments as to how high a goal he can be expected to achieve are naturally influenced by the rapidity of his progress toward that goal. A worker who had achieved the top operating position in his forties or fifties after a period of years of slow progress could not have been expected to feel such a sense of frustration at being blocked from the move into management.

There was also an important change over the years in the inherent interest the job held for Sloan. At first it was interesting and challenging; later it had become routine—except for occasions when a new product was to be made. (The tri-iso-butylene run must be viewed in this light.)

The importance of the new process and its experimental nature served to give the top operating job high status. As workers, foremen, and engineers together solved the usual operating problems, the poly operator's job became much more of a routine matter. As the process was mastered, management's evaluation of the poly operator job naturally underwent a decline. The magnitude of the decline in status over the years might be summed up in these words: from company men to watchmen. At first the poly operators were told that they were not regular workers, they were part of management—or almost part of management. Finally Masters told them that there was no skill to the job after all.

These changes served to create and intensify the negative sentiments Sloan held toward the job and the company. With these sentiments firmly established, he encountered a series of drastic changes during the last six weeks on the job.

First he was downgraded in status to serve as hydro-stillman three days a week—even though he retained his poly operator classification and earned more wages. Furthermore, this change for Sloan as well as for other poly operators resulted in the disruption of customary relations among members of work crews. For some months, Sloan had directed the work of Hudson and Swanson. He took great pride in getting performance from two men not highly regarded by fellow workers or supervisors. Now he had to adjust to different members of his crew each week; part of the week as #1 man and the other part as #2 man.

Martin's sick leave seemed to offer the opportunity to Sloan to become poly operator full time once more, but again he was passed over. At this point he initiated interaction with higher management people—

Plant Manager Douglas and Personnel Manager Franklin—hoping to get some reassurance as to his position and potential progress in the company. No such support was forthcoming.

The tri-iso-butylene run concentrated a number of important inter-action and activity changes, all within the same few days. Foreman Lloyd and Engineer Benton spent far more time in the plant than was customary, and Benton took over operations right out of the hands of the poly operator. A lower status man, Thompson, from the catalyst plant, with whom there had been previous friction, came into Hi-Test plant to run distillations and to tell the men how they were doing.

The tri-iso-butylene run presented the type of intellectual challenge that could give new meaning to the job for Sloan. This apparent oppor-tunity was denied him. During the first part of the week, he was in the hydro-stillman classification, where he had nothing to do with the process. When his turn as poly operator did come later in the week, Walling, his chief rival, was held over to direct the process. Thus Walling and not Sloan got whatever credit was due to the poly operators for the completion of the run.

It is noteworthy that on the day of the walkoff, Sloan was serving for the first time under his former hydro-stillman, Johnny Hudson. Was this reversal of the customary relationship too much to take?

Finally, we should note the significance of this particular safety hazard in the light of Sloan's experience. A man who has narrowly escaped injury or death through a tube blowout is naturally more appre-hensive of this hazard than one who has had no narrow escapes. On this score, Sloan was being realistic. A tube blowout at the time of venting the vapors was a very unlikely coincidence—yet such a coincidence could have had catastrophic results.

Nevertheless, we must remember that for some time the gases and vapors had been vented about once a month. Sloan had complained earlier, but at that time it had not seemed a matter of great consequence. I knew Sloan better than any of the Hi-Test workers, and he talked freely of many matters to me. My notes show no reference to the venting problem among all of his many criticisms of management—until after he walked off the job. It was the combination of the hazard with the mounting psychological pressures on Sloan that brought on the crisis.

Judging from the Joe Sloan case, we might venture certain generaliza-tions regarding the reactions of individuals.

The following changes experienced by a worker are likely to lead to erratic behavior and to negative sentiments toward the perceived source of the changes:

1. Loss in status.
2. Marked reductions in opportunities to initiate activities for others.
3. Instabilities and marked fluctuations in the interactions experienced (the tri-iso-butylene run).

The Joe Sloan case also suggests a generalization regarding age, progress in the organizational hierarchy, and level of aspiration. Other things being equal, the more rapidly the individual rises in the organizational hierarchy, the more serious is his adjustment problem when further advancement is blocked. Under these circumstances, blocking can be expected to lead to strong negative sentiments and to a desire to leave the organization. (While Sloan did not intend to quit on the day of the walkoff, note his statement that he would have resigned much earlier had he not wished to avoid conscription.)

This proposition suggests that if Joe Sloan had moved up at a slower pace, he would not have been so seriously disturbed by the blocking of his progress. Speculation as to what might have been does not, of course, provide any evidence in support of the proposition. It simply suggests a corollary for the proposition that might be tested in future research.

## 2. TECHNOLOGY, WORK PROCESS, AND SYMBOLS

Let us now look beyond Joe Sloan and see if we can draw from this case some tentative conclusions regarding technological environment and symbols, interactions, activities, and sentiments.

We have already noted that the technology tends to channel within certain limits the interactions and activities of workers and supervisors. This case suggests that the technology and work process also tend to establish the symbols men use in evaluating the rank or status of the job.

Management's initial evaluation of the technical difficulty of the position led to the symbolic placement of poly operators between workers and management.

Along with this symbolic separation from workers went certain activities and interactions of poly operators, not shared in by hydro-stillmen and fractionator operators. The poly operators met as a group for discussion with their foreman. They were also charged with supervision of the catalyst plant.

Along with this pattern of symbols, interactions, and activities went a complementary set of sentiments. Management people felt a high regard for the poly operators. The poly operators felt themselves superior to other workers. This did not mean that the poly operators held favorable sentiments toward their foreman in this early period. At least, at the time of our research, the poly operators were highly critical of these previous foremen. On the other hand, much of this criticism was directed at the way the foreman would "get down on" a given hydro-stillman or fractionator operator and would try to set the poly operators apart from their two immediate subordinates. At least, Sloan and Walling felt that Foremen Jones and Fitch had confidence in them. They did not feel the brunt of the foremen's criticism.

While the technology did not change substantially in the several years following the opening of the plant, the work process came under routine control. Management now introduced verbal symbols congruent to the changed situation: The poly operators were told they were now free to belong to the company union. While this did not serve to increase the interest of the poly operators in the company union, it tended to channelize their identification toward workers instead of toward management. A broad company policy announced in this period had the same identification effects: this was the decision that only college graduates would be promoted into management.

Interaction and activity changes accompanied these symbolic changes. The poly operator meetings with foremen were abandoned, and the poly operators were relieved of their responsibilities for supervising the catalyst plant.

In the early period, when constant difficulties were encountered, the poly operator had to initiate for hydro-stillmen and fractionator operators with a high frequency to coordinate the work of the plant. As the work became routine, the intervention of the poly operator was needed much less often. The other two men simply reported to him when they made changes in operations, and he seldom had to tell them what to do. This further served to reduce the perceived status of the poly operator.

If the poly operator had been responsible for the work of ten men, the sheer numbers involved would have made for significant interactional differences. In spreading his interactions over ten men, the poly operator would not have been able to interact with any individual with a high frequency. Thus, his position would have appeared to be separated from theirs both to himself and to his subordinates. When the poly operator had only two men with whom to interact in the Test Room (plus an occasional visit from the engine operator), and when he did not often interact with the foreman except in contacts shared with the other two workers, his interactions were bound to strengthen the poly operator's identification sentiments toward the workers. When you are thrown together for eight hours a day with two other men, with few other interactional opportunities, and with a technology that permits free interaction, you are bound to come to think of yourself as a member of that work group and to be so regarded by others.

The poly operators responded to this situation by changing their sentiments toward the job itself, toward other workers, and toward management. They came to recognize that the job had become more routine even as they resented this downgrading of its prestige. They came to identify themselves more with their subordinates and to look with unfavorable sentiments toward management in general, even when interpersonal relations with Foreman Tom Lloyd were harmonious.

In an effort to re-establish their lost superiority, poly operators asked for the title of "shift foreman" and then sought to equate their work with that of high status refinery operators. Having been rebuffed at these efforts of symbolic redress, the poly operators now received the heaviest symbolic blow of all: the watchman statement.

As Tom Lloyd pointed out, this word considerably exaggerated the loss of skill and status in the job, at least as viewed by local management. This made the symbol particularly offensive. On the other hand, it did clearly mark out the direction in which interactions, activities, and sentiments had moved since the opening of the plant.

Let us see if we can use the case to set up tentative propositions in a more general and abstract form.

Symbols tend to reflect the current pattern of interactions, activities, and sentiments in an organization. At the same time, the introduction of a new symbol may serve to signalize for participants that a change has taken place and thus to set off new interactions, activities, and sentiments in reaction to this change. More specifically, if managers apply to workers symbols implying a reduction of the status previously held by them, then these symbols can be expected to strengthen the workers' negative sentiments toward management and to set off interactions and activities directed toward re-establishing the status level the workers previously enjoyed.

The case of the poly operators suggests a general proposition regarding the relations among three levels in an organizational hierarchy. Let us refer to foreman level as A, the poly operators as B, the hydro-stillmen and fractionator operators as C.

As B's interactions with A (in situations not shared by C) are sharply reduced and B's interactions with C are increased, we can expect these changes in sentiments: (1) to all parties concerned, the status of B in the organization will be seen as having declined; (2) B will now tend to identify himself more with C and less with A.

Note the sequence of analysis we follow in such a case. We begin with such concretely observable items as the technology and the work activities. We see that management *sentiments* regarding technology and the complexity of the work activities, at the beginning of our case, tend to influence (1) the number of men placed in the plant, (2) the characteristics of the men placed there, (3) the status or rank of the poly operators, and (4) the interactions and activities of the top operators with the foremen and with fellow workers (including the catalyst plant).

Unfortunately, we have no observational data for the early period to compare poly operator interactions and activities in Hi-Test with what we observed in 1942–43. When workers and supervisors alike say that the job has become more routine, we infer that comparing the later with the earlier period, interactions and activities have become much more stable and subject to far fewer sharp fluctuations. Awareness of these changes affects management sentiments on all of the points noted above except the number of men in the plant. The characteristics of the men required for the job are seen as having changed (seniority replacing ability as the primary criterion of choice). The status of the poly operators is seen as markedly lower than before. Interactions and activities involving poly operators exclusively with the foremen are terminated, and the supervisory activity of the poly operator is sharply curtailed.

Such changes may bring forth from workers (1) compensatory interactions and activities or (2) withdrawal from the situation. In this case, we have seen examples of both types of responses. Joe Sloan's walkoff was clearly a withdrawal, but earlier he and his fellows had made several compensatory efforts (the shift foreman proposal, the claimed equivalence with refinery operators). In Chapter 14, "Enter the Union," we shall be examining a more far-reaching compensatory effort.

# Chapter 13 *TOWARD THE AUTOMATIC FACTORY*

AUTOMATION now seems the order of the day in American industry. We constantly hear speculations regarding the impact of automation upon workers and management and worker-management relations.

Is automation something new that is just now coming on the scene? In a sense it is, and in a sense it is not. Turning to the chemical and petroleum industries, we find that a large part of the work processes have been partially automated. As we saw in the case the Hi-Test plant, such a process runs without the intervention of manual labor. The workers observe the process as recorded on charts and make periodic tests of the state of the process. On the basis of what they learn from these observations and checks, the workers may adjust the equipment to vary the operating conditions. Otherwise they simply stand by and wait and watch.

In the Hi-Test case, just one aspect was lacking for the plant to be considered a fully automated unit. This was automatic feedback: the process whereby the unit produces information as to how it is performing and acts upon that information to make adjustments in operations without the intervention of man. Such feedback processes have since been developed in certain process industries.

What is entirely new is the development of automated or semi-automated plants in the field of mechanical manufacturing. Companies are beginning to develop manufacturing methods whereby material is moved from point to point and worked on automatically by machines. Instead of operating the machines directly, workers observe their operation, as in the Hi-Test case again, and intervene to make adjustments when they are required.

While much has been said and written about automation in manufacturing, we have very little research data on the subject. Our best chance to examine the impact of automation comes through the work of Charles R. Walker and his Technology Project at Yale University. The following discussion is drawn from Walker's book, *Toward the Automatic Factory: A Case Study of Men and Machines.*[1]

---

[1] New Haven: Yale University Press, 1957.

## TECHNOLOGY AND PHYSICAL CONDITIONS

We will examine the introduction of the first continuous, seamless tube mill in the United States in the Lorain, Ohio plant of the United States Steel Corporation. This change had important effects upon the nature of jobs and job classifications, and upon the relations among the men. In a broad sense, certain of these effects could be foreseen, and those we will note here. We will later describe effects that were not anticipated.

In contrast with the old steel tube mill with twenty-five men on a shift, the new mill was to produce four times as much with far fewer men. The original crew complement was eleven men, and this was later reduced to nine.

This reduction in the size of crew meant that the nine men were scattered over a large area of physical space. In the older mills, men worked together in groups of two to ten, forming a number of small work teams whose members could and did interact readily with each other. Members of the work crew in the new plant were so isolated physically that they had no opportunity to interact with one another during the time the mill was in operation, except through a public address system.

The new mill brought important changes in the physical and mental composition of the jobs. Except for one work station, manual labor was all but eliminated—and so was the manual skill of manipulating steel billets and tubing. A different kind of skill was being substituted, but until there was experience with the new plant, it was difficult to evaluate the skill required.

Changes in the jobs also involved changes in job classifications. The job classification system then in effect in the plant gave points to manual skill and to the heat and hazard of working conditions—all of these being considered greater in the old mill. For example, in the old mill, there had been a team of nine to eleven men for the operation of billet heating. The heater had job class 18, and his eight to ten helpers held classifications at job class 8. Only two men were required for this operation in the new mill; a furnace inlet man (class 4) and a furnace discharger (class 10).

On the average, men in the new mill were to receive less hourly pay than in their previous jobs. If the mill were placed on incentive, they might earn as much as they had before, or possibly more. Management expected to provide an incentive, but this could not be done until the mill had been in operation for some time.

Walker summarizes the work process in this way:

Three things will become evident: first, that the work flow is continuous; second, that the billet moves successively through five processes; third, that each of these processes is associated with a particular unit of machinery. The processes, and the five associated mechanical units, are: (1) heating to forging temperature in the *rotary hearth furnace*, (2) piercing into a hollow shell, in the *piercing mill*, (3) work on inner and outer walls of the pipe in the *mandrel mill*, (4) reheating in the *reheat furnace*, (5) final adjustment in size and length in the *stretch-reducing mill*. All five units are connected with each other by conveyors.

## EARLY REACTIONS

The mill went into operation in January of 1949. Walker and his associate, Robert Guest, conducted three series of interviews to get the men's reactions at spaced intervals of time. The first round of interviews was held during the late spring and summer of 1949. The second round was held in the spring of 1951; the third round toward the end of 1952. At other times, Walker was in touch with the mill, and these informal contacts provided information on developments that had taken place between periods of intensive study.

First we shall study the reactions manifested during the first period of interviewing, when the mill was still quite a new experience to the men. How did they respond it it?

It was generally reported that the work had become physically easier, as the following comments indicate:

The job on No. 4 is a cinch. It is two classes lower, but ten times easier. I just have to sit there. Once in a while I help out the reducer or nine-stand. . . .

Reason I'm glad about new job is that there is much less physical work than plugging the hi-mill—my old job. I look at it this way; as I get older I would want an easier physical job. . . .

It's easier; that is, there isn't much work to do; but you have to just stand there, and that's tiring, too.

On the other hand, there were a number of comments regarding the increased mental demands of the job. Two examples:

. . . You have to think more about the job you're doing. You can't look around. In the old mills, the job got so you didn't have to think—no mental effort. This job is very touchy—you have to *watch* all the time and think every minute. They should give a lot more credit to the thinking. Even when the mill is turned on automatic you still have to think all the time.

On the old sinking mill where I worked, you set it up and let it run . . . On No. 4 *concentrating* all the time in case something happens gets on your nerves.

While most men said that the job involved more nervous tension in this early stage, there were some who welcomed it as a challenge. As one man said:

I like it better on No. 4 because I have responsibility. I know my own work and I run the equipment by using my head and my eyes. I have exactly twenty-five buttons in the booth and one foot lever.

How did the men view the limitations on social contacts? No one preferred the new job in this respect. The majority of the men expressed indifference to the change, but a smaller group strongly disliked these new limitations. As one man said:

> In No. 1 we used to have a lot of fun—those on the furnace, anyhow. Over here in No. 4 there is too much tension. It was more like a home atmosphere in the old mills. You work alone in No. 4. It is against the rules for anybody to talk to me while I'm operating. On No. 1 there was a group of us on the furnace. We got to know each other good.

The public address system made it possible for the men to interact on the job, but at this point they were not accustomed to the equipment and made little use of it.

In the new mill, the men were seeing the foreman and assistant superintendent and superintendent much more frequently than they had in the old, and these interactions apparently were harmonious. The following two comments are representative of the new relationship:

> There's been a tremendous improvement in supervision in No. 4, as over the old mills. I like the superintendent, the assistant superintendent, and foreman X. With X I often talk over a problem. I tell him what I think; he tells me what he thinks.
>
> Relations with supervision are much better. They cooperate good and they help you out. In the old mill the foreman was always nagging you. They don't do that here. And they listen to what you have to say. I figure a man who's worked on a job a long time, the way I have, knows more about it than anybody. Knows more than the boss. Now on No. 4, if supervision asks you what's wrong with something, you can give him your idea of it. And he'll listen to you and be glad to get it. On the old mills, on No. 1, it wasn't like that. Something don't work right, you tell the foreman what you think is wrong, he says, "Oh, no, no, couldn't be, you're crazy." And then he goes and tells the superintendent what you tell him. Or maybe he does nothing about it. So after a while, when you get slapped down that way, you say to hell with him. Then you don't make any suggestions. You think if management don't care, you don't care. So you just put in your time.

On the earnings, the men had a uniform reaction, represented by the following comments:

> I was making a lot more money in No. 1. They should have us on bonus now. I know they are not signaling me to drop more billets out of the furnace because the piercer figures he ain't going to break his back for nothing.
>
> Coming over to No. 4 has made me lose a lot of money. I knew it when I came, but I thought by six months they would have jobs and bonus straightened out.
>
> The big gripe that men have now is bonus. Here is their opinion: "Why the hell should we work ourselves to death for their benefit?"

In general, there was an enthusiastic response to the physical conditions of the new mill, particularly as it contrasted with the old one. The following comments are representative of this sentiment:

> Tremendous improvement. It's clean, light, and safe. In the old mill it's so dark you can hardly see across the building in the daylight. In No. 4, it's as if you were out of doors, it's so light.

It's like living in a small, dark bedroom for years and then going into a nice big light bedroom. You would never want to go back to the old hole.

Conditions in the new mill were not regarded as ideal by any means. There were widespread complaints about the smoke that rose out of one of the work operations, but nearly all the men who complained about the smoke also said that management was doing everything it could to correct the condition. Apparently an adverse physical condition can be accepted by the men as long as they feel that management is aware of it and trying to do something about it.

Sentiments toward possibilities of job progression and promotion into supervision were predominantly negative. Since the average job classification in the new mill was lower than in the old, since there were fewer jobs, and since the spread from bottom to top classification was less, the men concluded that the chances of progress within the work ranks were reduced. They saw—and probably correctly—that they had less chance now for promotion into supervision. The new technology seemed to put a premium on college trained engineers for supervisory jobs.

How did the men view such a technological change as it affected working people? At this time, only two out of the twenty-two men interviewed (eleven men each on the two shifts then running) looked upon such changes as good for working people, without any qualification. Five of the workers expressed mixed reactions. It was all right for the men who had the new jobs, but what about people who were laid off because of these technological changes? Two-thirds of the men took a strong negative position. They saw the technological improvements as bad because they meant fewer jobs and too low a share of the gains of technological improvements to the workers.

## PAY AND PRODUCTION

While the men going into the new mill had expected to lose money for a time, they had not expected to wait almost two years for the incentive to be established. Over this period of time, the incentive became an increasingly pressing issue between workers and management.

From January to October, 1949, the production record showed marked fluctuations but a steady upward trend. After fluctuating between 70 and 85 pieces per hour for four months, production rose rapidly in September and early October to hit a peak of 100. The national steel strike intervened at this point. When work began again in November, the production curve, starting somewhat below 100, shot up rapidly to 110. While this was still far below the capacity management anticipated for the mill, the marked upward trend seemed to promise the end of the difficulties.

Production stabilized for three more months at slightly over 100, but the next movement was sharply down. In early March, 1950, production dropped to 80 an hour. The superintendent interpreted this as a concerted slowdown by the men, designed to pressure management into introducing the incentive. After meeting with higher management, the superintendent called in representatives of the local union and urged them to take action against the slowdown. At the same time, he promised that the incentive would be installed within six weeks. The union leaders responded by calling meetings of the mill crews to present to them management's pledge and also to ask them to raise production. The committeemen followed this with talks to each individual worker.

The result was that production bounced up just as rapidly as it had dropped—but only half way up—to 90.

Why did it take so long for management to introduce the incentive system? The industrial engineers quite naturally insisted that they were not in a position to set a sound rate until the mill was operating "normally," but what did "normally" mean? The men were prepared to suffer some losses for a period of time—perhaps six months—while they and management were learning how to operate the new plant and the engineers were making their studies. But the engineers felt that they could not base a sound rate upon studies made at a time when the mill was not operating properly. Therefore, they could hardly be ready with the new rate just as soon as the operating bugs were worked out of the mill. They claimed that they needed some months of reasonably smooth operation in order to carry on an adequate study. But when the major production difficulties were worked out of the mill, the workers quite naturally were not inclined to test out its potentialities to the fullest extent. They were holding back for the incentive to be set, and their holding back created further difficulties for the engineers in estimating what the rate should be.

On May 5, 1950, within the time promised at the March meeting, management presented its proposed rate to the officers of the local union. They responded by asking that management delay the installation of the rate until they had had a chance to refer it to specialists in the office of the international union.

On May 13, the crews of the new mill met with the local union officers. Representatives of other departments were also present, since the decision involved was seen to have wide implications. The outcome of the meeting was a decision to oppose the incentive plan. There were four major complaints leveled against it:

1. The plan called for reduction of crew size from eleven to nine men and the redistribution of the responsibilities of the men. This meant that six men would be dropped out of the mill. Management argued that this would make it possible to provide a more attractive incentive for those who remained. The workers would have none of this argument. They demanded that the old crews remain intact.

2. The men argued for more credit in the formula for delay time (time when the machines were down).

3. The union proposed that crane operators and maintenance men be included in the incentive, since they actually worked in the mill and contributed indirectly to its production.

4. The union asked for a better rate on heavy wall pipe, which did not move through the process so rapidly.

There followed a series of meetings between union and management at which these points were argued. Disagreements over this particular incentive plan led also to a discussion of the objections the international union was currently raising over the basic principles of the company's incentive programs in general.

At this point, the discussions bogged down, and no further union-management meetings on the incentive were held for a four-month period. During this time, production dropped gradually so that by early October it was down close to eighty, the point it had reached in the concerted slowdown of the previous March.

On September 28, local management again took the initiative, this time at a higher level, meeting with the union staff and district representatives. That meeting and events immediately following are described in this way by Walker:

Management offered to act upon two of the issues which appeared as major stumbling blocks: reduction in the size of the work group on each turn from eleven to nine under the incentive plan application; non-coverage by the plan of certain indirect workers. Management offered to train the six men for jobs of equal pay and to install a supplementary incentive plan to cover the jobs of hot mill crane man, billet crane man, and billet follower.

Union officers were receptive to the proposals, and the union's staff representative remarked: "This is the most generous offer I have ever heard the company make!"

What happened when this company proposal was brought by the union's leaders to our group is of great interest. The group rejected it flatly, against the union's advice. The union's staff representative reported back to management: "I have talked to the men and then to their committeeman, and they will not accept the proposal. They argue that 'taking care' of the men is not a solution. *No one*, they insist, should be eliminated."

Abandoning hope of a negotiated settlement, management now announced that the new incentive formula would go into effect on October 16. The management people recognized a risk of a strike, but they decided to take the risk. The superintendent called meetings with each crew and with the supervisors of each crew to explain the incentive formula. The union committeeman was present at each meeting. The reaction of the men is reported to have varied between hostility and curiosity about the possibilities of the incentive.

When October 16 came, the men did not walk out. One man describes their response in this way:

It was the men themselves that really started up production. They (management) put the incentive in last October, and then for about a month nobody thought they could put out anything. Then we started on No. 1 turn.

I guess it must have been the piercer operator, because he can control the speed more than anybody else. He decided to start moving a little faster. First thing you know, that crew saw they could make some bonus. Then my crew went along and pushed it. We got a little competition going between each other and then the third turn came in. I can't say the foremen or anybody in management told us exactly that we might as well give it a try, but it was the men themselves that really decided.

It is interesting to note that production started to jump only a week after the incentive came in—not a month as the worker said. Apparently the men liked to visualize themselves as holding out longer against management than actually was the case, and this colored their recollections.

Within two months production had gone over 140 an hour, and in late 1951 it leveled off between 150 and 160 an hour. As production rose in this manner, complaints on earnings subsided, though the men continued to note minor complaints regarding the incentive formula.

## CHANGES IN INTERACTION, ACTIVITIES, AND SENTIMENTS

The second round of intensive interviewing took place in the spring of 1951, about six months after the incentive system had been installed, and when productivity was fluctuating between 130 and 155 pieces an hour. However, there were still at times serious delays due to machine breakdown, and other sources of irritation between men and management, as we shall see.

To what extent had the men's sentiments changed, compared with the first period of interviewing? And how did these changes relate to changes in activities and interactions?

Regarding the job itself, certain reactions remained the same while others changed. The men continued to view the job as much lighter physically than their previous jobs—with the single exception of one of the men who had a good deal of manual work to perform and found it more difficult with this heavier production load. The mental aspects of the job were still emphasized, but the nervous tension seemed to have subsided. With experience, the men gained confidence in their ability to handle the automatic process, and they stopped worrying about it.

In the second period, the men were still physically isolated, but the social isolation had been modified. They had learned to use the public address system—and not only for emergency communication and technical problems. A certain amount of casual small talk also went into these channels. It was nothing like the amount of interaction that had prevailed when the men had worked together in small teams, but it was a distinct improvement from the isolation of the early months, and the men expressed satisfaction with the change.

Interviews showed a marked change in interactions between workers and management between the first and second periods. In the period when the mill was breaking in, there had been frequent interactions between the men and management as high up as the superintendent. Now two thirds of the men reported less frequent talks with supervision, with five of these making the distinction that they talked as often as before with the foreman but far less often with the superintendents. The men also reported a change in other aspects of interaction, as the following quotations indicate:

There's just that pressure, pressure, pressure, on the fellows all the time. You have the pressure of the machines and the pressure of the bosses. I just hate to go to work there every day. In the old mills when we knew we were going to have a good run coming up why I just couldn't wait to get in that mill and get things going. On No. 4 I just feel like I'm going in there to a concentration camp every day.

We were a lot closer to supervision when the mill started up. They wanted to help out. They asked us questions and we made suggestions. X (foreman) is one of the only ones who will talk about anything. He's one of the best. I suppose the reason supervision isn't around as much is that they have to get back in the office and do a lot of figuring on setting those rolls and a lot of other problems. They make a mistake, though, in not taking some time to talk to the men.

The higher-ups don't talk to us nearly as often as they used to. It's a funny thing, but they just don't seem to be the good fellows that we thought they were at first. They used to be really interested in the problems and come around and ask our advice. Now it is only when we have a breakdown that they come in and try to push us to get it fixed or give us dirty looks as if they thought it was our fault. A lot of the things that are wrong with that mill can be explained just by the attitude that is now built up between the bosses and the men.

In the second interviewing period, questions about working conditions showed the men much more preoccupied with the smoke than they had been in the first period. Walker describes their reactions in this way:

Only one worker still said unequivocally that working conditions were better. Six said they were better except for the smoke. Ten, in discussing working conditions, spoke only or chiefly of the smoke. Some of these felt so bitterly that the words "working conditions" provoked expression of general hostility to the company:
"I just can't stand that smoke, and I know the day is going to come when we say 'to hell with the contract' and pick up and walk out of the mill."

Regarding their chances of promotion, the men remained as pessimistic as in the first period. As to whether the development of such new mills was good for the working men, these workers were still concerned about possible unemployment and about what they considered the unfair share they received in the advantages of technological change. Perhaps they were particularly sensitive on this point because late in the second period one of the old mills was shut down; since the workers in that mill were in the same seniority unit with the new mill, some of these top seniority men from the old mill came in to bump out of the new mill men who had been on their jobs from the beginning. This naturally had an unsettling effect even for those who remained on the job.

Regarding pay, the men expressed a great deal more satisfaction, although they continued to complain about certain technical features of the incentive plan.

By the time of the third round of interviews in late 1952, we might say that a reasonably stable equilibrium had been reached. While during the second period production was fluctuating sharply between 130 and 155 an hour, in the third period the fluctuations were less sharp, and productivity was running between 160 and 180 per hour. Management people were now satisfied that the mill was operating at top efficiency. The men were now earning more than they had thought possible in the early months at the plant, and they were taking increased pride in their ability to get the maximum out of this plant.

According to Walker:

As to the "automatics as such," there were many comments reiterating the same sense of satisfaction and adjustment we found at the time of the second round of interviews. But a new refinement of worker knowledge and skill had added an ironical twist to the whole question of the automatics. When the mill was operating at high speed, the workers had found a way to run it faster—and hence earn a larger bonus—*on manual rather than on automatic.*

As one worker explained:

The engineers designed that mill to run automatic at a certain speed. When we go above that speed, the equipment prevents us from going any faster, because there are automatic kickoffs. So we have to throw it on manual if we want to reach really high speed, because throwing it into manual prevents the automatic kickoffs from working.

In the third period, the men reported far less "pressure" on them from management than they had noted in the second period. Negative sentiments toward individuals were no longer so strongly expressed, but the workers did express criticisms that are of some interest to us, as these three examples indicate:

At first supervision had to talk more with us because more things were going wrong. As a matter of fact *now* there are a lot of things they *could* ask us about—but they don't, and we're not going to tell them unless they do.

I think that we get along pretty good with our foreman. Of course his trouble is that he won't take any chances on things, and there are a lot of times when if he would ask us we could tell him whether he could take a chance or not. But that's one of the troubles with all those fellers out there—they don't ask us enough.

The foremen get along pretty good, but the men don't like the superintendent because he never asks what our opinion is about what went wrong. That's true of some of the others as well. And if they're not going to ask us, we're not going to tell them. So *the only time we let somebody know is when it might affect our production record.*

Regarding changing sentiments toward working conditions, Walker presents this summary:

> When the men first came to work on No. 4 mill, a whole series of fine features about their new work environment aroused their enthusiasm, and presumably explained in part a fairly good crew morale. The smoke was mentioned as almost the only blemish or exception to good working conditions.
>
> By the time of the second round the good factors were about half extinguished, psychologically speaking, by the one bad feature.
>
> By the time of the third round the good features were wholly extinguished. The men affected talked only of the one thing they hated, the smoke.

The third period study did not show any changes in interactions and sentiments among the workers themselves and in sentiments toward promotion and technological change generally.

## CONCLUSION

Any technological change, and particularly a change toward automation, involves movement from the known into the unknown. Just what the nature of the new jobs is to be cannot be visualized in any detail in advance.

Since the new jobs call for different types of skill, it is difficult to evaluate them and set wage rates on them on the basis of standards that were developed for the old jobs. Incentive rates present an even more difficult problem. If men accustomed to receiving incentive pay go on jobs at hourly rates substantially below their former earnings, they naturally want incentives to be applied as soon as possible. They recognize that incentives cannot be applied to the job immediately, that the industrial engineers must allow for time to provide experience for the men with the new machines and processes. Adequate studies can only be made when operations are running smoothly, but it may take many months on a radically new process to reach this point. As soon as operations begin to run smoothly, workers can see no reason for a further delay of installation of incentives, whereas the industrial engineers are just beginning their studies.

The ambiguity regarding the nature of the jobs provided for particular difficulties at the time management announced its incentive plan. The eleven men on each crew had naturally been thinking of an incentive to apply to an eleven-man crew. The incentive program applied to a crew of nine involved some redistribution of job functions, but more importantly, it threatened to drop out of the plant two of the men in each crew who had worked with it from the beginning. Over the months, working together and interacting together (even with reduced frequencies) the men came to look upon themselves as a crew and to build up sentiments of identification toward each other. An attack on any member of the crew became in their eyes an attack on the crew itself. This led them to resist strongly the proposal that crew size be reduced by two men.

When management offered no special provisions to meet the problems of the men to be dropped, the union leaders stood firmly behind the men in the mill. When management finally came forward with its promise to provide for the men in comparable jobs elsewhere, union leaders whose interactions and sentiments led them to see problems in terms of the broader perspective of the works as a whole could no longer see the crew size issue as one worth fighting about.

The workers themselves, even at the eleventh hour, rejected the management proposal verbally and by vote, but they accepted it in fact as it was put into operation. Why did they not express their sentiments in some drastic action such as a mill strike or a slowdown?

Several factors seem to have been involved in the *de facto* acceptance of the new rate.

1. Worker negative sentiments had been modified by management's promise to take care of the two men in each crew who were displaced. Accepting management's proposal now seemed no longer such an act of treason to fellow workers.

2. The risks of resistance now seemed much greater. Until management made the offer noted above, the men could count on the support of the international union. Now this support seemed to be withdrawn. Furthermore, the international union was in the midst of its annual contract negotiations, so that a local crisis would have been most unwelcome.

3. The men had already been making sacrifices for many months. Losing the possible gains of incentive earnings was a very concrete sacrifice. Less tangible but also important was the additional effort required of the men by the slowdown. It was actually easier to operate the equipment at the speed for which it had been planned.

We find worker sentiments toward people with whom they interact markedly affected by this interaction, whereas sentiments on other matters are much less closely tied to interaction.

In the first interviewing period, worker sentiments toward management, from foremen to superintendents, were highly favorable. At this time, there was frequent interaction of workers with these management individuals. There also developed a reciprocity in the initiation of activities between workers and management. Management people suggested actions to be taken by workers, and workers suggested actions to management people.

In the second period, worker sentiments toward management had become markedly less cordial, although some favorable reaction to the foremen remained. During this period, there was much less interaction between workers and management, particularly in those relations with members of management above the foremen. The workers also complained of the pressures they were under. This seemed to mean two things: that management people were no longer responsive to their criticisms and suggestions, and that management people had become more active in taking initiative toward them. Management people were also taking a more negative view of the workers, and worker perception of these negative sentiments tended to stir up a corresponding reaction from workers.

In the third period there seemed to be no change in the frequencies of interaction and no change in the ability of workers to initiate for management, but there was a marked reduction in what they called pressures from management. Sentiments at this time had become less negative toward management, but there were still pointed comments to the effect that the workers had much to contribute to plant operations that management people were not interested in and were not receiving.

It is interesting to note to what extent these interactional changes are related to technology and the progress of production. At the outset, the plant was as much of an unknown quantity to management as it was to the workers. To be sure, management had a detailed knowledge of the engineering aspects of the plant that workers did not possess, but day after day new and unanticipated operating problems came up. Not having the answers to these problems themselves, management people naturally asked for the help of the workers. Furthermore, until some of the initial production problems were worked out, there was nothing more important for foreman, assistant superintendent, and superintendent to do than to pay close attention to these problems and to seek help from the workers in solving them.

By the second period, the basic production problems seemed to have been worked out, but the long worker slowdown had just come to an end. Even as production rose, management people felt that the workers were not beginning to reach the potentialities of the plant. These negative sentiments led to a withdrawal of the higher management from the plant floor and particularly to a blocking of the channel of upward communication from workers to management.

In the third period, as Walker puts it, "The mill is rolling." At last the technology was paying off in terms of management expectations. As far as machines and automatic processes went, there was no need for management people to seek out interaction with workers and they felt no need to call upon them for help. The workers felt this change in the relaxation of "pressure" from above, but they continued to react negatively to the interaction frequencies that were so much lower than in the earlier period.

Worker reaction to working conditions over the three periods suggests that there is a tendency for workers to become accustomed to the favorable aspects of working conditions and come to take them for granted. The unfavorable aspects do not seem to be so readily taken for granted and may in fact increase in their impact over time. Such unfavorable aspects may come to symbolize worker-management relations. The smoke condition remained the same throughout, but at first the men could say that management was trying to do something about it. In fact, Walker points out that management was experimenting with different methods of control of the smoke problem throughout the period under study, but the fact that the condition did not change much seems to have led the workers to feel that management was not very concerned about it.

The men's opinions regarding their prospects for upgrading and promotion remained the same throughout a three-year period. Was this simply a recognition of the realities of the situation? Walker argues that this cannot be the complete explanation. To be sure, opportunities for upgrading and promotion within the mill were restricted, but the men were part of a much larger seniority unit that would have enabled them to bid into higher classifications in other mills and to seek promotion elsewhere. Apparently the men tend to evaluate their opportunities primarily in terms of their immediate working environment.

The same comment can be made regarding the men's reaction to the question of the benefits of technological change for workers. Management might well argue that technological change, in the long run, raises the standard of living of workers and provides new and better jobs as fast as it eliminates the old ones. Here again the workers judged primarily from their immediate environment. They saw themselves—just nine of them—putting out four times as much production as had been produced by a twenty-five-man crew in the old mills. In terms of that experience, technological change seemed to mean more production and fewer jobs; more money for management, less for workers.

Both on the questions of the prospects for up-grading and the benefits of technological change, we see that worker sentiments were not directly related to their interactions with management people. Interactions changed while sentiments on these broad questions remained stable.

Let us now put these conclusions in more general form.

Considering interactions and activities between workers and management we can make this statement: When there is a marked decline in the frequency of interaction between workers and management people, and when this is accompanied by a marked decline in the frequency of workers initiating activity for management people, then we can expect workers' sentiments toward management to become more negative.

Regarding interaction and identification sentiments within the work group: Individuals who interact frequently with each other are more likely to develop sentiments of positive identification with each other than are other individuals (union leaders, for example) whose interactions with them are much less frequent.

Regarding the relationship between technology and management interactions and activities: As the technical problems of technology and process become resolved and the operation becomes more routinized, management interactions with workers can be expected to decline in frequency, and the management people are likely to be less responsive to attempted initiations of activity from workers.

Regarding the relationship between sentiments and economic symbols, we see contrasting reactions on the part of workers and management people. Workers tend to regard their customary earnings as appropriate —until they improve—and are inclined to think that any sacrifice of earnings can only be justified on a short-run basis. Management people make a sharper distinction than do workers between base pay and incentive pay. Management people are likely to assume that workers have no *right* to anything beyond their base pay. The incentive must be justified in engineering terms before it is offered. Since the institution of an incentive system for a new operation is likely to take more time than workers will accept as appropriate for their sacrifice in earnings, these differing sentiments regarding time and economic symbols create the kind of clash we have been examining.

## Collateral Readings

MANN, FLOYD C., and HOFFMAN, L. RICHARD. *Automation and the Worker.* New York: Henry Holt and Co., Inc., 1960.

This study compares worker reactions to the job situation in two power stations, one of them an automated type.

WALKER, CHARLES R. *Toward the Automatic Factory.* New Haven, Conn.: Yale University Press, 1957.

———, and GUEST, ROBERT H. *The Man on the Assembly Line.* Cambridge, Mass.: Harvard University Press, 1952.

———, ———, and TURNER, ARTHUR N. *The Foreman on the Assembly Line.* Cambridge, Mass.: Harvard University Press, 1956.

The Yale Technology Project has taken the lead in exploring the human impact of technology.

## Discussion Questions

8    1. Suppose you were a restaurant manager, what steps would you take to reduce friction along the flow of work? More specifically, what would you do about friction between checkers and waitresses?

8    2. What seem to be the personality requirements of the job of waitress? Of hostess? What evidence would indicate a lack of fit between personality and the job?

9    3. Was Tom Walker a good foreman? Discuss.

9    4. Some students have classified foreman as "employee oriented" (concerned with motivation of workers and with his personal relations with them) or "production oriented" (concerned with output and technical aspects of job). Would you say Tom Walker was employee oriented or production oriented? Discuss.

9      5. Should it have been possible for Tom Walker's superiors to anticipate the difficulties he would find himself in in 1950? What knowledge would have been necessary in order to make such a prediction? How much was actually known by his superiors?

10      6. Consider the position of gaffer in the Benton plant. What special problems does he face by virtue of that position? What kinds of activities and interactions are required of him if he is to build up the support of team members? How did historical changes affect his position? What, if anything, could management do to strengthen that position?

10      7. Gaffer is a common type of position in industry, the job holders being known variously as working supervisor, group leader, straw boss, etc. Assume you are studying a different work situation where this type of position exists. Would you expect the man in this position to face the same problems encountered by the gaffer at Benton? Discuss.

11      8. The barrel department and motor line may both be known as assembly lines. Between the two departments, compare the jobs of worker. Of foreman. What similarities and differences do you see?

12      9. Compare the jobs of a first-line supervisor in a restaurant dining room, barrel department, glass blowing plant, motor line, and Hi-Test plant. What similarities and differences do you note? What does your answer suggest regarding the selection and training of supervisors? In order to make your comparisons systematic, you should put down the various dimensions along which you are making your comparisons. You will then find that a given case does not provide you with all the information you would like to have on one or more of these dimensions. Suppose you were making an analysis of the supervisor's job in one of these situations, for the purpose of understanding the problems the job holder might find in it. What further information (beyond what is in this book) should you have? Why would it be needed?

12      10. Why did Joe Sloan walk off the job? (Note that we are not asking why he was dissatisfied with his job. He had been dissatisfied for a long time. He walked off only once.)

12      11. Everyone agreed that the tri-iso-butylene run at Hi-Test plant had not been handled well. How should foreman Tom Lloyd have gone about it? What does your answer to that specific question suggest about the principles that should govern introduction of changes into organizations?

13      12. On the basis of the tube mill case, what seem to you the main human problems involved in the introduction of major technological change? How was each problem handled? In what ways, if any, could the handling have been improved?

13      13. Compare the installation of the automatic tube mill with the relatively minor change involved in the tri-iso-butylene run. Do the same principles of administration apply to both cases? Or are you dealing with different phenomena?

13      14. People often speak of "morale" as referring roughly to the sentiments men have toward their work situations. We see in these

chapters that men have sentiments toward a number of aspects of the work situation. Suppose you were asked to make a comprehensive analysis of the sentiments of workers toward their work situation in a given department. How would you classify such sentiments (sentiments toward what, in other words)? Would you expect a favorable sentiment toward one aspect of the work situation to be associated with a favorable sentiment toward another aspect of that situation? For example, if you know a man's sentiments toward his pay, would you be able to predict his sentiments toward his foreman? On the basis of your classification of sentiments and your analysis of the combination of sentiments found in each chapter of Part III, what do you suggest regarding the use of the term "morale"?

# PART IV   Union-Management Relations

SINCE unions have been involved in a number of cases already discussed, it has been impossible for us to ignore them. So far we have kept unions in the background of our story, but in Part IV we will bring them into the foreground and seek to give them systematic attention.

In a sense the union may be considered as part of the formal organization structure of the plant, for it has its own officially established positions and activities, which interlock closely with the positions and activities of the management organization. Most local unions are also part of larger labor organizations which are entirely independent of local management. For present purposes, our focus of interest will be on the union in its relations with its members in the plant and with members of the management organization.

"Enter the Union" examines the conditions and events that tend to promote or retard a unionization drive in a local situation. "Who Goes Union and Why?" seeks to explain the varying responses of workers during that particular unionization drive—why some men were for, some against, and others on the fence, and how changing situations changed voting intentions of some men.

It has often been noted that a given union-management relationship tends to change as the union wins recognition and the parties then gain experience in dealing with each other. This process of change is explored in "The Evolution of Union-Management Relations."

We find that the quality of union-management relations is not uniform throughout the plant. Some departments never seem to give rise to "trouble," whereas other work groups are constantly involved in maneuvering and putting pressure on management. We will examine such inter-departmental comparisons in "Work Group Cohesion and Union-Management Relations."

Collective bargaining is ordinarily thought to be in the fields of economics and law. So it is, and yet we find important human relations aspects to explore in "The Collective Bargaining Process."

Having considered various aspects of our subject, in "Patterns of Union-Management Relations" we seek to present a systematic framework for the analysis of the two interlocking organizations.

Our discussion so far has been limited to local situations. In "Human Problems of Large Scale Bargaining" we speculate as to how our knowledge of the local situation may help us to understand some of the great industrial relations crises of our times.

# Chapter 14 *ENTER THE UNION*

WE HAVE already met with unions in this book, for it has been impossible to discuss the response of workers to their environment without getting into some discussion of union activities. Up to now, unions have been an incidental part of our discussion. In Part IV of this book, unions and union-management relations will be our main focus of attention.

Why do workers join unions? I shall not seek to answer that question in general terms. The meaning of the union to workers can best be demonstrated by observing workers as they react to a union organization drive. In my first study in industry in 1942–43, I had the good fortune to spend five months, two to three days a week, with workers and management people of Blank Oil Company at a time when the Oil Workers International Union (CIO) was seeking to organize the workers of Hi-Test Plant and other surrounding installations in the city. I make no claim that this is a typical case, but we shall see that it involved many of the forces that actually do come to bear in such situations.

We have already met Hi-Test and Blank Oil Company in Oil City through our story of Joe Sloan. Joe will be one of the characters in this story, but a minor one, as we concentrate upon groups in conflict instead of upon the conflicts faced by any one particular individual.

This was the third attempt of the CIO union to organize the workers in this area. The two earlier attempts had won some supporters but had fallen far short of success. This third attempt culminated in a representation election in April, 1943, which the CIO union narrowly lost. Both workers and management people agreed that the union would have won if the election had been held just a few weeks earlier. With the decision thus hanging in the balance during the time of my field study, I had the opportunity to observe the forces that moved men for or against the union.

Why did the CIO union come so close to wining in 1943 when earlier drives had failed to provide any serious challenge to management's control? To answer this question, we need to look back upon the state of human relations in the organization in an earlier era.

## IN THE "GOOD OLD DAYS"

In the early days of the company, problems of supervision were relatively simple. Even in the manufacture of natural gasoline, where scientific knowledge was constantly applied to the processes, operations were of a rather routine nature. Men who had worked in the old type gasoline plants told me that an experienced worker in such an establishment required very little supervision. The operations of one day were just like those of the preceding day. Frequently the men would not see their immediate supervisor inside the plant from one day to the next. This, of course, minimized the opportunities for conflict over supervision.

In this stage of the company's development, both supervisors and men had the same social backgrounds. The supervisors were men who had worked their way up through the ranks, demonstrating their capacities on the job. The workers knew that a man who showed talent in handling men and equipment could look forward to graduating into supervision. No technical education was required. There was no sharp social line drawn between the men and their supervisors, and there were many social activities, such as picnics and stag parties, in which they all participated, looking upon themselves simply as fellow employees of Blank Oil Company.

Even for those who did not graduate into supervision, there was a road to distinction gained through long and loyal service to the company. The man who had been with the organization from its start—or shortly thereafter—enjoyed a special prestige and came to look upon it as his company. The executives cultivated this feeling of loyalty through awarding service badges of increasing distinction for each five years in the company's service. The long-time employee enjoyed a job security which was almost absolute. He could not be discharged by his foreman or plant superintendent, and the executives were careful to protect his interests in cases involving discrimination by those in immediate authority.

The great strength of the company's personnel work in this era was its informality. There was no special personnel department. The executives in the main office took pride in remaining in personal touch with their employees in the field. Long after the organization had become too large for its founder to keep up the personal contacts, the Natural Gasoline Department maintained those ties through General Superintendent of Field Operations Fred Fitzgerald.

As one worker put it:

All the men loved Fred. Any man that would work for the company a year, Fred knew him by his first name, and he knew something about him. When he came through the plant, he would stop and talk to the men. Then we used to have big picnics every summer. He would come down carrying some old clothes in a suit case. He would go off behind a tree and get into those old clothes and play ball with the boys. . . . You never heard anything about unions around here when Fred was alive.

Another man had this to say:

Fred Fitzgerald used to come around to these plants often. Yes, several times a year until a little while before his death, when the company was getting so big that he couldn't get around so much. He knew most of the men. He had grown up from ditch digger with the company. He would come around and ask you how your wife and kids were. He would know how many children you had, and if they had been sick, he would know about it. If you ever wanted to go see him, you could go up to his office and you could talk to him for an hour or two hours. He would never hurry you. If your story was right, you could depend on him to do something for you. If it wasn't right, he found out about it.

I will never forget one meeting where Fitzgerald spoke to us. There was some trouble in that field and the men were getting organized into a union. He called a meeting and he talked to us like this: "God damn it," he says, "What the hell do you guys want a union for? If you have some grievance, tell me and we'll fix it." After that the men got right up and cussed back at him. That's what he wanted. He wanted them to talk and they knew it. When a man would make some complaint, Fred would turn to the superintendent and say, "Why hasn't this been taken care of? Let's get some action on it."

From the standpoint of his living memory among the men, Fred Fitzgerald died just at the right time. In the last few years of his life, the company was expanding so rapidly that Fred was seen in Oil City less and less. In this era, he personally was the connecting link between the main office and the Oil City workers. A few years more of organizational growth might have strained this personal link to the breaking point.

So the era came to an end in 1939 with the funeral of Fred Fitzgerald in the main office city. At the time of the funeral, it was only with the greatest difficulty that local supervisors were able to persuade enough men to remain on their jobs to keep the operations going. From Oil City and in fact from all over the holdings of Blank Oil Company in the Natural Gasoline Department, the workers travelled at their own expense to the main office city to participate in the largest and most impressive funeral the town had ever known. Their grief at the loss was genuine and deep.

What would take the place of this communication channel between workers and higher management?

## THE COMPANY UNION

Several years before Fitzgerald's death and in response to an earlier CIO organization drive, management had given birth to a company union. How did the company union look to the men? The following picture was given to me by a man who was a representative of the company union in its early period:

The company called a big meeting of all of the men. The superintendents were there. They told us the organization was all ours. We could do with it whatever we wanted to. It was all their idea. The men hadn't any idea of starting an organization. For about a year and a half we held monthly meetings in the club house. The company would put up refreshments, and they furnished entertainment. We had some nice programs. We would get a hundred or a hundred-fifty out to each meeting. We set up a lot of committees and we were working on them. We did not have any grievances at that time.

We were well-satisfied, but we were just trying to work things out for the betterment of the men and for the company too. The superintendents did not hear nothing of it for a while and I guess they got suspicious so in one of our meetings all the superintendents and the division superintendent too came up. They held the floor for the whole meeting. There wasn't much that the men could say. They just told us that we should take more of an interest in the company. We had been taking an interest in the company. But they did not know what we were doing so they were suspicious. They told us that after that meeting the superintendents would have to come to every meeting. That really broke it up. I don't remember; we may have had a meeting or two after that, but we never got any real attendance. It was the company's fault. The company killed that company union.

The Hi-Test company union representative made these comments:

That company union is all right in a way. You can really get things with it when the (CIO) union puts on the pressure. It can't get anything when the company is not afraid of the CIO.

There was one man here that used to be a representative in the company union, and one time the superintendent called him into his office and told him, "You are spending too much time on that company union. I think you would be better off if you spent your nights home with your family." (He was referring to the man previously quoted.)

Our first informant tells us that management killed the company union in its early stages. Insofar as widespread membership participation and interest was concerned, this seems to be true, but as a paper organization—with occasional bursts of activity by some of its officers— the company union lived on and was to play an important role in the representation election of 1943.


## THE MASTERS CRACK-DOWN

Ed Masters took over the position of general superintendent of field operations upon the death of Fred Fitzgerald in 1939.

It would have been difficult for any man to step into the shoes of Fitzgerald, especially during this period of rapid expansion. The task was made doubly difficult by the nature of the situation which had developed in Oil City.

The company's operations there were marked by an exceptional laxity of supervision. The superintendent in charge was a competent gasoline man but an inveterate gambler. For months he had been organizing crap games in tool sheds, warehouses, and other secluded spots. With the encouragement of the superintendent, gambling activities grew completely out of control, and large numbers of men were neglecting their jobs to roll the dice.

The stealing of gasoline was also a problem. It had become a time-honored custom for men throughout the industry to help themselves to the gasoline they needed to run their cars. There was, of course, a rule against this practice, but the supervisors made no attempt to enforce the rule, and the employees, like human beings everywhere, judge rules more by the behavior they experience and observe than by official notices. There had been two cases of men being fired on this charge, but when the cases had been appealed, Fred Fitzgerald, in consideration for the long years of service of the culprits, had simply given them a warning and transferred them to another area.

The new general superintendent of field operations was sent in to clean up this situation. Since he had been working in another area, he had no personal ties to link him with the men in Oil City. He was entirely an unknown quantity to them.

The general superintendent's first move was to warn his immediate subordinate that the gasoline stealing practice was to be stopped. The response to this was the posting of warning notices in the plants. Some of the men took the notices seriously and stopped taking gasoline. One of them told me, "I figured that this time the company meant business." Others did not take this notice any more seriously than earlier ones which had made the same announcement.

Suddenly the blow fell. Seven men were caught stealing gasoline and were fired. The superintendent and the district superintendent were fired, and the top man in Oil City, the division (state) superintendent was transferred. Men who were completely unknown to the workers were brought in as plant superintendent and district and division superintendents.

The disruptive effects of this blow were impressive and far-reaching. Rumors of continued crack-down ran wild through the working force. There was endless speculation as to the character and policies of the new management people. The reorganization was so sudden and complete that for some days there were a number of employees who did not know to whom they were responsible and what they were supposed to do. There was a general feeling that the firings marked the end of an era of easy-going, friendly control in favor of harsh, impersonal action.

The workers took up a collection to pay for sending their company union representatives to the main office to plead with General Superintendent Masters that the seven workers be put back on their jobs. As one member of the delegation reported to me:

> We talked it over for a day and a half and finally he (Masters) agreed to put four of those men back to work. They did not go back on the same classifications so they really lost some, and those other men didn't go back at all. When we came home, we thought we had accomplished something, but when we talked to the men, we began to think we didn't do so much. They thought we had sold out. All those men should have been put back to work.

It must have seemed to the general superintendent that in view of the serious nature of the charges, he was leaning over backward to be lenient with the men; therefore, they should be satisfied. This view, however, overlooks the unsettling effects of the crack-down upon the organization of human relations in Oil City. The men had become accustomed to getting along with their superintendent, and they had built up ties of work cooperation and friendship with the employees who were fired. It took some time to become accustomed to the new supervisors and to the absence of old employees. The social situation was so disturbed that it is difficult to conceive of any settlement the company union representatives might have obtained that would have satisfied the men. One of the results of the trip, therefore, was to weaken the company union by making many of the men feel that they could not serve as representatives without being suspected of selling out the workers' interests.

Masters' first personal appearance in his new position in Oil City did nothing to reassure the men. He called a meeting of the local superintendents. At this meeting, one of the superintendents ventured to say something about cooperation with the men. According to both worker and local management informants, Masters stood up, shook the back of his chair angrily and said:

> To hell with cooperation! I don't want cooperation from the men. All I want is a good solid eight hours' work—on their feet.

The last phrase referred to the men's practice of sitting on packing boxes or benches at times during the course of their work. Since the work at Hi-Test, for example, mainly involved watching charts on the wall, the men felt that they could perform this part of the job just as well sitting down as standing up. Apparently Masters believed that sitting down did not constitute working, and the packing boxes and benches were thrown out immediately after this statement. During my five months at Hi-Test, I never once observed one of the workers sitting down except during the thirty-minute lunch period, and even then the men told me that this was probably contrary to Masters' orders, and if he ever visited the plant during the lunch period they would have to see to it that he found them eating lunch on their feet.

While four years had passed since the Oil City shake-up, it still loomed as a major landmark in the history of employee relations in this area. Nearly every man who discussed the causes of discontent with me would, without any prompting, carry his story back to that unsettled time. The shake-up did not leave scars only upon those who had been engaged in gambling and gasoline stealing. Joe Sloan said, "It changed me from a Republican to a Democrat, from anti-union to pro-union— overnight!"

## THE SITUATION AT HI-TEST

For this representation election, the bargaining unit involved over 200 men. Besides the Hi-Test plant, there was in the same plant yard the closely related catalyst plant and an older plant manufacturing natural gasoline. A few miles away there was another gasoline plant, and the company's labor gang was also included in the unit.

There were only seventeen men attached to Hi-Test, so we certainly cannot undertake to explain the whole campaign in terms of Hi-Test. Nevertheless, these men held the highest status jobs in the area and were in a strategic position throughout the struggle so that their experiences and reactions cast light upon the whole process. A further reason for dealing primarily with Hi-Test is that it is from this plant that I have solid research data, whereas my study touched only lightly on other units.

In telling the story of Joe Sloan, we have already covered some of the important factors involved in the struggle over the union at Hi-Test. We need only review them here.

This was a new plant producing by a relatively new process. The workers were not serving under the old-time, up-from-the-ranks foremen, but under technically trained college graduates. The workers who had moved into the plant first were young and ambitious and had fully expected to move up to higher levels.

We have seen how the status of the jobs at Hi-Test declined, and we have seen the ceiling close in against promotion into supervision of non-college men. Given this background, there should be nothing mysterious about the fact that some of the most dissatisfied men employed by the company in Oil City were also the most highly paid men.

While the plant was first staffed entirely without regard to seniority, a few months later half of the original working force was transferred to a new plant of the same type in another area. Positions thus opened up at Hi-Test were then filled according to the regular procedure, primarily upon a basis of seniority. The result was that of the original crew, only the poly operators and two hydro-stillmen remained.

This history accounts for the unusual distribution of seniority and age among the men. Though the average seniority varied insignificantly between poly operators and their subordinates, there were striking differences in the ages of the men at the time of my study. The poly operators averaged thirty-two and a half years, the hydro-stillman thirty-five and a half years, and the fractionator operators almost forty-five years.

This situation meant that the young poly operators had no place to go with supervision being closed to them, and the men at lower levels were discouraged because younger men were ahead of them.

For most of the time up to the entrance of Tom Lloyd in 1942, the Hi-Test plant had been under the supervision of Bill Jones and later, Tom Fitch, both of whom were chemical engineers. While Jones was finishing his college career, he put in some time as a worker in Hi-Test, and the change from worker to foreman made difficulties for him later. Perhaps the most understanding discussion of Jones' problems was furnished me by one operator in these words:

When Jones was on operations, he was no better than the rest of us. We used to have a bench in here and he would spend plenty of time on that bench. Then when we were supposed to clean up, he would just take a mop and push it around the pump and that was all. After he was foreman, one of the first things he had to do was throw that bench out. Now I happen to know that it was orders from the superintendent but the men don't consider that. They just said, "He used to spend more time on that bench than anybody and just as soon as he gets up there he takes it away."

One day I heard the division superintendent criticize the clean-up work. Then the next day Jones was on us for the cleaning up. The men were griping again. They would say, "Of all the lousy clean-up men he was the worst and now that he is up, he is getting after us."

They never should put a man above a group that he has been working with because those men don't like to think of him as a supervisor. It is all right if you send a man away for a couple of years and then bring him back. By that time they can get used to the idea.

I think the university and the company ruined Bill Jones. The university taught him the technical side but it did not teach him anything about handling people. The company put him in charge of operations because he was a smart man. He never could handle the men.

Another worker added, "We teach them (the technical engineers) all they know about operations, and then turn around and boss us."

Both Bill Jones and Tom Fitch delivered their orders down to the last detail. In many cases the men were not told the general objective of their work; they were simply ordered to make certain specified adjustments. Whatever the reasons for this procedure, it tended to reduce the work of the operators to mere mechanical manipulation and discouraged study and initiative.

The foremen went still further to discourage initiative. As one of the men reported:

Suppose you had a suggestion to improve operations. You might take it up with Tom Fitch. Before you got hardly started telling about it, he would begin shaking his head and tell you it was no good.

The men said that they sometimes found that the ideas they had suggested to Jones or Fitch were later put into effect—but they were given no credit for their suggestions. After several experiences of this kind, they stopped making suggestions.

Favoritism was the charge most frequently leveled against Jones and Fitch by the men. As one operator expressed it:

There was one poly operator that could never do anything wrong. That's the way Bill Jones looked at it. He would hold that man up to us as a model. Whenever he had anything new to try out, he would start it on that man's tour. He never gave the rest of us a chance. Now we didn't think that man was any better than we were, so naturally we resented it.

It was well known among the men that Jones and Fitch had confidence in some of them and placed no reliance on others. While he was holding monthly poly operator meetings, Jones used them as a forum to air his

views about the men. At one time he gave the names of three men that
he was "down on" and asked one of the poly operators to tell them of
their precarious position. The poly operator countered by saying that if
Jones had criticisms of his men he should make them to their faces. The
men thoroughly resented talk behind their backs.

One of the men discussed the problem in this way:

> Jones and Fitch used to get down on a man and then they would blame
> everything on him. There was one man here that they really ran off the
> place because he couldn't take it. Then at one time Bill Jones was down on
> X and X couldn't do anything right. Later Fitch was down on Y. It got so
> bad once Y almost hit him with a hammer.

Another man confessed that he had had difficulty restraining himself
from using his fists on Fitch when the foreman was "down" on him.

The men felt that these personal criticisms were unfair. They said that
they were all skilled men, and while they all made mistakes, there were
no operators so inferior to the others that they deserved to be especially
singled out. Furthermore, they felt that the foreman could be mistaken
in fixing personal responsibility because a man's difficulties might arise
from conditions left to him by the operator on the preceding tour. It was
the men's opinion that the foremen simply felt the need of having scape-
goats upon whom they could vent their feelings of irritation over any
operational difficulty.

This situation directly affected the technical side of operations. Tom
Fitch frequently gave detailed orders designed to meet certain operational
specifications. The operators, judging from their long experience with
the equipment, sometimes felt that the stipulated adjustments would not
yield the desired results. Knowing that they would be blamed if the
objective were not attained, the men simply operated the equipment so
as to reach that objective and "boiler-housed" the chart readings. That
is, they put down the readings that Fitch would think correct instead of
those actually obtained. This practice was exceedingly widespread. The
men looked upon it simply as a way of protecting themselves from unfair criticism. As a consequence, while Fitch may have suspected that
the men were "boiler-housing" their readings, he never knew exactly
how the plant was operating. His behavior prevented him from obtaining
the accurate records necessary for scientific experimentation and for
technical improvements in operations.

The men said that the records were falsified for another reason also.
There were certain men who, in order to escape criticism or win the
favor of the foreman, would cover up their own mistakes by recording
fictitious readings but would leave conditions such that their relief
operators were bound to get into difficulties.

Similarly, there were some who, when they got into difficulties, complained to the foreman that the men they relieved had left conditions in
a mess. The men all say that Jones and Fitch encouraged them to make

complaints about their fellow workers. This was one way of gaining favor with the supervisor. It created a problem even for those who did not "squeal" on their fellows, as Joe Sloan commented:

> Tom Fitch used to listen to what the men would say about other operators. He trusted me and so some of the men suspected that I was snitching on them. That is what X thought when Tom got down on him. When I found that out, I got Fitch to tell X the truth, that it wasn't me that squealed. Things like that gave me a lot of trouble.

In this period, Jones and Fitch were also in charge of the catalyst plant. We do not know in detail their effect upon that plant, but one event stands out in the memories of the men there. As a catalyst operator commented:

> When Bill Jones was down here he used to stay until 11 o'clock when we had lunch. Then he would go out. At 11:30 sharp, he would come down here on his bike. He would be off it and come a-running into the plant, before it stopped. He was such a lazy bastard himself, he couldn't believe that other men were not as lazy as he was. One time he called us a bunch of WPA workers. We had a meeting and were trying to get a better classification and get a road out of here. Masters was there too.

Tom Lloyd, who succeeded Fitch as foreman, made this comment:

> You can imagine how that hit the men. That was two years ago, and still sometimes when I try to get a man down here to do a better job, he tells me "What do you expect? I am nothing better than a WPA worker."

## NEW SUPERVISION AT HI-TEST

Had Jones or Fitch been in charge at Hi-Test and in the catalyst plant at the time of the representation election, a CIO victory would have been assured. Recognizing finally the difficulties arising between the men and supervision, management made some strategic replacements in 1942. Tom Lloyd came in as foreman, and Jess Douglas took over as plant manager over Lloyd and over the superintendent at the neighboring gasoline plant. By the time of my study, both Lloyd and Douglas had become popular and respected among the workers.

Tom Lloyd handled his men in a manner entirely different from that used by Jones and Fitch. He began with certain advantages. He was thirty-six years old. Some of his subordinates were older, but half of them were younger. He had not served alongside his men in operations. He gained his experience elsewhere, came in to win a good reputation supervising the catalyst plant, and made the transition to take over the Hi-Test plant without difficulty. He could not be looked upon as an inexperienced youth who had been taught his job by the men he was then called upon to boss.

Lloyd built skillfully upon this foundation. His relations with his men were carried on in an informal, friendly manner. While his predecessors were noted for "throwing their voices," I never heard him talk to his men in anything above a conversational tone.

Lloyd respected the ability of his men and had confidence in their judgment. One operator expressed it this way:

> Tom Lloyd is entirely different from Jones. Bill Jones would come down here and tell us what changes we had to make and that was all. If we could figure out from that what we were making, all right, but he never told us. Tom comes down here and tells us that we have to make a certain product and asks us how we think we ought to go about it. He will say to us, "You fellows know more about this than I do, what do you think?" Of course, he really knows a lot more than we do, but that flatters our egos, and we will figure out with him the way we ought to do it.

This did not mean that the foreman simply let the men run the plant as they saw fit. He set the objective and worked out the plans with them. He carefully checked the operating records of each day, as recorded by the men hour by hour on the Daily Operating Data Sheet. Since the records were no longer "boiler-housed," they furnished him with an accurate picture of operations.

The new foreman did not devote as much time to the details of operations as did Jones or Fitch. Lacking their experience of working on tour in this plant, he was not in a position to provide this detailed supervision. In general, he appeared in the plant only once or twice a day and sometimes not at all. Compared with the great frequency of supervisory activity by Jones and Fitch, this restraint of Lloyd's activity seems to have helped to re-establish the equilibrium of the working group.

The details of operation were not overlooked by the supervisor. They were entrusted to his assistant, Engineer Dan Benton. Since Benton had run tour in Hi-Test, he knew the equipment well. He was able to handle certain problems which could not be dealt with by the operators. For example, at one time one of the fractionating columns was giving a good deal of trouble. To solve the problem, it was necessary to give that column more concentrated attention than the fractionator operator could spare from his other duties. Besides, each operator might have had his special ideas as to what should be done, whereas the problem really required the experimental application of a uniform policy for more than the eight hours spent by any one operator on tour; Benton provided the uniform policy and the careful attention. Nevertheless, he did not simply take the column away from the operator. The problems were freely discussed and on occasion Benton tried out ideas suggested by the operators. When differences of opinion arose between Benton and the operators, I observed points being conceded on both sides. Benton recognized that the men had an intimate familiarity with operations which could not be gained by a technical engineer in a few months of running tour. The men recognized that Benton's technical background enabled him to gain an important perspective on operations which they necessarily lacked.

Bringing these two types of knowledge together on an informal, give-and-take basis was an immense aid toward building harmonious employee relations.

Lloyd checked up on his men in a manner quite different from that used by Jones and Fitch. In discussing with me his use of the Daily Operating Data Sheet, he said,

That sheet is not there primarily for my checking. The purpose of it is to enable the men to know what they are doing. By just looking over that sheet, I can tell how things are going. If something is wrong, I just ask the men to explain it to me. I never try to fix responsibility or say who is to blame. If a man's explanation is weak, he knows it as well as I do. I don't have to tell him. In telling me, he tells himself. That is all that is necessary. These men are very sensitive; they have thin skins, and they take great pride in their work.

Lloyd expected his men to do good work and they wanted to do their best for him. One of them expressed the feelings of the group when he said, "I never wanted to do anything for Bill Jones that I didn't have to do. I'll do anything I can to help Tom Lloyd."

The new management team had smoothed over relations at Hi-Test to a considerable extent. Without question, this served to weaken the interest of the men in the CIO union, but it did not kill their interest altogether. As Joe Sloan and others argued to me, Masters was still in power in the main office. Management's policy was to be good to the men while the CIO threat lasted. If the CIO lost the election, how long would Lloyd and Douglas last in their positions? What was to prevent Masters from sending in other men like Jones and Fitch? We see, therefore, as we have seen before, that the men's relation to the foremen is important but that it does not blot out all concern with higher management.

## THE CAMPAIGN

Since my research was carried on within the plant, I can only give a sketchy picture of union organizational activities outside of the plant. I shall report primarily the impact of the campaign upon developments among men on the job.

The two union organizers held monthly meetings and did a good deal of visiting of the men in their homes. Several company employees became informal organizers for the union, talking it up on the job. However, they distributed no literature inside the plant gates, so far as I could tell. One man just let his friends know that he had literature in his car outside the gate.

The literature passed out by the union emphasized that collective bargaining was a democratic process and pointed to the great gains that had been brought to workers through the labor movement. It also promised higher wages, increased job security, and stricter adherence to seniority in promotions.

These promised benefits did not seem to stir any great enthusiasm among the workers in the Hi-Test plant at least. Since some of these men had moved up very rapidly in classification and pay, wages were the last thing they complained about. In fact, while we can assume that these workers, like any others, would have been glad to have more pay, I found that wages were referred to very seldom in all of the discussions of unions that I heard. In a rapidly growing company, the men were more concerned about new jobs opening up than about losing their jobs. There was, however, a good deal of talk about the Masters crack-down, which involved the discharge of several men.

The seniority issue really cut both ways. Probably a majority of the men were in favor of having promotions follow seniority, but this had been the policy more and more adhered to by the company in recent months. Furthermore, there were a number of men who had risen rapidly because management had disregarded seniority earlier, and these men could hardly be enthusiastic for strict seniority.

The CIO drive seemed to have stalled well short of an assured majority when, at the beginning of February, Masters made his watchman statement, quoted in the chapter on Joe Sloan. Let us now provide the union-management setting into which that statement fitted.

It came at a time when management was negotiating with the company union on wages and several other matters. Lester Harper, company union president, described for me the past history of company union-management negotiations, leading up to the current activities:

In 1941 the men began to think that we had a general increase coming to us. The company union got out petitions and was beginning to circulate them around. Before we got the petitions to the company, we read in the newspapers that we were going to get an increase. Later on in the year, the men thought we had another increase coming and we got out the petitions again. The same thing happened. Before we could get the petitions to the company, we read in the papers that we were getting a second increase . . . Yes, it would have strengthened the company union if the company had gone through us on that.

Last February (1942) I wrote a letter to J. L. Weber (vice-president of the company) saying that the men thought we had another increase coming to us. He wrote back to tell us that he could meet with us to discuss it, but he was very much tied up on priorities and other questions and he would appreciate it if we did not insist on that meeting. He told us we could not get the increase anyway . . . It seems like when the men go up to Weber and he says no, they just back off and don't do nothing more. We just let it ride until August. By that time the cost of living had gone up some more and I wrote him a strong letter saying unless he met with us our representation plan would break down altogether. That was the beginning of these negotiations.

The possibility of the breakup of the company union apparently was not lost on Mr. Weber. Management met sporadically with the company union representatives through the late fall and winter.

The Hi-Test representative in these negotiations was Andy Taylor, a fractionator operator. Poly operator Mark Walling described to me the circumstances of Taylor's election to represent the men:

> Do you know how Andy got elected? They put a ballot box down here and it stayed here for three days without anybody putting any slips in it. Before that when we had to sign up whether we wanted the company union or not only two men out of fifteen voted for the company union and they crossed their names off when they learned they were the only ones. Well after that box had been there for three days, Ed Lester (hydro-stillman) and I got an idea. We took some slips of paper and wrote the name of Andy Taylor on them all, and we signed the different names of the men on all of them and that is how Andy was elected. We never thought he would take it seriously, but he did. Don't ever tell him because I think he doesn't know. Actually, he doesn't represent anybody but himself.

Whomever Taylor represented, by virtue of his election he was included in the negotiating meetings, and thus he became a channel of communication from the Hi-Test plant to the management negotiators and back again.

While the men at Hi-Test had little respect for the intelligence, dependability, or working skill of Taylor, they were naturally interested in whatever he had to report of the negotiations, and presumably some of them gave him suggestions as to things to bring up in the meeting. In fact, it was Andy Taylor who was making the argument for a higher classification for the poly operators when Masters broke up the meeting by calling them a bunch of watchmen (see Chapter 12).

The watchman statement had an immediately disturbing effect within Hi-Test. The day after it was made, the chief engineer of the division happened to drop in at the control room to ask the fractionator operator what was the trouble with the number four fractionating column. The operator replied curtly, "You're the engineer. You're supposed to tell us."

This embarrassed the chief engineer, because he had not the slightest idea what was wrong with the column, and only men who had worked closely with it could have been expected to know. The statement also upset relations of Dan Benton, the plant engineer, with the men. As he had been working primarily on the fractionating columns, sometimes, without thinking of the proper organizational channels, he had been directing the fractionator operator to make certain changes. No protest had come out of this until immediately after the watchman statement, when a poly operator complained to Foreman Tom Lloyd that his engineer was by-passing the poly operator.

For several days after the statement, Hi-Test men signed the Daily Operator Data Sheet as "the watchman," and there were a number of phone calls from other parts of the company's operations, asking to speak to the "chief watchman."

Several weeks later, a worker who had been very active for the CIO union made this comment upon the impact of the statement on the union drive.

After Masters made that statement about us all being watchmen, the CIO signed up 50 per cent of the men that it had. I signed up quite a few names myself. I signed up men that had been strong against it before. There was one man with the company twenty years. He was proud of his position as an operator, and he thought the company appreciated his work. He thought he could take care of himself. When Masters made that statement, this fellow got mad and signed a pledge card. He figured that if that was what the company really thought of him, he needed the protection of a union.

Had the election been held shortly after the watchman statement, it probably would have been a landslide for the CIO. In fact, the CIO organizers were reported to be jubilant at the time. For the first time they had an issue really capable of exciting the men—and presented to them by management. The union literature now reminded the workers of the watchman statement and played up General Superintendent of Field Operations Masters as the villain whose evil doings could be checked only by a strong union.

## LOCAL MANAGEMENT'S COUNTEROFFENSIVE

Local management people were disheartened and almost ready to concede the election to the CIO. Not so with Division Superintendent Al Wenzel, the immediate subordinate of Masters and the immediate superior of Plant Manager Douglas. The date for the representation election had not finally been set, and he hoped that, given a little time, the watchman statement would recede into the background and effective counteraction could be undertaken.

First Wenzel had to take steps to make sure that matters did not take still another turn for the worst. Reports coming back from the main office city indicated that Masters was angry at the reaction to his watchman statement. He was arguing that management was wasting its time negotiating with the company union. The workers really needed to be shown who was boss in this situation. Therefore he ordered that the surplus manpower in the Hi-Test plant and surrounding plant yard be bumped back immediately to lower classifications.

Some months earlier, when working hours had been lengthened from forty to forty-four per week, local management found itself with several more men than were actually needed to man the operations. The local management argued that there was no need to bump these men back immediately. The company was expanding rapidly. In the spring of 1943, a new large synthetic rubber plant was to be opened, and men from Oil City would be vitally needed to help man the new operations. Wenzel's plan was to hold the men in their current positions until the new jobs opened in the synthetic rubber plant. At that time, Oil City working hours would be further lengthened to forty-eight a week, and he hoped that this lengthening of hours, timed to coincide with the transfers to the rubber plant, would enable him to make personnel changes with a minimum of bumping back. In fact, if enough men volunteered to move to the new operation, there might not have to be any bumpings at all. But now Wenzel received the order to cut the men back immediately.

Foreman Tom Lloyd described the new "get tough" policy in this way. He laid the change in part to a decision of the National Labor Relations Board. The contract between the company and the company union had a provision regarding arbitration of matters on which the parties did not agree. Management claimed that this clause did not apply to wage rates. The company union representatives argued that it did, and the government had upheld this view.

It looks like Masters has got some backing from higher up. The old appeasement policy is out. From now on the company wants us to get tough. It seems that they did not think they had to abide by the contract with the company union and the company union did. Now they have found that they have to abide by that contract so they say, "If the men are going to cut all the corners they can on the contract, we are doing the same thing. We will show them who is running the company."

I guess they have given up on the company union. Franklin (Oil City personnel man) told us about the new policy. He and Wenzel had been up to the main office over the weekend, and when he came back he called local management together and he told us that we would have to get tough. From now on we are not supposed to make any concessions to the men . . . Now they are telling us that four men have to be bumped back. One out of Hi-Test and two out of the catalyst plant. If the men protest, we are supposed to can them. In the past I have never had the power of firing a man. I can only recommend it to my superiors. Now I can fire anybody I want to.

Of course, the local administration hates this like hell and Franklin doesn't like it either. He told us, "I'm afraid the men will think that I am the son of a bitch that brought up this policy. But they told me, if I didn't like it, they would put men down here that did."

This is really something new. In the past we have had the one big happy family policy. It never got this tough before.

Wenzel's first response to the cut-back order was to stall. He pretended not to understand it. After waiting a day so that he knew Masters would be out of the main office city, he called a personnel man in the main office to ask for clarification as to whether the bumpings had to be done at once. This gave him an opportunity to suggest the disruptive consequences of such a move. The personnel man said he would take the matter up with Vice-President Weber. Shortly the word came back from Weber that the bumpings could be postponed.

Now Wenzel could proceed to reactivate the company union, which had become dormant after the watchman statement. Wenzel explained to me that it was really his own fault that the CIO drive had gone so far. The great mistake he had made was in not keeping the company union alive. He said he knew that earlier superintendents had just not wanted to be bothered dealing with the company union and he had allowed them to discourage the men. He had had other things to do so he had not called regular meetings with the company union. But now he was going to stir things up again, if it was not too late. He called Franklin, the personnel man, and told him to get in touch with Les Harper, company union president, so that Les could "demand" another negotiating meeting with the company on the following Saturday.

Meanwhile Division Superintendent Wenzel and Personnel Man Franklin were keeping themselves informed about union developments. Did they have spies? One management man told me that on the morning following the last CIO meeting, Wenzel had a complete list of all the company employees who had attended. Wenzel denied this. He said, "We only had four of the names. We are not interested in all those names." Franklin added:

> We just felt that we ought to know what was going on there. How are we going to know if the CIO is a good thing for us or not unless we know about those things? Maybe we want to go in with the CIO. The man that brings us that information does it entirely voluntarily. He feels very strongly about this, and he thinks that it is in his own interest as well as for the company to find these things out.

In early March it was time for the annual election of representatives to the company union. In Hi-Test the first ballot showed two votes for Joe Sloan; two for Frank Kendall, a popular fractionator operator; one vote each for two other men; and the rest of the votes for "CIO," "Jesus Christ," and various obscenities.

The next day, when the run-off election between Kendall and Sloan was scheduled, Foreman Tom Lloyd urged the men to take it seriously. He argued that they had nothing to lose in doing so. If the CIO union won the representation election, the company union would be out, but if the company union did win, the men would at least have a representative in on the making of a new contract. The men did take the run-off more seriously, and they elected Frank Kendall.

While the campaign between the CIO and the company union was fought out on a day-to-day basis, the sentiments of the men corresponded to their anticipations of future situations. Suppose the CIO won, how would things be different? Suppose the CIO lost, how would the men fare without a CIO union? And if a man favored the CIO or the company union, how would this affect his future with the company? To some extent these considerations were inevitable among the men, but to some extent they were stimulated by contacts between the men and Division Superintendent Wenzel and Personnel Man Franklin.

To some of the men, the entrance of the CIO would mean a clarification of the relations between the men and management and an elimination of favoritism. As a Hi-Test hydro-stillman put it:

> If we had a union come in here, we could take care of things like that (promotions outside of seniority). The men wouldn't be so uncertain any

more. The company would have a line to walk, and the union would have a line to walk. The union could keep the company from getting out of line, and the company could keep the union from getting out of line.

But did the men really want an impersonal system? Would some of them rather prefer to take their chances with what management might offer them individually? In early March I had this report from poly operator Mark Walling:

Did you hear what Wenzel said to Jess Kemmerer? (poly operator). . . . Well this is what Wenzel said, and he probably meant for Jess to pass it on to us. He said, "Any one of those poly operators could have had the job that Tom Lloyd has now if they had just kept their noses clean." I went down to see what he meant about that. He told me the same thing, and when I asked him to explain, he just said, "Well, you know how conditions have been down there." It was obvious what he wanted to do. He wanted to make the poly operators ease off the CIO. Al is a good fellow, but he is a big bull artist. I happen to know because Tom Lloyd told me that he was promised his job almost six months before he finally got it. They had to wait all that time to make a job for Fitch somewhere else. If he was in line for that job, how would we have a chance at it?

Wenzel gave me his own version of the conversation:

I knew he would tell out there what I told him, but maybe I talked too much. I told him that he could get ahead himself if he just kept his nose clean and did his work. By that phrase, keep his nose clean, I just meant that he should keep out of trouble with the supervisor, and he felt guilty about the CIO, and he felt that I was referring to union activity. The outcome of that is just the man's personal business and I wouldn't interfere with that.

Is that all Wenzel meant? If so, why did he refuse to clarify the remark when Walling asked for an explanation? When the men were preoccupied with the CIO drive, it was inevitable that any such remark of Wenzel would be interpreted just as it was interpreted, and the division superintendent could hardly have been unaware of this.

Could such remarks discourage the men from supporting the CIO? I put this to Mark Walling.

Not a bit. We all know that Al is a big bull artist. We know that they wouldn't put a man in that position without a college education anyway.

But were the men actually that certain? The men knew the current company policy against promotion into management for non-college men, and yet several of these Hi-Test operators had told me that they had not entirely given up hope of somehow getting into supervision. Was it entirely an unrealistic hope? It certainly seemed so at the time, but before the war was over, management was finding such difficulty in getting enough college men to take foremen's jobs in its rapidly expanding operations that the policy against promotion of non-college men was rescinded. Whatever the facts of the case, the men listened avidly for reports from Wenzel about their promotion prospects even as they damned the division superintendent as a "bull artist."

A week later, Walling brought back another report on management's point of view, this time from a conversation with Personnel Man Franklin. He had asked Franklin what the company would do if the men went CIO.

> He said he thought it would be pretty rough. All the human side would go out of it. The company would just cut all the corners that it could. I wish I knew what was the best thing for us to do. Do you think the company will get rough?

I asked him if he had ever considered that possibility before.

> No, not until I talked with Franklin. I wonder what they might do? Maybe they will cut the poly operators out of here and just leave two men to run the plant. What do you think they could do?

I answered that different companies react in different ways and asked him what he thought he himself would do.

> I don't know. Just figuring out for myself, I think the union would be the best thing, but I wish I knew how it would affect the men.

I asked him if he thought his known connection with the union might handicap him personally with the company.

> "Yes, I think it has."

It is extraordinary that a poly operator such as Walling would consider the possibility of the company eliminating the poly operator position. The plant had originally been run with only two operators, but management had found it necessary to place a third man in charge in order to coordinate the work of the two. The poly operator position had not been created to please the men, and it is hard to imagine that it would be eliminated in order to punish them. But such were the tensions and anxieties in this situation that Walling was able to imagine the elimination of his own job.

Division Superintendent Wenzel had been able to stall off the Masters get-tough policy, so that no men were bumped back before the transfers to the rubber plant. Now he took the initiative to bid for full local control of the campaign in a meeting at the main office. He and Franklin had been called to the main office to discuss management strategy and tactics against the CIO in a meeting with Vice-President Weber and General Superintendent of Field Operations Masters. Wenzel reported to me that Masters did most of the talking at this meeting and seemed to be assuming that in the final weeks before the election, his assistant would be in Oil City taking command of the situation. Wenzel assumed—and probably correctly—that the mere presence of anyone identified with Masters in Oil City could be worth a number of additional CIO votes in the election. He therefore urged Vice-President Weber to leave the whole campaign to Franklin and himself. This was a local problem, he argued, and he knew how to handle it. Weber agreed. No one from the main office was seen in Oil City until after the election.

Having secured control over management action in the crisis, Wenzel now found events playing into his hands. It had come time to arrange the transfers to the rubber plant. If these had been handled autocratically or in a discriminatory manner, the transfers would have provided fuel to warm up CIO sentiment. As it was, several of the strongest CIO supporters among the men commented to me that management's handling of the situation had been perfectly fair and reasonable.

A company representative from the rubber plant had met with local management and with the company union representatives to describe the opportunities at the rubber plant, the nature of the community situation, and so on, and to respond to any questions. The men were then free to schedule individual appointments with him to explore the prospects the rubber plant might offer them. No one was required to transfer, and men were given time to make up their minds. On its side, management was not required to accept for the rubber plant everyone who was ready to transfer. However, I heard no criticism regarding individuals who wanted the rubber plant job and were refused the opportunity. Apparently, there turned out to be a pretty even balance between those wanting to make the transfer and those acceptable to the rubber plant representative. In Hi-Test, as one hydro-stillman transferred, it was only Joe Sloan whose job was affected.

The transfer activities had a striking affect on interest in the representation election. A sudden shift in topics of conversation among the men was reported to me by several informants. While before the transfer activities the progress of the union organization drive, and the various statements of the division superintendent bearing on that drive, had been a central focus of conversational interest, now the men were all talking about the rubber plant transfers. Each man had to ask himself whether he would be better off to stay or go. Not only did the men talk it over at home but they talked it over on the job. The men who decided to go found themselves suddenly in a situation where what happened locally no longer meant very much to them—even though they might still be around to vote in the representation election. The men who decided against leaving could not help but wonder whether they had made the right decision, and they were at least interested in hearing arguments that would provide reassurance on this score.

## THE FAREWELL PARTY

A final distraction was provided by poly operator Mark Walling himself—although he certainly did not plan it that way. It occurred to him that it was not right for the men to let several of their fellow workers leave for a new plant without having some kind of party in their honor. He telephoned Franklin and Wenzel regarding company support for such a party and found them uncooperative at first. Walling persisted and finally Wenzel agreed that management would furnish beer and pretzels for a party in the clubhouse. Walling then organized a collection among fellow workers to provide parting gifts for the men.

When I arrived at 8:15 at the clubhouse, the party was already well under way, and beer was beginning to flow. There was a crap game going on in one corner of the room and two poker games were starting, one for small stakes and the other for much higher stakes.

At one table, Mark Walling was playing checkers against an engineer, whom he beat four straight games. Throughout the room, there was a lively mixing of management and workers.

When Al Wenzel entered, he joined in the crap game and immediately became the center of attention, talking loudly with the men and joking about his prowess with the dice. Wenzel moved into one of the poker games later. Through the evening, he was circulating around the hall, radiating good fellowship. When he did stop to talk for any length of time, I noted him talking with Walling more than with anyone else.

For the speech-making, a popular worker served as master of ceremonies. All of the local management people were called on for remarks. Les Harper, company union president; Mark Walling; and the men going to the rubber plant all spoke briefly.

The speeches all followed very much the same pattern; the management people, Harper, and Walling told the men what good fellows they had been to work with and stressed the advantages they would have in the rubber plant. Wenzel provoked laughter with his heckling of some of the management speakers.

After the presentation of gifts from the men by one of the superintendents, Al Wenzel had the last word. Following the customary remarks about the men who were leaving, he went on to say:

> We wouldn't be here tonight if it had not been for that God damn Walling. He has the most persuasive telephone voice I ever heard. We had decided because of being afraid of being accused of this and that we couldn't come to this party tonight, but that God damn Walling wouldn't take no for an answer, and so we are here. I am glad to say that I haven't heard a word from anybody tonight about coming events, and the first man that mentions coming events will be thrown out.

The CIO organizational drive symbolized a division between the men and management. The men were on one side, management on the other. Did the men need a union to protect them against management? Some management people considered the organization as "one big happy family." In fact, the president of the company, in one of his rare visits to Oil City some weeks before the election, had said plaintively to local management people:

I want you to know this is the same organization that it has always been. We are the same men that we always were.

He recalled the days when he used to sign the payroll checks for all the company employees and when he used to visit the families of the men when somebody was sick. But, he went on:

We have grown so big I have to think of Washington all the time. They are doing so many things that I can't see the men as I used to. But my door is still always open to anybody that wants to talk to me.

The farewell party dramatized for the men as nothing else could have the conception of the company as one big happy family—with management in the parental role. Workers and management people met on the same social level. Good old Al Wenzel was there in vest and suspenders, making wisecracks at the men and encouraging them to joke back at him. The speeches all sounded a note of fellowship among all of these men working together. And interestingly enough, although the party had been organized by Mark Walling, one of the superintendents made the presentation of gifts, all of the management men were called upon to speak, and the final talk was reserved for the division superintendent himself. In spite of everything that had happened, the management people were acting out the one big happy family concept, and the men were enjoying it.

Did the farewell party affect votes in the representation election which took place less than two weeks later? That is a difficult question to answer. A man who exprsssed himself for the CIO before the party could hardly admit that such an apparently extraneous event as a farewell party had changed his mind. I am certain that it did not affect the votes of those who had previously stated to me strong CIO convictions. It may very well have affected a number of men who were on the fence, but some of these men had been wavering back and forth for a number of weeks, and it would be hard to weigh the significance of even so dramatic an event as this in the wavering process.

I assume that Mark Walling himself was the man most likely to have been influenced by the farewell party. When I saw him briefly a day or two later and asked him how he was voting, he said he was on the fence. In contrast to earlier discussions, he avoided further explanations. A week after the election he commented, "There are lots of crooked things about unions."

I asked if he knew anything crooked about the Oil Workers International Union. "No, but you read a lot of things in the newspaper about that sort of thing."

Why had the corruption issue suddenly come to Walling's attention? He was probably referring to the columns of Westbrook Pegler, which were syndicated in the Oil City's daily newspaper, but this was hardly a new theme for Mr. Pegler. Why had the Pegler remarks failed to impress Walling earlier? We must conclude that something had happened to Walling to increase his receptivity to this kind of argument. His involvement as a central figure in the farewell party may well have been such an influence. On the other hand, it might be argued that since the CIO had just lost the election, Walling was in the process of adjusting himself to the inevitable. However, the CIO had already entered a protest on the election, so a man did not have to accept its results as final unless he so desired.

## NEGOTIATING FOR THE COMPANY UNION

As the April 6 representation election date approached, management and the company union negotiators were meeting day after day to work out a new contract. It was management's idea to have at least a tentative draft of the contract finished before the representation election, so that word of its promised benefits could be spread before voting time. The final contract could then be worked out after the representation election— assuming that the company union won. A little more than a week before the representation election, the tentative contract was agreed upon and the negotiating meetings were terminated.

How this promise of a new company union contract affected the men I cannot document, but my record is clear as to the affect of the negotiating process upon Frank Kendall, who was the reluctant representative for Hi-Test plant. His remarks clearly show a change in sentiments accompanying the change in interactions and activities he had experienced during the negotiation period. It was noteworthy that in discussing the change of sentiments with me, he made no reference to any specific contract provisions. Here speaks a man whom I had identified earlier as one of the staunchest supporters of the CIO:

I used to think that the company was just out to get whatever it could from us. Now, I have been meeting with those men, and I have been studying them. I have come to the conclusion that they are really sincere. You can't be with a group of men for days like I was if they are hypocrites without you seeing that. I think they mean to be good to the men right now. If the company union wins this election I think they will do their level best to make things nice for the men—for a while. I think we would be better off if in the company union right now but the thing is, is it always going to be that way? I wish I knew.

After he had repeated himself several times on this theme, I asked him how he was going to vote.

I don't know. I am still on the fence. It wouldn't do for me to come back to these men and try to convert them to the company union. They would think that I was bought off. That's what they are looking for. I just don't know what I am going to do.

He told me that he had already been made the butt of jokes about the chicken barbecue dinners the management was buying for the company union negotiators. He assured me that although the men and management had eaten together, the worker representatives had bought their own lunches. He added that he had not got any enjoyment out of the experience of negotiating the contract. "It bores on me." He went on in this way:

> You know, I have changed my opinion of Masters a good deal since I have been seeing him. He talks right out and tells you what he thinks. He is a little blunt about it, but you know where he stands. Walter Gruber (employee relations director) is always trying to smooth things over. I don't like that so much.

> Tom Lloyd was talking to me yesterday. I didn't have the heart to tell him that I would vote for the CIO. No, it wasn't that I would be afraid to tell him. It just don't seem right to say that. It seems like we are letting the men down. Right now we have better bosses than we ever had before. The men are just beginning to appreciate them. That means a lot.

## MANAGEMENT'S ELEVENTH-HOUR EFFORT

Management did not wait out passively the last few days until the election. Tom Lloyd described to me the last moves that were contemplated:

> There will be plenty of dirty work. There will be no holds barred. The company wants to win this election at all costs. There are certain things we can do. These men that are supposed to go to the synthetic rubber plant on April 1—now we have just discovered that there are certain jobs that those men are to be kept here for until after the election. We know those men, and we know how they are going to vote. I don't think the union can protest that because these men were on the rolls March 1 when the union had a chance to go over the payroll. Then there is the district labor gang. Those men work all over the state, but it is just going to happen that on the day of the election they are all going to be working in Oil City. We don't think the CIO has been able to do much there. We are going to see to it that every man votes. I will go down on the job on Saturday and check up on all of my men. If a man has not voted, I will arrange to let him go off the job to get to the polls. If he does not want to go, I can say to him, "After all, this is a secret ballot and nobody is going to know how you vote, but it will be known whether you voted or not. And then whoever wins they can think that you were on their side. That sounds pretty logical, don't it?" Besides that we will work through certain men we can trust.

Local management people had met earlier, with each man going over the list of men under his supervision and indicating how he expected each man to vote. The summation of these estimates indicated a landslide for the company union. This suggests that we must not overestimate the accuracy of management information in such a situation. For example, I asked Lloyd to predict the votes of the Hi-Test men. He predicted nine votes for the company union, with five being on the fence and only three being definitely for the CIO. Among his nine for the company union were two men that I would have placed on the fence and two (Joe

Sloan and Johnny Hudson) that I was certain were going to vote for the CIO. When I asked Lloyd on what basis he predicted Sloan for the company union, he said:

I talked with him this morning and asked him how he thought it was going to go. He said he thought the company union might win it. I didn't ask him how he would vote himself, but from the way he talked, I think he is leaning that way.

Later that same day, Sloan told me flatly that he still intended to vote for the union—but he had told Lloyd that the company union might win, as indeed he thought it might.

The final blow for the company was wielded in the labor gang by Elmer Martin, welder and company union representative. Except for several welders, the labor gang was made up of men who had very little experience with the company. Furthermore, as Lloyd noted, the gang moved around to different locations in the state and thus was cut off from very much communication with the operating units in the Oil City area. The welders were not only the most experienced men in the labor gang, but also the only skilled ones. It was natural under the circumstances that they should have high status in the labor gang and that one of them should be elected company union representative.

During the week before election, Elmer Martin took it upon himself to explain the proposed company union contract to the labor gang. The meeting was held outside of the plant yard—but on company time. Martin claims that this was his own idea, but he had to have his superintendent's permission in order to make the time available to the men for this purpose.

I had no contacts with the labor gang and so no direct way of estimating the impact of Martin's meeting. However, given the prestige of the welder and the lack of experience of the labor gang members, it seems likely that this was indeed an influential move. And forty-five men in an electorate of two-hundred-odd were involved.

For the April 6 election, the workers had three choices; the CIO union, the company union, or no union. However, management had sent out word that the men who were against the CIO union should not divide their votes; they should vote for the company union, whatever their opinion of that organization. In reality, the election represented simply a vote for or against the CIO. The activities preceding the election had not convinced anyone that the company union was an effective organization. Thus in voting the men were expressing either their desire to put their faith exclusively in management, or to turn to representation which was not under management control.

The count in the April 6 vote showed 106 for the company union and 92 for the Oil Workers International Union. The CIO immediately challenged the election on a number of grounds, the two most important being Elmer Martin's meeting with the labor gang and Personnel Man Franklin's presence in an automobile near the polls throughout most of election day. (A CIO organizer had asked Franklin which side he was supporting, and the personnel man had refused to answer.)

While another election was scheduled for a later time, this was the end of my research, and I left Oil City a month later.

### ANALYSIS

Let us now see if we can put the case in a more general framework. The story told suggests that the progress of unionization can be considered as both a long-run and a short-run phenomonon. That is, we found that certain basic changes had taken place within the company and in the relations between company and environment to make unionization possible. We also saw how changes taking place day-to-day and week-by-week in the months leading up to the representation election served to increase or diminish the chances of the union.

Let us approach the unionization problem from a standpoint of the way the workers visualize the organization. In terms of the present question, there are two mutually incompatible ways of visualizing the organization: vertical versus horizontal integration. When management people speak of "one big happy family" they are presenting the vertical integration image. People at all different levels in the organization are alike in that they share a common membership.

The union organizer sees the situation in terms of horizontal integration: There are two classes of people in the organization; management and workers, with a sharp dividing line separating them horizontally.

I do not mean to suggest that there are workers who see the organization purely in terms of vertical integration or those who see it purely in terms of horizontal integration. We can expect nearly any worker to see the organization in terms of both concepts, but worker A may find vertical integration the predominant concept, worker B may find horizontal integration the predominant concept, while worker C may fluctuate between the two polls in response to events taking place in the course of the campaign.

Let us now examine the forces that lead to the strengthening of one or the other concept, thus resulting in a vote for or against the union.

### LONG-RUN CHANGES

If we consider the ten-year period leading up to the representation election of 1943, there were clearly important changes in the relation of the company to the environment of the country. At the beginning of the period, industrial unions were practically unknown. By 1943, they were an accepted part of the industrial scene, with legal protection and a federal governmental policy favoring collective bargaining. However, much the same could have been said about two earlier organizing attempts in the late 1930s, which failed to gain much headway. In other words, this environmental change does not seem to account for the 1942–43 drive coming so much nearer to success than the earlier ones.

It might be argued that the condition of the labor market provides part of our answer. In a period of wartime labor shortage, a worker need not have fears of prolonged unemployment if he is discharged for union activities. However, workers in this situation had strong claims for draft deferment, since they were considered to be working in an essential industry. As Joe Sloan himself commented, a man who quit his job or was discharged might be drafted. Therefore, while the labor market situation may be an important influence in some cases, it does not seem to be so here.

The major long-run influences seem to be two: career blocking and changes in worker-higher management relations.

The management policy of placing in supervision only college graduates served to divide the organization into two parts, with a sharp line drawn between them. The workers, thus cut off from advancement, were now less inclined to identify themselves with management and more inclined to feel, think, and act in terms of horizontal integration.

The change from Fitzgerald to Masters destroyed the connecting link between workers and the home office. Even while Fitzgerald still lived, there was from year to year a decrease in frequency of his interactions with workers, but there remained a feeling that you could go to Fred when you needed help, and he would help you. While Fitzgerald was alive, there also existed a system of reciprocity, which was well understood by the men. The exchange of activities was of this nature: The workers refrained from involvement with unions, and Fitzgerald acted on the problems they had with local management people. No such reciprocity was offered by Masters.

The change from Fitzgerald to Masters also involved drastic changes on the local management scene. Before the Masters' crack-down, what Alvin Gouldner has described as the "indulgency pattern" prevailed in the Oil City operations.[1] Discipline was lax and the men enjoyed certain benefits (free gasoline, time off for gambling, etc.) which were contrary to the official policy of the company. In return, they were expected to be loyal to the particular management people who provided the benefits. Now, I am not saying that all or most of the workers were happy with the particular set of personal relations involved in this indulgency pattern. I later heard many complaints about favoritism, but this simply pointed to a situation in which a certain number of workers might look to get

---

[1] Alvin Gouldner, *Patterns of Industrial Bureaucracy* (Glencoe, Illinois: The Free Press, 1954).

advantages through developing special relations with certain management people. While these channels were open, there was less likelihood of workers joining together on a basis that would establish uniform policies governing the position of individuals in the social system. When Masters stepped in, he destroyed the indulgency pattern with one blow.

The changes in potency of the company union also had a long-run impact. As worker interactions with higher management and sentiment ties to it became more attenuated, one might have expected the company union to step in and reestablish the relationship. In fact, this is apparently what higher management had in mind, and it is instructive to see how management's expectations were frustrated. As an organization with member support, the company union was destroyed at two levels. Local management found it inconvenient to have workers raising questions about its decisions before higher management people in the company, and so stepped in to discourage worker leadership activity and to take over the union meetings. Division Superintendent Wenzel recognized that he could have prolonged the life of the company union by encouraging regular meetings and taking action to assure workers that they would get responses to their complaints, even when those complaints embarrassed local management. But a dormant company union provided less immediate bother to Wenzel than did a live one, and he took no trouble to revive it until a greater threat appeared on the horizon.

Two types of action from the main office also served in the destruction process. The company union president noted higher management's tendency to anticipate company union demands and raise wages before negotiations had even been undertaken. He also cited a statement by the vice-president of the company who said, in effect: Don't bother me now; I have more important things to do in Washington, and you won't get anything anyway.

The company union therefore did not provide an institution through which workers were enabled to initiate activities for management on a regular and continuing basis. While this destroyed the company union as a real membership organization, the form persisted, as we have seen, and provided a vehicle through which management was later able to institute certain interactional changes that did have effects upon worker sentiments.

## CHANGES IN INTERPERSONAL RELATIONS

*Foremen-worker relations:* We can expect foremen-worker relations to affect worker sentiments toward the union to some extent. The experience of the Hi-Test workers under Jones and Fitch seemed to stimulate them in a pro-union direction. Their experiences under Lloyd seemed to modify this orientation. Some men expressed the sentiment that voting for the union seemed equivalent to letting the present good bosses down, and this was apparently a consideration even among those who continued to favor the union.

The two types of foremen-worker relations show marked contrasts in the frequency and direction of initiation of activity and in the presence or absence of a reciprocity relationship. For case one (Jones and Fitch), we can say that the following characteristics of the relationship promoted pro-union sentiments:

1. High rate of initiation of activity from foremen to workers.
2. Low rate of initiation from workers to foremen.
3. Absence of reciprocity between foremen and workers. Workers did not receive approval in exchange for work activity. We might say that a negative reciprocity existed with foremen penalizing to enforce standards and workers evading standards to escape punishment and get back at foremen.

Compared to the above situation, we can say that type two case (Lloyd) led workers toward a vertical integration concept through the following influences:

1. Decrease in the initiation of activity from foreman to the workers.
2. Increase of frequency of initiation of activity from workers to foreman.
3. Development of positive reciprocity with workers exchanging activities for approval.

The foreman-worker relationship may influence but does not fully determine worker sentiments regarding the union. As they talked about the union, Hi-Test workers talked a great deal about Masters and the home office. Some of them saw the decision of management to place Lloyd in this position as a temporary expedient to head off the CIO and argued that management might just as readily remove the "good" foreman at any time. Nevertheless, there did seem to be some influence along the lines I have indicated.

*Significant symbols:* In this case, we have a number of examples in which certain verbal symbols played a prominent role in affecting sentiments and interactions.

The use by management people of verbal symbols implying low status for workers tends to promote among workers the concept of horizontal integration, and thus encourages pro-union sentiments.

In this case we have two striking examples. One of the earlier foremen once referred to men in the catalyst plant as "WPA workers." We have Tom Lloyd's testimony that this stirred up such strong resentments that the men still talked about it years later. This obviously stirred resentment toward the management man who uttered the words and presumably toward management in general. We might also assume that it strengthened the horizontal integration concept and therefore promoted union sentiment, although we have no direct evidence on this point.

The "watchman" statement presents us with a more clear-cut case. This reawakened and fortified all the old sentiments of hostility toward

Masters and the main office. Workers and local management people alike reported that the incident had a sudden and far-reaching effect on pro-union sentiments.

*Worker-management off-the-job relations:* The case suggests that the following conditions will tend to strengthen the vertical integration concept and thus weaken pro-union sentiments:

1. Increase of interactions outside of the line of authority between workers and management, providing this is accompanied by
2. Increased opportunities for workers to initiate activities for management and
3. Management use of verbal symbols appropriate to the vertical integration concept.

In this case, we should note particularly two areas of worker-management off-the-job interaction. The company union negotiations with management provide the first example. We saw first that these increased interactions did not promote the vertical integration concept when a management man used a verbal symbol in striking contradiction of that concept. In effect, the watchman statement broke up the meetings. When they were resumed, we cannot testify that management did in fact use symbols implying vertical integration, for such evidence can only have been gained from observation of the meetings. However, we can say that management did not again introduce any verbal symbols which were sharply at variance with this concept of vertical integration.

In the case of the farewell party, I had an opportunity to observe the verbal symbols as well as the interaction. In the first place, we should note that the party itself arose out of worker initiative. It involved workers and management people interacting together, regardless of their sentiments toward the union. Managers and workers alike, in their speeches, used symbols implying vertical integration; referring to years of experience with each other within the same organization and remarking upon what a fine thing it was that all of the members could get together in such a good spirit.

One word of caution should be stressed. The reader should not assume that management people need only to speak in terms of "one big happy family" in order to stimulate workers to see the organization in vertical integration terms. When the appropriate interaction and activity patterns are lacking, such symbols will seem incongruous and be ineffective. In this case, the symbols were appropriate at least to the immediate interaction and activity situation. This combination of symbols with interaction and activities seemed to promote the concept of vertical integration at that time. Had the representation election come several months later, this momentary reorganization of interactions, activities, and symbols could not have been expected to have any effect upon votes. As it was, the farewell party took place within a few days of the election, and there is reason to believe that it had some influence in the vote.

So far we have been discussing worker visualizations of the organization in terms of two conflicting concepts: vertical and horizontal integration. This seems appropriate to the situation where a union organization drive is in progress. Where the union has become established, we shall see that the two concepts do not appear to be so conflicting to the workers as they do during the organizing period.

# Chapter 15 *WHO GOES UNION AND WHY*

WE HAVE now examined the evolution of human relations in the Blank Oil Company and the course of the CIO organizational drive as seen from the inside of the plant. We have noted that the vote went against the CIO union by a small margin and that it might have gone the other way if the election had taken place a few weeks earlier. Now let us look at the individuals who were the focus of union and management attention in the conflict. Why did worker A favor the CIO? Why did worker B favor the company union? And why did worker C swing first one way and then the other?[1]

My answers to these questions should be regarded as suggestive rather than conclusive. Systematic data to answer such questions are not easy to come by in the heat of a campaign. Since I was carrying on my interviews inside the company gates, the men knew that I had management's approval for my study, and some of them suspected me of being a company spy at the outset. Therefore it was some time before I felt confident enough in my position to raise any questions about the organizational problem. After I had been in the plant for several weeks, some of the men themselves took the initiative in bringing up the union question, and as time went on most of the men talked with me on the subject with increasing freedom. Nevertheless, I always felt that with all but a few of the men I had to take care how deeply I probed into this topic.

The researcher cannot approach this topic in the manner of a public opinion pollster who simply goes around asking people how they are going to vote. The approach must be much more casual and conversational. Furthermore, the mere statement of voting intention would not satisfy our interests. I would guess that approximately one third of the men were committed to the CIO and another third to an anti-CIO vote throughout the campaign; these men never wavering whatever happened. The most interesting are perhaps the remaining one third whose sentiments wavered during the campaign. In the case of these men, we need to examine not only the expression of voting intention at various times, but also

---

[1] This is based upon my article, "Who Goes Union and Why," *Personnel Journal*, Vol. XXIII, No. 6 (December, 1944).

the relationship between this intention and the flow of the events during the campaign.

The necessity of getting to know the men well before discussing their voting intentions limited the number of cases I could cover. A review of my notes shows that I gathered reasonably adequate data on only twenty-one men. Of these, eight were for the CIO, ten against, and three sufficiently undecided so that I would have no confidence in predicting their vote. The numbers are small. On the other hand, in parts of the oil industry relatively few men run large installations. There were seventeen men on the regular payroll of Hi-Test plant, and I was able to gather reasonably good data on thirteen of them. My other eight cases were distributed in this way: two catalyst operators, two operators of the neighboring gasoline plant, and four engine repairmen.

While thirteen out of seventeen cases might be accepted as presenting an adequate picture of Hi-Test, the scattered cases are statistically meaningless. As we shall see, however, they do point to certain common elements in the work environment that the various men faced and that were important in their voting decisions. Furthermore, the individual opinions are accompanied by statements about the voting intentions of fellow workers.

Let us look at the cases clinically and see what patterns appear to emerge.

The first thing we note is that the CIO union was perceived in drastically different ways by different workers. Engine Operator Borden put it this way:

I have a son and a nephew fighting in the army. I don't think it right when they are fighting for freedom abroad for us to have a dictatorship here. That is what the union is to me—just a dictatorship. Maybe I'm wrong, but they have to convince me. . . . No, I never attended any of their meetings. I didn't take no interest.

On the other hand, several men expressed their support for the CIO union to me in terms of their democratic beliefs: They said that this was a democratic organization, working to get the men what they themselves wanted and deserved. They saw the dictatorship on the management side, particularly in the person of General Superintendent Masters.

Why these contrasting perceptions? Were the pro-CIO men against the company and the anti-CIO men for the company? Apparently not. Joe Logan, Hi-Test hydro-stillman and one of the most active of the informal CIO organizers, had this to say:

This has always been a good company to work for. They have taken care of their men. In hard times other companies have laid off a lot of men, but if you have been on the payroll with Blank Oil, you could practically be certain you had a steady job as long as you did the work.

Did money or job security make the difference? While every worker would have happily accepted more money, the most highly paid men in

Hi-Test were also the most strongly for the CIO. No differences in degrees of job security could account for sentiments for or against the union.

I found three factors most influential in explaining voting intention:

1. The social background of the individual.
2. The social characteristics of the individual's job.
3. The presence or absence of special ties between the individual and members of management.

## 1. THE SOCIAL BACKGROUND IN VOTING INTENTION

I undertook no refined analysis of social background, but sought simply to distinguish three types of social situations which I called pure farm, mixed farm, and urban-industrial. In the pure farm case, the farm on which the individual grew up was isolated from town or city, and the individual had had little interaction with boys his own age in the process of growing up. The individual's father was in control of the family and farm at least until the boy reached his late teens. (Some of these men set themselves up as independent farmers after leaving the parental homestead and only went into industry in their mid-twenties.) For example, this is the way Engine Operator Borden (previously quoted) described his early life:

We were way out in the country. There wasn't anybody living close to us. When I was growing up, we all worked twelve to fourteen hours a day on that farm. We had to work hard to make it pay. The farm is just like a business. If you don't work hard to make it pay, you can't keep it going. Us kids just went to school maybe six to eight months of the year. . . . Yes, we went to church on Sunday. There wasn't much visiting between families where I lived. We just stayed on the farm, working all the time. . . . No, there wasn't much talking back and forth when we were on the farm doing our work. We had no time for that. My father told us what to do, and we just did our work.

Six of the pure farm types were in my sample, and five of these men were strongly anti-CIO and never attended a CIO meeting. In fact, they had never been active in the company union or in any grouping of men on the job. The sixth man was Mark Walling, Hi-Test poly operator, of whom we have already heard a good deal and whose personal background will be discussed later.

Joe Logan, the Hi-Test hydro-stillman who was so active for the CIO, confirmed my impression about the difficulty of organizing the pure farmers.

That's right, they sure are (difficult to organize). They don't know nothing about working in an industry unless they had been in it for a long time. On the farm they are used to working twelve to fourteen hours a day so eight hours don't mean a thing to them. I once worked on a construction gang with a bunch of farm boys. I grew up in the oil fields so I knew what a working day was supposed to be. But those men would turn out to work fifteen or twenty minutes ahead of time and when it got to be 5 o'clock—quitting time—they would still want to load another truck. And you couldn't stop them. Now I did as much work as any two of them, but when 5 o'clock came, I wanted to get off the job and get home. Another thing—those boys from the farm, when they get on to a job, they think they are going to get ahead quick by getting on the right side of the supervisor. I seen that many times. They always want to do just anything the supervisor says so that they can get ahead.

These pure farm men had had no experience in growing up with the frequent and regular interaction with boys their own age which often leads to group loyalties in opposition to formal authority. They had worked constantly under the direction of the formal authority in the family—the father—and now they seemed to accept authority from the foreman in industry just as if he were their father.

In mixed farm situations, although the individual was born on the farm and lived there during his early years, the full conditions of the pure farm had not been met. Several of these men had to leave the farm in their early teens due to the failure of the enterprise or to the death of the father. They then moved into farm labor or industrial jobs. In one case, the boy's father died when he was very young and the boy grew up on his grandfather's farm, but the grandfather had another man running the farm for him. Then there was the case of fractionator operator Frank Kendall, who became the Hi-Test company union representative. He was brought up on a farm, but his father also operated a sawmill and cotton gin and had little time to supervise the farm work. Kendall left the farm for factory work when he was fifteen.

Four of the eight mixed farm men were for the CIO, three were against, and one (Kendall) I classified as undecided. It is interesting to note, however, that not a single one of the four men whom I identified as for the CIO played any active part in the organization drive.

Of those with urban and industrial backgrounds, four out of seven were for the CIO, two definitely against, and one doubtful. I had expected a larger proportion of CIO men among those of this background, but one should note that two out of the three not committed to the CIO enjoyed special ties with management men, the significance of which will be discussed later. It is interesting to note also that the four men for the CIO in this group were also the only men in my sample who worked actively for the organization. Consider their backgrounds. Joe Logan, Hi-Test hydrostillman, was the son of an oil field worker, and his father was away at work much of the time that Joe was growing up. Joe started working in the petroleum industry while still in his teens. Another of the four was born on a farm, but his father began to follow the oil fields when he was a small boy. At the age of fifteen, this man went to work himself, holding several jobs before being hired by Blank Oil Company. The third man had grown up in a fair-sized town, coming of working age in the early depression years. For months he rode about the country in box cars, looking for work. When he got his first job, the work was unsteady and he had to make several changes before he finally came to work for Blank Oil Company. The fourth man had gone to work at the age of nine in a southern textile mill. He had worked steadily since that time in a wide variety of jobs and had been in many conflicts with the supervisors.

## 2. THE SOCIAL CHARACTERISTICS OF THE JOB

Support for the CIO was not evenly distributed throughout the plant yard. According to my informants, the strongest anti-CIO sentiment was concentrated among the engine operators and the engine repairmen. The engine operators were officially part of the Hi-Test plant, but their job contrasted with that of the men in the control room socially, technologically, and spatially. In the control room, the poly operator, hydro-stillman, and fractionator operator were all concerned with a chemical process, and their work involved watching various indicators and making periodic chemical tests. The engine operators worked, one to a shift, in a building about a hundred yards away from the control room, which housed six large engines that provided the power for the process. Engine Operator Borden described his work in this way:

> I like that job of operating engine. . . . Yes, the noise is bad, and it has hurt my hearing some, but I got so I didn't mind it. . . . No, there isn't much chance to talk with anybody down there. Supervisors never bother us much either.

The engine operators were socially isolated. The noise of the engines made it impossible for anyone to carry on a conversation with them in the engine room. They had practically no contact with other workers except that they might come up and spend half an hour at lunch with the men in the control room. For a man accustomed to frequent interaction, this could be an unendurable job, but two out of the three engine operators I interviewed were of the pure farm background, so the social isolation apparently seemed natural to them. I classified the third man as mixed farm, because he grew up on his grandfather's farm and the grandfather was not in close contact with him. This man, like the other two, was anti-CIO, but he was the only one among all of the engine operators who had at least attended a CIO union meeting. He differed also from the two pure farm engine operators I interviewed in that he was trying to get out of the engine room and become a fractionator operator.

Although these engine operators had served under Foremen Jones and Fitch, who had stirred up such antagonism in the control room, their relations with the foremen had been quite different. Note Borden's comment: "Supervisors never bother us much either." Men in the control room explained that Jones and Fitch had been chemical engineers with little interest in or knowledge of engine operation. Furthermore, the process in Hi-Test was constantly undergoing at least minor changes, whereas in the engine room, those six engines just kept hammering away. The only

thing to break the monotony was a breakdown of one of the engines, and
the engine operators had shown themselves fully capable of handling
such emergencies in cooperation with the control room men.

All four of the engine repairmen whom I interviewed were anti-CIO,
and nearly all of their fellow repairmen were reported to hold this sentiment. Two of my four were of pure farm background and one was of
mixed farm, while the fourth had grown up in town. While the town
man, like the others, was anti-CIO, he was the only one of the four who
had ever been organizationally active. Sometime earlier he had been a
representative of the company union.

For the engine repairmen, the nature of the work remained pretty
much the same year after year, and they had no problems with the supervision. While they worked on the Hi-Test equipment as well as elsewhere, they were not directly under the Hi-Test foreman. They had their
own chief repairman, a man who had spent the first twenty-five years of
his life on a farm and had only an eighth-grade education. They got along
with him with an easy informality growing out of similar backgrounds
and interests. Whenever I observed the chief operator with members of
his crew around Hi-Test, I did not find him giving orders to the men.
The usual relationship seemed to be one of discussion and consultation;
the repairmen and their chief would talk about the mechanical problem
at hand in an effort to reach a decision as to how it should be handled.

The men in the Hi-Test control room faced a social situation quite different from that experienced by the engine repairmen and the engine operators. They had served under Jones and Fitch and had borne the full
weight of that supervisory relationship. Six of the eleven control room
men that I was able to classify were for the CIO, three undecided, and
two probably against the CIO. Of the five men not committed to the CIO,
four enjoyed a special tie of some sort with management, and the fifth was
Joe Sloan's fractionator operator, the 53-year-old man who had recently
bid in on the job after many years as an engine repairman. He had not
served under Jones and Fitch.

Unfortunately, I neglected to gather systematic data on the educational
backgrounds of all the men interviewed. Therefore, while I cannot
document this conclusion, it is my strong impression that there were significant differences in the number of years of schooling between the control room men and the engine operators and engine repairmen. One of the
engine repairmen commented to me that for a man of his level of education, he had a good job, and he went on to add that he was not aspiring
to anything better. Having probably gone farther in school, the control
room men were more likely to aspire to higher jobs and to react against
management when promotion was blocked.

Even the two control room men that I have counted as probably voting
for the company union did not express themselves against the CIO union
as did some of the engine operators and repairmen. They just said that,

on balance, the men would be better off without the CIO union, and they acknowledged it was a difficult choice.

With only two informants each from the catalyst plant and the neighboring gasoline plant, and conflicting accounts as to sentiments among the men on these jobs, I can present no general comments regarding those work situations.

## 3. SPECIAL TIES WITH MANAGEMENT

By "special ties with members of management," I include family relationships and other influences which bring the individual into more frequent interaction with members of management than is characteristic for fellow workers.

Two men in the Hi-Test control room were related to members of management in another part of the Oil City operation. One of these men, Andy Taylor, also served as the Hi-Test company representative to the union during the first part of my study. I have already noted Mark Walling's statement that Taylor was elected to this position as a joke. Joke or not, the official position did bring him into frequent contact with members of management. This did not automatically make him opposed to CIO. Immediately after the Masters watchman statement, he said to me:

I tell you a company-dominated union aint worth a — —. What can we do? We are only one little group here. To get anything from the company, we have to get together representatives from all the other plants. We just can't get all those men together.

A month later, after he had participated in further negotiating meetings with management—which had run smoothly—Taylor said to me:

I think that the company union can do something for the men. Of course, I have been closely associated with the management in these discussions. I think that if the CIO came in, the company would just stick to the contract and would not deal with the man outside of that at all. In the company union we have a better chance to get things, I think.

Note that this was exactly the line being presented to the men by management.

One of the most strongly anti-CIO men in the plant yard was catalyst operator Martin Shockley. He had no farm background and was in fact the son of an oil worker, which might lead one to expect him to be favorable to the CIO; but note the special circumstances of his case as he tells us first his point of view and then his background:

I don't want to have anything to do with an organization that's run by Communists and racketeers. When I have to pay an organization in order to hold my job, I'll just quit. The way I look at it, if my supervisor don't want me to work for him, then I ought to get out and work some place else. If the men in here don't like working for Blank Oil Company, why don't they get out and get a job some place else instead of staying here and biting the hand that feeds them?

Of course, my case may be a little different from the rest of the men. My mother has always taught me to believe that Blank Oil Company was the only company in the world. My father worked for the company when I was about four years old. That was when Joe Blank was just getting started. My father knew him pretty good then. He had just worked for Blank for a few months when a fire broke out in the plant. In fighting that fire, my father got pneumonia and died. After that my mother got a check every month. It wasn't from the company, it was from Joe Blank's personal account. That check kept coming until my oldest brother was able to go to work for the company. Then the check was cut down some, and when I was able to go to work so that the two of us together could carry the load, the check was cut out. In those early days we used to spend some time on Joe Blank's estate. That hasn't happened for years, but he still remembers my mother every year with a Christmas card and a birthday card.

This early experience did not entirely insulate Shockley from labor organization. Other men claimed that in an earlier CIO drive, when he was in the midst of a conflict with Foreman Jones, Shockley signed a union pledge card. But then the popular foreman, Tom Lloyd, succeeded Jones, and Shockley was elected a company union representative, which involved frequent conferences with management. It was this change, together with his early background, which made Shockley so strongly anti-union.

Frank Kendall, Hi-Test fractionator operator, presents a striking case of the effects of a special relationship with management. At the time he was elected company union representative, he was considered by fellow workers as one of the strongest supporters of the CIO. After a long period of negotiations, Kendall was at least on the fence and perhaps leaning toward a company union vote.

In addition to Kendall's statements to me, quoted earlier, we have the report of Joe Sloan on two occasions shortly before the election. On March 30, Sloan told me that he had made a point of finding out from Kendall if he was still for the CIO. Frank had said he was.

When Kendall came in on evening tour on April 1, Sloan and another pro-CIO worker cornered him. Sloan said, "Are you going to make us any campaign speeches, Frank?" Kendall said he was not going to try to influence anybody. Both Sloan and the other worker tried unsuccessfully to get him to commit himself, but did not question him point blank. A CIO supporter from the other gasoline plant said flatly that Kendall had "sold out."

This was indeed a very difficult time for fractionator operator Kendall. If he had "sold out" for any tangible benefit promised by management, I was unable to discover what it was. His position with the company remained the same after the election as it had been before. His interactions had changed markedly, and his sentiments had adjusted to this change in interactions. This left Kendall a troubled man. He talked as if he would have been much happier if he had been left alone and had not been elected to represent the company union.

Perhaps the most interesting case of all is that of Mark Walling, who developed special interactions with management outside of any formal organization. We have seen Walling in action throughout the campaign. Let us now go back to his own statements about himself and his earlier experiences.

Walling worked on his father's farm until his late teens. As he put it:

> When I was growing up, I didn't think my father could do any wrong. I tried to do whatever he told me. When I went to work, I looked upon the foreman just like he was my father, and I tried to do everything just like he wanted it done. I didn't think the company could do any wrong.

I asked if other men had resented this attitude.

> Yes, they did. I didn't realize it at the time, but I know now that they considered me —— (subservient, and self-seeking). I didn't even know what that was then, but now that I look back on it, I can see that I didn't have any real friends among the men. I didn't know what the cause of it was. I was just doing the thing that I thought was right to do.

But then he was fired by one supervisor, and he said, "I learned my lesson. I don't act that way any more." However, the influence of the early years was stronger than Walling realized. Rehired by the company, he became an exceedingly capable and ambitious operator. He was friendly with Jones and Fitch, and was known as the foremen's favorite. One of the workers who was a foreman's scapegoat discovered that Walling had complained against him to Fitch. This "squealing to the boss" stirred up resentment against him among the men.

Probably this would not have disturbed Walling if he had been promoted into supervision, as he had been hoping. As it became increasingly evident that no non-college men would make this jump, he identified his interests more and more with his fellow workers and tried to win their friendship.

By this time Walling had found out that the foreman was not his father, and yet the mold of the early experiences still influenced his thinking on organizational relationships. Shortly before the election, he said to me, "There is no reason the company couldn't be like a father to the men." I never heard a worker of urban-industrial background liken a management man to his father or express a desire for having the company in the role of a father.

In the early stages of the campaign, Walling had been identified by management as actively for the CIO. In fact, he had attended one meeting in the company of CIO organizers.

The Masters watchman statement only served to reinforce Walling's pro-CIO sentiments. But then this event faded into the background, time passed, and Walling's natural tendency to seek out relations with his organizational superiors again asserted itself. This was to be observed even before the farewell party he organized. I learned from him of two occasions in which he had called on Division Superintendent Al Wenzel or Personnel Man Jess Franklin, ostensibly to get information from them. This information was brought back to fellow workers. Did he perhaps also give information to the management people?

The farewell party was of course a striking example of the upward initiation of interaction and activity changes. Walling had approached management people and they had responded to him. At the farewell party, he spent more time in conversation with Division Superintendent Wenzel than did any other worker. But here we are probably dealing with something more than just the simple quantity and duration of interaction, for interaction on a ceremonial occasion such as this seems likely to have a more pronounced affect upon men's sentiments than interaction as part of the day-to-day routine.

Even before the farewell party, Walling had given me indications of wavering in his CIO support. Right after that party, he told me he was on the fence. After the election, he was finding himself newly concerned about racketeers in the unions.

## ANALYSIS

Now that we have traced the varied reactions of workers, let us see if we can state some tentative conclusions regarding influences on the voting decision.

We shall review these three types of influence:

1. Personal background.
2. Interaction characteristics of the job.
3. Presence or absence of off-the-job relations with management.

We have been examining voting decisions in terms of ways of conceptualizing the organization. Those who think of it in terms of vertical integration tend to vote against the union. Those who consider it in terms of horizontal integration tend to vote in favor of the union. But then we must ask: What influences lead a man to visualize the organization in one or the other form?

In certain respects, the personal background a man brings to the organization predisposes him to one or the other view. Nor does this seem to be a matter of unique personal experiences. Our pure farm cases grew up in a social environment where the prevalent pattern of interaction symbolized vertical integration. The individual was isolated from peer group interactions and spent most of his time up to late adolescence in the family under the ever-present control of his father.

Men of such background tend to enter industry with an initial tendency to see the organization in terms of vertical integration. In fact, Mark

Walling makes this quite explicit when he says that in his first industrial job, "I looked upon the foreman just like he was my father." The later reactions of Walling indicate that such an orientation may be subject to change, and yet the Walling case also suggests that the early orientation is likely to have a more persistent effect than even as sophisticated a worker as Walling recognizes.

At the other extreme, we find those individuals whose early interactional experience could be symbolized in terms of horizontal integration: a town or city background involving frequent interaction with boys more or less the same age, with much less pervasive influence from the father. Such men were naturally more oriented toward horizontal integration, and the union fitted congenially into that picture.

Those who began life on the farm, but left it at an early age or went into farm labor, tended to fall between these two extremes in orientation. They seemed to take to the idea of a union much more readily than the pure farm boys, and yet not a single one of them played any active role in promoting the unionization movement.

Note the type of analysis being undertaken here. In a book concentrating on organizational problems, we begin this particular discussion with an analysis of personality. However, we do not undertake to present the full-scale type of discussion that would satisfy a student of personality theory. This discussion is based upon a simple proposition: that personality and behavior in organizations can be examined in the same terms. If we set side by side the pattern of interaction which the individual has experienced in growing up with the pattern to which he is exposed in industry, we can make certain predictions about his reactions in industry.

These predictions are not, of course, unconditional. The orientation the individual brings with him to the job situation may be strengthened or modified by the influences which we shall now consider.

The interactional characteristics of the job provide one such type of influence. Here we need to consider two aspects: (1) isolation versus peer group involvement, and (2) the nature of the relation between workers and immediate supervisors.

First we need to note that the personal background seems to exert a selective influence upon the type of job situation in which we find the worker. We find that the only engine operators who wished to remain in that position were the pure farm boys, who were accustomed to a low level of interaction and isolation from peer group relations. The only man of a different background was doing his best to get out of the engine operation job.

The pure farmers also tended to gravitate toward positions as engine repairmen, where they served under a former farmer like themselves, and developed a harmonious relationship with him.

Under Jones and Fitch, the workers in the control room had been subject to heavy pressure of initiation of activity downward with little opportunity to initiate in the other direction, and this experience seemed to influence them toward horizontal integration.

Off-the-job relations with management provided another influence to either strengthen or modify a given orientation. Here we can distinguish three degrees of influence.

Two of the men in our sample had relatives in the management of the company. While these particular men sometimes expressed the same anti-management sentiments as other workers in Hi-Test, in the minds of fellow workers there never seemed any doubt that they would finally cast their votes against the CIO union.

A weaker or at least more fluctuating type of anti-union influence is illustrated in the cases of individuals who developed off-the-job interactions with management. We have here the cases of company union representatives like Kendall for Hi-Test and Shockley for the catalyst plant. (Shockley had also experienced another kind of tie with management: the personal check from Blank to his mother to compensate for the death of his father on the job. Even so, in an earlier period, when he was under Jones and Fitch, Shockley is reported to have signed a pledge card. As he became active in the company union, his anti-union sentiments manifested themselves again.)

In the case of Walling, it was the farewell party which provided him with increased interactions with management and with opportunities to initiate activities for management.

For Kendall and Walling, I was able to chart fluctuations in sentiments which were apparently in direct relation to the growth of their interactions with and initiations of activities for management.

For those men who had no special ties with management, either through blood or off-the-job activities, the voting decision could be expected to be a product of the first and second categories of influence.

We can sum up the forces operating in the voting problem with these general statements:

1. The individual's personal background with family and peers tends to condition his sentiments toward what he considers to be a satisfactory job and toward the union and management.
2. The interactions and activities he experiences on the job will further influence his sentiments toward union and management.
3. The presence of special off-the-job relations with management will tend to draw the individual away from the union and toward management.

I have indicated earlier the direction of impact of the influences noted in the first two of these statements.

# Chapter 16 *THE EVOLUTION OF UNION-MANAGEMENT RELATIONS*

THE union organization drive necessarily represents an attack upon management control. The aim is to persuade workers that it is unwise for them to place their faith completely in the hands of management. Management is attacked. If it is to be effective, the nature of the attack must be adjusted to the existing state of worker-management relations. The first organizers at Blank Oil Company attacked the company so vigorously that they stirred up an adverse reaction among many of the men. It was only when Masters' watchman statement came out that they learned how to attack management without attacking worker loyalty to the company.

However much bitterness enters into the struggle, union organizers seek to cast the union in the role that Leonard Sayles has called "lawyer for the defense."[1] That is, they seek to give the impression that, whatever the individual's problem, he is to look to the union for its solution. The union will fight management to get for him what he needs and deserves.

At this point, the competing and conflicting interests among workers tend to be submerged. As the workers discuss various possible rules and regulations, they may be aware that a decision which will give advantage to one individual or group will also deny it to others, but until the union is in being, no one knows which people are to get which particular advantages, and stress can be placed upon general benefits such as wage increases.

As the union receives its first official recognition, its struggle is by no means finished. For the union to function effectively, management people must change their behavior and relations substantially. This is not easily done. In fact, the changes are often accompanied by sharp attacks on individual members of management and on management in general by the union leaders. As management people gradually adjust to this new relationship, the sentiments and interactions on both sides change, and this change is often accompanied by the emergence of a different type of local

---

[1] Except for other references noted, this chapter is based largely on Leonard Sayles and George Strauss, *The Local Union: Its Place in the Industrial Plant* (New York: Harper & Bros., 1951).

union leader. The first stage of fighting for recognition tends to bring to the fore what Max Weber calls the "charismatic" leader, the colorful individual who has a gift for expressing the sentiments of his people and for dramatizing the conflict situation. As relations between the parties settle down, the new situation tends to bring to the fore the bureaucratic leader, the individual who is skilled at negotiation and who prefers to work quietly rather than with great fanfare. Sometimes the same individual can change his own behavior sufficiently to serve as leader from one period into the next, but often the change in the relations among the parties leads also to a change in leadership personnel.

This sort of leadership change has been widely noted. Let us turn to a case to show how the process of changing relations brings with it a change in union leadership. Lois Dean has provided us with case studies of two union locals which she studied intensively.[2] Both of them showed the same shift from the charismatic to the bureaucratic leader. In one case, the charismatic leader was in the process of dying of cancer at the time when his control was challenged, so that we cannot attribute his downfall entirely to the changing social situation even though we can show that his successor behaved far differently from him. Let us look at the second case in which the downfall of the charismatic leader was not influenced by such a health problem.

## THE RISE AND FALL OF FRANK VITUCCI

The setting is a manufacturing plant that had been family owned, but shortly before World War II, it was taken over by the Truax Corporation. Employment rose to between six and eight thousand workers; in 1944 a union carried through a successful organizing drive. Top management also recognized the union in three other plants at much the same time. Elsewhere the adjustment to the union took place with little conflict, but in our Truax plant there were two years of struggle before the change took place.

The chief target for the union in this period was Industrial Relations Director O'Leary, a man who had been accustomed to running his own show and did not respond readily to suggestions or demands from the union.

The role opposite O'Leary was played by Frank Vitucci, a young man who had played a leading role in organizing the local. He had grown up in a poor Italian-American section of the city and had learned early in his life to settle arguments with his fists. As a teen-ager, he had had some success as an amateur boxer. In the union situation, he made little use of his fists, but he seemed to find the same sort of satisfaction in fighting management in other ways.

---

[2] "Front Office Leadership: The Decline of Militancy in Two Union Locals," (Ph.D. thesis, Cornell University, 1953).

One of Vitucci's admirers described him in this way several years later:

Frank wasn't the most intelligent man in the world, but he was militant. He was willing to *fight* for his rights and what he stood for. He was a low seniority man. He only had two years when he got active in the union. Ordinarily a person with so little seniority wouldn't want to stick his neck out. But Frank never cared for his own job. He liked to help the people. I can't help admiring a man like that.

A union committeeman of the later period described the two antagonists in this way:

O'Leary was a rough and tumble sort of man, always shouting and pounding the table, and making threats. You couldn't argue with him. Frank couldn't argue either, you see. All he knew was to shout and threaten strike. So he'd go in to O'Leary, and they'd yell and shout at each other, and finally reach a settlement that way.

The quotation certainly does not make clear how the men actually reached an agreement on anything, but we have a clue from Vitucci's own comment at the time when O'Leary lost his job several months later. Vitucci was the only one who expressed regrets. He said,

O'Leary was a good Joe. He was too soft. You could badger him into anything. We won all our big grievances.

Apparently O'Leary, for all his tough talk, often found himself in an untenable position and had to give way—if the union put on enough pressure. Vitucci was the man to apply the pressure.

The gains the union made against O'Leary were piecemeal. From the time of organization in 1944 through 1945 and early 1946, they were unable to reach agreement on a general contract. Instead, the parties worked together by means of agreements exacted on specific issues. In late 1945, the union was able to persuade top management to send in another negotiator to work with O'Leary, and at last the parties reached a temporary agreement.

During the early post-war months, the union was in a precarious situation. The union fought for its life primarily through finding and processing grievances. In this period, union officers did not wait for workers to come to them. They canvassed for grievances. Contrasting his own leadership with that of his successor, Abe Carter, Vitucci says:

Every grievance Carter's bunch has now, we had fifty. . . . Why I won grievances under O'Leary that I wouldn't even *call* a grievance now.

Harassment of the foremen was an important part of the union drive. One former union officer describes in this way the campaign to get old Dan McDougall:

There were a lot of those old birds around, and they caused the union a lot of trouble for a while. We had to act tough and we had to do a lot of bluffing to get around them and get grievances settled so the people would be satisfied.

We had to keep creating interest in the union, you see. I'll never forget one time—it was the first time I ever saw Bob Stevens (former Truax main office industrial relations director). What happened was, we had a grievance in the drives, and one of these old-time foremen, Dan McDougall, had that department. He was a hard-boiled son of a gun, and he bucked the condition up there in the drives. The girls on the line did this operation where they had a little stick of carbon and burred off the spring. That created a lot of sparks shooting all over, and some of them were pretty big sparks. Their hands were always getting burned, and the sparks burned holes in their aprons. One girl had a spark drop in her lap, and went right through her apron, through her dress, and she had one of those rubberized girdles on, and it went right through that, and it wasn't until it actually burned her skin that she knew it was there.

It was horrible that such conditions existed. You see, they had improper ventilation. There were open windows, but no cross-ventilation, so the wind just blew the sparks back in their faces. And the odor was terrible, because there was no ventilation. Well, when that one girl got burned, that's when the grievance came up. I was a committeeman and I went up there, mad as hops. I'm storming down the aisle looking for Dan McDougall, and along comes John Perkins (assistant industrial relations director) and Bob Stevens from the other direction. I didn't know Stevens, never seen him before. Perkins was showing him through the plant that day, and he was about to take over as industrial relations director. So I just went barging up to Perkins—we had to do a lot of bluffing in those days. I shook my finger at him, and I said, "What's the matter that such conditions as these are allowed to exist! If you don't get some decent ventilation in here, I'll take the whole damned department out on strike."

Well, what happened was, the company finally began to get rid of these old foremen, and although they didn't say so, I know it was because these old guys couldn't get along with the union, and the company realized the union was here to stay. They'd tell these foremen they had to play ball with the union, and if they still didn't, the company got rid of them. That's what happened to Dan McDougall. After the company told him to play ball with the union, he'd talk fine to the union officers—he and I got along swell. But as soon as we left, he'd go back to driving those people that were working for him. Well, finally, he was just having too many grievances. And we really needled him.

One time, there was a grievance on one of the lines up there, and instead of having just one of the girls write the grievance, we decided to have all sixty of them write the grievance. You see, the grievance procedure provides that when there's a certain grievance that applies to more than one person, one can write it out and you can turn in just one, but the settlement will apply to all the people that are affected. But in McDougall's case, we decided we'd have each person on the line write a separate grievance. Naturally, that would stop the line because it couldn't run unless everybody was working, and there'd always be somebody writing out a grievance.

Well, we did it that way, and by the time five or six had written, McDougall gets in touch with personnel, all excited, and says his line is down because everybody is writing a grievance. They then start hunting for me, but naturally I've made myself scarce. They're calling for me here and there, and meanwhile I'm hiding in an oil shed between the two plants. I had a spy out and when about fifty-seven of the grievances had been written, I decided it was time to come out of hiding. So I went up to McDougall's department and he was all upset and said, "Look what's happening here, everybody is

writing grievances!" All the time, I'm looking out of the corner of my eye to
see how they're doing with the grievances. When I see there are only two to
go, I say innocently, "Is that so? I wonder what could be the trouble. But
they're nearly through, it looks like, might as well let them finish up, and
then we'll go straighten it out." So we got all sixty of them. It wasn't long after
that they had to let McDougall go.

It took longer to get O'Leary, but that time came too. The grievances
at the foreman level, of course, piled up to the industrial relations director.
There were also plant-wide issues, the most important of which came to a
head in 1945. The workers had been eating their lunches on company
time. The company proposed to eliminate the paid lunch period, thus
lengthening by half an hour the time the workers were to be in the plant.
When O'Leary did not readily back down on this issue, Vitucci and his
bargaining committee decided the time had come for a show of strength.
As a committee member describes the situation:

> It had to come. We had to show O'Leary we meant business, and we had
> to show him we had the people behind us. O'Leary never believed that. He
> figured if it ever came to a strike, why, the people wouldn't go for it, and
> that would be the end of the union. Well, he got the surprise of his life.

One night as the second shift workers approached the plant, they were
greeted by Frank Vitucci and several committeemen, who said simply:
"We're hitting the bricks." When the day shift arrived, a picket line had
already been established and the plant was closed down tight. After
giving the strike order, Vitucci and his fellow workers had disappeared,
so the walkout appeared to be a spontaneous wildcat.

The strike lasted a week, being brought to an end by the intervention
of a representative of the international union and one from top management. The strike was settled on Vitucci's terms, and the victory strengthened his hold on the membership. In the 1946 election he won an easy
victory as president against a popular worker by the name of Ed Lynch.

The 1946 negotiations proceeded in two stages. First a master contract was negotiated for the four plants including our Truax local. The
understanding then was that local wage structures were to be further
negotiated on a local basis. O'Leary insisted that there was nothing further to negotiate. Vitucci was equally adamant in saying that the union
would strike unless an appropriate agreement was reached locally. In an
effort to avert the strike, top management at last replaced O'Leary with
Don Paxton, who had dealt successfully with unions elsewhere. (O'Leary
said in parting, "The union cost me my job," and no doubt he was right.)

If Paxton had entered the scene some months earlier, perhaps the
strike could have been avoided. A man who is unfamiliar with local
practices naturally is hesitant about making important commitments
rapidly. Vitucci was not the sort of man who could wait patiently. He led
the local out on strike, thinking of this as just another demonstration of
strength which would be over in a few days. The strike dragged on for
five and a half weeks. Out of it came a three-point agreement:

1. The union and management would work together to establish a joint system of job classifications.

2. Management would set aside an inequity equalization fund from which workers in the plant would ultimately get from one to ten cents an hour, depending upon decisions on the adjustments that were due them.

3. The union would have the authority to distribute the inequity fund.

A Vitucci committeeman described what happened in this way:

> We worked awfully hard on that wage structure. We worked on it for months. . . . Everybody was pretty short-tempered. We had an awful time getting that thing set up to everybody's satisfaction. And then when we finally did, and put it into effect, there wasn't half the people in the shop satisfied. Some of 'em were ready to cut our throats because they didn't get anything out of the adjustments.

Everyone in the plant got one cent an hour beyond the increase agreed upon in the master contract, but some of the workers, where the inequities were assumed to have been the greatest, received as much as ten cents. Most of the workers received little more than the one cent minimum. To many of these people, the wage structure was technical and confusing. All they knew was that they had struck for five and a half weeks for nearly nothing. As Vitucci put it:

> We should have had the company allocate the money. This way, the union took the blame. The people that got the ten cents were satisfied. The beefs came from the guys that got the cent.

This settlement was the beginning of the end for Frank Vitucci's control over the local union. It is interesting to note that his downfall was not directly due to a failure to make gains from management. He did indeed make gains but at a cost that seemed too high to a large segment of the working force. Furthermore, his whole leadership approach was based upon attacks upon management. He was not skilled for the negotiating and political maneuvering involved in balancing various issues among segments of the membership. He was equipped to represent the union in the "lawyer for the defense" era. When the problems increasingly became ones of balancing the interests of segments of the work group—in other words, intergroup relations problems—Vitucci lost his hold.

Vitucci's successor, Abe Carter, was a man of very different personality. He had taken no part in the organizing campaign. First as a steward and later as recording secretary, he worked quietly, conscientiously and inconspicuously for the union. After becoming recording secretary with the backing of Vitucci, he began to speak up in union meetings. He spoke in a measured and thoughtful manner, with an excellent command of the language. People began listening to him with respect.

Ed Lynch, who had lost out to Vitucci in the 1946 election, began to cultivate Carter, and persuaded him to run for president in 1947. Carter centered his attack on Vitucci, charging him with leading the union into an unnecessary strike. Vitucci's campaign consisted largely of defending himself and pointing to the gains the union had made. Carter won a decisive victory.

The shift from Vitucci to Carter brought about a marked change in the atmosphere of union-management discussions. There was no more pounding on the table and shouting. Carter organized his information carefully and systematically and presented it calmly and cogently. Don Paxton, successor to the table-pounding O'Leary, replied in the same vein. The excitement gradually faded out of labor relations at the Truax local.

Along with this change in union-management relations went a growing centralization of control within the local union.

There was a marked decline in the importance of the shop steward. A man who had served as steward in the Vitucci period made this comment:

The stewards don't amount to anything in the shop nowadays. They're just not important. About the only thing they do is to write the grievance out. After that, their job is done, and the committee handles the grievance from then on. In fact, the committeeman is usually in it from the beginning, anyway. The stewards *used* to be important, though. We handled more grievances right on the floor of the shop, instead of saving them up and meeting with the company once a week, the way they do now. As a matter of fact, they haven't *got* any grievances anymore. They'll go in and meet with the company every Friday morning, and maybe they've got one grievance. In our day, we *dug up* grievances. We went out and looked for them. One time, I remember, there was a fellow named Rockwell who'd been laid off unfairly and should've been reinstated with back pay. He was working some place else, but we went out and dug him up and brought a grievance. We won it, too, and got him his job back. Maybe that wasn't necessary, but you see, we had to show the union's strength.

## THE DECLINE OF THE STEWARD[3]

This seemed to be a common developmental trend. Furthermore, it came not simply from the decline in frequency of grievances but from at least four other factors.

First of all, there was *a change in the role of the foreman.* In the old days, the foreman really ruled the roost in his department. One of the first union attacks was on the foreman, as we have seen in the case of Dan McDougall. And so management generally was inclined to limit the foreman's freedom of action, to make him check with superiors before he gave an answer to a grievance. Management was afraid that if it let the foreman in department A make a settlement, this would result in a similar move by department X, and so a more uniform approach seemed necessary.

Since the steward was the man who handled the grievances with the

[3] This section, in revised form, is taken from my remarks on "The Grievance Process," *Proceedings of a Conference at the Labor and Industrial Relations Center,* Michigan State University, March 23–24, 1956.

foreman, the change in the role of the foreman had the effect of pulling the rug out from under the steward.

Second there was the *natural tendency of workers to appeal to the biggest shot that could be reached.* The steward was a fellow you knew too well. Somehow you felt that if you could contact the chairman of the grievance committee, the president of the local, or even the international representative, that would be much better. Just as in politics we think that if we can get to the United States senator rather than some local politician, we will do better, so it is in the plant. We see this not only inside the plants. When the local president, grievance man, or head of the grievance committee is out socially in the community, he may have a grievance put to him at any time. It doesn't matter what the occasion is or what the hour is. It is a twenty-four-hour job. When this happens, as union president or chairman of the grievance committee, you are supposed to tell the man gently but firmly, "Go to the steward first." In an organization that depends upon workers' votes, it is hard to do that. Many union presidents and other high local officials fear that workers will say about them as indeed they do say, "Well, Joe used to be a regular guy, but now he's too big for us."

Third, the *technical nature of many grievances became a problem.* Ten cents across the board is very simple, but grievances involving incentive rates, for example, are very technical indeed. There may be only one or two men in the local union who are qualified to argue and settle such grievances with management. Even they may need help from the international representative or some technically trained man in the international union.

And fourth, *many grievances are in fact inter-group problems.* For example, take the hypothetical case of a department made up of polishers and grinders. A new job comes into the plant. It is a better than average job. Should a polisher get it or should it go to a grinder? Is the steward a polisher or a grinder? In either case, his position is untenable. If he is a polisher and expresses the grinder's point of view, the polishers will accuse him of treason—if not lunacy. If he speaks for the polishers, the grinders will say he's looking after his own bread and butter. So the grievance by its very nature, has to be resolved by someone outside of the department. (Note that such a grievance has nothing to do with the time-honored argument of seniority versus ability. It is a question of which group gets the job.)

## THE UNION MEETING

This centralization of control reflected itself also in the local union meeting under Carter's regime. While no specific figures are available, all observers report that the turnout at the meetings under Vitucci was much larger than it was after Carter had become firmly established. In part, this was no doubt due to the atmosphere of excitement in the period in which the union was struggling for its life. In part it seems also to have been due to differences in the manner of conducting the meetings. If Vitucci had ever heard of *Roberts Rules of Order*, his meetings did not reflect the book. Anyone could get up and have his say. Grievances were freely brought up and argued on the floor of the union meeting. This sometimes made for long meetings. One wonders how interest could have been maintained when meetings lasted far into the night, and maybe some people were lost to the meetings because they took too much time. At the same time, people seemed to have a lively sense of participation. There was excitement in the union-management relationship then, and the worker could also look forward to excitement at the local union meeting.

The Abe Carter meeting was far different. He knew his *Roberts Rules of Order* by heart, and he enforced them. He had his agenda carefully prepared for each meeting, and he followed it. A member who tried to raise other topics might find himself called out of order. Carter insisted particularly that all discussion of grievances was out of order, since these were matters that should be referred to the grievance committee. In time it got so that only those close to the union officers turned out for meetings. The meetings that had drawn a hundred or more men regularly, and frequently much larger numbers, declined to thirty to thirty-five members per meeting.

There was some griping from the members about the way Abe Carter dominated the union, but there was no organized protest. Abe Carter ran the union, to be sure, but he worked diligently and he continued in his quiet and efficient way to make gains for the members.

### HOW MUCH CENTRALIZATION?

We have followed the process of centralization at the level of the local union. Does centralization go beyond this? Do we find that the top international officers have all the power in their own hands and that the local officers are little more than figureheads?

If we look at the determination of wages and fringe benefits, certainly it does appear that power is centralized at the top of the international union. In a large company, these matters are no longer negotiated at the local level. However, we must not exaggerate the degree of control that actually can be exercised from the top. Perhaps in an industry where there is very little technological change, so that work methods and procedures remain stable year after year, it would be possible to prescribe the rules and regulations from the top. In other situations, changes are constantly confronting local management and union people. Thus, they necessarily work out ways of getting together and resolving the immediate problems. If the solution that seems mutually advantageous to the local union and management people is not in accord with the written contract, this does not necessarily rule out the solution. The parties simply agree informally and take care that the agreement is not written down. In his discussion of "unofficial union-management relations," Melville Dalton makes these comments:

> In one of the plants a departmental superintendent declared:
> "(The plant manager and his assistant) have both said they don't give a damn what kind of arrangements are made with the union as long as things run smoothly and it's kept out of writing."
> Grievance committeemen made similar statements. Two of those whom I knew intimately were quite specific. One stated:
> "The top people (policy makers) lay down too many hard and fast rules to follow. But we get around the contract by doing a lot of things that we can work out and keep off the record."
> The other said:
> "Top union and management are always bothering the local plant. We can work out our own arrangements if they'll leave us alone. (The plant manager and assistant) told us they don't care what arrangements we make but if we get in trouble the contract will have to be followed to the letter right down the line."[4]

This was the only case in which a union officer admitted direct informal communication from management approving evasion of the contract, but actual behavior was similar in all the plants and had a character that could hardly have existed if local managerial and union officers had been opposed to evasion.

We see that in this way local union and management people retain a considerable amount of autonomy. At times each party has an interest in keeping the central office out of the local scene.


## THE MEANING OF GRIEVANCES

Years ago it was thought that a study of written grievances would cast light upon the state of union-management relations. Students even wrote theses on such data. Happily, this is seldom done any more. We have come to recognize that written grievances do not *clearly* tell us anything, though they can provide valuable data when combined with other types of data.

Does a large number of written grievances indicate widespread worker dissatisfaction? In general, this seems to be the case, yet we must not assume that every grievance represents a specific problem felt by a particular worker. As we have seen in the case of Foreman Dan McDougall, the submission of sixty grievances instead of one stemmed from a decision of a union officer. This was a way of putting pressure on management. A large number of grievances, therefore, may point to problems affecting union officers particularly and not just to problems experienced by rank

---

[4] See his "Unofficial Union-Management Relations," Robert Dubin, *Human Relations in Administration* (New York: Prentice-Hall, Inc., 1951), pp. 68–78.

and file members. This is not to say that the sentiments of the union officers are of no consequence. They are of obvious importance. I am simply
saying that a large volume of grievances does not point automatically to
the source or sources of the problems.

Suppose the rate of grievances is very low. Does this mean that the
workers are completely satisfied? No such simple conclusion can be
drawn, since a low rate can grow out of a variety of influences.

First, there may be a reluctance on the part of workers to express their
problems in terms of grievances. Why should this be so?

There are two factors to account for this. One is the old American
tradition of individualism and self-reliance, the belief that many of us
grow up with and which is reinforced in the schools, that one should be
able to take care of one's individual problems. We find workers talking
about this and saying in effect: "Somehow I ought to be able to handle
this matter myself, and I feel a little uneasy about going to anyone else
about it." It may not mean that they don't trust the union or that they
don't believe in the union. Many people, apparently even in well-established unions, view this turning to the union as an admission of the
helplessness of the individual.

There is another aspect: the workers' concern for management's reaction to the grievance. Workers don't like to be considered "trouble-
makers." Usually the worker does not fear a specific reprisal. However,
he has an uneasy feeling that if he puts in a grievance, management will
not forget it, and maybe somewhere along the line he will not get the
breaks to which he is entitled.

This presents a problem to union stewards and officers. We have run
into situations where union officers have been quite embarrassed to find
themselves in the middle of processing a grievance only to find that the
worker says, "Oh no. Let's forget about that. I didn't really mean it."
This gives management the impression that the officer is stirring up
trouble. The good worker just got talked into his grievance. Generally
we found it was the good worker who began to get a little leery about
this process when it came to a showdown, and decided that he would
rather back out. This eventually led union officers to require that the
worker sign his name to the grievance before submitting it for action.

A low rate of written grievances can also be a product of situational
influences—but it can grow out of quite different situations, as the following three cases will indicate.

Donald Roy has reported on a department in which he was a machine
operator.[5] The workers there had an intense distrust of management and
yet hardly ever put in a written grievance. They also thoroughly dis-
trusted the union and were convinced that it would do no good to process
grievances. Why this was so, Roy did not have the data to explain, but

---

[5] In my *Money and Motivation* (New York: Harper & Bros., 1955), chaps. iv,
v, and vii.

the important point for our purposes is that a distrust of the union can balance the pressures created by distrust of management, so that workers do not see the grievance procedure as a solution to their problems. This does not mean that they do nothing. In the Roy case, the men were very active in restriction of output.

In the case reported by Dalton earlier in this chapter, the distrust of management did not seem so intense—though we have no measures of this. There was enough confidence in the union to bring worker problems to the attention of union officers. However, the union officers and management people both felt that they had more freedom for maneuvering and striking bargains when nothing was put in writing. Thus many problems that were in effect grievances were handled informally without any written record.

In my study of the Chicago Inland Steel Container Company plant, I found a sharp change from many grievances to practically none at all.[6] The later situation was one of extraordinary harmony between union and management, and yet the absence of grievances did not mean that there were no worker problems being felt or handled. I found in fact that many worker problems were being taken up and resolved, but here again there was an avoidance of written records. In this case, the motivation was somewhat different from that reported in the Dalton case. The parties at Inland had come to take great pride in their harmonious relationship. They had come to think of grievances as symbolizing poor relations. For this reason, they simply avoided writing grievances on many problems that could have been written on grievance forms. The problems were resolved informally through discussion at whatever level seemed appropriate.

This suggests that the number of grievances raised—as well as the type of problems presented in grievance form—must always be considered in the social context of a particular union-management relationship.

## THE EVOLUTION OF RULES

The establishment of a union-management relationship involves also the development of a set of explicit rules for the governing of the industrial community. These rules limit the exercise of managerial judgment. For workers, they introduce important elements of predictability into a world that is largely beyond their own control. The effects are not entirely one-sided. While the rules limit managerial judgment, they can also ease the burden of decision-making through limiting the choice of alternatives.

Our whole book could be devoted to the evolution of rules in the union-management relationship. Here we will confine ourselves to one example: the seniority system.

While workers are by no means unanimous on this point, their prefer-

---

[6] *Pattern for Industrial Peace* (New York: Harper & Bros., 1951).

ences in general are for seniority clauses which give substantial weight to length of service in decisions regarding promotions, transfers, and layoffs. Why should this be so? While workers do not put it exactly in these terms, interviews suggest that they see themselves as investing their time in the service of the organization. The investment the worker makes should entitle him to some reward. More specifically, if Jones has invested more time than Smith, then Jones should have preference over Smith in promotions or in holding onto his job in layoffs. In general, management people share the same sentiments: that other things being equal, the preference should go to the man with greater length of service.

Differences arise regarding the relative weights to be given to length of service as opposed to ability, with management people, of course, emphasizing ability. The workers, too, recognize ability differences. Their desire to reduce the weight of ability in these judgments is due partly to their distrust of managerial standards of judgment. How is superior ability to be distinguished from mere favoritism in managerial judgment?

For example, consider the case of Walt Marshall in the catalyst plant of the Blank Oil Company. A catalyst plant worker told this story about Walt, and several others vouched for its accuracy:

When Al Manton (plant superintendent) was here, there was a job opening up as reclamation operator. It was a daylight job so everybody was interested in it. I had the most seniority so I thought I should get it, but when Al comes down here to post that job, he tells us, "There is no use anybody else bidding on that job. I am going to give it to Walt Marshall." Walt used to give him chickens, and he would sell the old man eggs. I have been down here when Al came down about those eggs. He would say, "Walt, how much do I owe you for those eggs?" And Walt would say, "Oh, anything you want to pay, Al, that's all right," so Al would pay him thirty-five or forty cents a dozen. Walt was open about it. He used to boast about the way he gave Al the chickens.

Of course, higher management did not approve of its foremen and superintendents becoming thus personally obligated to workers, but this kind of thing often does not come to the attention of higher management. Anyone who has interviewed workers about the plant situation before the union came in has picked up similar stories of the establishment of personal obligations which the supervisor has then sought to discharge by giving a worker preferential treatment.

When Tom Lloyd had become foreman of the Hi-Test plant, he described to me this experience from his period of supervising the catalyst plant:

I got into the most awful mess there I ever did in my life. After I had been there for a while, it was all a matter of routine. I went to Al Wenzel (the division superintendent) to tell him I wanted to quit and join the navy. I told him that there was no use having an engineer in that plant. One of the men could handle it. He said, "All right, can you recommend a man?" I picked out the man I thought was the best worker, and began to train him into the job.

As soon as the other men found out what was going on, they began to pick on Walt. They were just like a bunch of white roosters picking on a black one. They made things hard for him, and they complained over his head. So finally we couldn't give the job to Walt. . . . Of course, it was only my opinion that Walt Marshall was the best man, but then I was in the best position to judge.

Tom Lloyd had received neither chickens nor eggs from Walt Marshall. Granting his own fallibility, he was doing his best to select the most competent man for the job. Considering Marshall's past behavior, there was no possible way in which Lloyd could have convinced the men that the decision had been made on the basis of ability alone.

Many experienced management people have come to accept Tom Lloyd's view of seniority: that it is a good rule to follow in general but that there should be exceptions to it for jobs requiring special abilities. We must recognize that for many jobs in American industry, individual differences in skill have little meaning. For example, consider the men on the assembly line. Since the jobs require such a minimum of skill in the first place, it would be absurd to try to develop a promotional system based on estimates of the comparative abilities of the workers. The more abilities a job does require, the more inclined are the workers themselves to give some weight to ability in filling the job. However, they still demand some standards of evaluation in which they themselves can believe. This puts the responsibility on management to develop standards that will seem reasonably objective. In some cases the problem has been approached through a joint union-management administration of the standards. For example, we found in a study carried on in 1946 that union-management relations in the Tennessee Valley Authority were extraordinarily harmonious.[7] No one factor could be credited with this result, but it was interesting to note that unions and management had agreed upon a set of qualifications *and testing procedures,* jointly administered, to determine the qualifications of workers applying for positions demanding real skill. Management experience in this case showed that the union members of the promotion boards were even more exacting in their insistence that workers meet high standards in the tests before being promoted than the management people were inclined to be. This suggests that when workers and union leaders have some involvement in the establishment of promotional procedures and standards, so that possibilities of favoritism are reduced, it is possible to gain from workers some acceptance of ability as a criterion for promotion.

Seniority has been traditionally considered as an issue between unions and management. More recently we have come to recognize its broad significance as a system of rules placing individuals in the social system. Even where the placement of the individuals is to be determined by sen-

---

[7] William F. Whyte, "Patterns of Interaction in Union-Management Relations," *Human Organization,* Vol. VIII, No. 4 (1949).

iority alone, it remains to be decided in terms of what organizational units seniority shall be figured. For example, consider the cases of Jack Carter and several other Benton glassworkers who rose so rapidly to the top in the blowing room. If seniority at Benton had been calculated in terms of the plant or department, Jack Carter would never have been able to move over from another plant in the first place. It was only because seniority at Shawcross was figured in terms of service in all of the plants in that city that Carter was able to bring his seniority with him to Benton. The life we observed in Benton was strongly influenced by the seniority system which determined in part the characteristics of workers serving there.

While a seniority system provides workers with some security against arbitrary decisions of management, it should also be viewed as an influence on and a product of inter-group relations among the workers. Seniority involves not only the individual's current position in the department but also the structure of the promotion ladder: what job or jobs the individual can promote into, what job or jobs he can be bumped down to, in case of a reduction of the force. When forces are reduced, it is to the advantage of the individual to have as many jobs under him and as few over him as possible. This limits the number of people who can bump him to lower positions and provides ample bumping opportunities for him. To some extent, the nature of the promotional ladder will be determined by the technology and skills required, but where there are many jobs of approximately equal skill, there is considerable flexibility in setting up the promotional ladder. Furthermore, as technological changes take place so that new jobs are created and old jobs eliminated or modified, questions frequently arise as to possible rearrangements of the jobs and as to changes in the promotion ladder. We often see groups of workers struggling with each other over where a new job will fit.

As the union enters and establishes itself, inevitably it limits the free exercise of managerial prerogatives. As time goes on, the union may come to share in the discharge of a number of responsibilities. In some cases, the union may succeed in taking over control. This may seem like an important victory for the union, but let us note inter-group problems that may arise when the union does in fact assume control. In this chapter, we have noted how Frank Vitucci's victory in taking over, for the union, the distribution of the inequity equalization fund led to his downfall. In another plant we studied, the union had won a victory that gave it the power to determine seniority units and lines of promotion within the plant, subject only to the proviso that management be assured that individuals would be required to accept promotions offered. At the time of our study, we found the grievance committee of the local union more occupied with seniority disputes among its own members than with any other matter. In effect, the union had taken over this area of inter-group problems. When workers did not like a given decision, they could not blame management for it. It was their own union that had done it. This led to serious frustrations on the part of local union officers. They had to wrestle with very complicated matters through long hours of discussion, only to find that whatever they decided would be rejected by many of the workers.

## LOYALTY: DUAL OR DIVIDED

Many management people have been inclined to view the union-management relationship in terms of a competition for the loyalties of workers. The assumption seems to be that if the man is loyal to management, he cannot be loyal to the union, and vice versa. This may sound logical on the face of it, but is it in accord with reality?

It is at the time of organizing the union that the competition for loyalties appears to be most pronounced. In analyzing the campaign at Hi-Test, we talked in terms of vertical integration versus horizontal integration as alternative ways in which workers may conceptualize an organization. But even here, we drew attention to the case of a strongly pro-union worker who said, "This has always been a good company to work for," and went on to speak of the company in highly favorable terms. While in the organizing stage, sentiments tend to polarize, apparently even at this time some measure of dual loyalty is possible.

As the collective bargaining relationship becomes established, it is more likely to be accompanied by dual than by divided loyalty. This is perhaps the most thoroughly demonstrated proposition that we have in human relations in industry. The evidence comes from questionnaire survey studies of at least twelve union-management relationships. While the specific wording of the questions may have varied from study to study, the studies all had this in common: Workers were asked to express their sentiments toward the union and toward the company.

If loyalty toward one party necessarily involved alienation from the other, then we would expect workers who expressed favorable sentiments toward the company and management to express unfavorable sentiments toward the union and union leaders. By the same token, we would expect those who expressed favorable sentiments toward the union and union leaders to express negative sentiments toward the company and management.

So far this condition has never been reported. In one case, George W. England reports a complete absence of correlation—but *not* a negative correlation.[8] The Illini City study of five plants reports *positive* correlations in sentiments toward company and union running from .10 to .46.[9] While the two lowest correlations are not statistically significant, it is worth noting that all correlations are in the same direction. Furthermore,

---

[8] "Dual Allegiance to Company and Union," *Personnel Administration*, Vol. XXIII, No. 2 (March–April, 1960).

[9] Ross Stagner, "Dual Allegiance as a Problem in Modern Society," *Personnel Psychology*, Vol. VII, No. 1 (March, 1954).

the combined rank-and-file correlation of .32 for the five cases is significant at the 1 per cent level.

Willard A. Kerr, studying the Buchsbaum case so noted for harmonious relationships, reports "a positive Pearsonian coefficient of correlation
between the total scores on the management-oriented ballot and the
union-oriented ballot of .73."[10] That exceedingly high correlation suggests that dual loyalty will be most pronounced in situations marked by
cooperation among the leaders of both parties. On the other hand, Father
T. V. Purcell, in a study of the Swift local of the United Packinghouse
Workers of America, reports 73 per cent of the workers being favorable
to both organizations, with only 26 per cent being favorable to one and
unfavorable or neutral to the other.[11] The Swift situation was not noted
for union-management cooperation, and in fact, a strike had taken place
before the study. On the other hand, Father Purcell reports that the
workers were opposed to the strike and only went along as required by
the top officers of the international.

In a study of three local unions ranging from peaceable to contentious
relations with management, Lois R. Dean also finds dual loyalty expressed
by the workers as a whole in each situation.[12] When she then goes on to
check the relations among sentiments, interactions, and activities in each
case, she does find interesting differences. In the conflict case, the pro-
union, anti-management workers report themselves as attending union
meetings in far greater numbers than the dual loyalty or other categories
of respondents. A slight tendency in this direction was observed in the
in-between case, whereas the peaceable situation did not show the pro-
union, anti-management workers attending meetings in disproportionate
numbers at all.

The author gives this interpretation of her findings:

> Where management and the union are in continuous overt conflict, dual
> loyalty may still exist in the plant as a whole. The union meeting appears to
> attract, however, an entirely different sort of person; that is, the worker who
> does not see union and management as having compatible goals. This worker
> obtains further justification for this perception from what he learns at union
> meetings. For if relations between union and management are strained, the
> union leaders are likely to emphasize the conflict and insist that any benefits

---

[10] "Dual Allegiance and Emotional Acceptance-Rejection in Industry," *Personnel Psychology*, Vol. VII, No. 1 (March, 1954).

[11] "Dual Allegiance to Company and Union-Packinghouse Workers. A Swift–
UPWA Study in a Crisis Situation, 1949–52," *Personnel Psychology*, Vol. VII,
No. 1 (March, 1954), pp. 48–58. For a full report, see his book, *The Worker
Speaks His Mind on Company and Union* (Cambridge: Harvard University Press,
1954).

[12] "Union Activity and Dual Loyalty," *Industrial and Labor Relations Review*,
Vol. VII, No. 4 (July, 1954), pp. 526–36. Dean also reports similar findings from
Daniel Katz' University of Michigan Survey Research Center study of a large
automobile factory, and from Arnold Rose's study of a teamster's local. See his
*Union Solidarity* (Minneapolis: University of Minnesota Press, 1952).

the rank and file enjoy are due to the union's unremitting struggle against an obdurate management. Under these circumstances, dual loyalty breaks down, and the anti-management, pro-union worker predominates at the union meeting.

The union meeting, then, has a selection and reinforcement function. The workers it selects and the attitudes it reinforces depend, at least in part, on the degree of conflict in the union-management relationship. Apparently, management need not fear that the presence of a union in their plant will necessarily cause workers to become disloyal to the company; but if union-management conflict prevails, the most active unionists are likely to be the conflict-oriented workers with strongly one-sided loyalty. If the union-management relationship improves, our data suggest that control of the union may very well shift accordingly; so that, as at Amco, the active unionists will be those who look with favor on both management and the union.[13]

How do we explain this phenomenon of dual loyalty? It might be explained in personality terms. Perhaps the world is divided between "positive thinkers" and "negative thinkers." The positive thinkers tend to view things in a rosy light, whereas the negative thinkers see the world in more somber hues. While this is a possibility, it implies that the rosy responses of the positive thinker would not be limited to the union and management but would be seen in all of the questions, with an opposite tendency for the negative thinkers. Actually, the questionnaries do not seem to show this much uniformity.

Perhaps a more plausible explanation is provided by the integration of the union-management system itself. As the union-management relationship develops, the parties are no longer sharply separated in their spheres of activity. In effect, it is union and management together who administer the social system of the plant, even in cases where there is a good deal of friction between them. Furthermore, the workers come to realize that many of the problems they face are not problems separating union from management but rather problems in which union and management agree that one group and not another will receive a given benefit.

After the excitement of the organizing period has passed, we find that rank and file workers do not generally continue to speak of "we" in referring to the union. The union, like the management, is "they" to the workers. If a worker thinks that "they" are administering the system well, he checks favorable sentiments to both parties in the questionnaire. If he thinks "they" are doing poorly, he marks off the opposite conclusion, also for both parties.

So far little attention has been given to the possibility of the existence of dual loyalty among management people. Father Purcell reports 57 per cent of the Swift foremen manifesting this combination of sentiments (compared to 88 per cent of the stewards), but as yet we have no figures for higher management people.[14] If the logic of our analysis of dual

---

[13] *Ibid.*, p. 536.
[14] *Op. cit.*, p. 53.

loyalty among workers is correct, we should find the same phenomenon among management people—although perhaps in weaker form and less widely distributed. Indeed, as we talk with management people in a situation where the union is well established, we do find such evidences of dual loyalty. These men tend to accept the union organization as part of the whole institutional system and recognize an obligation to union leaders in their positions as leaders, in much the same way that they feel obligation toward fellow members of management.

### CONCLUSION

In this chapter, we have been following the evolution of a new institution, the union, and a new set of relations, those between management and union. We have noted the interdependence of the two institutions, as we have seen changes taking place within management affecting the union and vice versa.

As relations have evolved between union and management, we have noted three interrelated developments:

1. The issues between them become more complex.
2. Union officers become increasingly occupied with inter-group relations within the local.
3. A legal framework arises to regulate the relations between the parties. This consists of both the written law of contract clauses and the common law of past practices and understandings as to how things should be done.

These developments lead to the following two results:

1. A shift among industrial relations leaders from fighters to negotiators; from charismatic leaders to administrative leaders.
2. Centralization of decision-making activity toward the top level of local union and local management.

We also have recognized that many of the problems that previously were settled locally are now being settled on a company-wide or even industry-wide basis. We shall explore these implications particularly in Chapter 20, "Human Problems of Large-Scale Bargaining." However, our preoccupation with the drama of top level power struggles should not blind us to the fact that local union and management leaders may yet retain a good deal of *unofficial* autonomy in adjusting their relations to each other.

Finally, we have noted the evolution of a semi-integrated union-management institutional system. What may have appeared to the workers in the period of the struggle for recognition as two entirely separate and conflicting organizations, now seems to be an interlocking system, administered by management and union leaders together.

But a word of caution should be added to this interpretation. I do not mean to suggest that workers come to see union and management living together in perfect harmony. The fact that the parties are dependent upon each other and necessarily work together to at least a limited extent does not mean that they never fight. It only means that, after fighting, the parties come together again to continue their joint administration of the industrial relations system. In later chapters we shall examine the influences determining the degree of conflict or harmony we actually find within that industrial relations system.

# Chapter 17  *WORK GROUP COHESION AND MILITANCY*

SO FAR we have concentrated on union-management relations at the level of the local union. In this chapter, we shall probe below this level, looking at labor relations in departments or divisions of the local.

This view is necessary to avoid the tendency to oversimplify. We should not think of the local union as a homogeneous unit. Experienced union and management leaders recognize that labor relations behavior is far from uniform. Some groups appear to be militant while others are apathetic; some act in a cohesive fashion while others seem so disorganized that they are not able to present a united front to management.

What makes the difference? As we get below the level of the local and examine the technology and nature of the jobs, we find some of our answers.

This chapter presents for detailed examination cases from two local unions. The cases suggest certain tentative conclusions regarding work group cohesion, and Part VII will present a general, theoretical statement on the cohesion problem.

The first case involves a comparison between two divisions within a large local: one noted for the high level of activity and militancy and the other for comparative quiet in labor relations. We shall also explore certain changes which occurred within the militant division over the course of years.

The second case involves a small department which once was heavily involved in militant union activity, but later became so disorganized that no concerted effort could be successful. Here again we shall examine the impact of changes through time upon the level of cohesion and militancy within the department.

To understand the presence or absence of cohesion and militancy in each case, we need to begin our discussion with a description of certain aspects of the technology and the nature of the jobs as they affected the activities, interactions, and sentiments of the workers.

300

## 1. SMELTING VERSUS CHEMICAL DIVISION[1]

The study to be reported here involved a local union of over 6000 members encompassing a number of plants in the same city, all of them under the control of the works manager. The city was in French Canada, which meant that the higher management people were generally English Canadians. Workers, foremen, general foremen, and union leaders were almost exclusively French Canadians.

While our project was focused upon problems of relations within management, we were naturally interested in the forces involved in a four-month strike which was in progress during the course of our research. While the workers were out in all of the divisions and plants, it was evident that union militancy was not uniformly distributed. All the evidence indicated that the heart of union militancy was in the Smelting Division. This division had provided most of the labor relations crises leading up to the strike. However, the problems were not uniformly distributed through that division. It was on the vat lines, where most of the workers were concentrated, that the major labor relations problems arose. Furthermore, the man who was union president at that time had previously been a vat line worker, and the vice-president of the union for the division (who worked on the vat lines) was known locally as the most militant of the divisional representatives.

We will first compare the vat lines with the Chemical Division, where labor relations were markedly peaceable. Then, looking more closely within the Smelting Division, we will compare the vat lines with the caustic plant, where worker-management relations were quite harmonious. In each case, we shall ask what it is in the work situation that promotes or minimizes work group cohesion and militancy.

Let us compare the vat lines with the Chemical Division in terms of technology and the nature of the jobs.

1. *Working conditions.* Work on the vat lines was considered hot and heavy. The men had to work in close proximity to vats of molten metal, the extreme heat presenting a problem even in winter and making conditions exceedingly oppressive in the summer. In recognition of these difficult conditions, management provided air conditioned rest rooms in which workers spent up to half of the working day. Nevertheless, the working conditions generally were thought to be undesirable. Furthermore, most of the workers had to work close to the vats, so that this sort of experience was widely distributed.

In the Chemical Division, there was less of a problem involving excessive heat or heavy work. Certain working areas were rather dirty, but

---

[1] This section is based primarily on field studies carried out, under my general direction, by Laurent Picard and André Bisson.

there was a wide variation in conditions from location to location throughout the division. Working conditions were not uniform.

2. *Homogeneity versus heterogeneity.* We found a contrast between
the divisions in the nature of the jobs, and to some extent, this could be
described in terms of homogeneity versus heterogeneity.

On the vat lines, there was a day crew for each section. For operations
each section was divided into four parts, with crews working shifts in
each part. A general foreman was responsible for each section on a
twenty-four-hour basis. The jobs were closely similar in their skill requirements, and the spread between the lowest and the highest pay was
only about 13 per cent. As we have noted, all of these men worked close
to the vats, and this similarity in their jobs was of great importance to the
men.

Finally, for the vat lines, it could be said that the pattern repeated
itself over and over again from one end of the division to the other.
With very minor variations, one vat line was just like any other, with the
same complement of skills, positions, and working conditions.

The men here not only had the lowest average level of school grades
completed of any major section of the works, but they were also highly
homogeneous in educational and general social backgrounds.

The situation in the Chemical Division was much more heterogeneous.
There was a much wider variety of jobs and job classifications, and also
a greater range in pay (27 per cent) between the lowest and the highest
jobs. Since the top jobs were considered highly skilled, there was also
a much greater range in educational background within the division
—from very little schooling for some of the laborers to a high school
education for some of the top operators.

3. *Management flexibility.* The very heterogeneity of the situation
in the Chemical Division allowed for more management flexibility and a
greater degree of decentralization in the handling of labor relations
problems. What was done on one vat line naturally set a precedent for
the other lines, which tended to push labor problems up to high levels
for solution.

4. *Interactional opportunities.* While on the job, the men on the
vat lines worked together in teams. For roughly half of the working
day, the men were free to interact together without restraints in the
rest room. Furthermore, the men could leave their jobs for a period up to
three hours without causing a serious breakdown in operations. Beyond
the three hour point, the consequences of neglect would become exceedingly costly to management, but up to this point, management would
simply experience a drop in operating efficiencies. Thus it was easy for
one man to check with his fellows regarding his complaints, for groups
to meet with one another, and for demonstrations to build up involving
large areas or even the whole division. In other words, this was what

Leonard Sayles has called a high resonance situation, in which one individual facing a particular problem could readily find many others facing the same problem.[2] Such a situation is conducive to concerted group action. Far from inhibiting interactions among workers, the technology made it easy for such interactions to take place and for pair interactions to develop into group interactions and activities.

By contrast, most workers in the Chemical Division were widely separated in space, and they could not leave their work areas for any extended period of time without risking serious operational consequences. Furthermore, the worker in the Chemical Division who faced a given problem, even if he did seek out a fellow worker, might find that the other man did not share the same problem at all. In Sayles' terms, this was a low resonance situation.

5. *Strategic importance to the management.* While we could not argue that the Chemical Division was unimportant to management, it should be noted that the Smelting Division provided almost 40 per cent of the work force, whereas the Chemical Division provided less than half of that figure. Furthermore, management tended to think of the production of the works primarily in terms of the performance of the vat lines. It was said that most of the men in higher management had risen through the Smelting Division. Workers and union leaders seemed to recognize this sense of crucial importance in their division. Such a condition can be expected to encourage the workers to believe that concerted action on their part will bring concessions from management. The efforts of work group organization are likely to be rewarded.

6. *Job security.* Within this works, any reduction of the level of operations strikes the vat lines much more heavily than it does other divisions, including the Chemical Division. When the demand for the product drops off, vat lines are shut down and the men on those lines are transferred to other divisions or laid off. Having no transferable skills, the men in the vat lines are unable to make any special claim as to their value with management. They are thus inclined to look to the union for job protection.

Employment in the Chemical Division is generally much more stable. Even a reduction in the volume of liquids processed is not likely to reduce greatly the work force deployed through the plants. There is thus less need for the men in the Chemical Division to look to the union for job protection.

7. *The wage inequity issue.* The vat lines provided us with the case noted earlier, in which management had offered a production bonus during World War II to attract men during the existing labor shortage.

---

[2] *Behavior of Industrial Work Groups* (New York: John Wiley & Sons, 1958).

This production bonus made the total pay of the men on the vat lines higher than their skill justified. When the wartime labor shortage passed and management no longer needed a production bonus to attract new workers for the vat lines, management sought to reduce the size of the bonus during each contract negotiation. Thus the vat line workers found themselves sharing in each general increase, but losing a little of their bonus each time. Furthermore, the losses the vat line workers sustained were felt equally by all of them, and the threat of future losses affected all of them alike. An issue having a uniform effect on a group of workers is likely to stimulate a uniform response on their part.

## THE CASE OF THE CAUSTIC PLANT

The technological base for the differences in labor relations between the Smelting and the Chemical Division is further substantiated if we compare two parts within the Smelting Division: the large vat lines versus the small caustic plant. (The vat lines employed about 60 per cent of the workers of the division, whereas the caustic plant employed only a tiny fraction of this amount.)

While the caustic plant was formally within the Smelting Division, its technological and other characteristics were much closer to chemical operations than they were to the vat lines. The caustic plant offered a wide variety of working conditions and a high degree of heterogeneity in the job situation. The plant offered a pay range even somewhat greater than that found in the Chemical Division: the top job paid 32 per cent more than the bottom job (compared to 13 per cent on the vat lines). Since the plant was small and unique, most proposals for change initiated by workers or union officials could be carried through at low managerial levels. The caustic plant had smaller strategic importance to management than the vat lines, since it could be shut down for short periods without crippling company operations. This lessened the leverage the union and workers had in this unit. The interactional opportunities of workers in the caustic plant were also quite limited in comparison to those on the vat lines. Workers could not leave their jobs for more than a few minutes without incurring danger of explosions. No rest room facilities were provided for them. Since the caustic plant jobs were highly skilled at the top levels, and since the plant could operate economically even when other operations were reduced, the workers faced little problem of job insecurity. Finally, they were unaffected by the incentive rate inequity issue that was being fought out between management and vat line workers.

In all these respects, caustic plant workers resembled chemical plant workers much more than they did the men on the vat lines. Therefore, it is not surprising that management reported no labor relations problems with the caustic plant.

## POST-WAR ADJUSTMENTS

While we have reviewed some of the influences leading toward cohesion among vat line workers in contrast to the situation prevailing in the Chemical Division, this cohesion and militancy was not uniformly displayed. As we review developments through the first twelve post-war years, we will see how management sought to meet its vat line problems and how these management efforts led to counteractions on the part of the union in the vat lines.

Throughout this post-war period, there was no change in structure at the top levels. The division was divided into two departments, A and B, with a Superintendent for each department. Above the Superintendents was a General Superintendent for the division, who reported to the Works Manager. Changes in lower levels of the structure will be described presently.

During the period up to 1945, it appears that foremen and general foremen had had considerable authority in dealing with workers. The period 1945–52 was marked by a centralization of control. A general foreman describes the situation in this way:

Around 1945 and 1946, after the war, they took away completely the authority of the foremen. . . . Some time later, the union took account of the situation which was that the foreman was being neglected and had very little authority, and the union began to create problems that the foremen could no longer handle. They went to try to handle these problems at a higher level, and even at the level of Mr. S (works manager). At that time, the management did not permit the foremen to decide such matters. Even if the union did not understand this situation at the start, it is clear that after a certain time they saw what was going on, and it is also clear that they took advantage of it. For example, an employee might ask for a day off. The foreman would say no, and the grievance agent would then telephone directly to the superintendent without talking to the foreman, and would ask for the day off for the man. The superintendent would then telephone the foreman and tell him to give the man the day off. This sort of thing was happening right up to 1952.

This pattern of saying no at lower levels and saying yes at higher levels seems to have been maintained right up to the top.

The personnel manager at the time was the man who would say "no" for the works manager, but if the works manager himself could be reached and put under sufficient pressure, he would say "yes." At a lower level, the foremen seemed to be in the same situation as the personnel manager. They had no latitude for saying "yes." They could only say "no" and be reversed at a higher level.

This situation presented an open invitation to the union to put pressure on management and go on to the top for action.

This period also saw the establishment of the position of supervisor in the line of authority between general foreman and superintendent. A management man describes the situation in this way:

Four or five years ago, the organization chart was different. The foreman did not have any authority. It was the supervisor who decided everything. The general foremen were primarily messenger boys who took questions asked by their subordinates to the supervisor for answers, decisions, or favors. On the one hand, the general foremen did not have any authority, and on the other hand, the engineers (supervisors) were practically without experience. Up to this time, the engineers remained for a very short time in the same position. The situation was that the general foreman had to ask permission of an inexperienced engineer before making any change in the process.

The general foremen at this time had gone about as far as they could expect to go in the company, and were naturally concerned about maintaining their relations with subordinates. The supervisors, by contrast, were at the beginning of their careers and looked primarily upward toward establishing the relations that would enable them to advance. Furthermore, the supervisors changed positions so often that it was impossible to develop any continuity of operations in a given sector of the vat lines. Finally, most of the supervisors had little knowledge of the workers' language, so that language was a further block to good communication. Thus, there arose a serious cleavage between general foremen and supervisors. In this situation, the general foremen felt that they had little understanding or protection from above. They saw adjusting to the men and to the union as the only possible solution in such a situation. This led to setting up, each man for himself, a principality in which he developed his relations in whatever way would enable him to survive in this difficult environment. Each principality had its own norms of behavior. The supervisors, having very little communication with the general foremen, were unaware of these differences in operating practices, and had no way of effectively controlling the situation.

1948 marked the founding of a foreman's club in response to the unprotected and unintegrated situation in which the foremen and general foremen found themselves. Some of the men would have preferred to form a union of foremen, and the new club did, in fact, serve to present grievances to management.

The foreman's club raised two general grievances with management. Club representatives claimed that many foremen were receiving a smaller annual income than the workers whom they supervised. They also complained against the supervisors and urged that they be removed from the line of authority.

In 1952 and 1953, this structural change was made. With this change and the assumption of the position of works manager by John Black, we enter into a new period.

Before leaving the earlier period however, we should note that the 1942–52 decade was marked by an almost 50 per cent reduction in the labor force, accompanied by major construction programs and techno-

logical changes. Such changes no doubt complicated for managem
the handling of labor relations problems.

## THE NEW MANAGEMENT APPROACH: 1953–57

The new management approach was based upon a recognition that the foremen and general foremen were not really integrated into the management organization, and furthermore, that higher management had been exercising little control of the activities of the workers in the vat lines.

The structural change, involving the moving of supervisors out of the line and into staff positions, was the basic change which made possible the new management program.

Following the structural change, there arose these new developments:

1. The superintendent instituted weekly meetings with his staff and the general foremen to discuss policies and operations.

2. The general foremen were encouraged by the superintendent and his staff to visit lines other than their own in order to compare notes with other general foremen and have an exchange of ideas about operating practices. Up to this point, no such visits had taken place. It was only gradually, and with some difficulty, that this kind of visiting began to occur.

3. The general foremen were provided opportunities to visit another plant to observe the operation of the vat lines there and to see what ideas they could bring back. These visits seemed to provide an impetus to efforts toward improving efficiency throughout the division.

4. The superintendent set up promotion committees whose members, on a rotating basis, consisted of general foremen and staff. Previously, promotions had been made entirely from within a single vat line. Now, in the case of any vacancy, men were considered from all parts of a department. In the case of promotions from foreman to general foreman, the selection was no longer made simply in terms of men who had been moved up to serve as vacation relief for their particular general foreman. Three or four foremen were selected from various parts of a department to serve as vacation relief general foremen during a three-to-four month period, so that management could observe their abilities at length.

5. In an effort to clear up particular trouble spots, the superintendent arranged to transfer those general foremen who were thought to be particularly strong to take over the lines of general foremen who were not thought to be doing effective jobs.

I have commented on the tendency of the general foreman, in earlier years, to develop his own semi-autonomous principality as he sought to work out ways to live with the workers and the union. Management efforts to develop and improve uniform operating practices and to shift general foremen and foremen about in order to strengthen "weak spots" naturally had the effect of knocking down the walls separating the principalities and of disturbing the equilibrium of union-management relations.

This meant that problems between workers and management which

n settled at the principality level now became subject
ective control from higher management. To meet this
levels, the union leaders naturally tended to seek to
ce at the work level and exert pressure on management
the general foreman.

## CASES

The impact of these changes in the management approach can best be illustrated by description of two cases which precipitated worker-management and union-management conflict.

The first case grew out of the new practice of transferring foremen and general foremen from line to line. A general foreman, who was considered by his superintendent to have a very strong record, was transferred to take over the line of a general foreman thought to be weak and ineffectual. Along with the strong general foreman went a shift foreman by the name of Girard. Higher management knew Girard to be a very intelligent and conscientious individual, but one who had tended to be autocratic toward the workers and who had antagonized other foremen by his pretensions regarding his greater knowledge of operations. While they had cautioned him on these matters, his behavior had not seemed to change. Nevertheless, when he was among the men with whom he had worked for several years, he had no serious problems.

At the beginning of his new assignment Girard had no difficulties requiring the attention of higher management. Then he was away for several months, on loan to another plant. He came back to the line just at the time of heightened union-management tension. He ran into his first problem one Sunday morning when the union grievance man approached him and said: "You won't empty the vats on Sunday."

Girard replied: "The vats aren't emptied when we wish but when they are ready." The grievance man remained adamant on this point. Girard then called his department superintendent to ask whether he should force the issue. The superintendent replied that relations between union and management were then at a very delicate stage and that it would be well to hold off the pouring until the next day. (Actually, some of the vats were poured off on the following shift, still on a Sunday, without any difficulty.)

Somewhat later, management added new vats to the line, and this involved a redistribution of responsibilities. At the time of instituting a new schedule for cleaning up around the vats, higher management discovered that the cleaning-up duties on most of the lines had been abandoned from six months to two years earlier. The foremen were ordered to reinstitute the cleaning-up duties.

Girard, at this point, ordered one of the men to do some cleaning up. The grievance man told him that he could not issue such an order. Girard persisted. He told the man: "If you don't want to do the work, go on home." To this the man is reported to have replied: "I will not leave. The only one who can make me leave is the plant policeman."

Perhaps Girard thought the worker was just bluffing. When he still refused to follow orders, the foreman called the plant police and had the man ejected.

This action caused a stir throughout the division. The plant police were unpopular with the men, and Girard's action was bitterly resented. On this point, he did not even have the support of fellow foremen, who openly criticized him for not being able to handle disciplinary problems without bringing in such an outside force. Then several days later, Girard got into another argument with his men. Heated words finally led to drastic action; some of the men ejected the foreman from the plant.

This was regarded by management as an intolerable challenge to its prerogatives. Those considered to be ring leaders in the expulsion of Girard were discharged, and lesser disciplinary action was taken against several others. While the union leaders sought to defend the men, at least to the extent of decreasing the penalties, they were unable to provide an effective defense. The contract did not provide the workers with the right to eject the foreman.

The second case involved a change in working methods on a broader scale.

General foreman Daniel returned from a visit to another plant full of enthusiasm for the work methods he had seen there. Calling a meeting of his shift foremen, he convinced them that adoption of these new operating methods would result in improved efficiencies and also in less work for the men. Having convinced the shift foremen, Daniel then called a meeting with the workers on each shift to explain and endorse this new organization of work. The men evidenced at least a willingness to try out the plan.

As the new working methods were put into practice, Daniel's lines became a focal point of interest throughout the division. The department superintendent and the general superintendent visited the lines to observe progress. The general foreman felt the men were responding with pride to these evidences of attention and interest from higher management.

The new methods on Daniel's lines were also the subject for lively discussion among workers and union representatives in other parts of the division.

The union vice-president, Martin, now sought to intervene. He first tried to persuade the men and the grievance man on Daniel's lines to refuse to follow the new methods, but here he was unsuccessful. The men reported that they were satisfied that the methods were better for them as well as better for management. This resistance led to a period of ostracism for the men on Daniel's lines. For a short time other workers kept them out of the rest room or the lunch rooms. When this pressure failed to push the men back to the old working methods, this tactic was abandoned and the men were readmitted as before.

When the superintendent considered the methods to be firmly established on Girard's line, he took the first steps to introduce them elsewhere. Selecting another line for the change, he called a meeting of the workers on that line to explain to them what was to be done. According to the superintendent, one of the men got up and made the following statement:

> After all we would like to cooperate, but management should understand that the men have to take orders from the union. To have a strong union we must stick together. If there are to be changes made, the best thing probably would be to contact the union heads and then the union heads would give orders to the men.

The superintendent replied: "If there are changes to be made, it is written in the contract that management has the right to make them, and not the union."

The man replied in this way:

> Well, we don't know anything about that. You are an educated man and you can show us anything you wish and make us think you are right. If you have something to discuss, discuss it with the heads of the union.

According to the superintendent, the man acknowledged later that the union in the department had had a caucus on this matter and that he had been instructed by the union vice-president, Martin, to take this stand.

A short time later, the superintendent encountered Martin, who heatedly accused him of trying to break the union. The superintendent denied any desire to destroy the union and said that it was important to work together. After some further conversation, the superintendent asked for the cooperation of the union vice-president, who is reported to have replied in this manner:

> If you want to introduce your new system, there is only one way. Ask us and we will help you. Call a meeting with all the employees and explain it to them and we will help you.

The superintendent stated that he would be glad to do this.

Martin did not attend the meeting which the superintendent then called. Hardly had the superintendent begun his exposition when he was hooted and heckled by the men. Some of them got up and began pushing their chairs around on the floor, making such a noise that discussion was impossible.

That same evening the superintendent received a telephone call at his home from Martin, who apologized for the behavior of the men and promised cooperation in the future.

In consultation with his superiors, the superintendent had already decided to go ahead with further meetings with a change in approach. Now, instead of simply explaining the new methods to the men, he tried to elicit their suggestions for improvements in work methods which would get the new system under way. The second, third, and fourth meetings which the superintendent conducted went along without any disturbance and with a worker participation and discussion that was most encouraging to him.

When the superintendent next saw the union vice-president, he was told that if he intended to have any more meetings with the men, Martin was going to tell them to refuse to attend. The superintendent expressed surprise, saying that he had understood the vice-president was trying to help with the program. Martin said that he had wanted to help, but the program was dividing the union.

Blocked on the meetings, the superintendent decided to go ahead with the new program without further delay. He planned to introduce the new methods at first on those lines where he thought the general foremen had especially good relations with their men. He gave orders for the program to begin on one such line—and suddenly the other lines followed suit without waiting for similar instructions. The dam of resistance had broken, and in a short time the new methods were in use throughout the department. The superintendent reports that at this point he received a visit to his office from Vice-President Martin, who was extremely angry. According to the superintendent, Martin said to him:

> You have succeeded because you have control, but we will have our turn. We will stop this. The program is going because you have us by the throat.

Several months later, the whole works was shut down by a strike that lasted four months. Was there any connection between the union-management struggle in the vat lines and the outbreak of the strike? Since the strike grew out of the breakdown of negotiations on issues far transcending the vat lines, it is impossible to weigh the influence of relations within this division in the breakdown of negotiations. However, in the long series of negotiation meetings up to the strike, management people were convinced that Vice-President Martin was the most militant of the whole union negotiating group. The management negotiators were convinced that while some of the men on the union negotiating team were trying to avoid a strike, Martin actually seemed to welcome the prospect.

## ANALYSIS

These cases indicate the importance of the technology and nature of the job in channeling relations among workers and in stimulating high and low cohesion. The importance of a wage issue upon group activities is evident; however, we are not simply pointing out that money is important to workers. Note that the money issue affected all vat line workers alike, and therefore, inclined them to meet it in a like fashion.

The cases also illustrate ways in which management structures and policies may affect relations within a department or division and the ways those relations within a given unit may affect the union-management relationship as a whole. Let us explore these aspects of the program further through reviewing the management approach to the vat lines under the new works manager.

The works manager believed in decentralization. As far as the vat lines were concerned, should we describe the situation in terms of centralization or decentralization? Our case illustrates the difficulties we get into as we talk in a very general way about centralization or decentralization.

The case suggests that in the period 1953–57, control of operations became more centralized within the vat lines. At the same time, control of industrial relations became more decentralized. Management's efforts to move simultaneously in opposite directions may account for some of the difficulties management eventually faced. Let us explore further these conflicting movements.

Earlier we described the growth of the semi-autonomous principalities, with each general foreman and his foremen making explicit or implicit agreements with workers and union leaders regarding the way the lines would be administered. Management's program to increase efficiency led indirectly to the destruction of these principalities and to the increase of control in the hands of the superintendents and the general superintendent. This led, in effect, to more homogeneous conditions throughout the division. No longer could problems be resolved within the principality where they arose. A problem in one area of the division tended to become a general problem throughout the division. Thus, with increasing frequency, mass demonstrations and other concerted pressure efforts on the part of the union occurred in the division.

Decentralization in labor relations began with the works manager, who refused to respond to union grievances brought directly to him from lower levels in the vat lines. He believed that these problems should be resolved as close as possible to their point of origin. At first glance, this seemed to be a good human relations doctrine. But although it worked out very well in the Chemical Division, it did not work in the vat lines, where the impact of many of the problems touched the entire division. Furthermore, management efforts to centralize control of operations tended to transform principality problems into division-wide problems.

The role played by Martin, the union vice-president, must be viewed in the light of these conflicting trends. Management people explained his behavior in terms of adverse reflections upon his character and personality. While the situation did not provide opportunities for us to study Mr. Martin himself, even the management account of events and problems provides us with a possible line of explanation independent of any assessment of the personal qualities of the vice-president.

Under the principality form of organization, union leaders had been actively involved in the resolution of all sorts of problems. In developing the new efficiency program, the general superintendent and the superintendents were taking unilateral action. It was only when they encountered worker and union opposition, and when Vice-President Martin suggested more union involvement in the discussions, that management sought to include the union in the program. But then Martin did not attend the meeting at which he was expected, and he reasserted his opposition later.

This behavior seemed inconsistent, and therefore untrustworthy, to management people, but note that management was not really offering the union leader an active role in developing the new program. The superintendents had decided what they were going to do, and they were only asking Martin to come in to give his endorsement to their program. This represented such a radical change in union-management relations in the division and in the relations between Martin and the management people that one could hardly expect the union vice-president to accept it passively.

We should also note one important respect in which the decentralization program in labor relations was not in accord with the realities of organization structure. All our accounts of problems between Vice-President Martin and management in the division involved clashes with the superintendents. The general superintendent reported that he sometimes dropped in on meetings between the vice-president and superintendents, and other management people, but he appeared to view his role as that of an observer who threw in an occasional light comment designed to relieve tension. On the side of the union, Martin was responsible for affairs throughout the division. His position did not correspond with that of the superintendents. Rather, he was on the level of the general superintendent himself, and yet the two men rarely sat down to a serious discussion.

The same situation was observed at a still higher level. Except for the negotiating meetings immediately preceding the strike, for a period of many months the works manager had had only one contact with the union local president. That contact occurred at the time when a division-wide wildcat strike on the vat lines was coming dangerously close to the three-hour period at the end of which power on the lines would have been shut off and the lines would have gone down for a number of weeks. At that point the works manager warned the union president of the drastic consequences of continuation of the walkout and urged him to get the men back to work. This single contact, without discussion, hardly forms the basis for resolving industrial relations problems. The significance of the organization of interaction between union and management at various levels will be discussed in later chapters.

## 2. THE RISE AND FALL OF THE GRINDERS[3]

At the time of the organization of the union in 1941, the Grinding Department of 35 men in a work force of 1,200 provided the local union president and 3 members of the executive board. The grinders as a whole participated much more actively in union affairs than did members of the average department. Seven years later, the department provided no local union officers and few men who participated at all in union affairs. Whereas in the early period the men had been solidly united, now the department was divided against itself.

How do we explain these changes? Let us begin by placing the work group in its technological and physical and economic and social environments, and then let us look into the social system itself. The picture to be presented first represents the period around the time of union organization in 1941.

### THE ENVIRONMENT

The technology of centerless grinding provided a number of individual machines through which steel rods were run in a finishing process. The rods came into the department from an extrusion-type process that left a scaly, rough coating. The grinding finished them to a fine, mirror-like surface. In addition, errors in size that had developed at earlier stages in the process could be corrected through skillful grinding, thus saving waste materials and manpower.

The machines operated at automatically controlled speeds, but the men were required to set the machines up for each run and to adjust size tolerances to 1/100th of an inch and less. While the machine was operating, the worker generally had nothing to do except stand by, observe the process, and be ready to intervene if anything went wrong. When the machines were operating properly—which was most of the time —workers could leave their machines and move around the department for minutes at a time without any adverse effects upon operations.

Physically the workers were in an advantageous position. Their work space was light, clean, and airy. It was also located in the center of the plant, which put the grinders in a key position in the communications network. The work itself was light and the men did not get very dirty or tired on this job.

Since at this location all of the company's production of an important type of rod went through the grinding process, this department in 1941 had a strategic economic position. The workers' relations to the economic environment were reflected in their wages. They reported receiving the

---

[3] This case is based upon the article by Leonard Sayles, "A Case Study of Union Participation and Technological Change," *Human Organization*, Vol. XI, No. 1 (Spring, 1952).

highest pay of any group in the category of finishing operations. All of the men held the same job classification; they all received the same pay, except for the several "long grinders." There was just one machine that was larger and longer than the others, and men assigned to this machine received five cents an hour more than their fellows on the standard machines.

The grinders also received incentive pay. While management established the speed at which the machines operated, running the machines more continuously made the premium pay possible.

The economic importance of the job to management and its other characteristics combined to give the grinders a high status in the plant community. There were men involved in the production of steel who had higher classifications and received more pay, but in most cases their jobs were hot and heavy. These conditions gave the grinders some claim to social superiority.

As befits the favorable evaluation of their jobs, most of the grinders were long-service employees. Some of the newer men worked on a smaller second shift.

## THE SOCIAL SYSTEM: 1941

In this initial period, the sentiments of the men were reported to be quite similar on most important points. They took pride in their jobs and in their high status in the plant. They held strong feelings of friendship within the group. They were suspicious of management.

The technology and physical layout allowed for great freedom to interact on the job, and reports indicate that the men took full advantage of this freedom. The foreman was not seen on the floor very much. For the most part, these men just ran their own jobs. Most of the men lived in the same neighborhood. The men and their wives often got together for social activities, and family picnics were a common occurrence.

While the activities on the job called for setting up and tending the machines and reporting the production, it was possible for men whose machines were stationed near one another to share each other's work. In fact, when Joe Borse, who was to be first president of the union local, was out in other departments organizing for the union during working hours, other men "covered" the job for him. As already noted, the job activities, interactions, and sentiments growing up on the job led to the organization of social activities outside of working hours.

## THE UNION ENTERS

Why and how the workers in this plant were able to organize the union is not pertinent to our case. It is important to note how unionization affected leadership within the department.

At the time of unionization, there was no dominant leader in the department. The top seniority men held high prestige in the department, but with the exception of Straub and Salora, who were moderately active, the old-timers remained aloof from the conflict.

The leader of the organization drive, Joe Borse, had little seniority in the department. The two other grinders who were most active and influential in the organization drive were men of only moderate seniority: Korcz, who became an executive board member, and Silton, who became grievance man for several departments in the plant. Note that the union president and executive board members were elected from the plant-wide constituency, as was the grievance man, although his jurisdiction was limited to several departments besides his own. Thus these three men had achieved leadership not only within their own department, but also in the total plant community.

## THE FRUITS OF ORGANIZATION

Beyond the gains won by the workers as a whole through unionization, the grinders were able to take important steps to improve their own position in the early years of World War II.

As Sayles describes it:

With the outbreak of World War II, the demand for the company's product jumped sharply. The company, however, anxious to continue training replacements for this vital operation, refused to institute an overtime day, although this had become the policy in many other parts of the plant. The union supported a brief 24 hour strike that secured the coveted sixth day of work and the concomitant overtime payments. The company also demanded increased production but was unable to secure approval from the War Labor Board for an improved incentive plan. Adept bargaining by the union president achieved the results in practice if not in theory. The men were permitted to speed up their machines. At that time there was no change in the formula under which their earnings were computed, and this provided an automatic wage increase.

During the war, employment in the machine polishing department reached an all-time peak of 100, and there was increased confidence in the future. In the words of one of the men: "We felt we had the world by the tail. We were sure a cocky bunch then."

Later, as defense orders fell off, management undertook to change the incentive formula to take into account the increased machine speeds that had been authorized. This meant a substantial cut in earnings for the grinders. Led by Joe Borse, the men carried through a three-month-long slowdown which finally led management to re-establish the old incentive rate. In fact, the men did not just regain ground that they had lost. In the process of negotiation, the union was able to obtain from management a copy of the company's incentive formula, which had previously been confidential. With this knowledge, the men were able to increase their earnings without increasing production. They were paid for time spent on maintenance as well as on the piece rate for finished grinding. By writing on their time cards more maintenance time than was actually required, they achieved an actual pay increase.

## TECHNOLOGICAL, PHYSICAL, AND PERSONNEL CHANGES

Joe Borse became an international representative for the union in 1946. When he had been local union president, he had had union responsibilities for all of the company's operations at this location, but he had remained close to the grinders. As international representative, he could no longer work with them so closely. He was out of town a good deal of the time, and a new local president from another department was elected in his place.

Shortly thereafter, the department was hit by a combination of physical and technological changes. The old department was moved into a new plant a quarter of a mile away. If anything, the new surroundings were more physically desirable than the old, but the move disrupted the relations the grinders had had with men in other departments. No longer was their department the social crossroads of the plant.

As the men moved into the new plant, they were shocked to find that their process had been drastically devaluated by technological changes in preceding processes. In the new plant, management had installed greatly improved extrusion machines to produce a finished surface that required no further grinding. Many special orders still required the grinding operation, so all but a few of the oldest grinding machines were installed in the new location. As the department was by-passed on much of the production of the plant, the work available to the grinders was sharply reduced. With fewer polishing machines available to the men, some who had worked on the day shift for years had to drop back to the second shift.

According to the contract and past practice, the men with the least seniority were to drop back, but this affected men with as much as fifteen years of seniority, who had considered themselves fixtures on the day shift. This situation gave rise to seniority disputes that set the most influential men in the department against each other.

The most important case involved a written grievance signed by Korcz and Silton, who had played leading roles in organizing the union. They argued that because they operated the long grinders and had been receiving five cents an hour more than the men on the standard size machine, they were entitled to remain on the day shift and have men of somewhat greater departmental seniority drop to the night shift. The contract provided that in case of a curtailment of the work available, men of higher seniority bumped men of lower seniority down into a lower classification, or less desirable shift. It was specifically stated that at such a time of curtailment men were not allowed to bump up. Korcz and Silton were claiming in their grievance that the long grinder position represented a promotional step above the standard grinder, and therefore, they could not be bumped. The older seniority men naturally claimed that the job was in the same classification, no matter which machine was worked on, and that the long grinding job had never been considered a promotional step.

Management remained neutral in this case, allowing the men to fight it out among themselves. Straub, one of the top seniority men in the department, had just been elected steward, and he interpreted the grievance in favor of the high seniority men. Although no longer holding official union jobs, Korcz and Silton appealed the case from the department to the local grievance committee, to the district director, and even to the international president—but without success. The fact that the two men fought the case so hard and for so long contributed to the unsettled conditions of the department and to the suspicions which the men felt toward one another.

The second case involved the claim of a worker named Hoffman (then on the second shift) that another worker, listed as having more seniority, had achieved such seniority through a clerical error. Again management remained neutral and allowed the union to handle the case. After an investigation of the records, which yielded conflicting evidence, the union officials decided that the existing records had to be accepted as they were.

While Korcz, Silton, and Hoffman all lost their grievances, the cases left a heritage of bitterness that had important repercussions in later years.

In the years 1947–48, a decline in the volume of military orders, together with the new extrusion process, so reduced work for the grinders that all but the most senior men had to drop into the labor pool on a part or full time basis. Although the reduction of the total *number* of grinding jobs was not great, the work became irregular for most of the men. This lowered further the desirability of working in the grinding department, and men now began to transfer out into other departments. This also heightened conflict within the group, for some second shift men claimed that the first shift men were putting pressure on management to see to it that whenever work was short, the first shift people got to work full time and the second shift men bore the brunt of the shortage.

### A CUT IN PRICES

In the midst of internal bickerings, the department faced its most serious crisis—management again attempted to change the grinders' lucrative incentive formula. One day the superintendent appeared and without prior notice, tore down the old standard sheets (upon which incentive earnings were based) and posted new and more stringent ones.

The threat of a 30 per cent cut in earnings for everyone held some promise of reuniting the group that had been badly shaken by seniority disagreements. The succeeding events are described by one of the night shift men:

The same day we get together with the union president. Everyone gathers around and he tells us it's up to us and the union will back us. Whatever we do the company can't fire us. The day shift decides to hold a meeting that night. We men on the night shift knocked off to go to the meeting. Everyone was there. It was made pretty clear then that we were going to maintain our old speed. We weren't going to tell anybody but if management said anything to anybody, we were all going to walk off the job next day. We weren't going to take any threats.

Well, the next morning coming to work, three of the older men who ride to work on the bus together, three big shots, who always decide things, got together and decided that no, that wasn't the thing to do. They were going to go along with the new speed the company posted. The word soon got around and that was the end of our plan.

This resulted in general confusion in the department; with Borse no longer union president and other officers who once represented the grinders now inactive, the men lacked strong leadership. Bill Silton, who had been one of the department's ablest grievance men, recalled an exchange he had with one of the "older men:"

I was telling the men right then and there that the thing to do if we wanted to protect our incentive plan was to walk off the job. But then Salora turned to me and said, "Why are you telling us what to do. You haven't anything to lose. How do we know if these jobs will be waiting for us when we come back, that somebody else won't take them?" I tried to argue with him. I told him no good union man would take our jobs. We have a good union and they'll be behind us. But Salora and Dules and the others, they didn't care. They figured, five or six of them, they'd always be working anyhow. They didn't care what happened to the incentive plan or the rest of the men; so they didn't do anything about it and that was the end of our incentive plan, right there.

Of course the day shift men had another interpretation of the same events:

Sure, these younger guys wanted to strike. They were in favor of it right off the bat. But they had nothing to lose. Most of them by this time were in the labor pool doing unskilled work for low wages. We had a lot to lose. We figured we weren't going to strike. I'm sure it wouldn't have done any good anyhow.

The majority of the men apparently were not satisfied that the union leaders could really back them up once they started something.

The rest of us weren't clear either what we were risking, whether the company could get rid of us, so we followed the older ones instead of doing what we had originally planned.

Fears were also expressed that management might move the grinding operation out of the community to some other plant.

While in 1945 they had shown their unified determination to resist any changes by a prolonged slowdown, in 1948 the men merely went through the motions of filing a grievance. This soon became a dead issue, although the company promised a better plan "some time in the future." The men did little to pressure the union into action on their case.

### MANAGEMENT'S NEW OFFER

By the spring of 1951, the volume of orders involving grinding had again picked up, and management was concerned with increasing production in the department. This led the company to offer—for a trial period—a new and potentially rewarding incentive formula. The men on the first and second shifts decided informally that they would give only a moderate increase in production during this trial period so as not to give the company any excuse for another tightening of the rate. This time it was the men on the second shift who broke away from the informal agreement and joined the "youngsters" on the third shift in breaking all previous production records. Even management was surprised by the extent of the increase. It appeared likely that the new incentive formula would be drastically cut because of the lack of solidarity of the men.

On two critical occasions then, when standing firmly together might have seemed to be of advantage to all members of the department, that solidarity broke down in the face of distrust among the men.

### STATE OF THE SOCIAL SYSTEM

Let us now compare the state of the social system as we found it at the end of the case, with the picture presented at the beginning. We can summarize marked changes in sentiments, activities, and interactions.

So far as we can determine, worker sentiments toward management remained much the same throughout this case: distrust in the beginning and distrust at the end. This suggests, incidentally, that it is a gross oversimplification to assume any close relationship between worker sentiment toward management and aggressive or cooperative behavior in relation to management. Whether or not the workers act out their sentiments depends upon the other forces we have been examining.

Sentiments internal to the work group had drastically changed from harmonious to hostile. Along with this went a sharp decline in the confidence of group members in their ability to accomplish anything collectively. They also perceived themselves to have lost status and potentialities for the support of other groups in the rest of the plant. The grinders assumed that they could no longer get the support which had led all the workers in the plant to walk out with them to win them the sixth day of work.

We do not have the systematic data to show whether indeed workers in other departments had changed their sentiments toward the grinders, but scattered comments picked up by Sayles suggest that their perception of the situation was accurate. For example, one man said: "We're damn fools to have struck the plant so they could get a sixth day of work. What did we get out of it?" Whether or not the grinders interpreted community evaluations correctly, the important thing is that they acted in terms of their impressions of these evaluations.

There was little change in the strict sphere of job activities—though fewer men were on the first shift to perform these activities. The marked change came in out-of-plant activities, since the men no longer got together.

In interactions, the men no longer went out of their shift or departmental sphere to participate actively in the union. Their interactions with men in other departments had markedly declined. Having most of the men together for a departmental meeting became a rare event indeed, and broad social gatherings simply did not happen any more.

The changes in sentiments, interactions, and activities are reflected in the following comments. The first one comes from a man from the first shift:

In the old days, we were always having picnics and beer parties. One of the men had a cottage and we'd be down there having a wonderful time. But I don't know what's happened the past few years; no one seems to have any close friends in the department any more. We've all got interests outside, friends outside the plant; we just keep pretty busy without seeing the men we work with. The minute we leave the shop doors we sort of scatter in every direction.

The second is from a man from the second shift:

How could you have parties with those guys? Before it used to be 18 to 20 of us who were all working on Western Avenue together, and maybe we invited some fellows we worked with too. But now there's too much prejudice. Do you think we would go and have a party with that first shift? What do they care for us? What do we care for them?

## ANALYSIS

How did these changes come about?

Changes in the technological, physical, and economic environment of the group had the effect of transforming a once homogeneous group into one which was heterogeneous in important respects. Before the changes, the men thought of themselves as all doing pretty much the same job and getting the same pay. The fact that the long grinders received five cents an hour more and handled heavier jobs was not thought to be a significant difference by the men. Most men preferred the standard grinding machines, but a few men preferred to work on the long machines. There had been no competition for these assignments.

The group was not homogeneous as to shifts worked, but the smaller second shift at the outset was made up of younger men with less seniority, who apparently accepted the preferred position of the first shift men without any question. It was only when long service men of established social position in the plant and department were to be bumped back to the second shift that the equilibrium of the group was seriously disturbed.

Following Leonard Sayles' analysis, I am suggesting that if a group is homogeneous, it is likely to stick together in its relations with management; if it is heterogeneous, solidarity becomes more difficult to achieve. However, the case suggests that the degree of homogeneity cannot be assessed on an absolute basis. There are differences that matter and differences that do not matter. The differences that matter are those on which men in authority may make decisions that alter the relations of individuals to the environment. In the early period of our case, the difference between the long polishers and those on the standard machines simply did not matter. When Korcz and Silton made an issue of this difference as they struggled to hold their positions on the first shift, it began to matter very much indeed.

It is also important to note the positions of Korcz and Silton in the social structure of the department. We should not regard grievance handling as an impersonal, judicial process. It is always important to note which individuals are involved in a particular grievance and what positions they hold in status and in jobs in a department. Korcz and Silton had been leaders not only in the department but on a plant-wide basis. Their long and bitter fight to hold their first shift position lost them that leadership position not only in the department, but in the plant also. One man commented on Korcz, "He's lost every friend he had."

The downfall of Korcz and Silton threw the departmental leadership solidly into the hands of Straub, the steward, and others of the top seniority group.

The change in the department's relation to the economic and technological environment also affects the ability of the men to stick together on any given issue. Workers are not merely pawns who respond in a passive manner to management's manipulation of the environment. Workers also manipulate the economic and technological environment in an effort to induce changes in managerial behavior. The outcome of this mutual manipulation process depends not only upon cohesion within the work group. It also depends upon the leverage the group can exert upon its environment.

In the heyday of the grinders, they occupied a strategic position in regard to the technological and economic environment. A large part of the production of the plant had to go through their department. They could be confident that as long as they themselves stuck together, management would have to come to terms with them. This did not mean that management would have to give them everything they desired. It did mean that they had the strength to be sure that some important concessions would be made.

Changes in the technological and economic environment destroyed the strategic position of the grinders. One large part of the production that they had formerly processed now was produced in finished form without their operations. Their importance to the company was drastically reduced. No longer would a departmental strike or slowdown seriously cripple the company. If the workers threatened aggressive action, management could talk of transferring the grinding operations to another plant. Such a threat would not have been believed before the change in the economic and technological environment occurred, making the threat seem like a real possibility—particularly to the longest seniority men who had the greatest stake in continuance of the department.

We should note finally the relationship between the status of the group in the plant community and the importance of the operations it performed. When the grinding operations were essential, the grinders enjoyed high status and could rally support from other groups for their own interests. As the importance of grinding operations dropped drastically, there appeared to be a corresponding drop in the status of the group in the plant and a diminishing prospect of rallying support of other workers. The research of Leonard Sayles and George Strauss suggests that we can expect to find this relationship between status and influence, and the importance of the job performed, in local unions generally.[4]

---

[4] See *The Local Union: Its Place in the Industrial Plant* (New York: Harper & Bros., 1953).

# Chapter 18 *THE COLLECTIVE BARGAINING PROCESS*

ONCE there was a president of a small unorganized company who believed firmly in labor unions. He was, therefore, gratified when his employees notified him that they were joining a union and wished to bargain collectively with him. The negotiating committee submitted its demands in advance, and the president studied them carefully. As he compared those demands with contracts in other companies in his industry, he could find nothing that seemed unreasonable. The employees were simply asking for conditions that would put them in line with those existing in plants which had been organized for several years. So when the negotiating committee came in to bargain, he simply told them that he was prepared to accept their terms in full and sign a contract at once. Such a magnanimous attitude, he thought, would establish a firm basis for harmonious relations.

In legal and economic terms the union had won without effort the gains that had been achieved with great difficulty by other organizations. You would think, therefore, that the union people would have been very happy. This was not so. The employer's troubles began as soon as he had signed the contract. Productivity fell off, there were wildcat strikes in one department after another, and it was many months before relations settled down into the harmonious pattern that the employer's friendly attitude should have made possible.

What happened in this case? The union organization arose out of a variety of worker dissatisfactions, and the members of the negotiating committee found themselves in the unaccustomed but pleasingly prominent position of representing their fellows in the fight to eliminate these dissatisfactions. They took their mission very seriously, and prepared their arguments with care. The negotiators went into the conference with the employer under a full head of emotional steam. Then in the meeting with management there was simply nothing for them to do, and they went out of the conference with their emotions still awaiting expression. The whole thing simply had not been done right. They reasoned that since the president had given in so easily, they had been at fault in not demanding more of him. Things which he could give away so readily

324

must not be worth having. The same sentiments developed among the rank and file members.

The manufacturer made one fundamental and very costly mistake in this case. He looked at bargaining simply in legal and economic terms. He did not recognize that it is also a social process—a round of ceremonial activities.

He failed to recognize that bargaining involves dealing with emotions as well as with logic and economics. It is said by some authorities that emotions must be kept out of the collective bargaining process. This is nonsense. The emotions felt by people must find some expression. They simply cannot be ignored. If the emotions that are built up around the collective bargaining process are not expressed in that process, they will break out, as they did in this case, in other highly damaging ways.

This is an examination of the nature of the collective bargaining process. Bargaining involves technical questions of law and economics, but it also involves the emotions of workers, management people, and union officers, and the sentiments through which they give expression to those emotions.

To understand the process we must consider two important aspects: the network of human relations and the expression of the sentiments. For our purposes, this network of relations involves particularly those who sit around the bargaining table, but we must also consider the relations of union leaders with their members and of management negotiators with top management people who may not be directly involved in negotiations, but are often important in establishing limits and policies. All of these sets of relations I will be able to consider here, with one exception. My data come in large measure from collaboration with Sidney Garfield, late president of the International Chemical Worker's Union.[1] Accordingly, I cannot claim any knowledge regarding relations between management negotiators and top management in the bargaining process.

## SEVEN KEYS TO THE NEGOTIATING PROCESS

So as to face the maximum difficulty with our analysis, let us assume that a union and a management are entering upon negotiations in a period that has been marked by hostile sentiments and an exchange of negatively valued activities—such as slowdowns and work stoppages on the union's part. In such a situation, the actual negotiations often serve to intensify hostilities, yet occasionally we see parties utilizing the negotiations to effect a transition toward more harmonious relations. How is this done? Cases we have studied suggest seven general points.

---

[1] This chapter is based primarily on Garfield and Whyte, "The Collective Bargaining Process" (in four parts), *Human Organization*, Vol. IX, No. 2—Vol. X, No. 1 (1950–51).

*Bargaining*

*lic Equivalence of Status.*

ion leaders are to reach an adjustment with management,
arry on negotiations on a plane of symbolic status equality.
munity outside of the plant, this equality of status does not
management people even at the plant level are likely to be at
lea... r-middle class, with perhaps some holding upper-class positions.
If the international representative for the union is accepted in upper-
middle class circles in his home community, he would be the only one
of the negotiating team on his side so placed. Others would presumably
be classified as lower-middle and upper-lower.

When there are such disparities in social status between the parties,
it is quite natural for the management people to express themselves in
ways that symbolize their social superiority. If this is done, however, the
union people will react most vigorously against it.

The following case shows the disastrous consequences that can follow
from behavior symbolizing the status superiority of management.

The members of the local negotiating committee were preparing the
case they were to present in bargaining with the X plant of the ABC
Company. The annual contract still had six months to run, but there
was a clause allowing for discussion of wages at the half-year point. The
contract provided that if no agreement was reached during such interim
bargaining, the existing contract would continue to the end of the year.
Therefore, management did not have to act at this time. It was up to the
negotiating committee to persuade management that changes were necessary.

The negotiators took their duties very seriously. They prepared figures
on the rising cost of living and marshalled together all of the other common arguments in favor of a wage increase. They reviewed the plant's
production picture so that they could show that the union had been
playing an active role in the success of the company. They planned carefully among themselves and with the international representative as to
who was to make which arguments.

They went in and argued for a wage increase all afternoon long.
Finally the representative of top management stepped in and cut off the
discussion with these words:

Well, you fellows have done a lot of talking, and I must say I haven't
found your arguments very convincing. Still, I think you're a good bunch of
fellows, and I tell you what I'll do. I'll give you ten cents.

The union negotiators were temporarily stunned, but the international
representative recovered more quickly than the others. He said that ten
cents was a very good settlement, in line with the best that were then
being made around the country. He felt his organization should be happy
to have achieved such a settlement. And then, having spread this dash
of perfume, he quickly had the meeting adjourned.

Later, at the general membership meeting, the local union president gave this account of the negotiations:

Well, we talked and we talked and we talked. And in the wind-up, Mr. Jones says he don't think so much of our arguments, but we're a good bunch of fellows so he'll give us ten cents. . . . Oh, hell. . . .

The membership voted to accept the offer because there was nothing else they could do. The contract had six months to run. But next time it was not to be so easy.

When the contract ran out and the parties were again negotiating, management proposed a five cent general increase—making a total of fifteen cents for the year. The local union negotiators reported the offer to the membership meeting, where it was unanimously rejected. Anti-management feeling ran high at this time, and the members voted unanimously to strike unless the company came through with a better offer.

It was at this point that the international representative was again called in. He found the parties apparently hopelessly deadlocked. The management men were determined not to go above five cents. They were convinced that a total of fifteen cents for the year was on the generous side compared to what other companies were doing.

The international representative felt that a strike at this time might well be disastrous to the union. The company was in the process of re-organizing its staff and production lines and had no pressing backlog of orders. It would have been easy to shut that plant down and shift its orders to other plants for a considerable period, with little hardship to the company.

Furthermore, the international representative was convinced that a large majority of the workers did not really want to strike. The problem seemed to be that morale within the union had gone to pieces to such an extent that the members were not turning out in large numbers to their meetings even in a crisis. Only sixty-five of three hundred had come out for the strike vote. Attendance may not be high for every meeting, but a crisis meeting in a local of this size should be expected to bring out more than half of the members.

The local union officers wanted to avoid a strike they could not win, but they saw no way out of the impasse. Further discussions with the company brought nothing beyond the five cent offer. The state mediation service was then called in, but the mediator was able to make no progress. Finally, as a last resort, the international representative proposed that the mediator conduct another vote on the company's offer at the gates of the plant, to make sure every worker had a chance to vote on the issue. The vote was two to one in favor of accepting the five cent wage offer.

In that way, the strike was averted. But what of the underlying problems?

Let us ask why this highly favorable economic settlement led to such severe problems within the union. The case provides another example of the application of the old maxim: "It ain't what you do but the way you do it."

It is not often that a worker in the shop has a chance to sit down across the table with local management, or even with a representative of top management in a large corporation. That unusual experience makes a deep impression. The local officers had prepared themselves for it long and conscientiously. They felt, at last, that they were to sit down with management people, who would accept them as equals. But did they?

A relationship of even temporary equality requires expressions and indications of respect on both sides. It requires that concessions *be won*, not *given away*. You don't make gifts to equals except when they are in the position of making gifts in return. When the top management man said, "I'll give you ten cents," and took pains to show the men that they had done nothing to win this offer, he was in effect telling the local officers that they were beneath management—that they did not amount to much.

When the local president passed management's statement on to the membership, he was in effect letting them know management's opinion of the union. And he was telling them that their own leadership was unable to get anything except what management deigned to give. A more crushing blow to the morale of the union leadership could hardly be imagined. The leaders could have regained their standing with the people only through fighting to get more than management was going to give. With the contract still in force, they were blocked from this course of action.

When the end of the year came around and management offered five cents, the management representatives thought they were conceding a fifteen cent increase for the year. From the union standpoint, the picture looked far different. The ten cents at midyear had been given away, so that didn't count. It was only the five cents that was won by the union. And a five cent increase would not stand comparison with what other unions were doing. The union had to get more.

The maneuver of the international representative averted a disastrous strike, but it did not solve the underlying problems. It left the militant group completely frustrated, without any way of taking action, and it left the rest of the membership as apathetic as ever. In such a situation, we would not have to be crystal ball gazers in order to predict continuing unrest within the union and further friction between union and management.

The moral of the story might be put to management in these words: Don't give anything away! That does not mean that management made a mistake in offering ten cents. The mistake was in the way the offer was made. Instead of presenting a gift, management could have allowed itself to be persuaded that the union was entitled to ten cents.

### 2. *Attacking the Man Who Isn't There.*

In a society like ours, which puts an emphasis upon the values of frank expression, there is nothing quite like the satisfactions we get when we are able to express our hostile feelings directly at the target of our hostility. The difficulty of this approach is, of course, that a direct attack of A upon B nearly always serves to stimulate B to counterattack. Thus, even as A gets some satisfaction from his own expression, he receives new insults which fan the flames of resentment and demand further expression. And so it goes with B also.

Our studies suggest that on occasion, A can receive nearly the same measure of satisfaction—without the hazards—if he carries out an oblique attack: an attack upon the man who isn't there. I sometimes think that this man who isn't there plays one of the major roles in collective bargaining. Consider these several cases.

First, take the case of one plant of the Ajax Chemical Company, which employed about three hundred workers. When International Representative Shaw was called in to conduct negotiations for the local union, he was told by his committee that conditions in the plant were in an uproar.

Management negotiators claimed that the plant had been losing money. They had decided that the outdated technology and job methods were responsible for the backward condition of the plant and had called in an engineering firm to study the situation and to make improvements. The engineers moved in, and at a cost of approximately $30,000, carried out sweeping changes.

However, neither management nor the engineers made any effort to inform the union or the workers of what was to happen, and it soon became apparent that the foremen also knew nothing about the situation. When workers approached their foremen for explanations, they came away more confused than ever. The plant was so shaken up that nobody knew where he stood, and in their anxiety the workers expressed strong hostility to management.

In view of the financial condition of the plant, it seemed unlikely that the union would attain substantial economic gains in its bargaining with management. In fact, Shaw was told later by management that an increase of absolutely no more than three cents an hour had been predetermined.

Shaw decided that he would not attack on the economic front. At the meeting, after some preliminary fencing, he plunged directly into a long discussion of the engineering program. He spoke about the way the program had been introduced, and outlined the general effects that should be anticipated from a program of this nature. Then he continued by discussing in detail the problems that were cropping up in department after department. He even suggested that the foremen were as confused as the workers about the program.

So closely did Shaw's discussion hit home that it seemed to management that he must be possessed of remarkable insight. Actually, the facts he had were elementary to a man with experience in this field. He had seen enough of engineering and methods changes, introduced without proper preparation, to know exactly what was to be expected, and the reports of his local committee filled in all the necessary details.

Even after he saw that he had management on the defensive, Shaw continued to talk. Feeling it essential to avoid argument, he continued uninterruptedly for almost an hour and a half. He built up his case, stating that management had spent $30,000 only to find itself in a worse position than before the program had started.

As he talked, Shaw took careful note of the expressions of the men across the table. He saw that one of the vice-presidents had become exceedingly red in the face and seemed about to explode, and surmised that this was the man who had taken the initiative in calling in the engineering firm. But he made no personal charges against this vice-president either then or later.

Having put full pressure on this issue, Shaw eased up with a joking remark to the effect that his lecture should have been worth a seventeen cent an hour wage increase to the company. If the company offered them anything less than that, he said, the union would consider they were still owed the difference. This eased the tension somewhat.

Then Shaw said with emphasis: "You know who's to blame for what happened here? I don't blame you members of management at all. It's that engineering firm. I have seen cases like this before. It's the responsibility of the engineers. They just bungled the job." Immediately after that, he called a recess for lunch.

As soon as the meeting adjourned, the embarrassed and furious vice-president rushed to his office and put in a long distance call to the engineering firm. He gave them hell—unloading on them some of the pressure Shaw had placed on management.

The recess lasted for two hours, allowing plenty of time for Shaw's words to sink in and for management to reconsider its position.

When the meeting reconvened, it soon became apparent that management was making every effort to adjust the differences. One management man suggested bringing in the foremen to discuss the engineering and methods changes thoroughly. Shaw agreed that this would be an excellent idea. Another member of management asked whether it would not be a good idea to have joint meetings with the foremen and union officials. Shaw said that would be even better. Then, as they went on into the economic issues, management carried through in a very conciliatory manner, making an offer of an eight cent increase and two paid holidays, in addition to the six the union had already won. On the same day, many other substantial concessions were made, resulting in an agreement between management and the negotiating committee of the union.

Shaw and his committee were delighted with the contract, which was considerably better than the union had expected from the negotiations. The eight cent an hour increase met the general pattern in that area, and at that particular time, in that industry. No one else in the area had eight paid holidays and there were other features of the contract that were equally attractive.

The same approach can be utilized by management people. In studying the remarkable change in union-management relations at Inland Steel Container Company's Chicago plant (in *Pattern for Industrial Peace*[2]), I noted that early in the negotiations the management people expressed their concern on several occasions regarding slowdowns and work stoppages and other evidences of what management considered irresponsible actions. Each time, the management people were careful to state that they were not accusing any member of the union negotiating committee of being involved in these demonstrations. As a matter of fact, some of the local union negotiators had indeed been ringleaders in some of these activities. Furthermore, without being able to prove it, the management people were convinced that this sometimes had been the case. But what good could have come from direct accusations? If the union leaders had been so attacked, they would have felt impelled to defend themselves through attacking the management actions which they felt had made necessary this type of resistance.

By focusing attention on the man who wasn't there—on some unnamed and irresponsible union member—the management people could give full expression to their sentiments regarding the seriousness of the problem. Not being directly under attack, the union leaders could listen respectfully.

When they had their opportunity to reply, the union leaders fastened upon the same symbolic scapegoat. Complaining about some conditions their members faced, the negotiators placed the blame for these conditions upon the foremen. Here again, in most of the problems raised, union negotiators considered that higher management people were really more to blame than the foremen. Nevertheless, they too refrained from pinning the blame directly on the other side of the table.

At first glance, it may seem that this is an evasion of the real problems. We realize this is not the case when we distinguish between what people are thinking and what they are saying. When the management people heard the foremen attacked, they fully recognized that the problems being discussed were at least as much their own responsibility as that of the foremen. Furthermore, they realized that the union negotiators felt this way too—but were good enough not to say it.

By the same token, when management people attacked the irresponsi-

---

[2] New York: Harper & Bros., 1951.

bility of some unnamed workers, the union leaders fully recognized their
own personal involvement in these problems. They knew, moreover, that
the management people knew—but were good enough not to say it.

By means of such oblique attacks, the parties sometimes are able to
grapple constructively with problems that could not be handled by a
frontal attack.

*3. Encouraging Full Expression.*

When a man states a point of view on which you disagree, there are
two contrasting ways of meeting the situation. You can immediately
bring in counterarguments to show him that he is wrong. Or you can express interest (not approval) in his point of view and ask him to tell you
more about it. Why does he feel the way he does? What is behind his
thinking?

These two moves lead in opposite directions. The first move leads to
increasingly sharp disagreements, marked by brief and rapid inter-
changes, interruptions, and rising emotional tension.

The second move leads to relaxed tension and makes agreement possible. The man does not feel under pressure to get out his statement in a
hurry and prepare for counterattack. He is able to talk to the subject and
around it, in an informal, exploratory manner. Both parties are then
better able to size up possibilities of getting together.

This is illustrated by the opening of the discussion on the most difficult
issue in the Inland Steel Container Company case. For five meetings the
parties avoided the issue, but now they met it head on, with Attorney
Kaufman and General Factories Manager Novy speaking for management, and Shafer speaking for the union:

> *Kaufman:* All right. "The arbitration provisions of Section 2 shall not
> apply to the determination of wages, wage rates, or job classifications."
> Now, that is one that I believe we are going to have to insist on. I don't
> know how familiar you are with the history of our problems in this plant, and
> I can imagine, without knowing, what the union has said about it. If the union
> wants to explain why it wants that change, maybe we had better hear from
> them first on it. I want to tell you at the outset that that has been in there sev-
> eral years, I think, and we think that that provision is what has enabled us to
> beat several programs—when I say programs I am not mentioning a program
> that Lucius or Don or Ernie or anybody else are involved in—several con-
> certed efforts which were pretty clearly slowdowns.
> Is that a fair statement of our position, Bob?
> *Novy:* That is putting it very mildly.
> *Kaufman:* I am a mild fellow.
> *Shafer:* I am interested in Mr. Novy's statement. You say, "That is putting
> it very mildly."[3]

Instead of counterattacking immediately, Shafer encouraged the management people to state their position fully and freely. Only when they

---

[3] *Ibid.*, pp. 87–88.

had done so did Lucius Love speak for the union, and then management gave him a full and respectful hearing.

It took five more meetings to reach agreement on this issue (and on others too), but this manner of opening the discussion enabled the parties to explore their problems in an atmosphere of relaxed tensions that did not seem possible before Shafer encouraged management people to express themselves freely.

*4. Building a Pattern of Agreement.*

Where there are a number of issues to be negotiated between the parties, a few will be of major significance to both parties, and the rest will be of minor significance. If the parties discuss issues according to the sequence of the number of clauses in the contract, then it will be a matter of chance whether the minor or major issues are tackled first.

Even following this sequence of numbered clauses, I found in the Inland Steel Container Company case the possibilities of readjusting the sequence according to the weight of the issues. Without any conscious planning or agreement as to procedure, the parties in effect agreed that they would discuss the numerous minor points first. When they did come to a major issue, each party stated its own position briefly, which showed them that they were far apart. Then someone proposed that they move on to the next issue and leave this one until later.

In these negotiations, the question of whether the union should have a right to call for arbitration of grievances regarding a new or changed piece rate was the most important and explosive issue of all. After being passed over quickly in one of the early meetings, this issue did not come up for really intensive discussion until the sixth meeting, out of a total of eleven that made up the whole process. By the time this most explosive issue did come up for discussion, the emotional atmosphere in the bargaining had already undergone a substantial change. In the process of compromising on minor points, the parties were able to test each other out and establish the beginnings of an effective working relationship. This was particularly important in these meetings, for the key man, International Representative Lawrence G. (Jake) Shafer, had met the management people for the first time in the opening negotiation meeting in the 1947 contract talks. Before it could be determined whether an agreement was possible, he had to size up the men across the table from him, and they had to have an opportunity to size him up.

*5. Safety Valves.*

It is all very well to resolve that negotiation shall be conducted without emotional explosions, but what do you do when tempers rise—as they are bound to do when men disagree on issues important to them? At such points, the search for safety valves becomes important.

Jake Shafer found one in his interest in hunting and fishing. In the early stages of bargaining at Inland Steel Container Company, when the parties were still tense and wary of each other, Shafer interrupted the discussion with a casual comment that he had stopped on his way to the plant to pick up some pictures he had taken on a recent hunting and fishing trip. Would the men around the table like to see the photographs? The management men reported later that at first they had been mystified by this maneuver. Nevertheless, they agreed to inspect the pictures, and there followed an interlude of attention to hunting and fishing. When negotiations resumed, the tension seemed to be greatly relieved.

No standard set of safety valves can be offered. They must be developed to fit the particular situation. The skillful negotiator will recognize danger signals and be ready with some tension-easing diversion before men reach the point of making statements whose damage cannot be readily repaired.

*6. Personal Points in Common.*

In a conflict situation, the union and management negotiators are inclined to look at the men across the table as completely different types of individuals. Mutual trust cannot arise quickly; yet if the parties are exposed to symbols indicating certain personal points they have in common, they may be able to talk with each other more effectively than would otherwise be possible.

Since the parties appear to be in conflict on major issues, it is highly unlikely that these issues will provide potentially integrating symbols at the outset. Instead, the integrating symbols may be quite unconnected with the conflict situation, and perhaps for this very reason, provide a bridge toward understanding.

The hunting and fishing diversion of Jake Shafer did more than provide a cooling-off period. Robert Novy, general factories manager, commented later:

> It's been my experience that whenever you run into a real sportsman, you'll find that he is a pretty regular fellow. He's a man you can deal with straight from the shoulder. That's one of the things that sold me on Shafer.[4]

In the case of the Buchsbaum strike mentioned earlier (Chapter 3), integrating symbols of this sort helped to make it possible to bring the parties together so that bargaining discussions could begin. Another businessman provided the key symbols in a luncheon he had arranged with President Herbert Buchsbaum and Sam Laderman, union general manager. As Buchsbaum describes it:

> On the second day of the strike I had lunch with Laderman and with a business acquaintance of mine who had a contract with his union. Up to that time I thought all union people were a bunch of racketeers. My friend reassured me on this point. He said that you could count on Sam Laderman *keeping his word.* He told me that Sam was a real human being. He *liked opera.* He *disliked fights.* There would be nothing he would like better than being friends with the employer if it were possible. He assured me that the union was always willing to discuss things from a reasonable point of view. And

---

[4] *Ibid.,* p. 184.

Laderman assured me that our contract would contain the standard clause, that it would be no less advantageous to the employer than contracts the same union made with any other firm.

That made an impression on me. I still had no idea of settling the strike but I agreed to meet with Laderman and a committee of the employees on the third day. (The strike was actually settled at this meeting.)[5]

The mention of opera is particularly interesting. At first I assumed that Herbert Buchsbaum was a lover of opera. On the contrary, he told me that he never went unless his wife dragged him along. Nevertheless, he identified himself with the sort of cultivated people who are thought to enjoy opera. The opera symbol admitted Laderman to the company of cultivated men and therefore made it easier for the two men to talk together.

*7. Making the Institutional Framework Clear.*

Effective bargaining requires a flexibility of approach. The party that begins with a "final offer" or unalterable set of demands is simply inviting a strike, or else a humiliating surrender. The parties naturally begin with certain definite objectives and with plans as to how far they can go in meeting the demands of the other party. They size up what points can safely be yielded in return for concessions from the other party.

The first steps in bargaining involve an exploratory process on both sides. In the preliminary fencing, the bargainers size up the people across the table and try to sense the relative importance of each issue to the other party.

For effective negotiations, it is important for both parties to understand the limitations within which the other party must act. If this is not done, the union may push to the point of a strike an issue on which management cannot possibly yield, or management may precipitate a strike on an issue that the union negotiators cannot afford to yield.

Strikes are sometimes necessary and unavoidable, but there are strikes that arise simply because one party has pushed beyond the retreating point on a certain issue, through a failure to understand the crucial nature of the issue to the other party. If a strike is necessary, both sides should approach it with their eyes open. It is an evidence of bad leadership for one party to find itself trapped into a strike by having taken too early, too strong a stand on an issue that could not be won across the bargaining table. In such a case, the party must suffer a strike or else "lose face" on this issue.

Losing or saving face is not a peculiar oriental type of behavior, as it is sometimes supposed to be. It is of vital importance in bargaining and may strongly influence the emotions of individuals and the morale of their organizations. In fact, there may well be times when it is more important

---

[5] H. Whiteford, W. F. Whyte, and B. B. Gardner, "From Conflict to Cooperation: A Study in Union-Management Relations," special issue of *Applied Anthropology*, Vol. V, No. 4. (Italics used here to note key symbols.)

to the future solidarity of the organization to go through a strike than to lose face. But people cannot lose face unless they have put their face in the balance first—unless they have taken a strong, dogmatic stand. It is therefore a job of the negotiator to approach these points of possible impasse with the utmost care, to explore the situation thoroughly before taking any irrevocable stand, and to be ready with face-saving phraseology if the other party gets backed into a corner.

This exploration of the limits within which a bargain can be reached involves more than an estimate of the relative importance of the issues to each party. It involves an understanding of the reasons behind this importance. Such understanding cannot be conveyed simply through an argument concerning the issues themselves. The parties need to gain an understanding of the institutional framework within which the men across the table, think, feel, and act.

For example, International Representative Sutton found himself dealing with a peculiarly adamant plant manager. Sutton and his committee took pains to put forth the union's case for each demand in reasoned, unemotional language, but it was clear that they were making no progress. The plant manager's replies suggested that he considered these arguments simply an attractive cloak for personal ambitions.

Sutton then tried another tack. He placed the demands within the institutional framework of the union. He began talking about "the policy of our organization" and "the decisions of our executive board." He used words that had a familiar and pleasant ring to the executive. He suggested, by implication, that there were many similarities between the two organizations represented in that room.

At last the manager began to warm up, and it became possible for the parties to work out a contract that was a realistic adjustment of the problems of both organizations. The approach here was twofold. Sutton avoided red-flag words and used those that would not only sound familiar, but safe and respectable, to the executive. And then he used these words to place himself in the institutional structure of the union so as to make clear the limitations within which he acted. Management can apply the same principles in presenting its case to the union.

## THE ROLE OF THE INTERNATIONAL REPRESENTATIVE

As we consider relations within the union, let us look first at the international representative, who often is the key man in bargaining at the local plant level.

In many conflict situations, there is so much personal animosity between the local union leaders and the management people that, left alone, they would not be able to reach an agreement. If the international representative has not been involved in their previous struggles, he is in a strong strategic position in such a situation. While he does not qualify as a neutral, he is often able to view the local issues with a greater degree of objectivity than is possible for those on either side who are more intimately involved.

That does not mean, however, that the international representative can move right in and "call them the way he sees them." He represents the union and depends upon the committee and the rank and file for support. They don't expect him to act as an umpire; they want him to help win their objectives from management. Therefore, he cannot begin making adjustments to management's point of view until he has shown some ability to win concessions from management. He must establish himself with his own organization first. But, if management understands this problem, management can help him to take that step.

The case of International Representative Jones and Local XYZ will illustrate this point. Jones' union had just taken over a particular plant from another union. The convinced adherents of the ousted union presented a difficult problem to the new organization.

Previously, relations between union and management had been terribly strained. In the preceding four years, the workers had been out on strike for a total of fifty-two weeks. Management had been fighting the union tooth and nail, and had followed a practice of stalling at all times.

When the new union took over, Jones met with the management people in a room where the tabulation was being made of the representation election. He let the local people pay attention to the tabulation, and he himself concentrated his attention upon Carter, the district superintendent who represented top management. Jones tried to be affable and kid the management man in order to establish some sort of casual relationship. Finally, he was able to persuade Carter to meet him at breakfast the following morning. After a little preliminary small talk, Jones said that he wanted to smooth out relations between the company and the new union, but he could do it only if he could show his people that he was able to get action from management. He suggested that management agree to a meeting with the union negotiating committee the following day; then a week later, meet with the union again to submit management's answer to the union's demands; and the following week, set aside two days in which to negotiate the contract. Jones added that the company was under no legal obligation to meet with the union at this time because it would take ten days or two weeks for the certification to come through from Washington; but he wanted to have something to take back to the people to show that the company was willing to take the first step. He also felt that keeping to a close time schedule was important in view of the dragged-out nature of previous negotiations.

Carter said he'd think it over, and commented, "You talk just like a businessman." Later in the day, Carter called Jones and said that he had secured top management's agreement to go ahead with the time schedule Jones had outlined. That night Jones was able to go before a meeting and surprise the members with the statement that the company had agreed to a negotiation meeting the following day—when they were not even required to do so by law. He also laid out the schedule of meetings that were to follow. In view of past history, this impressed everyone, and kept to a minimum criticism leveled by people who had been closely associated with the previous union. When union and management were able to carry through this schedule and reach an agreement after two days of negotiating, that agreement was accepted by the membership with considerable enthusiasm, and thus the first steps were taken toward establishing a harmonious relationship. In this case the international representative could not have made any moves toward cooperation if management had not agreed to make certain concessions that strengthened his hand with the membership.

In the Inland Steel Container Company case, Jake Shafer held a strong hand with the local union from the very beginning of negotiations, even though he entered shortly before the first meeting with management as a complete stranger to the local people. Here it appears that the situation played into his hands. The local union negotiators were bitterly hostile to management and convinced that no worthwhile agreement was possible. At the same time, the membership had gone through a 199-day strike the previous year, and the plant had been shut down for about 55 days in a complicated labor dispute the year before that. Clearly, a strike was to be avoided if at all possible. Jake Shafer, as a new man, could set out to explore the possibilities. The local union people in this situation could afford to sit back and let Shafer make his try for an agreement. When negotiations broke down, the local leaders could resume control. As negotiations progressed, however, the local union officers began to see evidences of real progress even long before a final settlement was reached, and this added steadily to their confidence in Shafer.

### GETTING THE CONTRACT ACCEPTED

In our form of collective bargaining, it is not enough for the negotiators themselves to reach agreement. The agreement must then be ratified by the membership, and sometimes an apparently good settlement is voted down. Upon what does acceptance or rejection of the settlement depend? Let us consider the following four questions:

1. How good is the contract, in terms of member expectations?
2. What has been the pre-existing pattern of human relations in the local union?
3. What has been the customary sequence of activities in the past in working out a contract?
4. To what extent are the achievements of the contract dramatized to the members?

The following case shows the influence of the first two factors together. The plant in this case was located in a semi-rural area of declining industries. It manufactured charcoal and wood alcohol, both of which were in declining demand. The union's research department showed that the industry was sick and that management could not stand any wage increase at that time. In fact, in that particular area, no contract had carried a wage increase and there had been two negotiated wage cuts. The plant under review was part of a corporation that could close this unit with little disturbance to the total operation. The union, therefore, was in an exceedingly weak bargaining position.

Nevertheless, the local union negotiating committee was pushing vigorously for a fifteen cent increase. After four fruitless meetings with management, the international representative was called in.

Now the workers not only did not want a strike, they did not expect an increase. In a small town, there are inevitably enough informal contacts between workers and foremen, or friends or relatives of workers with friends or relatives of foremen, for the workers' feelings to be public knowledge. In this case, the workers were saying to each other: "We'll be lucky if we get the same damn contract again." And management knew it.

Why then the aggressive demand for a fifteen cent increase? First, because of the bitter resentment of the workers toward management. The local people felt that management had resisted the union at every opportunity and in every possible way. They were constantly on guard against management, and had fought out a strike only two years previously. And second, because two factions were fighting for control of the local union. Although they were not divided on any ideological lines, the two contending leaders disagreed on all sorts of issues within the plant. They could agree on only one thing; the boss was their chief enemy and must be fought aggressively.

The union leaders in power felt compelled to make strong demands. Anything less, they felt, would be interpreted as weakness and would result in political suicide. They probably were afraid that management would demand a wage decrease, and their demand for a fifteen cent raise was only a tactic to head off such a move on management's part. But management did not propose a decrease. And as the local officers argued for the fifteen cents, they found themselves so committed to this figure that they were powerless to back down. The opposition leaders were forced to agree that fifteen cents was a very strong union demand, so while the argument continued the local officers had no opposition. But they knew that if they agreed not to take an increase, the opposition would immediately jump into action and gain adherents for the local union election to be held only six weeks hence.

When the local negotiating committee and management finally reached an impasse, the international representative came in for three meetings. Each time he argued the union's case vigorously—with no real hope of success.

Finally, in his third meeting, the international representative called a recess and announced to his committee:

Look, I'm tired. I don't think we can get any further. The company refuses to budge. I think you ought to go back and recommend a strike to the people. Let's break off negotiations, call a special meeting, and call for a strike. I will clear it with the International Union. You already have strike sanction. I say it's okay—go ahead, call the strike!

The committee members argued back:

No, no, let's not break off negotiations. . . . Let's keep it going. We don't want to take a strike vote. . . . Let's keep talking.

The international representative stood pat:

Look, you're wasting my time, you're wasting your time, you're wasting the conciliator's time. You just can't get anywhere. You know it and I know it.

The local people still wanted to keep the negotiations going and kept arguing until the international representative came forward with a new proposal:

I would suggest that we go back in and negotiate now and say that we will accept the same contract, but with a thirty-day wage opener. And I'm willing to go to the membership and sell that.

The local officers accepted this proposal immediately. The right to reopen wage negotiations at any time, on thirty days' notice, could hardly mean anything concrete, since the economic picture for the plant was not likely to change much within the year. But the proposal did have face-saving value. Furthermore, the international representative's offer to take responsibility for the settlement seemed to take the local officers out of the line of fire.

When the international representative went before the membership meeting, he was faced with a dual task. He wanted to sell the contract, and he also wanted to protect the position of the local officers. This he did by making a strong attack upon the membership—for letting the negotiating committee down.

He began by complimenting the local committee members for the efficiency with which they had handled the negotiations. They had really done their part, he said. But the rank and file members had forgotten that they, too, played an important role in negotiations, although they did not sit around the bargaining table. In his words:

Every single person in this hall and every single person within management knew, number one, that you weren't going to strike, that you didn't want to strike, and number two, that you felt you would be lucky to get the same contract. Whenever you talked about the negotiations, inside the plant or outside, you blabbed, every one of you. You said, "We'll be lucky if we get the same damn contract." Top management knew it. You gave guns to your committee, and then you forgot to give them the ammunition.

You were fighting a losing battle from the beginning, but you do have a thirty-day wage opener. I don't know if it's going to do you any good, but if conditions change, and you fellows really mean business, then you have a chance to redeem yourselves. You can't blame anybody but yourselves for what has happened.

Besides, you have to be conscious of certain things. First, you have a sick industry. You know as well as I that nobody in this area has gotten a raise—and as a matter of fact, two outfits got a cut of 15 per cent. You know it and management knows it. And one more thing, throughout the country, our union has been getting increases in only 40 per cent of our contracts. We just haven't been getting many increases this year. So I wouldn't feel too bad about the fact that you didn't get an increase.

The membership voted unanimously—but with no enthusiasm—to accept the contract.

When the elections were held, all the incumbent officers were voted out, and the opposition group took over. We have no evidence as to what happened, but we assume that the opposition faction campaigned on the issue that the officers in power had been too easy on management and that the new group would be more aggressive and more effective in its demands. That conclusion is supported by subsequent events. Immediately the new officers took over, they invoked the thirty-day notice for reopening wage negotiations. (I have no information on this second effort.)

In this case the difficulties in worker-management relations were compounded by the declining economic picture. Since relations between workers and management had been fraught with conflict, there was a good deal of emotional support for a tough policy toward management. If he had been dealing with a prosperous plant, the international representative could have sought to negotiate enough out of management so that the settlement would not only be accepted by workers but so that the incumbent union leadership could support it without fear of losing control. The unfortunate economic situation provided no rewards that the local leaders could bring back to the membership.

The international representative also had to deal with the conflict between worker expectations and their sentiments toward management. The fifteen-cent-an-hour demand grew out of their hostile sentiments toward management. At the same time, as Shaw pointed out to them, they really had no expectation at all of getting anything like fifteen cents. By bringing dramatically before them the conflict between their sentiments towards management and their expectations, with a face-saving clause thrown in, Shaw was able to meet the immediate crisis and get a contract settlement. While meeting their expectations, the settlement did not express worker sentiments toward management, and therefore it could be used against the incumbent leadership as a means of voting the old crowd out.

We must not assume from this story that the union leaders can strengthen their bargaining position simply by telling the members to

talk militantly. An occasional individual may be able to put up a bold
front and convincingly portray an impression of confidence he does not
feel, but this is not possible for a large body of workers. If the members
as a whole do not feel this confidence, sooner or later the impression is going to get out to management.

This does not mean that if the negotiators begin by asking for fifty
cents an hour and the members generally believe that nothing better than
fifteen cents will be possible, that the opening demand serves no function.
It is well recognized in those bargaining situations that the union opens
with larger demands than it really expects to settle for and that management opens with smaller offers—if any—than it expects to have to grant.
If the members really believe that in terms of what workers elsewhere
are gaining and in terms of the profitability of the plant, they have about
fifteen cents coming to them, it would be hard indeed for management to
get them to settle for much less. On the other hand, if their expectations
give them no hope for an increase, then it won't make much difference
whether the negotiating committee is talking about fifteen cents or fifty
cents.

The solidarity and militancy of the union is not demonstrated in conversation alone. It may also be shown in certain activity changes.

Perhaps in certain departments there has been a great deal of overtime
work and it has been the accepted practice for the foreman simply to
ask certain workers to stay beyond the regular time to finish up important
jobs. He may suddenly find that this is no longer possible. If a strike is in
the offing, the workers may willingly forfeit their time-and-a-half overtime pay on the grounds that they do not want to help management get
ahead with its production schedule. This type of pressure sometimes may
result in an actual slowdown in the plant, but more often it means that
workers are being extremely careful not to do any more than usual. The
effects of increased tension may also be visible in the grievance process,
where stewards and other union officials may push grievances much
more energetically than they have in the past, showing that they are
militantly behind their leadership.

It is important to demonstrate this unity in order to strengthen the
position of the union negotiators and to give the rank and file a sense of
participation. But it is not always necessary for such a demonstration to
restrict and hamper management. Sometimes the demonstration can be
accomplished with as much if not greater effect in terms of a constructive
contribution to the efficiency of the enterprise. For example, we observed
one case where a marked transition toward cooperation was effected
through negotiations carried on over a period of four months. Among
other things, management was concerned with a serious problem of absenteeism. Following discussions of this problem, the union leadership
went before a membership meeting and put a strong case to the members.
They were told that they were hurting themselves and the position of their

union through their absenteeism record. It was suggested that if the record could be improved, it would be a demonstration of the effectiveness of the union leadership and would enable the leadership to win greater gains from management. The record of later negotiation sessions reveals that management gave credit to the union leadership for a substantial improvement in the absenteeism record. This seems to have been an important factor in giving management confidence in the union leadership, and stimulating a willingness to make concessions in return for the improvements that it suddenly discovered the union leadership could bring about.

The power of the union to carry out such activities will, of course, be affected by the particular environmental situation in which it finds itself. This is particularly true for the organization of activities that will be negatively valued by management. For example, if the plant is operating well below capacity and a number of workers have already been laid off, there will be no overtime for workers to refuse to do. Slowdowns will also tend to be difficult to organize, for workers will feel that management might shut down a given operation altogether. The same anxieties tend to hold workers back against the more militant expression of grievances.

Let us now illustrate the importance of the third and fourth questions raised above. If, in the past, workers have voted down one or two proposed contracts and have then found management coming forward with a better offer, they naturally find it hard to believe that the contract offered the first time is the best they can do. At least they will not accept the first contract offer unless it is put to them in the form of a dramatic presentation.

We see both of these points in the further adventures of International Representative Shaw, who thought he had arrived at a good settlement in the situation involving the engineering changes. A few days later he received a telegram from his negotiating committee urgently demanding that he come back to help them. The membership meeting had voted not to accept the contract.

Upon his return, Shaw found the union negotiators and management quite depressed. The union negotiators still felt that the contract offer was an excellent one, but they had not sold it. The members were still so hostile toward management that they could see nothing good in the contract.

In a joint meeting, Shaw told the union negotiators and the company executives that he still felt the contract offer was a fair one. However, he would have to insist that the company make a new offer, an offer to be made in a way that would not hurt the company financially. He suggested a cost of living adjustment, and told the company to pick out the points of the cost of living index beyond which the cost of living would have to rise in order for the adjustment to go into effect. He suggested that they should not choose a ridiculously high figure, but one on which they could count on not having to pay anything. Since the cost of living at that time appeared to have leveled off, this seemed to offer no practical difficulties.

The management people objected, saying that this would lead the workers to expect gains that would never materialize. Shaw replied that this was not the case; he would tell the membership that they were not getting anything, but he did need an excuse to go back to them. Management accepted this deal, picked an index point ten points above the one prevailing at that time, and wrote this into the contract. Armed with the amended contract, Shaw then faced the general membership meeting.

Prior to the meeting, the atmosphere had been full of tension and the local negotiating committee members were only too eager to turn the complete responsibility over to Shaw. Shaw stood up to address the members and began by saying, "I don't know whether I should say I'm glad or sorry to be here. I understand you've come here tonight to take the hide off me." This brought a laugh from the crowd, and Shaw felt the tension ease somewhat. Then he said he had had a new offer from the company, but he added that the union wouldn't really get anything concrete out of it. Before he laid the offer on the table, however, he wanted the members to understand what had taken place at the initial negotiations.

Shaw began by describing the lecture he had given the management people on the engineering and methods changes. Not only did he repeat what he had said to management, but he stated which management people had been present, describing how they had looked and how they had reacted. He was particularly careful to describe the vice-president who had become so upset. As he told his story, he found the crowd coming with him. They tittered and laughed at certain spots, and he could hear them saying, "That's telling them," or "That's what I tried to tell them, but they wouldn't listen!" and similar remarks that indicated that he was really expressing what they felt.

At the end of this discussion, Shaw announced that he was not there to try to persuade the members to accept the contract. It was up to them to make their decision, but they should consider the alternative. Were they ready for a strike? He emphasized that few strikes recently had been successful, and suggested that if they were going to strike they had better be prepared for it to be long and costly. He then sat down, leaving the decision up to the members.

Two or three of the old-time workers spoke up, saying that they had been through a strike and knew what it meant. They thought the members should take the matter very seriously and not jump into it without a great deal of thought. When the vote was finally taken, it was 175 to 5 in favor of accepting the contract, which was essentially the same as the one they had turned down earlier.

The action of the membership in voting down the original contract suggests that Shaw and his committee overlooked an important part of the bargaining process.

Compared to the achievements of other locals, this was a good contract. The union's skill in bargaining had won a wage increase of five cents an hour more than management had expected to concede—and in a situation where management could not easily make financial concessions.

But a contract with economic concessions was not enough. The engineering program had completely destroyed the equilibrium of the union-management social system. Until that problem was solved, the members would remain in a state of anxiety and tension.

Furthermore, in past dealings, the union had adopted the procedure of voting down the first two management offers and accepting the third. The management people were aware of this pattern, but in their desire to make amends for the engineering disturbances, they overlooked this point and offered every possible concession in the first round.

If it had been handled effectively, perhaps the members could have been won over in one meeting. But in presenting the contract to the members, the local officers did little more than lay it on the table and outline its good points.

The local officers who had participated in the bargaining were satisfied that the problems were worked out. But the rank and file had not experienced the bargaining first hand and they were still experiencing the serious disturbances caused by the engineering program.

Shaw's major contribution was to allow the members to share vicariously the experiences of the local officers and himself. Their cheers and laughter and shouts of "That's telling them!" and their almost unanimous vote prove that he brought this experience home to them quite vividly.

We do not mean to suggest that the union's acceptance of the agreement solved the problems growing out of the engineering program. A disturbance of that nature must be treated with patience and skill over a period of time. But at least Shaw was able to establish an emotional basis between management and union, upon which the necessary adjustments could be built. As they left the meeting, the workers were ready to believe that improvements were in prospect.

All too often, the chairman of the union negotiating committee does little beyond placing the new contract on the table and inviting the members to inspect its favorable points. He may say: "We had a tough fight with management to get this for you," but he seldom gives the members a sufficiently vivid picture of what went on around the bargaining table for them to feel as he does about it. He merely concentrates on the technical details of the contract and then asks the members to trust him and his committee because of their past service to the union. It is as if the members were presented with a box score of a baseball game, without being given an account of the plays that went to make up the score.

## LAUNCHING THE AGREEMENT

Let us assume now that the members are ready and willing to sign the contract. How should the actual signing be carried out? It can simply be a routine matter, or it can be made into an impressive ceremony. Where relations have been reasonably stable and harmonious, there will be no need for such a ceremony. But in the signing of a first contract, or when the parties have reached an agreement that they hope will effect a transition from conflict to cooperation, the situation is quite different. Throughout the world, ceremonies are used to accompany transitions in people's relations.

Benjamin M. Selekman has reported on a very interesting use of ceremony in a case involving the Commonwealth Edison Company of Chicago and the International Brotherhood of Electrical Workers.[6] The union had finally succeeded in organizing the company and was ready to sign the first contract with management. While management officials were not pleased with this development, they were determined to meet it realistically. They wished to establish a basis for cooperative relations with the union and hoped to avoid the period of confusion and friction that generally accompanies the initial recognition of a union. The international representative suggested that this might be accomplished if management would agree to a joint ceremony at the signing of the contract.

The ceremony was held in the union hall, before a large audience of members. On the stage were top union and management officials who addressed the members, telling them what their sentiments were toward each other and how they hoped their relations would develop. The members were tremendously impressed to hear the president of the company give his endorsement to the new relationship right in their union hall. This carried a conviction that would never have come from a printed statement or even from an address limited to top officials. For the members, this scene dramatized the ushering-in of a new era in union-management relations and destroyed the very common suspicion that management did not really believe in the contract and would try to by-pass it wherever possible.

Once the contract has been signed, it must be put into effect by both parties. Here, again, is an opportunity for action on a group basis. If the parties wait to interpret the contract only as specific cases arise, people will not understand the changes that have taken place.

The annual round of collective bargaining presents the most favorable opportunity for effecting changes in union-management relations. The entire process builds up so that people are led to expect changes and to be ready to adjust to them. The changes, therefore, must be put into effect

---

[6] See his *Labor Relations and Human Relations* (New York: McGraw-Hill Book Co., Inc., 1947).

as an integral part of the process. The contract must not be allowed to drift—it must be launched.

Selekman refers to the "technical launching" and the "emotional launching." The contract is a technical document that must be studied and discussed by those who will administer it, from top management down to foreman, from top union official down to steward. Such technical knowledge is essential—but it is not enough. A contract is also a statement of the pattern of human relations that the parties wish to develop —a purpose for which the written word is particularly inadequate. One can have two situations in which the contracts are identical, and yet there are vast differences in the way the parties get along together.

Since, beyond the formalities, the contract says so little about the relations that are to be developed, it is important for the people who will be responsible for shaping these relations to get together and discuss their plans for the future.

It is now common practice for top management to hold meetings and to explain and interpret the new contract to its foremen and superintendents. Similarly, high union officials discuss these matters with their stewards.

Such meetings are essential, but in some cases they do not go far enough. We have seen cases where these separate meetings failed to clear up misunderstandings on technical points, particularly on "the spirit of the contract." These misunderstandings were cleared up most effectively through joint foreman-steward meetings.

Regardless of what the discussion leader says, a separate meeting gives the impression that there is a separate union or management position regarding the contract. On the other hand, the joint meeting dramatizes for all involved that the parties are mutually concerned with building up the relationship between them.

## THE PROBLEM OF MANIPULATION

In this discussion, I have emphasized the ceremonial nature of the collective bargaining process. I have suggested that certain aspects of the process need to be acted out dramatically, if the process is to work through to a successful conclusion.

Many people will find this point of view hard to accept. They will consider it insincere and involving the manipulation of men. They may also regard these statements as very dangerous advice, perhaps assuming that if the leaders of management and unions just develop enough manipulative skill, they can get the workers to accept anything that the leaders desire.

Nothing could be farther from the truth. Contracts are not negotiated in a vacuum. Workers as well as union and management leaders know what kinds of contracts are being negotiated in related industries as they set out to negotiate their own contracts. They know a good deal about the financial situation of the company. They are also aware of certain problems involving friction within the plant—whether the problems revolve around incentive rates, job evaluation, or promotional ladders. The situation is rarely so structured that the contract that will result is completely predetermined. On the other hand, the situation is always structured to a considerable extent so that agreement must be reached within certain limits. Skill in handling the collective bargaining process—on both sides —can often make the difference between reaching an agreement within these limits and failure to reach agreement, with resulting losses to both sides.

Nor am I saying, as is sometimes assumed, that good human relations in collective bargaining simply means arranging somehow to have the parties like and trust each other. The problem goes much deeper than the sentiments of Mr. A for Mr. B. Consider this case in which a high degree of trust had already been established.

The president of the company was embarrassed. He pointed out to the union negotiators that their harmonious relations were well known throughout the industry; that the union had always been able to trust him in the past. Now he asked that they trust him once more by not asking for a wage increase at that time, but instead, reopening discussion in ninety days. He stated that by then, he hoped the company would be able to offer the increase it was unable to give at present; he offered no further explanation.

The union negotiators were sympathetic but unmoved. They agreed that their relations had always been satisfactory and that they had been able to trust the president. The chief negotiator even went so far as to say he trusted the president now—without question. But, he added, the union negotiators had had several years of personal experience with the president and their trust had been built up thereby. On the other hand, the hundreds of workers in the plant, having had no such direct experience, did not have the same personal trust in management. So it was not conceivable that the union negotiators could simply ask the membership to take the president on faith. There had to be some explanation that they could pass on to the members.

The president's feelings were hurt by this apparent lack of faith, but he went on to tell the story that he had been embarrassed to reveal. The company's financial problems were not due entirely to the general business situation. Management had made serious mistakes in its buying policy and in the general operation of some departments. The president felt that steps were being taken to repair the damage and that he could reasonably expect the company to be in a more favorable position within three months. But at the moment, management was in a very difficult position.

The union negotiators accepted this explanation. In fact, only a few of the details were news to them, since the "grape vine" in the plants had reported some of management's blunders. So while it embarrassed the president to make such admissions, his story served to bring out into the open officially, what was common knowledge to the union leaders and to many employees. In such a situation, the president could not have asked the union to go along on faith. However, when he revealed the full story— including a convincing account of steps being taken to meet the crisis—he placed himself and the management in a much better position in relation to the union. He also gave the union negotiators a story they could carry back to the members. Instead of having to apologize for failing to get an increase and asking that the members trust a man whom they knew only as a remote symbol, the negotiators were able to make a strong and reasoned case for the ninety-day extension. On the strength of this case, backed by the years of harmonious relations with management, the union members voted overwhelmingly for the extension. The story has a happy ending, for three months later, the parties were able to negotiate an increase that fitted in very well with current trends in the industry.

The principle involved in this case can be stated in this way: the sentiments people have towards a company, a union, an individual, or a group, are strongly colored by the personal relations they experience. The union negotiators had had frequent interaction with the president, mostly of a mutually satisfying nature. They therefore had a high personal regard for him and would have been inclined to accept his word without question. But they were intelligent enough to recognize that the members did not enjoy similar interactions with the president and could not be expected to have the same sentiments toward him. To ask them to take him on faith would have placed a dangerous strain on leader-follower relations within the union. In that event, there certainly would have been protests that the leaders were selling out to management.

Successful negotiation is not just a matter of winning the personal regard of men across the table. The negotiator can make trouble for himself through his very successes, and the man who is won over often finds himself in a most difficult personal situation.

When the union leader decides that the top executive is, after all, honest and well meaning in his dealings with the union, his problems may very well be starting instead of ending. Will the top executive have the intelligence and perseverance to carry agreed-upon solutions right through his organization? Is the management organization functioning in such a way as to make it possible for a top policy decision to be carried out effectively down to the plant level? These questions indicate the folly of accepting the top executive simply on a personality basis.

The workers in the plant don't know the big boss. Their daily contacts with management are with foremen, superintendents, personnel men, time study men, engineers, and so on. If relations at that personal contact level continue to be unsatisfactory to the workers, the personal respect of top union for top management cannot be turned to the advantage of either party.

Industrial relations problems are too complicated to be solved simply by "good men" who approach them with "good will." The union man who allows himself to be won over on this basis alone is asking for trouble for himself and his union. Unless the negotiator can foresee changes in the whole union-management system of human relations as a result of the new relationship between himself and the management negotiator, he must proceed with the utmost caution and not allow himself to be sidetracked by attractive personalities.

In short, no relationship can be treated realistically in isolation. The union negotiator must see his relations with management from the perspective of his relations with other union officers and members. The management man must be sure that by winning over a union representative, he does not isolate that man from the rank and file, thus rendering him useless to both union and management. Management must think not only of its relationship with the men across the table, but of protecting and improving the positions of those men with the rank and file.

## CONCLUSION

Collective bargaining presents an emotional as well as an intellectual problem. We assume that the skillful bargainer needs to have thorough knowledge of the past application of given contract clauses in his own situation, coupled with knowledge of trends in other bargaining situations that may affect the contract he is seeking to obtain. These aspects we have taken for granted. Our focus has been upon the emotional aspects of the problem.

We see the bargaining process as involving the channeling of emotions in such a way that the parties can work through to a mutually acceptable solution. Note that we speak of channeling rather than suppressing, for we assume that if the situation is fraught with hostile sentiments, the parties cannot work through to a solution if they simply undertake to suppress expression of those sentiments. The problem is to find means of expression that will not destroy the possibilities of reaching agreement.

Here we have given attention to the meaning of verbal symbols, concentrating particularly upon the status parity problem. We have argued that in many cases the refusal of management, consciously or unconsciously, to accept union negotiators on an equal footing has made agreement impossible. We have examined the symbols that tend to equalize relations along with those which tend to subordinate the other party.

We have also suggested that the course of bargaining must be seen in the perspective of the past pattern of activities and interactions, and the current network of interpersonal relations. When in the past the parties have reached an agreement only after two or three management offers have been turned down by the membership, it will be very difficult to gain acceptance for the first management offer, no matter how good it is.

This does not mean that the past pattern must be continued forever. It does mean that the parties should recognize when they are making a major departure from past practice and should do something to dramatize the value of their new approach.

Concerning the network of interpersonal relations, we need to recognize that it is not only the parties around the table who have to get together, but the union negotiators and the rank and file as well, for it is the rank and file who will have to vote upon the settlement. We have shown cases in which failure to recognize problems in this area has led to rejection of a good management offer, and we have shown some ways in which the members may be influenced to accept an offer that the negotiators feel is a good one.

Finally, while we have given particular attention to the human relations aspects of bargaining, we must be careful not to overemphasize this side of the picture as against economic conditions and forces. The current economic situation of the firm involved in contract negotiations, together with the pattern of settlements being reached in the same industry during that time, will tend to establish certain limits on the behavior of both parties. However, we must not assume that the parties will always act in terms of the long-run economic health of the firm.

There are times when the parties fail to reach an agreement that would be economically advantageous to both sides. There are also times when the parties reach an agreement that has unfortunate economic consequences.

We therefore cannot assume that the economic forces will just automatically work themselves out. It is the task of the negotiator to exercise such human relations skills as will bring about a contract that is economically sound. At the same time, we need to recognize that the use of such skills will not guarantee an economically sound settlement. Men may be led to disaster with great skill. We are simply saying that skills in human relations need to go together with skills in economic analysis in order to arrive at solutions that may be accepted in the long run by both parties.

# Chapter 19 *PATTERNS IN UNION-MANAGEMENT RELATIONS*

CAN we discern any patterns which prevail from group to group in examining union-management relations? That is, do we see any similarities among cases where harmonious relations are reported on both sides? Do we see any similarities in cases where conflicts are reported on both sides?

Our efforts in the past to find these patterns have been obscured by a tendency to concentrate attention exclusively on sentiments. It is observed that in apparently harmonious situations union and management leaders express faith in each other, whereas in apparently conflict-laden situations, they cast bitter aspersions on the point of view, trustworthiness, and motivation of members of the other party. It is noted that in conflict situations people have little confidence in being able to settle their problems without coercion, whereas in harmonious situations they are inclined to feel that all problems can be worked out without resort to strikes.

We cannot proceed very far along this line of thinking before recognizing that we are dealing in tautologies. We define a harmonious relationship in terms of the sentiments the parties feel toward each other, and then we try to explain the harmony of the relationship by reference to these same sentiments. Obviously, this is a futile pastime.

In seeking patterns, I suggest that we continue to look at the sentiments, but seek to determine what interactions and activities are associated with what sentiments.

In the preceding chapter, I have sought to show how the negotiation process itself may serve to effect a transition from one pattern of relations to another. In this chapter, I am seeking to demonstrate some of the chief patterns that are to be observed.

The scheme to be presented grew out of study of a very small number of cases, so that it must be regarded as highly tentative. On the other hand, since the first statement of this scheme appeared in 1949, I have had occasion to apply it to an increasing number of cases and have found it a distinct help in analyzing the behavior observed.[1] Furthermore, I have

---

[1] William F. Whyte, "Patterns of Interaction in Union-Management Relations," *Human Organization*, Vol. VIII, No. 4 (Fall, 1949), pp. 13–19.

encountered no case which violates the scheme—where, for example, a pattern of harmonious sentiments is associated with the interaction and activity pattern characteristic of conflict situations. I therefore suggest with some confidence that this way of looking at things can be helpful to any student or practitioner in the field of union-management relations.

Before getting down to cases, certain limitations should be pointed out. The scheme is based upon a study of relations involving industrial unions. Its possibilities of application to craft union situations are not known. Furthermore, the scheme purports to explain behavior at the level of the industrial plant and the local union. It includes the behavior of the union's international representative and of representatives of main office management who enter into activities at the local plant level. It does not deal with the total range of union-management relations from the local plant up to the top management of the corporation and of the international union. On the other hand, even where contracts are negotiated on a company-wide or industry-wide basis—which is becoming an increasingly common practice—there are still many cases in which local union officers and plant management officials have a good deal of autonomy in working out their relations with each other within broad limits set by the contract, company policy, and union policy. The scheme should apply to such local plant situations.

While the scheme does not purport to explain what happens when the United Steel Workers Union negotiates with the steel industry, for example, it may perhaps cast some light—at least by contrast—upon this area of relations. After we have examined the plant level relations in some detail, we shall go on in the next chapter to consider the implications of the scheme for larger scale relations.

## A SCHEME FOR ANALYSIS

This scheme is sketched in the accompanying diagrams. The arrows in the diagrams refer not to the simple frequencies of interaction but to the frequencies of origination of activity (or action) between points of the organization structures.

The diagrams are very much oversimplified. They describe only four levels of organization, leaving out staff organizations in order to concentrate upon the relations between the line organization of management and the union—except for one diagram in which it has been necessary to include staff. In studying any particular case it will, of course, be necessary for the researcher to draw his diagrams in terms of the actual number of levels of organization and to tie in staff with line.

These diagrams are not intended to cover all possibilities of union-management relationships, even within the limitations already stated. They represent merely an outline of a few of the common types to be observed. If the scheme proves to be of value, other researchers may introduce other observed patterns.

The analysis begins with the period before the union enters the plant, Diagram A, concentrating here as in the other diagrams upon the frequency of interaction and the origination of activity. In a non-union plant there are many varieties of interaction patterns, but emphasis here is placed on one very common type. Origination of action proceeds with a very high frequency down the line from top management to the worker, with very little action being originated up the line. As noted in the key, the thickness of the arrows indicates a rough estimate of the relative frequency of origination.

Diagram B, representing the situation when the union enters, shows what a drastic change is introduced into the social system of management

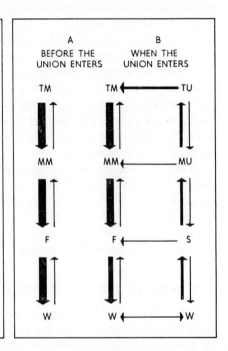

KEY

THICKNESS OF ARROWS REPRESENTS
RELATIVE FREQUENCIES OF
ORIGINATION OF ACTION

TM   TOP MANAGEMENT

MM   MIDDLE MANAGEMENT

F    FOREMEN

W    WORKERS

S    UNION STEWARDS

MU   MIDDLE UNION

TU   TOP UNION

A
BEFORE THE
UNION ENTERS

B
WHEN THE
UNION ENTERS

when this occurs. New and unfamiliar people enter the picture to originate action for management at various levels. Furthermore, one of the chief effects of the union organization is to place limitations upon the frequency with which the foremen can originate action for the workers. The foreman thus finds himself in a position whose difficulty will be elaborated upon later.

Various studies have shown that such a drastic change in the pattern of origination presents a difficult adjustment problem to those concerned. The top management, accustomed to unilateral control, finds it difficult to respond to the origination of a new group of people. Management's efforts to cope with this situation will be described in terms of two common patterns.

Diagram C depicts management's "soft policy." By following this policy, management men adhere to the theory that they can win peace and a harmonious adjustment with the union through satisfying the demands of the union leadership as often as possible. They look fondly toward the day when their generosity will be rewarded—the day the union leaders will cease pushing their demands. Unfortunately for management that day never dawns, and if we regard the problem in terms of the pattern of origination, we recognize that such an outcome is impossible. The union leaders, accustomed to originating action for management at a relatively high frequency, will not adjust easily to a situation calling for a cessation

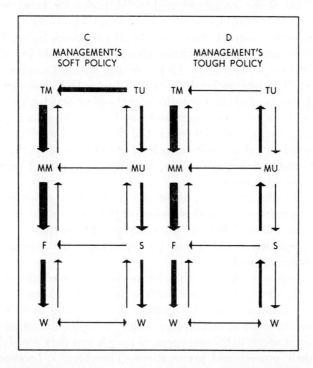

of their origination. Also, we should note in this diagram the strong control exercised upon the rank and file by the union leadership. As their demands are granted by management, the union leaders are able to offer constant rewards to the rank and file, thus strengthening their efforts to originate action down the line in the union.

As long as management continues to give in, trouble may be avoided, but such behavior on management's part is not unlimited. For example, we may take the case of the Blank Manufacturing Company which operated a chemical plant employing about 350 workers. The president of the company had given in to the union leaders so often and so readily that wages in his plant had become the highest in the industry, approximately 25 per cent above the level of his competitors. The men also had the finest working conditions in the industry. At the same time, however, costs were high and productivity within the plant compared unfavorably with competitive plants. Consequently, the Blank Company was losing money. The president reluctantly decided that the time had come to say "no" to union demands. Since he did not feel able to take this step himself, he hired an industrial relations man to act for him. The first time the new executive put his foot down, the union went out on strike. The strike was unauthorized, in violation of the contract, and the international officers of the union exercised all their influence to persuade the men to return to work, but the control of the local leadership over the rank and file was so tight that the strike continued with solid ranks for many weeks.

At the end of the fifth week, the international officers ruled the strike a clear violation of contract, and wrote to all employees telling them that unless they returned to work within ten days, they would lose their jobs. Even under this pressure, only 10 per cent of the 350 workers returned to the plant. The international union then began to recruit new workers to break the strike, and three months later the plant was back in operation —but with a highly inexperienced and unskilled working force. Throughout this entire period, only 10 per cent of the original work force showed a willingness to break away from its local union leadership, thus illustrating the strength of that leadership, built up over years of gaining concessions from management.

This strike was, of course, disastrous for the local union leaders and for the nine tenths of the workers who lost their jobs in the plant. It was also a terrible financial blow to the company. Furthermore, it indicated to management that its policy with the union for so many years had been basically misconceived.

If a soft policy is impracticable, let us observe the results of a "tough policy." In Diagram D, we see such a situation. To maintain union-management relations, the management must respond to origination of action from the union at certain times. But each time the union demands some action, it seems to the management people that they are giving away some of their powers and prerogatives. Therefore, it becomes highly important in management thinking to draw the line between those powers and prerogatives that can be safely yielded or shared with the union and those that must remain sacred to management. The tough policy management then seeks to draw this line in order to protect its prerogatives and takes a strong defensive position behind it, defending its privileges in an elaborate, legalistic manner. As a result, there is much pressure up the union structure toward management, the union leaders feeling compelled to originate action upon management, but with only limited success because of the narrowly defined areas in which management is willing to give ground. In a situation of this kind we find that management generally takes firm steps on questions of discipline. Within the union this approach may generate much antagonism toward management, but if the punishments are followed through fairly consistently, there are not likely to be many undisciplined outbreaks. Wildcat strikes may be more a product of confusion and inconsistency than of a tough management. However, the management that pursues a tough policy builds up strong hostilities toward itself within the union, and those strikes that are authorized may be long and bitter. In such situations it may be found that the workers are not particularly interested in stepping up productivity for management, the latter achieving production through technology and the various controls it exercises over the job.

Many management people have surveyed the results of both a soft policy and a tough policy and recognize the drawbacks in each approach. In making their decision to be neither tough nor soft, they resolve to be "firm but fair." For the analysis of behavior, this policy has one basic difficulty: it is meaningless. One may announce that one is being firm, but to others one's attitude may appear stubborn and unyielding. One may believe one is being fair, but the reaction of others may be that they are being badly cheated. The terms "firm" and "fair" are so vague and are subject to so many different interpretations that no particular pattern of interaction and activities is defined. They are simply a set of symbols which may be described as a management ideal.

## UNION-MANAGEMENT RECIPROCITY

There is, nevertheless, an alternative to the tough and soft policies. This can be seen from examining the diagrams. As we compare C and D, we note one striking similarity: Management rarely originates action directly for the union. Management has only one channel through which to originate action: through its own structure. Whether they are acting tough or soft, the managerial people in these situations feel themselves in a defensive position, and regard any move on the part of the union as an attempt to take away ground from management. For them it is a highly unrewarding position and does not augur well for harmonious relations with the union. A way out of this problem is shown in the diagram called "Union-Management Reciprocity."

While most of the observations in this article are rather tentative and based upon a small number of cases, one generalization can be made with considerable confidence: Wherever union and management in industry get along well together and express favorable sentiments toward each other, we find management originating action directly for the union to some degree, as well as originating down its own management structure. What arises may be termed a *reciprocity in the origination of action*, and when this develops we also find what is generally described as a sharing of responsibilities between union and management.

Tough managements constantly talk about union irresponsibility and demand that the union leaders become more responsible. But what do they mean by responsibility? We find that according to their conception, management has the responsibility of organizing production, effecting technological changes, setting up the marketing and advertising facilities, and so on, through a wide range of vital and interesting activities. On the other hand, the union leaders are responsible for preventing their members from going on strikes or participating in slowdowns, and for encouraging them to follow the plant rules in general. The union leaders are supposed to make their position felt only in the grievance procedure. Their responsibilities, therefore, are entirely of a negative character. That is, the union leaders, in exercising their "responsibilities," have a punishing effect upon the members. This is hardly the foundation upon which to build a harmonious union-management relationship. If the leaders are to hold their positions, they cannot follow through on this negative conception of responsibility desired by management.

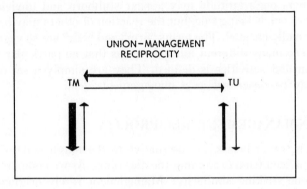

A sharing of responsibilities does not necessarily mean that the management must have the full concurrence of the union before acting upon every problem. There are varieties of adjustments in this area, but in the major problems affecting the union, no new action is taken by management without a thorough discussion with the key union people.

With the development of reciprocity between union and management at the top levels, we find the people concerned expressing favorable sentiments toward each other and speaking with some pride about the way they get along together. However, the fact that an adjustment has been reached at top levels does not necessarily mean that relations will flow harmoniously at the lower levels. Since the social systems are made up of interdependent parts, changes in one part will affect other parts; however, a change that leads to more harmonious relations at one point will not in itself necessarily have the same impact at other points. Further compensatory changes at many points in each system are essential.

## PROBLEMS AT LOWER LEVELS

To illustrate this observation, let us look at the situation in Diagram E, "Foremen Under Pressure." Here we see that it is possible to work out a harmonious relationship at top levels in such a manner that the foremen feel themselves under increasing pressure from above as well as from the union. For a complete understanding of this situation, we should consider the pressure of staff organizations, for in recent years the foreman's freedom of action has been seriously curtailed by the development of staff activities in engineering departments, in industrial relations staffs, and so on. The foreman's situation today often means that while the union is originating action for him, the very presence of the union limits his freedom to originate action for his subordinates. Moreover, the presence of the union may also lead to increasing pressures on the foreman from the top down. We often find top management regarding the foreman as something of a scapegoat. As union-management frictions chiefly crop up at this point, some top management people regard the whole problem as one of foreman-training; therefore, they seek to devise more elaborate methods of telling the foreman what to do. With all these pressures converging upon him, the foreman finds himself limited in his opportunities to compensate for them. Consequently it is not unusual to find him complaining that he has become a bumping-post between labor and management, and expressing in many ways the feeling that he is what we have described as "The Man in the Middle."

How is the foreman to re-establish his own personal equilibrium in the face of these pressures? One answer is shown in Diagram F, "Foreman Organization." Here we find foremen joining organizations such as The Foreman's Association of America, which enables them to originate action up the line of management as far as the highest levels, if necessary. The Foreman's Association of America has declined in strength considerably in post-war years for reasons beyond the scope of this study. Still, we often find foremen expressing the desire for a representative to convey their wants to the higher levels of management.

It is not suggested that an organization of foremen is the only method by which they can re-establish their equilibrium in management's system of relationships. Diagram G shows the possibilities of adjustment in three directions. Foremen may be encouraged to increase the frequency with which they originate action upon their superiors. The origination of action from superiors to foremen may be decreased. The foreman may be encouraged to originate action for the union steward. To put this statement of possibilities into subjective language, high levels of management should encourage foremen to make their needs felt, and should allow them more freedom to organize and operate their departments. The foremen should also consult with union stewards before taking action on disciplinary and other problems involving the union within their departments. In general, we find that where a situation giving scope to these adjustments prevails, the foremen have high morale and express favorable sentiments toward both management and the union.

Cooperation between top union and top management presents hazards for union organization also, as shown by the situation in Diagram H. In

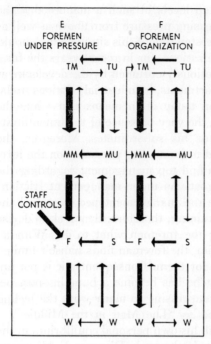

E
**FOREMEN
UNDER PRESSURE**

F
**FOREMEN
ORGANIZATION**

STAFF
CONTROLS

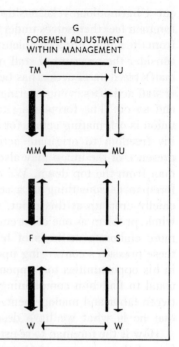

G
**FOREMEN ADJUSTMENT
WITHIN MANAGEMENT**

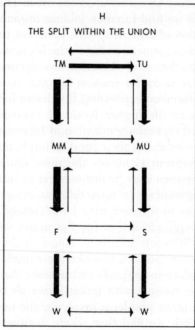

H
**THE SPLIT WITHIN THE UNION**

this diagram we find management originating action for top union with a relatively high frequency and top union originating action down the line inside the union with similar frequency. Here, also, originations of action up the union line and from top union to top management have been relatively curtailed. This situation has certain definite characteristics in terms of symbols and sentiments. We find that after a certain number of encounters, both top union and top management people establish personal ties and a feeling of mutual trust. Union leaders become aware of and interested in management's problems, such as costs and productivity, and realize that the management people are not the ogres they expected to find. There is awakened in the union leaders a sympathetic attitude toward management's point of view. Furthermore, they begin to use the same symbols used by management to describe union-management problems. As these symbols fail to win a response from the rank and file, the union leaders come to feel that the workers don't understand sufficiently what is going on and need to have "the true picture" described to them. We sometimes hear top union leaders speak in the same disparaging terms management people use regarding the intelligence and understanding of the rank and file. The management man who hears such talk should not regard it as a healthy sign, but rather as a danger signal pointing to a possible future split within the union. In several cases a situation of this kind led to a rank and file uprising during which the top union officers were voted out of office; in other cases we found top union leaders making commitments for the rank and file which they were then unable to carry out.

The union-management men who see this danger approaching may find a possible solution by referring back to Diagram G, in which relatively high frequency of origination of action prevails within the union from the bottom up. Origination within the union in these two directions (up and down) are closely related. When top union and top management get together to increase the frequency with which top union originates down the line of its structure, they should not ignore the necessity to increase activity up the line of the union. If this is not done, the equilibrium of the system will be destroyed.

## THE SCHEME AS A GUIDE TO DATA

This scheme not only suggests how to organize the data; it also tells us exactly what data we need to explain conditions we discover.

For example, a study by Orvis Collins of union-management relations in the Tennessee Valley Authority showed that relations between foremen and stewards were remarkably good, both sides speaking favorably of those they dealt with in the opposite structure. According to this framework of analysis, we would then expect to find the foremen originating action for the stewards on matters of discipline and in other areas, in addition to their normal activity of responding to the stewards. When we conducted interviews on the topic, that was precisely what we found. On the other hand, although Collins found that over-all union-management relations in TVA were remarkably harmonious, he did find some minor tension between members of middle management and the union. Indeed in TVA the middle management people alone seemed to feel themselves in a defensive position, fearing that the union was depriving them of some power. The union men spoke highly of most members of management, but were critical of many middle management people. According to our conceptual scheme, we should expect to find that members of middle management did not originate for the union to any appreciable extent, while their opposite numbers in the union originated action for them with a relatively high frequency. When we interviewed to test this hypothesis, we found it amply substantiated by the data. Applying the scheme in this manner points out tension areas and gives some explanation of how these tensions are related to the social system, as well as indicating possible changes that would relieve the tensions.

This case suggests one of the values of a conceptual scheme. It indicates the types of data that should be gathered and how they should be put together. It leads us to believe that when we find a certain pattern of sentiments between two points in an organizational system, we should then expect to find a certain pattern of interactions and activities, and it is there that we can direct our attention.

# Chapter 20 *HUMAN PROBLEMS OF LARGE-SCALE BARGAINING*

THE discussion in Part IV has so far been focused on relations between the local union and the management of the plant in which it is organized, with some incidental attention being given to the roles played by the international representative and home office management in the local situation. I have concentrated attention here because it is primarily here that we have human relations research data.

We must recognize that increasingly, union contracts are bargained on a company-wide and even industry-wide basis. Does this mean that the topics discussed so far have no relevance to the major industrial relations problems of the day? To what extent can we apply what we have learned so far about local situations to large-scale union-management relations? This chapter seeks answers to such questions.

In the preceding two chapters, we have also made one important assumption which should be stated explicitly: that management's goal in union relations is to achieve cooperative relations with union officers at all levels. Once this goal is assumed, then we can consider as scientifically as possible the means whereby the goal may be achieved. It is important to recognize that the goal itself has no scientific standing. The goals selected by individuals are matters of their own value judgments. We cannot determine, in any scientific sense, what goal in labor relations a given management *should* seek.

If that is true, then it follows that each different goal to which management people aspire would require a different set of means for reaching that goal.

In this chapter, we shall seek to analyze conditions prevailing when varying goals are desired. Management people may decide that establishing harmonious relations with a given set of union leaders is not a desirable goal. Or perhaps management people decide that in their particular situation, cooperation with union leaders is a goal impossible to achieve —impossible, at least, without sacrificing other goals that are important to management.

Let us now proceed to re-examine union-management relations, without making any assumption that cooperation is desirable, or even possible.

## IS LARGE-SCALE COOPERATION POSSIBLE?

Cooperative relations are not ends in themselves. For cooperation to persist, the parties to the relationship must feel that they are gaining certain advantages out of that type of relationship. So we do not ask management: Do you want cooperation with union leaders? We ask: What do you get out of such a relationship?

Let us re-examine local level relations first, so that we can try to fit this pattern to company-wide or industry-wide bargaining.

In the harmonious situations observed, we noted the development of reciprocities between union and management. The union at various points was able to originate activities for management that were positively valued by the union. Management, by the same token, was able to originate activities for the union that were positively valued by management. Out of this exchange grew the positive sentiments.

To make this more concrete, let us consider two illustrative cases. Since we are accustomed to thinking of the union originating for management, let us concentrate upon the reciprocal aspect of this relationship. This is a way of asking what the union can do for management.

After the Chicago plant of Inland Steel Container Company had passed through a bitter period of conflict between management and the United Steel Workers Union, the valued activities provided by union for management had become an important aspect of the harmonious relationship. These ranged all the way from the relatively simple case of overtime on the receiving dock to the much more complex case of the reorganization of the maintenance department.

In the receiving dock case, the men were refusing to accept overtime. Since a half-unloaded truck could not be left overnight, this meant that when there was not time in the regular working day to complete unloading of the whole shipment, the truck had to be dispatched back to the steel mill. This occurred at a time when steel was in short supply, so that a delay in receiving the shipments could cause disruption of production schedules in the container plant and consequent losses to management and workers both.

Studying arbitrators' decisions in such matters, the management people were convinced that they could insist on overtime work in specific instances and discipline workers who refused to comply. In other words, management felt that it had a legal right to take this unilateral action. This was indeed the way such a problem would have been handled in the conflict period, but now the general factories manager simply called upon the international representative, discussed the problem with him, and asked his cooperation. Jake Shafer, international representative, called in Don Hanes, local vice-president (the president being on leave of absence), and the two of them discussed the matter. Hanes got in touch with the steward in the receiving department and scheduled a departmental meeting. At the departmental meeting, Hanes urged the workers to abandon their refusal to take overtime. He pledged that if they continued to feel they were being unfairly treated, they should take the matter up in the grievance procedure, and the union would seek to protect their interests in grievance discussions. The result was that the refusal to accept overtime was abandoned—and management received a further example of the valued activities that could be provided by the union.

The maintenance department presented a variety of problems. Costs were so high that management was seriously considering contracting out a large part of the work. There was friction within the management organization in the department. There was widespread dissatisfaction among workers, centering particularly on charges of favoritism on the part of the foreman. Discipline was exceedingly lax.

International Representative Shafer had been discussing this departmental situation with Don Hanes (now president), who worked in that department, when General Factories Manager Novy took the initiative in calling upon the union for help. He outlined the problems as he saw them to Shafer. It was evident even in this first discussion that the men were dealing with a complex problem that needed considerable exploration. Therefore, the parties agreed upon a joint union-management study of the maintenance department situation. This led to an extraordinary amount of discussion activity for a period of slightly over a month.

"Novy's record for the May 12–June 13 period shows twenty-three meetings jointly with the union or within management. Fifteen of the twenty-three meetings were joint ones. These meetings consumed fifty hours, fifteen within management and thirty-five joint. If we had figures on the time spent within the union, the total would be considerably larger."[1]

What came out of these meetings? A few examples will indicate the scope of the agreement:

1. A decision that the department was overstaffed. Two workers were laid off.

2. A complete reclassification of jobs. This made for greater efficiency and also greater earnings for the remaining men.

3. Discharge of the foreman; appointment as foreman of a group leader in whom the workers had expressed confidence.

4. Redistribution of the men so that the number on the second shift was raised from six to sixteen. The foreman was placed in charge of that shift with his superior, the supervisor, being in charge of the twenty-four-man day shift. This made it possible to do more maintenance work at night when the production machines were shut down.

5. A statement on departmental rules and discipline. This will be presented in detail in Chapter 22.

---

[1] From William F. Whyte, *Pattern for Industrial Peace* (New York: Harper & Bros., 1951), p. 145.

Management people expressed great satisfaction with what had been accomplished. They reported that costs had been cut substantially. Increased efficiency showed up in a sharp reduction in the amount of overtime hours, even with two fewer men. It was also felt that worker-management and union-management relations in the department had been greatly improved.

While the union leaders were not happy about the dropping of two workers, they had recognized that the high costs of the department presented a real threat of a large layoff. The remaining men enjoyed increased earnings and also more secure jobs.

While some management people might not approve of the approach the Inland management took in these cases, there can be no denying that management did receive concrete gains. These gains were possible in the local situation because the international representative, in responding to management, could organize interactions and activities right down to the worker level.

In industry-wide or even company-wide bargaining, what the company can offer the union is quite clear, but what the union can offer the company is not at all clear. The union can always seek benefits of increased wages and various fringe benefits. If these are won, they will be reacted to favorably all down the line to the worker level. Management may sometimes be rewarded through having top union officials intervene to help smooth out troubled local situations or crises such as wildcat strikes. But does this provide enough reciprocity to make for favorable sentiments?

Suppose management seeks a major change from the union—such as a change in the working rules, as in the 1959 steel industry negotiations which resulted in a strike. Working rules are a very delicate matter in any local situation, depending as much upon local customs as they do upon contract provisions. Quite analogous changes were worked out in the Inland Steel Container Case within the machine shop, but here the problem involved people accustomed to working closely together and within a well-established framework of the exchange of valued activities. If the president of the international union and his chief co-negotiators agreed to a change in the master contract regarding working rules, just what would happen at the level of hundreds of plants, each having its own patterns of local customs?

In this situation, then, we see the union bargaining for gains which can be clearly registered without any significant changes in behavior at the plant level. At the same time, management is bargaining at the top level for changes in patterns of work activities that need to be effected many levels below the negotiating committee. Management cannot make its demand specific as to the precise changes that are to be made because the clause must apply to an endless variety of local situations. Therefore, a work rules clause must be stated broadly, and yet this very generality of the statement gives union negotiators and workers the impression that long-standing patterns of activities and rights in jobs are to be disrupted without the union having any recourse. Interpretations of this strike from both management and union spokesmen make it clear that it was this generalized threat to job conditions which united workers behind their union leaders and solidified union ranks through a long strike. In the end, management settled without any contractual changes on the work rules issue.

If management people conclude that top level union leaders cannot provide management with gains at the shop level where the work is done, then management people may be inclined to feel that there is no positive value in cordial relations at the top level. In that case, the aim may become to limit insofar as is possible the losses the top union leaders can cause management; in other words, to devise a strategy which will tend to neutralize the power of top union leaders so that management will be freer to work out its problems directly with workers and local union leaders. The most articulate spokesman of this point of view has been Lemuel Boulware of the General Electric Company. So strongly has this individual stamped his mark upon the company philosophy in labor relations that it is widely known as "Boulwarism."

It will be worth our while to give special attention to the General Electric approach for two main reasons which suggest its general significance.

1. However one may seek to measure the long-run gains and losses growing out of a given policy, in the summer and fall of 1960 the General Electric approach achieved what seemed to many observers a spectacular victory.

The leaders of the IUE turned down management's contract offer and called a strike. The company continued to operate the plants—with difficulty at first, but with growing success in getting workers to come back to their jobs. In a short time the union leaders were forced to call off the strike and to sign a contract essentially the same as that offered to them before the strike.

In recent years, few companies have sought to operate during a strike. So far as I know, this was the first time (since the early days of organization) that a major multi-plant company, in a clash with a major industrial union, kept its plants open during the strike.

2. This apparent success is likely to have an important influence upon policies and procedures of other managements. In fact, shortly after the strike I happened to be with a management group which included one General Electric man. After the GE man had explained the policy and related procedures, a top management man in another company said flatly: "That is going to be the management approach from now on." Others nodded assent.

What then are the policies and procedures we are talking about? First, it should be noted that we are dealing here with a highly controversial topic. Our aim is not to pass judgment on the ethical values in the policies, but rather to explain what the policy looks like in action and examine its implications for the future of collective bargaining.

## THE GENERAL ELECTRIC APPROACH

The company approach can be summed up under the following points:

1. *Community relations activities.* Wherever the company operates, management aims to develop a broad community relations program designed to discharge what it considers to be its obligations to the community and to develop favorable community sentiments toward GE. This approach is thought to be helpful to the company in many respects. For our present discussion, its chief significance lies in strengthening management's position in the local community in such a way that in case of a strike, the local law enforcement agencies will be likely to enforce the law regarding mass picketing, picket line violence, and other activities that might keep employees from going back to work. Whatever other values the company may seek and achieve through its community relations program, there is no denying that the program strengthens the company's hand at a time of crisis.

2. *Systematic studies.* Long before collective bargaining begins, GE industrial relations men begin studies leading them toward the kind of offer they will eventually make at the bargaining table. This includes. of course, study of the demands likely to be presented by the union. While managements generally are giving more attention to the work of preparing to bargain, few companies have gone as far in this respect as General Electric.

3. *Direct communication with workers.* GE management people carry on direct communication with workers in the various plants periodically during times of normal business conditions. There is an extensive survey program to determine what the workers want and expect from the company. For example, are they primarily interested in cents per hour or in a major medical insurance program?

The company presents its point of view through direct mail pieces going to workers' homes, as well as in the weekly employee newsletter published locally at each plant. These communications cover matters of controversy with the union, but are by no means limited to such issues. In other words, management communicates with employees whether or not union issues are being argued. Management also gives special attention to the first-line supervisors in the hopes that they will be able to represent the company's point of view.

When management is prepared to make its offer to the union, that offer, in full detail, goes to all of the workers through the mail within a few hours up to a day after it is presented across the table to the union leaders.

4. *Bargaining strategy.* Management refuses to do what it calls

"haggling." Management refuses to introduce a small offer in the early stages of bargaining to balance an astronomical demand, and then to approach a settlement through a series of compromises.

Early in negotiations, management lays its full offer on the table. The intention is not to change this offer except insofar as discussions bring out information management had not previously considered.

On the other hand, while holding firm to the over-all level of benefits, management is willing to bargain regarding the elements that should go into making up this cost to the company. For example, if the offer should be ten cents an hour, management is willing to bargain as to whether all or none of this goes into a direct wage increase, whether one or another fringe benefit is added, and so on. At this point, management is not willing to consider union proposals that the package add up to twelve cents, fifteen cents, or any other figure beyond ten cents.

The distribution among the elements in the final package may be bargained centrally, but it can also be bargained locally. In fact, though this generally escaped notice in the heat of the 1960 strike, the distribution of these elements in the package settlement was locally negotiated, with the thought that the local management and union people could in that way better fit the settlement to the needs of the situation.

5. *Attractiveness of the offer.* It is management's aim to make an offer that will be so attractive to workers that they will be exceedingly reluctant to strike or remain out on strike when urged to do so by union leaders. The nature of the offer is arrived at on the basis of studies of what workers want, of what other unions and managements are agreeing to, and of what management estimates the company can afford to pay. Through direct communication to workers, management seeks to persuade them that the offer is indeed attractive and that a strike cannot win them anything beyond the offer.

In the 1960 situation, there was ample evidence that management had been successful on this point. The strike vote, which is little more than a formality in many situations, actually yielded a relatively small majority in favor of a strike, and some of the largest locals voted against striking. Local union leaders in the mammoth Schenectady local did not bring their workers out immediately and only a few days later they called off the strike well before the national officers had capitulated.

6. *Operating the plants.* If the strike finally does come, management makes every effort to keep the plants operating by securing the assistance of local authorities in getting workers through picket lines and making newspaper, radio, television, and direct mail appeals to workers to come back to work.

## IMPACT ON UNION LEADERS

It is no surprise to find the top union leaders of IUE holding bitterly hostile sentiments toward General Electric. The management practice of communicating directly with the workers on industrial relations matters tends to undermine the position the leaders have with the workers. Furthermore, the bargaining strategy prevents the top union leaders from working up to the final offer in successive stages and thus being able to dramatize to the membership the union contribution in securing the gains involved in this final offer.

Top union leaders are naturally inclined to hold more favorable sentiments toward management people when management leaders limit their industrial relations communications primarily to the union leaders, do not seek out direct contacts with the workers, and give union leaders the opportunity to participate in the process of shaping up the final settlement. In effect, the General Electric management people have decided to emphasize their direct relations with workers, whatever effects this may have upon their relations with top union leaders.

## SUCCESS UNDER WHAT CONDITIONS?

While from one standpoint the General Electric approach seems to have been highly successful, this does not mean that it would work for every management. We must consider the particular conditions prevailing in this situation which may have strengthened the company's hand in dealing with the union.

It is often said that among the major unions, IUE is relatively weak. The assessment of the strength or weakness of a union is not an easy matter, but at least we can point to certain objective factors in such an assessment.

The International Union of Electrical Workers, led by James Carey, arose out of a bitter struggle against the leadership of the allegedly Communist-dominated United Electrical Workers. While IUE was able to win over a majority of the UE locals, the long struggle no doubt left deep-seated factional divisions which might have weakened the loyalty of workers to any leadership that finally emerged. Furthermore, there are now large numbers of General Electric plants organized by unions other than IUE: IBEW, UE, and UAW particularly. This means that IUE can shut down well under half of the GE plants by its own direct action. To this extent, strength may depend upon building up and maintaining a united front among the several unions. IUE claimed to have established such a united front before the 1960 negotiations began, but the other unions accepted the General Electric offer within a few hours after it was made. Under these circumstances, IUE members might well ask themselves, "If the offer is good enough for the other unions, why isn't it good enough for us?" And they would recognize that it would be extremely difficult for General Electric to improve on an offer that other unions had already accepted.

Against unions stronger and more skillfully led than IUE, the General

Electric approach might be ineffective. Nevertheless, we can expect that some other managements will try to apply what they think they have learned from the apparent success of the General Electric Company.

## CONCLUSION

For this book, the General Electric experience is significant only insofar as it highlights some of the problems of large-scale bargaining.

We have shown how reciprocity may—and sometimes does—develop in union-management relations at the local level. We have shown how this reciprocity may break down at the top level. There the exchange may take the form of management offering a reward in order to escape a threatened penalty (the strike). Let us put this situation in more general terms. In the relations between A and B, if A rewards B in exchange for B's withholding a penalty, and this exchange continues, then we can expect A to develop negative sentiments toward B and to seek ways of escaping the penalty without continuing to reward B.

This suggests that if cooperative relations are to develop at top levels between large companies and unions, the parties must explore to find new possibilities of reciprocity at those top levels. Note that this is intended to be a scientific statement: If X is the goal, then Y is the pathway to that goal. Many management and union leaders will reject the goal. But if they do, they will continue to contend with the instabilities and tensions of the relationship in which A is called upon to reward B in order to escape the penalty B can impose on A.

## Collateral Readings

JAQUES, ELLIOTT. *The Changing Culture of a Factory.* New York: The Dryden Press, Inc., 1952.

A study, by a psychiatrist, of the evolution of worker-management and union-management consultation in a British plant.

GOULDNER, ALVIN. *Wildcat Strike.* Yellow Springs, Ohio: Antioch College Press, 1954.

Case study of a strike.

KARSH, BERNARD. *Diary of a Strike.* Urbana: University of Illinois Press, 1958.

Case study with particular emphasis on varying reactions of workers.

SAYLES, LEONARD. *Behavior of Industrial Work Groups: Prediction and Control.* New York: John Wiley & Sons, Inc., 1958.

A study of the forces that lead to work group militancy or apathy.

———, and STRAUSS, GEORGE. *The Local Union: Its Place in the Industrial Plant.* New York: Harper & Bros., 1953.

An analysis of human relation in unions, based upon twenty-odd case studies.

WHYTE, WILLIAM FOOTE. *Pattern for Industrial Peace.* New York: Harper & Bros., 1951.

> A case study of a union-management relationship which changed from bitter conflict to warm cooperation.

## Discussion Questions

14      1. Suppose you are a union leader, looking for ways to make your organizing efforts more effective. What lessons would you draw from the Hi-Test case?

14      2. Suppose you were representing management, looking for ways to keep the union out. What lessons would you draw from the Hi-Test case?

15      3. Suppose you wished to predict, during an organizing drive, whether a given worker would vote for or against unionization. What information would you need to have?

15      4. What relationships between job satisfaction and personality are suggested by Chapter 15?

16      5. What changes in behavior are required of the foreman as the union becomes established? What changes are required of the local union leader? Should it be possible to predict which individual foreman or union leaders will make successful adjustments to the changing relationship? What indications would you look for in making such a prediction?

16      6. What are the possibilities and limitations in using the analysis of grievances to cast light upon the union-management relationship?

16      7. You are consulted by union officials who tell you that their stewards (1) are not doing a good job and (2) don't seem eager to take on the responsibilities of the job. They want you to plan a steward training program for them. What would you recommend?

17      8. Compare the cases of Chapter 17 ("Work Group Cohesion and Militancy") with cases presented in earlier chapters. What general statements would you make regarding factors leading to high or low work group cohesion?

18      9. In collective bargaining, what is the influence of economic information upon the discussion process?

18      10. "The Collective Bargaining Process" focuses attention primarily upon relations within the union and between union and management negotiators. What problems of relations within management would you expect to have accompany the collective bargaining relationship? How would you advise management to meet these problems?

19      11. What possibilities for reciprocity between union and management do you see? Illustrate with examples taken from several levels in the organization, from foreman up to plant manager. Use a case from your experience or from your reading.

19      12. Are there any pitfalls for the union leader in the development of reciprocity with management? If so, can they be avoided? How?

20      13. What possibilities do you see for the development of reciprocity between union and management at the top levels of large organizations?

20      14. Select a large company and large union with which it deals (other than GE and IUE). Suppose management decided to try out the GE approach. What results would you predict? On what information would your prediction depend?

# PART V  THE MANAGERIAL PROCESS

IN EACH chapter up to this point, we have encountered members of management in action, but so far we have been considering them in relation to the environment of the plant and to the union. In Part V, we make the company hierarchy the focus of our attention. We consider relations among the various levels of the line of authority and examine the forces that make for effective or ineffective managerial leadership.

We begin with the first-line supervisor and then move on to consider more generally the man-boss relationship.

We find that this pair relationship can only be understood when it is placed in the context of the social system as a whole; therefore, in Chapter 23, we undertake to examine a plant where we see some of the inter-relations among five levels in the hierarchy. More specifically, we see how a change in managers leads to successive changes at each level down to the bottom. This case also gives us an opportunity to observe some of the inter-relations between personality and organization.

In the last two chapters we consider one of the basic problems of bureaucratic organizations. Many people have claimed that large organizations tend to stifle individual initiative, to elevate the ability to follow detailed rules over creativity. We will consider some of the conditions of formal organization structure and managerial leadership which may make for the development of greater individual initiative.

# Chapter 21 *THE FIRST-LINE SUPERVISORY POSITION*

WE BEGIN our examination of the management process by considering the role of the foreman. It is often said that the foreman is the key man in management from the worker's point of view, that he represents the company to the workers. We shall have occasion to question this emphasis as we go along. But the foreman, who directs the work of production or process in the plant, is at least a convenient point at which to begin.

## THE FOREMAN DOES NOT EXIST

First, a caution against a very common semantic fallacy: mistaking a word for a thing. We often unconsciously assume that because we can speak of *the* foreman, such an individual and such a position actually exist. This leads people to try to discover how *the* foreman should be selected, how *the* foreman should be trained, and how *the* foreman's behavior should be evaluated. This leads further to the assumption that *the* good foreman will have the same abilities and skills regardless of differences in first-line supervisory job situations. Nothing could be farther from the truth.

We must begin our analysis by recognizing that the technology and the nature of the tasks performed by the workers tend to shape the role and influence the behavior of the foreman. Comparisons among the cases already described will show something of the range of possibilities.

We have seen that the foreman on the assembly line has large numbers of very brief interactions with his workers individually and very rarely interacts with more than one individual at a time. By contrast, the foreman in the Benton blowing room has extended conversations with individuals and sometimes with groups of men. On one occasion, we noted the Benton foreman spending more than two hours with Jack Carter, observing him at work and discussing his work problems with him. Such an extended period of interaction would be completely out of the question on the assembly line.

In our study of the Blank Oil Company, we noted that the foreman of the engine repair crew also related himself to his men in a way that would have been impossible on the assembly line. The men worked in small groups, and at times the foreman would be observed standing with a group of men, carrying on a lively discussion involving the diagnosis of mechanical problems, with items of small talk thrown in.

The foreman's interactions may vary markedly even within the same organizational unit. While the men in the Hi-Test control room complained bitterly about their former foremen, Jones and Fitch, and reported being under constant pressure from them, the engine operators reported that they rarely saw these foremen and were simply left alone by them.

The foreman's job may also change markedly through time. In examining the problems of Tom Walker in the Barrel Department, we have seen how the changing nature of the production in the department drastically affected his relations with other organizational units, and then with his own workers.

The Tom Walker case also underlines the importance of looking at the foreman's job in terms of a whole network of relations. We customarily think simply of the foreman's relations to his subordinates, and sometimes we consider his relations with his own immediate boss. In examining the foreman's job, we need to consider also the relations he needs to develop and maintain with other foremen in related departments and with staff and control people. In the assembly line studies, we have seen the foreman interacting more with people outside his department than with his workers. Changes in his relations with the people outside his own department often affect the foreman's relations with his workers.

While all of these distinctions need to be noted, we can make some general statements regarding the historical evolution of the first-line supervisor's position, and also, regarding the social characteristics of the men we find in that position.

## THE CHANGING NATURE OF FOREMAN POSITIONS

It is often said that the foreman's position is weaker today than it was many years ago. What is meant by this statement?

While there were differences from company to company and even department to department, in manufacturing plants fifty years ago the foreman really ran his own department. He had the authority to hire whomever he pleased and to place workers wherever he wished in the department. He also had a free rein on disciplining workers, including firing them. His sovereignty was only beginning to be disturbed by the growth of staff specialists, and he had no union to question his decisions.

All this has changed in most plants. Industrial engineers come in to study and change job methods, and in some cases, to set incentive rates. Design engineers move in to introduce technological changes at a rate much faster than fifty years ago. Cost accountants establish much more elaborate systems of record keeping and paper work than the old foreman faced. The union provides a channel of appeal against the foreman's decisions, and it is this force which has helped to bring the personnel man into the foreman's sphere of action. Between them, union leaders and personnel men see to it that a system of job classification and orderly progression from job to job is developed, so that the discretionary powers of the foreman are severely curtailed.

## MOVING UP FROM WORKER TO FOREMAN

Years ago it was the universal rule to choose foremen from among the workers. This picture has been steadily changing, so that company after company is recruiting its supervisors from among college-trained men; even when promotion to the foreman level is left open to workers, we are likely to find that there is a ceiling one or two levels higher up on promotions of ex-workers.

In part this has been a natural development of advancing technology, which tends to require special training for management positions. We must explain it also in terms of the widening social cleavage between management and the workers, which makes it increasingly difficult for management to find workers who can function in the middle of a latent conflict situation.

We find in some cases that the workers who are promoted are unable to handle a foreman's job and must be dropped back to the work level. How can we explain such failures?

We must first examine the basis of selection. In going through the personnel records of one plant, we picked out the following estimates of two workers written by the plant superintendent:

Employee has the ability but lacks courage to face criticisms of fellow employees. Was considered as supervisory material until further consideration exposed above trait.

Employee has an excellent knowledge of machine operation and could become pace setter if he so desired, but is influenced by his group and lack of determination to force his crew.

Here two men were denied promotions because they were considered to be loyal to their work group, and it was assumed that such loyalty was not compatible with management's objectives. This is a very common management reaction. The worker who fits with the group is ruled out on those grounds. But what alternative is there for management? If the promoted worker has not been a respected member of the work group, then naturally the workers resent him intensely in his new position and resist his authority. Many foremen have been defeated by such opposition.

Nor can the problem be solved simply by promoting the leader of the gang, as is sometimes done by management. If management and workers were on the same team, pulling in the same direction, then the informal leader would obviously be the best choice. When a marked social cleavage separates workers from management, then the man who crosses the line must immediately ask himself whose side he is on. If he tries to keep close to the work group, then management looks upon him with distrust. If he conforms to management's expectations, then the workers feel he has sold them out. Some foremen we have observed try to "ride the fence," playing the workers' game when among them and conforming to management's logics when in contact with higher management. When the pressures on the foreman from above are not too severe, it seems possible to maintain this position—and we have seen it done—but the foreman always runs the risk of losing the confidence of both sides. At best, this is hardly an effective approach to the problem.

There are other factors which make for difficulty in the adjustment of the ex-worker foreman. At best, this is a difficult transition to make. In many cases a man will take ten years or more to work up to the highest non-supervisory job, so that he will have become thoroughly habituated to the work routines by the time he is faced with an entirely different sort of job. The job of handling men is quite different from that of handling machines. The new foreman must break away from hand-and-body manipulation of machines and from close concentration upon the details of a narrowly restricted job. He must see the pattern of jobs and men in relation to each other. He must learn to think in somewhat more abstract terms.

Many men fail to make this adjustment. They apparently do not feel secure unless they have their hands on a machine, and they pitch in to do jobs themselves to the extent that direction and coordination suffer.

A promotion clearly involves changes in the thought processes of the new foreman. It also involves a very important transition in human relations. It is in facilitating this transition that many managements are particularly inadequate.

Anthropologists have shown that all well-integrated societies have ceremonial ways of handling such social transitions. When, for example, the boy approaches the age of maturity, it is not left to him to become a man by himself. The society organizes an elaborate *rite of passage* to channel and support this change. While the content of the ceremonials varies widely from tribe to tribe, the form and function are much the same. First the individual is removed from the ordinary associations of his daily life—together with others making the transition at the same time—and brought into intimate and frequent contact with the adult males of the tribe. There follows a period in which the novice is ceremonially instructed in the technical and social aspects of the new role he is to play. The rite comes to a close when the novice is reintroduced to the society, and ceremonies are performed to give recognition to his new role.

Such rites are essential for the handling of social transitions. They help the individual to think, feel, and act in terms of the new role, and they help the total society to recognize the transition that has been made and to give recognition to the new role.

While ceremonials tend to be much less emphasized in our own society, we do give some attention to celebrating such transitions as marriage and school graduation. Unfortunately, with certain notable exceptions, ceremonials play a very small role in the life of the modern factory. It is perhaps at this point that management experimentation should be encouraged.

While we cannot expect a system of ceremonials to establish harmony within the factory when other important factors stimulate conflict, the transition from worker to foreman is of profound significance to the individual and to the whole factory. This suggests that more attention should be given by management to exploring the nature of the transition and to experimenting toward the development of more effective ways of bringing it about.

Perhaps some companies have been providing such ceremonials without planning it that way. Harrison Trice reports this experience with a company that had an elaborate program for the selection and training of foremen.[1] At management's invitation, he spent a summer studying both the company's testing program for potential supervisors and the two-week training program provided for those selected. Trice could find neither a relationship between the men's test scores and their subsequent performance as foremen, nor any evidence of the effectiveness of the two-week training program. Trice expected that management would be discouraged by his negative report, but the personnel manager accepted it with equanimity. He said that he had thought for some time that the facts would turn out to be what Trice had reported. Nevertheless, the program's real value might lie in the effect it had in making the new foremen feel that they were really foremen and making the workers feel that it was indeed something to become a foreman. He explained that in fact management gave little attention to the test scores in making its selection of foremen but that the candidates took the process most seriously and reported that they had really gone through an ordeal when they had finished the testing program. Similarly, whatever other effect it might have, the two-week training program did isolate the new foremen from workers and perhaps helped them to get adjusted to their new role.

The ceremonials appropriate to a primitive society could hardly be accepted in the United States. We would regard them as meaningless evidences of superstition. In a society oriented toward science and hard

---

[1] Through personal communication.

practical facts, it may well be that we need to develop ceremonials that will *appear* to be based upon science and practical concerns, even when they have no such demonstrated connection. In a period when the personality testers are under fire for not being able to prove their claims, this approach to testing may give them a new lease on life.

## THE COLLEGE-TRAINED FOREMAN

Today, while the opportunities of advancement for workers are narrowing, supervisors are being recruited in large numbers from men who are graduates of colleges and universities with degrees in engineering or chemistry, business management or non-professional subjects.

These "outsiders" have a difficult adjustment to make. In the first place, they are members of the middle class, and family background—or at least the educational process—has given them a social outlook far different from that of the workers. Furthermore, they generally come in to supervise experienced workers who are older than they and who feel keenly that the supervisory jobs should not be given to "outsiders." As one worker put it:

> You want to know what's the matter with this place? There's no hope! It's just like we were beating our heads against a brick wall. We're stopped where we are. If they need a foreman, they bring him in from the outside.

The college-trained foreman, therefore, is under pressure from the moment he starts work. Of course, he does not begin to supervise as soon as he sets foot inside the plant. If this is his first supervisory job, management generally provides him with a training program which involves observation of machines and processes as well as some formal instruction from management. The man may be provided with some reading matter on problems of human relations, but the emphasis is generally upon study of technology and of management procedures. Even where human problems are emphasized, we find that people cannot readily learn new ways of behaving by reading subject matter which is not closely tied to practice.

When these new men move into supervision, we frequently find conflict arising over the problem of *knowledge.* How much does the supervisor know about the jobs performed by workers? How much does he need to know?

Here we must distinguish between the college-trained engineer or chemist and the college man without this technical and scientific background.

The well-trained technical man knows a good deal about machines and processes. His problem is that he often fails to recognize the limits of his knowledge. He does not realize that the skilled and experienced operator inevitably has a more intimate, detailed knowledge of his machine or process than the foreman can or should have. Thus the foreman tries to impose tight controls over the operations, making no provision for the skill or judgment of the workers. This sort of approach is self-defeating.

We have seen this problem in the Hi-Test plant. Former Foremen Jones and Fitch had always given their operating instructions in great detail and were highly critical of the men when the operating results did not come up to what the foremen predicted on the basis of their instructions. Through their day-to-day experience, the men learned that often the detailed instructions issued by the foremen would not in fact lead to results that the foremen called for. The workers could not point this out to the foremen because the foremen, being technically trained, refused to acknowledge that the workers might know more about some aspects of operations than they did. Therefore, in order to escape criticism from the foremen, the workers took to "boiler-housing" their record of operations on the Daily Operating Data Sheet. They wrote down in full detail the operating steps the foreman had directed but then went ahead to operate the plant so as to come out with the result that the foreman required. In many cases this meant that the actual operating steps were far different from those indicated on the data sheets. These foremen thus never knew exactly how the plant was operating. Their relations with the workers prevented them from obtaining the accurate records necessary for scientific experimentation and for technical improvements in operation.

The successor to Jones and Fitch, Tom Lloyd, recognized that efficient operations, as well as good morale, depended upon supervisory recognition of the knowledge and skill possessed by the workers. How he provided such recognition is analyzed in the following chapter.

Lloyd's evaluation of the skills of his men is best shown in this comment upon the Masters "watchman statement":

> Masters told the truth, but that was only part of the story. He said that the men were only watchmen, that they had to watch the charts and call in specialists for anything they needed done. It is true they have all these indicators, but they have to do more than just watch. A man has to know that if he sees one thing on a chart over here, he has to look at another chart to see how that fits in. He uses those charts to diagnose the situation. He acts like a doctor. The doctor doesn't only read your temperature and check your pulse. He uses those things to tell him what needs to be done. A man in operations needs experience to do that. The engineers can't do it for him.

The experience of the tri-isobutylene run demonstrated the soundness of Lloyd's statement—even though at the time he failed to apply it to his problem. Somehow, when the crisis was upon him, he believed that the technical man (Dan Benton) could operate better than the workers. By having Benton supersede the operators, Lloyd upset the relations among the men and between men and management, and also failed to achieve his operating goals.

In college, the engineer is not taught how to operate fractionating column number 4 at the Hi-Test plant. He learns the basic principles of

chemical engineering that will enable him to understand the fraction-
ation process and perhaps to make basic improvements in the process.
But somehow a complex piece of equipment never acts just exactly as
theory dictates. The skillful operator, through long hours of experience
on his job, learns things about it that no engineer with a much broader
range of duties can ever possibly grasp. Even in much simpler jobs, we
have found this to be the case. Therefore, the problem of efficiency as
well as the problem of cooperation depends upon an effective combination
of technical knowledge and worker-operating skills.

In such a situation, some workers will learn what adjustments to make
without understanding why. There will be at least a few others, like Joe
Sloan, who develop both the "feel" of the job and some of its scientific
foundations. Even in the growing complexities of modern technical
processes, these men seem qualified to move up into management. In
fact, there are other companies in the same industry with the same
processes which have not had a flat policy against selecting foremen out
of the ranks. In one company, for example, while the management people are largely college trained, there has been a practice of teaming the
college and non-college man together out in the fields and plants. In one
place, the superintendent will be a college graduate and his assistant a
man up from the ranks; in another installation, it will be the other way
around. In this way, the necessity for combining job knowledge with
technical knowledge and with a variety of social experience has been
recognized.

The college graduate in business management or other non-engineer-
ing subjects faces a similar problem, but one which is more difficult in
some respects. He does not go in equipped with scientific and technical
knowledge. He is chosen because he is thought to have "supervisory ability." According to this theory, if he has such ability, he will be able to
pick up on the job the technical knowledge he needs. However, he runs
into immediate worker resistance on this score.

One worker expressed his resentment in this way:

> They put in men as foremen who don't know anything about the machines.
> The idea behind that is that knowledge about the work isn't necessary, that all
> the boss needs to know is how to supervise men. Supervise what? How can you
> supervise a man if you can't tell him what to do?

Another worker made this comment:

> They'll send in a foreman that doesn't know a damn thing about the work.
> We'll show him a little about the work. Then he'll come around and give us
> orders. Maybe then he knows something, but he doesn't know all of it. He'll
> jump on you just to show his authority.

It is not easy to learn the job this way. A worker told us this story
of worker resistance:

The other day we were having trouble, and finally we got the job to running right. The foreman came out and asked what we did. I told him, "Oh, just some minor changes." All we did was tighten up the screws, but if I'd told him that, the next time we had trouble, he'd come out and tell us to tighten up the screws.

And maybe the next time the trouble wouldn't be the same thing, but he'd be telling us to tighten up the screws and getting us all fouled up.

If we tell them anything, they'll be sure to be using it on us later. Either getting us fouled up doing the wrong things or trying out their God-damned experiments. The way to do is to keep things to ourselves for our own protection.

And so the workers do their best to keep the new foreman from learning the job. They answer questions either in a non-committal manner, or else they simply feign ignorance.

We have seen foremen react to this situation in two ways. First, they may believe that the workers really do not know the answers to the questions. And yet it is clear that any man of average intelligence who has operated a machine for several years should know the answers. Therefore, it follows that the workers are stupid. This sentiment, of course, leads to a further deterioration of supervisor-worker relations.

Or the supervisor may recognize that workers know more than they are willing to tell. Then the problem becomes one of finding ways of forcing workers to divulge information. As one worker told us,

These guys think I'm supposed to teach them. That foreman said to me, "I want you to tell me what I want to know! If you won't tell me, I can make it tough for you!"

The worker who told this story spoke with intense bitterness. And all the other workers in the plant, of course, had heard the story and reacted against the foreman.

Clearly these foremen are in an exceedingly difficult position. They lack the support of a technical background, and their training period does not provide them with anything beyond superficial knowledge of machines and processes. They are supposed to have "supervisory ability," and yet they have very inadequate knowledge of the activities they are expected to supervise. Perhaps they could pick it up in time, but they want to make a showing with management by carrying on the supervisory activity their role demands. Therefore, we often find them stepping in and giving orders based on very incomplete knowledge. This antagonizes workers and stimulates them to withhold their knowledge to make it as difficult as possible for the supervisor to learn his job.

And finally, workers do not believe that a college education creates "supervisory ability." They feel that the supervisory jobs rightfully belong to them, and they have no incentive to help the "outsider" make good as foreman.

## STATUS SYMBOLS IN THE SUPERVISORY RELATIONSHIP

Status symbols play an important role in the supervisory relationship. The workers are quick to catch any attitude of social superiority on the part of foremen, and any such manifestations are hotly resented.

One worker said of a new foreman:

He wants us to call him *Mister* Thomas. Every time he walks past I feel like walking up to him and punching him in the jaw. One of these days I'm going to do it.

Another worker made this statement:

These bosses run around here acting as if they're better than we are. We had a foreman here that used to take a drink with some of the fellows after work. The superintendent told him that he shouldn't mix with us, that he was supposed to belong to *a different class.*

When workers describe a good foreman, they speak in these terms:

One thing about Jessup, he didn't go around in a suit and white collar. He changed his clothes, and five minutes after seven he was out on the floor with the men. . . .

He spent his time out on the floor, not in the office. He used to wear work clothes, and when anything went wrong, he wasn't afraid to step in and get dirty. . . .

I'll tell you why Taylor was a good foreman. He knew these machines, and when the boys got into trouble, he'd step right in and help them out of it. He'd lend a helping hand. I've seen him outside on a cold day, helping a couple of fellows push a truck.

These points raise some fundamental problems in supervision. The workers' comments run directly counter to well-entrenched theories held by some management people. According to these theories, the supervisor's job is to direct work activities; it is not his job to help operate the machines, except insofar as the help is offered in the form of instruction and advice. Furthermore, to maintain the respect and dignity due management, supervisors should emphasize the status distinctions setting them off from workers. Management thinking here follows the "familiarity breeds contempt" adage: If workers get to know foremen as people, they cannot give them the respect due management.

We find these theories to be unsound. We must question first the assumption that workers will respect superiors who emphasize status distinctions and who are careful not to meet them on an equal plane. All our evidence indicates that this is simply not true.

This does not mean that the foreman should participate on an intimate basis in the social activities of his workers. If he becomes too close to some men in his department, he will be suspected of playing favorites. The foreman must seek to avoid becoming closely identified with any worker clique. However, it is quite possible to establish good informal relations with workers without joining any faction.

It is well recognized by management that the foreman who can't keep his hands off the machines is not doing the supervisory job for which he was hired. The mistake is made when this sound observation is extended into a total prohibition of manual work on the part of the foreman. The foreman who lends a hand in emergencies and is not above helping out occasionally on an unpleasant job does not jeopardize his supervisory activity. On the contrary, he builds the cooperation which makes for effective supervision.

Workers recognize that the foreman's responsibilities do not allow him to be constantly at hand when they need help. They do not expect him to do the work of a worker, nor will they respect him for doing the work they feel they should be doing. The time and effort he spends in lending a hand may be very small, and yet it can serve to build the loyalties upon which effective organizations depend.

Furthermore, the foreman, in showing that he is not above getting his hands dirty, makes an important status point. He narrows the gap between himself and the workers and demonstrates in this way his regard for them and their jobs.

This does not mean that all status distinctions between workers and supervisors should be wiped out. In large organizations especially, gradations of status are important in organizing the relations of the members to each other. The clothes worn, the size, location, and furnishing of the work or office space, and many other points serve to place people in the structure. If men do not behave in accord with the status symbols attached to their positions, they are subjected to criticism from subordinates as well as superiors.

The question is not whether status distinctions should or should not exist. The foreman's desk, telephone, paper work, etc., all serve to set him apart from workers, even when he does not make a point of distinguishing himself in the clothes he wears on the job. The question is: Does the foreman accentuate or minimize these status distinctions?

There are two compelling reasons for minimizing such distinctions between foremen and workers. First, American workers like other Americans are brought up to believe that all men are created free and equal, that they are "just as good as anybody." Therefore, while they will accept status symbols that seem to be a natural part of the supervisory job, they deeply resent those which smack of social pretensions. They have no respect for the man who tries to set himself above them as if he belonged to an entirely different species.

Second, if status distinctions between any two adjoining levels of an organization are too large, effective communication between them breaks down. According to this view, the organization can function effectively with a very great spread in status symbols between worker and company president—providing the levels in between are separated step by step by far smaller graduations in status. If management insists that there shall be a sharp break in status between bottom supervision and the workers, then of course we have a social cleavage under which cooperation breaks down.

It is not easy to generalize upon the handling of status symbols. For example, we cannot make a flat rule as to the sort of clothes the foreman should wear, for clothes do not have an absolute meaning apart from the social context. They are symbols whose meaning will vary from organization to organization according to the social experience of the members. To adjust successfully to his job, the foreman must learn how people react to these status symbols and govern his own behavior accordingly.

Probably an examination of his *functions* will serve as the best guide to his behavior on the job. He should get across the idea that he acts differently from the workers not because he belongs to a different social class, but because his job requires a different sort of activity. Since his functions call for the direction and organization of work, it is obvious that he cannot afford to spend large parts of his time at machine or work bench; on the other hand, it is perfectly reasonable for him to give the occasional help over rough spots which builds loyalty and adds to the effectiveness of his supervision. Other status questions can be answered by applying the same yardstick.

This is, of course, no automatic formula. There is always room for the exercise of judgment—as there is in most of the foreman's activities. Nevertheless, if the foreman follows this general approach, it will be possible for him to build up a close and effective working relationship with his men.

In conclusion, however, we should not fail to note that the foreman's ability to follow such an approach will depend upon the sentiments and behavior of his superiors. If management feels that the foreman must maintain considerable social distance in order to get respect from workers, then the foreman who narrows this gap will be subject to severe criticism from his superiors. The primary responsibilities for narrowing the supervisor-worker social cleavage therefore rests with the higher levels of management.

### CONCLUSION

The points discussed in this chapter may be summarized in the following way.

1. We find few uniformities in the interactions and activities required as we compare the foreman's position in situations where there are marked differences in technology and work flow.

2. In general, foremen do not have the power of unilateral decision making that was more commonly observed among them half a century ago. Their power has been checked by the growth of unions and also by the growth of staff and control groups within management. The foreman

now faces the major problem of integrating his interactions and activities with those of other management personnel.

3. The process of moving up from worker to foreman involves a difficult social adjustment. The worker who is well integrated into his work group finds it hard to initiate activities for this group which have not been customary with them. The man who has not been well integrated may find it easier to attempt such initiation but is likely to run into strong resistance.

4. As technology and applied science advance in industry, there is an increasing tendency for management to appoint college graduates even to first-line supervisory positions. These men are likely to face a serious problem of status cleavage in their relations with the workers. The conflict often arises around their failure to recognize the knowledge workers gain through experience.

5. Symbols tend to draw people together or to push them apart. In a society like ours, which tends to de-emphasize status symbols, worker responses to foremen are likely to be more readily obtained when symbolic status distinctions are minimized. However, this de-emphasis upon status distinctions cannot be carried out by the foremen alone. The inclination and ability of the foremen to de-emphasize distinctions may depend importantly upon behavior of higher management people.

# Chapter 22 *THE MAN-BOSS RELATIONSHIP*

LET us now examine the supervisor in action with his immediate subordinates. We shall first look upon the relationship in terms of reciprocities: exchanges in what men do for each other and in the initiations of activity, one for the other. We shall then go on to consider certain aspects of the communication process that is involved in getting the work done, in evaluating subordinates, and in rewarding or punishing them on the basis of results.

## RECIPROCITY IN REWARDS AND PUNISHMENTS

As we pointed out in Chapter 2, relations among individuals may be looked upon as involving a series of exchanges. The idea applies to the supervisory relationship. Note these three comments from restaurant workers:

> Miss Nelson is always ready to do little favors for us when she can, so naturally we're glad to help her out.
> I like Mr. Jennings a lot. He's always ready to do a favor for you if he can.
> Miss Loomis was really a wonderful supervisor. She was always willing to do us a favor whenever she could. So naturally we wanted to do everything we could possibly do to help her. You know, it didn't seem like work to help Miss Loomis. I was always glad to do anything I could for her. We didn't want to let her down.[1]

We have cited other cases in previous chapters. When the foreman in the Benton blowing room spent two hours with Jack Carter, helping him to master his technical problems, this contributed toward forming the strongly favorable sentiments Carter held toward that foreman. With the workers on the assembly line, we have seen that perhaps the most important point in their evaluation of a foreman was his willingness or unwillingness to step in and help them when they got into difficulties. In the case of Tom Walker, we noted that when the workers held favorable sentiments toward him, they did favors for him—such as letting him

---

[1] These quotations and much other material from this chapter are from Part IV, "Human Elements in Supervision," of my *Human Relations in the Restaurant Industry* (New York: McGraw-Hill Book Co., Inc., 1948).

know regarding a mistake in the production orders. When their sentiments toward the foreman became unfavorable, they withheld these
personal favors.

Note the function of sentiments in the exchange. If A does a favor for
B, B then holds more favorable sentiments toward A, but the cycle is
only completed when B turns these favorable sentiments into a favor he
does for A.

Along with this exchange must go some sort of balance. We cannot
exactly measure the importance of favors performed, so we can strike
no precise balance, but we can say that the maintenance of favorable
sentiments between A and B depends upon some sort of approximation of
a balance in the exchange of favors. If A is the only one to do favors,
this places B under obligations to A—obligations that he cannot discharge. This tends to change B's sentiments towards A. He may still
welcome the favors and yet at the same time resent his dependent position.
This is the kind of problem we find in a paternalistic relationship between workers and management, and this may explain why in some such
cases we get sudden shifts from a situation in which workers seem to be
quite happy to a situation in which they have turned against management.

While the obligations in favors are generally felt and even consciously
recognized, they must not be stated directly as interpersonal claims. The
supervisor who says, "I did X for you so you have to do Y for me,"
changes the nature of the action he is calling for by that statement.
However strong are the obligations we feel, we like to believe that doing a
favor in return is a voluntary action. When we are told that it is something we owe, we are inclined to challenge the debt and find reasons for
persuading ourselves and others that the claim against us is not legitimate.

It is of course not only favors that are exchanged. You do X against me,
and I will do Y against you. The exchange of favors builds up positive
sentiments that encourage a further exchange of favors. The exchange of
penalties builds up negative sentiments that promote further negative
exchanges. How can management short-circuit this negative cycle and
get it moving in a positive direction? This is a question to which we shall
return at various points.

As we have seen in our discussion of incentive problems, in some situations penalties are two-edged swords, hurting the instigator as well as the
one against whom the action is directed. This suggests a three-fold classification of penalizing actions initiated by workers, and the same scheme
should hold for actions originated by management:

1. The act does not penalize Self (or does so to a very minor degree) and
does penalize Other. As long as sentiments toward management remain negative, we can expect workers to continue this line of action.
2. The act does hurt Self and does not hurt Other (or hurts Other to a
relatively minor degree). This line of action is soon abandoned by the workers.
3. The act hurts Self and also hurts Other. This is the case when workers

are carrying out a concerted slowdown, trying to pressure management into establishing a higher piece rate. Such situations are likely to be unstable, as we have seen in the case of the Steel Tubing Mill.

The employment contract itself represents an exhange: a certain quantity and quality of work in return for a specified amount of money in wages, incentive pay, and fringe benefits. Many managements have struggled for years to work this equation out in exact terms. The aim is to exact from workers just the amount and quality of work that management determines it has a right to receive in return for the benefits given. In other words, what the worker gives in return for the benefits should not be a voluntary matter on his part but should be determined as completely as possible by management.

Research and experience suggest that this approach to the problem of "a fair day's work for a fair day's pay" is not productive from management's point of view. Workers generally seem to view their obligations to management in terms of two levels of performance. There is a minimum level of performance that workers owe simply as a result of being members of the organization, being assigned to certain jobs, and being rewarded with certain material benefits. Management has no *right* to *demand* any more than this. There is a higher level of performance that workers are willing to give as their contribution to an exchange of favors with management. It is up to management to encourage this contribution. In some cases, more money will be offered by management as at least part of its additional contribution, and in other cases a relationship between management and workers that increases workers' favorable sentiments towards management will bring forth this additional contribution.

The Tom Walker case provides us with an illustration of this point. We noted that Walker had called upon the departmental steward to get the workers to do the amount of work Walker felt they owed him and the company. After carefully observing the men who were allegedly failing to meet their obligation, the steward reported to Walker that they were indeed performing up to the minimum required by their employment contract. Neither the foreman nor the steward could demand that they contribute more. Only an improved relationship between the foreman and workers would motivate the workers to increase their contribution. In other words, Walker had to do more for the workers in certain respects before he could get them to want to do more for him. Since, instead, he had become involved in a cycle of exchanging penalties, he was powerless to bring about this increased contribution.

## RECIPROCITY IN INITIATING ACTIVITY

The relations between superior and subordinate depend to some extent upon the relative frequency of initiations downward compared with those going upward. In the next section, we will discuss initiating in a downward direction.

As we interview workers regarding their relations with their superiors, their comments suggest two interrelated types of response on the part of the superior. These two types are illustrated by the two questions: Does he listen to me? Do I get action from him?

Behavior relevant to the first question is related to sentiments of interpersonal understanding. I once spent some months studying a restaurant whose manager prided himself upon being a great student of people. He had psychology books on his office shelf and told me he had learned so much about people that he could discern what a waitress' sentiments towards her supervisor were just by observing the girl momentarily in interaction with this supervisor. As I interviewed the waitresses, I found that none of them considered the manager an understanding person, and that furthermore, his judgments about their sentiments were far from their own statements in this field. Why didn't they regard him as an understanding person? In a variety of words, their comments on the subject added up to one point: "He won't listen to us. He isn't interested in what we have to say." I also found this reaction among supervisors reporting directly to the manager.

Listening behavior serves several human values for the subordinate. Often workers need to get something off their chests—to have a catharsis experience. There is also a frequent need to feel that you control the situation you are in to some degree, especially when you feel most helpless. At least while the worker is talking to his superior about a topic initiated by the worker, he can feel in control of the situation. The listening behavior of the superior also has an important symbolic significance. It says, in effect, "I respect you as a person. I think you have something worthwhile to say."

Listening, alone, is not enough. There are some times when a subordinate simply wants to get something off his chest and expects nothing more than a respectful hearing. There are other times when a subordinate is proposing that his superior take a certain action. In such cases, it is not enough for the foreman to nod his head sympathetically, saying, "Isn't that interesting," and giving other evidences of respect and understanding. The subordinate wants something done, and he is not content with merely having the opportunity to talk about it. We sometimes hear workers saying something like this about a superior: "He is a nice fellow to talk to, all right, but nothing ever comes out of it. He'll listen to you, but that's as far as it goes."

These two types of responses to subordinates are not completely independent of each other. Subordinates report that after a few experiences in bringing problems to the superior who listens sympathetically but does nothing about them, they lose interest in further interactions of this nature. They then stop taking the initiative in bringing problems to the individual, and their sentiments toward him become more negative. He is no longer regarded as an understanding sort of person.

When workers report that their supervisors do not take any action in response to complaints and suggestions, they also express negative sentiments toward him. This upward initiation on the part of workers depends upon more than the response the supervisor gives when the worker takes the initiative on a complaint or suggestion. The supervisors who seem to have the most wholehearted support of subordinates do not just wait for these complaints and suggestions to come to them. They go out calling for consultations. Recall worker comments on Tom Lloyd at Hi-Test. They expressed appreciation that he consulted them, listened to them, and responded to their suggestions.

Many management people recognize the value of calling on subordinates for suggestions, but are concerned as to what happens when they cannot act on such suggestions. As one executive said:

> That's one trouble about asking for suggestions. People will give you a suggestion, and they may be entirely wrong. From your angle, you can see that, so you cannot act on it. Then what are you going to do? They think you don't pay any attention to their ideas.

We took this question up with a skilled worker in the restaurant industry. Suppose he and his fellows were consulted on an idea but then the supervisor did something different from what they recommended:

> Well, that's O. K. After all, the supervisor has the responsibility of deciding what shall be done. All we can ask is that we get consulted on the idea. Then I'd be willing to go along and try anything. Miss Thompson (present supervisor) is good that way. Supervisors aren't all that way, I can tell you. I had to work under a woman once that wanted us to understand right from the beginning that her word was law. She actually told us that if she said black was white one day and that black was black the next, we had to change around. You couldn't tell her anything. Well, that was some time ago—when I was a busboy. I didn't have much responsibility then. It was just a routine job, so it wasn't bad. I just yessed her and went along with her on it.

I asked, "I suppose you'd have a difficult time under such a supervisor now?"

> I wouldn't work under such a supervisor now. I'd quit. You see, now I know what I'm doing. When you know your job, you resent it when they just tell you what to do. You know, management could learn a lot just asking the workers the way they think the work should be done. They'd get a lot of good ideas, and even if they didn't, they'd get a lot better cooperation that way. That's what I like about this place. They want to know what we think.

So far, we have been discussing the behavior of the supervisor as if this were simply the product of his own personality. We must recognize, of course, that the supervisor is not a free agent. Whatever his position, he has to fit it in with the policies of the organization and with the directives coming to him from above. The first-line supervisor in many cases has little latitude at all. Suppose, for example, a worker complains to his foreman about a particular incentive rate. Perhaps the foreman is a very understanding sort of fellow and listens sympathetically to what the worker has to say. But let us assume, furthermore, that the worker is not just interested in a sympathetic hearing, but actually wants that rate changed. The foreman will almost never have the power to change the rate himself. The most he can do is take up the complaint at a higher level in the organization. In some cases, it may be that men he can talk to personally, such as the general foreman and the superintendent, will have the power to initiate discussions with the time study people, leading to a possible rate change. In other cases, these matters are resolved at a still higher level, and the foreman can only pass the complaint up the line and hope for the best.

The initiative coming up from below must be seen in relation to the initiative coming down from above. We find everywhere a worker reaction against foremen who "breathe down our necks." This phrase appears to refer to frequent interactions to workers initiated by foremen, and interactions involving (1) giving detailed work directions, (2) adversely criticizing work being done, and (3) calling for a higher quantity or quality of work. Workers frequently describe what they call a good foreman as one who "lets us alone," or "doesn't bother us." The reaction seems to be that no interactions are better than a large number of those in the categories noted above. However, it must not be thought that frequency of interaction is all that is involved here. We often find foremen having a high rate of initiation of interaction with workers and yet enjoying a favorable response from them. These are the foremen who circulate around a good deal, mainly raising questions about how the worker is getting along and what he thinks might be done concerning the work situation, and engaging in a good deal of small talk quite unrelated to the work.

## CONDITIONS FOR EFFECTIVE INITIATION

However understanding a supervisor may appear to be, he cannot do his job unless he has some skill in initiating activity for subordinates. A restaurant worker made the point in this way:

> I suppose we should be more orderly and attentive, but I don't know. You just don't feel like paying any attention to Miss Bronson. You know, it might sound funny to say this, but I think a good supervisor should be able to keep the girls in line. She shouldn't let them run all over her.

The people who have the opportunity to "run all over" their supervisor are not very happy about it. It is not a pleasant experience to work for a supervisor for whom you have no respect.

For effective action, orders and directions must be definite and clear as to what is to be done, how and when it is to be done, and who is to do it. If the order does not fit in with the regular routine, then the why of it should also be stated. This seems an obvious point, and yet there are supervisors who have trouble with it. We talked with one who was very worried because the workers did not seem to be responding properly to her authority. She gave this example:

Well, just the other day I noticed that the "blueberry pie" sign in our cafeteria was soiled, and we needed to get another one to put on the bulletin board. I went up to the checkers. They were standing together by one of the counters. I told them about the sign and told them to change it. I said it four or five times. I said, "I don't care who does it, but somebody's got to do it." I certainly wasn't going to do it myself. Well, finally I walked away from them, and a couple of minutes later one of them walked over and did what I told her to do, but it shouldn't have taken that much time. I should have gotten results the first time. I kept asking myself, what would I do if they just refused to do anything for me?

Putting up the sign was a one-man job. It could not have been done efficiently by two people working together, and yet the supervisor failed to specify who was to take action. This introduced a new and confusing step into the course of action. At first, neither girl acknowledged that the supervisor was giving her an order. Then, when the supervisor went away, the two girls had to decide between themselves which one was to act. Why should the job be done by one rather than by the other? If B took action, then it would appear that A was in a superior position and could make B follow orders. And why should B acknowledge A's superiority? All these questions of status inevitably come to the fore and interfere with the course of action.

In this case, the surprising thing is not that there was a delay, but rather that the order was finally carried out at all. When the supervisor gives a clear and direct order that fits in with the regular course of work, the tendency is for workers to respond automatically, without giving the matter any thought. If the order is confusing as to what, how, when, why, and who, then the worker necessarily stops to think things over and has to decide what he ought to do. When this happens, the original impact of the order is lost, action breaks down, and authority disintegrates.

This does not mean that the worker should be just a machine, giving no thought to his work. We simply have to recognize that the work of complex modern industry cannot be carried forward if every move must be thought through carefully by everyone involved in the action. There is a time for discussion and consultation, but there is also a time for direct orders and automatic responses.

In giving orders, it is well to recognize Chester Barnard's "zone of indifference."[2] He argues that in any stable authority relationship, there will be no need for discussion with the subordinate, or for serious consideration on his part in response to orders, regarding actions that are customary parts of his job. In fact, the subordinate would rather not have to think about these matters. It is important for the superior to recognize

---

[2] *The Functions of the Executive* (Cambridge, Mass.: Harvard University Press, 1938), pp. 167–70.

at what point an order he has in mind goes beyond the zone of indifference. In any industrial organization, workers develop sentiments as to what activities are appropriate parts of their jobs and what fall outside of these limits. In some unionized situations, job content may be specified in detail. Even when there are no explicit understandings on this point, workers inevitably develop sentiments regarding the nature of their jobs.

This does not mean that a skillful supervisor cannot get workers to go beyond the customary limits. It does mean that he needs to recognize what the customary limits are and to adjust his behavior as he approaches and reaches beyond those limits. The adjustment involves verbal symbols and also the exchange of favors. If the supervisor simply orders the men to do something beyond these limits, he is likely to find his orders disobeyed, indirectly sabotaged—or carried out, accompanied by the filing of a grievance. The supervisor's behavior should symbolize the fact that he knows the order he is issuing goes beyond customary understandings. This requires at least an explanation and some time for discussion to encourage compliance. It also involves assumption of an obligation on the part of the supervisor. He asks the workers to do a little extra for him. The exchange of favors requires that he be prepared to provide a little extra reward for them in the future.

The manner of issuing orders must also be seen in terms of symbolism. In our democratic society in general, with our emphasis upon social equality, the supervisor may find it helpful to phrase his orders as if they were requests—except in cases of emergencies. The tone of voice is expected to be conversational. As in the Hi-Test case, many workers objected to supervisors who "throw their voices." However, this is by no means uniform even in our own society. There are types of work situations in which abrupt orders and loud voices may be taken for granted. In more authoritarian societies, the supervisor who gave his orders in conversational tone might fear that he would appear weak to his workers.

How much direction does the worker need from the supervisor? This question cannot be answered in exactly that form because there is more than one way to direct the work. Consider the contrasting cases of General Foremen Black and Thomas. Black issued his orders in detail—and only for a brief time period. That is, he would tell his subordinates what he wanted done next. When he expected that operation to be nearing completion, he would come back to check on progress, then issue another order. By contrast, Thomas thought in terms of a longer time perspective. Considering a sequence of work operations, he would outline to subordinates what they were to do and discuss with them the problems that they might face in the future. The amount of time each general foreman spent with his subordinates may have been approximately the same, but interaction patterns were quite different. Black interacted with his foreman perhaps half a dozen times a day, nearly always for very brief periods and nearly always the pattern within a given interaction was the same. Black told the subordinates what to do and they acquiesced. Thomas did not average more than one interaction a day with a given foreman, but that often involved a discussion of from fifteen minutes to a half hour in length. Furthermore, the foreman had frequent opportunity to raise questions, to make suggestions, and to get a response to these efforts. The foremen under Black complained to the researcher that they were not having any chance to develop, whereas the foremen under Thomas spoke with confidence about their abilities and chances to progress.

## CRITICIZING SUBORDINATES

Criticizing subordinates is perhaps the most difficult task the supervisor has to undertake. He recognizes he is dealing with very touchy problems. Too much criticism is demoralizing, and unless the criticism is administered skillfully, it may disrupt the relationship between supervisor and subordinate. On the other hand, if there is no criticism at all, the subordinate may continue inferior performance without being motivated to improve and perhaps without being aware that his supervisor considers the performance inferior.

When we were studying the restaurant industry some fifteen years ago, what was known as "the criticism sandwich" was then in vogue. This called for sandwiching the adverse criticism in between two items of praise. The supervisor would call the worker into his office and then figuratively give him a pat on the head, a kick in the pants, and finally another pat on the head. I have never observed the criticism sandwich being served, nor have I been able to interview workers who have had it served to them. Therefore, my conclusion is not based upon research data. It is based upon the assumption that when a worker is (infrequently) called into a management office, he probably knows that some serious problem has arisen. His anxiety will remain high until the supervisor gets to the point. The initial and final pats on the head will strike him as insincere and contrived.

The most effective supervisors I have observed have taken a frontal approach to administering criticism but have at the same time sought to leave the maximum initiative in the hands of the individual being criticized. This is illustrated in the comments of two supervisors, both of whom were exceedingly well regarded by subordinates.

Restaurant Manager Potter described his approach in this way:

> When some mistake is made, I go up to the worker and ask him to explain to me how it happened. A lot of times it won't be his fault. There may be something wrong with the ingredients, and I ought to know that.
> When you go to them that way and let them explain, they feel a lot better. Sometimes they will come to you and tell you when they make a mistake, and

you can really talk it over. You get to know what's going on. That's very important.

When we have some trouble, I call the person into my office, and I tell him that things haven't been going right in certain ways, and I say to him, "Here's the problem. What do you think we can do about this?" I have him try to tell me what the solution is.

The same point is illustrated in Tom Lloyd's handling of his relations with the Hi-Test men. Recall his comment on the Daily Operating Data sheet. It communicated a great deal to him, but he did not use the information to criticize subordinates directly. Instead, he raised questions as to what had happened, then let the individual explain it himself. Lloyd was convinced that the worker, in giving a weak explanation, would be just as aware of its weakness as was the foreman. He could accept responsibility better if he talked the problem through himself, rather than if the foreman just tried to pin it on him. Under his predecessors, the symbols on the sheet represented primarily the struggle over control. Under Lloyd, they came to represent operating reality.

I observed one occasion in which Joe Sloan made an error in operating which was serious enough to prompt him to call it to Lloyd's attention. Sloan and I walked up to the foreman's office together. Sloan explained what he had done and what had happened. Lloyd listened with interest, made a joking comment about taking it out of Sloan's next paycheck, and delivered no criticism at all. The worker had acknowledged the mistake and accepted responsibility for it. His behavior indicated that he felt very badly about the mistake. Should the foreman have tried to make him feel worse?

This case also shows that the foreman who handles criticism in this manner gets a much more accurate picture of operations than one who takes a punitive approach. The error Sloan made might have been one that could have been concealed from the foreman. Perhaps under Jones or Fitch, a worker making such a mistake would have done his best to conceal it. Then the foreman would either have been unaware of what had happened or might well have ended up by blaming the wrong man.

Noting the difficulty most supervisors have in criticizing their subordinates, management people have undertaken to formalize the process. Company policy calls for an annual or semi-annual evaluation interview.[3] The supervisor calls in the subordinate and talks to him about his performance since the last evaluation period. The supervisor points out his strengths and weaknesses and also fills out a rating form in which the strengths and weaknesses are checked off. In some systems, it is recommended that he go over this rating form with the subordinate.

The rating form serves a dual purpose from the standpoint of higher

---

[3] For a penetrating analysis of performance appraisal, see Douglas McGregor, "A Critique of Performance Appraisal," *The Human Side of Enterprise* (New York: McGraw-Hill Book Co., Inc., 1960), chap. 6.

management. It furnishes documentary evidence that the evaluation interview has taken place, and it also furnishes data which may be used later when the subordinate is considered for transfer or promotion.

These procedures are based upon the notion that subordinates feel a need to know what is expected of them and how they are measuring up to these expectations. The procedures developed, however, have other effects which need to be weighed.

In the first place, if the supervisor in the course of a year has never given the subordinate any inkling of how he is doing, then the evaluation interview becomes a very formidable experience for both men. On the other hand, if superior and subordinate have talked casually on many occasions about work performance and problems, then an evaluation discussion will be much easier to undertake—but will add little to what has previously passed between the two men. Something indeed may be added since the review period may provide for a more summary approach to work performance, in which it is easier to put a number of separate items into perspective.

I have never sat in on a management discussion of evaluation interviewing programs in which management people were expressing any satisfaction as to the way the programs were proceeding. Either the evaluation interviews are not being made, or else the management people have reason to believe that they are being so poorly handled as to have adverse affects upon both morale and performance.

The universality of such reactions suggests that the procedures pose some difficult problems in human relations. There are two distinct parts of the evaluation interview. In the face-to-face situation, the superior discusses strengths and weaknesses with the subordinate. Then, he has to go on and put in some kind of a written report on this subordinate to higher management. He faces difficulty in both parts of this assignment.

In many settings, the evaluation interview seems to proceed in the social atmosphere of a trial. The superior has all of the initiative. He tells the subordinate what is good about him and what is bad about him. If the subordinate does not accept the adverse criticisms, then he is being "defensive," and this is a bad sign in itself. Furthermore, it is always the subordinate who is the problem case. It is not appropriate for him to suggest that some of the difficulties he has been having are due to the inadequacies of his superior.

The written evaluation report presents a still more difficult psychological problem for the superior. As we have seen especially in the case of Jack Carter and the men on his glass-blowing team, subordinates value highly a boss who works out his criticisms directly with them and does not pass them on to higher levels. Many supervisors feel this same sentiment and are inclined to talk to their subordinates in ways that express this thought: "This problem is just between you and me. Let us work it out together, and no one else has to hear about it." In the evaluation interview, the supervisor is figuratively looking over his shoulder at his superior, and the subordinate feels betrayed, knowing that a report on his weaknesses will go to higher levels. Of course, subordinates know that their superiors talk about their performance when questioned by higher-ups, but somehow the written document seems much more cold and forbidding than what passes in conversation.

The supervisor faces another difficulty as he considers his ratings in relative terms. Suppose he rates his men objectively and really points out weaknesses as well as strengths. But suppose other men in his position just gloss over weaknesses and rate all their men highly. In that case, he may be penalizing his own men and causing them to fall behind less capable individuals in the competition for promotion. He may feel therefore, that the safest thing to do is to rate every man high. But one can't afford to rate all his men as perfect, because this would indicate that no real evaluation has been carried out. Certain slight faults must be pointed out, but these can be dwarfed by the great strengths of the subordinate—at least up until the point at which the supervisor becomes so disgusted with the subordinate's incompetence that he decides to fire him. (At that point, past rating forms become very awkward for the supervisor.)

Quite a different approach to the appraisal interview has been outlined by Douglas McGregor.[4] In this approach, the subordinate is asked to plan for himself and his organizational unit for the coming six months. This involves setting targets and also means of reaching those targets. Following some discussion with his superior, he puts these ideas in written form. At the end of the six-month period, superior and subordinate get together again to compare earlier plans with the progress actually achieved. Here again it is the subordinate who takes the initiative. He reports how he feels he progressed or failed to progress toward certain objectives. The superior participates in the discussion—to ask questions and to suggest certain possible explanations—but he is expected to encourage his subordinate to carry the brunt of the discussion.

The goal-setting aspect of this type of evaluation is extremely important. If a goal is stated in terms of units of production, it can readily be determined whether or not the individual has reached this goal, and it is not necessary for the superior to point out a failure. If another goal is the improvement of relations between the individual and an official in another department, then it is not so easy to measure results, but the subordinate can be encouraged to talk about specific inter-personal events and not just about vague feelings. If he thinks that the other department

---

[4] *Op. cit.*, chap. 5, "Management by Integration and Self Control." Robert Hood, President of Ansul Chemical Co., first pointed out to me the possibilities of this approach.

is cooperating with him better than before, on what does he base this opinion? If the expected cooperation has not been forthcoming, what seem to be the reasons behind this failure?

As the subordinate reviews with his superior his performance in relation to the goals he himself established, he goes on to establish goals for the next evaluation period.

Another important aspect of the procedure is the requirement that the subordinate take up the question: How can you, my superior, help me more effectively to progress toward these goals? Facing this question helps to keep the discussion on a plane of symbolic equality. The subordinate does not feel as subordinated as he does in situations where his superior is telling him what is wrong with him and providing no opportunity for him to express his own initiative or criticism of his superior. Keeping the initiative with the subordinate also helps him to internalize the goals which are being discussed. That is, he not only states but actually feels his responsibility for progressing along the lines he indicates. He does not just passively accept the demands placed upon him by a superior.

## COMMUNICATION: WRITTEN OR ORAL?

So far we have been considering only oral, face-to-face communication between superior and subordinate. The two may also communicate in writing. Shall we consider a written memorandum just as if it were a face-to-face interaction? My thesis is that the two types of communication have very different effects and therefore should be considered separately. The supervisor needs to learn what can and cannot be done in writing. Let us consider several cases and then seek to arrive at some general principles.

We will begin with the memorandum Jim Dayton placed on the bulletin board for workers in the blowing room of the Benton plant. So as to have this before us for later comparisons, I quote it once more:

Within recent weeks there has been an increase in the number of finished and unfinished pieces missing. To help eliminate this deplorable condition, we must prohibit all unauthorized persons from entering the finishing area. In the future, if there are pieces of ware which in the foreman's judgment should be shown to blowing room personnel, those pieces of ware should be shown by the foreman to the person or that person should be escorted by the foreman into the finishing area.

Let us consider also a notice placed by management on the bulletin board for the employees of one department of Inland Steel Container Company. The notice read as follows:

You are hereby advised that you, along with other employees of the Machine Shop and Electrical Department, have been observed, at one time or another, violating one or more of the company rules in the following manner:

Washing up and changing clothes before ten-minute time limit.

Congregating in washroom and smoking at time other than relief period.

Overstaying relief with stock answer "I forgot" and neglecting to punch off of relief.

Union representatives talking to employees or vice versa about union business without requesting permission.

Riding elevators as passengers.

Smoking on job.

Departmental maintenance men in Machine Shop as much as thirty minutes before quitting time.

Going to canteen before lunch time.

Neglecting to use safety glasses or goggles.

Failure to report back when jobs are finished.

Cleaning machinery with high pressure guns with oleum spray.

Working on personal jobs on company time without permission.

Consider this due notification that in the future you will be expected to adhere to company rules and regulations as outlined in the small booklet which you received some time ago entitled "Your Job," which you should have in your possession.

You will also be held personally responsible to see to it that the above-noted violations shall not exist in the future on your part.

Any further violations of company rules and regulations shall be followed by verbal and/or written reprimands depending upon the nature and repetition of such violations on your part. In accordance with company policy, continued violations will end in discharge.

Suppose we were asked to predict worker reactions to the two memos and had only one item of information beyond the written text: the knowledge that the union was weak in the Benton plant and that it was very strong and militant in the Inland Steel Container Company plant. What would we predict?

If we look at the tone of the two memoranda, we may see little to choose between them. Both may appear abrupt and dictatorial. If we look at the background situations, the meaning of the notices seems quite different.

The second notice grew out of union-management consultation over the problems of the Maintenance Department—the case described earlier, in Chapter 20. Note that this process took a little over a month and included numerous meetings between union and management, accompanied by meetings within management and within the union, particularly at the departmental level. By the time the notice was written, all of the issues to which it referred had been thoroughly discussed, and the parties had come to agreement on each one. While the notice called for far-reaching changes in worker behavior, it only served to put in the form of written symbols what had been arrived at through the interactions and activities of the preceding month.

The Hi-Test notice regarding the stealing of gasoline provides another case for our analysis. Unfortunately, we do not have the wording of this notice, but we do know how the men reacted to it. Some men apparently decided that this time the company meant business, but many of the men carried on with their customary pattern of supplying their own gasoline from company facilities. The drastic measures taken by General Superintendent Masters brought the gasoline stealing to a stop, but they also had unfortunate effects on human relations in the organization, as we have already pointed out.

These three cases suggest some general conclusions:

1. Written communication alone is not an effective means of introducing significant changes in interactions and/or activities. There are two difficulties here. Written communication goes just one way. The recipient is not offered any means of replying while the message is being presented to him. A problem of any complexity cannot be resolved through a single written statement. It needs a working-through process.

2. Written communication can be used effectively—and without hazard—to set off interactions and activities that are within the customary pattern for the people receiving the communication.

3. Written communication can be used to confirm or make official what has already been worked through in other ways. We should not assume that this is an incidental or unimportant step. If the written notice does not appear, with the passage of time participants in the discussion may come to have differing interpretations as to what was decided. The written communication, then, has the function of providing a set of stable symbols around which future interactions and activities can be organized.

To what extent can we use written communication to deal out praise or blame? I have found no problems in written compliments. While these may not perhaps convey the personal warmth that comes with a spoken word of praise, I have never heard of anyone objecting to them. For adverse criticisms, the situation is quite different, as the following two cases will indicate.

The manager of a plant of 1,200 employees received a letter from one of his superiors regarding the performance of the plant in the preceding half year. The letter began by complimenting the manager for having got out 20 per cent more production than had been budgeted for the period. It then went on to point out that the manager had exceeded his budget on long distance telephone calls by over $400, requesting that he exercise more restraint on this matter in the future. A management consultant happened to meet the plant manager several days after he had received this letter and had a chance to observe the effects upon him. The plant manager expressed a vigorous sense of outrage. He had done a spectacular job of increasing the productivity of the plant. To be sure, this had been noted in the letter, but what really stuck in his craw was the comment upon the long distance telephone expenditures. The letter had taken his attention completely away from present and future activities of the plant. For more than a day's time, with the help of his secretary, he had been digging through the records of long distance telephone calls in the preceding six months. On the basis of what he found, he had dictated a ten-page letter to his superior, listing each telephone call and pointing out at length why it was essential. The letter was never actually sent, for the management consultant advised against it, and perhaps by this time the experience of writing the letter and telling the management consultant about the problem had got it off the manager's chest sufficiently so that he could get on to other matters. For us, the important point is the intense concern that the manager showed with just a brief but adversely critical comment in a letter from his superior. Was this a neurotic response? We cannot report on the state of mental health of the manager, but it is significant to note that he was indeed doing an effective job in his position, as the over-all record of the plant showed.

Consider this case in a university setting. The dean wrote a memo to one of his professors requesting a statement about the plans the professor had developed for an off-campus adult education program that was to take place during the summer—for which the professor was to receive part of a regular summer salary. The professor responded with a brief memo that simply indicated the subject matter of each day's discussion. The dean carried the correspondence further with another brief note expressing the opinion that judging from the professor's report, this was not the carefully planned and solid type of program for which the university was accustomed to paying a part of a professor's summer salary.

Receipt of this note brought forth an explosive reaction from the professor. It seemed to him that the dean was saying, in effect, two things: that the professor did not know what he was doing, and that he was taking advantage of the institution through trying to get by with slipshod work.

The professor immediately called to seek an appointment with the dean in order to thrash the matter out. The secretary reported that the dean was out of town for two days. During the waiting period, the professor had ample opportunity to role play (in his imagination) his forthcoming encounter with the dean. He would begin by demanding that the dean explain the memorandum. This certainly would put the dean on the defensive. The professor would then bring in further information to show that the program scheduled was indeed more carefully designed and organized than most programs offered by the institution. The dean would counter with some weak response, and so it would go. After the professor had rehearsed once what he was going to say, there was no need to go over it again. Nevertheless, during the next two days the professor found his mind constantly wandering from the work immediately at hand toward the encounter that he was going to have with the dean. If we had had any objective measure of the professor's productivity in this period, the loss that could have been charged up to the memorandum would have been substantial.

When the two men finally got together, some of the professor's anger had died down. He presented the case for his program as calmly as he could, and the dean replied by expressing satisfaction with what had been planned. The end of the meeting left no issue between the two men. But this does not mean that no harm was done. We have already noted more than two days of reduced efficiency on the part of the professor, and it should also be noted that the incident reinforced the negative sentiments the professor already had toward the dean.

It might be argued that the professor should have been able to avoid this unpleasant incident. Knowing the dean as well as he did, he should have known the dean's tendency to want to see things spelled out in detail, and he should have presented a more complete report in the first place. However, in this book we are concentrating upon what the superior can do to build good relations with his subordinates. Another book could be written about what subordinates can do to get along with superiors.

These cases suggest that if the superior anticipates a continuing relationship with his subordinate, he should avoid putting adverse criticisms in written form. Such expressed criticisms seem to demand an answer. Until they are answered, the incident is not closed. Therefore, since some face-to-face discussion is required in order to handle the criticism effectively, why put it in writing in the first place?

In the case of the plant manager, let's see how the whole matter might have been handled in discussion. The superior could have complimented the manager in person on the production record and then might casually have gone on to raise a question regarding the telephone expenditures. No doubt the manager would have given a general explanation and a defense. Whatever the superior had to say to this, the fact that he had raised the question would have indicated to the manager his concern about expenditures in this category, but the manager would have felt rewarded at having a chance to present his point of view on these expenditures.

In the university case, the dean might have called the professor in and said simply, "The outline you have sent me doesn't present a very full picture of what you plan for the program. I wonder if you would mind telling me more about it." This could have led—in a more pleasant atmosphere—to the kind of conversational content that did in fact finally take place between the two men. It would have taken no more of the dean's time. It would have saved a serious waste of time on the part of the professor and a worsening of relations between the two men.

## CONCLUSION

The conclusions of the present chapter may be summarized as follows:

1. The man-boss relationship is built upon a series of exchanges. To understand this relationship or to modify it in action, we need to know what values are being exchanged. We may also think of an exchange in the initiation of activities. A sharp change in the frequency of initiation from superiors to subordinates, without any compensating increase from

subordinates to superiors, is likely to give rise to disturbances within the organization.

2. Effective initiation of activities requires the use of verbal symbols that are (a) appropriate to the culture pattern and past pattern of activities, and (b) clear in specifying who does what, with whom, when, and where. (Of course, in what detail the instruction is specified will depend upon the relation of the present directive to past activities.)

3. The evaluation interview, as ordinarily practiced, tends to subordinate the person being evaluated and stimulate defensive reactions. These adverse effects can be minimized by an approach which places maximum initiative in the hands of the subordinate.

4. Written communication cannot be used, without adverse effects, to initiate unaccustomed interactions and activities. On the other hand, written communications may be of vital importance in symbolically stabilizing a new pattern of interactions and activities which has grown out of previous interactions and activities.

# Chapter 23 *MANAGERIAL SUCCESSION*

WHEN we examine the pattern of relations between superior and subordinate, it is not enough to see these solely in the present. How subordinates respond to a superior will depend in part upon the pattern previously established with this particular superior. If the superior is new in this position, the reactions he receives will depend in part upon the pattern of relations established with his predecessor. It is for this reason that we need to study problems of managerial succession, of what happens when manager B succeeds manager A.

This discussion is drawn from a large restaurant that we shall call Chandlers. The restaurant provided service on two floors out of a main kitchen, linking kitchen to dining room with two service pantries and a bar on each floor. There were approximately two hundred employees, but we shall confine our attention largely to what is known as the front of the house: the dining rooms. The study was done in 1944 in a period of booming business and labor shortage that made for difficulties in supervisory relations.

Our case involves a change in managers from Mr. Potter to Mr. Stanton. As is so often the case, the change in personnel did not stop at this point. When Mr. Potter was manager, his immediate subordinate in the front of the house was Miss Ellis, supervisor of service. In a staff position at the same level was Miss Geiger, training supervisor.

Mrs. Schultz was assistant supervisor of service, reporting to Miss Ellis. All of the hostesses reported to Mrs. Schultz particularly, and also to Miss Ellis. Under the hostesses were the waitresses.

The organization structure is shown in the accompanying figure.

Mr. Potter left on January 1, 1944. Within an eight-month period, the change in managers had been followed by personnel changes all the way down to waitressess. The changes with which we shall particularly deal seem all closely related to the change in managers. In fact, we shall observe a change taking place at the top being followed by changes at successively lower levels.

In June, Miss Ellis, supervisor of service, and Mrs. Schultz, her assistant, quit their jobs. Mr. Stanton appointed Miss Geiger supervisor of service and abolished the training position. In July Mrs. Loomis, one of the hostesses, left her job. Within another month, Ann Lindstrom, Rita Carey, and her sister and several other waitresses quit.

Let us begin by examining the situation under Potter, particularly as

CHANDLERS: THE FRONT OF THE HOUSE UNDER MANAGER POTTER

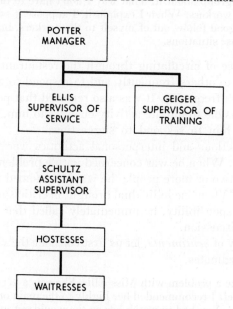

it affected his immediate subordinates. We will examine the changes that took place at lower levels step by step as new people moved into these positions. For each of the key individuals in this case, we shall examine the pattern of activities, interactions, and sentiments that developed.

## THE MANAGERIAL PROCESS UNDER POTTER

*Activities and Interactions:* Potter spent little time in his office. He was inclined to circulate about the restaurant, observing as he went, and also stopping to chat with people all the way down the line from his immediate subordinates to the work level.

He did not initiate changes in activities directly to people below his immediate subordinates. He described his behavior in this respect by citing an incident that arose in the restaurant to which he went upon resigning from Chandlers.

The other day I happened to be walking through the dining room when I ran into a waitress just as she was tossing off a glass of orange juice over in a corner. I couldn't help seeing it, and she knew I saw it, but I just stopped and chatted with her for a few moments on other things, and then I walked away. I looked up Miss Loring (head hostess) and mentioned the incident to her. I

said if the girls were coming on the floor hungry, we ought to work that problem out, but in any case we would have to check up on picking on the food. I
left the problem in her hands. That's what I do when I happen to notice something wrong. Sometimes I tell the supervisor which employee it was, but other
times, I just tell what I saw without mentioning any names and let the supervisor speak to the group about it. That way I don't have to take on the job of
reprimanding the workers. When I explain it, I suppose it sounds just like a
way of making a good fellow out of myself to the workers, but that's the way
I like to handle those situations.

Potter's practice of circulating through the restaurant led him to initiate interaction to others frequently and to respond to the initiative of
others with a high frequency. It was also reported that people below his
level found it possible to initiate activity changes to him. They could go
to him and get him to respond to suggestions.

Potter's interactions and interpersonal activities were not limited to
the pair situation. When he was concerned with a problem in the area of
responsibility of two or more people, he was accustomed to calling them
in to talk it over. When one individual brought in criticisms in the area of
someone else's responsibility, he immediately called that person in for a
three-cornered discussion.

In the category of *sentiments*, let us first consider the view Potter held
of his key subordinates.

Well, I did have a problem with Miss Ellis. She was a very efficient supervisor and when I left I recommended her highly to the main office, but she had
certain weaknesses. You had to watch her or she would get away with things.
She would take advantage of you. I worked with her in the Y store. I knew
what to expect of her and when I came out here I knew how to handle the
situation.

Regarding Miss Ellis' weaknesses, he made three points: (1) She
would sometimes leave the job earlier in the evening than her official
quitting time, and he had to check her on this. (2) "She did a little drinking during working hours, and that was bad." (3) She was on terms of
close personal friendship with some of her subordinates. They would go
out together to parties after work. He felt that some of the hostesses who
were not in on these activities felt that the personal associations led her
to play favorites on the job. The manager felt he had to check her on this.

Potter continued with some remarks regarding Mrs. Schultz and Miss
Geiger:

Now, Mrs. Schultz was a high-strung tempermental girl, but the new girls
were very fond of her. She did a good job. The only thing was that she was
rather unstable. At least five times she came into my office to tell me that she
was going to quit, and I had to talk her out of it. If I could talk her out of
it, probably someone else could talk her into it.

When Miss Geiger was assistant service supervisor, I felt she had an even
temper and that the girls would go to her with their problems. I thought we
needed somebody like that on training because we had such a high turnover
that I was afraid that if we didn't keep teaching good service we would forget

how we did things. That's why I gave her that training position and took her off the floor altogether.

Now, if Mr. Stanton couldn't keep Miss Ellis in line, he is certainly better off without her. I had no trouble with her, but that was because I had worked with her before and knew what to expect.

These statements suggest that Potter had faith in his subordinates, and yet it was not a blind faith. The criticisms he raised regarding Miss Ellis could be considered quite serious, but yet he felt that her strengths more than balanced her weaknesses—as long as he was on the job to keep the weaknesses in check.

The *sentiments* of subordinates toward Potter are best summed up in this statement by Miss Ellis:

He was a wonderful manager. He knew everybody on the staff and you felt that you could go to him with any problem that you had. You always felt that he was behind you. He'd do whatever he could for you.

Such sentiments seemed to prevail all down the line. In fact, waitress reactions to Potter bordered on hero worship. After he left Chandlers, he found he could not come into the restaurant any more to have dinner because word of his presence would spread rapidly throughout the house, and many of the waitresses would want to come down and greet him. Potter realized that this public display was embarrassing to his successor.

## THE MANAGERIAL PROCESS UNDER STANTON

*Activities and Interactions:* Stanton spent most of each day in his office. He did little circulating throughout the restaurant, and when he did move about, he did not stop to talk with people. Employees commented that when Stanton went by, he generally seemed preoccupied and unaware of their presence.

Stanton initiated interaction to subordinates, particularly at the lower levels, with greatly reduced frequency, compared to his predecessor. Employees reported that they hesitated to initiate interaction with him. This also led to far fewer efforts to initiate activity changes for Stanton than had been the case with Potter.

Since Stanton did not seem generally accessible to approaches from subordinates, he received his information primarily from those few who did take the initiative in interaction with him. When I asked him how he was able to know how his subordinates were functioning, he gave this response:

It's not so hard when you've had some experience. There was a manager in our Z store. He's one of the best managers in the chain. He told me once that there wasn't anything that went on in his store that he ought to know that he didn't know within twenty-four hours. Not that he had stool pigeons working for him either. There were just some people that really had the best interests of the store at heart. If they see some people do something that was going to hurt the store, they'd take him aside and say, "Now, look here. You ought not to do that." If that didn't work, they'd take it to the manager. I feel the same way here. There's not much that goes on in the store that concerns me that doesn't get to me in a pretty short time.

Miss Ellis seldom initiated interaction with Stanton. Miss Geiger did not hesitate to do so. The significance of this difference will be noted shortly.

Stanton also contrasted with Potter in the matter of set events or interaction in group situations. When one subordinate approached him to discuss the problem in the area of another subordinate, Stanton did not follow the practice of calling in the other person and having a three-way discussion. We shall see later the importance of this difference to Miss Ellis.

Stanton's *sentiments* toward subordinates can be inferred from comments he made to me regarding individuals from the level of his immediate subordinates down to the waitresses.

Of Miss Ellis, he said, "I think she is worried about getting married. I've had some trouble with her." (He paused long, he did not look at me.) "I can't say that I like her. It seems that she has been out to make things tough for me."

He then went on to describe how Miss Ellis had talked of quitting several times and always changed her mind, of how she selected the time of finally quitting for a period which would make the maximum difficulty with him (when he was off on vacation), and of how she took certain others with her. He went on:

> One thing you can tell about Miss Ellis from what happened after she left was that she was just working for Miss Ellis. She was only building up loyalty to herself, not to the store. If she had been working in the best interest of Chandler's, why would those other two have quit just because she left? Just because they were all friends doesn't seem to me to be any reason for all of them leaving. Why do they all have to go just because one goes?

Regarding Miss Ellis' possible sources of dissatisfaction, he said:

> I heard that she had been talking before she left, telling people that she wouldn't work from nine in the morning till nine at night for anybody. Now, it's true that the work was temporarily pretty hard for a month, but I thought that was a very poor attitude to take. If it was too hard for her, why didn't she come in and talk it over and we could have worked something out?

One evening, almost a month later, as I was having dinner with Mr. Stanton, I told him I had heard that Mrs. Loomis was leaving. He nodded:

> I think that when a person doesn't think for themselves, they aren't hardly qualified to think for a group of girls. We might just as well get rid of her now. You know, she's one of the ones that was going to quit when Ellis threatened to quit last January. When Ellis decided to stay, she decided to

stay too. She must have been talking with Ellis now, and Ellis probably got her to pull out of here.

The following day, I told Mr. Stanton that I hoped to talk with Mrs. Loomis before she left. He said he didn't think she was in that day. "She probably went to one of Ellis' parties last night and had a hangover this morning and didn't come in." He picked up the phone and called Miss Geiger, who reported that Mrs. Loomis was indeed at work.

Stanton talked a good deal about the "cliques" among the employees. Ann Lindstrom, the informal leader among the younger waitresses, seemed to him aggressive, insubordinate, and a corrupting influence among the other girls.

Stanton also saw the evil influences of cliques among several of the men employees, who quit at about the same time as Ann Lindstrom and several of the other waitresses. Regarding the downfall of Jonesy, his assistant maintenance man, he commented, "Everything was all right until Jonesy moved in with Lou and Fred. That was when the trouble started. You know, in the crowd you just have one fellow with the wrong attitude and he can change the mind of the others."

Stanton's prevalent distrust of subordinates was illustrated one afternoon. As I was leaving the restaurant, he followed me downstairs to tell me that he suspected a certain recently hired man was the same individual who had been discharged for stealing in another unit of the chain in another city. He said he was investigating this. Later I learned from him that his suspicion had proved to be unfounded.

In this case, Stanton was not conjuring up imaginary problems. Some employees do steal from restaurants. What struck me was the emphasis that Stanton gave to the case as evidenced by his taking the initiative to bring it to my attention and to follow me down the stairs with the story. This occurred at a time when he was apparently feeling some anxieties regarding my talking with disaffected employees, and he seemed to be concerned with showing me what a hard time employees were giving him.

We can sum up Stanton's view by saying that he was inclined to expect the worst of subordinates. When they once got off the track of good behavior, he saw no possibility of bringing them back, and he suspected informal groupings of undermining loyalty to the organization.

For the *sentiments* of subordinates toward Stanton, let us begin with Miss Ellis:

Mr. Stanton just doesn't seem to care. He sits in his office with his own work and you don't feel that you want to go in and bother him. You think it's just up to you to handle your job in the best way you can. But I have nothing against him personally. I think that Mr. Stanton is a nice person.

Note that Stanton has already confirmed Miss Ellis' statement that she was not inclined to take the initiative with him. We find him saying, ". . . why didn't she come in and talk it over . . .?" In other words, he expected subordinates to take the initiative with him, and he took no steps to facilitate this when it did not happen.

Comments of other supervisors and workers had the same general meaning as the Ellis statement. Subordinates viewed Stanton as unapproachable and uninterested in them and their problems. Miss Geiger was an exception to this. I was unable to get her to make a direct statement regarding either of the two managers, and yet it is clear from her behavior that she did not regard Stanton as unapproachable.

## IMPACT OF THE CHANGE IN MANAGERS

In assessing the impact of the change in managers, let us focus first on Miss Ellis and Miss Geiger.

For Miss Ellis the change meant a sharp reduction in her interactions with the manager, accompanied by a marked change in her sentiments. No longer did she feel supported by the manager. Instead, she felt entirely on her own and being challenged by an aggressive rival.

For Miss Geiger, interactions with the manager did not change nearly so much, for Miss Geiger was inclined to initiate these herself.

The abandonment of Potter's three-way discussions of interdepartmental problems had a particularly threatening effect upon Miss Ellis, as we shall see shortly in her own words.

The Ellis-Geiger relationship may be considered in three time periods. (1) Miss Geiger was the direct subordinate of Miss Ellis. (2) Miss Geiger held a staff position on the same level with Miss Ellis, under Manager Potter. (3) Positions remained the same but the two women worked under Stanton.

How did the two women view their relationship? Unfortunately, I was unable to get Miss Geiger to give me her views. This is the way it looked to Miss Ellis:

Well, frankly, she was the main reason why I left. I liked her and we were very friendly when she was my assistant. I think it was a mistake to put her in charge of training just for that one store. Here Miss Geiger had been used to being on the floor and she wanted to keep active on the floor. There were times when she'd come out and tell the girls something that was just the opposite from what I had told them. That made a very awkward situation when we were contradicting each other. It was bad for both of us. One time I found her bawling out Mrs. Schultz. She was furious, and she slammed her fist right down on the table. Now, that was no business of hers at all. Mrs. Schultz was under me, not under Miss Geiger. Anything like that she should have taken up with me first. I just walked away. What else could I do? But that made a terrible impression upon the girls.

Then she used to go in to Mr. Stanton every now and then with some criticism of the way my department was being run. Of course, I was interested in improving anything that could be improved in my department, so I would have been glad to have her come to me; but it was really none of her business to take those tales to the manager. I resented that very much. It seemed a sneaking thing to do to talk behind my back.

I asked whether Miss Geiger had taken such criticisms to Mr. Potter:

No, she hardly ever did that. You see, just as soon as she went in to Mr. Potter with any criticism, he would call me in and we'd talk it over. That way, everything was open and aboveboard. It was entirely different under Mr. Stanton. She could go in and talk to him, but I wouldn't hear about it until later.

## THE MANAGERIAL PROCESS UNDER ELLIS AND GEIGER

Let us now compare the managerial process as exercised by the two supervisors of service.

Miss Ellis interacted frequently with subordinates, both on and off the job. A number of them reported that they felt free to go to her and seek to initiate activity for her.

She developed with subordinates a reciprocal relationship, involving the exchange of activities for interpersonal loyalties, as her own comments and those of her subordinates will show.

Miss Ellis gave her views of her subordinates in this way:

I liked the girls very much, every one of them. Maybe I liked them better than was good for me.

I asked her what she meant by that:

Oh, I think Mr. Stanton resented a little the way I got along with the waitresses. You see, I'm not so old myself but I felt as though I were like a mother to them. They used to come to me with all their problems—all kinds of things; trouble at home or in their work or what they should do about their boy friends. They expected me to be a regular Dorothy Dix (she laughed). Oh, I didn't know all the answers by any means. In fact, most of the time I didn't give any advice at all or wouldn't have known what to advise, but it seemed to help some kids to get it off their chests when they had somebody to talk to.

One thing I enjoyed about that job was working with the girls to help them do a better job. Some of those girls changed a good deal after coming to work for Chandler's. You could tell from the beginning that they had been used to being pushed around. They acted as if they had to assert themselves or they wouldn't get anywhere, as if they were afraid of people pouncing on them. After a while, they learned that they didn't have to act that way. You know, I don't care how good a waitress is, there are always some times when she gets stuck and can't handle the job herself. Then she needs somebody to help her. We tried to teach the girls that if they cooperate with each other, then they get along better themselves. When we had all old girls who had been with Chandler's from five to ten years, it was easy to break in the new girl. The waitresses would do the teaching themselves, and the new girl would fit in in a short time and cooperate very well. Now it's a little harder because there is so much turnover, but still you can expect the girls to handle it themselves to a very large extent.

I asked her how she got the girls to cooperate with her:

If the girls just see that you are doing everything you can to help them, they'll break their necks for you. When they were having trouble getting food out of the service bar, I would go back there and see if I couldn't speed up the service. If we were out of something and the guest wanted to wait for it, I'd try to find out how much time it would take; and sometimes the girls would have more than they could carry out, and they'd ask me to take the food out for them. I would always do that. Then I gave them time off when they wanted it just as much as I could. I tried to cooperate with them on that as much as I could. Except for a month at the end of this spring when we were so terribly shorthanded, I was able to let the girls off quite a lot. Even in that month, if some emergency came up, I arranged things so that the girls did get off. Sometimes it meant taking tables off the floor, but I thought it was better to do that than to overwork the girls. When they see that you're in there pitching for them all the time, then they want to do whatever they can do for you.

Subordinates generally responded to Miss Ellis with favorable and friendly interpersonal sentiments. I heard no charges of favoritism against her, and yet it should be acknowledged that I did not have a random sample of subordinate reactions to Miss Ellis. There may well have been, as Mr. Potter thought, certain ones who considered that she played favorites. At least we can say that among certain groups of hostesses and waitresses, Miss Ellis had warm and enthusiastic support. Some of these waitresses said of her, as they did of Mrs. Schultz and Mrs. Loomis also, "She was always ready to do us a favor, so naturally we wanted to do anything we could for her." There was also a general feeling that Miss Ellis was highly approachable and sympathetic to the problems of subordinates.

Regarding Miss Geiger, we did not find her involved in any *interactions* with subordinates off the job. Subordinates generally hesitated to approach her on the job also. There was a widespread feeling that she would not respond to complaints and suggestions. In other words, subordinates seldom sought to initiate activity for her.

We heard no reports, either from Miss Geiger or from her subordinates, regarding any reciprocal relationship in which there was an exchange of favors and interpersonal loyalties. Miss Geiger was inclined to think of her work in terms of "pressing" (her own word) to enforce the standards of the restaurant. A good part of her activity involved inspecting the work being done and correcting people who were doing it.

Miss Geiger describes her relations with subordinates in this way:

I talk to the girls here. I try to explain to them that it doesn't make it any harder for me when they don't come in, but it just means doubling up for the other girls and it really isn't fair to them. But that doesn't seem to make much impression. They call in and they say that they're sick and I can't say they are lying, but I know very well that lots of times they aren't sick at all. Miss Ellis and I have tried to meet the problem in every way we know how. We have given out a lot of requested time; that is, when they let us know in advance that they want to be off on a certain day, we arrange the schedule for them. For example, maybe a girl has a husband in the army coming home for a ten-day furlough. We'll see that she gets some time off. We try to do that so that when they can't come in they'll play fair with us and let us know. But it doesn't seem to work at all. This morning I hired a girl who had worked for seven years for a woman who ran a small tea room. In all that time she had not taken any requested time off. I asked her why not and she said, "The woman just didn't want us to take any time off." That made me wonder, maybe we were being too lenient with the girls. Maybe we should tell them we wouldn't let them take time off. I don't know what the answer is.

Mrs. Schultz, former assistant service supervisor, gave this report on her relations with Miss Geiger:

I got along well with her at first. In the end, she got too high up for me. I think I knew her better than anyone else has ever known her. I had the privilege to see her outside work, and I mean it's a privilege. No, she just doesn't have any friends. I don't think she wants any. She just withdraws inside herself. I remember one time, I had Thanksgiving dinner with her. I can remember writing to my husband and telling him that we had had such a wonderful Thanksgiving dinner together. We had a good dinner and talked about our experiences at Chandlers. He wrote back, "I'm happy to hear that your Thanksgiving dinner came up to the Chandler standard." (she laughed) Well, that was the first time I began to see that maybe I shouldn't take the Chandler standard so seriously. I didn't see it at first, but now I can see that Miss Geiger wanted to use me for her ends all the time. She told me right from the start that I mustn't associate with Alice Ellis. She told me that she was the sort of person that I ought to have nothing to do with. Once she told me, "One of these days, Alice is going to hang herself and then I'll have that job." She confided in me more than she did in anyone else. One time she broke down and told me a good deal about her life. She's had a very unhappy life. Her husband is dead. She was very worried at one time and wanted to see a doctor. I asked her why she didn't go see my uncle. Well, my uncle is the type of person that puts people at their ease and gets them to talk. She really unburdened herself to him. There were lots of things that he wouldn't tell me. You know once, a little while before I left there, I saw Miss Geiger crying one time. Yes, I wouldn't expect you to believe that right off. She was actually crying. Then she came to me and said, "Louisa, listen to me. I need somebody to talk to." But by that time, she had done so many bad things to me that I just turned to her and said, "If I could help you, I'd be glad to do anything I could, but there's nothing I can do for you now," and I turned and walked away. Wasn't that terrible?

The *sentiments* of the waitresses toward Miss Geiger will be presented more fully later.

## THE ROLE OF THE ASSISTANT SUPERVISOR

While we are not in a position to make a systematic comparison between the managerial approach of Mrs. Schultz and that of her successor, we can provide some background regarding the supervisory pattern practiced by Mrs. Schultz and that of her closest subordinates. This will give us some estimate of the meaning of her withdrawal from the organization.

Mrs. Schultz' relations with her superiors, Miss Ellis and Miss Geiger, have already been described.

In considering the relations with subordinates, we might consider Mrs. Schultz and Mrs. Loomis, a hostess, together, for I interviewed them together after they had left Chandlers. They described their relations with subordinates similarly, and they were similarly viewed by subordinates.

Mrs. Schultz expressed her *sentiments* toward waitresses in this way:

> You know, I really loved those girls on my floor. They needed somebody to help them so much. There would be one girl who had an unhappy home, another girl who wanted to get married, another didn't know what to do about her boy-friend. They all had problems that they would have to unload on somebody and I was always there to listen to them. It really hurt me to have to go, but my health was very bad at the time and the strain of the work was just too much for me.

Note the striking similarity of this view with the one expressed by Miss Ellis. Both expressed concern about the girls as individuals and about their problems away from the job. By contrast, Miss Geiger was particularly concerned with the way these off-the-job problems affected their work.

Both Mrs. Schultz and Mrs. Loomis talked more specifically about their relations with workers. It began when I told them that Ann Lindstrom had recently quit the restaurant, and I wondered whether they had known Ann very well. Mrs. Loomis spoke first:

> Yes, I did. At first, I didn't have much time to give her because as floor hostess I had to cover the whole floor. I noticed her from the start. It seemed that in the beginning, she was a little on the defensive and she had that sarcastic way about her. When I got to know her better though, we got along very well. She was a good little waitress. You know, she isn't very strong, but when we gave her that station near the doorway, she was perfectly satisfied. I think she worked out her problems pretty well, and I felt that she was reasonably happy. I could always call on Ann to do anything for me in a pinch. She was good about that. I knew that the girls got to like her a great deal too. You know, she was quite a bright girl.

Mrs. Schultz said:

> Did you know that she writes very well? Yes, she's showed me a couple of her things. Now, I can tell you a story about Ann Lindstrom that might interest you. You know, Ann is rather outspoken. It happened that time when they put in that new system in the kitchen. Well, that was terrible. Remember, Kathleen, it was so hard for the girls. They complained about it and complained about it, but it seemed that no one would pay any attention to them. Finally Ann decided to write in a suggestion and put it in the suggestion box. She didn't sign her name to it, but I guess they checked up on her handwriting in the office. She worded it pretty sharply. It went something like this: "We've complained and complained about the new system in the kitchen, but it looks like management is just taking care of their own interest and doesn't care about how the girls feel. Maybe if this is put down in black and white somebody might pay some attention to it."

Now, you know the way Mr. Stanton is. He'll just take a dislike to somebody and right away he wants to get that person fired. He called Miss Ellis and me into the office and said, "Miss Ellis, Mrs. Schultz, I want you to fire Ann Lindstrom within the next twenty-four hours. I don't want to see her around here any more. Get rid of that girl." He just sat there with that grim expression on his face and we knew that there was nothing we could say to him about it. Alice and I just looked at each other and then we went out of the office. Well, we decided to forget about it at present, so we didn't fire Ann. And I guess he forgot about it too.

Up to that time, I didn't really know Ann, but I took her aside and I didn't tell her about what had happened in the office, but I said to her, "Ann, I want to give you some advice. After this, if you have some complaints, don't put them in where you'll get into trouble. Just come talk to me about them and you'll be better off." She responded to that right away and we were on a friendly basis from that time on. That was the last time she put a suggestion into the box.

Especially for the younger girls who had not yet come to think of themselves as professional waitresses, the links with Mrs. Loomis and Mrs. Schultz were important in keeping them within the restaurant.

## THE IMPACT HITS BOTTOM

Beginning with a change in managers, we have been following a series of changes down the line until we reach the worker level. We are not in a position to trace the impact of these changes upon waitresses throughout the restaurant, but we can see it particularly among the younger waitresses, whom I knew best.

This is best characterized by reporting a discussion I had with Ann Lindstrom and her close friends, Rita Carey and Marie Pappas. I opened the discussion by saying to Ann that I had heard she was quitting and asking her to tell me more about it:

*Ann:* Well, last night I was just getting ready to go home when Miss Geiger opened the door and calls down the stairs, "Ann, I want to see you." Well, can you imagine that? Just when I was on my way home. I wondered what was the matter. The trouble with Miss Geiger is that she just doesn't know how to talk with the girls. Oh, she had a lot of things on her mind, and she had an idea that I'd been talking back to the guests. But I don't recall anything like that. I try to treat them all the same no matter how they treat me. Then she had an idea that I was dissatisfied with my work. You see the other day there were four deuces in our section that came open and I asked Miss Taylor (hostess) if I could take over that station. She said she'd see Miss Geiger about it. Another thing, you know they tell us around here, if you don't get along with a girl in your section, ask either to have her transferred or have yourself transferred. (A section consists of three stations.) Rita and I always got along together and this was the only time that it ever happened, we just couldn't get along with this girl and I spoke to Miss Taylor about her to get her transferred. Well, Miss Geiger held that up against me. So she said she wouldn't give me the four deuces because I'm not strong enough to carry them. Well, I'm carrying a square (table for four) and two deuces now; what's the difference?

*Marie:* That's right, it's the same thing.

*Ann:* Well, Miss Taylor was trying to get me the four deuces. You see, she's really for the girls, but Miss Geiger wouldn't listen to her and then Miss Geiger brought up this thing about our complaining about the girl in our section. She said she didn't like to have girls that didn't get along with some of the other girls. Now can you imagine that? First they tell us if we don't get along with a girl, we should complain; and then when we do complain they hold it against us. She said to me, "Ann, I don't believe you look upon waitress work as a career." I said, "Miss Geiger, you're right there; I certainly do not. I don't care for the work. There's no advancement in it." Well she said to me that some of the girls here have worked for seven or eight years and are just working for their ten year ring. I said, "That's all right for them but not for me. I don't look upon it as a career." Well, she didn't like that at all. She said to me, "If you don't like it here, why don't you quit?" "All right," I said, "I think I will quit." I didn't tell her when; I'm going to tell her that later.

You know one thing she didn't like. She told me she thought I was a disturbing influence among the girls. I said to her, "Miss Geiger, you don't have any idea how many girls were going to quit that I persuaded to stay here." She didn't like that at all.

*Rita:* Ann, stop talking about quitting. Cut out that nonsense. You got me to stay and now it's not fair for you to get out.

*Marie:* If you quit, I'll quit too. I really mean it.

*Rita:* I used to like Miss Geiger. I used to think she was all right but now I don't like her any more.

*Marie:* Miss Geiger is two-faced. She comes up and fusses around you, straightens your collar and smiles at you and then she tells you something. Something real sarcastic. I'd give anything in the world to have Miss Ellis back. She was really good. She'd tell you straight from the shoulder but you could talk to her. You can't talk to Miss Geiger. She isn't interested. She just wants to tell you.

These reactions suggest that we can view the impact of a series of changes as involving increasing pressures from the top down accompanied by a closing off of channels to initiate activity changes upward. Note the reports of frustrated efforts to get action from Miss Geiger.

## PERSONALITY AND MANAGERIAL BEHAVIOR

So far we have been describing the changing patterns of human relations growing out of a change in managers. We have discussed why subordinates responded in a given manner to a certain superior, but we have given little attention to determining why the superior acted in a given fashion. That question takes us into the field of personality. For lack of competence and data, we cannot undertake any exhaustive analysis of the personality of individuals involved in this case. What we have to say will seem incomplete and superficial to students of clinical psychology. Nevertheless, we do have one important advantage over clinical psychologists. Rarely do they have an opportunity to see the individuals they analyze in action in an organization. Taking advantage of this opportunity, we shall seek to compare the past patterns of interaction, activities, and sentiments of the two managers and the two supervisors of service with their patterns of interaction, activities, and sentiments within the organization.

I shall first present the cases, with a minimum of interpretation. At the end of the chapter, we shall see what general statements can be made about the personalities of the four individuals and the functioning of the organization.

Potter grew up in a small town. His father worked in a hotel. "I remember him as a nice fellow, and I did find that he was well liked by those who worked under him in the hotel." The father died when Potter was twelve, and, for four years before that, he was drinking so heavily that "he didn't really count as a father around the house. . . . It was almost as if I didn't have a father at all."

The mother was the dominant person in the household. Potter speaks of her in this way:

I never got along with my mother. She was the sort of person that fussed at you all the time. . . . My mother was a nagger. Everything had to be just right—to her way of thinking—or she would pick on you for it. Suppose you put down this piece of paper here (indicating on desk) and she would tell you it really belonged here (indicating position inch away), and she would really insist on it. . . . She often spanked me.

After the punishment had been administered, did he generally think it was justified or unjustified? He laughed. "I didn't ever think she was justified."

After his father's death, he and his mother and an older sister were desperately poor. He worked at whatever odd jobs he could find, and the money he brought in was important to the family. He recalls having an argument with his mother at the age of sixteen and ending by telling her, "I don't care what you think about, I am going to do it anyway." While he continued to live at home until he went to college, he felt that his mother had no control over him after that.

He does credit his mother with one lasting influence:

She always drummed into me that I was better than other people because I was a Potter. I don't mean better in the sense that I shouldn't talk to other boys and be friendly with them, but she would insist that I didn't have to act like them. She would say, "Maybe that is all right for him because he doesn't know any better, but you are a Potter and you do know better. You must act better." It's a funny thing, but somehow I did accept it.

The only warm and strong family relationship he enjoyed was with his grandmother. He ate many of his meals with his grandparents and always felt that his grandmother understood him and had a warm interest in him. He recalls that she always had a full cookie jar and never set any limits upon what he might take from it.

As he grew up, Potter had one exceedingly close friend, Jeff Thomas, the star athlete in high school. Potter went out for the team in all sports without success in any of them. In neighborhood and school athletic activities, Thomas was the dominant one of the pair, but in school work, it was Potter who helped Thomas.

In high school, Potter's activities were not limited to sports. He won a public speaking prize, acted in all of the plays for which he was eligible, and participated in all of the social events. He was surprised to find, shortly before graduation, that he was to be the valedictorian. He had put little time into studying.

With the help of relatives, Potter went to a large ivy league college, and there he found himself much less at home than he had been in his small-town high school. He joined a fraternity, and again he started participating in a wide variety of activities, but here he encountered "a drinking problem."

> I would drink until I got drunk and then would do the most ridiculous things, and the next day I wouldn't know what I had done. I got into all sorts of trouble and I nearly got thrown out of college.
> I had a few good friends who stuck by me in the fraternity. The people outside wouldn't have anything to do with me. No girl wanted to go out with me because you couldn't tell what I might do. I suppose I drank to get my nerve up.

What did he mean by that? He acknowledged feeling shy and ill at ease. Wasn't this strange for one who had been so socially active in high school? "Yes, but in high school I was with people I had known all of my life. This was a new world for me, and I didn't quite feel a part of it."

Potter had been raised a Catholic and had served as an altar boy, but while in college, he dropped out of church.

At the end of his third year in college, Potter left to take a job. Shortly after this, he found new elements of stability in his life. He gave up drinking completely. He got married and joined the Protestant church in which his wife was an active member.

Potter's early years present a picture of personal insecurity which he apparently sought to balance with a very high level of social participation. Marriage, a family, and the job have seemed to provide him with a sense of security so that the frantic social participation is no longer necessary. He regards himself as an introvert and reports feeling still ill at ease on social occasions when he is with people he does not know very well. He seems to concentrate his social activity on the job. "I am very much interested in my work, and I enjoy it thoroughly. I don't have any trouble talking with people on the job."

Stanton's father was an insurance man. He began this way telling me of his early life:

> I came from a very religious family. There were three of us. An older brother and a younger sister. I won't say that my parents were very strict with discipline, but they had very definite ideas. They wouldn't stand for any drinking, smoking, card playing, or dancing. Now, I don't think that that was

right. I know in bringing up my own children, I want to be entirely different. They could do what they wanted to do within reason. We'll talk it over and if I don't think they should do something, I'll just tell them what the consequences are likely to be. I don't want them going out somewhere to smoke or have a drink. When they start to smoke and drink, I want it to be in the house.

I asked how the parents' ideas were enforced:

They weren't very severe about it. I can only remember being spanked once. No, I can't remember what it was for. Oh, sometimes I would go out and try a smoke or drink or sneak out to a dance but I didn't do that very much. I didn't get much kick out of it.

I said that I recognized that now he saw that his parents' ideas were mistaken, but did he feel at the time that they were right?

Yes, I think I did. I just took it for granted. Oh, once in a while, I would do something out of line and get punished for it, but when they punished me I thought that was all right, that I had been in the wrong.

I asked whether he had confided in his father and mother very much:

I talked to my father some. We'd go fishing together and things like that, but I don't think that I was so close to my parents as some people are. I know some of my friends were a lot closer to their parents than I was.

I asked whether there was any gang of fellows that he used to hang around with:

No, I wouldn't say that. I had some friends in school, but I always had to come home right after school unless there was some good reason. Oh, if there would be a ball game or something like that it would be all right with my parents, but outside of that, they expected me home. I didn't hang around the way a lot of kids do.

Miss Ellis told me that she was the third of four children, having a younger sister and an older sister and brother. She was born and brought up in V, a large city several hundred miles away from the Chandlers Restaurant we studied:

I didn't have to go to work. It was just something to do. I didn't want to sit around home doing nothing. You see, we had been quite well off until the depression. Then my father lost a lot of money. We moved out of V to W— that's a few miles out. We stayed there for two years. Then one winter when we were in Florida, my father got double pneumonia and the doctors told us we couldn't take him back north until he had spent more time in the South; so we were there for a whole year. After I came back to V, I had been away and traveling around for so long that I hardly had any friends left any more. That was the main reason why I went to work.

One time, I was having dinner in the V Athletic Club with a girl I knew and two men. I said something about looking around for a job. The girl was secretary to Mr. Thompson, manager of the V Chandlers Restaurant. She liked Mr. Thompson very much and she said, "Why don't you come in to the store and see if you could get a job?" I thought I'd try. I thought I'd probably work a few weeks and probably have enough of it, but I went in and worked as a hostess. After a while, I was made assistant supervisor in the V store, and then they had an opening for a supervisor in Z. They asked me if I would go there. I had a very good friend at Chandlers at the time. We'd always been together. We were very close, so I decided that if we could both go, that would be all right. We worked in Z for a time and then the girl got married and I went back to V for a couple of months to be with my family. At that time, this store needed a supervisor. They got in touch with me and I came out here and settled down.

My father always joked about me supporting myself because I never have. He's always helped me out. He was swell when I wanted to quit Chandlers. I was so deeply in debt that I couldn't have got out if he hadn't paid my debts for me. But he had always been against me working in the restaurant at all. He doesn't like restaurants, so he was very happy when I decided to get out.

I asked her what sort of discipline there had been in her family. "Not very much, I'm afraid. Mostly, I got my own way. My mother was very easy on me."

I asked her how her mother went about getting her to do the things she was supposed to do:

She would just say, "Do it for me," the way mothers do, and most of the time I just made up my mind what I wanted to do. My father used to say, "What's the use of telling her? She'll make up her own mind anyway." I was very headstrong.

I asked her what part her father played in the discipline:

He left most of that to my mother. Oh, sometimes he would put his foot down and then we would know that we had to obey. I think we were a little afraid of my father. He was a stubborn redhead.

I asked her whether she confided in her mother and father:

I did in my mother. I suppose I talked to my mother as much as the average girl does. I'd tell her about the people I was going out with and the things I wanted to do. Oh yes, she'd listen to me. She was wrapped up in her children. She just lived for her children. My father was different. It would never have occurred to me to confide in him.

A few years ago, my father sold the coal mine that he owned, invested the money, and now he's retired and lives on his investments. My mother has been an invalid for the last eight years. I think her illness has kept the family close together.

She told me about her school experience:

My family sent me away to Parker. You know, that school is a sort of prep school and finishing school and junior college outside of V. The first month there, I just hated it. I'd been used to having my own way and I didn't like the discipline, but after that I got to like it very much. Miss Roland was the woman in charge. She was very strict, but we all respected and admired her. Whenever we went out of the room when she was there we had to curtsey when we left. No, we didn't confide in her. We would never have thought of going to her, but we thought she was very fair. We did confide in some of the teachers. We had some grand teachers there.

I made a lot of friends at Parker and I was active in all sorts of sports. I went out for just everything all the time.

You know, when I took my job at Chandlers, I thought I would stay just a short time. If anyone had told me that I would be working for them for six years, I would have thought that they were crazy. I think it was that I just got interested in working with people. I've always enjoyed working with people and trying to size them up. Sometimes I go out to the beach in the afternoon and just spend all afternoon watching the people who come out on the beach. It's a regular circus.

I asked her what she looked for in the people:

Oh, I try to guess which people are related to each other, what people are members of a family, things like that.

I approached the life story of Miss Geiger with some trepidation, since I had felt that always in the past she had talked to me with great reserve. To my surprise, the mere statement of my interest in her early life served to set her off. She talked more animatedly than in any situation where I had been able to observe her. She began in this way:

I can say that I had a very happy home life. Of course, we had difficulty, but we were a happy family. My parents were strictly religious. I had a religious training all the way through.

Since my mother was sick for a good many years, she had to have her children do most of the work in the house. She had to have it organized in a good system or else the work wouldn't have gotten done at all. There were three of us girls to take care of the house and at the start of each day she would lay out the work for each one of us. She tried to make it like a game so that we wouldn't mind the work, but it had to be done. If we didn't finish with our task in the morning we had to stay in in the afternoon until the work was done before we could go out for our leisure or to play. My mother was a good manager. When she went to school she studied things like that so she would be able to take care of her home when she got married. I attribute a lot of my success to the training I got from my mother.

She got us to take a lot of interest in our work around the house. We would try to outdo our older sister and she would try to keep ahead of us. It was like a game.

I asked her how her mother had stimulated such competition:

She'd tell us, "Now, you don't want your older sister to do a better job than you, do you?" And she'd tell our older sister, "Now, you're older than they are so it's up to you to set a good example." She was supposed to help us in our work too.

I asked how her mother had enforced her orders:

We weren't punished very much. You know, I think it's because my mother was sick and had to depend on us and because of religious training; we had such a respect and consideration for my mother that it would have seemed a terrible thing not to obey her.

You know, my father often threatened to whip us, but he never did. Still we were always afraid that sometime he would. My father was a stern person. When we did things we weren't supposed to do, he'd remember it. Maybe a couple of weeks later, we'd go to him and ask him for money for something we wanted to buy and he'd remember something we'd done not long ago and wouldn't give it to us. I remember one time, I threw a stone at a girl and hit her on the ankle. That was when I was about eleven years old. I didn't mean to hit the girl. I only wanted to scare her. I wanted to be friends with her, and after that, she'd have nothing to do with me. She wasn't badly hurt. Her ankle was sore for a couple of days, and I felt terrible about it. A little while after that, we went to the fair and I asked my father for some money to buy some ice cream. He said that he'd give me ten cents if I'd spend five of it for that girl. I refused to do it, so he didn't give me the money. Yes, I remember, I thought that that was terribly unfair. I thought that other girls were a lot luckier than I was in their fathers. But then at other times, I'd look at it differently and think that it was wonderful to have a father like ours.

I asked what occasions would give rise to those sentiments:

Well, he'd play with us sometimes, and then you know, we had a horse and buggy to ride to town in. Sometimes he'd sit up with us but let us do the driving. We had a lot of fun that way.

I asked her whether she confided much in her father and mother:

Not so much in my father as I did in my mother. We girls were much closer to our mother than we were to our father. I think that's the way it usually is, so we would take things up with her whenever we had anything that worried us. Whenever we had done anything wrong, we'd go and tell my mother first and let her tell my father about it. We knew that my father would find out about it sooner or later, but we thought that we'd get off easier if we spoke to my mother first. As I look back on it, it seems that my mother did most of the disciplining in our family.

I asked whether she would confide to her mother any problems that she might have with boys she thought of dating:

No, my parents really selected the boys we could go with. We used to have parties at home.

I asked her to tell me about her friends and the group in which she played in growing up:

We lived in a little town. There were no big cities near where we grew up in southern Illinois. All the people in town knew each other and most of them were related in one way or another. They were cousins and friends from the old country, yes, Germany. I did have four girl friends that I knew pretty well; they were all classmates of mine. But the really biggest activities that we had there were the church socials and the church clubs. We'd get together to make patchwork quilts and bake cakes—things like that to be sold or raffled off for the church—and then we'd have big parties in the church. There were four or five older women in the club that conducted our meeting and got us organized. No, you couldn't take a leading part in a club like that until you were middle-aged.

I asked her to tell me about her religious training. She said that she had belonged to the Lutheran Church:

We went to church and Sunday school in the morning and then after lunch, we'd sit around and then my father would read the Bible to us. We were taught how to behave out of the Bible. That we should respect the old and the sick, that we should not hate people, but instead forgive them even when they had done wrong. Things like that.

In assessing the stories of these four individuals, what common points of analysis can we bring out? I suggest that we view the upward or downward orientation of the individuals as a central point in our analysis. Note here how this relates to the earlier discussion of vertical versus horizontal integration in chapter 15 on "Who Goes Union and Why." We need also to ask what past pattern of activities and interactions led to one or the other direction of orientation.

With Potter we see this pattern: (1) parental control was never firmly established, (2) young Potter did not accept parental disciplinary action as justified, even at the time, and (3) he grew up with very active peer group relations. The lack of either firm or supportive relations with parents may have contributed to the personal insecurity he suffered in college. Together with his strong peer group associations, it may have helped to build the sensitivity to the thoughts and feelings of others that was so marked in his managerial behavior.

Stanton's story shows very tight and very consistent control exercised from parents throughout his life at home and little peer group association at any time. Though Stanton now states disapproval of these parental standards, he accepted them as reasonable at the time. The existence of this tight control and Stanton's acceptance of it apparently conditioned him toward an upward orientation and made him ineffective in relating to subordinates except to those who took initiative toward him.

Miss Ellis' story makes it clear that she had a great degree of freedom from parental control in the home. It was only in the school situation that she experienced any firm control from authority figures. Miss Ellis' account also clearly shows the importance of peer group relations throughout her working life. Note that she would not even move from one city to another unless her closest friend came with her. This orientation is also manifested in the interest she takes in the personal problems of her subordinates. She was apparently oriented toward those on her level and toward subordinates, having difficulties in initiating interaction upward unless this relationship was facilitated for her.

With Miss Geiger, we see tight parental control which, as in Stanton's case, was fully accepted as long as Miss Geiger remained at home. Rewards were offered her from above, even for competition with her own sisters. She reports no close peer group ties, pointing out that even in the church club situation, it was the middle-aged women who exercised all of the leadership. This sort of personal background tended to orient Miss Geiger in an upward direction, so that she saw possible rewards from adjusting herself to superiors and was inclined to seek out interaction with superiors.

Comparing Miss Ellis with Miss Geiger on upward initiation of interaction, we find Miss Geiger moving quite readily in this direction, whereas it does not seem the natural thing to do to Miss Ellis. This presented no problem with Potter who was so readily accessible with the interactions he frequently initiated throughout the organization. The problem only arose under Mr. Stanton, who withdrew to his office.

This analysis suggests a hypothesis regarding the relationship of personal background to managerial behavior: The individual who grows up under tight family control and (1) accepts this authority exercised by parents and (2) lacks frequent peer group interaction, tends to be oriented upward, and to be unencumbered by sentiments of loyalty to peer group members or to subordinates.

Just on the basis of four cases, I would not urge this hypothesis. I offer it simply to illustrate the possibilities for relating personal background data to behavior in organizations.

We view organizations in terms of patterns of interactions, activities, and sentiments. We view the individual in similar terms. Therefore, when we substitute B for A at a key point in the organization, knowing that the two men have markedly different patterns of interaction, activities, and sentiments, we can expect this to lead to significant changes in interpersonal relations and in the functioning of the organization. Since the social system is made up of mutually dependent parts, a marked change in one part is bound to have repercussions throughout the system, as it did in this case.

# Chapter 24 *BUILDING INITIATIVE IN MANAGEMENT*

"WE CAN'T seem to get our foremen and general foremen to show much initiative and sense of responsibility." This is a familiar complaint voiced by many people in higher management.

What can be done about it? Let us consider the case of John Dyer, general superintendent of a production division, who did a remarkable job in building up the initiative and sense of responsibility of his lower management people. This report is based primarily upon field work of André Bisson.

Dyer directed a division of about 700 men in the same company and location as reported on in the "Smelting versus Chemical Division" section of Chapter 17, "Work Group Cohesion and Militancy." We may recall that this was a situation in which foremen and general foremen as well as workers were predominantly French Canadian, whereas higher management people were predominantly English Canadian. It may be that the culture of French Canada, with its strong emphasis upon authority in family, church, and community, predisposes supervisors toward the passive acceptance of authority from above. Whatever the impact of this cultural influence, the management organization in earlier years had certainly functioned to encourage passivity. Control was highly centralized. Higher management people had little confidence in the capacity of their French Canadian foremen and general foremen. This was recognized by the foremen and general foremen and necessarily diminished their own confidence in themselves.

What could a general superintendent do to reverse this pattern? Management took action along four lines. The first two points can be briefly stated, and the last two will require more extended discussion.

1. *Change in organization structure.* In the earlier period, in the Production Division as in the Smelting Division, there had been "supervisors" between the general foremen and the superintendents. As part of general management policy of the works manager, this position was eliminated. Staff assistants were provided for technical consultation, but the general foremen began reporting directly to the superintendents, who in turn reported to the general superintendent. In this case, General Superintendent Dyer simply implemented the approach favored by his im-

mediate superior. Whatever the origin of the idea, this change in organization structure was necessary for the building of morale, as we shall note.

2. *Delegation of authority and responsibility to general foremen.* Dyer made specific decisions lowering the point of decision making within his division. General foremen were authorized to requisition materials and new employees on their own signature. They were also authorized to write and sign purchase orders for new equipment on any given item not to exceed a cost of one thousand dollars. Previously all of these powers had been in the hands of the superintendent. Only the works manager himself was authorized to sign requisitions for new items of equipment totalling more than a thousand dollars. At first, men in the personnel department, purchasing department, and warehouse were not inclined to accept the signatures of the general foremen in this division, since they were accustomed only to slips signed by superintendents. However, the general foremen insisted on their rights, and their own superintendents and the general superintendent backed them up, so that in a short time the new procedure was in effect.

3. *Stimulation of upward communication.* The general superintendent embarked on a campaign to stimulate upward communication.

4. *Introduction of rewards and penalties.* The general superintendent developed a system of rewarding those individuals who behaved in the new management pattern and of penalizing those who failed to show the initiative and sense of responsibility he was seeking.

## STIMULATING  UPWARD  COMMUNICATION

John Dyer had the impression as he began that relations between lower and higher management were on a very formal plane. Foremen and general foremen seemed to be ill at ease in the presence of higher management people, and this posed a barrier to communication. Dyer set out in various ways to informalize the relations.

The production division had a number of social functions during the year. The annual supervisors' party was attended by everyone. Here members of higher divisional management and their wives met with the foremen and general foremen and their wives. There were always some farewell parties during the year, when engineers or supervisors were transferred to other plants.

Dyer attended these functions and also made it a practice to accept any invitation to a gathering of his foremen or workers. A tall, broad-built man in his late thirties, he organized a hockey league for young boys which became very popular. Having played for a university team in his younger days, he had a real interest in hockey and he coached some of the teams. His interests also included curling in the winter and golf in the summer.

An important part of the management program in this division consisted of the pattern of meetings. Considering first the mechanics of the arrangements, we find that the meetings were marked by two characteristic features: their regularity and their structure—in terms of the organizational positions of those attending.

Each meeting group spanned three levels in the organizational hierarchy. Each meeting was held once a month.

The general superintendent's meeting included his two superintendents and their staff, and all the general foremen. The meeting was conducted in English and lasted up to two and a half hours. The general superintendent was chairman of the meeting and began by presenting any information he had about general management policy and about developments that might affect the division. He then asked members of the group to bring up their problems and undertook to spend most of the rest of the time discussing problems so presented. If a problem seemed limited in its impact to one particular department, he suggested that it be handled in that departmental meeting rather than in the divisional meeting. While he made efforts, as will be described, to stimulate full participation in the meetings, the general superintendent wanted it understood that the purpose of these meetings was not to reach decisions. They were for the purpose of consultation.

Midway in time between the monthly meetings of the general superintendent were the departmental meetings. Here the superintendent was in charge, and the meetings were also attended by his staff members, the general foremen and the foremen. The meetings were conducted in French and lasted up to an hour and a half.

There was also a monthly meeting led at first by each general foreman and attended by his foremen and the workers of the section. This took place the last half hour of a working day, and production was shut down for that purpose. The meeting was conducted in French. (After these meetings had become established, the shift foreman took them over.)

The structure of the meetings, with their overlapping and interlocking memberships seems an important factor in facilitating communication and understanding among different levels and in eliminating communication bottlenecks. However, this structure only provides the mechanics within which effective communication can take place. We must now examine how management built an atmosphere which took advantage of the opportunities provided by this structure.

At the outset, the general superintendent made it clear to his superintendents that he wanted to build an atmosphere in which authority was questioned and individual ideas expressed. Whenever they disagreed with anything he said in his monthly meeting, he encouraged them to come right out and express this disagreement forcefully. Perhaps the general foremen looked on somewhat incredulously the first few times this happened. However, as they saw that the general superintendent accepted and even welcomed disagreement, they gradually took this as an invitation to express themselves.

The general superintendent also sought to stimulate self-expression by carrying over into the meetings the same informal atmosphere that he fostered in his individual contacts in the plant and on social occasions. He sought to leaven the discussion of serious topics with a relaxed and casual approach, so that meetings were marked not only by serious talk but by occasional merriment.

John Dyer felt some people had a perverted idea of human relations. They thought that you should be careful to express yourself in a subtle manner when you disagreed with others:

> I don't believe in that at all. If a man disagrees with me, I am much happier when he comes into my office and says, "John, I think you are full of crap, and here is why I think so." than if he says, "John, I have been thinking over what you said, and I think that maybe there are some points that maybe need a little further consideration."

Dyer added that he tried to build an atmosphere in which people could say right straight from the shoulder what they thought. Since he showed that he could take what he called "straight talk" and even welcome it, he also found that he could express his opinions forcefully to his subordinates without intimidating them or suppressing their own opinion.

This is the way the top-level meetings appeared to three men at the general foremen level:

> The general superintendent told us that he is never sure of a man who says yes. But he likes a man who says no and who says why he is saying no.

> He never imposes his own idea. He never gives an order. He always asks what we think and if our idea seems better than his, he always accepts it. Another thing that we like about him is that we know that he is ready to fight for our ideas even up to the works manager. He has done that already.

> Everyone speaks French around here and besides, it is so easy to get to see the general superintendent that I don't see why there should be any problem of communication with us. Besides, we have these meetings very frequently and everyone is free to ask questions. We are even invited to make the questions just as embarrassing as possible. And we respond to that invitation. John invites us openly to argue with his opinions. He always says that his own idea is probably not the best and that our thoughts have great value. Besides it has often happened that he has abandoned his idea in order to take one of ours, recognizing that his own was not so practical. Now that really invites us to think and scratch our heads and rack our brains. That is why I think the discussions are so profitable.

It is interesting to note that the meetings with workers were not ordered by the general superintendent but were a natural outgrowth of the pattern that management set at higher levels. One general foreman, who became quite convinced of the values of meetings in which he participated, began to wonder why the program should not be carried down to the worker level. He raised the question somewhat tentatively to the general superintendent. He pointed out at the same time that such meetings would involve a direct loss in production to the company. The general superintendent stated the conviction that the value of the meetings would far outweigh the lost production time.

The general foreman then proceeded to experiment with the monthly meeting with his foremen and the workers in his section. At first, the workers seemed apprehensive about voicing their opinions. Therefore, he asked them to get together and appoint a spokesman so that neither he nor his foremen would be able to identify the source of any complaints. In a short time, this initial anxiety of the workers had been overcome, so that complaints and suggestions were freely voiced by workers and no elected spokesman was necessary.

After the general foreman had several months of experience with these meetings, the genral superintendent called upon him to report on them at the general superintendent's monthly meeting. This led to a lively discussion, and all of the general foremen then proceeded to institute meetings with workers in their own sections. We cannot be sure to what extent the other general foremen were convinced at the outset of the desirability of this procedure and to what extent they saw it simply as a way of gaining favor from higher management. However, on other issues, they had not been reluctant to challenge points of view expressed by their superiors. In any case, as they became involved in these meetings with workers, most of them became convinced that this was an important approach to communication.

These workers were unionized, but this seemed to provide no barrier to communication. The first spokesmen chosen by workers were generally stewards, but even when spokesmen were no longer chosen, there were no objections from the union. In fact, Dyer reported that one grievance committeeman criticized a general foreman to him for allowing the meetings to lapse. (Dyer then suggested that the general foreman reinstate the meetings, which he did.)

## REWARDING AND PENALIZING

Dyer sought to encourage a risk-taking approach among his subordinates. He told them on numerous occasions that he wanted them to feel free to make mistakes. He argued that anyone who never made a mistake could not be trying very hard to improve his performance, because the man who was trying to develop his organization would be trying out new things, and not all of the new ideas would work out. Dyer told his men that he would never jump on them for making a mistake. It was only if they made the same mistake the second time that he would give them a hard time. Their reports to us indicate that his behavior matched his words.

Some of the most important rewards and penalties cannot be administered at frequent intervals. The decisions a manager makes regarding promotion, demotion, and transfer of his subordinates naturally have an important influence upon them in indicating what behavior is to be rewarded and what is to be penalized.

In the early months of his new regime, with the expansion of the managerial organization, Dyer was able to make a number of promotions and thus give some early indication of the types of behavior that would be rewarded. In the Reprocessing Department, which constituted one half of his total area of responsibility, the number of products produced rose from approximately 1,000 to something over 6,000. While the number of workers employed remained the same and even dropped slightly through Dyer's period, this great increase in complexity of operation suggested the desirability of dividing each of the reprocessing units into two parts. Therefore, it was necessary to appoint two new general foremen and (with the four-shift operation to cover twenty-four hours and Saturday and Sunday) eight new foremen.

Dyer also changed the promotional ladder for supervisory appointments. In the past it had been assumed that promotion would go to an individual within the particular unit to be supervised. Dyer made it known that anyone within the division might be considered for any position for which he might be qualified. This enabled management to look much more widely for its supervisory talent.

Dyer sought to involve in promotional decisions the men who had the best opportunity to observe those who were under consideration for promotion. When a new general foreman was to be selected, the existing general foremen met with the superintendents and the general superintendent to discuss possibilities. When a new foreman was to be chosen, the existing foremen met with the general foremen to develop a list of possibilities to be submitted to a superintendent.

One general foreman described the selection of new foremen in this way:

We had a meeting where all the foremen got together and had an open discussion. In these discussions, everyone brought in the name of a fellow that he thought was ready to be able to take the position in his own department. After we had discussed the problem for quite a while, we got together on a choice of five names. I went with those five suggestions of the foremen to discuss the matter with the superintendent. It was with him that we finally agreed on three of these five men to fill the three jobs open as foremen. I believe that it was well accepted by the foremen that were leaving the section as well as those who were remaining in it because they had contributed to it.

In other divisions our interviews with foremen and general foremen on the one hand and with higher management people on the other indicated that the two groups tended to have different criteria in mind when they considered which individuals should be promoted. This was not the case in the Production Division. There, while a general foreman and the superintendent might disagree as to which individual should be promoted, they appeared to be applying the same standards of judgment. Disagreement was based upon opinions of the qualities possessed by an individual and not upon differences in standards of judgment.

This type of consensus seemed to grow out of the management program of discussion meetings, which gave the foremen and general foremen a much clearer idea of what higher management people were looking for than we found elsewhere. In effect, the men learned to value initiative and sense of responsibility in their associates, just as higher management did. Furthermore, the discussion meetings provided each foreman and general foreman with a much better idea of some of the capacities of their fellows than would have been available to them without exposure to these meetings. The meetings offered an exchange of information and ideas, so that men had a real opportunity to size up the abilities of individuals with whom they otherwise had little contact.

Dyer announced that ability would be the sole criterion for promotion to positions of foreman, general foreman, and higher levels. This statement of policy did not, of course, have any effect by itself. It is customary for management people to announce that promotions will be based on ability. Subordinates respond to the way promotions are actually made rather than to any statement of policy.

In this situation, earlier promotional decisions had not been in accord with this type of policy statement. In the works as a whole as well as in this division, there had been a tendency to promote to the foreman and general foreman level primarily in terms of seniority. An examination of Dyer's sentiments toward people and their expected performance will show why he was more inclined than many of his fellows to emphasize the search for ability. Some management people tended to regard French Canadians as being very much alike. If one starts with this assumption, then the small differences in abilities one may expect to find would hardly be worth the trouble involved in disregarding seniority. By contrast, Dyer believed that the differences among French Canadians were far greater than any differences between French Canadians and English Canadians. Believing that the differences were large and important, he felt compelled to search for distinctions in ability.

The new requirements Dyer imposed upon his subordinates also made it more important for him to evaluate differences in ability. The man who expects a new foreman to be a "good soldier," who simply carries out orders from higher levels, will find many men who can meet this expectation adequately. The man who is looking for imagination and initiative will find much greater differences among men in this respect, and therefore, will feel compelled to evaluate these differences more carefully.

To subordinates, the meaning of management policy tends to be shaped in terms of certain key decisions. In this case, there seemed to be two promotions to general foreman that were particularly influential in shaping opinion.

The first case involved an immigrant from the British Isles who began in the division as a sweeper. In a few months he was transferred into the planning department and worked his way up there. From that department he was moved over into production as a general foreman. This occurred at a time when all the previous general foremen had been appointed from the ranks of foreman. Furthermore, all previous general foremen in the division had been French Canadian. Dyer commented:

> We wished to hell then that he was a French Canadian, but we had to stick by our policy of appointing the most capable man regardless of where he came from. Within a short time, he was running the most efficient line in the division.

The second case involved the question of language ability. It was the official policy of the division that foremen would be judged on ability in performing the job, without regard to their ability to speak English. However, the French Canadians were not convinced as to the real meaning of this policy until they observed a "test case." A general foreman described the situation in this way:

> The test case came up last winter when they named X. We knew that X was the best man to become general foreman. But we were wondering whether he was going to be named because he did not speak English. In fact, X was named. We were much surprised but much pleased also. We were further reassured by what happened when X got into some difficulties because he didn't know English. He went to his superintendent and offered to resign. The superintendent said to him that it wasn't up to him to learn English but up to the engineers and the superintendents to learn French. Since that time, we have believed that French Canadians will not be barred from advancing in the organization. That gave confidence to everybody.

Let's see how the situation looked to the man who received the promotion:

> After being on the new job three or four months, I went to see my superintendent and said to him, "I want to return to my old job because this new one isn't going well at all." The superintendent asked me what it was that wasn't going well and I said that it was English—that it was a really serious problem not to be able to express myself in English. I have to have almost everything translated by my clerk and have him translate into English the letters and notes that I send out. The superintendent answered immediately that I was not in England but in French Canada, and he told me that French was my language, and it was understandable that I should have difficulty in speaking English. He added that it was a good idea, in fact almost obligatory for me to learn English, but that I was not to make such a problem of it. He told me to keep on doing my best and to let the other problems take care of themselves. He added that most of the engineers were making efforts to learn French and

that before long everyone would be able to talk easily enough with me. As for me, I am taking steps to learn English as fast as possible. I have begun evening courses and I am going to continue them. In the autumn, I am continuing a course two evenings a week that I began last year. I intend to take another one one evening a week. I am determined to speak English more easily so that I can be comfortable with it. On the other hand, people around here are very friendly and sympathetic. Everyone now speaks a little French and we can get along with each other easily enough.

It is interesting to note that while the man was in fact promoted, at the same time he was urged to learn English. This is only a realistic response to the actual situation. In that particular division, a man could perform quite effectively as a foreman with no knowledge of English. But for a general foreman, the knowledge of English is a decided asset.

Without some fluency in English, it would be absolutely impossible to rise above the general foreman position, for beyond that point, jobs require dealing primarily with people whose native language is English and who, in many cases, are not very fluent in French.

In this discussion, I am therefore suggesting that John Dyer and his superintendents made determined efforts to base their promotions upon judgments of ability. I am not suggesting that their judgments were infallible. In fact, about 40 per cent of those promoted to shift foremen within the first year were judged later not to be competent in their jobs and were demoted to the worker level. There were also appointments of general foremen which did not work out. In some of these cases, the men were named staff assistants, which was nominally a promotion, but unless they performed well in this position, they were transferred into another part of the division. (The percentage of successful choices became markedly higher after the first year.)

The human cost of this sort of movement will be considered later. At this point, we should note that Dyer and his superintendents were following their approach to its logical conclusion. If the executive planned to have the most able man for each job, and if his judgment for each selection was not always correct, then it followed that he had to make a change when he found he had made a mistake. If he had not done this, he could not have continued to claim that he was promoting the best men that could be found.

## EXTENDING THE PATTERN DOWN THE LINE

We have already discussed some of the ways in which John Dyer extended his pattern of leadership down the line, but now let us look more specifically at three of the key positions involved: superintendent, general foreman, and foreman.

While we have noted the enthusiasm with which foremen and general foremen accepted Dyer's leadership, we may well wonder whether the superintendents were equally enthusiastic. As they sat in the three-level meetings in which either their superior or their subordinates—or both— might express disagreement with them, did they feel undermined? As the general superintendent circulated through their departments, conversing with general foremen and foremen, did they feel by-passed?

Dyer was aware of these possibilities, and he sought to avoid undermining the superintendent. In his conversations with individual foremen or general foremen, he was careful to avoid giving any orders or instructions. If a foreman or general foreman asked what he should do, Dyer always referred him to his superior. On the other hand, whenever Dyer was asked for his opinion on a certain matter, he did not hesitate to give it. Although he always qualified such a statement by advising the man to take the question up with his own superior, this approach quite clearly exposed the foreman or general foreman, from time to time, to ideas that were contrary to those of his immediate superior.

Some superintendents might find such differences of opinion alarming. For example, one superintendent was worried to find that at the top level meeting he and one of his general foremen were arguing at times for different points of view. The superintendent came to the general superintendent to propose that he and Dyer should get together in advance of the monthly meeting to discuss what ideas would be presented in that meeting and to be sure the general superintendent and the superintendent were in agreement. Dyer replied in this way: "Like hell I will. This is a free speech policy. I'll say what I think, and you say what you think. I want to know what people are thinking."

This particular superintendent did not get along very well under Dyer, and the general superintendent eventually offered him a choice of several jobs outside of the division. No such position was to the man's liking, and he quit the company.

Bob Foster, who later succeeded Dyer as general superintendent, did not feel so threatened when he occupied the superintendent's position. When I cross-questioned him regarding this possibility, he said that the only time he was upset by Dyer's approach would be when the general superintendent, in the top-level divisional meeting, would casually mention a situation in Foster's own department which the superintendent was unaware of. However, Foster insisted that he did not resent this behavior on the part of his superior. He said that such reports simply indicated that he should get on the ball himself and see to it that he was even more fully informed about affairs in his department than was his superior.

These two cases suggest there were differential reactions to the general superintendent at the next level below him. Clearly, it is no accident that it was a superintendent who could fit into the Dyer pattern who was promoted to succeed Dyer and to carry on the same pattern.

A story told us regarding one of the general foremen suggests the extent to which Dyer's approach carried down to that level. A general foreman, who was disturbed about a certain problem, called in two of his foremen. He told them, "I don't like this situation. Why don't you do X?" Without any hesitation, the two men turned and started out of his office, whereupon he called them back and asked them what they were going to do. They said they were going to do X. He asked them why. They said that they were just doing what he had told them to do. He then rebuked them for responding in this way, saying that they were not to take any action unless they themselves believed it was the thing to do. Whatever the general foreman said, it was they themselves that must take responsibility for their own actions. If they acted in response to his suggestion, this would be no excuse if the action turned out to be a mistake. Here, the general foreman was applying the Dyer policy of fixing responsibility with the men who acted, regardless of what superiors might say to them.

Our second general foreman case involves the transformation of the mill. At the time, the mill was operating under a general foreman who had a high degree of technical competence, but who was unable to raise production beyond 12,500 pounds an hour when the engineers rated the mill's capacity at 15,000 pounds. The general superintendent and superintendent assumed that the problem was a human one and not a technical one, and therefore, began casting about for a man who might have the human skills to raise the mill to a higher level of achievement. Foster proposed André Tremblay, a general foreman whose only experience was in the Reprocessing Department, and who knew nothing whatsoever regarding the technical side of the mill. Dyer first argued against this selection, but finally went along with his superintendent.

Tremblay took over in the middle of the working day. Walking into the mill, he ordered all the lines shut down and invited the whole crew to meet with him in the cafeteria. He then told the men that the superintendent had appointed him to get more production out of the mill and that he intended to do it. At the same time, he said he had no technical knowledge of the mill. He was going to count on the crew to help him with the technical side, and he promised them he would do everything he could to support them in return.

Within three months, production was up to 15,000 pounds an hour. Within a year it had reached 20,000 pounds—one third more than the mill's rated capacity.

How did he do it? The most significant part of the story to me was that Tremblay was allowed, and indeed insisted upon, freedom to do the job in his own way. Dyer commented that during the first few days on the job, the general foreman seemed to be on the telephone all the time; "We didn't know what the hell he was doing." It turned out that he was calling friends and relatives all over the area who might have knowledge regarding members of his crew. He wanted to learn as much as he could about every individual and his family.

Tremblay also emphasized results as opposed to outward forms. When he first came on the job, he noted that foremen or workers would snuff

out their cigarettes when they saw him coming, although there were no
safety regulations that called for this. He bought several packs of cigarettes and went around among his crew. With each man, he would stop,
offer a cigarette, light up and smoke with him and then say something
like this:

> I don't want ever again to see you snuff out a cigarette when you see me
> coming. When things are going well in the mill, I want you to relax and
> smoke a cigarette. If things aren't going right, I want you to snuff out that
> cigarette and plunge in to straighten things out.

Tremblay took a similar approach regarding relaxation on the part of
the men. He noticed that when they had been sitting down and he appeared on the scene, they would immediately stand up and try to look
busy. He ordered some iron chairs made and had them distributed
throughout the mill. He explained to the men that he didn't want any
more of this jumping around and looking busy when he appeared on the
scene. If things were going well, he wanted the men to relax, and he
provided chairs for that purpose. When the mill got into trouble he
expected the men to get off those chairs in a hurry and do everything
possible to get the mill rolling again. Note here the contrast with Masters (in Chapter 14) who ordered the chairs out of the Hi-Test control
room because he believed that the men were not paid to relax.

Tremblay also displayed his independence in his evaluation of his
subordinates. When they appointed him, the general superintendent and
superintendent told him that they did not think that any of the shift
foremen under him were adequate, and that he would probably have to
replace them all. However, he was to work with them until he made up
his own mind and then come to them with his recommendation. Three
months later he came in to say:

> You couldn't possibly have been more wrong. Those three are all first-rate
> men. Two of them are top-shift foremen. The third man is not a good foreman,
> but he knows the machines thoroughly and could be an invaluable man to me.
> I want him for my assistant.

Higher management accepted his recommendation.

So effective was Tremblay in building up team spirit among his crew
that the men now were not content to leave on their annual vacation without first having a picnic together. While their wives were preparing
things at home for the trip, the men left work together, went out to a
recreation area, and just sat around drinking beer, eating sandwiches,
and talking about the things that had happened on the crew during the
preceding year.

To what extent has the spirit of initiative reached down to the foreman
level?

Consider the following statement by a general foreman:

> I encourage my men to come with their own ideas and to discuss my ideas.

Whenever a man agrees to do something that I mentioned to him by saying, "Okay, you're the boss," I immediately call him back to my office and tell him that I do not like his attitude at all. I usually tell him, "You're doing the job. I am not doing it. I am only suggesting something. If you're not convinced, you don't have to do it. I want you to do things that you are sure of."

I feel that I have succeeded to some extent because I have seen incidents to prove to me that my men show some sense of responsibility. For instance, one Sunday morning on the twelve to eight shift, the crane broke down. My shift foreman called the mechanical department, and asked them to repair the crane immediately. The mechanical people said they could not do the job, that they would have to call in the millwrights, pipe-fitters, and so on. They said, "We cannot do that without the approval of our superintendent." He said, "You call those men right away because this crane is stopping the production, and I can't afford to lose that production." There was some reluctance from the mechanical people to do that, but my foreman insisted that he was taking on himself the whole responsibility of this decision. Finally, the mechanical people decided to call the repair crew and the whole thing was repaired before eight in the morning. I congratulated that foreman on Monday morning for his decision.

We did not have enough data to say how typical such a reaction on the part of the foreman would be in this division. On the basis of fragmentary information, we would guess that only a minority of the foremen would have taken the initiative when such heavy commitments were involved. If only a few foremen responded in this way, that was still a marked gain over previous experience in this division, and a marked advance over other divisions observed in the company. The case is also interesting because it shows how a general foreman modeled his behavior after John Dyer.

### RESULTS ACHIEVED

The most obvious result of John Dyer's management approach has been the extraordinarily high morale of lower management people. I have never seen such high morale at this level anywhere else. Since morale is a general term that means different things to different people, I must clarify how I apply the term to this case.

In the first place, the men universally expressed sentiments of liking and admiration for the general superintendent. The superintendents were also viewed in a favorable light in both these respects—one more than the other, and both of them somewhat overshadowed by the general superintendent. Sentiments toward the company were also more favorable here than in other divisions we studied. This did not mean that the foreman and general foreman were uncritical in accepting company policies and procedures. We picked up a number of criticisms, but none of them seemed to be matters of serious concern for the men who talked to us.

Morale is often thought of solely in terms of the sentiments men have toward their superiors in the organization and toward the organization itself. This case suggests that we should look at the sentiments the men have toward themselves. In general, these men expressed confidence in themselves and their abilities that was far beyond anything we found elsewhere in the company. Along with this heightened self-regard had come a rise in both the level of expectation as to possible advancement in the company and the level of aspiration of these men—which leads to a problem to be discussed in the next section.

The development of the human resources of the division must be considered one of the most important results achieved. I have already described the way in which foremen and general foremen responded to the stimulating atmosphere created by the general superintendent. It is noteworthy that this achievement in management development was realized without the institution of any formal training program. The new pattern of management provided an atmosphere in which men could grow in skill and understanding. More specifically, the program of management meetings contributed to the training of superintendents and general foremen in discussion leadership. John Dyer set a pattern in the meetings he conducted. The superintendents, having observed him in action in those meetings, patterned their own approach to discussion leadership on his. The general foremen had both the general superintendent and their superintendent as models for discussion leadership, to be applied to their own behavior in the meetings that they conducted with foremen and workers. As they took over meetings with their workers, the foremen had experience in the superintendent's meeting to guide them.

While discussion leadership is only one area of skills important to a management man, it is a significant area. I am also assuming that the experience the general foremen had in participating in meetings conducted by their superiors, and then in conducting meetings themselves, provided them with more valuable training in discussion leadership than could have been provided by any formal training course alone. This is not to say that such courses are of no value. I am simply making the rather obvious point that men's behavior on the job is much more influenced by their experience in actually performing the job than it can be by any detached training program. The most effective training will be that which builds onto the experience that the men are actually acquiring in job performance.

So far we have been looking at the values of this management approach primarily as they affect the general foremen and foremen. We see another dimension as we view the process from the standpoint of General Superintendent Dyer. He said to us:

> I want people to question my ideas. If I am not confident that a man will question my ideas, I am afraid to give him any idea until I have had a chance to study it out in full detail. That slows us all up. It is much better if I can feel free to pass along an idea and be confident that the man will use any part of it

that seems sound to him or reject it altogether if he feels it does not make sense in his situation.

We often hear higher management people express surprise when one of their casually intended remarks turn out later to have set off a chain of activity on the part of one or more subordinates. Some higher management people seem to regard this as a peculiarity on the part of their subordinates. To avoid the problems caused by this peculiarity, they try to be more careful about expressing any casual ideas that might be mistakenly interpreted as directives. This means that the subordinates do not get the possible benefits of casual ideas that have real potentialities.

This type of response on the part of subordinates should not be looked at in terms of the peculiarities of individual personalities. It is the function of the type of relationship built up between superior and subordinate. John Dyer could freely express to subordinates any idea that popped into his head, with confidence that no such idea would be put into effect without being tested by critical thinking and challenging discussion. This meant that John Dyer did not have to hold back on his ideas. Being an imaginative man, he had many valuable ideas to contribute to the organization, and he had organized the management process in such a way that his ideas were effectively used. In fact, we can look upon the management process in this situation in terms of the generation, refinement, and implementation of ideas. From this standpoint, the process was highly effective.

Did the productivity of the division increase under John Dyer? All the men we talked to were convinced that it did, and yet there was no easy way of measuring it. In particular units, large and even spectacular increases could be shown, as we have noted in the case of the mill under General Foreman Tremblay, who raised output from 12,500 to 20,000 pounds an hour. However, as the production of the division increased greatly in complexity (from roughly 1,000 to 6,000 products), there were only a few units whose production remained sufficiently similar so that reasonable comparisons could be made. The figures themselves did not provide any good measure of productivity changes.

## COSTS OF SUCCESS

Success is not without its costs. In this case, some of the costs are obvious, whereas others are more subtle. Let us examine both types.

Immediately apparent are the costs of human failure. As John Dyer developed a new set of standards for managerial performance, some men who would have performed at least acceptably under a different management pattern now found themselves experiencing failure. Foremen were demoted back to the worker level, general foremen to the foremen level—or shifted laterally to get them off the job. One superintendent left the company. While there was a very real human cost involved in Dyer's approach, we should not assume that a more traditional approach would have been without cost. Under that more traditional approach, some of the men who failed under Dyer would have succeeded—but those who grew in strength and resourcefulness under Dyer would have been frustrated. In other words, there is a cost to be paid with either approach, but the cost is paid by different people.

Less obvious but equally important is the potential cost of raising the level of aspiration among lower management people. It seems to us a deferred cost, one which had not been paid at the time of completion of our field work, but which might have to be paid at a later time.

By building up the confidence of foremen and general foremen in themselves, management also built up their aspirations as to what they wanted to achieve and their expectations as to the possibilities of advancement. When we add to this that, on the average, many of the foremen and general foremen in this division were younger and better educated than their peers in other divisions, we can expect to find still further pressures toward advancement—or greater frustrations when blocked by management, as we saw in the case of Joe Sloan (in Chapter 12).

Some of the general foremen were looking toward higher positions— including that of superintendent. Some of the foremen told us that they would not be satisfied to rise simply to the position of general foreman or staff assistant.

The very close relationship of foremen and general foremen with superintendents and general superintendent led them to feel that they understood the jobs performed by these individuals much better than they would have been able to understand them had they been working elsewhere. They were impressed by the administrative skill they had seen the superintendents exercising. This naturally led them to define the positions held by these men primarily in administrative terms. For example, one general foreman said:

> The superintendent must direct men, make plans, and hold meetings. He administers. He does not do the work of an engineer or he does it very rarely. Besides, there is always a staff of engineers at his side in case of need. The superintendent is first and foremost an administrator. I don't see why a good general foreman who has experience in the plant would not be just as good a superintendent as any engineer.

On the other hand, the men recognized that a superintendent was expected to be an engineer. Another general foreman said:

> That is not surprising because it is a tendency everywhere to name engineers. On the other hand, you have here a group of young general foremen coming up. There are several of us general foremen between the ages of twenty-five and thirty-five. If this were really the last position to which we could aspire, that would be extremely discouraging. We would not care to stand here marking time in this position until our retirement. Well then, in the next few years, we will really see if we can move higher.

In our meetings with management to discuss our findings in this division, we argued that if some of these men were not able to advance to higher levels within two or three years, the high morale situation would begin to go sour, even with the continuation of the same kind of personal relations we had observed. John Dyer had already been transferred to a bigger job elsewhere, and it seemed entirely possible that his successors might have to suffer the penalties of Dyer's success.

Was it realistic to think that French Canadians without a college education might expect to move, on the basis of ability alone, to higher levels of management? Since our research terminated just at the point where promotions of general foremen into jobs at recognizably higher levels were just beginning, we cannot report to what extent promotional opportunities balanced the aspirations of the men who have been so stimulated. We can only report one interesting comment of Bob Foster, the new general superintendent. When he found a promotional opening for one of his general foremen, he received many favorable comments from other general foremen. This move had seemed to them all symbolic of the opening up of new possibilities. When the second general foreman was promoted, the situation changed markedly. A number of the general foremen came in to talk with the general superintendent. Each man began by saying that he was not criticizing the choices of the two individuals who had already been promoted, but he just wanted to know if he himself was being considered as a promotional possibility and what he ought to be doing to improve his chances.

The first promotions were to staff positions (above the staff assistant level). To this writing, no French Canadian general foreman without a college education has attained the position of superintendent in this division—or in any other division of the company at this location. As we have seen, the superintendent's position has been looked upon as symbolic of the most important type of advancement in the organization, and it remains to be seen whether or not French Canadian general foremen will reach this position and how they will respond in the long run if they do not reach it.

It may be interesting to report reactions of John Dyer and Bob Foster to this potential problem. After reviewing a draft of this chapter, they argued vigorously that I was creating a problem which did not—or did not need to—exist. In their arguments, they stressed three main points:

1. There is always a shortage of good men within management. It is unlikely that executives can help men to develop so fast as to create a surplus.

2. Superior performance can itself be a reward to the individual quite apart his promotional possibilities. They see men appreciating the opportunities they have had to develop themselves.

3. The men have a realistic appreciation of their own limitations. In some cases, they can be expected to recognize that they do not possess

some of the requirements for higher positions and will, therefore, adjust their sights to a career without large advances from their present level. For example, take the case of the general foreman who was promoted to that position when he could hardly speak English at all. In spite of his diligent efforts to learn the language, his command of it is still far short of what would be required to operate effectively at a higher level where most of the communication would be in English. The man is unlikely ever to acquire sufficient language competence to be qualified for promotion, and the executives assume that he realizes this himself.

4. They do not consider a college degree in engineering a necessary requirement for advancement to positions of superintendent and above. Recognizing that a man is handicapped without a college degree, they nevertheless feel that a noncollege man of outstanding ability could perform acceptedly at higher levels than general foreman.

The merits of the first point are difficult to weigh. This strikes one as a very familiar management sentiment: ability is always desired, and you can never have too much of it. The second and third points do indeed seem to have some weight. As to the fourth point, we should recognize that its impact depends in a substantial degree upon the sentiments of executives in the division and in the works as a whole. Under Dyer and Foster, noncollege men did indeed advance markedly, but both men acknowledged that their own point of view regarding formal education was distinctly a minority opinion in management. They reported that the more prevalent management view was that a college degree was well-nigh essential for advancing beyond the lower levels of management, and indeed, that a man who did not have an engineering degree was likely to be sorely handicapped in competition.

John Dyer had left the division at the time of our study. Three years later, Bob Foster had also received a promotion to another location. Have they been succeeded by men who have the common sentiments regarding the formal educational requirements for management? If so, raising the level of aspiration of foremen and general foremen indeed remains a cost to be paid later in frustration of hopes. In other words, what might not turn out to be a cost eventually in an organization led by Dyer or Foster may well turn out to be a heavy cost should another management point of view prevail.

## PLANNING FOR ORGANIZATIONAL DEVELOPMENT

As we reviewed a draft of this chapter, John Dyer told me that the steps he had taken had not all been as carefully planned as I have implied. For example, the three-level meeting program had not at first been part of his plan. He believed that it was important to have some discussion meetings within management. He thought of calling together his two superintendents and his top staff people, a total of five or six men. He felt that this group was too small for the exchange of views that he wished to promote. Therefore, he decided to add the general foremen to the group. As the three-level meeting was established at the top, the pattern was then naturally extended down to the bottom.

While we can accept John Dyer's interpretation, this does not affect in any way our analysis of the effectiveness of his managerial approach. We are concerned with what he did, with how other people responded to his actions, and with the way in which he achieved his results. A man who is casting about for new and better ways to manage an organization is bound to discover possibilities that he did not visualize in advance. As in the medical sciences, we can assume that some important innovations will develop accidentally. On the other hand, these accidents do not happen to just anyone. They happen to the people who are actively searching for new solutions.

However much of the program described was consciously planned at the outset, we can insist that the effort to plan for the development of the human resources of his division was an important feature of John Dyer's leadership. We suspect that it is those men who undertake to plan for organizational development who will achieve the most satisfactory combination of results in personnel development and in organizational effectiveness.

## CONCLUSION

Let us seek to summarize here the actions responsible for the gains made in this case.

1. *Changing the formal organization structure.* We have noted the elimination of the position of supervisor. The delegating of specific decision-making authority on certain problems to general foremen was also a change in formal organization—in the officially established activities attached to positions.

2. *Breaking the barriers to communication.* John Dyer promoted his "free speech policy" in every possible way by providing ample opportunities for communication and an informal atmosphere in which to talk. This was reinforced by the next point:

3. *Rewarding and penalizing.* Dyer set up a system in which original ideas and dissenting opinions were rewarded with personal recognition, and in the long run, those voicing them were rewarded with promotion. The same system penalized conformity through various expressions of disapproval, and in the long run, through demotion or transfer.

4. *Involving lower management in discussions of management problems, from technical matters to personnel.* But note that this did *not* involve group decisions. The responsibility for decision making continued to rest with the individual.

5. *Fostering freedom of action.* Men were not only encouraged to

speak freely. They were encouraged to act in terms of their individual judgments, within broad policy limits. This carried down at least to the general foreman level. Note that in the case of André Tremblay, the steps the general foreman took to establish his leadership were entirely his own idea, and his superiors only later learned what he had been doing. Note also, certain costs involved in this approach to management. Publicly recognized failure became more common. However, this was balanced off by the more spectacular successes achieved by members of lower management who did survive, and by the satisfaction they could get in calling their successes their own.

6. *Raising the levels of aspiration among lower management people.* To encourage ambition may appear as a profit at one time, and yet may later involve a cost if aspirations are not satisfied.

# Chapter 25 *ON THE MEANING OF DELEGATION*

THE plant manager was talking about his experiences under a previous manager:

Of course, he talked about delegation. I suppose he went home and told his wife, "We're doing things differently now in the plant. We're delegating."

One day he called me into the office and he said, "Damn it, Ed, we've gotta delegate around here. Now you take this letter from the telephone company and handle it for me. They want to put six more lines in here. Hell, we can't afford it. You tell them that."

I told him I would handle it, but I felt like asking him whether I should bring the letter back for him to sign.

Ridiculous as this case sounds, it illustrates a common problem within management. I have never met an executive who did not believe that he delegated. Most subordinates report that their bosses do not delegate to them enough. Why these opposing interpretations?

The differences arise because the term "delegation" has no commonly accepted *behavioral* definition. If the parties could get together as to the observable items of behavior referred to by "delegation," then it might be possible for them and us to know what they are talking about.

The last chapter dealt with some aspects of managerial delegation. In this chapter, we shall examine a second case, and then seek to arrive at some general conclusions—and our own definition of the word.

This is the story of "Food World," a large and growing chain of supermarkets.[1] As the organization grew, top management came to feel farther and farther removed from the stores. Since they were unable to keep in close touch with the stores, it seemed reasonable to believe that the organization would function more effectively if more authority and responsibility could be delegated to the store level.

Before any significant degree of decentralization and delegation could take place, it was necessary to change the organization structure. Before the change, there was no single responsible head in the store. Each store had a produce manager, a grocery manager, and a meat manager. At the level above them was the district manager, with his two assistants.

---

[1] Paul R. Lawrence, *The Changing of Organizational Behavior Patterns* (Boston: Harvard University Graduate School of Business Administration, 1958).

The district manager supervised the grocery manager, while one of his assistants supervised the produce manager and the other directed the meat manager.

Under the new organization structure, the district manager had no assistants at the district level. The new position of store manager was created, and he supervised the meat manager, produce manager, and other personnel in his own store. The central office provided men with the titles of meat merchandiser and produce merchandiser, but they were thought to function in purely an advisory capacity to the appropriate departmental managers in the store. It was emphasized in management planning that the store manager was really to be in charge of his store.

PARTIAL ORGANIZATION CHART, 1955

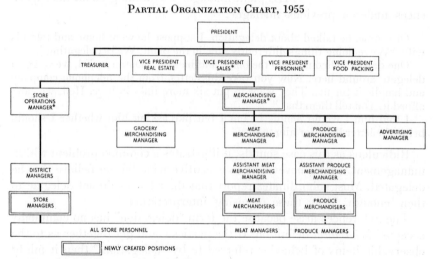

\* Men with major roles in planning organization.

## MEASURING DELEGATION

The philosophy of delegation required that district managers refrain from detailed supervision of the store managers and encourage their initiative. To what extent did it work out in that fashion? Paul Lawrence and his research associate, James V. Clark, undertook to answer that question through field observations and measurements. After some preliminary work, they concentrated upon three district managers (DM1, 2, and 3) in their relations each with three store managers. DM1 fell in with the new pattern as if it had been made for him. He avoided detailed supervision and took pride in developing the store managers. DM3 seemed still to be involved in every detail of store operation. DM2 was inconsistent, sometimes directing in detail and sometimes holding back.

The observers now sought to classify and measure the content of conversations between district managers and store managers. They divided all of the conversation into the following five topics: people, merchandise, records systems, physical plant, and small talk. The following table gives their findings:

PER CENT TALKING TIME BY TOPICS IN DM-SM CONVERSATIONS

|  | DM1 | DM2 | DM3 |
|---|---|---|---|
| People | 48 | 17 | 11 |
| Merchandise | 16 | 41 | 32 |
| Records systems | 22 | 25 | 47 |
| Physical plant | 7 | 11 | 10 |
| Small talk | 7 | 6 | 0.5 |

Several items catch our attention in this table. We note a sharp difference between DM3 and the two others in percentage of time devoted to small talk. Apparently DM3 was all business while he was in the store.

We also note that each DM had his own favorite topic to which he devoted almost half of the conversational time. While we have no comparable measurements for other studies, this may well be typical of managers. We may find that the manager typically devotes a disproportionate amount of time to the topic of particular interest to him, and this may not bear any relationship to the needs of the subordinate or the characteristics of the situation. We find in general that most new topics were initiated by the district manager—the percentages ranging from 77 for DM1 to 86 for DM3.

Does the choice of topic which receives most conversational attention have any effect upon the degree of delegation? I would argue that it does. In the fields of *merchandise* and *records systems*, the favorite topics of DM2 and DM3, the district manager could well assume that he knew far more than the less experienced store manager, and this assumption would probably be accepted by the store manager. We would then expect the district manager to dominate the conversation on these topics. The topic of *people* seems to be different in its effects. While the superior might dominate a conversation on the abstract nature of people, most of the talk about specific individuals would probably concern those who were working in the particular store. It would be obvious to both parties that the store manager knows more than the district manager about the people who work in the store. The topic of *people* therefore is likely to be conducive to the display of considerable initiative on the part of the store manager.

The researchers also sought to classify conversational units by types of utterances and measure the amounts of talking time on each type. Here the classification system divided utterances into these four categories: questions, information, opinions, and directions or suggestions. The following table summarizes the results of this effort:

PERCENTAGE OF DM AND SM TALKING TIME BY CATEGORIES

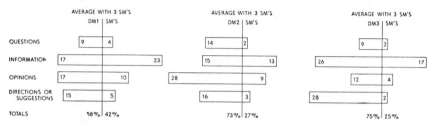

The distribution of talking time shows a significant difference between DM1 on the one hand and DM2 and DM3 on the other, with DM1 talking less than three fifths of the time and the other two talking approximately three quarters of the time. As we compare the two extremes, we see that DM3 offered three times as many opinions as his store managers, whereas DM1 offered less than twice as many; DM3 offered fourteen times as many suggestions or directions as his subordinates, whereas DM1 offered only three times as many.

## THE PICTURE TWO YEARS LATER

The researchers also made a followup study of the district manager–store manager relationship two years later. They assumed that some real changes that did not appear at the outset might become evident after a period of time, and this indeed proved to be the case.

Unfortunately, they could not give the followup data on all three district managers because in the meantime, DM1 had been promoted. This promotion, of course, was related to DM1's superior ability to fit the new management pattern.

The figures on DM2 and DM3 for the two periods show striking changes. These are summarized in the following table:

Here we find a marked reduction in the proportion of talking time on the part of the superior. We also note much more of a balance between superior and subordinate in offering opinions and suggestions or directions.

## WHAT ACCOUNTS FOR THE CHANGES?

As Lawrence put the case, the changes are not due to any one factor, but rather to a combination of factors. With his guidance, we can enumerate a number of these factors.

1. *Organization structure.* Without a fundamental change of organization structure, there would have been no store manager to whom authority might have been delegated. This is obvious on the face of it, and yet we are often inclined to overlook the obvious. This case suggests

COMPARISON OF DM-SM TALKING TIME BY CATEGORIES IN 1955 AND 1957

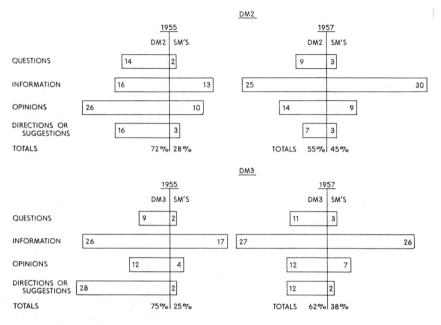

that we are likely to find changes in organization structure going along with a program of delegation and decentralization.

2. *Top management endorsement of the program.* No one was fired in establishing the program, but several men who had been district managers were demoted because it was thought that they could not handle the job according to the new pattern. Higher management people, both in pair situations and group discussions, made it quite clear that they were behind the program and thus strengthened the impression that district managers who were able to fit into the new pattern would be rewarded, whereas those who failed to fit into it would not. The promotion of DM1, who best fitted the pattern among the three men studied, probably made the criteria of management rewards and punishments even more clear to the men.

3. *Budgeting and employee rating procedures.* Higher management developed a new program whereby district managers were required to get from store managers estimates of their own store budgets and ratings on their employees. The district manager could dominate the process of preparing these estimates and evaluations, but the way the procedure was established made it clear that initiative was expected to flow up from the store manager.

4. *Status supports for the store manager.* The researchers report upon a meeting in which the vice-president for sales discussed with district managers current union negotiations, raising the question of whether or not management should undertake to keep store managers informed

regarding the process of negotiations. Some district managers opposed this on the grounds that the store managers were too close to the employees and should not be trusted with confidential information. The sales vice-president argued that if the store managers were ever going to consider themselves part of management, they must be trusted, which meant bringing them in on confidential information. He decided that this should be done. Probably there were other examples of status enhancement for the store manager, although this was the only one reported by the researchers.

5. *Top management's consultative approach.* Before the changes were announced, higher management people spent considerable time visiting in the stores and consulting with men farther down the line regarding possibilities of organizational changes. This helped to develop receptivity on the part of men below the district manager level.

The authors note that the district managers were not consulted— except for DM1, who was brought in on a confidential basis. Probably DM1 was consulted individually because his views were known to be compatible with the new approach. Nevertheless, the authors correctly point out that this involvement in consultation made it easier for him to adjust to the new system. Similarly, the exclusion of the other district managers from this consultation made the adjustment more difficult for them.

6. *Influence of superior's behavior.* The store operations manager (SOM) was the immediate superior of all the district managers. The researchers made a number of observations of him in pair situations with a district manager and also in group meetings with his district managers. They found that SOM talked only 43 per cent of the time in the pair situation and only 29 per cent of the time in a group situation. In superior-subordinate relations, it is common to find instances in which the superior talks 75 per cent of the time or more in a pair situation and close to 50 per cent in a group situation. The figures for SOM suggest that he did indeed display a pattern which threw the initiative to subordinates.

SOM exerted further influence in his annual session in which he conducted an evaluation discussion with each immediate subordinate. The authors report that in the early period he told DM3 that he was making progress but was upsetting subordinates by the way in which he criticized them. They also report that DM3 was very defensive in his reactions and would not admit this fault. The fact of defensiveness, nevertheless, does not mean that the criticism had no effect. At least DM3 became aware that he was not pleasing his superior in an important matter.

7. *Peer group influence.* In discussions with SOM, most of the district managers spoke favorably of the new system and gave an optimistic picture of the development of the store managers. DM3 was

the only one who painted a rather negative picture of the store managers. Finding himself in this minority position, he may well have wondered whether some of the fault was not on his side.

8. *Influence by subordinates.* Store managers recognized that the new program called for them to display more initiative and sense of responsibility. In general, they responded favorably when opportunities were offered along this line. On occasion, they claimed responsibilities that were not offered to them by district managers. The authors report instances where the store manager said, in effect, to his superior, "You let me handle this."

9. *The organized training program.* The company also carried through an ambitious training program for the district managers. While some of this dealt with technical matters, there was a good deal of emphasis upon the new management approach. The author describes one meeting in which DM2 described quite movingly the difficulties in adjustment he was having—and yet was apparently accepting the new approach. DM3 blurted out, "Speak for yourself." The comment suggested strong resistance. Nevertheless, at the end of this particular session, DM3 came up to the instructor and said, "Don't be discouraged about me. I've got some things to learn, and I am learning some of them."

If we examine the problems of DM3 in particular, we seem to see this type of progression. At first, he was highly confident, considering himself a first-rate district manager. The combination of factors described above undermined his confidence in his own acquired pattern of managerial behavior. The new approach structured a new way to proceed and win managerial rewards, and gradually and gropingly he was moving in this direction.

10. *Time, techniques, and personal adjustment.* When systems and procedures are new, the superior naturally feels some anxieties about the abilities of subordinates to take appropriate actions. As precedents for handling certain types of problems become established, behavior becomes more routinized. The superior is then less likely to feel that the store will go to pot if he does not exert firm control.

## TOWARD A DEFINITION OF DELEGATION

On the basis of this chapter and the last, let us see if we can arrive at a behavioral definition of "delegation." Let me first note that I do not intend to define my term in relation to "authority" or "responsibility." Those terms themselves need definition in behavioral terms.

Delegation involves the level of the hierarchy at which a given activity may be initiated, independent of clearance from above, with respect to that activity. That is, we can say that the activity has been delegated to B when he characteristically initiates this activity with associates and subordinates without prior interaction with A, his superior. Comparing a later with an earlier period in an organization, we can say that some degree of delegation has taken place for a given activity when that activity is characteristically initiated at a lower level than it was in the earlier period.

Note that the degree of delegation, according to this definition, can only be assessed with regard to a given type of activity. In Chapter 17, "Work Group Cohesion and Militancy," we noted concurrent efforts to raise the level of initiation for operating decisions and lower the level for industrial relations decisions.

There seem to be three main conditions favoring delegation:

1. *Changes in formal organization structure.* A reduction in the number of levels in the hierarchy tends to make it more difficult for superiors to initiate activity in all the details of operations for their subordinates and, therefore, tends to encourage subordinates to initiate at their level. In John Dyer's case, we noted that the encouragement of initiation at the general foreman level would have been impossible without the elimination of the position of supervisor between general foreman and superintendent.

The individual can initiate activities at his level, without consulting superiors, most effectively when the activities assigned to him cover the total operations of his particular organizational unit. If he can take action in one sphere only when other individuals at his same level take related actions, then on many occasions he will need to go to his superior before taking the action in question. We have seen this in the Food World case. Before the reorganization, there were three men sharing top operating responsibilities in a given store, with each man reporting to a superior from the district office. This meant that problems of coordination among the three individuals often had to be referred to one or more levels above the store. Only when the store manager position was established, with the manager being assigned direction of all of the activities of the store, was it possible to build up the initiation of activities at the store level.

Delegation can also be fostered by specific managerial decisions that call for certain activities being initiated at lower levels. In the Production Division case, we have seen Dyer arranging to have the general foremen initiate the activities of hiring and purchasing that formerly had been initiated by the superintendents. In the Food World case, we have noted that the store managers were required to develop the store budgets and annual plans, which had previously been prepared at higher levels.

2. *Changes in face-to-face relations.* The changes in formal organization structure, noted above, actually have their effects in changes in face-to-face relations, but they only tend to channel those relations. They do not determine in detail the characteristics of face-to-face relations. Within the framework of the formal organization structure, we can see

certain ways that the superior, in interaction with his subordinate, can stimulate the subordinate to initiate more activities at his own level. In other words, it is not enough to announce the policy that such-and-such a decision shall be made at such-and-such a level. The pattern of interactions within the organization will determine whether the man at that level actually initiates the activity on his own or takes it first to his superior for approval.

Based upon the Food World data, we can say that delegation is fostered when, in the relations between superior and subordinate, the superior reduces his percentage of total talking time—and particularly the proportion of opinions, directions, and suggestions that he offers—compared to those of his subordinates. Note that we are here dealing with proportions. The proposition may not require an absolute reduction of the number of opinions A expresses in conversation with B. We found John Dyer very free in expressing opinions to subordinates, and yet he had developed a relationship such that subordinates were equally free to express their opinions to him.

3. *Rewards and penalties.* Whether B will feel free to initiate activities without checking with A will depend in part upon how A responds when B actually does so. Is B rewarded or penalized for such initiative? We have seen John Dyer developing a relationship in which subordinates were rewarded for exercising this initiative and discouraged from checking with superiors on some of these areas of activity. In many cases, when we hear superiors complain that the subordinates are not showing any initiative, we find that whatever the subordinate does, the superior tends to find something wrong with it. This type of penalizing behavior will wipe out any positive effects from verbal encouragement of initiative.

## Collateral Readings

BARNARD, CHESTER I. *The Functions of the Executive.* Cambridge: Harvard University Press, 1938.
    Difficult reading but worth the effort. An executive analyzes organization structure, authority, and cooperation in business organizations.

BROWN, WILFRED. *Explanation in Management.* New York: John Wiley & Sons., Inc., 1960.
    A challenging analysis of organization theory and practice by the Chairman and Managing Director of Glacier Metal Company, the organization reported upon by Elliott Jaques in *The Changing Culture of a Factory.*

DALTON, MELVILLE. *Men Who Manage.* New York: John Wiley & Sons, Inc., 1959.
    An intimate picture of reciprocities and struggles for power within management.

GARDNER, BURLEIGH B. and MOORE, DAVID G. *Human Relations in Industry*. 3d ed. Homewood, Ill.: Richard D. Irwin, Inc., 1955.
See especially chapters 5–8.

GOULDNER, ALVIN W. *Patterns of Industrial Bureaucracy*. Glencoe, Ill.: The Free Press, 1954.
A study of managerial succession in an industrial plant.

LAWRENCE, PAUL. *The Changing of Organizational Behavior Patterns*. Boston: Harvard Graduate School of Business Administration, 1958.
A case study of decentralization, with methods to measure the degree of delegation actually achieved.

McGREGOR, DOUGLAS. *The Human Side of Enterprise*. New York: McGraw-Hill Book Co., 1960.
An attack on traditional theories of organization and an attempt to develop a theory that is based on research findings.

STRAUSS, GEORGE, and SAYLES, LEONARD. *Personnel: The Human Problems of Management*. Englewood Cliffs, N.J.: Prentice-Hall, Inc., 1960.
See especially chapters 5–17.

WHYTE, WILLIAM FOOTE. *Human Relations in the Restaurant Industry*. New York: McGraw-Hill Book Co., Inc., 1948.
See especially Part IV, "Human Elements in Supervision."

## Discussion Questions

21    1. It is often said that the foreman is the "key man in management" as far as workers are concerned—that he is the primary influence upon the sentiments and productivity of workers. To what extent is this true? Present evidence for your conclusion.

21    2. You are called in to advise an executive who is considering problems at the foreman level. He wants to know about the advisability and possibility of strengthening the foreman's position. What would you reply?

22    3. Have you ever worked under a boss who practiced "close supervision"? "General supervision"? Describe as systematically as you can the supervisory behavior of such a "close" supervisor; of such a "general" supervisor, on the basis of your own experience and observation. Indicate any difficulties you encounter in classifying a boss in such terms. What reactions did you and fellow workers have to the "close" supervisor? To the "general" supervisor? (If you have not had such experience directly, you may report on other work situations known to you.)

22    4. Suppose you are recommending to a subordinate that he practice "general supervision." He says he does not know what you mean. Explain it to him in such a way that he himself can tell whether he is following your recommendation.

22    5. A supervisor's relations with his subordinates may change in response to changes outside of the immediate supervisor-subordinate relationship. Give examples. In general terms, how do you take these outside influences into account in analyzing the supervisor-subordinate relationship?

22    6. Reciprocity may be all very well between supervisor and subordinate when the values being exchanged are stable, but what happens when management feels called upon to ask for a marked

increase in worker productivity? Does reciprocity then break down?

22    7. Management is planning to introduce a major technological change into the plant. What role, if any, should be played by written communication in this change process?

23    8. You have appointed a new plant manager. He has had previous experience in manufacturing with your company but is new to this particular plant. How would you advise him to go about establishing his position?

23    9. In what ways did the sentiments held by the two managers and the two supervisors of service (in Chapter 23) toward their subordinates affect the course of events?

23    10. You are a plant manager. It comes to your attention that some of your subordinates think you "play favorites," that you are more sympathetic to some individuals and groups than to others at the same organizational level. You take this seriously. In an effort to determine what has given rise to these sentiments, you review your behavior in the recent past. What kinds of evidence would you look for, and how would you interpret it?

23    11. To what extent were personnel changes at the bottom of Chandlers related to the change in managers? Trace the links from position to position.

24    12. The boss says to you, "I hate yes-men!" What does this mean? How do you find out?

24    13. Chapter 24 indicates that John Dyer had a well worked out philosophy regarding the extent of and limitations to authority possessed by himself and others in management down to the foreman level. How would you state this philosophy? What evidence for your statement do you find in the case?

25    14. Considering particularly Chapters 24 and 25, what is meant by the delegation of authority? If you were observing an organization yourself, how would you estimate the degree of delegation existing?

25    15. What influences can be brought to bear upon an executive to further his delegation of authority?

# PART VI Service, Staff, and Control Activities

IN OUR discussions of management, we have been dealing with the vertical dimension of the line organization and the intergroup dimension of union-management relations. Other officials, such as personnel men, engineers, and maintenance supervisors, have been considered only as they affected the line organization. Let us now try to deal with them more systematically in their own right as well as in relation with the line.

I will begin without formal definitions of a staff function, service function, or control function. I do this because the definitions usually given do not coincide readily with reality. For example, it is commonly said that a staff man does not have authority but is simply an advisor to a line. The difficulty with this definition is that we actually see the staff man doing many things that hardly fit under any definition of the word "advice," and we see many staff men who are rarely observed doing anything that could be called advising.

The word "authority" presents the same problem. We may say that a staff man does not have authority over a line man, but what are we to say when we observe a staff man initiating activities for a line man— as we often do?

The difficulty with established definitions is that they did not arise out of any observation of behavior in organizations. They are essentially normative definitions: statements by authorities of the way life in an organization *should* be organized. In this book, we are disregarding this normative approach. We aim first to observe the behavior that is to be found in organizations, and then to seek systematic ways of describing that behavior.

We shall examine the functioning of so-called staff, control, and service groups according to concepts which apply to behavior that can be observed or to indices of behavior that may be discovered through research:

1. *Evaluation of activities.* We assume that the activities performed by a given department will be given a certain value by other members of the organization—that value being particularly influenced by the

461

evaluation held by organization members of high rank. The value of the activities carried on in this department will have effects upon the department's relations with other departments. It will also affect the perceived status of those individuals performing the activities.

2. *Initiation of activities.* As between individuals or groups in an organization, it is important to know whether activities tend to be initiated primarily from A to B or from B to A.

3. *Blocking of activities.* Activities are not only initiated; they may also be blocked. That is, B may propose to take a certain step, then A may veto this step. It is important for us to know who can veto what for whom.

4. *Channels for the exercise of sanctions.* Rewards and punishments may be administered *directly* by a superior to his subordinates or *indirectly* through a third party who establishes for a superior and subordinate standards on the basis of which rewards and penalties will be administered. There may be important differences in organizational functioning according to whether the individual holds direct or indirect control of sanctions. This leads us to:

5. *Symbols of organizational performance.* We need to discover what the symbols pointing to organizational performance are, how they are established, and who controls their measurement.

6. *Organizational rank.* When we talk, for example, of the relations between the line and staff man, it is important to know how they stand relative to each other in the organizational hierarchy. It makes a difference whether the plant personnel director is talking to the plant manager or to the foreman.

7. *Reciprocity.* The relations among representatives of different groups may be viewed in terms of reciprocities. We need to know what values are being exchanged in order to predict the responses of participants.

In Part VI, in successive chapters, we shall consider the roles and organizational activities of these functionaries: maintenance supervisors, engineers, accountants and cost control men, and personnel or industrial relations men. For each type of function, we shall examine some case materials, which we will then seek to interpret in terms of the seven-point framework noted above. A more general analysis of the integration of the line organization with service, staff, and control activities will be reserved for our chapter on "The Organization" in Part VII.

# Chapter 26  *MAINTENANCE AND OPERATING ORGANIZATIONS*

MAINTENANCE organizations must be examined in the context of intergroup relations. The effectiveness of a maintenance organization is judged in terms of the way it serves the operating division and departments. In this respect, maintenance organizations have problems distinctively different from those of most production organizations.

In maintenance, it is exceedingly difficult to plan a steady flow of work. If the operation is large enough, management can make estimates of the load of repair work to be expected from month to month, so as to make possible some routinization of activities. Preventive maintenance can be scheduled even more precisely. Nevertheless, even in the largest maintenance organizations there will be unavoidable and sudden changes in the work load, which make for difficult administrative and human problems. Even when the work from one unit to the next appears to be the same, there may be wide differences in the amount of labor and cost of materials required. Two specimens of the same machine seldom break down in an identical manner. Furthermore, the efficiency of repair work depends in large measure upon skill of diagnosis. A mechanic may spend hours making repairs indicated in his initial diagnosis, only to find that the "repaired" machine still does not run properly and that a different approach is required. This is one of the reasons why cost estimates of repair work are notoriously unreliable.

Given these difficulties, how shall management organize its maintenance activities? There seem to be two main approaches to this problem, with many variations in between.

1. *Decentralization.* Here a small maintenance group is attached to each operating unit. This has the advantage of making maintenance assistance readily available so that a minimum of operating time is lost. But how large should this maintenance group be? If it is large enough to take care of most of the problems that can be expected to arise in the department, then there are bound to be many times when there are idle maintenance men in the department, just waiting around between machine breakdowns. If the maintenance force is reduced to the point

463

where the men can be kept busy most of the time, then there are bound to be peak load periods when they cannot handle the problems without causing serious delays in the operations.

Any company which decentralizes its maintenance can be expected nevertheless to retain some central maintenance unit to cope with the problems that cannot be handled within the departments. The problem then becomes one of balance: How much should be done by departmental forces? How much should be done by a central force? Some companies fluctuate back and forth between centralization and decentralization.

2. *Centralization.* There will be few cases of complete centralization. Wherever interruptions of operations are costly, it is the usual practice to keep at least one maintenance man in the department, so that minor repairs can be made quickly.

Within a pattern of centralization, there are two general types of controls exercised on the scheduling of maintenance. According to one system, maintenance work is scheduled by the maintenance supervisors themselves; thus, the head of the machine shop schedules the work for his shop, the head of the heavy equipment repair shop makes work schedules for his group, and so on. No doubt, there is something to be said for combining, all together, the complementary activities of directing work, requisitioning men and materials, and scheduling work. At the same time, this puts the maintenance supervision in the middle of a difficult area of interdepartmental problems.

The machine shop or the heavy equipment shop work not for one department but for a number of them. This raises the question of priorities in getting the work out. Should the work be done strictly in the order that the jobs come into the shop? This seems like the fairest system, and yet it fails to allow for differences in degrees of urgency. Suppose a routine job for department A is next in line, but then an urgent job comes in from department B—with the supervisor from department B claiming that his production is crippled until he can get the job done. Then it would seem that the department B job should be done first. But how are differing degrees of urgency to be weighed? The maintenance man who has discretionary powers in these matters is bound to be the focal point for pressures from operating people.

To avoid these pressures and the inequities that may arise in servicing different departments, management may establish a department charged with centralizing the scheduling of maintenance work. All orders for maintenance must then come into this department, and the departmental personnel would then go out to the appropriate shops to tie in each new order with the existing schedule for each shop. To do this efficiently requires much more than simply marking down a sequence in the order of jobs. The schedule cannot be a realistic guide unless the person making out the schedule estimates the number of men required on the job, the number of hours of labor required, the parts and equipment needed, the expected speed of their availability, and so on. This may also necessitate establishing cost estimates on each job, and even determining the exact number of men who are to work on the job. In other words, this involves a division of managerial functions—which traditionally rest with the foreman—between the man making up the schedule and foreman. Some friction is to be expected from this division, as we shall see.

The management of maintenance activities also raises some interesting questions involving the relations of craftsmen and engineers. In maintenance organizations, craftsmen without college training are likely to rise to higher levels than in many operating units. These status differences may give rise to frictions, and we also find that engineers and craftsmen tend to have far different views of machines and mechanical problems, which again can be a source of friction.

Some of these problems will be illustrated in the cases described below.

## THE STANDARDIZATION PROGRAM

First let us consider the problem of standardization in purchasing. As a rule, we find that when decisions are made by people who are to be directly involved in carrying out the decisions, those individuals respond with higher morale than is the case when the decisions are made above their level. Other things being equal, decentralization in decision-making seems to contribute to high morale. But decentralization can also lead to problems.

In the case of the Overseas Corporation, the general foremen had been given the responsibility of making decisions regarding the tools and equipment they needed in their units. Depending upon the amount of money involved in the given purchase, some of these purchase orders had to be approved at higher levels, but no standards had been imposed on a company-wide basis.

Since different general foremen had different ideas about the best machines and tools for particular jobs, management found itself with a wide variety of machines and tools spread throughout its operations, even when the same type of job was involved.

This approach presented management with a financial and a warehousing problem. Having available replacement machines and parts for all the machines then in use led to a very high inventory. This was aggravated by the distance of the company from the United States, whence came most of the machines. Since freight shipments would be several weeks enroute, and since air freight would be prohibitively expensive if not impossible, Overseas Corporation had to maintain many more spare units on hand than would have been necessary at a United States location.

This also involved a serious problem of obsolescence. There was a good deal of movement of personnel from job to job and from area to area within the company's operations. Thus, General Foreman Smith might be convinced that the ABC machine was the best possible one for his needs and would therefore insist that spare units and parts be locally warehoused. Then his place would be taken by General Foreman Jones, who firmly believed that the XYZ machine was more adequate, and therefore insisted that extra units should be provided for this machine. This meant that the spare units for ABC would simply remain in dead storage. By the time that a new general foreman succeeded Jones and reconsidered the use of the ABC machine, that machine was likely to have become obsolescent through technical progress within the ABC or other companies.

This type of system led the company into an inventory of many millions of dollars. When higher management began looking into the problem, it was apparent that a large proportion of this inventory would never be used.

Recognition of this problem led to a standardization program. Standardization committees were established in the main office and in each division. The aim was to establish a standard approved list of machines and tools that would cover all the major parts of the company's operations. Once this list was put into force, a general foreman could order something which was not on the list only if he received approval from the divisional Standardization Committee or from a member of that committee who was delegated the responsibility of judging such requests. There was also a provision for carrying some of these requests as high as the main office Standardization Committee, but what distinguished the requests that went all the way to the top from those that were handled in the division office is not clear from our records.

From the standpoint of higher management, the new system was exceedingly effective. Some months after its installation, the inventory of machines and parts was down to less than half the figure that had been reached before standardization. Results could be shown in dollars and cents. On the other hand, the new system carried with it certain costs in friction and increased demand on supervisory time and effort—though these were never directly measured.

Let us see how the new system worked, from the point of view of the general foreman. While he might agree that standardization was a good thing as a general principle, he often complained against the judgment of those who made the standardization decisions, and often felt that he badly needed some item that was not on the approved list. In such a case, his first step was to check with the warehouse to see if by chance the type of item he wanted was still in stock. If he did not find it— and usually it was not there—he then had to draw up a written request and justification for the purchase. Before and after taking the step, he generally spent a good deal of time consulting with local management people about his proposal, marshalling his own arguments and trying to persuade those who might be consulted by the divisional Standardization Committee.

Ordinarily it took some weeks for the written request to go from a general foreman to the stage of final action at divisional headquarters. In the meantime, the general foreman had to wait and possibly substitute some makeshift arrangement while he was waiting. This sometimes led him to place an order with the machine shop to have the item in question manufactured. This was, of course, a costly procedure, for the machine shop was not set up to manufacture such items in quantity.

As often as not, the general foreman's request would be turned down by the divisional committee. In fact, the standardization program cannot be expected to work unless most requests for substitute items are turned down. But what does a general foreman do when his request is vetoed? Let us consider "The Case of the Tool Kits" for illustrative purposes.

Our story begins on a November 8, when a general foreman submitted a requisition for the purchase of four tool kits to be used in the servicing of a unit of a certain type of machine. The cost involved was approximately fifty dollars.

On January 6, the requisition was approved by local management. (Why it took almost two months for the requisition to get out of the local organization we have no idea.)

On January 12, the requisition was received in the division office. On February 8, the Standardization Committee raised a question as to whether the use of the kits would affect the manufacturer's warranty on the machines. It was requested that the requisition be held up for the decision of the engineer, who was then out of the city. When he was able to give his attention to this matter, the engineer recommended against accepting the local requisition. His decision was upheld by a representative of division management. The cancelled requisition was returned to the local unit on April 4.

Almost six months had passed since the original request, but our story is not over yet. On May 27, the general foreman resubmitted the requisition, together with a more elaborate statement justifying the order.

By August, when I left the local scene, a final disposition of the tool kit case had not been made, so I cannot tell the end of the story. However, I can provide this information regarding the bases of decision making, both in the divisional office and in the local situation.

I learned that the division turned down the requisition not only on the question of the manufacturer's warranty. The action was also taken in line with general company policy to have repair and servicing of machines done outside of the company whenever adequate facilities were available and there seemed a good chance of saving money. This seemed like a case in point because there was a service agency in the division office city for the machines in question.

At the local level, the situation looked entirely different. The manufacturer's warranty was brushed aside on these points:

1. Most of the machines in question were so old that they did not come within the warranty period.
2. Anyway, a warranty can apply only if the machine is sent back to the manufacturer (in the United States), and then only if he is convinced that the difficulty is due to faulty materials or workmanship. This is a costly and long, drawn out procedure at best.

Regarding the possibility of having the servicing done in the division office city, the craft people made this point. With the tool kit, the unit could easily be serviced without being removed from the machine. The job took no more than half an hour. If the unit were sent out, it had to be removed from the machine, which took at least two hours time. In other words, having the work done outside would cost the company more before the unit even got out of the local shop.

Obviously, this is an extreme case. It does not represent the average situation. Rather, it represents the situation as viewed by some of the general foremen. As one foreman sought to explain his point of view to me, he brought up this case to symbolize everything that was objectionable about the system. Thus the case is highly significant—even though it is not typical—in that it exemplifies the point of view of the general foremen.

The hostile sentiments of the general foremen toward the system were directed particularly against the engineers, whom they saw as being in control of the standardization committees and procedures. The prevailing sentiments of many of them can be summed up in these terms (paraphrased from my interviews): "The engineers don't really understand our problems. Furthermore, they aren't interested in our problems. If the engineer who is making the decision doesn't accept my reasoning, why doesn't he call me up and try out his answer on me or ask to explain it further? The trouble is, engineers think they know it all. They think we are stupid. Now they have set up all this complicated system so that the general foremen are pinned down in useless paper work more than they ever were before."

The engineers in division headquarters had a different view of standardization problems and a matching set of sentiments toward the general foreman. They regarded the average craft supervisor as an illogical individual, who was inclined to develop strong personal attachments to particular machines. He was also thought to be a stubborn individual, inclined to resist change even when it was obviously indicated.

It is not my intention to finish this case with a balance of profits and losses under the new system. There was no such balance available. The gains achieved under the new system were to a large extent measurable—and measured—in the reduction of the inventory. The costs of the new system were not measured, but some of them were potentially measurable. If management were concerned with striking a more realistic balance, other sets of figures could be gathered. For example, it could be found how much time each member of a standardization committee was spending on this task and this could be charged as a fraction of his salary. Field studies could at least bring forth some useful estimates of the time being spent by general foremen on the new procedures. (Ideally, we should be able to compare this with the time they were spending in acquiring tools and equipment under the earlier system.) No direct dollar value can be put on the increasing frictions between craft supervisors and engineers or on the increasing frustrations felt by craft supervisors, but these two costs are obviously incurred in achieving the gains of the new system. Quite apart from dollar values, management had no way of registering these changes in interpersonal sentiments and thus considering them in management decision making. This matter of factors measured and factors unmeasured presents a problem in management to which we shall return later.

## THE AREA COORDINATION SYSTEM

The Overseas Corporation provides us with another problem in organizational structure and relations as we examine the operation of the Area Coordination System.

The Maintenance and Construction Organization of the corporation was a new structure designed to achieve better coordination of maintenance and construction activities. It must be viewed against the background of the type of organization which preceded it. In the old days the craft organizations were supreme. Each craft was headed by a general foreman. The general foreman reported to a master mechanic or craft coordinator.

Under this type of organization, craft supervisors received work orders from the "owners" of equipment and the supervisors themselves had considerable freedom of action in scheduling the work in their shops. This led to an emphasis upon the relationship between a man and his boss from the bottom to the top of the line of authority. Such an organization may be well adapted to putting out high quality work in each craft.

However, the basic problems of maintenance and construction cannot be solved in terms of a man-boss relationship. Nearly every job that comes in to maintenance and construction requires the work of more than one craft, and some jobs may call for the work of half a dozen. Under these circumstances, the efficiency of the work depends at least as much upon intergroup relations as it does upon the relations within each craft group.

Furthermore, as we have already noted, it is characteristic of work in maintenance and construction that the flow of production is not even and steady. There will be shortages of men in some shops, while others find themselves with surpluses, and sometimes these shortages and surpluses occur simultaneously within the same craft but in different installations operated by this craft. Efficiency obviously depends upon a full utilization of man power, and in maintenance and construction this seems to require the ability to move men from shop to shop to meet the fluctuating needs.

The new Maintenance and Construction Organization, then, was designed to increase efficiency through the coordination of inter-group relations and through a more flexible assignment of workers.

The Maintenance and Construction Organization established what were, in effect, two parallel lines of authority. Under the chief of the Maintenance and Construction Organization was the Area Coordination Organization, and under the craft coordinator, a number of craft groups. The area coordinator and his assistants were responsible for receiving orders for work from the "owners" of equipment and for preparing a production schedule. This schedule was supposed to determine on what day a given craft should start work on job X, how many men would be assigned to the job, and how long the job should take. The assignment of men also involved the power to shift workers from place to place to meet work requirements.

The area foremen and the supervisors below them were responsible for determining the best methods of doing the work, for training their men, for directly supervising the work, and for evaluating workers and determining job classifications and pay increases. Since they did not have control over the number assigned to them from week to week or the freedom to decide when a particular job should be done or how many men should be assigned to it, they had given up certain important functions they previously performed.

The job description stated that area coordination and craft supervision groups were to work together as a team. However, the description also clearly stated that the area coordinator was the captain of the area team.

We found a good deal of friction between the area coordination and craft supervision groups, with the craft supervisors feeling that they were the underdogs in that situation. Although the assistant area coordinators and the area foremen appeared on the same level on the organization chart, many craft people felt that the assistant area coordinator had the higher status with management as well as more power.

It was quite natural for craft people to have these sentiments regarding status and power, because the craft people no longer had the full control over the work that was once theirs. Furthermore, in planning the work schedule, the assistant area coordinator was frequently in the position of telling the foreman what to do, while the official distribution of functions and responsibilities provided the foreman with no opportunity to tell the assistant area coordinator what to do.

Craft supervisors also complained that the area coordination people were so preoccupied with the equipment and paper work that they neglected the "human element." What did this mean? This question is best answered by a story that was told us by a craft supervisor:

I think this problem we had about Holy Week really shows you the point of view of those people. Thursday and Friday of that week are religious holidays. Instead of that, Area Coordination told us that we were going to have to work those days—to get an emergency job done. Besides, we weren't going to work just one shift; we were going to have to work three shifts right around the clock. Spread as thin as we are, that would have meant that all of the expatriates and all the national foremen would have had extra hours to cover the job. Besides, we couldn't have required the men to work on those holidays. We would have had to ask for volunteers, and we knew damned well that we couldn't get enough men to come out and work on those days and those hours to be worth the effort.

I argued with Area Coordination. I told them just what I thought of their point of view. I told them there were other ways of getting that job done. But I might just as well have been talking to a stone wall. Their attitude was that they were running things around here, and we just had to do whatever they told us. They couldn't think of anything but the jobs to be done and their pieces of paper. The human element didn't enter into their calculations at all. The Area Coordinator even said to me that he didn't have to worry about personnel. That was my problem.

Well, I argued with them until I saw it was just going to do no good. Then I went to my general foreman and told him what I thought about it. He took it on upstairs and now we hear that the plan has been called off. But the fact that they told us they were going to carry on such a work schedule gives you an idea of their point of view.

Another craft supervisor made this comment:

Some of these people in Area Coordination don't consider the individual at all. Lately here they came through with a schedule that would have required Sunday work out of us every Sunday for a period of two months. Now, of course, I am supposed to be on call twenty-four hours a day, seven days a week, but outside of my six regular days, I am only supposed to be called in if it is an emergency. How can it be an emergency if you can schedule the work two months ahead?

While something like the Holy Week work schedule problem or the Sunday work problem only come up occasionally, such incidents made craft supervisors feel that they were at the mercy of the area people. To be sure, if the area man pushed you too far, you could appeal to your general foreman, and he could go upstairs and perhaps get the decision changed. However, this possibility seemed open only on a large and dramatic issue. In the normal routine, the craft supervisor might feel subjected to many unnecessary inconveniences in the personnel field without being able to do anything about it.

Was this area-craft friction inevitable? Apparently not, for we found several cases where the assistant area coordinator and the craft supervisor were getting along well.

We looked into one such relationship and discovered two possible explanations for the harmony we observed. In the first place, the men had worked closely together before the Maintenance and Construction Organization was set up and they had always been good friends. In the second place, the actual procedures that the assistant area coordinator used were different from those that were customary.

We heard many complaints from craft supervisors that the area people would give them a work schedule already completed without consulting them at any point. They often felt that the area people were young upstarts who did not really understand the craft problems. They found that the work schedules were often impractical, but to institute a change when a schedule was already made out involved an argument with the assistant area coordinator and possibly even an appeal to a general foreman.

In the case of the area foreman and the assistant area coordinator who got along so well, the work schedule really could be called a joint product. Before he took his first steps in making up the schedule, the assistant area coordinator would go to the foreman to discuss the work in prospect for the coming week, the technical problems that might be involved, the number of men that would be required, and so on. Whenever possible, they would go out to look over the jobs together—and on these occasions the United States foreman generally took his national foreman with him, so that all supervision was involved in this planning process.

Next, the assistant area coordinator would prepare a tentative work schedule for the week and bring this in to the area foreman for discussion. At times the area foreman would disagree with the assistant area coordinator as to the number of men required for a particular job. In such cases, he told us, sometimes the assistant area coordinator would accept the foreman's estimate, sometimes they would agree on a compromise, and sometimes the foreman would agree to go along with the scheduled number of men. Since he felt he played an important part in making up this work schedule, the area foreman never found it difficult to come to an agreement regarding the various aspects of scheduling.

As the last step, the assistant area coordinator presented the completed and official work schedule to the area foreman. Since this only put in final form what the two men had already thoroughly discussed and agreed upon, there was never any problem at this point.

When two men work together well in a situation where friction might be expected, it is often said that the harmony is due to their particular personalities. In this case, while their past association certainly helped the two men to learn how to get along with each other, we should emphasize that the procedures they followed and the ways in which they organized their relationship were objectively different from what we observed in cases of friction.

The harmonious relationship did not arise simply by accident, because the two men happened to like each other. At the same time, we should note that the procedures they worked out were not based upon management directives.

Could management resolve the conflicts without scrapping the Maintenance and Construction Organization? I cannot provide a good answer to that question because our research and reports to management terminated just at the time local management was beginning to work seriously on this problem. Nevertheless, two points should be raised in concluding this case.

We should not assume that the craft supervisors were opposed to the Maintenance and Construction structure in principle. At first, this was my assumption as I listened to their many complaints regarding the operation of the new system. But when I put to a number of them this question: "Would you like to be able to discard the Maintenance and Construction Organization?" The answer was almost unanimously: "No!"

As one said: "The basic idea is good. It just isn't working like it should."

How, then, should it work? As our study was terminating, the head of Maintenance and Construction had decided to concentrate management attention on the resolution of frictions. For this purpose, he had relieved his craft coordinator (the executive in charge of supervision of craft work) from all of his administrative duties for a six-month period. This executive was then to spend the six months in intimate association with craft general foremen, foremen, national foremen, area coordinators, and assistant area coordinators, observing them as they worked together and talking with them about the problems they faced. It was hoped that this would lead to the discovery of points of friction and development of methods of smoothing out relations.

## THE STRUGGLE AT MILO

*Men Who Manage*, by Melville Dalton, provides us with the most intensive study available of relations within management, of the exchange of favors and penalties, of factional maneuvering and power struggles.[1] One of Dalton's cases, taken from Milo, a very large manufacturing plant, involved the relations between maintenance and operations.

Dalton sets the stage for us in this way:

For a decade the records of all repair work were prepared by the maintenance shops in which the work was done. This record included time and materials for doing the work. The shops sent a copy to the Auditing Department, which charged the cost to the given head. Over a period of several years friction developed between operation and maintenance groups. Some heads of operation complained about the backlog of over 1,500 uncompleted orders in the various shops, while foremen of maintenance protested about being "pushed around" by operation executives.

Hardy (assistant plant manager) and the assistants to Stevens (plant manager) investigated and found that some heads had hundreds of unfinished orders while others had none. The condition was hushed up to prevent invidious ascription of good or poor leadership, when obviously there could be no poor leaders.

The backlog belonged almost entirely to the less aggressive and less astute heads. Once their orders and worn equipment were delivered to the shops, they assumed that the work would be done as soon as possible, and attended to more urgent matters. Or if they did inquire at the shops, they put no pressure on maintenance foremen. On the other hand, the chiefs abreast of their repair work were there because they checked constantly on the progress of their orders. They expedited the work by use of friendships, by bullying, and by implied threats. As all the heads had the same formal rank, one could say that an inverse relation existed between a given officer's personal influence and his volume of uncompleted repairs.

For example, a dominant chief would appear in person and tell the maintenance foreman that certain jobs were "hot" and were holding up production. Some operation chiefs threatened to block their flow of informal favors to maintenance officers. These favors included (1) cooperation to "cover up" errors made by maintenance machinists, or at least to share responsibility for them; (2) defense for the need of new maintenance personnel; (3) support in meetings against changes recommended by staff groups that maintenance forces opposed; (4) consideration, and justification to top management, of material needed by maintenance for its success and survival in meeting the demands of operation.

Confronted by an aggressive executive demanding special service, the foreman would look about his shop for machines with jobs that could be removed with least danger of offending other executives concerned. He would "pull" the partially repaired job of some less bellicose supervisor and replace it with that of the demanding head.[2]

This problem led to a good deal of discussion within local management ranks and between the top local management people and men from the central office.

Working with the main office, top local management developed a two-point plan to deal with the problem. One part of the plan was the installation of a piecework incentive system for maintenance workers—

---

[1] New York: John Wiley & Sons, 1959.

[2] *Ibid.*, p. 34.

which will not be discussed here. The part that will receive our attention was a new organization structure and control system.

The Field Work Department was designed to take over the estimating and scheduling of all maintenance work. The staff of FWD, nearly one hundred strong, was drawn from a pool of experienced operations and maintenance men. In addition to having a general familiarity with Milo technology and production processes, each FWD man was a specialist in some aspect of maintenance work, such as boiler repair, motor repair, carpentry, and so on. The large staff was placed under a superintendent of maintenance who had earlier been in operations himself. The FWD was housed in a new building, which was isolated from other structures, so that the planners would be removed from the immediate pressures of operations or maintenance men.

The new system gave each operations department a specific annual series of numbers for use in writing maintenance orders. If one department had a series from 5,000 to 10,000, an order number anywhere within that range would identify the order as to the department of origin and place it in a time sequence, so that job 5070 would be begun before job 5071. Each order was punched on a time clock as it entered FWD, so that an order from one department would take its chronological place in line ahead of an order from another department that came in later. In other words, the scheme was designed to function completely on an impersonal basis, with order numbers and time clock numbers being substituted for personal relations.

For each job, FWD specialists in materials, routing, and machines, would estimate the cost of materials and labor and indicate the shops and routes among machines and operations that the job should follow. Before the maintenance work was actually begun, the cost estimate was submitted to the executive who had issued the maintenance order, for his signature. The order was then placed in a pouch with blueprints and instructions and sent to the shop assigned to the job or to the first point of the job. The actual cost of the job was later computed on the basis of records of materials used and labor supplied at each phase of the work.

The FWD system was remarkably successful in breaking the log jam of maintenance orders. However, the new system produced results which had not been anticipated by the plant manager and assistant plant manager.

In effect, the new system reversed the performance scores of competing groups of superintendents. In group A were those superintendents who had been most aggressive towards maintenance in the past and most successful in getting work out of maintenance ahead of their less aggressive competitors (who were also more inclined to follow the rules). Group A men now found that their actual costs were running well above estimated costs, and these discrepancies were a source of considerable embarrassment.

The superintendents in what Dalton calls group B enjoyed a sharply contrasting experience. These were the individuals who had previously exerted no pressures on maintenance and had dropped far behind in their maintenance work. According to Dalton's evidence, they seemed to be outsiders as far as the informal power system was involved. But now, thanks to the operation of the FWD system, they were not only getting their work done much more rapidly, but their actual costs were running well below estimated costs.

The group A men now began to express resentment against FWD. This began with sarcastic remarks regarding "pencil pushing," "red tape," and so on.

The group B superintendents were not as strong partisans of the new system as might have been expected, according to Dalton, because their actual job costs in some cases were so far below estimates that they too feared embarrassing questions from higher management.

What is the explanation for the discrepancies between estimated and actual costs? As I have already noted, the estimation of maintenance costs is extremely difficult, so that discrepancies will certainly be expected—but to find one group of superintendents consistently overestimating costs and the other group consistently underestimating them is unexpected.

Dalton found the explanation in the behavior of maintenance foremen. Apparently in the period before FWD, these foremen had been exceedingly resentful of the pressures that the group A operations superintendents placed upon them. They received exceedingly few favors and many threats and penalties from these superintendents. Apparently, it was only at the higher level of maintenance department management that there existed any exchange of favors with the department A superintendents. Since the group A superintendents had the most powerful positions in the informal organization of the works, maintenance department management could gain increased appropriations and other favors through cooperating with these superintendents.

Protected by FWD from the direct pressures of group A superintendents, the foremen were now in the position to pay off on some old scores. This they could do by charging to group A jobs, working time which their men actually spent on group B jobs.

As the pattern of excess costs for group A superintendents developed, those individuals naturally became suspicious and began to investigate. While they were not able to prove the existence of a general pattern, they did discover several cases of improper charges and used these with top local management to discredit the system. Apart from these few cases of proven violations, the group A superintendents were no doubt able to gain additional support for their point by view by pointing out that the very inaccuracy of cost estimates by FWD was evidence of inefficiency. The FWD organization was set up to provide better cost estimates as well as to provide for better scheduling, so that the gross inaccuracy of the FWD cost estimates became a source of embarrassment to the proponents of this system.

The fight over FWD also became involved in a problem of maintenance piece rate incentives. These had been introduced, at the same time as FWD, as another means of speeding up the work. The speed with which the incentives were introduced resulted in an unusually large number of "loose" rates being established. Group A superintendents attributed some of their cost problems to this source also. They were unable to get the incentive program thrown out, but the FWD did fall before their attack.

For some time several of the departments had had their own small maintenance crews to handle simple repairs that needed to be done quickly. Now top local management decided to place large crews within the departments to handle all maintenance problems. FWD was reduced to a "skeleton crew" of less than a dozen men, and its personnel was absorbed elsewhere in the plant. Relatively large maintenance groups were then attached to each of the major operating departments and placed under the direct control of the departmental management.

Friction between maintenance and operations now shifted to within the operating departments. Dalton reports this complaint by an operations foreman:

> It was bad enough when we had to put up with central maintenance. We at least felt free to run our production the way we wanted to. Now it's worse than ever. Higgins comes around and sticks his nose in to tell you your men aren't taking care of the equipment. He thinks they should work with one hand and hold an oil can in the other. He tried to tell me last week when we had a breakdown, that it was my fault—that I hadn't let the line stay down long enough the last time to let him do a good job! What the hell does he expect? That line is supposed to be moving, not standing idle. He comes nosin' around and tries to pass the buck. Jesus Christ! I know my equipment. We never had any trouble in here till they sent him over from the shop.

The following day Dalton encountered the maintenance foreman and opened the conversation by saying that he had heard that the two men had had an argument the day before and wondered whether the production foreman had landed any punches "below the belt." The maintenance foreman replied in this way:

> You're damned right he did! That's the only way he knows how to fight. He skips on his maintenance costs to get a little extra production. Hell, he could get a damn sight more production if he'd keep his line lubricated. Go over and look at his cranes—the wheels and gears shine like the sun!
> In the long run he's going to get less production and more costs. But you can't tell him a damn thing. He knows it all. I came out a while last night to see that everything was all right. And it's a damn good thing I did. I saved him a thousand dollars in maintenance costs by spotting the leaky line and defective gauge on his ——— tank. He might have had a blowup with lost time cases. And if he hadn't, he'd at least have damaged enough material so that

the reprocessing would have cost over a thousand dollars and would have cut hell out of his production. And that's not all. He's in the hole on his costs now —I saved him from an ass-eating. But hell, he never has a kind word for maintenance, and least of all for me. It's always "gimme, gimme," with nothing ever coming back.

When these frictions came to the attention of management at higher levels, the assistant plant manager suggested that in the future responsibility for maintenance costs would rest with the maintenance foreman. This encouraged operations people to give even less thought to maintenance and to concentrate on production regardless of cost.

We have now followed maintenance foremen through a complete cycle. Our story began before FWD, when they were the harassed victims of the aggressive operations superintendents. FWD gave the maintenance foremen protection from these aggressions and put them in a real power position so that they could markedly affect the performance records of the various operating departments. Having used their power with more freedom than discretion, they found themselves at last shorn of the protection of FWD and placed under the direct control of operational management.

While this is the end of our present story, there is no reason to believe that this cyclical rise and fall of maintenance in relation to operations may not have continued in this organization and is not to be found in many another. Our data suggest that the relations between operations and maintenance are often fraught with friction and instability.

### CONCLUSIONS

Let us see now what general conclusions we can draw from these cases, focusing particularly on the relations between maintenance and operating organizations.

We see first a problem in the evaluation of the two activities.

Although maintenance is essential in most companies, it is usually thought to be of less importance, and therefore of lesser status, than operations.

There are other differences in the evaluation of activities not directly related to status. As Dalton points out, the maintenance men tend to view their work from a craft point of view, which means that they place particular weight upon the way work is done. Operations people tend to emphasize the end product and to be impatient with the maintenance man's concern for the proper care of equipment and the proper operating methods.

We see status problems also in the characteristics people bring to their jobs. In general, the maintenance people tend to have somewhat lower educational backgrounds and community status than men at the same level in operations. This makes it easier for outsiders to establish control over what would seem to be maintenance functions, and more difficult for maintenance supervisors to initiate activity toward these outsiders. This we have seen in the standardization case of the Overseas Corporation, where the important functions of choosing materials and equipment for maintenance work were strictly limited by controls established outside of the maintenance organization. We encountered consistent and bitter complaints from maintenance people regarding their inability to initiate for these outsiders.

While we encounter problems of low organizational status in maintenance in all of these cases, we see one significant difference between the Overseas Corporation and the Milo Corporation in this respect. In Milo the maintenance shops constituted just a small part of a large complex of plants, with most of the activities being concentrated in production. This may help to explain why the FWD collapsed at Milo, whereas the Area Coordination System survived at Overseas. We have noted the resentments the maintenance supervisors expressed toward the Area Coordination System and their sentiments favoring continuation of the system. Presumably the supervisors within maintenance at Milo also favored the continuation of FWD. The difference was that at Milo the production superintendents were in a sufficiently powerful position to undermine FWD, whereas only one third of the personnel of Overseas Corporation in this area was devoted to operations, which gave the top operating people less opportunity to exercise influence upon the high level managerial decisions that would have been necessary to change the organization structure.

Also, the nature of maintenance activities generally tends to place operations in the position of initiating activity for maintenance. This also tends to fix the status of maintenance below operations. When Group A consistently initiates for Group B and Group B has little opportunity to initiate in return, we find people evaluating Group A as having higher status than Group B.

If we were dealing with only one operating department and one maintenance shop, this pattern of one-way initiation might be expected to stir negative sentiments of maintenance people toward operating people, but it would not give rise to the serious problems of coordination we have seen. When several operating groups are trying simultaneously to initiate activities for maintenance, serious problems of coordination do arise. Given the pattern of rare initiation of activity, together with the low status accorded to maintenance, a situation results in which it is difficult for maintenance people to resist the pressures placed upon them and to establish their own independent system of priorities.

The establishment of the Area Coordination System and of FWD both had the same effect in one respect: They blocked off direct initiations from operations to maintenance. The new approach still provided for one-way initiation of activities, but this time from the planning group to maintenance. We have noted in the Overseas case, however, at least one example where a planning man and a maintenance supervisor developed a reciprocal relationship and positive sentiments toward each other instead of the negative sentiments that generally prevailed in such a relationship. This provides us with an example of a phenomonon we have often noted: The parties involved reorganize their activities and interactions together, so that they work out a harmonious adjustment when strict adherence to management's plans would cause conflict. As I took leave of the Overseas Corporation, management was just beginning a study to discover the nature of these informal adjustments and to find ways that the formal organization structure and established procedures might be modified so as to promote such adjustments rather than just leaving them to chance.

Through what channels were sanctions exercised? Here we only have data from the Milo case. We have seen how the powerful group A superintendents were able to initiate activities with a high degree of success upon maintenance foremen because the group A people were thought to be highly influential in determining the size of the maintenance budget and in decisions regarding advancement of personnel within maintenance.

The symbols of organization performance played an important role in the changes observed in the FWD case. An operating superintendent was evaluated by his superiors partly in terms of maintenance costs. Before FWD, the high status group A superintendents were in a favorable position to get favors from maintenance which resulted in a good maintenance cost record. Under the FWD system, their favorable cost position was suddenly reversed and this generated activities which eventually led to the abandonment of FWD.

Possibilities for reciprocity differed at different organizational levels. Before FWD, there was a well-established exchange of favors between group A operating superintendents and the maintenance superintendent. This exchange did not involve the maintenance foremen, who only received negatively valued activities from the group A superintendents. In terms of our theory of exchange, we might say that upon the installation of FWD the maintenance foremen owed some negative activities to the group A superintendents. They proceeded to express their negative sentiments through these negative activities, thereby threatening the status of the group A superintendents—and thus indirectly bringing down the FWD.

# Chapter 27 *ENGINEERS AND THEIR INNOVATIONS*

WE FIND engineers almost everywhere in American industry. They are influential figures in most organizations and dominant in some. We cannot begin to give a comprehensive treatment to the role that engineers play in industry, but this chapter should serve to indicate some of the human relations problems involved in engineering activities.

First we should note a terminological problem. When people speak of engineers, it is not always clear to what they are referring. The word "engineer" is used in two senses. In the professional sense, it refers to a man who has a college degree in engineering. In the functional sense, it refers to men who are carrying on engineering activities in industry. Many—but not all—of these will be professional engineers. At the same time, there are many professional engineers in industry who are no longer doing technical engineering work, but are carrying on supervisory or managerial jobs.

In this chapter, I shall be concentrating upon technical engineering activities and the way they are integrated into the operations of a firm.

The engineer, in his engineering function, is one of the chief innovators in industry. In this chapter, we shall examine in detail one such innovation, from the original idea to commercial production. This is the story of the Amicon tube.[1] The first problem was to design the tube. Then a model had to be built. The final steps involved setting up a production line, determining the job methods involved in producing the tube, and getting the line running to produce the tube on a mass basis.

The first step was taken in August, 1948. It was not until January, 1950, that the project was functioning on an efficient mass production basis. How long a time should be allowed between the first design work and the establishment of efficient production depends of course upon the complexity of the technical problems involved. The Ronken and Lawrence book gives us no evidence of this nature. However, the report contains considerable evidence of failure to develop an effective social

---

[1] This discussion and analysis is taken from Harriet Ronken and Paul Lawrence, *Administering Changes: A Case Study of Human Relations in a Factory* (Boston: Harvard University Graduate School of Business Administration, 1952).

process. Our assumption, therefore, is that if the social problems of introducing the new product had been more effectively handled, it would have taken management and workers a much shorter time to solve the technical problems.

Let us first review the chronology of events in this case.

## FRED FISHER'S GROUP

The idea for the Amicon tube was the brain child of an industrial engineer, Fred Fisher. Ordinarily, the industrial engineers began work when the product had been designed by the development engineers. It was then the task of the industrial engineers to establish the methods of production, to design the production line, and so on. In other words, the usual sequence of activity began with the development engineers, with the industrial engineers coming in next, and the product being finally turned over to the manufacturing organization.

However, since Fred Fisher himself sold the idea of the Amicon tube to management, he was given the responsibility of doing the developmental work. In August, 1948, he began experimental work in his own small cubicle, assisted by George Ames, who was also an industrial engineer.

By November, experimentation had proceeded to the point where a pilot production unit could be established. Claire Cochrane and Alice Nagle were hired as workers for the new unit and the project was given a small workplace on the factory floor.

From November to February, 1949, Fred, George, Claire, and Alice worked closely together. They were working on the same body of activities; they were interacting almost constantly within the group, but only infrequently with people outside of the group. Furthermore, relations were not structured along the usual authority lines. Fred encouraged the girls to make criticisms and suggestions regarding any phase of their work. They responded by displaying considerable initiative and developing a very keen interest in their work.

As we should expect, this pattern of interactions and activities led to strong positive sentiments of the girls towards the engineers, particularly toward Fred Fisher. The girls also identified themselves strongly with the company, taking great pride in their own contributions to it. The work they were doing received far more attention from higher management than did the work of other girls of the same seniority and rate of pay. Fred Fisher responded to the sentiments of the girls with sentiments favorable to them. He had a high regard for their intelligence, initiative, and dedication to the project—and let them know it.

## GOING INTO PRODUCTION

On February 7, 1949, higher management made the decision to put the Amicon tube into production. Fred Fisher protested he had not had time to work all of the bugs out of the operation. Management was nevertheless impatient to push ahead.

Lou Corriveau was selected as foreman for the new line. At first he was to supervise only Claire and Alice, but new girls were to be added to the line as soon as he was ready.

Fred Fisher was given the responsibility of telling the girls that they were now under Lou's supervision. Fred commented to the researchers that this was "just a paper change," and at first he continued to interact with the girls almost as much as before.

When Lou was given the new job, he was told that this was his chance to "get somewhere" in the company. He naturally felt that his success would be measured by the productivity of the new unit and was impatient to get ahead with it.

At first, the Amicon tube appeared to be only a minor part of Lou's responsibilities. He retained the duties and title of foreman of an established production line in the neighboring work area. Apparently management people assumed that it would take only a small amount of Lou's time to supervise just two individuals; therefore they felt no necessity to relieve him from the other production line until the Amicon tube line had a few more girls on it.

Low now found himself in a difficult situation. He felt completely at home on his old production line and was well accepted by the girls there. His duties on that line could easily fill up his day and there was a natural tendency for him to spend time in the area of his customary pattern of interactions and activities.

Lou realized that his progress required him to spend increasing amounts of time with the Amicon tube project, but Fred Fisher appeared to be in control there as much as before. Lou recognized that the girls were strongly loyal to Fred and regarded the foreman as an outsider. Furthermore, Lou found the process of production much more complicated than he had been led to expect, and he recognized that Claire and Alice knew a good deal more about it than he himself did. How could he supervise two girls when he did not have the knowledge necessary to direct their production activities? In a large department, a foreman may be able to maintain his position when some workers have more technical knowledge than he does, providing he can handle adequately the problems of organizing the work of the department. But when he is dealing with only two people, the problems of organization can hardly justify full-time attention. Technical production problems dominated the situation on the new line at this point, and here Lou was at a decided disadvantage.

When Lou did appear on the scene, he had the impression that the girls were paying little attention to him and continuing to seek guidance from Fred Fisher.

In response to a complaint from Lou, Production Manager Davis

ordered Fred Fisher to stop dealing directly with the girls. Any concern
he had with the line was to be taken up through Foreman Corriveau.

Almost immediately after this order, Claire was absent for an extended period and Alice continued to work on her own. Her production
decreased greatly, and she claimed to find the materials unsatisfactory.
She complained to Fred, not to Lou.

Lou's next moves against Fred Fisher occurred during the meetings
of the "Amicon Tube Management Team." Beginning in February,
1949, weekly meetings of this management group were held for the
purpose of discussing progress of the project and any problems connected with it. As these meetings proceeded, it became apparent that
the tube production was not moving ahead as rapidly as higher management expected, and the discussions naturally appeared to revolve
around the question of whose fault it was that progress was so slow.
Lou argued that most of his difficulty stemmed from the lack of adequate tools and supplies—these being the responsibility of the industrial
engineers. He also complained that the industrial engineering studies had
rated the "spacing" job as less skilled than Lou felt justified, so Lou was
anticipating later difficulties with workers that he might bring to the
job.

During the management meetings, Fred lost further ground to the
design engineers. He had been carrying on the "grid experiment,"
which he hoped would lead to some solution of the production problems
of the line. Keller, chief of the Industrial Engineering Department and
Fred's immediate superior, ruled that this experiment should be turned
over to the development engineers. Presumably this decision arose out
of protests from the development engineers that industrial engineers had
taken over developmental work.

Before moving on, let us give more detailed attention to the weekly
meetings of the "Amicon Tube Management Team," for they had important effects on the social atmosphere of the production lines. The
most remarkable features of these meetings were the number of people
present and their ranks in the organization. In the first meeting attended
by Lou Corriveau, the following individuals were also present: Barnes
(plant manager), Heity (production control chief and chairman of the
committee on the Amicon Tube Project), Davis (production manager),
Keller (chief of Industrial Engineering), Fisher and Ames (industrial
engineers), Parent (development engineer), McKay (chief of purchasing), Downing (chief of personnel), Quigley (chief of accounting), plus
five staff specialists who are not otherwise identified by the researchers.
Sixteen people, many of them of high rank in the organization, were
involved in this discussion. No one could say that the Amicon Tube
Project was not receiving management attention.

The authors make these observations regarding the conduct of this
particular meeting:

1. Most of the talking was done by high-ranking management officials. Lou and Fred spoke only in response to occasional questions directed at them.

2. Production Manager Davis expressed interest primarily in production schedules.

3. Keller, Heity, Quigley, and Parent contributed technical engineering ideas. Lou and Fred, the men closest to the technical problems, were not asked for such ideas and did not volunteer them.

4. Heity asked the industrial engineers about industrial engineering aspects of the project, although they had been involved in all phases of the project up to this point.

In all of February, only 198 units were produced, and yet 7,500 were scheduled for March; 800 were actually produced.

The development engineers now began to become more active on the project—but with little immediate success. Dick Gantos asked Alice to try out on the line an experiment that had already been tried and discarded by Fred Fisher. Alice responded with apparent reluctance, and Gantos could not tell whether the failure of the experiment was due to technical imperfections or to a lack of effort on her part.

Now at last Lou was relieved of responsibility for his old line and free to spend all of his time on the Amicon tube. Lou greeted this change by staying overtime for a number of nights so that he could make tubes himself without being observed by Alice. He kept at this until he finally felt quite competent at it and was able to increase his confidence for handling the project.

At this point Claire returned to work, and the two girls were back together again. Claire found out that she was unable to work with acid, so "spacing" was taken away from Alice and assigned to Claire. Spacing had come to be thought of as the prestige part of the job, and Alice resented being put on "little jobs." Now for the first time there arose friction between Alice and Claire. Claire resumed her frequent interactions with Fred; Alice, for the first time, began to approach Lou, for which she received his encouragement.

Fred now reported to the researchers that he felt "frustrated" and "blocked."

During April, production rose to 2,500 units—but 20,000 had been scheduled.

April was marked by two important management changes. Metcalf succeeded Barnes as plant manager, and Hurtig replaced Davis as production manager. Lou had the impression that neither Metcalf nor Hurtig considered the Amicon tube an important project. Lou's first reaction to these changes was a greater feeling of insecurity. But the lessening of top management's interest perhaps opened up the way to progress that was not possible when so many management people were expressing such a vital concern.

At last the production line began to expand. Lou brought in three girls who had worked with him on the old production line. He considered them more capable and cooperative than Alice and Claire. Naturally he felt more secure with them, and the researchers had the impression that he was beginning to relax and appear more confident.

Alice began to make friends with the new girls on the line. As they had favorable sentiments toward Lou, her own sentiments began to change. The observers reported that she no longer was constantly criticizing Lou in conversations with them. Her interactions with Fred Fisher also decreased sharply. Claire became more hostile to Lou and Alice.

At this point Fred tried to get Lou to accept the machine that he had developed for the production process, but Lou continued to insist that it was unsatisfactory. Trying to make good the technical deficiencies, Lou began working on them himself.

In this period, friction between the development engineers and the industrial engineers came out into the open. Fred confided to the researchers that he thought that Development Engineer Gantos was deliberately sabotaging the efforts of the industrial engineers. Vronska, a mechanic working for Fred, accused Gantos of this to his face.

Heity, head of production control and chairman of the Amicon tube team, now became very concerned about the obvious friction among the groups concerned with the project. He urged the production, industrial engineering, and development engineering people to cooperate, but what this meant other than that they should all say favorable things about the progress of the project was not clear to anyone. Lou interpreted Heity's statements as simply a demand for increased production.

In May, 5,000 units were produced—still far below management's expectations.

Claire now requested a merit increase in pay. Lou discussed the matter with Personnel Manager Downing and Production Manager Hurtig, and they agreed to turn her down on the grounds that her performance was not exceptional enough for this "out of season" attention. Note that in the early period of the four-man group, Claire had been considered an exceptional person by all concerned with the project. The change in sentiments toward Claire followed upon the changes in interactions and activities we have noted.

In the early period, Claire had looked upon the Amicon tube project as belonging in part to her. Now she commented that it was "Lou's baby." Shortly after her merit increase request was declined, she requested a transfer out of the department. A month later, Claire's request was granted.

In May, Lou finally accepted the machine that Fred had been working on, and the observers noted the beginning of improvement of relations between Lou and Fred and between the two engineering groups.

This improvement was choked off by a change in organization structure introduced by Production Manager Hurtig. The production manager replaced the foreman of the nearby ignition control line with a new man who had considerable production experience. Lou now heard indirectly that he was supposed to report to this new man instead of directly to Hurtig. Hurtig felt that the new man would be able to give Lou more help on the project, but, strangely enough, he made no effort to explain this to Lou, and Lou naturally looked upon the move as a demotion for himself.

Lou now complained to Production Manager Hurtig that Fred Fisher was again on the floor too much. The complaint went from Hurtig to Chief Industrial Engineer Keller. Keller passed on the criticism to Fred, who was very upset about it. Lou reported later the impression that Fred was now beginning to become more cooperative.

In June, 100,000 units were scheduled, and production came to only 3,000, a substantial drop compared to May.

Fred now told the researchers that he was making a deliberate effort to improve his relations with Lou. He did this by building up the frequency of his informal interactions—contacts when he just dropped in to talk with Lou, without having anything that he wanted Lou to do. Shortly Lou was reporting that their relations were improved.

Lou was now spending more time talking with his girls and particularly explaining to them the technical details of tube production. The tube production group was expanded by the addition of four more girls. Although they were not handpicked choices from his former line, all of the girls—with the exception of Claire—were now saying that Lou was a wonderful boss. As Claire transferred out, there were no remaining points of friction between workers and foreman.

## DEVELOPMENT ENGINEERS TAKE OVER

In July, after a series of months in which production constituted only a small fraction of the production schedule, Hurtig decided that the Amicon tube was not ready for production after all. He turned the project over entirely to the development engineers and directed them to work the bugs out of it.

Lou greeted the change with a sense of relief. The removal of the impossibly high production quotas took the psychological heat off him.

This change in responsibility was accompanied by a discontinuation of the large meetings of the "Amicon Tube Management Team." Now the only ones who were meeting together were those who were intimately involved in the project: Lou and several of the development engineers. They met as a group daily for a brief discussion of progress and problems. They also interacted freely in group situations during the working day.

The development engineers were pleased by their new responsibilities and relationships. Parent, the head of development engineering, said,

"This is the sort of thing that should have been done a long time ago."

Fred Fisher was extremely annoyed by the change and confessed to the researchers that he was on the point of resigning. He said:

> The (development) engineers would not have anything to do with the Amicon tube in the beginning. They were afraid of it because they thought it was going to fizzle. Now they see it is going to amount to something and so they want to take it over.[2]

Fred Fisher withdrew from the situation in order to work on another project. Perhaps Fred's involvement in activities and interactions away from the Amicon tube project enabled him to view that project with more detachment. In any case, about six weeks later he was saying to the researchers that perhaps the behavior of the development engineers and the foreman could be accepted as legitimate. They just had a different frame of reference on these matters. In late August, Fred was offering his help to the development engineers on the industrial engineering aspects of the problem. Parent told the researchers that he thought Fred had some useful ideas after all, and he encouraged Fred's approach. The relations between the two engineering groups gradually became as amicable as they had been before the issue of the Amicon tube project.

On September 1, 1949, Fred Fisher was promoted to head of industrial engineering. Several months later, profiting by his Amicon tube experience, he undertook to work with development engineers in redefining the responsibilities of the two engineering groups. Relations between the two groups continued to improve.

On December 1, the production organization was once again made responsible for the Amicon tube. By January of 1950, production at last reached the level considered reasonably satisfactory by higher management.

It is fitting to end our story with Fred Fisher's perception of the situation in early 1950. At that time he told the observers that industrial engineers really had no business doing research on product development. He stated that it would have been better if he had been made to report to the development engineers during his months of research on the Amicon tube project.

Note that Fred's point of view on the role of the development engineer shifted with changes in his pattern of interactions and activities. Throughout the time when industrial engineers were in fact competing with the development engineers for control of the project, Fred's sentiments toward the development engineers were highly negative. When the development engineers were given full control over the project, Fred spoke most bitterly of their motives and was on the verge of resigning. As he became involved in interactions and activities on an-

---

[2] *Ibid.*, p. 262.

other project, his sentiments changed so that he was able to say that the development engineers had a legitimate point of view after all. When he became head of industrial engineering, he was able to initiate interactions and activities to the head of the development engineers, as well as to respond to Parent's initiations. Fred at last came around to the view that the way the project had been initially organized was basically wrong and that his once deadly rivals should have had control from the beginning.

## ANALYSIS

Why did it take so long to get the Amicon tube into production? Was this a case of resistance to technological change? Calling it resistance is an oversimplification. Calling it technological is also an oversimplification.[3]

The slow progress from idea to product may be explained in terms of three areas of disturbance: (1) among engineering groups, (2) between engineering and production, and (3) between higher and lower management. Let us examine each area in turn.

1. *Among engineering groups.* In this company, as in others, there was a customary work flow among engineering groups. The development engineers customarily carried the process from initial idea through drawings, the construction of models, and testing of those models. It was only when the development engineers thought that they had an item about ready for production that the industrial engineers came in. It was then up to the industrial engineers to adapt the model for production, to design the production lines, and to work out the methods of production. This customary flow involved the development engineers to some extent in telling the industrial engineers what to do, while industrial engineers told the foreman what to do.

This flow also helped to establish the relative status positions of the two engineering groups, with the development engineers occupying a markedly superior status. Perhaps this had something to do with the desire of the ambitious young industrial engineer to undertake the development work.

As the tube project was initially organized, the development engineers were by-passed altogether. When they were finally brought in, it was first to test the equipment developed by Fred Fisher. In the normal sequence of development activities, testing comes toward the end. The tests showed that the equipment was faulty. Fred countered with the claim that the tests had been improperly carried out. This conflict is an interesting example of the way in which men can disagree about even

---

[3] For some of the main points in this analysis, I am indebted to Michael Stewart. See his "Resistance to Technological Change in Industry," *Human Organization*, Vol. XVI, No. 3 (1957).

apparently scientific data when their customary relations have been disturbed.

2. *Between engineering and production.* The flow of work from engineering development into production involves a series of transition points at which changes in interactions and activities are required of the participants. The efficiency of the process will depend in large measure upon the smoothness with which these transitions are worked out. In this case, higher management either overlooked the necessity of these transitional adjustments or else assumed that they would take place by management order. In any case, management made no provision to facilitate these transitions, so that we see outbursts of negative sentiments at each transition point and many evidences of technical inefficiency. Following are some of the transition problems encountered from the beginning and on into production.

Let us begin with the closely knit original four: Fred and George, Claire and Alice. They carried on their activities together and interacted with a high frequency. Fred encouraged the girls to take initiative in proposing activity changes. The predictable result was strongly favorable sentiments among the members of the group to each other and a strong identification of each member to the group and to the project.

When the project was turned over to the foreman, apparently no one stopped to consider the changes in interactions and activities necessarily involved for the original four and to plan how these changes might be made without an outburst of negative sentiments. As Lou came between Fred and the girls, and their established patterns of interactions and activities were thereby disrupted, the development of negative sentiments of the girls toward Lou and of Fred toward Lou was a natural and a predictable outcome.

Now let us examine the problem Lou faced in establishing his supervision over the project. He enjoyed the positive sentiments of the girls on his old production line, where he continued to feel secure. As he was placed by higher management in between Fred and the girls, he recognized the negative sentiments they came to hold toward him. This led him to want to avoid the situation altogether, and yet his future depended upon mastering it. Mastering it came to mean in his own mind gaining control of the project away from Fred.

In this early period, Lou faced severe technical problems, for he simply did not know enough about production of the tube to initiate activity changes for the girls. The only one who had the organizational position and the requisite knowledge to help Lou master the technical aspects of the job was Fred Fisher. What was technically possible become socially impossible. Given the prevailing negative sentiments between the two men, Lou could not bring himself to ask for help from Fred and any offer Fred might make to help would have been looked upon by Lou as a maneuver to resume control of the project.

This case also illustrates a failure in the integration of technical and practical knowledge, a problem we have discussed in Chapter 21. No plans were made to help Fred Fisher to impart what he had learned to the foreman or to help the foreman communicate his knowledge of operations and supervision to Fred, so that the two together might integrate the different types of knowledge.

3. *Between higher and lower management.* In this case, neither Fred Fisher nor Lou Corriveau felt that he received any help from higher management. Both men regarded higher management simply as a source of pressure. What happened to give these men the impression of pressure? The management meetings and the symbols of organization performance were two of the major sources of perceived pressure.

The so-called management team was entirely too large to make for an effective problem-solving discussion. As we have seen in the John Dyer case (Chapter 24), it may be appropriate to bring together sixteen or more men from time to time to present information or to arrange for an exchange of ideas. Sixteen men can hardly be an effective working group.

Lawrence and Ronken point to an interesting correlation between the organizational status of the individual and his participation in discussion in these meetings. The higher his status, the more the man had to say. This meant that the men who were actually working on the problem and knew most about it contributed least to the meetings. In effect, higher management people were simply talking at Fred and Lou without providing a setting within which they could effectively respond.

The symbols of organization performance are here represented by the estimates higher management made each month for the production that was to be achieved in the following month. We have noted that these symbols were ridiculously out of line with reality—that the department did not for many months come anywhere near meeting the standards set.

Why did higher management set such high standards? What functions did those symbols serve?

For higher management, we may interpret the setting of the high estimates as a means of relieving anxieties they felt regarding the unsatisfactory performance up to each time of estimate setting.

In primitive societies, magical practices have this function of relieving anxiety in the face of the unknown and apparently uncontrollable. Facing the uncertainties of the present and the immediate future, without any concrete and obvious means of changing the world around them, primitive people engage in magical practices. When they have carried through the magical rituals, they feel more secure and confident. So it was with the magical rituals performed by higher management in setting the production estimates.

Unfortunately, while the setting of high production estimates may have relieved anxiety for higher management, it served to intensify anxiety at lower levels. Each month higher management placed the foreman and all those associated directly with him in the project in what psychologists call a failure situation—working under goals they knew they could not reach.

## ON THE PROCESS OF INNOVATION

This analysis suggests certain ways in which the work of engineers may be organized more effectively and the process of innovation be carried through more smoothly.

The case suggests, first, that in planning for technical innovation, management should not think primarily in terms of the line of authority. Effectiveness in the innovation of new processes and products depends upon the organization of a flow of work involving the development of certain regularities in interactions and activities. At points where marked changes in interactions and activities need to take place, management must give attention to the way these transitions can be effected.

Next, the case illustrates the futility of management pressures as a means of getting things done. Attempts to initiate activities exclusively down the line of authority can hardly be effective when the problems involve horizontal coordination among various work groups and departments.

Finally, the case also suggests that symbols of organizational performance should have some relation to the real world of here and now and not be set mainly in order to make higher management feel better. How can estimates be established more realistically? In the field of innovation, no one can predict the future accurately, but it appears that higher management overlooked one step that might have made for more accurate predictions and also for better morale at the lower level. Why was the foreman never asked what he might be able to produce the next month?

# Chapter 28 COST CONTROL, PRODUCTION, AND PEOPLE

BUDGETS and the budgeting process are central features of our highly industrialized society. To produce a product at a profit, management needs more than machines and technical processes. Management also needs a means of keeping score—calculating the score for the total organization at appropriate time intervals and also calculating the score for each unit making up that total, so that the contributions of the units can be evaluated.

Budgets are generally prepared annually, and they are often broken down into monthly and weekly totals. Each budget can be looked upon as a goal for the organization, as determined by top management. The goal is based in part upon past experience but also represents a projection of a future desired state of affairs. The budget may specify goals for production, labor costs, maintenance costs, materials costs, amount of waste or scrap, and so on.

In terms of our scheme of analysis, what are budgets? They are symbols designed to represent a planned state of organizational performance. The symbols have effects upon the sentiments of people and in turn affect their activities and interactions. In this way, the impact of budgets is felt throughout the social system even by those who give little direct attention to budgets. The purpose of this chapter is to explore some of the ways in which budgets affect sentiments, interactions, and activities in the social system.

Most of the material in the present chapter is drawn from *The Impact of Budgets on People*.[1]

## WHAT DO BUDGET SYMBOLS MEAN TO PEOPLE?

In a study of four plants, Argyris and Miller asked each factory supervisor to name the department which affected him most and then the

---

[1] Prepared by Chris Argyris for Controllership Foundation, Inc., under the direction of Schuyler Dean Hoslett, with the assistance of Frank B. Miller, Jr. (Ithaca, N.Y.: Cornell University School of Business and Public Administration, 1952).

second most important department. A total of 56 per cent considered production control as most important and 44 per cent named the budget department; *all* but one supervisor who named production control first chose the budget department as the second most important department.

These sentiments should be interpreted in terms of the flow of interactions and activities within the plants. If we just looked at the efficient functioning of production departments, we might assume that their supervisors would consider the maintenance department as the most important one for them. One could argue that without efficient maintenance, production would break down. However, as a general rule the production departments initiate interactions and activity changes for the maintenance department, whereas production control and cost control constantly initiate interactions and activity changes for the production departments. The budget people also have control of one of the key sets of symbols in the organization and thereby indirectly bring rewards and penalties to the production supervisors.

How do the budget people see their own role? One man says, "If I see an inconsistency, I'll go to top management and report it. No, I never go to the supervisor in charge. It is our job to report any inconsistencies to the top management."

Another man gives this picture:

As soon as we examine the budget results and see a fellow is slipping, we immediately call the factory manager and point out, "Look, Joe, you're behind on the budget. What do you expect to do about it?"

True, he may be batting his brains out already on the problem, but our phone call adds a little more pressure—er—well, you know, we let them know we're interested.

The important thing for us to do is follow up. The supervisor's interest lags unless someone is constantly checking up on him. A little pressure. If you don't, the tendency is to lag. You can't blame supervisors. They are interested in the machines.

I think there is a need for more pressure. People need to be needled a bit. I think man is inherently lazy and if we could only increase the pressure . . . I think budgets would be more effective.

The factory managers, superintendents, and higher level supervisors see budgets in much the same light. Consider these two comments:

The job of budgets is to see to it that we *never forget* we've got a job to do. Sure, we apply pressure with budgets. I guess budgets aren't worth much unless they have a kick in them.

I go to the office and check that budget every day. I can then see how we're meeting the budget. If it's O.K., I don't say anything. But, if it's no good, then I come back here (smiles) and give the boys a little . . . Well, you know. I needle them a bit. I give them the old . . . hm . . . well . . . you know what . . . the old needle.

The factory foremen take quite a different view of budgets. Budgets represent pressures on them—that they cannot pass down to the workers.

These two comments are illustrative:

You can't use budgets with the people. Just can't do anything like that. People have to be handled carefully and in our plant, carefully doesn't mean budgets. Besides, I don't think *my* people are lazy.

No sir, I can't use budgets to increase production. I don't dare go up and say to a man, "My budget is *up* $5,000 this year, John." He'd look at me in scorn. No sir, anything like that is using a *whip*. And the men *don't like it*.

How do the workers see budgets? They often recognize that management people are worried about costs, but with the foremen afraid to put the cost situation to them, they remain uninvolved in the struggle.

## PROBLEMS WITH BUDGETS

This discussion suggests several important problems involved in the application of this set of symbols.

1. *Pressure.* The budgets are seen as sources of severe psychological pressure on the part of management people. This problem may be perhaps most acute at the foreman level, because the foreman receives the pressure and has no one to whom he can pass it on without fear of damaging reactions.

2. *Budget results indicate the score but do not reveal the plays that went into making up the score.* As one factory supervisor said:

Let's say the budget tells me I was off. I didn't make it. That's of interest. But it doesn't tell me the important thing of why I didn't make it, or how I am going to make it the next time. Oh sure, they might say all I need to do is increase production and cut out waste. Well, I know that. The question is how to do it.

3. *The goal is always rising.* As one man commented:

If I meet this budget, those guys up there will only raise it. Oh, you can't let them know that you made the budget without too much trouble. If you do they'll up it as sure as hell.

4. It is often charged that *the goal is too high*. One factory supervisor made this comment:

Budgets should be realistic. They should reflect the true picture. Take the error budget for example. There is something. The error figure is way too low. I know it. The people know it and so do the financial people know it.

So I suggested to the financial people that they should increase it. They refused. They feel that if they increase the budget to a realistic level and the people meet it, they'll have no reason to cut down errors.

We, on the other hand, feel differently. Our people see the figure and they know it is ridiculously low. So they say, "Oh, those financial guys do that so they can have the opportunity to wave the flag."

5. In many situations, *production management people do not participate in the goal-setting process.* At least this is true at the level of factory superintendent and below.

Most of the controllers interviewed spoke about encouraging the participation of the line people in the budget-making process, but they seemed to view the budget people as the active agents and the supervisory people as the passive accepters in this so-called participation process. Argyris paraphrases the comments of a number of controllers in this way:

> We bring them in, we *tell* them that we want their frank opinion, but most of them just sit there and nod their heads. We know they're not coming out with exactly how they feel. I guess budgets scare them. . . . Some of them don't have too much education. . . .

Similarly, the controllers refer to another phase of the participation process as they outline what happens when they present the budget to the supervisor:

> Then we request the line supervisor to sign the new budget. Then he can't tell us he didn't accept it. We found the signature helps an awful lot. If anything goes wrong, they can't come to us, as they often do, and complain. We just show them their signature and remind them they were shown exactly what the budget was made up of. . . .

Needless to say, the supervisor who is asked to sign on the dotted line— and knows he has no alternative—can hardly feel that he is participating in the budget-setting process.


## THE IMPACT ON PEOPLE

What impact do these problems have upon the sentiments, activities, and interactions of people?

1. *The budget man achieves his successes by pointing out the failures of departmental managements.* Note, furthermore, that these failures are not generally pointed out to the man immediately in charge of the unit. The problem is located there but exposed at a much higher level. Thus, the factory supervisor finds negative sanctions brought down upon him as a result of the checking of the budget man. There is no doubt that this system stimulates the supervisor to take budgets and costs very seriously, so that it has a strong motivating effect. At the same time, we can expect it to lead to strongly negative sentiments toward the budget people on the part of factory supervisors. We must ask: Is this a necessary price that must be paid for developing an efficient and cost-conscious organization? Or can this result be achieved with less cost of interpersonal friction and negative sentiments? This question will be discussed in Part VII.

2. *Budget and cost control procedures, as often used, tend to put supervisors in a failure situation.* In fact, some controllers and higher management people seem to feel that the only way to get supervisors highly motivated regarding costs is to have the budgets so tight that supervisors are nearly always falling at least somewhat short of meeting the budgets.

The assumption seems to be that men are naturally lazy and will relax as soon as they have reached a goal set before them. If this assumption were true, it would then follow that great care must be taken to set goals that are rarely reached.

On the other hand, if we assume that most people in industry are concerned with doing a conscientious job and would get especially strong satisfaction in meeting or exceeding the goal set before them, then it is obviously a mistake to set goals that can rarely be met.

Research suggests that constant failure to meet goals has a depressing effect upon both the morale and productivity of the individuals involved. This does not, however, suggest that the lower the goal, the better the morale and performance. People seem to perform best and to achieve the greatest satisfactions when they are called upon to put forth special efforts to meet the goal, but then do find it within their reach.

3. As often administered, *budgets promote interdepartmental friction and an orientation toward the past.* That is, budgets provide supervisors with an incentive to discover faults in other departments so that they and their departments may escape blame. Wherever the blame is finally placed, the effort to pin down responsibility involves a canvassing of past events and may divert considerable time from current activities and planning for the future.

An illustration of this effect is provided by a case presented by Argyris in these words as he describes a management meeting and the events that followed:

Present at the meeting were the supervisors of the two departments, two budget people, the supervisor of the department that supplies the material, and the top executive whom we shall call the leader.

Leader: I've called you fellows down to get some ideas about this waste. I can't see why we're having so much waste. I just can't see it.

Now (turns to one of the supervisors), I've called in these two budget men to get some ideas about this waste. Maybe they can give us an idea of how much some of the arguments you're going to give are worth.

Cost Man 1 to Leader: (Slightly red—seems to realize he is putting the supervisors "on the spot.") Well, er—we might be wrong, but I can't see how. There's an entire 1 per cent difference and that's a lot.

Supervisor A to Supervisor B: (Trying to see if he could place the blame on Supervisor B.) Well, maybe—maybe—some of your boys are throwing away the extra material I sent back to your department.

Supervisor B: (Becomes red, answers quickly and curtly.) No, no. We're reworking the extra material and getting it ready to use over again.

Supervisor A: (Realizing that the argument wasn't going to hold much water.) Well—you know—I've been thinking, maybe it's those new trainees we have in the plant. Maybe they're the cause for all the waste.

Leader: I can't understand that. Look here—look at their budget, their (trainees') waste is low.

The meeting continued for another twenty minutes. It was primarily concerned with the efforts of Supervisors A and B to fix the blame on someone except themselves. The leader terminated the meeting as follows:

Leader: All right, look here, let's get busy on this—all of you—all of us, let's do something about it.

Supervisor B left the meeting, flushed, tense, and obviously unhappy. As he passed through the door, he muttered to himself, "Those g—— d—— budgets!" (Note that the budgets are immediately blamed for the unhappiness.)

Supervisor B hurried down to his area of the plant. He rushed in the office and called his subordinates abruptly—e.g., "Joe—get over here—I want to speak to you—something up."

The subordinates came in, all wondering what had occurred. As soon as they had all assembled, the supervisor started:

Supervisor B: Look, we've just got to get at this waste. It makes me look like ——. Now let's put our heads together and get on the ball.

The supervisors set to work to locate the causes for the waste. Their methods were interesting. Each one of them first checked to see, as one of them put it, "that the other guys (departments) aren't cheating us." A confidential statement finally arrived in Supervisor B's hands from one of the subordinates to the effect that he had located the cause for waste in another department.

Supervisor B became elated, but at the same time was angry at the fact that he had been made to look "sick" at the meeting with the leader.

Supervisor B: . . . I'm going to find out why they are making the waste. I don't mind taking a little ——, as long as it's me that's doing the trouble.

Supervisor B roared out of his office and headed straight for the office of Supervisor A, where the confidential sources had reported the waste. Supervisor A saw him coming, and braced himself for the onslaught.

Supervisor B: ——, I found out that it's your boys causing the waste. ——, I want to know why——. . . .

Supervisor A: (Cuts off Supervisor B . . . spits out some tobacco and says)—Now, just hold on to your water. Don't get your blood up. I'll tell you. . . .

Briefly, we have tried to show, by a running account of one small problem, the effects budgets can have upon people. In this cost-conscious plant, five or six people on the supervisory level spent many man-hours trying to place the blame on someone else.

4. As usually administered, *the budget process does not involve workers*. As the foremen point out, it is probably fortunate for management that the process does not reach workers—as it is ordinarily carried out. If the foremen did indeed transmit to workers the cost pressures they themselves feel, the losses incurred by management would certainly outweigh any gains that could be made. On the other hand, the behavior of workers is certainly of great importance in creating the figures that the budget

process reports. Therefore, it does seem ironic that workers are left out of the process altogether. We may ask whether there might not be some way of involving workers in the process without incurring the losses that would normally be expected.

## THE BUDGET-MAKING PROCESS

The process by which the budget is made up has important consequences for the reactions of operating people to that budget. Let us consider two contrasting cases.

The first is taken from the company in the Argyris-Miller study, where production supervisors reported feeling under the most extreme budget pressures. Here we found a common belief that accountants were running the company. In fact we found that a very high proportion of the men in top management were accountants by educational background.

Let me digress to point out the general significance of this phenomenon. While most large companies recruit men of a variety of educational backgrounds and promote to higher management levels men from the several functional specialties, we often do find that one particular category of men has much more than its proportionate share in the higher positions. Thus we find members reporting that company A is run by engineers, company B by salesmen, company C by accountants, and so on.

The effects of such a promotional emphasis may go far beyond the careers of individual members. Men of a given category are likely to see the organization and its problems in similar ways, and when they hold the dominant positions, they are able to impose their own views upon the structure and procedures of the organization.

In the accountant-dominated company, the controller in the main office was naturally a powerful figure. Furthermore, his power extended into every plant. Reporting directly to the controller, and independent of the plant manager, the plant controller was responsible for the direction of the plant office and also for the budgets for office and plant. The controller would hand down to each plant controller the targets they should seek to establish so that the figures for each plant would fit into the overall company budget the controller was to recommend to the president and board of directors. The plant controller would then work out the figures for departments and the plant as a whole.

In this process, the plant controller was not required to seek out the collaboration of operating management. As I have noted in earlier references to this company in Chapter 6, "Formal Organization Structure," collaboration did not generally take place, and sharp conflicts between plant manager and plant controller were commonly observed. In the one case where we found collaboration, it seemed something more than a coincidence that the plant manager himself was an accountant. While this may have helped to smooth relations between the two men, it did nothing to relieve budget pressures perceived at lower operating levels. In fact, we see the plant manager calling cost men into meetings with superintendents to help him apply the pressure to them.

In the second case, while we have much less systematic information, the process seemed to be quite different. In this company, the vice-president and controller was considered to be a staff man responsible for establishing the cost control and accounting procedures for the company as a whole. He was also looked upon as a technical consultant to the cost control people in the plant. However, each plant manager had a plant controller reporting directly to him. It was the plant manager who presented the preliminary budget for his plant to the general manager and the president of the company. At least in some cases, this preliminary budget grew out of considerable discussion that the plant manager held with his superintendents and with his controller.

The president then reviewed with his general manager the preliminary budgets submitted from the plants. He reported that he sometimes acted to tighten up a plant budget but at least as often decided that the goals set were unrealistically high and should be somewhat reduced. It was his aim to establish budgets that *could be met.* The involvement of the supervisors in the budget-making process and the establishment of goals that seemed reasonable to them combined to make them feel under less budget pressures than the supervisors in the first case reported.

# Chapter 29 *THE ROLE OF THE*
##          *PERSONNEL MAN*

WHO is the personnel man? What does he do? Where does he fit into the organization?

In this chapter, I am not trying to provide technical answers to those questions. The student must turn to text books in personnel administration to find the detailed specifications of the personnel man's job and the directions as to how he goes about developing programs of wage and salary administration, merit rating, and so on. I shall seek rather to provide a social answer to those questions: to examine the role of the personnel man and the way he plays that role in the organization.

## THE EVOLUTION OF THE PERSONNEL DEPARTMENT

Personnel departments, as we find them today, should be seen against the background of their evolution. They have arisen primarily in response to certain pressures upon the management organization. In large measure, these pressures have been generated by unions.[1]

The industrial relations department is one of the union's chief contributions to the management organization. Even some of these departments in non-union companies must be considered in large measure a response to the push of unionization. There were specialized industrial relations functionaries in the mass production industries before the advent of unions, but in most cases their activities in the twenties and early thirties were confined to the process of initial employment.

By the 1940's, industrial relations activities had expanded greatly, and the top man now generally carried the title of manager of industrial relations or of employee relations or personnel. He was still outranked by the vice-presidents of sales, engineering, manufacturing, and so on. By the 1950's, in most large companies the top industrial relations man had attained the rank of vice-president.

The union created an obvious need for the development of negotiators within the industrial relations department. In some companies with many

---

[1] The rest of this section is from my chapter on "The Impact of the Union on the Management Organization," in Conrad M. Arensberg, et al., editors, *Research in Industrial Human Relations* (New York: Harper & Bros., 1957), pp. 171–74.

plants and many different contracts, a group of men can spend all of their time throughout the year in preparing for negotiations and in negotiating contracts. But this is not all. Unions create other needs involved in the day-to-day administration of the work force.

Unions have weakened the workers' dependent relationship upon management. Years ago, many management people prided themselves upon taking personal interest in the welfare of their workers. This meant that they might grant special consideration to workers beset with personal difficulties or unable by reason of health or age to carry on their regular jobs. But these favors were generally based as much upon attitude toward management as upon need. The "loyal" employee might expect to be "taken care of," whereas there would be no favors for the "troublemaker."

Union pressure has generally put an end to this sort of situation. Unions insist that what a man receives in pay, in hospitalization benefits, in his retirement plan, and so on, shall not be subject to the discretion of management, but shall be determined by policies established to some degree through contract negotiations.

On all fronts, the union has demanded standardization, and management has had to hire specialists and develop special activities in order to meet these demands.

To justify its wage and promotion system, management has had to develop procedures for job descriptions and job evaluations. Taylor's scientific management movement began such activity before large-scale unionization, but it was immensely stimulated by union pressure.

Unions have exercised heavy pressure through the grievance procedure on matters of discipline and promotion. This has led not only to the creation of a set of functionaries to deal with the union on grievance procedures, but also to efforts to standardize management's policies and to build up the necessary paper records for dealing with the union.

In the past, management has claimed the right to promote the ablest individual, regardless of seniority. But how is ability to be determined? Before unionization, in some cases promotions simply went to the workers who were able to ingratiate themselves with the foremen. Such favoritism accounts for much of the union pressure to establish seniority as a basis for promotion. Even before unionization, many managements followed seniority in promotion in most cases, and today most managements seem willing to promote by seniority in relatively unskilled jobs. However, most managements seek to retain the right to consider ability on skilled jobs. In some cases, unions are willing to agree on this in principle, but they demand proof of relative qualifications. This has forced management to examine its jobs carefully and to keep more adequate records upon the performance of individual workers.

Unionization frequently released a flood of grievances and complaints against foremen. Often this led higher management people to see the foreman as a scapegoat for all the ills of worker-management relations. If this were true, then something had to be done to train the foreman to establish better human relations with his workers. This interest led to the widespread development of training programs in American industry. The union influence did not stop at this point, for as the more sophisticated management people began to recognize that some of the problems had their roots above the foreman level, the emphasis in training shifted toward higher levels in the organization.

Union pressure for fringe benefits created a need for a new type of specialist within the industrial relations organization: a man who knew something about principles of insurance and actuarial problems.

These new activities have led to a professionalization of the personnel field. In making its first response to the union, management often looked toward some individual whose sole or main qualification was that he got along well with people. Such an individual may find favor with workers and union officials at the outset, but management soon finds that just "knowing how to get along with people" is not enough. Including as it does contract negotiation, wage and salary administration, selection and employment, safety, merit rating, job description, job evaluation, grievance handling, training, benefit programs, and so on, the field of industrial relations has become highly technical. The industrial relations administrator does not need to know the technical details in all of these areas, but he must have a general familiarity with them sufficient to know whether his subordinates are talking sense or nonsense. Furthermore, the stakes in industrial relations have become so high that management cannot tolerate the well-meaning bungler who merely happens to "like people."

We now have college and graduate school programs designed to train men in industrial relations, and industrial relations men in industry are seeking to enhance the standing of their field through clothing it with professional regalia. While this urge toward professionalization may have some roots in a desire to add to the prestige of the field, nevertheless the job functions have become sufficiently technical and specialized to lead naturally in the direction of professionalization.

While noting the influence of unions, we should not think in terms of a simple cause–effect relationship. Before the advent of unions, there were people in management who would have liked to develop an improved human relations program but found themselves blocked by management's preoccupation with the "practical" matters of costs, technology, etc. Possible slowdowns and strikes being matters of obvious practical concern, unions have greatly strengthened the hand of many people who were privately (but ineffectually) committed to a broader social viewpoint.

## A CASE OF ORGANIZATIONAL MOBILITY

We have shown how forces outside the personnel department may serve to stimulate the growth of that department and make it possible for its leading officials to rise in status within the organization. While these forces may make such changes possible, we should not think that the changes follow automatically. A bungler in a top personnel job can retard the growth of a department—until he is replaced. By the same token, a skillful man may accelerate the growth of personnel activities and advance the status of personnel officials within management.

Let us watch such a skillful man in action. Warren Hawkins was brought in to head personnel activities for the Overseas Corporation at a time when its personnel program consisted of little more than recruitment, selection, and placement of workers.

Less than ten years later I found the company so well organized with programs thought to be representative of the most modern personnel thinking that Overseas was often referred to as a model in this field.

How did Hawkins do it?

In a sense, we might say that he was given a free hand to set up a modern industrial relations program, but he was wise enough to realize that a free hand from above can never secure cooperation from below. His first weeks and months on the job were spent in observation and consultation. He went around and talked with operating people from high to low levels about their problems and what he and his department might do to help them. On the basis of this experience he developed a list of priorities—approximately ten activities that he hoped eventually to establish. But—and this is important—he did not then start by instituting number one, which he considered the most important. The first move he made was on the point that ranked number five or six on his list: a safety program.

It came about in this way: One day, as Hawkins was talking with a key man in top management, that executive expressed great concern over safety problems. He had just heard a report from the field that a worker had been killed in an accident. At this particular time, Overseas' safety record was not good, and the executive expressed himself vehemently that these fatal accidents were occurring entirely too often. What to do about it? Through what he had learned in his period of consultation and observation, Hawkins had a plan ready, and he now laid it out on the table.

The first step would be to demonstrate top management's great concern for safety. This would be done through a series of meetings throughout the operating areas. These would be conducted by this key man, assisted by Hawkins and by the district superintendents in the particular areas. The meetings would be concerned not only with showing top management's interest but also in canvassing the men in the field for ideas regarding an action program. On the basis of what came out in these meetings, the Industrial Relations Department would undertake to develop a specialized safety program, working closely with operating management. Needless to say, Hawkins already had a number of ideas as to what would constitute a good safety program, but he withheld these until there had been a full opportunity to canvass the problem in the field discussions.

The result of this development of a safety program was a drastic reduction in lost time and fatal accidents, so that today Overseas has an exceptionally good safety record. We are not so much concerned with what was accomplished as we are with the way it was accomplished. The approach that built the safety program led to effective action in other fields also. As the industrial relations people showed that they could respond to needs expressed by operating management, they found opportunities to institute the other programs on Hawkins' original list of priorities—and still others that he and his associates conceived later.

The story of Warren Hawkins demonstrates a way in which a skillful staff man may expand the activities of his department and increase the acceptance of that department with operating management. But let us not assume that such a growth of staff activities is an end in itself. Let us now raise some questions regarding the value of the staff contribution to the organization.

## THE PARADOX OF THE PERSONNEL DEPARTMENT

Some years ago I was engaged in a study of relations within a management organization in one of the main operating areas of a large company. I encountered evidences of serious problems of internal friction and widespread statements to the effect that the morale of the lower and middle management people had sharply declined in the preceding months.

While in the midst of this study, I was invited to sit in on a day-long meeting in which representatives of the Personnel Department of this company presented for a group of visitors an account of the personnel program of the company.

The formal presentations and discussions all gave a glowing picture of the personnel program. Not only was this an outstanding program, but also it was improving all of the time.

Of course, some of this would naturally be discounted as the picture one presents to outsiders. However, as I looked around the table at the local personnel men and listened to them talk, I became convinced that they actually believed what they were saying. As I reflected further upon the matter, I found I believed it myself.

How do we explain this apparent paradox of declining management morale on the one hand and an excellent and improving program on the other? The answer becomes apparent as we note the substance of what was reported at the personnel meeting.

The personnel men pointed with pride to the safety program. My own observations indicated that their pride was well justified. I had found supervisors highly safety conscious, and the exceedingly low and declining rate of accidents was a very tangible evidence of success.

The personnel men described the suggestion program, whereby management gave out financial awards for the worthwhile suggestions that were dropped in the suggestion box. While I have never considered a formal suggestion program as a very important part of good management, there seems no doubt that, as such plans go, this was a good one. The number of suggestions submitted and the amounts of money being paid out were increasing.

The personnel men reported also on the training program for foremen. Within the preceding two years, all of the foremen in the area had gone through an extensive series of discussion meetings, examining cases and discussing principles of human relations. I could report that this had been effective at least to the extent of getting foremen to talk about human relations in terms consonant with the philosophy of the training program. Whether this program had had any effect upon changing the behavior of supervisors and their relations with subordinates was quite another question. On the other hand, research has shown that it is exceedingly difficult to demonstrate the effects of such training programs. Without having such a research measure, all I could say was that this program looked as good as any I had seen.

The personnel men went on to discuss job evaluation, wage and salary administration, and other matters much in the same terms. It was apparent that this company had all of the personnel programs that a good textbook in personnel describes, and so far as I could tell, the programs were run in the manner that the textbook specifies. The personnel men, therefore, had good reason to speak with pride of the variety and excellence of their programs.

Why then the low morale within management? The major problems here could be charged to a drastic change in organization structure that had been instituted a year earlier. The dissatisfaction was due partly to the manner in which the program was introduced. The middle and lower management people felt that the new structure and procedures had just been imposed upon them without taking into account their problems and their ideas about those problems. There were also strong feelings that the structure itself, which involved a radical change in the relations among the people, was not providing either for efficient operations or for good human relations.

What part had the personnel department played in the introduction of this new organization structure? No part at all. Higher management had sent in two engineers who were familiar with the new type of structure from past experience. These men spent some months working out plans. The top personnel man in the area knew nothing about these plans until he sat in on the management meeting at which the completed plans were announced. He played no part in this meeting except to suggest that these new men should take pains to explain the program carefully at lower levels. (It is always a safe thing for the personnel man to suggest that communication is important and more attention should be paid to it. Such a statement will always elicit agreement—whether or not any further action results.)

The personnel man, in describing this meeting to me, did not seem to be expressing any dissatisfaction with his own role and that of his department. In this particular company, there was another department which handled problems of organization structure. The personnel department kept itself busy with personnel programs.

Research has shown that organization structure, technology, and work flow have impressive effects upon the state of human relations in any organization. Thus we often find that the personnel man is assumed to have some responsibility for the morale of the organization but no responsibility for some of the major influences upon the morale.

## THE PERSONNEL MAN AS HUMAN RELATIONS CONSULTANT

It might be argued that there is another side of this picture. The personnel man is expected to be a consultant to line management on human relations problems. If he plays the role effectively, he can indeed meet some of his responsibilities for the morale of the organization.

This is true enough, but how often does the personnel man really play this role? And how effectively does he play it? My experience suggests that there is far more talk about staff advising, in this field, than there is of actual advisory behavior. What are some of the main obstacles against the utilization of this advisory role?

### 1. *The Need for Justification.*

Personnel men seem still to need ammunition to justify the value of their contribution to the organization. The production man can point to the volume of production, to costs, and so on. The engineer can point to new machines and processes developed and installed. All this is very concrete. On the other hand, the effective consultant performs in a manner which makes it very difficult to measure his contribution. He stimulates other people so that they may come to look upon some of his contributions as their own ideas—and then how does the personnel man get credit for his contribution? Furthermore, it is hard to imagine how the personnel department, in its annual report, could make a case for the value of its advice. We are inclined to expect the receiver of advice to report how helpful it was (which he often fails to do). When the man who gives advice publicly places a value on that advice, this seems boastful and is resented by those receiving the advice.

There is therefore a sense of security in personnel programs. The personnel man can report the number of training programs given, the number of supervisors involved in them, the accident record, the new wage and salary classification system, and so on. There is a natural tendency to concentrate on those aspects of the job that can concretely be reported to higher management. For the personnel man, they become the symbols of organizational performance.

### 2. *The Confidentiality Problem.*

For the personnel man to function effectively as a consultant, people must be willing to talk with him freely and frankly. Their willingness to do this will be determined in part by their estimate of what he will do with the information they give him. Will the information be treated confidentially? Just what does confidentiality mean?

This problem is illustrated by comments I received in one study from a superintendent of field operations. He explained his failure to call upon personnel men for help in this way:

> They tell me that they are just a staff organization. They are here to help you, and you are supposed to bring any problem you want to them. Several times I had a problem somewhere in my group and wanted to consult somebody, so I went up to personnel and told one of them my story. The answer I would get would be, "Let me think about that one. I'll get in touch with you on it."
>
> The next thing I would know, the big boss would call me on the phone, and he would want to know what I was doing about such-and-such. Well, I would tell him I was working on the problem and thought I had it under control. Now the first time that happened, it might have been just a coincidence. But the second time was just once too often. When things like that happen you feel that you just can't trust them. Now, I feel the less they know about my problems, the better off I am.

When I reported this incident to the personnel people in the central office (without identifying either informant or the man he complained against), the story was greeted with a great sense of outrage. Such a violation of confidences was considered reprehensible, but also extremely rare.

I wonder how rare it actually is. In this case, the man complained against was considered one of the leading district personnel men in the company and shortly went on to a higher position. His close relations with the district manager, to whom he apparently gave the information, might help to explain his advancement. I do not intend to give the impression that this passing of confidential information was a calculated move to win the favor of higher management. The field superintendent worked in a building some distance removed from the district manager and his chief personnel man. The personnel man had an office almost adjoining that of the district manager, and the two were frequently together. The district manager felt rather isolated from the field situation and looked upon his chief personnel man as an individual who really had his finger on the pulse of the organization. Given the fact that the personnel man spent much time with the district manager and little time with the field superintendent, it is easy to understand how the personnel man could let slip comments regarding the field superintendent's problems without even stopping to think of the possible effects on the field superintendent or of the problem of confidentiality.

I suspect, further, that confidences will not be respected within an organization unless certain standards regarding what is and is not confidential have been made explicit. Along with this must go a rationale for the protection of certain information. If confidentiality just depends on the personal ethics of an individual, then there are bound to be varying interpretations of what confidentiality means.

### 3. *Inspector versus Consultant.*

Who enforces personnel policy?

In one case I studied, top management became aware of certain difficulties out in the districts that seemed to stem from failures of local management to act in accordance with the contract and company personnel policies. After several problems had arisen over a period of several months in various districts, the president of the company expressed his concern to a personnel man and told him that his department should conduct an "audit" regarding the application of the company's employee relations policy in each plant.

Since the event took place in the elevator of the main office building and since the personnel man was not in charge of his department, he hoped he was safe in forgetting about it. In fact, the president took no further action to require an "audit." However, the fact that the personnel people were so concerned about the possibility of this undertaking suggests that they recognized a problem of role conflict.

It is clearly impossible to be an inspector and a consultant at one and the same time. If the functions are divided within the department so that some men are inspectors and others are consultants, will the consultants be accepted by the operating organization? Or will their identification with the inspecting department render them impotent as consultants? I do not know the answer to these questions, but any management that wishes to develop the role of *consultant* for the personnel man must also be concerned about what, if any, responsibilities he has as *inspector.*

### 4. *Training for the Consultant.*

What training does the personnel man have to serve as a consultant in human relations? He may know much of the technical aspects of personnel, but in all too many cases we find he is just a nice chap who likes people, remembers the golden rule, and is in favor of "good communication." If those items represent the sum of his human relations equipment, then it is fortunate that he has little opportunity to give advice. An advisor needs some tools to analyze the situations on which he is giving advice.

### 5. The Advisor without Data.

The accountant, the engineer, and other specialists have data that they use to back up their recommendations to management. Unfortunately, everyone in management considers himself a natural hand at human relations. Furthermore, much of the data that the personnel man has is also common knowledge to the rest of the organization, whereas the accountant and the engineer have command of data which is not known to other people until they themselves present it. How is the personnel man going to serve as an advisor to management on human relations when he has no data of his own on which to base his advice?

### CONCLUSION

In raising these questions regarding personnel activities, I have not been trying to discredit them. It seems to me that most of the activities I have noted perform useful functions for operating management. I am simply pointing out that there are other influences beyond the scope of most personnel programs which may powerfully affect organizational morale—for better or worse.

While accepted theory regarding the functions of the personnel man depicts him as playing an important role in analyzing the human relations problems of the organization, interpreting his findings to line management people, and advising them on administrative practices, I have rarely seen personnel men carrying out such functions. If they are to perform such functions, a redefinition of the role of the personnel man is necessary. The next chapter will present a case in which such a redefinition was attempted.

# Chapter 30 *AN ACTION RESEARCH PROGRAM FOR THE PERSONNEL MAN*

THIS chapter describes a program designed to create a specialist's role on organization and human relations for the personnel man.

The organization involved was a 500-room hotel in a large metropolitan center. The project had its inception some years ago, when I gave a talk in the Tremont Hotel on the findings of a research program on human relations in the restaurant industry. James Smith, vice-president, general manager, and active operating head of the Tremont, was in the audience. He was a self-made man who had worked as a dishwasher at the age of thirteen and had risen so rapidly as to become half-owner of the hotel before he was forty. Smith was a man who liked to try out new ideas, and what I had to say was apparently quite new and unfamiliar to him. Furthermore, while the hotel was immensely profitable in that war boom year of 1945, it was also beset with severe human relations problems.

Smith approached me after the meeting to talk about these problems. He told me that the hotel was currently without a personnel manager. Would it be possible for me to recommend a man who had been trained in the kind of research I was then involved in at the University of Chicago? Further conversation revealed the fact that there had been three men in the personnel manager's position in little more than a year's time, which suggested that the job was a rather hazardous one. I told him that I was not prepared to recommend anyone simply for the personnel manager's position, but that I would make him a counter-proposal. If he would agree to—and finance—an action research program, I would recommend one person to carry on the research and one to implement the action program. I would be willing to serve as director of the research and consultant to hotel management in connection with this program. Smith agreed to the proposal, and we began work in mid-July of 1945.

## THE ACTION-RESEARCH TEAM

As a result of this agreement, Meredith Wiley became responsible for the action program and received his salary directly from the hotel.

511

In view of all of the difficulties previously described in the role of the personnel man, the project initially called for Wiley to be an assistant to Mr. Smith and to have no direct responsibilities for the usual personnel functions. We began with the assumption that the routine personnel functions of recruitment, hiring, payroll, and so on could be handled in the personnel office without much attention from Wiley. This might possibly have worked if there had been an experienced personnel man on the job. Actually, the office was being held down by a secretary who had had no training in personnel work at all.

It soon became apparent that Meredith Wiley would be held responsible for the functioning of the personnel office, no matter what his title. Therefore, within a month after the beginning of the project, we arranged with Smith to have Wiley's title changed to personnel manager. For the rest of the year, then, we were engaged in exploring this new role for the personnel man.

The field research staff consisted of Edith Lentz, who spent full time at the hotel but was on the payroll of the University of Chicago— on funds provided by the hotel.[1]

We decided that Edith Lentz's field research notes should be made available to Wiley and sent to me at Chicago—but should be seen by no one else. Similarly, whatever notes Wiley was able to find time to write, under the pressure of his personnel duties, would be available only to Edith Lentz and to me.

As research director and consultant, I spent a day each month at the hotel. Miss Lentz spent two days each month at the University of Chicago, except on occasion when Mr. Wiley came down for a consultation. This meant that the research director and staff people were together every two weeks. There were also frequent communications by letter, along with research reports.

### WHAT WERE THE PROBLEMS?

The main problems of the Hotel Tremont at the time of the launching of our study can be summed up under five headings:

1. *Labor turnover.* During the preceding twelve months, labor turnover in the hotel had been 250 per cent, or slightly over 20 per cent per month. There was, of course, a wide range of variation from department to department. In some groups, such as dishwashers and miscellaneous kitchen help, the hotel was hard-pressed to keep anyone on the job for more than a few days. However the figures might have been explained, it was evident that the working force was too unstable to make for efficient operation. The high turnover was also symptomatic of a low level of employee satisfaction. Absenteeism was also a serious problem.

2. *Factional strife.* When Mr. Smith came in to take over as top

---

[1] Meredith Wiley and Edith Lentz are the actual names of the people involved. All other names are fictitious.

operating manager of the hotel, he brought with him a number of executives who had served under him in the hotel he had left. These people were widely referred to as "the Smith crowd," and those who were not a part of it assumed that this "crowd" had the inside track with Mr. Smith.

3. *Interdepartmental friction.* A hotel is a complex organism with highly interdependent departments—which, at the Tremont, were often at war with each other.

4. *Autocratic supervision.* Management's direction was autocratic at the higher levels. Some of this autocratic approach was also observed at lower levels in the organization, but many lower-level supervisors were weak and indecisive, apparently feeling caught between pressure from the top and resistance from the workers. Organizational channels were not observed—at least on the way down.

5. *Unclear lines of authority.* Many people did not know to whom they were responsible. In some cases, two or more people were giving orders—sometimes conflicting—to the same individual.

6. *Union grievances.* It was not so much existence of grievances as the lack of any adequate means of handling them that presented a problem. Stewards in the various departments felt powerless to take action, and therefore the grievances all went to business agents who had responsibilities all over the large city. These men in turn had difficulty in handling problems with hotel personnel, so that often a grievance, after a long delay, would reach the office of the hotel association, where a man who knew very little about the Tremont would try to handle it.

## BEGINNING IN FOOD SERVICE DEPARTMENTS

We began the project work within the Food Service Departments for two main reasons. In the first place, Edith Lentz and I were fresh from a year of field research studying restaurants. In the second place, we learned that two thirds of the hotel's revenues came in from food and drinks, which suggested that a start in this area would bring us to grips with important problems.

After our general introduction to the hotel personnel, Edith Lentz began work in the Coffee Shop, the lowest priced of the three dining rooms. She observed the waitresses at work and interviewed them and their supervisor to learn their conception of their problems.

On the average, the girls in this room were younger and had less restaurant experience than those in the other two dining rooms. They were attempting to cope with a steadily expanding volume of business without any formal training for the job and under heavy pressure of disapproval of Mr. Kraus, resident manager and immediate subordinate of Mr. Smith. He considered their performance inadequate and told them so flatly in several departmental meetings.

Miss Paris, the dining room supervisor, was fairly popular with most of the girls, but she was working under extreme nervous tension. She reported that she knew Mr. Kraus considered her too soft on the girls, and she was trying to speak to them more sharply about their short-comings, but this was not easy for her.

The waitresses felt that management had no interest in their problems. Symbolic of this lack of management interest was the problem of the water spigot. Every time the waitresses needed to fill up their water pitchers, they had to walk about one hundred feet from the dining room to the nearest water spigot. They had raised this problem months before but had been told that nothing could be done until the hotel's ambitious renovation program had been completed. Meanwhile, as business steadily increased, the girls had to make more and more trips to the distant water spigot at every meal.

It was not our aim to have the research findings simply presented to Miss Paris or to anyone at a higher level. Since one of the main problems involved the pattern of interaction between supervisor and subordinates, we felt it important that actions taken by the supervisor should grow out of her face-to-face discussions with her subordinates.

Armed with Miss Lentz's notes and analyses of the Coffee Shop situation, Wiley began interviewing Miss Paris and consulting with her on what she might do. When she suggested that she might try con-ducting a weekly discussion meeting with her girls—although she doubted her ability to do this effectively—Wiley encouraged her strongly and discussed with her how such meetings might be handled. He also sat in on the first meetings, so that he was in the position later to compliment her on the way she conducted them and also to provide further sugges-tions regarding techniques.

Later, the waitresses reported to Miss Lentz that their weekly meet-ings had completely changed the emotional atmosphere of the dining room. They felt under less tension and able to do a more efficient job. They also commented that improvements in the organization of their work had grown out of their discussions.

The new water spigot was the most concrete achievement. After this problem had come up during the first meetings, and after Wiley had dis-cussed it further with Miss Paris and with the hotel engineer, Wiley went directly to Smith to present the case for a spigot that would be conveniently located at the edge of the dining room. Wiley was able to make Smith see that the spigot had a symbolic as well as a technological function. As long as nothing was done about this pressing problem, the girls would be convinced that management did not really care about their problems.

Smith readily saw this point and added that perhaps the planned renovation of the hotel had been used as an excuse for failing to pay attention to immediate problems. There was no need for the spigot to await the whole program, and he ordered it immediately installed.

While relations improved within the dining room itself, the waitresses continued to complain about friction in the kitchen. Miss Paris wondered whether a discussion meeting with the chef might help. While he encouraged her to think along these lines, Wiley recognized that such a meeting would only be effective if the chef knew how to respond to the girls' criticisms. The first time Wiley discussed the possibility of such a meeting with the chef, he found that the chef had no conception of the problems of the girls or of the possibility of such a meeting. Wiley therefore let the matter rest for a short time. Only after he had had two more meetings with the chef and had discussed the matter thoroughly did he feel that such an interdepartmental meeting should be undertaken.

This interdepartmental meeting turned out to be a turning point in relations between the Coffee Shop and the kitchen. Thanks to Wiley's preparatory work, the chef entered the meeting with some conception of the types of criticisms that would be directed at him, and he was able to receive these criticisms in a receptive and unemotional manner. Wherever he could promise action to remedy a problem, he did so; later, he followed through. On some problems, he felt there was no action he could possibly take. In these cases, he responded by explaining to the girls the kitchen situation that prevented him from taking action.

Even in the course of this single meeting, a remarkable change took place. The girls began the meeting by voicing their complaints with a great deal of vigor. As the meeting proceeded and the chef responded skillfully, the emotional level of the meeting appeared to drop. The waitresses accepted without question the chef's statements in those cases where he said he was unable to act. Furthermore, toward the end of the meeting they were suggesting to each other actions they might take in the kitchen to make the job easier for the kitchen personnel. The girls testified later that their relations in the kitchen were markedly improved, and the chef spoke with great satisfaction about the improvements that he himself saw.

The roles played by Lentz and Wiley in this discussion process become clearer when we compare developments in the Coffee Shop, and between Coffee Shop and kitchen, with the situation in the Zebra Room, the hotel's top status dining room. Before Miss Lentz had had an opportunity to undertake any interviewing there, and at a time when Wiley still was a relative stranger to the department, the department head arranged a meeting at which his waiters and waitresses directed their own complaints to the chef. While they reported feeling better after this meeting, the chef felt quite bitter about the way he had been taken to task, and we were unable to find any concrete changes that had grown out of the meeting. It appeared that the waiters and waitresses, not having had the opportunity to drain any of their feelings off in interviews and in their own group meetings, had poured on to the chef such an aggressive attack that he was unable to respond as he had in the Coffee

Shop. This suggests that just calling meetings is hardly an answer.

Later in the course of the project, we found serious problems involving the food checkers and waiters and waitresses. As we found in our restaurant industry study, the checker tends to be a focal point of friction. While this is often explained as due to the personality of the given checker, we feel that the nature of the job itself can account for most of the friction observed.

The checker performs two functions, which differ substantially from one another. On the one hand, she does the clerical job of ringing up on her machine the various items on a girl's tray and recording the amount of the bill on the check given her by the waitress. On the other hand, she is an inspector, empowered by management to inspect the tray to see that the food and utensils are arranged properly, that the portion of meat has parsley on it, if that is called for, and so on. If she finds anything wrong, she can send the waitress back to the kitchen.

This combination of functions may give the waitresses little difficulty at times of slow business, but at the height of a rush hour in a busy restaurant, the situation becomes quite different. The waitresses are standing in line to get through the checker stand. The mere waiting process can allow the hot food to cool and the cold food to warm up. If, in addition, the girl is sent back to the kitchen, her whole work schedule is thrown off, and she may fear trouble with customers and her supervisor.

In the Tremont case, this particular friction point was made much more serious by a lack of adjustment to the steadily growing volume of business. Three checkers worked at one checker stand serving three busy dining rooms. In addition, the checkers answered the room service telephone and wrote the orders for that department on checks which they passed along to waiters or waitresses in that department.

A few hours of observation by Miss Lentz at the checker stand during rush periods was enough to reveal the work flow problems. In addition, she interviewed the checkers and their supervisor to get their ideas about possible improvements. Following the brief study period, Wiley began consulting with the immediate supervisor and with other management people regarding the changes that might be made. Out of these discussions, backed up by the research findings, grew two main changes. A second checker stand was established so that the traffic could be divided and rush hour pile-ups avoided. The room service telephone was located elsewhere, so the checkers were not burdened with this duty.

The effects of these changes were immediately apparent. The most experienced and efficient checker had been on the verge of quitting before this study began. Now she commented:

Honestly, you have no idea how different it is. It's just a new job altogether, that's all. It isn't only that the work is cut almost in half, either, but the confusion is so much less. You see when all the dining rooms were busy at once, before this new stand opened, half the waitresses would go in one direction when they left the stand and the others would want to go the other. They were forever getting into each others' way and we were always afraid of trays upsetting or food splashing over the dishes. Not only that, but we didn't have time to be polite to people. The room service phone would ring all the time and we were just too busy to be courteous. I admit it, I know myself I just *had* to be short with people. We tried to cut out all unnecessary work to save time. Now—oh, I feel swell today. It is like heaven, really it is.

A waitress reported the prevailing view of the waiters and waitresses in this fashion:

Say, that new checker's stand is swell, isn't it? That certainly made a big difference in our service. Gee, we used to have to stand around and all the food would get cold while we waited. Then the customers would gripe. It wasn't our fault, it was just that we had to wait out at that checker's desk. I'm sure glad this new desk is in operation.

## OTHER STUDIES

From the food service departments, the research moved on into the Housekeeping Department and then into the Front Office. I shall not undertake to review these particular studies in detail, since they involved some of the same aspects already dealt with.

The housekeeping study added one new element worthy of attention: a resolution of a problem of conflict within department management through altering the organization structure. This seemed to be an instance of "the Smith crowd" problem, since Mr. Kane had come in with Mr. Smith from the previous hotel to assume a superior position over Mrs. Grellis, the former manager of the Housekeeping Department. Miss Lentz and Wiley worked very closely with both individuals as the departmental study progressed, and they finally arrived at a solution of one of the conflict problems through a change in the structure. While Mr. Kane retained over-all responsibility for the department as a whole, he devoted his attention primarily to the house men and the cleaning of the public rooms, while Mrs. Grellis carried on the direction of the work of the maids in the sleeping rooms. Presumably this change would have been strongly resisted by Kane if it had been proposed without consultation, but the process of discussion led him to accept it and to be happy with it.

While the project undertook no special study of union-management relations, that problem area came up in nearly every department studied. As our understanding of the organization increased, Wiley was able to take initiative in the union relations, so that grievances now were brought directly to him, and he worked with the supervisors and department managers in resolving them. This new organizational procedure was greeted with satisfaction on the part of the stewards and business agents for the union and on the part of the hotel management. Grievance pile-ups were no more.

## TOP LEVEL PROBLEMS

Constructive changes in organizations at low levels usually can only be made if changes are also introduced in behavior at higher levels. At the same time, our ability to induce changes at higher levels may depend in large part upon our ability to effect constructive changes at lower levels. In a project such as this, we were working simultaneously at department levels and at the levels of resident manager, and vice-president and general manager. Since both areas of activity cannot be described simultaneously, I have begun with the departmental studies. I now proceed to describe the problems and the changes introduced at the higher levels, but the reader should recognize that we were concerned with these top level activities at the same time as we were operating directly at the departmental levels.

Smith was an impatient, imaginative, and hard driving executive. Every now and then he took actions that resulted in serious human relations disturbances, and yet it was he who brought our program in and it was his support throughout that was the necessary condition for its effectiveness.

The resident manager, Mr. Kraus, first seemed to us the primary stumbling block in our progress. A former Austrian army officer in World War I, he had later had twenty-odd years of experience with a hotel auditing firm. This had involved moving around from place to place, spending a week or two with each hotel, inspecting the books, revising the accounting and cost control system, and telling management people who should be fired or transferred. Kraus had never had to stay in an organization to carry out these changes until, shortly before we began our work, he was brought in by Smith as resident manager. A more inappropriate background of experience for management is hard to imagine.

Kraus used to spend at least half of each working day patrolling the hotel. When he observed anything not to his liking, he took immediate action, issuing direct orders to anyone from the lowest employee to his immediate subordinates and sometimes discharging employees on the spot. We found cases where the immediate supervisor of the discharged employee did not discover for several hours that the individual was not just absent.

Kraus believed that people were inherently lazy and had to have the riot act read to them every now and then, individually or collectively. To get the flavor of Kraus, consider what happened during one meeting of the Coffee Shop waitresses.

The meeting was called for three o'clock but it was twenty minutes after three when Kraus finally arrived. His face was red and he came in without a smile and started speaking before he sat down. The girls were jittery and none of them had eaten since before eleven o'clock that morning:

Kraus: Well, let's get this thing going. I have another meeting after this one. (He sat down.) We're spending a lot of money to make this place over and to improve the service to the customers. So far as I can see, our efforts have been positively wasted. We ask for your cooperation and what do we get? Nothing! This has got to stop. All of you are making good money here and you seem to think, "Why should I worry about the customers?" Things have got to change around here. This hotel is not going to be run for the employee's benefit anymore. It is a place of business and it's going to be run that way. If any of you don't like it, get out! We don't want you here! etc., etc., etc.

He went on to warn them of specific sins, such as swearing in the kitchen, forgetting to present the customers with a sales check, and so forth. With each recital of their wrongs, he would say they must do better or be fired.

After he relieved his mind, he called on Miss Paris to speak. She was trying her best to imitate his attitude, but being by nature a gentle person, it seemed completely incongruous. She said in bullying tones:

I have a setup here on the table. Please study it. Goodness knows you ought to know by now how to set a table, but evidently some of you must be reminded. Another thing, I want you to cooperate with each other more. Why can't you work together? You should help each other without being urged.

Kraus interrupted:

Don't make that a request; it's an absolute command! No cooperation, out you go. Is that clear? And don't think I don't mean it, because I do!

We were anxious to see what effect, if any, this meeting had on the Coffee Shop and so hung around to get repercussions.

The person most strongly affected by it was the supervisor, Miss Paris. She took to heart every word Kraus had spoken. Instead of being a pillar of strength and calm, which was her usual contribution to the department's welfare, she became highly nervous and demanding. Several days later, she commented:

I know Mr. Kraus was right the other day. We don't do as good a job as we should. I don't know what to do; I keep telling them over and over but they never seem to change. Mr. Kraus said we must keep pounding till the girls finally learn right from wrong. I have tried to be nice to the girls. I don't know; I just don't know. They have been so upset since the meeting the other day, and yet they have had it coming. They don't do as well as they could. Mr. Kraus thinks I'm too soft and I believe I am too, but what are you going to do?

What she did was to begin "pounding" on the girls at every possible occasion. She jumped them for lateness, for untidy appearance, for slow service. The girls in turn became jittery and began to make more mistakes than ever. All the things that Mr. Kraus had warned them specifically about, began recurring. For instance, swearing at the cooks. He had been adamant about that and had pointed his finger at one culprit, roaring, "and I mean you!" Three days later this same girl broke down in the kitchen again, got into a fight with the cooks, and ended up telling the chef off. Another waitress, who had wondered (with tears in her eyes) why Mr. Kraus had stared at her the whole time during the meeting (he hadn't), simply failed to show up for work several days later and didn't even phone in. One of her closest friends said:

That isn't like Helen. It just isn't Helenish. I was out with her last night and she seemed all right then. The only thing she said was just that there had been so much tension this week.

Asked what she meant by tension, she said:

Oh, having a person watch you all the time, that makes you nervous. It has been worse in the kitchen lately, too.

One of the most capable waitresses started going to the doctor:

It's that throat of mine again. It was all better, I thought, but I've been so nervous all week and I couldn't imagine what ailed me. Then I talked to my doctor and he said it was probably my throat so I'm going over to see him again today.

The next day this girl tripped and fell with a heavy tray of dishes. All the girls complained of tension and it was a good week before the normal equilibrium was restored.

The project's first effort to reform Kraus took place a month after work had begun. For one of my monthly visits to the hotel, Smith called a meeting of his management people and asked me to talk to the group. Ostensibly my remarks were drawn from our restaurant research, but they were specifically aimed to meet the problem of Kraus. On a blackboard, I sketched the pressures affecting the waitresses from customers, cooks, checkers, and from the whole line of authority above them. I dwelt at some length upon the nervous tension experienced by waitresses and the effect this had upon their performance as well as upon their satisfaction with the job. I emphasized strongly that waitresses needed to be relieved of pressures from higher levels and to have open to them a channel for communicating on their problems up the line.

Following this presentation, there was a group discussion. Kraus himself had little to say, but Smith strongly endorsed the point of view I had expressed, and others followed his lead.

Apparently this meeting indicated to Kraus that his reading the riot act approach was no longer in his favor. This behavior ceased. Up to this point, we had succeeded in blocking Kraus but not in rechanneling his behavior. For weeks, Wiley sought to establish a relationship such that the two men could work together. Our theory at this point was that Kraus himself had problems within the organization. Particularly, we knew that he was not a member of "the Smith crowd" and must be insecure with some members of that "crowd" at lower levels who bypassed him in reporting to Smith. We reasoned that if Wiley could encourage Kraus to talk out his problems, the two men would be able to reach an understanding.

This personnel counseling approach simply did not work. Kraus would not stand still long enough to be interviewed.

At first, Kraus had been wary of Wiley, apparently wondering what kind of a threat the new man could pose to him. When weeks passed and Wiley took no aggressive action, Kraus concluded that Wiley was a weak individual and that he need pay no further attention to him. In fact, he began telling other executives, "If you want something out of the personnel office, don't go to Wiley. He's a dope. Take it up with Miss Dickson (personnel assistant)."

Wiley at last decided to take the bull by the horns. The immediate occasion for the encounter was an order Kraus had given to transfer the Zebra Room waitresses into the King Cole Room and to transfer the King Cole waiters into the Zebra Room. It was a Kraus theory that a really high class restaurant required waiters. This move had been taken without any consultation. The waiters and waitresses who were affected were up in arms and protesting to the union. Wiley necessarily became involved in the problem at this point, but he used the problem as a means of pointing out to Kraus that the personnel department could not straighten out personnel problems when such arbitrary actions were taken without any consultation. Things would run more smoothly if the two men could work together. The meeting continued stormily for some minutes, but the final outcome was an implicit treaty of peace, with Kraus agreeing to work with Wiley. (Wiley dictated his recollection of this encounter immediately afterward, and this will appear in the appendix of the book we are publishing on the case as a whole.[2])

From this point on, Kraus and Wiley worked closely together. We cannot say that Kraus became transformed into an outstanding executive, and yet the changes achieved were indeed sweeping. No longer did he read the riot act to individuals or groups. He was now willing to let his subordinate supervisors hold discussion meetings without his presence. When he did attend, we found him actually learning to listen to what people said and to respond to their problems. Furthermore, he now observed the channels of the organization so that workers and supervisors no longer had to fear the direct intervention of the big boss. These changes in Kraus were essential for the process of stabilizing the organization and for working effectively with supervisors at lower levels.

---

[2] Whyte, Lentz, and Wiley, *An Action-Research Program for Management*, to be published in 1962.

## RESULTS

We cannot show results in productivity in such a case, for the revenues of the hotel depended to such a large extent upon the state of general business activity in the community and responded to many other factors besides the state of relations within the organization. Perhaps the most marked index of change is found in the records of the labor turnover. Within eighteen months after the beginning of the project, turnover had dropped from over 20 per cent per month to 6 per cent, at about which point it levelled off. So far as we know, other hotels in the city did not experience a similar drop in the same period, but we cannot prove this, for other hotels did not keep turnover records at that time.

Perhaps the best demonstration of effectiveness is found in the comments Edith Lentz picked up from workers right up to the top level. There was an almost universal appreciation of an improvement in the quality of interpersonal relations. People reported that their jobs were more satisfying, that they experienced less nervous tension. Without having any direct measure, Smith was convinced that these changes also contributed to better relations with hotel guests and, therefore, to the profitability of the enterprise.

## THE NEW ROLE OF THE PERSONNEL MAN

The project evolved a new role for the personnel man. On the one hand, he handled the routine functions of his office, delegating as much as possible to his assistant. On the other hand, he served as a consultant on human relations problems.

We defined human relations problems broadly. The personnel man dealt with changes in the organization structure, altering or clarifying lines of authority. He dealt with changes in the work flow and in the technology—as in the cases of the water spigot and the checker stands. He rechanneled the handling of union-management relations.

There was no formal training program in the hotel during one year of research, and yet it might be said that the personnel director was functioning as a trainer a large part of the time. The group meetings he stimulated can be regarded as training sessions. Training was by the case method, but in this instance the cases did not come from Harvard or Cornell but grew out of the research project itself. The cases discussed were those cases that immediately concerned the people carrying on the discussion. Wiley coached the supervisors so that they would be able to handle these training sessions more effectively.

Wiley and Lentz, working together, were able to provide supervisors with feedback on the effectiveness of their own supervisory efforts. For example, after sitting in on the first group discussion meetings in the Housekeeping Department, Edith Lentz interviewed a number of the maids. On the whole, they were enthusiastic about the new approach, but some of them felt embarrassed and put on the spot by certain remarks that had been made by Mr. Kane or Mrs. Grellis. Wiley was able to report to Kane and Mrs. Grellis just what it was that had upset these women—without revealing which individuals had given them this criticism. Observation of later meetings indicated that the organization of the discussion was much improved in these respects.

Looking back over this case, I would describe the personnel man's role in the following six respects:

1. *Keeping confidences.* The notes of the field researcher and of the personnel man were not available to anyone within the organization, no matter what his authority position. (Mr. Kraus made several attempts to see the notes and was refused.) Similarly, neither Miss Lentz nor Wiley ever identified a particular individual as the source of a complaint. Reports to higher management or to supervisors always involved the presentation of general ideas, distilled out of observation and the statements of individuals. If such confidential relations cannot be maintained, then employees, supervisors, and managers themselves will not be willing to talk their problems over freely with the personnel man or with the research worker.

2. *Blame or interpretation?* The personnel man seeks to avoid laying the blame for the problems he finds on particular individuals. Instead, he seeks to understand the bases of human problems and to interpret this understanding to supervisors and managers. His first responsibility is to understand *why* people behave as they do and to communicate this understanding to those having responsibility for parts of the organization.

3. *Working with the man most immediately responsible.* Wiley, at all times, worked primarily with that supervisor immediately responsible for the problem area. As much as possible, he avoided placing himself in the position of reporting errors and inefficiencies to the top. Through working closely with the departmental supervisor, he was able to help that supervisor to improve the performance of his department. Then Wiley, in reporting to the top, was able to describe progress being made as well as problems encountered. This made it possible for supervisors to look upon Wiley as someone who could help them to do a better job.

4. *Consultation with the top man.* Mr. Smith naturally wanted to be kept informed regarding the progress of his program. Wiley sought to meet this need by letting the boss know what department he was working in at a given time and what he hoped to accomplish. He sought to avoid pressure from the boss to give him information regarding the details of any given study or action program. He led Smith to expect that fuller reports would be presented when the action program was underway.

Wiley also sought to alert Smith regarding any anticipated developments of major importance to the hotel. For example, on one occasion,

Wiley advised Smith that he should be prepared for a major clash between Resident Manager Kraus and the new chef. Smith appeared to pay no particular attention at the time, but when, several weeks later, the clash did occur, Smith recalled the prediction and gave Wiley credit for it. This appeared to be a major turning point in the relations between the two men. Wiley gained prestige as a man able to foretell the future. (Actually, this was not a very difficult feat, for anyone who was close enough to observe the two men in action would have realized that a major clash was unavoidable. However, the fact that Wiley did not have a special crystal ball does not affect our analysis. The prediction had its effect.)

Wiley also sought to help the top executive to understand his own impact upon the organization. In this he was not as completely successful as in some other respects, as we shall discuss in the book on the case.

5. *Presentation of data.* With Wiley, consultation did not involve simply presentation of advice on the supervisor's problems. Direct advice from the personnel man was minimized. Instead, he emphasized the presentation of data illustrating the problems of the department. He then discussed these problems with the supervisor and encouraged the supervisor himself to suggest what might be done. In many cases, it was the supervisor who came out with an idea that formed the keystone to the action program in his department. Wiley did not aim to solve the human problems himself. His objective was to build a problem-solving organization.

6. *Responsibility for rewards and punishments.* Wiley avoided getting directly involved in the administration of rewards and punishments for supervisory and management personnel. We believed that it should be the responsibility of the operating executives to administer the rewards and punishments. Of course, our program had an important impact on the administration of rewards and punishments. As we got our program established, it became apparent that those who were able to lead their units according to the pattern we were seeking to establish would be rewarded, whereas those who did not follow the pattern would run into negative sanctions. However, it was Wiley's constant effort to help people fit into this pattern so that they themselves could earn the rewards from the operating executives.

## THE ROLE OF THE RESEARCH DIRECTOR

In the beginning the research director was vital to the progress of the personnel program. As Wiley became more firmly established, my role became less and less important. It was important that I could discuss things with Smith at a time when Wiley was still seeking to establish a sound relationship with the top man. This consultation was particularly important in meeting Smith's impatience. I had told him at the outset that it would take several months before he could see any results. Each time I visited the hotel, he wanted to know what had been accomplished. In the early stages, I sought to give him the impression that things were indeed moving even before results were apparent, and he was willing to wait and to withhold pressure from his personnel man.

The outsider also performed an important role—particularly in the early stages of the project—in giving the research worker and the personnel man some perspective on what they were doing and also some encouragement. They were at first in a very lonely situation where outside support seemed important.

I sought to dramatize for the hotel management the kind of program we were developing. The first important move came with my first management meeting in which I discussed the pressures coming down on the waitresses and thus sought to insulate them from the pressures of Kraus. Smith's strong endorsement of this presentation meant that our approach was accepted as company policy. In later meetings, whenever we had something to report from our research, I made an effort to give as much credit as possible to the supervisors and executives who had worked with us. Smith followed suit, openly congratulating them on what they had accomplished. In other words, I sought to show people that if they fitted in with the pattern we were developing, they would be rewarded. This apparently helped to assure general cooperation.

## Collateral Readings

BROWN, WILFRED. *Exploration in Management.* New York: John Wiley & Sons, Inc., 1960.
See especially Part 4, "Specialist Work."

CHAPPLE, ELIOT D., and SAYLES, LEONARD. *The Measurement of Management.* New York: Macmillan & Co., 1961.
See especially Chapter 4.

DALTON, MELVILLE. *Men Who Manage.* New York: John Wiley & Sons, Inc., 1959.
See especially Chapters 3 and 6.

DRUCKER, PETER. *The Practice of Management.* New York: Harper & Bros., 1954.
See especially Chapters 16, 17, and 23.

McGREGOR, DOUGLAS. *The Human Side of Enterprise.* New York: McGraw-Hill Book Co., Inc., 1960.

RONKEN, HARRIETT, and LAWRENCE, PAUL. *Administering Changes.* Boston: Harvard Graduate School of Business Administration, 1952.
A case study of a new product, from invention all the way into production.

STRAUSS, GEORGE, and SAYLES, LEONARD. *Personnel: The Human Problems of Management.* Englewood Cliffs, N.J.: Prentice-Hall, Inc., 1960.
See especially Chapter 18.

## Discussion Questions

26    1. As plant manager, you receive from your maintenance superintendent a proposal for establishing a program of preventive maintenance for the various production departments. For what reasons might such a proposal arise? How would you expect the production superintendents to respond to it? Why?

26    2. You are the superintendent of a new department that his been given control of scheduling of maintenance work. What steps would you take to seek to win the cooperation of maintenance foremen while carrying on the scheduling work efficiently?

27    3. Suppose you could carry out the Amicon Tube project all over again, profiting from what you have learned in Chapter 27. Begin at the point where Fred Fischer approaches you with his idea for the Amicon Tube. How would you organize the project?

27    4. John Dyer used meetings of twelve or more people to good effect, whereas the "management team" meetings on the Amicon Tube seemed to do more harm than good. How do you explain the difference?

28    5. Cost control systems, as often operated, seem to put severe pressure on production people and to accentuate intergroup competition, at the expense of cooperation. Can you think of new approaches that might reduce perceived pressure and promote cooperation—without losing productivity?

28    6. For maximum motivational effect, should a goal be (*a*) out of reach, (*b*) reachable with extraordinary performance, (*c*) reachable with somewhat above average performance, (*d*) reachable with average performance, or (*e*) easily reachable? How do you know?

29    7. We have pointed out that a management man tends to get rewarded for results that can be reported concretely and that this leads the personnel man to concentrate on *programs*. Can you devise ways in which other aspects of his performance might be made more readily reportable?

30    8. It might be argued that the Tremont Hotel action research program worked well because the organization was so disorganized when we began that anything was bound to be an improvement. Do you agree? Consider how such a program might be applied to an organization that already had a highly developed personnel department.

30    9. Suppose you were asked to design a personnel research program for a large organization that already had highly developed personnel activities and technological and scientific research and development activities. Where would you recommend that the personnel research director and his group be placed in the organization? In the personnel department, reporting to the vice-president for personnel? In the research and development department, reporting to the vice-president for research and development? Or would you have the personnel research director reporting to a newly established vice-president for administration, whose responsibilities would include application of the research findings? Or would you consider other possibilities? What seem to be the possible advantages and disadvantages of each decision?

# PART VII  A Theoretical Restatement

I HAVE built this book out of cases. Case analysis is not an end in itself. I have undertaken to suggest the general significance of each case and to develop from it some tentative general propositions regarding human relations in industry. No doubt so far the cases have overshadowed the general propositions. Part VII provides us with an opportunity to view the cases in perspective, to pull together the propositions they suggest, and to assess the state of theoretical development represented by this book.

No grand theoretical scheme will now emerge, but some parts of such a scheme seem to have jelled sufficiently so as to be worth examination. Crude though this theoretical effort may be, we hope that it will illustrate one of the virtues we claim for this book: that it makes possible fruitful arguments between the reader and the writer. The reader who is dissatisfied with my theoretical approach need not content himself with an attack upon the reasoning that lies behind it. As fully as I can, I have tried to lay before the reader the data from which I seek to draw my theoretical conclusions. I invite the reader to use the same data to supplement, modify, or undermine my conclusions.

Of course, no student who sees the possibility of proving his professor in grievous error will want to limit himself to the data the professor lays before him. That reader will want to go beyond the text, to examine the recommended collateral readings—and other readings not recommended at all. He may even want to go out into the field to see for himself. If so, more power to him! The progress of knowledge depends upon this confrontation of theory by data: the discovery of data that do not fit the theory and the discovery out of theory of new types of data that we need to gather.

Throughout this book, we have been considering the individual, the group, and the organization. We have not been able to write for long about individuals without bringing in groups and organizations, or to write of organizations without bringing in individuals and groups. Even now we cannot achieve a complete separation, but we conclude Part VII with these three large questions:

1. What have we learned about the individual at work?
2. What have we learned about groups in work organizations?
3. What have we learned about work organizations?

Since we cannot answer one of those questions without attempting partial answers to the other two, we shall also seek to integrate what we have learned.

# Chapter 31 *THE INDIVIDUAL*

FOR purposes of understanding organizations, what do we need to know about the individual?

Whenever we consider the behavior of an individual on a particular job, we are concerned with personality—and with the nature of the job. In our analysis, we need to keep three interrelated aspects of the problem in mind:

1. *The fit between personality and job.* Since not everyone can do every job, this is, in its practical aspects, a selection question. Can we specify, in personality terms, what the job requires of the job holder? If so, can we then select individuals who meet these personality specifications? Beyond selection, can we predict how a given individual will behave on a specified job? What are the consequences of fit or lack of fit in the behavior of the job holder?

2. *Possibilities of personality modification.* Suppose the individual's personality does not fit the job very well. What are the possibilities of personality change in order to achieve a better fit?

3. *Possibilities of job modification.* Again, suppose the individual's personality does not fit the job very well. What are the possibilities of changing the nature of the job in order to achieve a better fit? Within management, there may be much flexibility in adjusting a job to an individual personality. When we are concerned with large numbers of workers on the same job, clearly the job cannot be modified to fit each individual personality. However, we can ask whether the job is of such a nature that the average worker cannot adjust well to it. If we find that only a small minority of the available personnel can so adjust, clearly management needs to explore possible modifications in the job.

Answers to all of these questions depend upon our definition of the nature of personality and of the social requirements of the job—and also upon the data called for by such a definition, so that we can analyze the personality-job fit in each case.

What do we mean by personality? For our purposes, the term refers to the characteristic pattern of interactions, activities, and sentiments of the individual.

Under interaction, we are concerned with the frequency, range, and initiation-response ratio. There are some individuals accustomed to interacting almost constantly, whereas there are others who feel at ease only when they are alone most of the time. We note also wide differences in interaction range, with some individuals interacting with a wide variety of people and others confining their interactions to a very small circle. In initiation, we find some individuals readily initiate interaction with others, whereas others rarely interact unless someone else approaches them first.

Under activities, we are particularly concerned with the individual's tendency to initiate activity changes for others. In any persisting group we find a few individuals who initiate activities for others, whereas the others characteristically only respond.

Under sentiments, we must distinguish between those that form a relatively stable part of the individual's personality and those which are largely determined by the situation. The worker's sentiments toward his foreman may shift with changes in the relations with his foreman. His level of aspiration, growing out of his family and community background, will be much less subject to change.

We look at the nature of jobs in the same way. Some provide for frequent interaction, while others place workers in social isolation. Job A may require the individual to initiate activities for others, whereas job B may require him mainly to respond to the initiative of others. The position a job holds in the organizational hierarchy will be related to the sentiments the job holder has toward himself and his fellows.

The analysis we shall now undertake is a crude one. We lack the measures of personality and of job social requirements that would enable us to make precise statements regarding this relationship. For the present, we must be content with rough generalizations and with showing the possibilities for more systematic work.

We shall deal successively with the personalities of workers and of supervisors or managers. This separation is not due to any conclusions regarding general personality differences between workers and supervisors. Since we are concerned with the individual-job relationships, we find it useful to recognize differences in jobs at least to the extent of separating out those at the bottom level from those involving supervising and directing the activities of others.

## THE PERSONALITY OF WORKERS

Let us begin with our cases of workers.

Melville Dalton's rate-busters (in Chapter 7, "Impact of the Economic Environment") show the effects of both a low interaction rate and community social status. These were the nine men who refused to accept the group norms regarding production and were totally isolated from the work group. In eight of these cases, Dalton found that the individuals also interacted with a very low frequency outside of work, which suggested that a low interaction rate was natural for them, so that exclusion from the work group could not be regarded by them as a penalty. The one socially active individual was a member of the Masons, and thus associated with people of a distinctly higher social level than his fellow workers. Dalton's data for all nine indicate that, in terms of social origins and also in terms of their own evaluations of their status, these men occupied a somewhat higher social level than the other workers. They considered it beneath themselves to associate with fellow workers.

We have noted the severe constraints placed upon both interaction and activities by the automotive assembly line. We have also noted in Chapter 11 that these constraints do not affect all workers equally. Frank Jasinski has found a relationship between the expressed need for interaction and satisfaction with the assembly line job. Those who adjust best to the assembly line are also those who report little need for interaction.

The engine operators in the Hi-Test plant (Chapter 12) present another case of acceptable social isolation. Here we found that the men who had grown up on the farm and were accustomed to spending long hours alone had no difficulty in adjusting to the isolation of engine operations, whereas those whose background provided more sociability looked upon the engine operating job as completely unacceptable.

The Hi-Test case also illustrates the influence of authority figures and peer groups upon the later sentiments, interactions, and activities of the individual. We have seen (Chapter 15) that the man who grew up under the firm (and accepted) control of his father and experienced very little in the way of peer group interactions tended to be anti-union and to avoid much involvement in any sort of group. The individual who had a smaller proportion of his activities under the direction of his parents and who built up an active peer group life tended to be much more receptive to the unions. Of course, these personality factors do not in themselves determine the vote of an individual in a representation election. That vote is a product of situational influences as well as personality factors.

Our examination of the nervous tensions experienced by waitresses (Chapter 8) indicated that the waitress in a busy restaurant must not only be able to handle a high frequency and range of interactions; she must also be able to initiate interactions and activities to customers and fellow employees. We found that those who had active leadership roles in their own social groups were able to carry this role over into the work situation and thus effectively manage the pressures of the job. The girl who had been a follower in her social activities had difficulties withstanding the pressures unless she happened to be teamed up with other waitresses who helped her to establish control over the situation.

## THE PERSONALITY OF MANAGERS AND SUPERVISORS

We can also view personality in terms of the fit between personal background and behavior on the job in the case of supervisors and managers. Let us begin with Jack Carter, the gaffer in the Benton plant (Chapter 10), who occupied a quasi-supervisory position.

While we did not present the data in the chapter, our evidence clearly indicates that Carter's behavior on the job fitted closely with his social experiences in the process of growing up. He had always been a highly active individual, initiating interaction freely with a relatively large number of individuals and being often sought out by others. In his informal social life, he was clearly the leader. It was he who initiated changes in activity for others. He carried this pattern over into the work situation, establishing himself solidly as the informal leader of the work group of which he was titular head.

This correspondence between informal and formal leadership was not found on some of the other shops. We may recall, for example, the young gaffer who was unable to bring himself to tell his gatherer what he thought the gatherer was doing wrong. On this particular shop, it was clearly the number two man, the servitor, who was the informal leader. The gaffer was described by his friends as a rather shy and retiring fellow who had always hesitated to exert any leadership in social activities.

As we have seen, where there was a fit between personality patterns and formal leadership position, the work went smoothly and relations among the men were harmonious. Where such a fit was lacking, the work tended to be less coordinated and the relations among the members was marked by friction.

While this fit between personality and job requirements is of practical as well as theoretical interest, we must recognize certain practical limitations to the application of these ideas. While it is certainly desirable to have an informal leader in the position of working supervisor or straw boss, management will often find itself called upon to promote into these positions men with high seniority or high technical skill, even when these men do not show marked social abilities. If promotions to working supervisor position have customarily gone by seniority, workers themselves are likely to protest when management promotes an informal leader to this position, outside of seniority. Workers may find that they enjoy working under such an informal leader when they do experience it, but they are not likely to place the harmonious relations and team spirit that might be forthcoming very high in their scale of values in advance of the experience.

Thus management must expect to find in these positions many men who have little leadership skill. It just is not possible to staff all of these positions with Jack Carters, even if there were enough like him to go around.

Management must therefore look to see what can be done to support the position so that men with modest leadership talents can function adequately. As we have pointed out in our Chapter 10 on "Teams of

Artisans," in an earlier period men of modest social abilities but high technical skill were able to function as gaffers without difficulty because of the support provided that position in the organization at that time. We have seen how the withdrawal of such support gave rise to incoordination and interpersonal difficulties on a number of the shops, so that it took an individual with exceptional social skills like Jack Carter to build the strong position he held. In our final chapter, we will return to a more complete consideration of possibilities of changing jobs so as to enable people to function more effectively in them.

Our Chapter 23 on "Managerial Succession" provided illustrations of the way in which the pre-job social experience of individuals tends to influence their relations with superiors and subordinates. We have seen that individuals who have grown up under tight parental control (without ever rebelling against it) and have not experienced active peer group associations tend to accept authority readily and to adjust less adequately to relations with subordinates. On the other hand, those who enjoyed more freedom from parental control and led an active peer group life tend to be more responsive to subordinates.

## HOW FIXED IS PERSONALITY?

How malleable is the adult personality?

While we need not accept the views of some psychoanalysts that the personality is completely formed in the early childhood years, nevertheless, the evidence does seem to indicate that the personality characteristics an individual has acquired by the time he reaches mature years are not subject to ready and rapid change.

This general conclusion is supported by our ability to cite a number of cases in which the personality pattern developed in family and community has clearly carried over into the work situation. On the other hand, we must not assume that change is impossible—that if individual does not fit job, we can only change the job or get another individual into it.

In Chapter 25, "On the Meaning of Delegation," Paul Lawrence has provided us with cases in which measurable changes in personality have taken place. We find, for example, that in a two-year period District Manager 3 reduced his proportion of talking time with subordinates from 75 per cent to 62 per cent and reduced his proportion of opinions expressed and suggestions and directions given also. His superior provided him with a model for the new approach, and he found that he was rewarded when he was able to follow this approach and penalized when he deviated from it.

Just how far the adult personality can be changed so as to fit the interactional requirements of a job is a question that cannot be given any general answer. To speak very systematically on this topic, we need better measures of personality and of the interactional requirements of jobs than those now in general use. We have noted in Chapter 2 that Chapple's Interaction Chronograph may enable us to move ahead in personality measurement.

Whatever the possibilities of personality change, the manager would do well not to make this his primary focus of attention as he examines the man-job fit. When men are said to have failed because of their personalities, we often find that in fact they were trying to do jobs with such conflicting requirements that no one could have been expected to perform them adequately. It is therefore good practice for the manager to examine the stresses and strains that are part of the job before he draws conclusions regarding the personality of the job holder.

## THE INDIVIDUAL AND THE ORGANIZATIONAL ENVIRONMENT

Up to this point we have been considering the adjustment of the individual to his immediate interpersonal situation. While we must recognize that a lack of fit between the personality pattern of the individual and the social requirements of the job will lead to negative sentiments toward certain aspects of the job, we cannot assume that a harmonious situation in interpersonal relations will necessarily make the individual happy with his job.

Joe Sloan (Chapter 12) provides us with a case in point. Up to the time of the tri-iso-butylene run and the day of his walk-off, Joe was enjoying very good relations with his foreman. While he expressed some dissatisfaction with his position in the work group, he also expressed many positive sentiments regarding his work associates. Nevertheless, we have recorded him as seriously dissatisfied with his job. What is it beyond interpersonal relations that affects the individual's sentiments toward his work situation?

To understand Joe Sloan, we need to relate the position he held in the organization with his social background. We may say that satisfaction with the position held depends upon the relationship between that position and the individual's level of aspiration. That is only another way of making the obvious point that if an individual has a level of aspiration markedly higher than his current position—and seems to have no prospects for moving higher—he will be dissatisfied.

The notion becomes more useful as we specify the influences determining the level of aspiration. That level will depend in part upon the social background the individual brings into the organization—particularly the status of his family and his level of educational achievement. Other things being equal, the individual of higher family status will tend to have higher aspirations in the organization than the individual who comes from a lower social background. Similarly, the individual who is a high school graduate will tend to have a higher level than the one who has only completed eight grades. Of course, such statements hold only on the average. We all know of cases of individuals of very inferior family status and low level of formal educational achievement who have had exceedingly high levels of aspiration. Such cases would need to be explained through examination of the individual personality particularly in relation to the family. However, these striking cases should not obscure the general conclusion. In fact, we often hear it made explicit for us by informants who say to us, "For a man of my education, this is a good job," or "A man of my education ought to be able to get a better job than this." (People find it easier to be explicit about educational level than about general social status.)

We would also expect to find a relationship between level of aspiration and age and rate of progress in the organization. The individual may find a given job satisfying at age twenty-five, whereas he might consider himself defeated if he held the same job at age thirty-five. The French-Canadian foremen and general foremen serving under John Dyer (Chapter 24, "Building Initiative in Management") were pointing to this relationship when they told us that they were happy with their current positions because they were still young but that the same positions would not look nearly so good to them a few years later. We see the impact of age and rate of progress particularly in Joe Sloan's case. When an individual moves up exceedingly rapidly so that he holds the top operating position at age twenty-seven, his level of aspiration is bound to rise along with such rapid forward progress.

This does not mean that, apart from his social and educational background, a worker who does not move up at all eventually becomes satisfied with his current position. In Chapter 11 on "Men on the Motor Line," we have seen workers continuing to dislike assembly line operation as the years go on and yet also renouncing hopes of progress in the organization, beyond the modest goals of getting a job that would take them off the line. Blocked on the job, they come to equate personal progress with out-of-work activities: buying a better car, paying off the mortgage on the home, buying a new television set, and so on.

The satisfaction of the individual with his job also depends upon his relation to the technological, economic, and physical environment.

As we have pointed out in Chapter 7, "Impact of the Economic Environment," money has a relative as well as an absolute value. Everyone wants more money—though the strength of this urge varies from man to man—but most people can be satisfied without unlimited amounts of money. The individual evaluates the adequacy of the money paid him in terms of what his associates are receiving. If his job ranks high in the scale of skill and status, he is concerned to find a low-ranking job paying more money.

The relation between man and money is a complicated one, for we do not have any opportunities to observe men responding to money alone. Always the response occurs in a social situation so that worker behavior depends as much on the way in which the money system is administered by management as upon the absolute amounts of money offered. In our final chapter, we shall return to a consideration of ways in which economic rewards may be better integrated into organizations.

We have already illustrated the impact of the technology upon job satisfaction in noting the relationship between personality and assembly line jobs. The impact of other physical conditions of work is illustrated in Chapter 13, "Toward the Automatic Factory." Here we have argued that conditions of work must also be viewed in relative terms. Workers in other countries might take for granted conditions that would be considered highly objectionable by American workers. Even an objectionable condition must be seen in a social context. The smoke problem in the tube mill provides us with a good example of this proposition. At first the workers spoke enthusiastically about the fine physical conditions of the plant. They noted that the smoke at one job site was the only drawback and that management was trying to do something about this. While management indeed did try to remedy the situation, workers observed no improvement in the course of months. They therefore came to the conclusion that management did not really care about them, and the objectionable condition came to symbolize this lack of concern.

This suggests that workers will accept difficult physical conditions when those conditions seem clearly necessary in the job situation. When the conditions do not seem necessary, they come to symbolize a lack of concern of management for workers.

### THE ORGANIZATION MAN PROBLEM

Can man maintain his individuality as he works within the organization?

Readers will recognize this as one of the controversial questions of the day.

Principal spokesman concerning the conformist pressures of organizations on individuals has been William H. Whyte, Jr.—with whom I am often confused. *The Organization Man* presents a picture of the individuality of people being suppressed under organizational pressures.[1] Whyte claims that the superiors and associates of organization members consciously or unconsciously demand conformity to the ways of thinking and acting found within that particular organizational sub-culture.

Whyte actually makes a two-pronged attack. On the one hand he attacks the organization for suppressing individuality. On the other hand he attacks members for being all too ready to conform, to accept

---

[1] New York: Simon & Schuster, 1956.

the rewards that come from approval by associates and superiors in exchange for giving up free expression of one's individuality. People are not only seduced by organizations. They actually get to enjoy the seduction process.

How shall we evaluate this picture of organizational life? In the first place, we should note that a question as large as the impact of the organization on man's individuality can have no satisfactory research answer. If we were to attack the question through research, we would first have to define *individuality*, establish ways of measuring it, apply these measures to people before and after they go to work in a given organization, and then carry out these operations in a large sample of organizations so as to be able to generalize about the United States at least. While it might be possible to develop the appropriate research methods, we doubt whether the tremendous efforts involved would be justified by the results that might be obtained.

Lacking the data for a full answer, we can nevertheless draw from research several points of caution regarding such a large generalization.

In the first place, let us not assume that this is a new problem. Ever since human society began, the individual has faced a necessity of making some sort of adjustment to the group and the organization. We may be inclined to think that men were freer to express their individuality in some golden age of long ago, but we must be wary about romanticizing the past.

As we look at the present situation, we find several difficulties in applying the Whyte claims in a broad and general fashion.

In the first place, we must recognize that it is not men alone who make up the oppressive or liberating atmosphere of the organization. The task the organization is set up to accomplish and the technology and work flow through which this task is accomplished may have important impacts upon individual freedom of action. The individual on the automotive assembly line has very little freedom of action indeed, but note that it is not the foreman who directly enforces this conformity upon him. We find the skilled glass workers in the Benton plant feeling that they have a good deal of freedom to express their individuality; here again, it is not the leadership of the foreman or the assistant plant manager which creates this atmosphere of free expression. At the bottom levels of the organization, the freedoms and constraints may be in large measure built into the job situation by the nature of the task performed and the way the technology and work flow are organized.

The conformity argument also makes the implicit assumption that success in the organization depends largely upon maintaining pleasant personal relations among superiors and work associates. We cannot afford to overlook the fact that an organization is set up for the purpose of getting work done. Superiors try to judge their subordinates in terms of the work results they obtain. Of course, this is not an easy judgment to make, but the least we can say is that performance is never entirely irrelevant. We can say somewhat more if we distinguish between organizations in terms of the measurability of results. As was pointed out in Chapter 6, "Formal Organization Structure," it is good practice to "supervise by results" because this gives the subordinate the maximum freedom to try to get results in the ways he thinks best. This approach may be relatively easy to apply in some organizations (department stores, for example) where the various organizational units can function with a high degree of independence of each other and performance figures are readily supplied. It is much more difficult to follow this approach in organizations where various units are highly interdependent and many individuals and groups are performing functions that are not subject to any direct measurement. Thus, we might expect closer supervision and more pressure toward conformity in those organizations where results of individual and group effort are difficult to measure than in those where results are more readily measured.

Finally, we should note that it is not only differences in organizational mission and technology that have differential impacts upon individual self-expression. The freedom of the individual to develop his own initiative may depend also in large measure upon the leadership skill of the individual responsible for his unit. We have shown that John Dyer, within a large corporation, was able to operate his 700-man division in such a way as to bring forth a vertible flowering of personal initiative.

To be sure, Dyer was a man of unusual skills. We would not expect the average executive to duplicate his results. However, in science we are not so much concerned in determining what the average situation is like. We want to know what conditions yield what results. If we study John Dyer's division and other organizational units where initiative seems to flourish, we may be able to discover the knowledge that will increase individual self-expression in organizational life.

# Chapter 32 *THE GROUP*

THE individual does not meet the organization alone. Whether he is at the work level or is a member of management, he is likely to fit into some group. His adjustment to the organization will be influenced by his group membership. The functioning of the organization will be influenced by the behavior of the groups within it.

In this chapter, we shall consider the role of groups both at the worker and managerial levels. We shall begin with a theory of work group cohesion and later consider the utilization of groups within management.

## A THEORY OF WORK GROUP COHESION

The Western Electric Research Program, with its major publications coming out between 1935 and 1939, drew the attention of research men toward the work group. People began to talk and write about "informal organization." This was a useful counter-balance to the prevailing views of "scientific management" which tended to look upon organization in a highly formalistic manner and made no allowance for the relations arising among men working together.

When Roethlisberger and Dickson described and analyzed the men of the Bank Wiring Room, they presented us with a case of a work group that was tightly organized and whose organization served to insulate it against pressures from management.

For some time, this study colored our thinking. We tended to think of *the* work group (in the model of the Bank Wiring Room) and unconsciously assumed that all work groups were similarly marked by strong internal cohesion. More recent studies have suggested that this is a highly misleading view. We are indebted primarily to Leonard Sayles for giving us a more realistic picture of work group organization.

We now recognize that, just as there are work groups marked by strong bonds of cohesion, so are there work groups of men who are so badly divided against each other that they are unable to stand together defending any group point of view. Of course, there are all sorts of variations in between these extremes.

What makes the difference? What are the forces that lead to strong cohesion and what are the forces that tend to destroy work group cohesion?

First, we need a working definition of group cohesion. In the literature, there have been two main approaches to the study of group cohesion. In one approach, cohesion is measured by the responses workers give to questionnaires addressed to their sentiments. Does the worker feel he is a member of a good group? How would he feel about being transferred, at the same rate of pay, to another work group? And so on. The groups in which the members express positive sentiments toward the group and negative reactions toward the possibility of being transferred out of it are judged to be highly cohesive. The major study along this line is that of Stanley Seashore.[1]

The other approach, taken by Leonard Sayles, judges cohesion in terms of concerted group activity.[2] Cohesive groups are ones in which the members act together toward some common goal. Groups low in cohesion are those in which the members rarely if ever get together for concerted group activity.

We might assume that groups in which members express strong positive sentiments toward the group and negative sentiments toward the possibility of leaving it would also be those groups whose members would act together toward common group goals. Until this relationship has been tested, we cannot be sure that the two researchers are talking about different aspects of the same thing. My own approach will be based primarily upon Sayles, but I shall make some reference to Seashore, assuming tentatively that the two sets of findings are indeed congruent.

We shall deal here with four sets of influences upon group cohesion:

1. The personal and social characteristics of individuals.
2. The structure of jobs.
3. Uniform or differentiated impact of issues.
4. Management responses to group pressures.

Following our consideration of the way in which these influences affect group cohesion, we shall consider some practical implications for management and union action.

1. The Personal and Social Characteristics of Individuals.

Two types of factors seem to be involved here: homogeneity or heterogeneity of social characteristics and horizontal versus vertical orientation.

A. *Homogeneity or heterogeneity of social characteristics.* We might assume that people who are homogeneous in social characteristics are more likely to stick together than those who are heterogeneous. If this is so, it remains for us to specify those characteristics that would be particularly relevant.

---

[1] *Group Cohesiveness in the Industrial Work Group* (Ann Arbor, Michigan: Survey Research Center, 1954).

[2] *Behavior of Industrial Work Groups* (New York: John Wiley & Sons, Inc., 1958).

Ethnic affiliation seems to be of importance even today, and was probably of much greater importance in the past. Particularly in the heavy industries, some U.S. managements in the late nineteenth and early twentieth centuries encouraged immigration of workers from a number of different countries and sought to mix the ethnic backgrounds of the workers at any given work site on the assumption that people from different parts of the world would have trouble communicating with each other and would be sufficiently suspicious of each other so they would have difficulty in developing any common front against management. It seems significant that some of the first strong unions were marked by homogeneity of ethnic background.

While the sharp lines of cleavage have been blurred by succeeding generations, we still often find in local union elections that ethnic affiliation is the unstated issue dividing the leading candidates. A recent study by Zaleznik, Christenson, and Roethlisberger shows the significance of this factor in work groups.[3] In the department they studied, the informal work groups were dominated by Irish Americans. The intensive analysis of this department of fifty workers suggests a qualification to our statement regarding ethnic homogeneity. High cohesion on a departmental level may not necessarily require that all who work in a given situation are tightly integrated into one or another work group. Insofar as concerted action goes, cohesion may exist in a department when there are one or more dominant groups whose leadership is accepted by the other individuals even when they are not integrated with these groups.

Although there have been no studies focused on this point in particular, we may assume that, other things being equal, a one-sex work group is likely to be more cohesive than one in which both sexes are represented. In order to combat division along sex lines, unions commonly insist upon "equal pay for equal work." Where women are treated differently from men and particularly where they are paid less than men in the same classification, there always appears to be the possibility that management will seek to save money by substituting women workers for men. If such a move develops, a possible advantage to women is at the same time a disadvantage to men. Hence the union effort to insist upon equality of treatment.

While the question of homogeneity of social class background has not been raised regarding work group cohesion, evidence from community studies suggests that people of different social class backgrounds have more problems in communicating with each other than those of similar backgrounds. Within a group at the work level, we will not

---

[3] A. Zaleznik, C. R. Christenson, and F. J. Roethlisberger, with the assistance and collaboration of George C. Homans, *The Motivation, Productivity, and Satisfaction of Workers: A Prediction Study* (Boston: Harvard University Graduate School of Business Administration, 1958).

expect to find the complete range of social class backgrounds that appears in a community, but we often do find sufficient range of differences for the individuals in question to be very conscious of them. If the work group is divided between upper-lower and lower-lower, we are likely to find that the upper-lower people consider the lower-lower individuals dirty, unreliable, and generally possessed of unpleasant characteristics, while the lower-lower people feel discriminated against by the other workers. Where we find a downwardly mobile individual of middle-class origin in such a work group, we are likely also to find a problem of personal adjustment and lack of integration. Those we encountered in the restaurant industry study seemed to keep themselves apart from the work group, as if to say that they really belonged to a superior class.[4] This is naturally resented by the other workers.

If the members are close together in age, is this likely to lead to greater cohesion? Our study of "Teams of Artisans" (Chapter 10) shows the Benton glass blowers rather sharply divided on an age basis. The statistics of the Seashore study show no such effect. Perhaps we may conclude that while age cleavages are possible, they are not common. We must bear in mind that our own culture tends to de-emphasize age differences, so that they may be less important for work group cohesion than they might be in a society where age differences are closely associated with differences in status.

There seems to be no reason to expect that groups whose members are close together in seniority will tend toward cohesion—unless the group is in competition with some other group for promotions based upon seniority. Seniority presents a sharp cutting point. If promotions or demotions depend upon seniority within the department, then the man who has one day more employment than another has an absolute superiority over the other in this respect. Furthermore, if seniority dates are close together, there is greater likelihood of disputes arising as to whether an individual seniority date is accurate—as we have seen in the case of the centerless grinders (Chapter 17, "Work Group Cohesion and Militancy"). Such disagreements can readily lead to conflict.

B. *Horizontal versus vertical orientation.* Some people seem to look primarily to their organizational superiors for approval, whereas other people seem to look primarily to their peers—people on the same organizational level. These two orientations represent two extremes: of course, many people seem to fall somewhere in between, being pulled in both directions. A work group consisting of members who are oriented toward their peers will naturally be more cohesive than one in which a substantial proportion of the members are oriented toward their organizational superiors.

In the previous chapter, we have discussed this aspect of the indi-

---

[4] See "Moving Up and Down in the World," in my *Human Relations in the Restaurant Industry* (New York: McGraw-Hill Book Co., Inc., 1948), chap. 11.

vidual personality. The argument may be summed up in this way: The individual who grows up under the firm (and accepted) control of his parents and who has little peer group experience will tend to be vertically oriented; the individual who does not experience such parental control and who has led an active peer group life will tend to be horizontally oriented.

"Who Goes Union and Why" (Chapter 15) showed us one case which does not seem to fit this pattern, but closer observation shows the same underlying relationship. We noted that Mark Walling had grown up on a farm, under the firm control of his father, until he went to work in the oil industry; yet we have further noted that at the time of the beginning of my observations, he was leaning toward the union. But note that Walling himself commented that when he first went into industrial work he "looked on the foreman like he was my father." When Walling was fired from the first company he worked for, this identification of the father with the foreman was weakened. Nevertheless, when the showdown came, he could not take a strong position for the union. Furthermore, he still saw the organization in vertical terms—or wished to believe it could be that way. Witness his statement just after the election to the effect that there was "no reason the company couldn't be like a father to the men." In the many long discussions I had with some of the men who were strongly for the union, I never had one of them use the father–child analogy either in referring to his own industrial experience or to the management-worker relationship.

Vertical or horizontal orientation may also depend upon one aspect of the foreman-worker relationship. The individual who finds he can initiate activity for the foreman is more likely to be vertically oriented than the individual who cannot. Thus, within a department, a *general* inability to initiate for the foreman is likely to promote a horizontal orientation.

2. Structure of Jobs.

Here again, we may emphasize two aspects: homogeneity versus heterogeneity and interactional opportunities.

A. *Homogeneity versus heterogeneity in characteristics of the job situation.* The characteristics which tend to unify or divide men include, at least, pay, skill, working conditions, and type of job. The assumption is that people who are on jobs which are objectively similar in these various respects will tend to view the world around them in similar terms, and this will facilitate cohesive group action. Conversely, those who are in jobs that are dissimilar in these respects are likely to view the world in dissimilar ways and have difficulty in pulling together.

B. *Interactional opportunities.* The assumption here is that individuals whose job situation permits them to interact readily will tend to be more cohesive than those whose job situation makes interaction difficult. This is not to say that physical proximity will be a controlling factor, for people may work close together under conditions (severe noise, for example) which make interaction difficult. On the other hand, the work may allow people who are ordinarily physically separated to come together and interact. For example, in a study of the unionization of utility workers, by George Strauss, we find one of the most cohesive groups being the meter readers who worked all over the city and surrounding communities.[5] Nevertheless, they had sufficient freedom of action so that they were able to develop a social pattern of meeting at certain restaurants for coffee at certain times of the day, and this possibility was essential to the concerted action they displayed. They were also isolated from interaction with other groups of workers, which may have provided a further impetus toward cohesion.

We have explored the impact of these two factors particularly in Chapter 17 ("Work Group Cohesion and Militancy"). Sayles points toward a possible relationship between factors A and B in his discrimination between strategic and erratic groups. The strategic are the groups that stick together over a long period of time and push their interests with a well-developed strategy and tactics. The erratic groups are those which are likely to erupt in sudden and unexpected protest after a period of apparent apathy. He suggests that in some cases of the erratic groups, we have the combination of individuals doing the identical thing on a *group* basis, which means that they are working in close proximity with unlimited opportunities to interact. Without any restraining barriers, there seems to be the possibility of an irritation exciting emotional support from group members so rapidly as to lead to uncontrolled outbursts.

3. Uniform or Differentiated Impact of Issues.

Issues are ordinarily classified as to subject matter—seniority, pay rates, vacations, and so on. Here we are classifying them as to whether they affect the work group in a uniform fashion or affect different individuals in different ways. An issue which strikes everyone alike tends to stimulate a concerted group reaction, whereas an issue which affects members differently tends to make it more difficult to carry out concerted group action.

Inequity payments present a classic type of issue with a built-in divisive force, as we have seen in Chapter 16, "The Evolution of Union-Management Relations."

Uniformity of impact tends to be associated with homogeneity of social characteristics of jobs, but not necessarily so. In Chapter 10, "Teams of Artisans," we found a great heterogeneity of job characteristics, but the two issues of Sunday work and election day pay affected everyone alike, and on these issues the individuals were able to unite.

---

[5] "Factors in the Unionization of a Utilities Company: A Case Study," *Human Organization*, Vol. XII, No. 3 (1953).

4. Management Responses to Group Pressures.

The tendency of a group to resort to concerted action depends in part upon the history of past management reactions to such concerted group efforts. If past concerted group activity has yielded rewards to the members, they will have a greater tendency to act together in the future. Conversely, if past concerted activities have yielded no rewards to the members and have even yielded penalties, the members will be less likely to pull together in a common effort in the future. If past results have been mixed, with a combination of rewards and penalties, then the degree of cohesion shown at any time will be more problematical.

In this form, it sounds as if we are talking exclusively about interpersonal relations: the leadership of the work group in relation to management's willingness and ability to respond with rewards or penalties. Beyond this, can we point to forces that tend to make the group more cohesive in action and tend to make management more or less inclined to give ground? In this respect we should consider *leverage* and *management policy.*

*Leverage* refers to the importance of the work performed by the group to management—how much management can be helped by the cooperation of the group, how much management can be hurt by the withholding of cooperation. If the group's work is exceedingly important to management, the group is likely to perceive this importance and assume that management is more likely to respond to this group's collective pressures than it would to the pressures of some work group whose operations seemed more peripheral to the enterprise.

Technological change may change the *leverage* of a given work group on management. We saw this in the case of the centerless grinders (Chapter 17). In the period when most of the production of the plant necessarily went through this department, the centerless grinders were a very cohesive group, exercising effective pressures on management. Technological changes that enabled management to finish a large part of its production without putting it through the grinding department drastically reduced this group's leverage on management. While other changes were also involved, we note that the men did recognize that the technological change had sharply reduced the importance of their department to management. They therefore felt that the chances of getting rewards for concerted presures were reduced, whereas the chances of incurring penalties were greatly increased. The successes the men had achieved in earlier efforts to put the pressure on management might have been expected to encourage them toward further concerted group activity. Indeed, the men often referred to this past history as they discussed what they might do in the future. They recognized, nevertheless, that the leverage situation had drastically changed, and this change placed difficult barriers in the direction of concerted activity.

The management response to group pressure efforts must also be considered, independently of leverage. Without any management plan-ning and policy, we might assume that management would tend to yield gains to cohesively organized groups with strong leverage positions. In general, this does seem to be the case, and we commonly find that such groups enjoy somewhat better wages and working conditions than a detached evaluation of their skills and responsibilities would indicate. However, this obviously cannot go on forever. Experienced management people have come to realize that yielding to one group effort serves symbolically as a potential reward for the next effort of that group. The management which responds in an impromptu fashion to such group efforts is simply building the power of the work group and losing its own control. This realization leads management to develop a policy and program of action.

We see the effect of this approach particularly in relation to wildcat strikes. Years ago, we may have been inclined to assume a simple re-lationship between the frequency of wildcat strikes and worker senti-ments: the more frequent the wildcat strikes, the more negative the sentiments of the workers toward management. Research has convinc-ingly shown that the relationship is more complex. The prevalence of wildcat strikes may indeed point to strong anti-management sentiments, but the absence of these strikes does not necessarily indicate more favor-able sentiments of workers toward management. Presence or absence of wildcat strikes seem to be more closely related to management responses to these collective group activities than to worker sentiments themselves.

Where wildcat strikes have been prevalent, experience appears to have shown the workers that they were an effective technique for making gains. It has not mattered whether management has talked tough if, in the crisis, management has been prone to yield to pressure.

Where wildcat strikes are infrequent, we tend to find that manage-ment has evolved a consistent policy and program for meeting them. This may involve points along this line:

1. Management refuses to negotiate any issue while the men are on strike. Management will only talk to union representatives regarding getting the men back to work.

2. Management refuses to accelerate or in any other way change the han-dling of grievances then being processed. In other words, not only does man-agement refuse to give the wildcatters an immediate reward. Management also takes steps to see to it that the technique is not indirectly rewarded.

3. Management undertakes to administer disciplinary action upon those chiefly responsible for the wildcat. Clearly, this is a hazardous move, particu-larly since management may be mistaken regarding the leadership responsi-bility and may thus become involved in unforeseen consequences.

The transition from frequent to infrequent wildcat strikes seems bound to be a painful one. No matter what management people say, workers who have found wildcats rewarding in the past are not likely to assume that they will be unrewarding in the future. Management's firm stand may in fact provoke a larger and longer stoppage in the immediate situation, so that a change in policy and program in this field is likely to be costly. The management that is not prepared to pay the cost had better not try to take a firm stand.

This is not to suggest that a management program which ends wild-cat strikes thereby resolves outstanding differences between workers, union, and management. Clearly, where worker negative sentiments are involved, there need to be ways of dealing with the issues giving rise to these sentiments. I am simply pointing out that the frequency of wildcat strikes seems to depend in large measure upon the rewards or penalties that follow from them.

## WHO GAINS FROM COHESION?

The discussion so far may seem to imply that a high level of cohesion within a work group is disadvantageous to management. Indeed, we have given examples in which cohesive groups were able to fight very effectively against management. However, we should not assume that cohesion necessarily leads to conflict between the group and management. We have noted in Seashore's study that there were high cohesive groups that were high in productivity as well as high cohesive groups low in productivity. The common element in both types of cases is closer adherence to a group *norm* regarding productivity than we find in groups low in cohesion. Cohesion, then, can be an advantage or a disadvantage to management, according to the relations between the group and management.

In fact, internal conflict in a group may not be advantageous to management even in a situation marked by some conflict between workers and management. As we have seen in one point in the center-less grinders case (Chapter 17), management was handicapped because of its inability to achieve any consensus within the work group regarding a new incentive. Low cohesion may involve confusion and disorganization, which are hardly conducive to efficient operations.

The value to be attached to high cohesion by workers or management can only be determined as we consider the relation between the work group and the larger organization. In our final chapter, we shall consider possibilities of achieving a more integrated organization.

## THE UTILIZATION OF MANAGEMENT GROUPS

In examining groups within management, we can take two possible approaches. In one approach, we recognize that management to some extent represents a political organization with individuals jockeying for prestige and power. This approach has been very effectively taken by Melville Dalton, but very few people have written systematically about the politics of management; therefore we are at a loss to proceed very far with this topic.[6] The other approach involves considering the way groups are used in management operations. The issue is brought into focus by the question we hear asked these days: Should management have more or fewer group meetings?

Consider the case of an engineer who once told me that he never wanted to attend any more management meetings. This extreme reaction was brought on by a recent experience in a three-hour meeting conducted by the head of his engineering department. The meeting had been called together by the department head in order to discuss some new types of accounting reports that were being required by higher management. The first fifteen minutes of the meeting were taken up by a representative of the accounting department, who presented the rationale behind the department's new forms and gave an explanation of the information which was needed. My informant had no quarrel with this segment of the meeting.

Following the accounting presentation, the department head announced that the new forms would require a new set of reports from his department, which meant that the old assignments as to who prepared which reports could no longer be in effect. He then invited discussion as to which individual should prepare which report under the new procedure. The group spent the rest of the afternoon on this topic. The discussion led into endless arguments. No one objected strenuously to a particular assignment he might be given, but no one wanted to be stuck with a particular report when he thought someone else was at least as good a candidate as he for that assignment.

As we review this case, it should be apparent that discussion in terms of more or fewer management meetings is beside the point. Here a manager was using a meeting for two purposes, only one of which could be performed effectively in that meeting. The provision of information went smoothly enough. The members then assumed that the boss would perform his customary supervisory duties and make the individual assignments himself. They would have been pleased if he had announced that he would be glad to reconsider his decisions if they seemed inequitable, but they considered it a waste of time and an aggravating experience to have to spend almost three hours on a task that they felt it was up to their supervisor to perform.

For another example, consider the Amicon tube case discussed in Chapter 27 ("Engineers and Their Innovations"). We found examples of both the use and misuse of groups within management. The so-called management team of sixteen men, ranging from foreman up to plant manager, clearly did more harm than good. Too many people were involved for an effective discussion of a localized technical problem. Since

---

[6] *Men Who Manage* (New York: John Wiley & Sons, Inc., 1959).

a number of status levels were involved and no steps were taken to avoid this outcome, the natural result of the composition of the group was dominance of the discussion by the higher status people who knew the least about the problem in question.

It was only when this so-called management team approach was abandoned in favor of a small group meeting limited to men directly involved in the problem that the tube project began to make headway.

John Dyer, the general superintendent discussed in Chapter 24, on "Building Initiative in Management," provides impressive examples of the effective use of management groups. His three-level meetings contained approximately the same number of people as were involved in the "management team" in the Amicon tube case, and yet he managed to avoid the unfortunate results of the Amicon group. How so?

In the first place, he used his meetings for quite a different purpose. The Amicon group was set up to examine a specific technical and human problem and to arrive at a decision on it. While the plant manager would announce the decision, he hoped that the group discussion would shape it for him. John Dyer's purposes were quite different. He made it clear that decisions would be taken by each individual in his own area of responsibility and that the meetings were designed simply to stimulate everyone's thinking. Furthermore, he limited discussion to matters that were of division-wide significance, which avoided the effect found in the Amicon tube case, where men were talking about matters on which they had little knowledge. While his meeting contained three levels instead of the five represented at Amicon, even this three would have been enough to show the natural status effect if he had not taken steps to set a different pattern. In other words, we would ordinarily expect the top two levels in a three-level meeting to dominate the discussion, but John Dyer used the meeting for the specific purpose of stimulating the initiative of the men at the third level. As we have seen, his leadership skill in this respect was extraordinary.

Concluding our examples with John Dyer suggests a necessary emphasis upon the leadership skill of the man conducting the management meeting. Holding constant the number of individuals and number of organizational levels represented, a meeting can still be effective or ineffective, according to the skill displayed by the leader.

In complex modern industry, the interrelations among individuals and departments will necessarily require a certain amount of group discussion. It is fruitless for the executive to ask whether there should be more or fewer group meetings. He should rather concern himself with questions such as these:

What questions can be effectively handled in a group meeting? What questions do not lend themselves to a group approach? Since meetings can be used to transmit information, to arrive at decisions, or to exchange ideas, what are the possibilities and limitations of each management use? For each purpose just noted, what is the maximum number of participants that may be effectively involved? For a given problem to be discussed, what should be the composition of the discussion group, according to organizational levels and functional specialties? What differences in the nature of the discussion can we expect according to whether the group is homogeneous or heterogeneous (1) as to status levels, and (2) as to functional specialties?

Finally, how should the meeting be conducted? Out of that one large question we could derive a large number of specific questions regarding the role of the discussion leader.

It is not my purpose to try to answer any of these questions in this book. A whole book could be written about the use and misuse of groups in management. I sketch out a few of the questions that might be asked simply to emphasize the folly of attempting to answer the general question: should management have more or fewer group meetings?

# Chapter 33 *THE ORGANIZATION*

IN THIS final chapter, we shall take a broad look at the organization as a whole, considering both its possibilities and its problems. Most of the ideas to be presented here have already appeared in the book, but this final chapter presents us with an opportunity to bring them together and focus them upon the main object of our concern: the organization.

I shall also undertake to integrate the observations of this book with other research findings, particularly with those of the Survey Research Center at the University of Michigan.[1] I concentrate on this one body of research because it has been highly influential in affecting the thinking of all those concerned with human relations in industry.

## ORGANIZATIONAL PRODUCTS

What are the products of an organization?

In a manufacturing or process organization, the products are concrete and obvious, and even in a service organization we can speak of so much work to be done and therefore of the productivity of the organization. We can thus be concerned with the conditions that lead to high or low productivity.

While work organizations are established to get jobs done, the product is not the only output of the organization. The experience of working in an organization gives rise to sentiments among the members: satisfaction or dissatisfaction with the immediate job, sentiments toward the supervisor, toward the company, toward working conditions, and so on.

While everyone realizes that organizations are set up to get work done, in a democratic society we like to think that happy workers are the best producers and that favorable sentiments between supervisor and supervised lead to high productivity. As we shall see, the relationship is not nearly that simple.

Early work concentrated on the sentiments the foreman held toward his job and toward the workers in relation to the productivity achieved

---

[1] I am greatly indebted to David Sirota for stimulating my thinking along these lines. However, he is not to be held responsible for any specific conclusion presented.

by this unit. On the basis of interviews held with them, foremen were classified as either "employee oriented" or "production oriented," the first category consisting of those who talked about problems of workers, about the need for motivating them, and the second category being made up of those who talked about the job primarily in technical terms and in terms of the need of getting out production.

In a Prudential Insurance Company study, it was found that six out of the nine "employee oriented" supervisors had high productivity groups, whereas seven out of eight of the "production oriented" supervisors had low productivity groups.[2] There was also evidence of more favorable sentiments toward the supervisor among those under employee oriented supervisors. This confirmed the comforting notion that a supervisor who thinks in terms of his people gets better production as well as more favorable sentiments.

There were three problems in connection with such an interpretation:

(1) *The hen and egg problem.* Which comes first: the orientation or the results in productivity? If this seems an idle question, let us apply it to Tom Walker, the Barrel Department foreman in Chapter 9. Was he employee oriented or production oriented? We cannot answer that question without attaching a date to it. While I did not ask Tom Walker the same questions as the Survey Research Center used when making its judgment of orientation, my data suggest a classification of Walker as employee oriented in 1948 (when production was going very well) and production oriented in 1950 (when production was down).

(2) *The sentiments-behavior problem.* Here we have a two-fold problem, that of relating the sentiments the supervisor verbalizes to those he "really" feels. While this is a problem common to all studies of sentiments, it may be particularly difficult here because of supervisory exposure to human relations training programs. Although these programs have shown little effect upon supervisory behavior, as perceived by subordinates, they do provide the supervisor with the accepted verbiage as to what represents "good human relations." But even if we assume we have good data on sentiments, subordinates do not react directly to the sentiments of the supervisor but only to the way those sentiments are manifested in behavior.

(3) *Conflicting results of later studies.* This simple relationship did not always show up in subsequent studies, as we shall see.

What is the productivity effect of close versus general supervision? Here closeness is understood as issuing of detailed instructions and fre-

---

[2] Daniel Katz, Nathan Maccoby, and Nancy C. Morse, *Productivity, Supervision, and Morale in an Office Situation* (Ann Arbor, Michigan: Survey Research Center, 1950).

quent checking on progress, whereas general supervision involves issuing general instructions and avoiding detailed and frequent checking on progress. In the Prudential study, the supervisors practicing general supervision got better production results than those who supervised closely. However, a study of railroad section gangs revealed no correlation between closeness of supervision and productivity.[3] The discrepancy is explained in terms of the differences in the nature of the two jobs. The Prudential work groups were involved in routine clerical operations of little skill, where the supervisor's knowledge of operations could contribute little to employee performance. There seems to have been more skill involved in the section gang operation, so that a foreman who checked closely on his men might be able to move the work ahead —even if the men resented his surveillance.

Whatever the validity of this explanation, note that it refers to a difference in the nature of jobs—a factor that has never been thoroughly explored in the Survey Research Center studies and to which we will return later.

One of the most daring of the Center's studies involved an experiment in changing the decision-making level in clerical departments of the Prudential.[4] In one set of work groups, the research staff worked systematically with management people to have them lower the level at which decisions were made and to involve employees in the discussion of these decisions. In a matched set of work groups, the decision-making level was systematically raised, and the work methods studies associated with scientific management were brought into play. Productivity was measured in each work group before the experiment and after it had been carried out for a year. Questionnaires were used to elicit employee sentiments.

The questionnaires showed workers responding much more favorably toward their supervisors and toward the job itself in the groups where decision making had been decentralized, but the productivity results were not nearly so clear-cut. Productivity went up in the groups where the level of decision making had been lowered, but it went up even more in those groups where the level had been raised. This suggests that centralization of authority may elicit even more productivity than decentralization but at a possibly heavy cost in negative sentiments. However, the generalization regarding productivity must be questioned in this case as we note the nature of the productivity measure. In these

---

[3] Daniel Katz, Nathan Maccoby, Gerald Gurin, and Lucretia G. Floor, *Productivity, Supervision, and Morale Among Railroad Workers* (Ann Arbor, Michigan: Survey Research Center, 1951).

[4] See Nancy C. Morse, and E. Reimer, "The Experimental Manipulation of a Major Organizational Variable," *Journal of Abnormal and Social Psychology*, Vol. LII, No. 1 (1956).

particular work groups, the amount of the work to be done was fixed so that working harder or more efficiently would not increase productivity. Productivity could only be increased through reducing the number of employees performing this fixed volume of work. The involvement of employees in discussions with management is likely to strengthen sentiments of employee loyalty to each other as well as to management, so it is hardly to be expected that the employees will suggest that some of their numbers be laid off or transferred to other departments. In this type of situation, the work force is only reduced as new employees are not hired to replace those who quit their jobs. On job operations where the amount of work to be done was not fixed, the participative approach might have proved superior in productivity as well as in worker satisfaction. This would fit in with our observations on the John Dyer case (Chapter 24, "Building Initiative in Management").

What is the relationship between intrinsic job satisfaction and productivity? To measure intrinsic job satisfaction, the researchers used the direct question: "How about the work itself, how well do you like that?" Here, comparing workers in high producing and low producing sections, the researchers found those in the low producing sections responding more favorably in both the railroad study and the clerical study, though the difference was not statistically significant in the clerical study. In both studies, workers in high producing groups expressed more pride in their groups. In neither study was there any correlation between group productivity and expressed satisfaction with the company.

The authors note that the inverse correlation between productivity and intrinsic job satisfaction was found in two situations where the work required little skill. We assume that the higher producers might be also those who felt entitled to a higher level job. We might therefore expect to find a positive correlation between intrinsic job satisfaction and productivity on highly skilled jobs. This remains for further investigation.

So far the studies we have reported do not seem to fall in any neat pattern. The more recent Michigan studies suggest that the earlier work had assumed too simple a relationship between supervisor orientation and productivity or between worker participation in decision making and productivity. More recent research points to the importance of *conditioning* variables. In other words, we no longer expect to be able to say flatly that employee orientation of the supervisor correlates with high productivity—or even with high worker satisfaction with the supervisor. We expect to find these relationships only under certain specified conditions.

Finding inconclusive results as he related employee orientation of supervisor to worker satisfaction with supervisor, Donald Pelz continued to cast about for meaningful ways to organize his data.[5] He classified his foremen into those having high power and those having low power in relation to their superiors. He now found that among those foremen having high power with their superiors there was a positive correlation between employee orientation and high satisfaction with supervisor. For foremen having low power, there was little if any relationship between employee orientation and high satisfaction with supervisor—some of the indicators even showing a negative relationship.

Note how this finding is in accord with the point of view expressed in this book, where we have argued that the foreman-worker relationship cannot be considered in isolation. The high power foreman, in Pelz's terms, is presumably the man we would characterize as being able to initiate activity for his superiors. If his employee orientation indicates that he is receptive to initiative from below, then we have a situation where worker initiative can carry up the line at least two levels, leading to higher productivity and to favorable sentiments toward the supervisor. (Pelz does not report productivity results in this study.) In the low power situation, the foreman is presumably not able to initiate activity up the line, so workers who bring their problems to him may find a sympathetic ear but no response on those proposals that require action at higher levels.

In a study of worker response to participative management—where workers were permitted to discuss their problems with superiors—Victor Vroom generally found that subordinates held favorable sentiments toward supervisors in such a work situation.[6] However, when he divided these subordinates into two groups, according to personality measures of their reactions to authority, he found that those he classified as highly authoritarian did not respond nearly so favorably as those in the lower group.

Note how this finding fits in with our study of John Dyer's division. While Dyer achieved spectacular results with supervisors—both in productivity and in sentiments toward the job—we have noted that this came about only at the cost of replacing a number of men at positions of foreman, general foreman, and superintendent. While we do not have personality studies of the men so relieved, it is apparent that at least some of them failed because they were not at home in the management environment built by Dyer. They seemed to need more detailed direction than they received.

---

[5] *Power and Leadership in the First Line Supervisor* (Ann Arbor, Michigan: Survey Research Center, 1951). See also his "Leadership Within a Hierarchical Organization," Albert H. Rubenstein and Chadwick J. Haberstroh (eds.), *Some Theories of Organization* (Homewood, Illinois: The Dorsey Press, Inc., and Richard D. Irwin, Inc., 1960).

[6] *Some Personality Determinants of the Effects of Participation* (Englewood Cliffs, N.J.: Prentice-Hall, 1960).

Culture as well as personality may condition responses of individuals to participative management. This is suggested by a Norwegian replication of experimental studies carried on earlier at the Harwood Manufacturing Company. In the Harwood studies, it was found that when employee groups were involved in discussion regarding both the introduction of new production methods and the amount they wanted to produce, productivity results were better than in cases where employees were not so involved.[7] The researchers also found more favorable sentiments toward supervisors and a lower labor turnover in the participative situations.

In the Norwegian study comparisons of the experimental groups with control groups, in which no participative efforts were made, indicated no differences in productivity.[8] We should note, however, that the amounts to be produced were not discussed in the experimental groups as they had been in some of the Harwood studies. The workers' expressions of satisfaction with participation did not show any consistent picture until workers were divided into those who expressed a belief in the legitimacy of participation and those who did not. Those who felt it was legitimate for workers to be consulted regarding the work situation responded favorably to the participation experience, whereas those who had expressed a different opinion showed no such favorable reaction. This comparison of one Norwegian with another does suggest that cultures may differ markedly in the proportion of people who feel that subordinates should have some say in their work situation. In the culture of the United States, we should expect a large proportion of workers to desire and expect such involvement, whereas in many other countries the proportion may be much smaller.

What do all these studies indicate? While we find a number of exceedingly interesting items, the over-all picture is more tantalizing than satisfying, for the problems seem much more complicated that they appeared to be earlier, and clear patterns are only beginning to emerge.

Why has progress been so slow? I would argue that the researchers have been handicapped by an oversimplified conception of human relations. As long as attention was focused exclusively on the man–boss relationship, we could hardly expect to have any solid findings emerge. Thus, Pelz's introduction of the relation between the foreman and his superiors—giving us three levels to deal with instead of two—represents an important advance. But why stop at three levels in an organization that has many more?

The inconsistency between the Prudential and railroad findings sug-

---

[7] Lester Coch and John R. P. French, Jr., "Overcoming Resistance to Change," in Dorwin Cartwright and Alvin Zander (eds.), *Group Dynamics* (Evanston, Ill.: Row, Peterson & Co., 1953 and 1960).

[8] John R. P. French, Jr., J. Israel, D. As, "An Experiment in Participation in a Norwegian Factory," *Human Relations*, Vol. XIII, No. 1 (1960), pp. 13–19.

gests that there must be something in the difference between the two types of jobs to account for different responses. This is hardly a surprising conclusion when we are comparing jobs so disparate as that of the office clerk and of the worker on a section gang. But recognizing the importance of differences in jobs is only the first step. We need to explore systematically the impact of a given technology and pattern of job duties upon workers and upon the relations between workers and management. We have tried to take some steps in this direction in the present volume. Furthermore, while it is better to study relations among three hierarchical levels instead of two, and better still to extend our focus to further levels, we cannot be satisfied with the hierarchical picture alone. As I have tried to show in this book, the organization is far more than a line of authority. A study of it must involve an examination of important horizontal relations of work flow from department to department and within a given department. Without considering such work flow relations, how can we explain the problems of Tom Walker and his Barrel Department (Chapter 9)?

Within many organizations there exist important relations between the line management people and staff, service, and control departments. These relations have received little attention, and yet their importance cannot be doubted. We have tried to deal with some of them in this book, and in the next section of this chapter, we will attempt some generalizations upon these relations.

Research has also faced difficulties in its concentration upon "morale." However the term is defined, it refers to the sentiments of organization members, but there are various classes of sentiments that do not necessarily fit together. In each class of sentiments to be discussed below, it is possible for workers to have a favorable or negative reaction without necessarily involving the same degree of positive or negative reaction in another class.

We may begin with sentiments workers have toward the job itself and toward the working conditions surrounding the job. Here we have seen assembly line workers holding strong negative sentiments to the job itself. These seem to be associated with negative sentiments toward the company as a whole, and yet we may find positive sentiments toward the foreman. On the other hand, the Benton glass blowers showed strongly favorable sentiments toward the job itself, were generally favorable toward the company, and had highly negative sentiments toward the assistant production manager.

What sentiments do workers have toward their particular work group? As we have seen in the case of the centerless grinders, discussed in Chapter 17, the men maintained negative sentiments toward management throughout the period covered. However, at the beginning of that period they held strongly positive sentiments toward their own work associates, while at the end of that period their sentiments toward those

associates were strongly negative. In more general terms, Stanley Seashore's studies of work group cohesion have shown that strongly favorable interpersonal sentiments within a work group can be found in situations where groups are either highly favorable or unfavorable toward
management.[9]

What about relations to the immediate supervisor and to higher management? The workers in the Hi-Test plant were strongly favorable to
their immediate foreman, Tom Lloyd, and to his boss, while they displayed strongly negative sentiments toward General Superintendent
Masters. When the Barrel Department workers turned against Tom
Walker, this did not affect their favorable sentiments toward higher
management in general.

These observations point to the folly of attempting to sum up scores
on all these sentiments and call the result "morale." This is not to suggest
that the Survey Research Center makes this error. However, popular discussions often jump from a conclusion about a specific sentiment to
generalizations about "morale," when it is most important to ask which
class of sentiments moves in which way in response to what conditions.

Since none of these classes of sentiments seems clearly related to
productivity, we might focus attention on sentiments toward productivity
itself. We will then say that those people with high morale have a high
motivation to produce. In other words, people who want to be productive are more likely to be productive. While this is no doubt true, the
statement only rephrases the problem for us. We must now ask: What
makes people want to be productive? The answer to that question is not
to be found in any single class of sentiments. Motivation to produce is an
outcome of a combination of interactions, activities, and sentiments in
relation to a set of symbols. We shall explore further the nature of this
combination in the remaining sections of this chapter.

## AUTHORITY OR INTEGRATION?

Our review of the literature has concentrated upon the man–boss relationship. Before we can generalize about organizations, we must consider other types of relationships.

A large, complex organization depends upon the integration of the
operating groups with specialist groups. How is this brought about?

The traditional approach involves trying to define the functions and
relationships among groups in terms of authority, responsibility, coordination, advice, and so on—with none of these terms being given any
precise behavioral referents.

For example, it is said that the staff man is an adviser to the line man

---

[9] *Group Cohesiveness in the Industrial Work Group* (Ann Arbor, Michigan:
Survey Research Center, 1954).

and does not exercise authority over him. Such a statement hardly conveys a realistic picture of behavior we often see in industry between line and staff people.

This is illustrated by the case of Harry Holmes, a vice-president for industrial relations, and one of his plant managers. Harry was a man in his sixties who had come up through the ranks in the company and acquired a tremendous respect on the part of workers and managers alike. The plant manager was consulting Harry on an action he wanted to take. Harry advised him against it. The plant manager persisted, rephrased all his arguments, and said he was determined to proceed. Harry shook his head once again and said: "If that's the way you feel about it, go ahead. It's your decision to make. But that sure is going to get you into a lot of trouble." The plant manager thought it over some more and decided not to do it after all.

Harry Holmes told us the story to show that he only served in an advisory capacity to the line. The plant manager was free to accept or reject his advice. Now, I don't know how this exchange looked to the plant manager, but I know that situation well enough to imagine the plant manager's reaction. If he went ahead, he knew very well that Harry Holmes would take no action to stop him, because Harry was very conscientious about avoiding the exercise of authority. If the plan worked all right, then there was nothing to worry about. On the other hand, if he went ahead and the labor relations difficulties anticipated by Harry Holmes did materialize, what then? The general manager would ask him why he hadn't consulted Harry Holmes, and he would have to admit that he had consulted Holmes but had refused to take his advice. Or the general manager would ask old Harry why he hadn't advised the plant manager. Harry wouldn't want to hurt the plant manager, but he was an honest man, and he would have to say, "Well, I told Joe that that would lead to trouble, but he was determined to go ahead anyway." Or words to that effect.

In this example, merely saying that Harry Holmes served in an advisory capacity does not explain the situation. On the other hand, it is equally misleading to say that Harry Holmes exercised authority.

If we define authority in terms of the direct exercise of sanctions, then Harry Holmes was not exercising authority. However, he was in the position where, whether he wanted to or not, he brought sanctions to bear upon the situation indirectly. Harry Holmes' sanctioning power was derived only in part from the formal position he held. At least as important was the set of relations he had developed with the top management people and union leaders over the years.

Still, let us not overlook the importance of formal rank in our advice–authority problem. Suppose the plant manager had received the exact same advice from the plant personnel manager, his immediate subordinate. Would he have responded in the same way? Hardly. The plant personnel manager was in no position to bring sanctions to bear directly or indirectly upon the plant manager.

The proposition may be stated in this form: The staff man who holds an organizational rank superior to that of the line man will initiate activity for the line man or block the line man's initiations more often than will the staff man whose rank is inferior. In terms of people's perceptions, this explains why the plant manager is likely to classify a statement from his plant personnel manager as "advice," whereas the foreman is likely to interpret the same statement as "orders." This proposition sounds almost too obvious to state, and yet how often do we read discussions of the staff–line relationship in which the authors fail to specify the organizational rank held by each of the individuals involved? Clearly, a discussion of staff–line relations which omits these status considerations is bound to be misleading.

Let us consider other specialist functions beyond giving advice: inspection, innovation, service, and goal-setting.

Often the inspection function is not explicitly part of a specialist's job, and yet the activity may take place anyway. In the nature of his responsibilities, the specialist is often free to roam widely through the plant and thus has an opportunity to notice many things relevant to his specialty—as well as many other things not so relevant but of possible interest to higher management. The specialist is generally attached to a hierarchy much shorter than that of the line foreman; observing a problem in a foreman's department, he can readily bring it to the attention of people at the top of his specialist group, from which point the problem may be presented to the line organization far above the level of foreman. The foreman may then find himself suddenly called upon to explain a condition on which he had presented no report up the line and, in fact, one which he hoped would not come to higher management's attention. Thus, the specialist may be rewarded by his superiors for providing them with information they consider valuable, while the foreman may be penalized in such a situation. We then may find higher management wondering if the personalities of the foreman and the specialist are responsible for their inability to cooperate very well on projects where they are supposed to work together. Of course, personalities give us no answer in this case. We can characterize the relationship in terms of the following proposition: When A is rewarded for activities that result in penalizing B, then (1) A will be inclined to continue these activities, (2) B will have negative sentiments toward A, and (3) other activities in which they are expected to work together will be marked by failure of cooperation and mutual recriminations.

This does not mean that the inspection function should be eliminated from the organization. Unfortunately, very little research attention has been given to the organization of inspection activities, so we are not ready to generalize regarding their reorganization or elimination. However, two points are clear even at this early stage. The same individual cannot carry out the inspection function as described above and still get the cooperation of those whose work he inspects in other activities. Not all activities are compatible with each other in the organization, and it is up to management to see to it that individuals are not given incompatible activities to perform.

The second point involves the level at which the observations are reported. If the specialist reports his observations directly to the foreman— and then offers to help him to correct the condition—quite a different relationship is possible between the two men. This will be explored further as we consider the innovating function.

Engineers in particular, but also personnel men and some other specialists, are expected to be innovators, to get operating people to adopt new products, machines, processes, and systems of doing work or of organizing relations among people. If the innovation process is to proceed smoothly, it must be fitted into the existing pattern of interactions and activities.

People tend to become accustomed to a certain pattern of activities. We also find a tendency toward a patterning of interactions. This means that the individual becomes accustomed to interacting with a certain number of other individuals with a certain frequency from day to day and with a certain balance between the interactions he initiates and those to which he responds, and so on. This is not to say that A must interact with B exactly six times per day if their sentiments toward each other are to be maintained. It does mean that if several days go by without any interactions at all and then A initiates twelve interactions to B in one day and twenty the next, we would anticipate difficulties between them.

One aspect of the common difficulties between specialists and operating men is that the intervention of the specialist upon operations tends to be sporadic.

The operating man develops his own pattern of daily activities and his own pattern of interactions with superior and subordinates. In many situations, the specialist is free to move over a wide geographical and social area so that he may interact little if at all with a given operating man over a long period of time. If he then suddenly begins concentrating on this operating man's area, with frequent initiations of interaction and frequent efforts to induce changes in activity, it is only natural to expect the operating man to react negatively.

We are accustomed to thinking of the specialist as the innovator. He may often be regarded as the disrupter, but, we may ask, is this disruption a necessary concomitant of innovation?

In innovation, the specialist is trying to get the operating man to do something differently, or at least to accept some changed process, machine, or method, in his area of responsibility. Who gets the rewards and penalties in this type of situation? Frequently, we find that the

penalty of having to go through a difficult adjustment process is monopolized by the operating man, whereas the reward of credit for generating and implementing a new idea is monopolized by the specialist.

If we examine the relationship in these terms, it is a wonder that
cooperative activities between operating men and specialists ever develop. Indeed, they do not when the specialist carries out his role in the
terms just described.

Fortunately, there seems to be a different way of going about it. As I
have examined those specialists who did seem to get along with operating people, I have found that they have proceeded in a manner that can
be described in terms of five general points:

1. The specialist builds up a certain frequency and regularity of interaction with the operating man before seeking to bring about any innovations.

2. This means, in effect, that the specialist does not simply cook up his innovation in his own mind and then move right in and try to bring it about.
Instead, he deliberately withholds his innovating efforts until he has established a personal relationship which will make them more acceptable.

3. Before he seeks to innovate, the specialist concentrates on familiarizing
himself with the operating man's situation and problems. Some of this is done
through observation, but a good deal of it is done through interviewing. This
means, in effect, that the specialist gets the operating man to explain his situation as he views it himself, and to take the initiative in their relationship.

4. The specialist tries to build his innovations into a pattern of reciprocal
initiations and exchange of valued activities. That is, he is not exclusively asking the operating man to change his behavior. He is also providing opportunities for the operating man to call for help from the specialist.

5. The specialist helps the operating man with activities for which the
operating man receives rewards.

We have seen this approach illustrated in the case of Warren Hawkins as he built up the personnel organization described in Chapter 29.
This is also the procedure used by Meredith Wiley in the action research
program at the Hotel Tremont. Note that he made his first reports to
the top of the organization highly general and reported in more detail
only as the supervisors, with his help, were able to show progress, and
for this they received recognition from Mr. Smith.

Specialist groups themselves have the same need as operating groups
to develop a regular pattern of interactions and activities. In the Amicon
tube case (Chapter 27) we saw the customary sequence of activities and
interactions of development engineers and industrial engineers completely disrupted. This disruption seems to have accounted in large
measure for the painfully slow progress of the tube from idea to production.

Compared to the innovating specialists, a service organization such
as maintenance is in quite a different position in relation to the operating
organization. As we have seen in Chapter 26, "Maintenance and Operating Organizations," maintenance tends to have a low value relative to
operations and to be constantly on the receiving end of initiations of

activity from operating people. There also tends to be a lack of reciprocity between the two groups, with operating people calling on maintenance for service and maintenance generally not being able to call upon operating people for anything in return.

This condition leads maintenance people to feel that they are in a subordinate position and under pressure from the operating people. When this general pressure situation is compounded by conflicting demands on maintenance from various operating groups, management may establish an independent scheduling organization to serve as a buffer between operations and maintenance as well as to plan the work. While this may eliminate the conflicting pressures on maintenance, it may also serve simply to substitute for operating people the scheduling group as the constant initiators to maintenance. We have cited one case in which a work scheduler and a maintenance foreman developed a reciprocal relationship, which indicates that this sort of thing is possible. If management people were more aware of the needs for reciprocity, such work organization systems might be better planned and better administered.

We might note one further situation in which maintenance people may initiate for operating people: establishment of preventive maintenance programs. No doubt there are good technical engineering reasons to support such programs, but our concern here is with the changes they bring about in the interactions and activities between operations and maintenance. In a preventive program, maintenance people must schedule for a given department regular periods when machines will be overhauled and when checks on their operations will be carried out. This clearly involves maintenance people in initiating changes in activity for operating people—perhaps a welcome opportunity for maintenance but a change likely to be resisted by operations.

The significance of organizational goals will be considered further in our next section. At this point we need simply to note that the goal-setting process tends to establish the sentiments of the specialist and the operating people toward each other. If the operating people at lower levels have no part in establishing the goals for which they are to work, they necessarily develop negative sentiments toward the specialists who set these goals and feel under pressure from them and from higher management people who utilize the set of symbols in evaluating their performance.

Let us now see how this approach to the relations between specialists and operating people may be applied to the building of an efficient and effective organization.

It is customary to plan organizations in terms of the authority and responsibility to be distributed to each position. As I have tried to show, this approach leads to all sorts of difficulties. Particularly in a large and complex organization, it is simply not practical to specify in any detail who has authority over what. Attempts to do so will result either in overlapping of functions or failures of coordination.

In such organizations, we must begin by saying that numbers of people must work together in a variety of ways—and then we must go on to specify the ways that are required, without attempting to define the authority involved in the various positions.

We begin by examining the work that needs to be done—at the level of production or process itself. We note how the work flow may be best organized for the most effective utilization of men and machines. We then seek to answer questions such as these, for any given activity:

Who should initiate the activity? Who interacts with whom in carrying it out? What symbols are established for the evaluation of performance? Through what channels of interaction are these symbols established? What rewards or penalties are provided for superior or inferior performance?

The answers to such questions will tend to establish for us the activities and interactions that are required and the incentives that bring them forth. To establish further control over the sentiments of the people involved, we also need to look for possibilities of reciprocity in the exchange of valued activities. If we specify that cooperation is to take place between A and B, we need also to ask what each is expected to do *for* the other and whether we have established a system in which both will be rewarded for the results of their cooperative activity.

## REWARDS AND PENALTIES

It is often assumed that man is an inert animal who will only become active when prodded or lured by specific rewards or penalties. This is not the case. Man is naturally an active animal. Most times he would rather be doing something than nothing. Furthermore, he gets certain intrinsic satisfactions from the job he does.

Jobs vary in the intrinsic satisfactions they can provide. As we have seen, the Benton glass blowers found great intrinsic satisfaction in their work, while the automotive assembly line workers found little if any such satisfaction in their jobs.

While management would do well to recognize the possibility of intrinsic satisfactions in work and to seek to find (through job enlargement) increased possibilities of such satisfaction, we must recognize that intrinsic satisfactions alone cannot be enough even for highly skilled workers, and they will fall far short of motivating workers on routine jobs.

Looking beyond the intrinsic satisfactions or dissatisfactions of the job itself, let us begin with penalties. On this subject we can make two points, the first being rather obvious and the second requiring more elaboration.

An organization requires some balance between penalties and rewards. If rewards appear to be sparse and penalties frequent and heavy, the participants will either leave the organization or else develop their own strategies for evading penalties without doing what their superiors expect of them. The reciprocity developed in this type of situation involves an exchange of penalties.

The second point is that penalties and the authority to impose them should remain implicit. When penalties are made explicit—before they are invoked—the result is likely to be a generation of negative sentiments and resistance to those in authority.

Consider the following case in which a foreman describes the way an organizational change had been announced to his group in a management meeting conducted by Manager Smith:

I have never known a time when a change was looked forward to with such enthusiasm. Often you find people just bucking against the change because it is a change, but here the general feeling was that the old type of organization for our group had outlived its usefulness and the time was ripe for a change.

But I'll never forget that meeting when Smith talked to us about the plan for the new setup. Right in that meeting he said to us that this new organization had to succeed and he said, "If there is anyone who doesn't get in there and buck to make this new organization a success, why we will just run him off." He actually used those words: "run him off." You could feel the chill in the atmosphere right then and there. There was not much enthusiasm left after that meeting.

Now why did he have to say that? You can't get anywhere frightening a group of men. Besides, most of us were ready to pitch in and cooperate anyway. Later on if you had found that some individual wasn't pitching in, you could have called him aside and warned him that he ought to get in there and do a job. It certainly does no good to try to frighten a whole group of men.

We may well ask, with the foremen, why the manager made the possible penalty explicit. In doing so, he conveyed no new information to these men. They knew that they were working under authority, that they were not free to reject directives from their superiors. That being the nature of a work organization, there is nothing to be gained from making it explicit, and much to be lost. There may perhaps be differences from one culture to another in this respect, but at least in our own culture, men like to feel that they are voluntarily doing the things that they do, even within a work organization. We expect the boss to *ask* us to do something, not to issue a peremptory order—with stated penalty attached. The most effective organization is one in which the possible penalties are understood but rarely mentioned or imposed.

Let us turn now to rewards. Here the organizational problem is three-fold: to establish a set of symbols to represent rewards, to relate those symbols to types of behavior, and to relate types of behavior to the productivity of the organization.

We must first recognize that unless management develops symbols that can be rather concretely expressed and related to behavior, the hoped for behavior is not likely to arise. Let us say that the performance of the foreman is measured in terms of costs, volume of output, and scrap record. He is also told that he will be evaluated in terms of his ability to maintain "good human relations." If no symbols are provided whereby "good human relations" can be recognized and rewarded, then we can expect the foreman to concentrate on those items where concrete symbols are provided and give little attention to "good human relations"—whatever that phrase means.

Management not only has a problem of providing symbols that will motivate behavior but also of ascertaining that the motivation will be in the direction of organizational effectiveness. As long as symbols are provided and penalties or rewards attached to them, we can be sure that they will have an effect upon behavior, but that effect will not automatically be in the direction management intends. For example, Peter Blau cites a case involving employees in a government employment agency, whose task was to interview unemployed workers and to send them out to job openings.[10] In order to stimulate productivity, the supervisor began keeping records of the number of referrals made by each interviewer. This had the effect of increasing the number of referrals, but whether it served the over-all purposes of the organization was questionable. In concentrating upon numbers, the interviewers tended to cut short their exploratory conversations with applicants and so derived a lesser understanding of them and their problems. The interviewers also tended to refer workers back to employers who had promised to re-employ them in any case, thus getting credit without having really served any function. Interviewers also tended to try to avoid cases they knew to be difficult to place. This kind of phenomenon is often found in industry: The set of symbols does motivate behavior but the behavior does not necessarily serve the purposes of the organization.

We also have cases where two sets of symbols point workers in opposite directions. Consider the example of an incentive system and a suggestion system.[11] In one plant having both in effect, workers on incentive were required to report to management any improvements they themselves had worked out on the job. If they did this, they were rewarded through the suggestion system—but then the job was restudied and the piece rate lowered. On the other hand, if the worker decided to try to keep his improvement secret, he ran the risk that an industrial engineer might catch him at the job with the new method and institute a restudy of the job, thus penalizing the worker and his fellows without giving them any reward at all for the invention. Clearly, the two systems

---

[10] *The Dynamics of Bureaucracy* (Chicago: The University of Chicago Press, 1955), especially pp. 40–48.

[11] See my *Money and Motivation* (New York: Harper & Bros., 1955), pp. 255–56.

pulled workers in opposite directions. It was not a question of whether workers would respond to the offer of money. The situation provided money rewards and penalties in two opposite directions.

We find another problem in the customary lack of integration of the symbol system with the work flow of the plant. Accounting and cost control records are generally provided department by department. The over-all effectiveness of one plant we studied depended in large measure upon smooth coordination among departments along the flow of work, and yet the symbol system provided absolutely no direct rewards for this and in fact encouraged behavior which broke down cooperation. It was often unclear just where a given mistake had been made. Since each cost had to be charged to some department, department heads spent a great deal of their time devising ways to pin such costs on somebody else. As we conducted a supervisory training program for department heads and foremen in this plant, we found them much preoccupied with this cost allocation problem. They had their own expression for it. They would speak of "throwing the dead cat over the fence and into the other fellow's yard." Their description of the situation gave us a picture of dead cats being heaved in all directions.[12]

If economic symbols can serve to motivate people toward competition and conflict, can they also be used to symbolize a common goal for the total organization? Some efforts have been made along this line, the best known of them going under the name of the Scanlon Plan, named for Joseph Scanlon, a brilliant innovator who began this work for the United Steel Workers and, until his death, continued setting up union-management cooperation plans while on the faculty of Massachusetts Institute of Technology.

The Scanlon Plan is an incentive system in which the pay-off is based upon the performance of the plant as a whole. In the area of symbols, this involves attaching the incentive to improvements in labor costs as compared to some base period. If, for the given period, labor costs in relation to the sales dollar are below the base period, the difference is paid out according to a formula previously agreed upon between union and management.

Compared to individual or group piece rate systems, this approach has some notable advantages. It avoids the constant wrangling we often find under piece rate systems. It also avoids the problems of intergroup conflict, with one group complaining that its own incentive is not as favorable as that of another group or with the skilled maintenance workers arguing that they are not as favorably treated on incentive as the production workers. The Scanlon Plan does not of itself eliminate perceived inequities in pay rates, but it does not introduce new inequities as a piece rate program is almost certain to do. It also provides people with an in-

[12] See Chris Argyris, *Executive Leadership* (New York: Harper & Bros., 1953).

centive to improve intergroup relations, for any improvements in the
effective working relations of groups and departments to each other are
reflected in the plant-wide performance figures.

The plant-wide performance symbols will have no automatic effect.
They are like a flag around which all members of the organization may
rally, but whether they rally or not depends upon the organization of
interactions and activities in relation to these symbols.

Under the individual incentive plan, the individual can readily see the
connection between his skill and effort and the pay-off. Under a group
piece rate plan, the connection is somewhat more removed, but nevertheless the worker can measure his own progress in relation to the group
effort. If he slackens, others may urge him onward, and he similarly
may prod a fellow group member who is not pulling his load. Under the
plant-wide set of symbols, the connection between individual performance
and incentive earnings is exceedingly remote. The plantwide symbols
can have meaning only to the individual insofar as he is integrated in a
group and is actively participating in the system and insofar as the
groups are integrated at higher levels.

It is not so much increased physical effort as the generation and implementation of ideas and the better integration of parts of the organization that lead to the payoff under the Scanlon Plan. This means
that the system must provide for a canvass of ideas regarding improvements in every department and for a regular program of union and management discussions at the top local level to screen the ideas and to give
management the opportunity to put them into effect.

The Scanlon Plan is discussed in much detail elsewhere.[13] For present
purposes, its significance is particularly that of providing incentives and
channels for the initiation of activities from the bottom levels up to the
top in the plant. In some cases the Plan has been a spectacular success,
and management people have been amazed at the fruitfulness of the ideas
held by workers or that workers have been able to develop when challenged. It is this reversal of the customary direction for the initiation of
activities that provides the major explanation of success in these cases.
Here, the plant-wide set of symbols could not work by itself, but without
such a plant-wide symbol system, it would be impossible to generate the
active participation in the development of ideas by workers and lower
management people that has been observed in these cases.

## A SYSTEMS APPROACH TO ORGANIZATION

In this section, I shall attempt to sum up the point of view of this book
regarding analysis of organizational problems. We might characterize it

---

[13] See "The Scanlon Plan," in my *Money and Motivation* (New York: Harper
& Bros., 1955). See also Frederick Lesieur, *The Scanlon Plan* (Cambridge,
Mass.: The Technology Press of Massachusetts Institute of Technology, 1958).

as a systems approach to organization and contrast it with a cause–effect approach to the analysis of organization.

The student who pursues the cause–effect approach tries to find one or more factors which can be taken as the "causes" of certain other phenomena. He may try to show, for example, that a certain type of foreman activity or sentiment is the "cause" of high productivity. Another man might try to demonstrate that a given incentive system was the "cause" of high productivity. As we have seen, a number of these factors could be cited as causes, individually or in combination, of organizational behavior; yet every presumed cause can be shown to have the given effect only in a certain type of context and not in another.

If we acknowledge that the impact of a given force depends in part upon the context within which it operates, then this recognition should lead us to see the necessity of building a scheme of analysis in which forces and contexts are integrated. This is what I mean by a systems approach to organization. My system involves the interactions, activities, and sentiments of the members in relation to the social, economic, and technological environment. I assume a state of *mutual dependence* among the elements of the social system, which means that a change introduced into interactions will be accompanied by change in activities and sentiments; a change introduced into activities will be accompanied by changes in interactions and sentiments, and so on. I also assume a state of mutual dependence between the environment and the social system, which means that a change introduced into the environment will have its effects upon the social system, and changes that occur within the social system may have their effects upon the environment. In this book, in considering the environment–social system relationship, we have been primarily concerned with the impact of environment on social system.

The systems approach points us towards significant data that would otherwise be overlooked, and it also gives us some preliminary notions as to how the relations among these bodies of data might be analyzed. For example, in the case of Tom Walker, the Barrel Department foreman (Chapter 9), our problem was to explain why the productivity of his department had fallen off, his relations with his workers had worsened, and management had lost faith in his ability. To solve the problem, we examined his relations with his workers, but we did not stop there. We also examined his relations with his organizational superiors, noting the impact of changes in personnel. We also looked at his changing relations with the union representatives. We placed him in the management work flow, noting with which management people he interacted. Finally, we examined the nature of the work flow and production process within Walker's department, noting particularly the changes that had taken place within the two-year period.

Furthermore, we did not just add up our findings for each problem area. We tried to trace out the interrelations among these areas. We noted the pervasive impact of the change in the volume and type of orders going through the department. We pointed out that the new situation required Walker to multiply his interactions with other management people who even in 1948 held negative sentiments toward him. We showed how this change in production affected the work available within the department and how Walker's response to this situation led to a division in the work group and growing friction among workers and between workers and the foreman. We also noted how the removal from the situation of the union president and the production manager, with whom Walker had been accustomed to working out his problems, made it more difficult for him to cope with the new situation.

The systems approach can also be applied on a larger scale to the organization as a whole. In Chapter 19, "Patterns in Union-Management Relations," we dealt with four levels of the company's organization and four levels of the local union and their interrelations. We did not seek to explain union–management harmony or conflict in terms of relations among the parties at any single level, nor did we confine ourselves to examining the sentiments of the parties. Instead, we sought to show how changes in the frequency of initiation of activities at one particular point would be accompanied by changes at other points in the system and by changes in the sentiments of the parties.

This systems approach assumes that an organization tends to develop a pattern of interactions and activities of such a nature that changes in this pattern are accompanied by changes in sentiments. What do we mean by pattern? We mean that there is some regularity to be observed. Joe does not interact with Tom precisely twelve times every day, but observation shows his *interactions* with Tom ranging between eight and sixteen. If we suddenly observe that the two men are not interacting at all or that they are interacting thirty times a day, we can then assume that a significant change has taken place within the social system.

Similarly, we may observe the foreman initiating *activity* for Joe between four and eight times a day, and Joe initiating for the foreman between two and six times a day. If suddenly we observe the foreman initiating to Joe between fifteen and twenty times a day, whereas Joe does not increase his initiating to the foreman, then we expect to find evidences of disturbance between the two men. In other words, it is departures from the observed pattern that alert us to significant changes taking place in the social system.

We further assume that the interactions and activities initiated in one direction are not independent of those initiated in another direction. That is, we assume that there is a necessary relationship between the foreman's initiation toward the worker and the worker's initiation toward the foreman. While we have observed a number of cases in which favorable sentiments of workers toward their foremen were associated with worker opportunity to initiate activities for foremen, we cannot predict sentiments from observing this direction of initiation alone. Chris Argyris has reported a case in which workers held favorable sentiments toward their foremen, yet rarely initiated activity for them.[14] At the same time, he reported that the foremen very rarely initiated activities for the workers. The sentiments seem to be associated with a *ratio* of initiations going up to those coming down. This would assume that a marked increase in frequency of initiations from foreman to workers will be accompanied by the growth of worker negative sentiments toward the foreman, *unless* the workers increased their initiations to the foreman in a roughly comparable amount. This is an abstract way of saying that when a foreman wishes to introduce changes in the activities of his workers without getting them upset with him and resisting his efforts, he should encourage them to suggest to him adjustments that he might make.

We have been speaking of compensatory initiations between foremen and workers, increases down balanced by increases up. In one sense and on a larger scale, the union can be considered as a compensatory mechanism in relation to the management organization. As management increases its initiation of activity down the line, the disturbances felt at the work level may be expressed in increased initiations up the line in the union and from union at several levels to management. Upon management's ability to respond effectively to these compensatory initiations from the union may depend the effectiveness of management's administration of the organization.

We have also pointed out that when initiations go exclusively or almost exclusively from A to B, with no provision for B initiating back at A, then negative sentiments arise between the parties. This seems to hold true whether we are talking about foreman–worker, production man–maintenance man, or manager–union official. Union–management cooperation depends not only upon the responses of management people to initiations from union officers. It depends also upon the ability of management people to initiate to their opposite numbers in the union.

We have been talking about reciprocity in the initiation of activities. We should note also that there is something to activities beyond just the number of them. They tend to be valued, positively or negatively, and the exchange of these values tends to channelize interactions, activities, and sentiments. When two men are expected to work together, we need to ask whether there are valued activities they can exchange with each other. We have noted instances where the activity for which B is rewarded serves to penalize A. Under these circumstances, we can hardly expect positive sentiments between the parties.

## THE STRATEGY OF ORGANIZATIONAL CHANGE

What has been said so far about the way organizations function tells the reader by implication all that I have to say regarding problems of

---

[14] *Understanding Organizational Behavior* (Homewood, Illinois: The Dorsey Press, Inc., 1960).

introducing change in organizations. In this concluding section, I simply try to make explicit the principles involved and apply them to the problem of change.

Let us begin with a new man moving into an organization with a mandate from his superiors to introduce changes. How should he proceed?

Consider the case of Mr. Jackson, who came in from another district to take over a particular management group. A few months later his subordinates had forgotten everything Jackson had said on the occasion of his first meeting with them—except for his opening statement. They would never forget that. He said, "I have been sent in to straighten things out around here."

Resistance to change was born at this moment. Some of the men in this group had been with the company in this kind of work for years. They prided themselves on their skills and on their loyalty to the company. They were not aware that they were in bad shape. If you had asked them, any one of them could have suggested changes that he thought would have improved the organization. But Mr. Jackson did not ask them. He told them. They resisted every change he sought to introduce.

If we assume that a manager should seek to win the favorable sentiments of his subordinates, clearly Jackson's first move was a blunder. Before we go on to consider further the problems of winning and maintaining favorable sentiments, let us recognize that such favorable sentiments may not be a necessary condition for carrying out certain types of changes. Now and then we hear that things had gotten into bad shape in a particular plant, and home office management had sent in one or two "hatchet men" to straighten out the situation. Some times it seems that "hatchet men" are sent in just for a brief time to make drastic changes that they will not have to live with, and higher management later sends in managers whose assignment it is to smooth out the disturbed situation.

The hatchet man approach has one notable advantage when it comes to making drastic changes, such as firing and demoting people. The man who comes in from the outside and begins to make changes quickly does not become encumbered by positive sentiments toward his management associates. He may make the drastic and apparently brutal decisions that another manager who has lived and worked with a particular group would find it exceedingly difficult to make. On the other hand, we must wonder whether this one advantage is enough to compensate for the serious and long-lived disruptions that follow in the wake of decisions by the hatchet man. If it is possible to introduce far-reaching changes into the organization and at the same time build and maintain positive sentiments among organizational members toward their superiors clearly this is the optimum approach. How do you do it?

Consider the following statement by Restaurant Manager Potter:

There is one thing I try to impress on my new managers. I tell them, "When you go in to take over a new place, don't make any changes in the first three months. The store can run itself for that length of time without you. Now maybe your predecessor was a poor manager and the employees didn't like him. Still, if you come in and change things around right away, they will remember your predecessor, and they will be thinking that his ways were the right ways.

I tell them, "Carry a notebook around with you, and when you see something that should be changed, go back into your office and make a note of it. And don't let anybody see you writing in that notebook. Don't make any changes at first, but spend three months letting the supervisors and employees get to know you. When they get used to you you can begin making your changes—gradually."[15]

The same point is illustrated in a study by Merei of children's play groups.[16] He observed groups of children for a period of time until they had developed stable patterns of interaction and initiation of activity. He then picked out the leader of each group and removed that child from the group for a period of two weeks. Within this two-week period, a new leader had taken over, and the group had evolved its own regular set of activities. When Merei reintroduced the previously established leaders, they were not immediately able to take over. The customary sequence went something like this. The former leader would attempt to initiate a new activity for the group. He would be resisted or ignored. Afer several such unsuccessful efforts, he would modify his behavior. First he would fit himself into the established activities that were going on. Then he would begin more and more to take the initiative in those particular activities. As he found the other children beginning to respond to him, he was able to introduce modifications into the established activities and even eventually to introduce entirely new activities to the group. Note that he was not able to introduce any changes at all until he had fitted himself into the group's activities.

The advice of Potter and the experiment of Merei illustrate the same point. The man who wishes to introduce changes must win personal acceptance first. That is, he must fit himself into the framework of interactions and activities of the organization before he can be effective in changing that pattern. This is obvious enough when we are discussing a social group. We are likely to overlook the point in a formal organization because we may assume that when a man has been given a position of manager, he automatically becomes able to initiate activities for his subordinates. This is not the case. Unless he wins acceptance first, his efforts to introduce change will be frustrated.

The fitting-in process is not limited to activities and interactions. Re-

---

[15] In my *Human Relations in the Restaurant Industry* (New York: McGraw-Hill Book Co., Inc., 1948), pp. 332–33.

[16] Ferenc Merei, "Group Leadership and Institutionalization," in E. Maccoby, T. Newcomb, E. Hartley (eds.), *Readings in Social Psychology* (New York: Henry Holt & Co., 1958).

calling (in Chapter 2) the case of Gregory the Great and his advice to his missionaries in Britain, let us consider symbols also. Gregory was telling the missionaries that they should accept the existing symbols of the pagan religion but fit themselves into the interactions and activities of the people organized around those symbols, and in this way, gradually get into the position where they could reinterpret the meaning of the symbols in terms of Christian doctrine. In effect, he was pointing out that an attack upon the symbols would simply alienate the people and make it impossible to win them to the Christian church.

Let us assume that the manager has now established his position so that he has a chance of success in introducing changes. What does he now try to change?

Does he seek to change sentiments directly? A good deal of experience and some research on training programs indicates that this is a futile pastime. In training foremen, do we tell them, "You should be more employee oriented?" Of course, the admonitions are never put in that terminology, and yet this is the import of many training efforts. The trainers are trying to get the foremen to think and feel differently about their subordinates. When this is done by the lecture method, we certainly would expect no results, but even when the approach is through a discussion technique, the results seem disappointing, as we have noted in Chapter 1.

Why should this be? Since sentiments grow out of experience in interaction and activity, it seems difficult if not impossible for trainers to change these sentiments of foremen to subordinates directly through admonition or discussion. Even should the approach be effective with foremen, they are in a most unstrategic position in the organization, so that significant changes have to be introduced at higher levels. But even a training program focused on sentiments but aimed at all levels would not seem to promise much progress.

More leverage for a change can be gained through working directly on interactions and activities. If the manager really believes in increasing the delegation of authority, he can reorganize the distribution of activities so that certain of them which previously required specific approval at higher levels may now be initiated and terminated at lower levels without such clearance. The manager can build up the initiative of subordinates in both interactions and activities, as John Dyer did, through discussion meetings in which he encourages full participation and especially encourages those who have new ideas and dissenting opinions to express themselves. In this way, he may establish a pattern that will carry on down to lower levels. The experience of John Dyer and of Meredith Wiley at the Tremont Hotel suggests that the most effective discussion training sessions for subordinates are provided when the discussions are skillfully led and organized around the actual problems of the organization.

While we emphasize the importance of the job situation itself for training purposes, we do not consider off-the-job training as useless. Some modifications may be introduced into the interaction patterns of individuals through a type of training in which the individual is subjected to an intensive group experience, such as that provided by the National Training Laboratory for Group Development at Bethel, Maine, and through further training approaches based upon free discussion and attempts to build up the sensitivity of members to reactions others have to them. For example, we may have a manager who tends to dominate all discussions with his subordinates. Since they are his subordinates, they are hardly in a position to put much pressure upon him to reduce his dominating behavior. When, for several weeks, he is part of a discussion group in which no one takes orders from him, he soon finds that he is resisted when he attempts to dominate the conversation. Other members show subtle and then more obvious signs of disapproval of him, and, if he persists, he may finally be told that he is talking too much. This is an upsetting experience, and, in some cases, it may upset the individual without leading to any change in his behavior in the organization. On the other hand, there have been some individuals who have found such an intensive discussion group experience highly illuminating in enabling them for the first time to understand how others react to them and to begin to modify their interactions in response to this understanding.

Suppose the manager seeks to introduce changes in behavior through changing some of the *symbols* of the organization. In the preceding section, we have pointed to some of the possibilities. While symbols may indeed present powerful tools for organizational change, we find that many people in recent years have come to overestimate the potency of these tools. For example, having suddenly discovered status symbols, they feel that these symbols are almost magical formulae that can be used to change human relations in any desired direction. Consider this case provided us by Dale Carnegie:

> This mechanic's job was to keep scores of typewriters and other hard-driven machines functioning smoothly night and day. He was always complaining that the hours were too long, that there was too much work, that he needed an assistant.
>
> J. A. Want (the boss) didn't give him an assistant, didn't give him shorter hours or less work, and yet he made the mechanic happy. How? This mechanic was given a private office. His name appeared on the door, and with it his title—"Manager of the Service Department."[17]

As far as Dale Carnegie was concerned, this was the end of the story, but I can let my readers in on certain developments that took place

---

[17] Dale Carnegie, *How to Win Friends and Influence People* (New York: Pocket Books, Inc.) I found this on p. 241 of Copy 2, 365, 447 of "The most popular work of non-fiction of our time." (It had reached this figure in 1942. Is it still going strong?)

later. A day or two after the events described, the mechanic was approached by a fellow worker, and the following conversation ensued:

"Congratulations, Joe, I see you are a department manager now. How many people in your department?"

"Well, there is just me. Nobody else."

"You mean you are a manager, but you got nobody to manage?"

"Yeah, I guess the boss just gave me the title."

"At least you must have got a good raise out of it?"

"Well, not exactly. The boss didn't say anything about more money."

After Joe had been subjected to variations of this conversation with several of the workers and had overheard conversations about him in which the word "sucker" kept recurring, he approached J. A. Want again. This time he reported that he felt more overworked than ever and needed *two* assistants. He wanted more money also. As he put it, "I figure that a manager should be worth a lot more to you than just a plain mechanic."

I should add that my sequel is imaginary, but can anyone really believe in the happy ending of this story provided by Dale Carnegie? The point is that symbols are not arbitrary. They bear some relation to the organizational world around them. The symbol of the title of manager implies supervisory activity, some people to supervise, and a job that should pay more money than one without such a high-sounding title. The possibilities of substituting status symbols for money are actually quite limited, and the man who tries to make such substitution is likely to find that he gets into more trouble than the effort is worth.

This does not mean that there is nothing to be gained through changing the symbols. In some cases, we can change an objectionable title to one that is more acceptable to the job holder and still is in line with his functions in the organization. For example, one hospital superintendent mentioned to me a job classification that had existed in his hospital: "bulb snatcher." In this large hospital, there was one man employed full time to patrol the halls and replace worn-out light bulbs with new ones. The title was indeed descriptive of the man's functions, and yet we can hardly imagine that employee answering the questions of acquaintances and friends by saying, "I am a bulb snatcher." In this case, we can hardly change the title to "electrician" because that title is customarily given to skilled craftsmen who would resent having their classification shared by an unskilled man. Perhaps something like "electrical maintenance man" or "assistant electrical maintenance man" might be more satisfying to the jobholder without giving rise to any adverse reactions on the part of others.

Consider the title of "dishwasher." We have noted in Chapter 2 the case of the woman who was at the point of quitting because a relative had addressed her with scorn, calling her simply, "You dishwasher!" In this case we find the job itself has so changed over the years that the usual title is no longer really appropriate. In any large and modern restaurant, dishes are no longer washed by hand. They are fed into a machine that does the washing. In some restaurants now, employees involved with this function are called "dishmachine operators"—a title which not only has more favorable status connotations but is actually more descriptive of the functions performed. Of course, this does not mean that the employee will never again be called a "dishwasher" outside of the restaurant. Nevertheless, he can say to himself and others, "I am a dishmachine operator," and hold his head just a little bit higher in so doing.

While there are indeed certain constructive steps that can be taken in the manipulation of status symbols, the manager should recognize that these are symbols that tend to place individuals in relation to each other and do not have an integrating effect upon the organization as a whole. If a manager wishes to increase the degree of what he calls "teamwork," he would be well advised to give even greater attention to the establishment of integrating symbols than he does to the manipulation of status symbols. Some of the possibilities of integrating symbols have been indicated in the preceding section, especially in our discussion of the Scanlon Plan.

Finally, the manager should give special attention to the possibilities of introducing concrete changes into the working environment. He must recognize that changes in technology, work flow, and organization structure will necessarily bring about changes in interactions, activities, and sentiments. The skillful manager will think of such changes not only in terms of technical efficiency but also in terms of making more effective the relations among organizational members.

For example, consider the case of the checkers in the restaurant division of the Tremont Hotel (Chapter 30, "An Action Research Program for the Personnel Man"). How might one have gone about improving the relations between checkers and waitresses? We can imagine training approaches involving group discussions of waitresses and checkers together, so that the waitress would get to understand better the point of view of the checker and vice versa. Any skillful trainer could readily imagine role-playing situations in which the waitress plays the role of a checker and the checker the role of a waitress and so on.

In the Tremont Hotel, no such training efforts were made. Edith Lentz worked out some physical changes at the checker stands, rerouted the lines of waitresses, and proposed certain changes in the duties of the checkers. This reduced greatly the frictions about which all of those affected had been complaining.

We should note further a change in organization structure that could have eliminated such frictions completely. If we abolish the position of checker, we eliminate this particular friction point. The suggestion is not at all farfetched. In fact, there are many large and busy restaurants that function without checkers. The waitresses take over the responsibility of totaling their own checks, and hostesses assume the responsibility of seeing to it that the waitresses are serving the food in the proper manner.

Let me conclude with a note on the way an effective manager thinks about his organization. Concerned though he may be about improving the relations among the members, he does not see human relations in a vacuum. He recognizes that the technology, work flow, and organization structure tend to channel relations in certain ways. He recognizes that the economic and other symbols tend to place people in relation to each other and to motivate them to work together or to fight against each other. Even holding constant these environmental forces and sets of symbols, he recognizes that he can still introduce certain changes through operating directly on the interactions and activities of his subordinates. He does not preach to the members about the sentiments they should have toward each other and their superiors in the organization. He recognizes that if he is skillful in organizing the environmental forces, the symbols, and the interactions and activities of his organization, the sentiments will take care of themselves.

## Collateral Readings

For readings, see those recommended for theory under Part I.

## Discussion Questions

31      1. Regarding the fit between personality and the job, pick out three jobs known to you from this book, other readings, or your experience. Describe these jobs in such a way as to indicate the personality requirements for each job. How would you size up the potential job holders to determine whether they would fit one of these jobs? What manifestations of personality would you look for?

31      2. If a given job seems incompatible with the personalities of most potential job holders, how would you go about changing the job? Give examples of possible changes.

32      3. What difference does it make in the supervisor's job whether he supervises a high or low cohesive group? What implications does this have for the selection of supervisors?

33      4. Consider the theoretical approach used in this book. What are its major strengths?

33      5. What are the major weaknesses of this theoretical approach?

33      6. There are many points in this book where the evidence presented has been fragmentary and the conclusions therefore tentative. Design a research project that would enable you to check one of the conclusions reached here or to test out further what seem to you the weaknesses of this approach.

# INDEX

# INDEX

## A

**ABC** Company, 326–30
Abegglen, James, 66
Absentee ownership, 78–80
Achievement, craftsmen's feeling of, 173–74
Action research, 511–25
Activities
  in automated factory, 225–28
  budgets and, 496–99
  delegation and, 455–56
  in developing new product, 482–89
  direct and symbolic aspects of, 47
  distinguished from interaction, 22
  effect on workers' sentiments, 231
  group cohesion and, 315–21
  individual evaluation of, 19–20
  of individual worker, 17–18
  initiation of
    concern with, 18
    conditions for effective, 395–98, 407
    distinguished from initiation of interaction, 22
    increase in number of, 147
    in maintenance and operation, 479–80
    personality and, 529–30
    reciprocity in, 392–95, 406–7
    reduction in opportunities, 213
    by staff man for line man, 560
    union-management relations and, 353–57
  on innovating project, 490
  and interactions and sentiments, 17–21
  mutual dependence with interactions and sentiments, 51, 569–71
  pattern of
    defined, 51
    habitual, 561
    past and current, 420–28
  of restaurant manager before and after change of managers, 409–14
  stimuli to symbols, 148
  strategy for changing, 572–78
  as symbols, 33–34
  technology and, 214–17
  in union-management relations, 352
  in the workplace, 47

Age
  group cohesion and, 542
  level of aspiration and, 212, 214, 535
Ajax Chemical Company, 329
Amicon tube, 481–92, 548–49, 562
Analysis of data
  in cases presented, 3
  plan of this book, 50–51
  tools for, 17–37
Arensberg, Conrad, 15
Argyris, Chris, 13, 493, 496–97, 499, 570–71
Artisans, teams of, 149–78; see also Craftsmen
Aspiration, level of
  education and, 534–35
  individual, 18–19
  job satisfaction and, 534–35
  management initiative and, 444–46, 448
  technology and, 242–43
Assembly line
  characteristics of work on, 179–80
  described, 181–84
  diagram of, 182
  frustrations and tensions of workers on, 186–89, 197
  leadership structure and, 194–97
  men on, 179–97
  role of the foreman, 190–94, 197
  sentiments toward jobs and, 184–90, 197
  work groups and social groups, 194–97
  workers' attitudes toward management and, 189–90, 197
  workers' attitudes toward union and, 190, 197
Authority
  delegation
    initiative of management and, 430
    integration of groups and, 558–64
    meaning of, 449–57
Automatic factory
  case study of, 218–34
  reactions of men to change to, 220–22, 225–28
  technology and physical conditions in, 219–20

**B**

Bakke, E. Wight, 10
Bales, R. Freed, 29
Bargaining, large-scale; *see also* Collective bargaining
    General Electric Company approach, 368–71
    human problems of, 363–73
Barnard, Chester, 396
Barrel department, 136–48, 552, 557–58, 569–70
Benton Division, Shawcross Corporation, 149–78, 294, 377, 390, 402–3, 532, 537, 542, 557, 564
Blank Oil Company, Hi-Test Plant; *see* Hi-Test Plant
Blau, Peter, 566
Boulware, Lemuel, 367
Buchsbaum, Herbert J., 26–27, 334–35
Buchsbaum, S., & Company, 26, 296, 334
Budgets
    people and, 493–95, 496–99
    problems with, 495–96
    process of making, 499–500
    as symbols, 493
Burtt, Harold E., 12

**C**

Canada, French, case study of plant in, 301–13, 429
Career blocking; *see also* Aspiration, level of
    union drive and, 263
Carey, James, 370
Carnegie, Dale, 575–76
Case studies
    analysis of, 3
    basis of selecting, 2
Center for International Studies; *see* Massachusetts Institute of Technology
Centralization of maintenance, 464–65
Chandler's restaurant, 408–28
Chapple, Eliot, 15, 40, 96, 534
Charts; *see* Diagrams
Chemical Division, post-war adjustments in, 305–7
Chemical and smelting divisions, union militancy in, 301–13
Chinoy, Ely, 187
Christenson, Robert, 77, 541
Chronograph; *see* Interaction Chronograph
CIO, 200, 209, 237–63, 268–77
Clark, James V., 450
Class system; *see* Social structure; Yankee City study

Cohesion, group
    militancy and, 300–323
    of workers, 162–68
Collective bargaining
    contract
        carrying out, 347
        getting ratification, 338–45
        signing, 346
    emotional aspects of, 324–25, 350
    human relations in, 348–51
    influence of past activities and interactions, 338, 345, 350–51
    keys to negotiating process, 325–36
    problem of manipulation, 347–50
    process, 324–51
    role of international union representative, 336–38
Collins, Orvis, 76–77, 361–62
Colombia, economic innovators in, 60–61
Committee on Human Relations in Industry, 10
Commonwealth Edison Company, 346
Communication
    culture and, 63–66
    Latin-American culture and, 63–66
    stimulating upward, 430–33, 447
    systems of in large restaurants, 129–31
    with workers, General Electric Company's plan, 368
    written or oral, 402–6, 407
Community
    absentee ownership and, 78–80
    human relations and organization of, 11–12
    industry and, 9–10, 68–80
    responsibilities of local management, 79
    unions and, 79
Community relations of General Electric Co., 368
Company union
    danger of breakup, 249–50
    in Hi-Test Plant, 239–40
    impact on union drive, 264
    negotiating for, 259–60
    vs. CIO, 251–56
Concepts, clarification of, 22–23
Conceptual tools
    for analysis of data, 17–37
    in effective thinking, 3
Conflict and union militancy, 308–11
Conformity, pressure on individual for, 536–38
Congress of Industrial Relations; *see* CIO

Control
method of examining activities, 461–62
setting up system of maintenance and, 475–78
Cooperation in industry, factors determining, 11–12
Cost control
people and, 493–500
production and, 493–500
size of enterprise and, 86
Craftsmen
job satisfaction
from creative opportunities, 172–75
variety of work and, 175
workers' contribution to company and, 175
maintenance problems and, 469–73
in modern glassware production, 149–78
Culture
communication and, 63–66
concept of, 57–58
impact on Japanese industrial organization, 66–67
Latin-American and communication, 63–66
meaning of work in different kinds of, 59–63
Customers
relations with in large restaurant, 125–27
size of business and relations with, 84

**D**

Dalton, Melville, 99–101, 289, 291, 473–74, 476–78, 530–31, 547
Dartmouth Manufacturing Corporation, 73–74
Dean, Lois R., 281, 296–97
Decentralization of maintenance, 463–64
Delegation
definition of, 455–57
factors determining effects of, 452–56
management initiative and, 430
on the meaning of, 449–57
measuring, 450–52
Detroit Edison Company, 12–13
Diagrams
sentiments, interactions, and activities of Joe, 50
relation between organization structure and size of restaurant, 83
work flow and organization structure in large restaurant, 126

Diagrams—*Cont.*
the motor line, 182
union-management relations before and after union enters, 354
union-management relations under soft and tough management policies, 355
union-management reciprocity, 358
foremen under pressure, 360
foremen adjustment within management, 360
Chandler's restaurant under Manager Potter, 409
organization chart, 1955, for supermarket chain, 450
percentage of district manager and store manager talking time by categories, 452
comparison of district manager and store manager talking time in 1955 and 1957, 453
Dickson, W. J., 8–9, 539
Discipline, effect of sudden tightening, 240–42, 249
Division of labor
to increase efficiency, 6
required by expanding business, 82–84

**E**

Economic environment
group cohesion and, 322–23
impact of, 98–121
job satisfaction and, 535–36
mutual dependence with interactions, activities, and sentiments, 569–71
social system and, 119–20
work flow relations and, 140–41
Economic progress and social structure, 72–76
Economic symbols; *see also* Symbols
as motivation, 567–68
Education and level of aspiration, 534–35
Engineers and their innovations, 481–92
England, George W., 295
England, Industrial Revolution in, 61
Environment; *see also* Economic environment; Organizational environment; Physical environment; Social environment; Technological environment
adjustment to process and, 198–217
group cohesion and, 314–15
individual in his organizational, 38–53, 534–36
technological and physical, 123–234

Environment—*Cont.*
  union militancy and, 314–15, 317–18
Equipment and employee relations in restaurant, 127–29
Ethnic affiliation
  group cohesion and, 541
  influence of in industry, 76–78
Evaluation interview; *see* Performance rating
Everbest Restaurant, 35–36
Executives, training in human relations for, 12–13

F

Failure situation, placing people in, 492, 496–97
Fleishmann, Edwin A., 12
Food World, 449–57
Foreman; *see also* Supervision; Supervisors
  adjustment within management (diagram), 360
  on assembly line
    interactions of, 191–93, 197
    personal relations with men, 193–94
    role of, 190–94, 197
  change in role of, 286–87
  college-trained, 382–85, 389
  decline in authority as factor in union militancy, 305–8
  delegation of authority, 430
  nature of position
    change in, 378–79, 388
    conclusions concerning, 388–89
    lack of uniformity, 377–78, 388
  under pressure (diagram), 360
  productivity and attitudes, 551–54
  promotion to
    ceremonial aspects of, 380–82
    chance of workers for, 379–80
    difficulties in adjusting after, 379–80, 389
  success and failure of a, 136–48
  union-management relations and, 358–61
  worker satisfaction with and productivity, 551–58
Foreman-worker relations
  in glassware factory, 170–72
  incentive system and, 111–13
  initiation of activities and, 141–42, 147
  social status and, 386–88
  union drive and, 264–67
Foreman's Association of America, 359
French Canada; *see* Canada, French

Functional vs. product organization, 93–95

G

Gardner, Burleigh B., 10, 32
Garfield, Sidney, 27, 325
Gasoline plant; *see* Hi-Test Plant, Blank Oil Company
General Electric Company, 367–71
Gestural interaction, categorizing, 28–31
Glassware; *see also* Benton Division, Shawcross Corporation
  changes in social organization of workers, 151–58, 159
  craftsmen producing, 149–78
  technology in production of, 151
Goal-setting function of specialist, 560, 563
Gossett, John, 26
Gouldner, Alvin, 263
Gregory VII, Pope, 36, 574
Grievances
  meaning of, 289–91
  union and, 286–87
Grinding department, union interest in, 314–23
Group
  behavior
    concept of external and internal systems, 22–23
    in a piece rate system, 102
  cohesion
    differences from group to group, 49
    factors influencing, 311–13, 321–23
    gains and losses from, 547
    individual characteristics and, 540–43
    a theory of, 539–46
    union militancy and, 300–323
  high or low resonance of a, 49
  individual and the, 49
  integration of operating group with specialist group, 558–64
  leverage, 545–47
  processes ignored in early studies, 9
  in work organizations, 539–50
Guest, Robert H., 185, 220

H

Hagen, Everett, 60–61
Harris, Edwin F., 12
Harvard Business School, 7–11
Harwood Manufacturing Company, 556
Hawthorne effect, 8
Henderson, Lawrence J., 1–2

Heterogeneity
  group cohesion and, 168, 540, 543
  union militancy and, 302, 304, 322
Historical background of book, 1–53
Hi-Test Plant, Blank Oil Company,
  198–218, 237–63, 269–73, 280,
  292, 377, 378, 383, 394, 397,
  399, 403, 440, 531, 558
Homans, George C., 15, 22–23, 44–45,
  77
Homogeneity
  group cohesion and, 168, 540, 543
  union militancy and, 302, 322
Horizontal orientation
  group cohesion and, 542–43
  individual mobility and, 427
  toward the organization, 262, 263,
  267
  union voting and, 277–79
Hotel Tremont, 511–25, 562, 574, 577
Human relations
  change of managers and, 420–28
  in collective bargaining, 348–50,
  351
  community organization and, 11–12
  early study of, 10–11
  in industry; *see also* Committee on
    Human Relations in Industry
  evolution as field of study, 5–16
  factors important in study of, 2–3
  job structure and, 11–12
  in large-scale bargaining, 363–73
  personality and, 175–76
  personnel man as consultant in, 507–
  10
  status and, 175–76
  training high executives in, 12–13
  training supervisors in, 11
  visualizing, 50
  in the workplace, 46–49

### I

Identification of self with others and
  with group, 20
Illini City study of loyalty, 295
Impersonal forces acting on individual
  economic reward system, 42
  legal framework, 43
  organization structure, 42
  work flow and technology, 42–43
Incentive pay; *see also* Piece rate system
  in automatic factory, 222–25, 228–
  29, 232
  as economic symbol, 98–99
  foreman-worker relations and, 111–
  13
  group cohesion and, 318–20

Incentive pay—*Cont.*
  individual responses to, 99–102
  systems of
    based on performance of entire
     plant, 117–18, 567–68
    intergroup relations and, 113–17
    union conflict resulting from,
     115–17
Individual, the; *see also* Worker, the
  diagram showing sources of senti-
    ments, interactions, and activi-
    ties of, 50
  group cohesion and personal charac-
    teristics of, 540–43
  in his organizational environment,
    38–53, 534–36
  at his work, 47–49, 529–38
  impact of impersonal forces on, 42–
    43
  personal identification of self, 18–20
  responses to money rewards, 99–102
Industrial relations department
  development of an effective, 504–5
  union influence on development,
    501–3
Industrial sociology as a field of study,
  5–16
Industry and the community, 68–80
Inequities
  in piece rates, 114–15, 118
  union militancy and, 303–4
Initiation
  of activities
    conditions for effective, 395–98,
     407
    delegation and, 455–56
    distinguished from initiation of
     interaction, 22
    equipment and, 127–29
    increase in number of and, 147
    interaction and, 47
    layout and, 127–29
    in maintenance and operation,
     479–80
    person responsible for, 18
    reciprocity in, 392–95, 406–7
    reduction in opportunities for, 213
    sentiments toward union and, 265
    sex and, 127–29
    by staff man with line man, 560
    status and, 127–29
    systems approach to study of,
     570–71
    union-management relations and,
     353–57
  of interaction
    distinguished from initiation of
     activities, 22
    person responsible for, 18

Initiative, management
   building, 429–48
   costs of success in building, 443–46
   at lower levels, 437–40, 447
   results of an effort to build, 441–43
Inland Steel Container Company, 26,
      110–11, 291, 331–33, 338, 364–
      66, 402–3
Innovation
   effective organization of process, 492
   by engineers, 481–92
   function of specialist, 560, 561–62
   origination and development of new
      product, 482–89
Inspection, function of specialist, 560–
      61
Institute for Social Research; *see* Uni-
      versity of Michigan
Interaction
   assembly line and, 184–85, 191–93,
      197
   automation and, 221, 225–30
   budgets and, 496–99
   defined, 18
   delegation and, 456–57
   in developing new product, 482–89
   direct and symbolic aspects of, 47–
      49
   distinguished from activities, 22
   disturbances caused by changes in
      on an innovating project, 490
   in glassware factory, 159–60, 161–
      62
   group cohesion and, 315, 321, 543–
      44
   of individual worker, 18–21
   initiation of, 18, 22
   instabilities and fluctuations in, 213
   between kitchen and dining room,
      515–16
   mutual dependence with activities
      and sentiments, 51, 569–71
   oral and gestural, 28–31
   pattern of
      defined, 51
      habitual, 561
      relation of past and current, 420–
         28
   personality and, 529–30
   of restaurant manager before and
      after change of managers, 409–
      14
   between restaurant supervisors and
      workers, 133–34, 415–17
   sentiments and, 231
   strategy for changing, 572–78
   symbols and, 47–49, 148, 265–66
   technology and, 214–17

Interaction—*Cont.*
   theory of applied in this book, 15–
      16
   in union-management relations,
      352–54
   union militancy and, 302, 304
   union voting and, 277–79
   verbal symbols and, 265–66
   in the workplace, 47
Interaction Chronograph, 40–41, 534
Intercultural perspective, the work
      world in, 57–67
Interest in job in relation to number of
      operations performed, 185–86
Intergroup relations
   in a barrel department, 137–38
   incentive system and, 113–17
   on an innovating project, 487–92
   maintenance and, 463, 468–69
International Brotherhood of Electrical
      Workers, 346
International Chemical Worker's Un-
      ion, 325
International Harvester Company, 12
International Union of Electrical
      Workers, 367, 369–70
Interpersonal relations and union
      drive, 264–67
Ireland, field study in, 15
Issues, impact on group cohesion, 544

**J**

Japanese industrial organization, 66–
      67
Jasinski, Frank J., 185, 531
Job, the
   evaluation of, 118–19
   fit between personality and, 529,
      532
   group cohesion and structure of,
      543–44
   nature of
      personality and, 529
      relation to interaction, activities,
         and sentiments, 530
   pressure and timing of the, 174
   satisfaction
      economic environment and, 535–
         36
      in glassware factory, 177–78
      and the individual, 534–36
      physical environment and, 535–
         36
      productivity and, 554
      technological environment and,
         535–36
      worker reaction to process, 176
   security
      union militancy and, 303–4

Job—*Cont.*
security—*Cont.*
union promises, 248–49
structure and human relations, 11–12
union voting and characteristics, of, 272–74, 277–79
working conditions in glassware factory and, 172–75

**K**

Kerr, Clark, 11
Kerr, Willard A., 296
Kettering, Charles F., 58–59
Knowledge
systematic
needed by sociologist, 1
in study of human relations in industry, 2–3
technical and practical, failure to integrate, 491

**L**

Labor, division of
to increase efficiency, 6
required by expanding business, 82–84
Labor and Management Center; *see* Yale University
Laderman, Sam, 334–35
Langshaw, Walter, 73–75
Latin America, 60–63
Lawrence, Paul, 29, 450, 452, 481, 491, 533
Layout of work space and employee relations, 127–29
Leadership
assembly line and structure of, 194–97
quantitative measures of, 161–62
of team in glassware production, 153–58
types of union, 280–81
Lentz, Edith, 512–17, 522–23, 577
Likert, Rensis, 10
Love, Lucius, 26, 333
Loyalty of worker, 295–98

**M**

MacGregor, Douglas, 15, 401
Maintenance and operation
centralization of, 464–65
coordinating activities, 469–73
decentralization of, 463–64
Milo's struggle with, 473–78
organizations, 463–80
relations between, 478–80, 562–63
relative evaluations of, 478
setting up system of, 475–78

Man
in industry, 13
and process, 198–217
relation of boss and, 390–407
Management; *see also* Managerial process; Managerial succession; Manager
action research on problems, 518–21
assembly line workers and, 189–90, 197
building initiative at lower level, 437–41, 447
conflict with workers as factors in union militancy, 308–11
costs of success in building initiative in, 443–46
counteroffensive against union drive, 251–59
delegation
approach to, 454
in budgeting and operating procedures, 453
endorsement of program and success of, 453
in supermarket chain, 449–57
friction between higher and lower, 491
group cohesion and responses of, 545–47
initiative and, 429–48, 441–43
participative and worker reaction, 555–56
structure
militancy and, 305–8
union-management relationships and, 235–373
Management groups, utilization of, 547–50
Management-worker relations
in glassware factory, 168–72
union drive and, 263–67, 277–79
Manager; *see also* Foreman; Management; Managerial succession
attitudes of effective, 578
impact of change of, 414–15, 419-20
personality of, 531–33
relations with subordinates affected by size, 83, 85–86
Managerial process; *see also* Foreman; Management; Manager
before and after change of managers, 409–14
discussion of, 375–459
exercised by restaurant supervisors, 415–17
personality and, 420–28
Managerial succession, 408–28

Manipulation of men in collective bargaining, 347–50
Massachusetts Institute of Technology, Center for International Studies, 60–61, 567
Mauss, Marcel, 45
Mayo, Elton, 8, 10
Merei, Ferenc, 573
Miller, Frank, 77, 149, 159–61
Miller, Frank B., Jr., 493, 499
Milo Corporation, 473–80
Money
  automation and, 222–25
  culture and, 98
  impact on men, 42
  individual differences in response to, 99–102
  job satisfaction and, 535–36
  motivation of men, 6
  response to incentive pay and, 100–102
  valued as reward, 45
Morale; *see* Sentiments
Motivation of worker, early studies of, 9
Motor line; *see* Assembly line

**N**

National Labor Relations Board, 252
National Training Laboratory for Group Development, 575
New Bedford, Massachusetts, 72–76, 78

**O**

Oil Workers International Union, 237, 258, 261
Operating organization; *see* Maintenance and operation
Oral and gestural interaction, 28–31
Organization, the
  authority or integration in, 558–64
  behavior of men in
    early assumptions concerning, 9
    factors affecting, 13
  functional vs. product, 93–95
  specialization and, 95–97
  strategy for change in, 571–78
  structure
    activities and changes in, 577–78
    conflict and, 517
    delegation and, 452–53, 456
    formal
      defined, 81–82
      human behavior and, 10–11, 81–97
    initiative of management and, 429–30, 447

Organization—*Cont.*
  structure—*Cont.*
    interaction and changes in, 577–78
    maintenance and, 475–78
    patterns of supervision and, 88–93
    planning for development of, 446–47
    sentiments and changes in, 577–78
    size
      case of a restaurant, 82–88
      diagram showing relations between, 83
    symbols for, 34–37
    systems approach to, 568–71
    tendency of human beings to develop informal, 10
    vertical vs. horizontal integration, 262–67
    as a whole, 551–78
Organization man problem, 536–38
Organizational environment, the individual in his, 38–53, 534–36
Organizational products, 551–58
Organizational relations as field of study, 5–16
Origination of activities and interaction; *see* Initiation
Overseas Corporation, 465–73, 479–80, 504
Ownership, absentee, and community power, 78–80

**P**

Pavlov, Ivan, 102–4
Pay; *see* Incentive pay
Pelz, Donald, 554–56
Penalties; *see* Rewards and penalties
People
  budgets and, 493–95, 496–99
  cost control and, 493–500
  production and, 493–500
Performance rating, 399–402, 407
Personal background
  organizational behavior and, 278
  union voting and, 277–79
Personal identification, 20
Personal worth, self-concept of, 18–20
Personality
  fit between job and, 529, 532
  group cohesion and, 540–43
  human relations and, 175–76
  managerial behavior and, 420–28
  of managers and supervisors, 531–33
  modification of, 529, 533–34
  nature of the job and, 529

Personality—*Cont.*
  pattern of, and individual behavior, 38–42
  status and, 175–76
  of workers, 530–31
Personnel
  action research on problems of, 518–21
  changes in barrel department, 138–40
  department
    evolution of, 501–3
    limitations on concerns of, 505–7
  group cohesion and changes in, 317–18
  man
    action research program for, 511–25
    as human relations consultant, 507–10
    new role at Hotel Tremont, 522–24
    role of, 501–10
  problems in Hotel Tremont, 512–13
Physical environment
  in automatic factory, 219–20
  group cohesion and changes in, 317–18
  job satisfaction and, 535–36
  and technological environment, 123–234
Piece rate system; *see also* Incentive pay
  case study of use as incentive, 99–102
  conditioned-response theory and, 102–4
  conflict and, 102–8
  foreman-worker relations and, 111–13
  motivation of productivity, 6
  rate-change problems, 108–11
  setting rates, 104–8
Politics
  piece rate incentives and, 100–102
  unionization and, 78–79
Process
  man and, 198–217
  of work
    symbols and, 214–17
    technology and, 201–2, 214–17
Production
  cost control and, 493–500
  and pay in automatic factory, 222–25
  people and, 493–500
Productivity
  lighting and, 7
  motivating through piece rates, 6

Productivity—*Cont.*
  rest periods and refreshments and, 7–8
  social influences and, 8–9
Promotion by ability, 434–37
Prudential Insurance Company, 552–53, 557
Psychologists in industry, early studies by, 7, 9
Public relations responsibility of management, 79–80
Punishments; *see* Rewards and penalties
Purcell, Father T. V., 296–97
Purchasing, standardization of, 465–69

R

Rank, individual's own and prestige of others, 20–21
Reciprocity
  in initiation of activities, 265, 392–95, 406–7, 560, 571
  in maintenance and operation, 480
  organizational behavior of individual and, 43–46
  in rewards and punishments, 390–92
  union and management, 357–58, 371
  in the workplace, 48–49
Religion
  attitude toward work and, 59
  response to incentive pay and, 100–102
Research; *see also* Action research
  methods used in this study, 16
Restaurants
  communication systems in large, 129–31
  crying and noncrying waitresses, 131–33
  diagram of work flow and organization structure, 126
  factors affecting employee relations, 127–29
  relation of size and organization structure, 82–88
  technological and physical environment in, 125–35
  work flow in, 125–35
Rewards
  delegation and, 457
  group cohesion and, 545–47
  organizational behavior and, 43–46
  and penalties
    management initiative and, 430, 433–37, 447
    principle of, 564–68

Rewards—*Cont.*
  and penalties—*Cont.*
    reciprocity in, 390–92
    relation between, 560–62
Roethlisberger, F. J., 8–9, 77, 539,
    541
Ronken, Harriet, 481, 491
Roy, Donald, 106–7, 290

## S

Sayles, Leonard, 49, 280, 316, 321–
    23, 539–40, 544
Scanlon, Joseph, 567
Scanlon Plan, 117–18, 567–68
Scientific management
  early assumptions, 9
  Taylor's ideas of, 6–7
  union pressure and, 502
Sears, Roebuck & Company, 88–93
Seashore, Stanley, 540, 542, 547, 558
Selekman, Benjamin, 346
Self-concept, 18–20
Seniority
  assembly lines and, 184
  evolution of rules, 291–94
  in gasoline plant, 243
  in glassware production, 152–53
  group cohesion and, 542
  resentments caused by, 141, 146
  union promises concerning, 248–49
Sentiments
  toward assembly line jobs, 184–90,
    197
  of assistant supervisor toward res-
    taurant workers, 418–19
  automation and changes in, 225–28,
    229–30
  budgets and, 496–99
  economic symbols and, 232
  group cohesion and, 315, 320
  group productivity and foreman's,
    551–52
  of individual worker, 18–22
  on innovating project, 482, 490
  and interaction, 231
  concerning limits of the job, 397
  morale and, 557–58
  mutual dependence with interactions
    and activities, 51, 569–71
  organizational change and, 572–74
  pattern of, 51, 420–28
  personality and, 529–30
  of restaurant managers and workers,
    410–14
  technological environment and, 214–
    17
  toward union, 268–79
  in union-management relations, 352
  verbal symbols and, 265–66

Sentiments—*Cont.*
  walkout of operator and, 211–14
  of workers toward restaurant super-
    visor, 416–17
Service
  function of specialists, 560, 562–63
  method of examining activities in,
    461–62
  staff and control activities and, 461–
    526
Sex
  employee relations in restaurant and,
    127–29
  group cohesion and, 541
  initiation of activities and, 127–29
Shawcross Corporation; *see* Benton Di-
    vision, Shawcross Corporation
Siegel, Abraham, 11
Size and organizational structure in a
    restaurant, 82–88
Smelting and chemical divisions, union
    militancy in, 301–13
Social background
  group cohesion, 541–42
  level of aspiration and, 534–35
  response to incentive pay and, 100–
    102
  union vote and, 270–72
Social contacts
  response to incentive pay and, 100–
    102
  union drive and, 256–59
Social environment, mutual dependence
    with interactions, activities, and
    sentiment, 569–71
Social groups and work groups, 194–
    97
Social structure
  economic environment and, 119–20
  economic progress and, 72–76
  in glassware factory, 151–59
  group cohesion and, 320–21
  relation to industrial organization,
    68–72
  technology and, 68–72
  unionization and, 68–72
Specialists
  functions of, 95, 560
  integrating with line organization,
    96–97
Specialization
  to increase efficiency, 6–7
  organization structure and, 95–97
Staff, activities of, 461–62
Standardization
  to increase efficiency, 6–7
  in maintenance, 465–69
  of purchasing, 465–69
  size and, 86–88

Status
  delegation and, 453–54
  employee relations in restaurant and, 127–29
  human relations and, 175–76
  on an innovating project, 489, 491
  level of aspiration and family, 534–35
  in maintenance and operation, 478–80
  negative sentiments resulting from loss in, 207–8, 212–13
  of negotiators in collective bargaining, 326–28
  personality and, 175–76
  routine operations and, 204
  self-concept of, 18–19
  symbols and, 386–89, 575–77
  technology and, 214–17
Steel fabricating plant; see Barrel department
Steel Workers Organizing Committee, 78
Strauss, George, 323, 544
Supermarket
  comparison of talking time of district manager and store manager in 1955 and 1957 (diagram), 453
  delegation in, 449–57
  distribution of talking time between district manager and store manager (diagram), 452
  organization in 1955 (diagram), 450
Supervision
  close vs. general, 552–54
  criticizing subordinates, 398–402, 407
  first-line position of, 377–89
  friendly, 246–48
  functional, 7
  organization structure and patterns of, 88–93
  relation between man and boss, 390–407
  status symbols and, 386–88, 389
  technology and, 243–46
  before union drive, 243–46
Supervisors
  first-line, 377–89
  managerial process under two, 415–17
  personality of, 531–33
  role of assistant in restaurant, 417–19
  role of in restaurant, 133–34
  size of business and responsibilities of, 85–86

Supervisors—*Cont.*
  training programs for, 11–13
  union militancy and, 305–8
Survey Research Center; see University of Michigan
Swift and Company, 296–97
Symbols
  behavior change through change in, 575–78
  economic
    incentive pay as, 98–99
    sentiments and, 232
  giving orders and, 397, 407
  on an innovating project, 491–92
  interaction and, 47–49
  in maintenance and operation, 480
  motivating behavior, 565–67
  for the organization, 34–37
  role of in success and failure of foreman, 148
  situational determinants of meaning of, 31–32
  status
    in collective bargaining, 326–28
    in supervisory relationship, 386–88
  summary on, 37
  technological environment and, 214–17
  verbal
    interaction and, 265–66
    sentiments and, 265–66
    union drive and, 265–66
  water spigot as, 514
  to which men respond, 24–37
Systems approach to organization, 568–71

**T**

Taylor, Frederick W., 6–7, 9, 502
Team
  leadership of in glassware production, 153–58
  work operations and composition of, 149–51
Technical knowledge, integration of practical and, 491
Technological environment
  group cohesion and, 322–23
  job satisfaction and, 535–36
  mutual dependence with interactions, activities, and sentiments, 569–71
  physical environment and, 123–234
Technology
  in automatic factory, 219–20
  changes
    activities and, 577–78
    interactions and, 577–78

Technology—*Cont.*
  changes—*Cont.*
    sentiments and, 577–78
    group cohesion and, 317–18
    social structure and, 68–72
    symbols and, 214–17
    work flow and
      on assembly line, 181–84
      in steel fabricating plant, 137,
        147
    work process and, 201–2, 214–17
Technology Project; *see* Yale University
Tennessee Valley Authority, 293,
  361–62
Theory
  background of in this book, 1–53
  restatement of, 527–28
Thinking, effective way of, 1, 3
Time study problems, 105–8
Timing of the job, 174
Titles as symbols, 30
Tools for analysis of data, 17–37
Tremont Hotel; *see* Hotel Tremont
Trice, Harrison, 381
Truax Corporation, 281–86
Turner, Arthur N., 181–84, 186, 188–
  91, 194–95

## U

Union; *see also* Company union
  assembly line workers and, 190, 197
  centralization of power in, 288–89
  community and growth of, 79
  decline of importance of steward,
    286–87
  diagram of split in, 360
  drive
    analysis of, 262–67
    farewell party and, 256–59
    in a gasoline plant, 206–8
    in grinding department, 315–23
    in local situation, 237–67
    management's counteroffensive,
      251–62
    organizing campaign, 248–51
    social structure and, 68–72
    supervision before, 243–46
    voting decisions in, 277–79
    working conditions before, 237–
      39, 242–43
  foreman's relations with, 141–43
  in glassware factory, 152–53
  grievances and, 286–87, 289–91
  group cohesion and militancy, 300–
    323
  incentive pay and, 115–17
  international representative in collective bargaining, 336–38

Union—*Cont.*
  leader
    General Electric Company approach and, 369–70
    meeting attendance and type of,
      287–88
    rise and fall of a, 281–86
    types of, 280–81
  personnel departments and, 501–3
  rules, 291–95
  social background and sentiments
    toward, 270–72
  wages and promises by, 248–49
  who goes and why, 268–79
Union-management relations
  change in organization structure
    and, 517
  conclusions on, 298–99
  cooperation possibilities, 364–68
  data needed for study of, 361–62
  early study of, 9–10
  evolution of, 280–99
  factors affecting in French Canadian plant, 311–13
  introduction, 235–36
  management policies
    diagram of, 355
    firm but fair, 357
    goal of, 363
    soft, 355–56
    tough, 356–57
  militancy and conflict in, 308–11
  patterns in, 352–62
  problems at lower levels, 358–61
  reciprocity in, 357–58
  scheme for analysis of (diagrams),
    353–57, 354–55
United Chemical Workers Union, 26
United Electrical Workers, 370
United Packinghouse Workers, 296
United States Steel Corporation, 219–
  28
United Steel Workers Union, 353,
  364–66, 567
University of Michigan
  Institute for Social Research, 10, 12
  Survey Research Center, 551, 553–
    54, 558

## V

Venezuela, culture and communication
  in, 64–66
Vertical orientation
  group cohesion and, 542–43
  intergroup relations and, 137–38
  to the organization, 262, 265–67,
    427
  union voting and, 277–79
Vroom, Victor, 555

## W

Wages; *see* Incentive pay; Piece rate system

Waitress
crying and noncrying, 131–33
work flow and, 125–27

Walker, Charles, 181, 185, 218–20, 224, 226–27, 230–31

Walkout
of operator in gasoline plant, 198–201, 211–17
personal history of the man, 202–8

Warner, W. Lloyd, 9–10, 15, 68, 72

Weber, Max, 59, 281

Western Electric Company, 7–11, 16, 539

Whyte, William H., Jr., 536

Wiley, Meredith, 511–12, 514–17, 520–24, 562, 574

Wolfbein, Seymour, 72–74, 76

Words as symbols, 28–31

Work
job satisfaction and amount of, 175
meaning of
class differences in views on, 59
in different cultures, 59–63
factors influencing views on, 58–63
status distinctions, 62–63
operations and team composition, 149–51
piece rate system and measurement of, 104–8
reactions to process, 176

Work flow
activities and changes in, 577–78
economic environment and, 140–41
on an innovating project, 489–90
interactions and changes in, 577–78
organization structure in restaurant and (diagram), 126
problems in glassware production, 158–61
in a restaurant, 125–35
sentiments and changes in, 577–78
technology and, 137, 147, 181–84

Work group
cohesion in, 162–68

Work group—*Cont.*
heterogeneity vs. homogeneity in, 168
social groups and, 194–97
theory of cohesion in, 539–46

Worker, the; *see also* Individual, the
on assembly line, 186–89, 197
criticism by supervisor, 398–401, 407
factors affecting behavior of, 13
impact of change of managers on, 414–15, 419–20
loyalty to company and to union, 295–98
meaning of work to, 10
personality of, 530–31
reaction to automation, 220–22, 230–31
unemployment and, 10
what is he like? 38–42

Worker-management relations
between a foreman and workers, 141–43, 147
in glassware factory, 168–72
between man and boss, 390–407
off-the-job
sentiments about union and, 266–67
union voting and, 277–79
special ties and union voting, 274–77
union drive and, 263–67
union militancy and, 308–11

Working conditions
in glassware factory, 172–75
as symbols, 33–34
before union drive, 242–43
union militancy and, 301–2, 304

Workplace, human relations in, 46–49

Worthy, James C., 89–90

## Y

Yale University
Labor and Management Center, 10
Technology Project, 181, 218

Yankee City study, 9, 15, 68–72, 78

## Z

Zaleznik, Abraham, 77, 541

*This book has been set on the Linotype in 10 point Monticello, leaded 2 points, and 9 point Monticello, leaded 1 point. Chapter numbers and titles are in 18 point Bodoni #275. The size of the type page is 27 by 47 picas.*